A Practical Logic of Cognitive Systems
Volume 1

Agenda Relevance
A Study in Formal Pragmatics

A Practical Logic of Cognitive Systems
Volume 1

Agenda Relevance
A Study in Formal Pragmatics

Dov M. Gabbay
Department of Computer Science
King's College London
London, UK

and

John Woods
The Abductive Systems Group
University of British Columbia
Vancouver BC, Canada

2003

ELSEVIER

Amsterdam - Boston - London - New York - Oxford - Paris
San Diego - San Francisco - Singapore - Sydney - Tokyo

ELSEVIER SCIENCE B.V.
Sara Burgerhartstraat 25
P.O. Box 211, 1000 AE Amsterdam, The Netherlands

First edition 2003

Library of Congress Cataloging in Publication Data
A catalog record from the Library of Congress has been applied for.
British Library Cataloguing in Publication Data
A catalogue record from the British Library has been applied for.
ISBN: 0-444-51385-X
∞ The paper used in this publication meets the requirements of ANSI/NISO Z39.48-1992 (Permanence of Paper). Printed in The Netherlands.

We dedicate this volume to the memory of our mothers

Flora Sassoon Gabbay

and

Gertrude Mary Woods

Contents

Preface

This work originated from lectures given in 1989 at the University of Amsterdam. An early suggestion was that relevance is not fruitfully thought of as a merely propositional relation, or at least not in the first instance. Thinking so revived an interest in pragmatics provoked by some penetrating remarks by Richmond Thomason, at a talk attended by Gabbay and Woods at Stanford in 1971. Thomason may be startled to learn that he is the remote cause of the present work, but it is true all the same.

Material that eventuated in chapter 5 was first presented at the World Congress of Philosophy in the summer of 1989, in Brighton. Ralph Johnson, David Hitchcock and Timothy Williamson were generous with their suggestions. Chapter 6 made a callow appearance as an ISSA Lecture (International Society for the Study of Argumentation) at the University of Amsterdam in April 1990. Tjark Kruiger and Susanne Gerritsen made helpful criticisms. The main idea, the principal business of chapter 7 and beyond, was floated in 1988 in Amsterdam. Francisca Snoeck Henkemans, Fransica Jungslager and Eveline Feteris performed a valuable service in disbelieving most of it. An attenuated version was presented at the Third International Symposium on Informal Logic, at the University of Windsor in June 1989. Michael Scriven, Harvey Siegel, Jonathan Adler and Jonathan Berg subjected the effort to helpful scrutiny. Scriven wanted to know where the normative theory was; and chapter 10 eventually took shape. Some of this was read to a joint session of the Eastern Division of the American Philosophical and the Association for Informal Logic and Critical Thinking in December 1991 in New York. William Lycan and L.J. Cohen commented to good effect, leading to a better idea of what to do about a normative theory of relevance. Mark Weinstien and Jonathan Adler also assisted in the process of critical self-discovery. An earlier version still had been read the summer before at the International Conference at McMaster University. Joining the list of benefactors were Robert Pinto, George Bowles, and Erik Krabbe.

Material that has found its way into the latter half of chapter 6 was first delivered at the University of Groningen in the Spring Term of 1988. Searching criticism was provided by E.M. Barth, Jeanne Peijnenburg and Pier Smit. A redraft was read to the Southwest Logic Group, in Seattle in July 1991. Stephen Thomason, Brian Chellas, Ray Jennings and Charles Daniels made generous suggestions.

The book underwent a substantial *perestroika* in the Fall Term of 1992 in Amsterdam. (Friendly wags spoke of the Dutch Book that was in the making.)

For most of the 1990s the relevance project was set aside under the press of other research obligations and a particularly heavy adminstrative load for Woods. The project was revived when Gabbay and Woods were writing *The Reach of Abduction: Insight and Trial.* In preparing that work, it was necessary to give an account of relevance. The authors were pleased to discover an attractive fit between Woods' conceptual analysis and Gabbay's work on Labelled Deductive Systems (LDS) and Time, Action and Revision (TAR) logics. The conformity of these two approaches called for joint authorship, and this book is the result. In writing it, we have found ourselves attracted to writing a comprehensive work on the practical logic of cognitive systems; and we are pleased to offer *Agenda Relevance* as the first volume of this larger work.

Research for this work has been supported by a Fellowship-in-Residence at the Netherlands Institute for Advanced Study for the first half of 1990. Dirk J. Van de Kaa was Director of NIAS and Frans van Eemeren was leader of the research group. We are greatly indebted to them for their support. The Social Sciences and Humanities Research Council of Canada has favoured Woods' work with a series of Research Grants, as has Professor Bhagwan Dua. This work was also supported by a research award to Gabbay from the Alexander von Humboldt Foundation at DFKI Saarbrücken and an EPSRC research project GR/R award to Woods. Our sincere thanks to all.

We have also benefited richly from correspondence and conversation with: Peter Alward, Johan van Benthem, J. Anthony Blair, Kenneth Boessenkool, Michael Bratman, Bryson Brown, Peter Bruza, Jim Cunningham, Frans H. van Eemeren, Kevin Gaudet, Peter Godfrey-Smith, Rob Grootendorst, Sally Jackson, Scott Jacobs, Ruth Kempson, Peter McBurney, Ruth Millikan, Rolf Nossum, Agnes van Rees, George Schlesinger, Timothy Schroeder, Hartley Slater, Patrick Suppes, Agnes Verbiest, Mark Vorobej, and Ronald Yoshida. For superb technical assistance, we also thank Jane Spurr in London, and Randa Stone and Dawn Collins in Canada. We especially wish to thank Douglas Walton for permission to cite his forth-

A stylistic note: we adopt the convention in which generic reference via singular personal pronouns be in the grammatically masculine form.

Part I

Logic

Chapter 1

Introduction

Omne ignotum pro magnifico.

Tacitus

The great advances in logic in the last century and a quarter saw a turn from its historical preoccupation with arguing and reasoning in favour of quite particular contributions to mathematics. It made possible important gains in both the *foundations* and the *methodology* of mathematics. The foundational contribution was largely of philosophical interest. It sought to establish a basis for logicism, for the reduction of mathematics to logic. The methodological contribution also has its philosophical significance, but it threw its net more widely, capturing the interest of those who thought that mathematics could only benefit from the rigour and the standards of exact proof that the new logic was in process of articulating.

It is difficult to overestimate the significance of the mathematical turn in logic. Not only did the new logic greatly narrow logic's former range of interests, it was able to do so only after determining that the traditional syllogistic approach to logic was inadequate for logic's new ambitions. Ever since its inception, 2500 years thence, logic had been in all essentials the logic of the syllogism. The mathematical turn brought a surprisingly abrupt end to Aristotle's long-lived hegemony.

Given the venerability and sheer persistence of that influence, it is perhaps not wholly inexplicable that mathematical logicians did not entirely break with the traditional line that logic is about reasoning and about arguing. There are plenty of textbooks on mathematical logic, including some of the best and most senior, in which we find it said, without a shred of irony or embarrassment, that mathematical logic is the most general, or the basic theory of reasoning. Those of greater circumspection would claim that the new symbolic logic was the theory of *mathematical* reasoning.

It would be quite wrong to overlook the fact that mathematical logicians have been quick to recognize various respects in which the claim of logic to be a theory of (mathematical) reasoning is implausible. To that end, various distinctions have been invoked:

- *process/product*
- *descriptive adequacy/normative legitimacy*
- *actual circumstances/ideal conditions*

What these distinctions were thought to have had in common was that (a) while mathematical logic misdescribed the left side and properly described the right side, nevertheless, (b) left side circumstances could be thought of as *approximating* to right hand conditions in ways that would make it accurate to say that logic makes fruitful provision for the left side too.

Ever since its inception, and throughout the mathematical revolution, logic has been conceived of as a highly specialized investigation of *language*. In Aristotle's hands, the language of logic was Greek; in the hands of Frege, the language was the stylized notation of the *Begriffsschrift*. We see in this passage from natural to ideal languages a not inconsiderable development. But here, too, there were common constants. One was that all the target properties that a logic would seek to elucidate were represented as properties of linguistic structures. As Quine would say, with characteristic verve, 'Logic is linguistics on purpose'.

If modern mathematical logic attaches its findings to languages that no one speaks, or could, the complaint recurs that logic can't be about reasoning and arguing. Here, too, distinctions were invoked. Chief among them was that between

an actual sentence of a real language/its logical form in an ideal language

Considerable effort was expended to show that when conditions are right, *some* at least of the properties of ideal linguistic structures map to certain natural language structures in a principled way [Woods, 2002c, sec. 6]; for sober reconsideration, see [Woods, 2003, chapter 15].

We might refer collectively to these myriad efforts to support the claim that mathematical logic is a theory of reasoning and arguing as the *Standard Defence*. The Standard Defence is not lightly dismissible. It is closely patterned on widely accepted methods for showing that the empirical inaccuracies of our best scientific theories are discountable under the appropriate approximation relations. No one dismisses the physics of frictionless surfaces just because its laws fail in nature, even as regards the pre-game, freshly Zambonied ice of Maple Leaf Gardens. All the same, the Standard Defence of mathematical logic has come under scrutiny from two largely unconnected sources, *computer science* (including AI) and *informal logic* and *argumentation theory*. A common reservation is captured by this question: Are the approximations postulated by the Standard Defence sufficiently intimate to justify its claim that logical theory may be seen as overriding empirical inaccuracy on the ground? Their answer, severally and jointly, is No. Informal logicians would observe that mathematical logic isn't particularly adept at modelling fallacious reasoning; computer scientists would point out the difficulties in getting plausible AI models out of standard logic. Some AI theorists would also note that certain features of reasoning and cognition generally are *sublinguistic* and thus lie exposed to systematic misdecription by theories that concentrate on investigating various properties of linguistic structures.[1]

Out of this welter of criticism certain themes have come to dominate. The authors of the present volume have particular interest in the following two:

1. Mathematical logic makes inadequate provision for the investigation of *practical reasoning*;

2. In its decontextual preoccupation with language, mathematical logic makes inadequate provision for the analysis of *cognitive structures*.

It is not to our purpose in this Introduction to adjudicate these claims; we want rather to *motivate* the book that follows. But we say in passing that much of the work in mainline logic itself these past thirty years has been to modify the standard or classical expression of logic in ways that take such criticisms seriously into account. The sheer scope and intensity of these adjustments is discernible in the fecund pluralism of the present-day research programme. Suffice it here to note developments in modal, deontic and epistemic logic; relevant and linear logic; dynamic and temporal logic; logics of action and labelled deduction; adaptive and preservationist logics; dialethic logic; dialogue and interrogative logic; and many more. To the extent possible, our approach in this book is to preserve the spirit of this collective attempt at logical self-reform in the cause of 'user-friendliness'. But we also wish to emphasize what many of these otherwise attractive

[1] Alternatively, some theorists take subdoxastic processes to involve symbol manipulation, but in a different representational system than that in which doxastic reasoning occurs.

systems of logic do not. We wish to respond positively and constructively to the challenges implied by the two basic complaints noted just above. Accordingly, what we expressly seek for is

1. a logic of *practical reasoning*; and

2. a logic of *cognitive systems*.

The present book is the first volume of *A Practical Logic of Cognitive Systems* (*PLCS*), of which three further volumes are forthcoming. One is in an advanced state of readiness, *The Reach of Abduction: Insight and Trial*, and a second is well underway, *Seductions and Shortcuts: Fallacies in the Cognitive Economy*. Following these will be a volume provisionally entitled *Formal Models of Practical Reasoning*. In each case our choice has been motivated by the conviction that these matters are of essential importance to practical logic, and that they are in need of further theoretical attention than they have hitherto received (and so cannot be thought of as closed parts of the research programme).

In most approaches, practical reasoning is distinguished in one or other of two ways. One sees its distinctive mark in the *content* of the reasoning; the other sees it in its *standards of rigour*. On the content side, practical reasoning is often said to be reasoning about what to do or how to solve problems; on the standards side, practical reasoning is thought of as governed by standards both less theoretical and less strict than those of 'pure' or 'formal' logic. We do not dispute these conceptions of the practical, but we do favour an alternative. We find it both intuitively attractive and theoretically fruitful to conceive of practical reasoning as reasoning done by practical agents, and in turn to conceive of practical agency in terms of the degree of access to key cognitive resources such as *information, time* and *computational capacity*. Given that such access is a matter of degree, practical agency is a comparative concept. As access enlarges, practicality recedes in favour of the theoretical, as we shall say. Intuitively, individual agents are paradigms of practical agency, whereas institutional agents such as NASA or Italian physics in the 1930s are theoretical agents par excellence.

This, the *resource-bound* approach to agency gives a conception of the practical that while different from, is not hostile to, either the subject matter or standards approach. It may be that practical agents in our sense deal rather more with matters of common or everyday interest to human beings than theoretical agents in our sense do; it may also be true that, since individual agents usually operate under press of scarce resources, the standards against which to assess their cognitive performance would be less rigorous and exacting as those required in retrofitting the Concorde. Even so, it is clear that the subject matter, standards and resources approaches to practical agency are disjoint.

We have it, then, that a logic of practical reasoning is a certain kind of aspects of description of a practical agent. But not everything a practical agent does or is capable of doing is grist for the mill of practical logic. We shall therefore say that a practical logic is a description of certain aspects of the behaviour of practical agents under conditions that qualify it broadly as cognitive. Accordingly, we shall also find it useful to deploy the notion of *cognitive system.*

A cognitive system is a 3-tuple of a cognitive agent, cognitive resources, and cognitive tasks performed dynamically in real time. A cognitive agent is a being capable of perception, memory, belief, desire, reflection, deliberation, decision and inference. A practical cognitive system is a cognitive system whose cognitive agent is a practical agent in our sense, that is, an individual. A practical logic of the sort we are describing gives 'a certain kind of description' of a practical cognitive system. It is necessary to say something more about this.

Writing as logicians, we are interested in those aspects of cognitive behaviour for which a logician's more or less standard repertoire of target properties are instantiable in illuminating ways. In addition to properties such as *inference*, *consquence*, *consistency* and *validity*, we shall in due course add to the list notions such as *revision*, and, of course, *relevance*. Writing as logicians who have an interest in theories of reasoning that score well on the score of empirical adequacy, we seek descriptions of the behaviour of logial agents that deploy our logical vocabulary systematically and unsuperficially, but not in ways that take us to distant idealizations for which plausible approximation relations are hard to find.

On the face of it, our conception of a practical logic echoes a conviction of Bacon, who took logic to be a part of rational psychology. Although we stop well short of Bacon, ours is avowedly an approach to logic that could be called *psychologistic.* This will offend purists who, entirely correctly, have been quick to appreciate that model theory, proof theory, set theory and recursion theory have nothing to do with psychology [Barwise, 1977]. But there is more to our conception than is to be found in the four central domains of mathematical logic. In as much as we want our logic to give an account of aspects of the cognitive behaviour of practical agents, it is essential that psychological parameters not be overlooked entirely. In consequence, we find ourselves in agreement with those for whom the distinction between logic and psychology is neither exact nor exhaustive (see, e.g. Thagard [1982]).

There is an important sense, therefore, in which the logic of practical cognitive systems is not psychology. The relevant distinction is characterized best in *operational* terms, concerning which an analogy with mathematical logic is revealing. Mathematical logic gives an account of various properties (such as entailment, deducibility and consistency) of linguistic structures. Recall here Quine's quip: 'Logic is linguistics on purpose'. This should trigger an obvious question. *Why isn't logic linguistics?* Although some logicians have attempted to meet this question head-on (e.g. Quine [1960]), the answer for the most part is to be found by examining the different things that logicians and linguists actually *do* with the common matters that bind them. In each case the boundary between logic and linguistics is operationally discernible in the different things that logicians and linguists are *interested in* and *good at.*

It is the same way with the distinction between logic and psychology. Here, too, the difference is an operational thing. Even when, as in our case, the logician and the psychologist share a good many interests, our respective methodologies (what we are respectively *good at*) will serve to preserve the distinction non-trivially. If a logician has been mathematically trained, or has imbibed something of what goes on in computer science, he will bring to the table a competency in *formal modelling.* If the logician has been philosophically trained, he will bring to the table competency in *conceptual analysis.* In our approach, the two are systematically linked. In giving 'a certain kind of description' of aspects of the cognitive behaviour of practical agents, we do the following two things in order. First we give an analysis of the concepts that are central to the identification and basic description of such behaviour. A conceptual analysis may be interesting in its own right, but on our approach it is also input to a process of formal modelling. The logic in question is a linked partnership between *conceptual models* and *formal models.*[2]

We note in passing that there is nothing in what we are proposing with which to reprove, still less ignore, the extraordinary success of the modern logic of linguistic structures. What it may lack in psychological reality or applicability, it more than compensates for in results that are both indispensable in describing a cognitive agent's resources (for example, his ability to draw *consequences* or his partiality for *consistency*), and of obvious help to the theorist who describes such behaviour. So we disavow entirely the anti-formalist apostasy indulged in by some members of the informal logic community.

[2]So we do not cast our lot with John Cohen: 'if there is such a thing as psychology, it should consist (to paraphrase Bertrand Russell) of propositions which do not occur in any other discipline.' [Cohen, 1972, 9].

We have, in effect, re-pledged ourselves to the proposition that the laws of logic are the laws of thought. We are not alone in this:

> This is a doctrine which was popular in the last [=19th] century, but is now [=1979] very much out of favour. Nevertheless, I think it is true ... My thesis is that laws of logic are like [... scientific laws]. They are laws governing the structure of ideally rational belief systems ... They can be used to explain at least some of the features of ordinary belief systems, and the theory of rational belief systems in which they are embedded provides a framework for determining what remains to be explained about of belief systems. It thus defines a research programme. Ellis, [1979, v]

A logic that is practical in our sense falls within the ambit of the *pragmatic*. Historically, pragmatics is that branch of the theory of signs in which there is irreducible and non-trivial reference to agents, to entities that receive and interpret messages. By an easy extension, a pragmatic theory of reasoning is a theory in which there is express irreducible and non-trivial reference to cognitive agents. If in turn a cognitive agent is conceived of as a certain kind of information-processor, then a pragmatic theory of cognitive agency will provide descriptions of processors of information. Given that a logic is a principled account of certain aspects of practical reasoning, logic too is a pragmatic affair. If we ask, 'which aspects of practical reasoning are the proper province of logic?', we say again that the answer lies in operational arrangements. Practical logic is that part of pragmatics that investigates practical agency from the point of view of properties the logician finds interesting and is adept at analysing and modelling. Thus, again, properties such as implication, deducibility, generalization, relevance, analogy, plausibility and hypothesis, as studied by the methods of conceptual and formal analysis. The present work, *Agenda Relevance*, is an exercise in pragmatics in this sense. Given that the pragmatic enquiry that it triggers is subject to the methods of formal modelling, it may also be said that the book is an exercise in *formal pragmatics*; hence the work's subtitle.

As understood by a number of theorists, pragmatics is always a branch of the investigation of language. In the approach we take here, the importance of language can hardly be gainsaid. But since our emphasis is on cognitive systems, and since there are aspects of cognition that occur sublinguistically (or anyhow, subdoxastically), we are faced with a decision. One option is to reserve the *logic* of cognitive systems for those aspects of cognition that are linguistically manifest and to leave all else to the other branches of cognitive science. The alternative is to include the pre- or sublinguistic in logic's reach. We do not suppose that this is a knockdown argument that decisively dismisses either of these two possibilities. Even so, the choice need not be arbitrary. Counting for the first option is the comparative *manifestness* of language, and the efficiencies engendered by this fact. Counting for the second option is the fact (or apparent fact) that the logician's target properties are also definable for structures that are not in the requisite ways linguistic. So, for example, it appears that some of our inferences are sublinguistic (or subdoxastic) and that, for beings like us, evasions of irrelevant information are largely automatic. Our own inclination, therefore, is to embrace (with appropriate caution) the more generous option. Accordingly, a practical logic is that part of a pragmatic theory that deals with the requisite aspects of practical cognitive agency at both linguistic and sublinguistic levels, and for which a suitably flexible notion of information will prove necessary.

It is well to emphasize that, in taking logic into a practical turn, we are not alone. Our approach, although developed independently, also shows a certain affinity to work done under the rubric of 'the dynamic turn', an approach to logic that emphasizes the 'interfaces with cognitive science, and the experimental study of how information and cognition works in humans once we set ourselves to study the psychological and neurological realities underneath ...' [van Benthem, 2001, p. 5].

Chapter 2

The Practical Logic of Cognitive Systems

> ... [T]he human brain is a highly parallel setup. It has to be.
>
> John Nash, [1954]

2.1 PLCS and Cognitive Systems

The present work is the first volume of *A Practical Logic of Cognitive Systems*. We here concentrate on the analysis of a notion which lies at the very heart of cognitive competence. The notion is relevance, and its centrality is attested to by the considerable facility with which beings like us ignore irrelevancies and 'stay on point' in the performance of our cognitive tasks. In so saying, we have a particular conception of what it is to *be* a cognitive agent, and accordingly, of how we should think of a logic of cognitive agency. Offering a rudimentary description of this logic, *PLCS*, is the principal business of the present chapter.

We wish to lay some emphasis on the fact that we are here attempting to run on two tracks concurrently. We want, of course, to get relevance right. But we also wish to develop *PLCS*, indeed, to embed the theory of relevance in it. For various reasons, both expository and tactical, we do not wade right in with the account of relevance, but rather we devote some time to describing and motivating *PLCS*. Relevance takes over in Chapter 5, and holds centre-stage for the remainder of the book. Readers who are impatient to be getting on with relevance can skip the preamble on *PLCS* and move directly to page 69.

Even so, it is possible to say now in a wholly general and informal way that information is relevant when it helps things get done. *Relevant information is information that is helpful in certain ways.*

We begin with the notion of a cognitive system. Intuitively, a cognitive system is any functioning reader of this book, or institutional agent, such as NASA, The Abductive Systems Group, or present-day neurobiology. Fundamental to the idea of a cognitive agent is that of a being or a device that processes information under conditions that qualifies the output as one or more of a class of states typified by belief restructuring and decision. In so doing, the cognitive agent exploits available cognitive assets or resources, thus facilitating the end-performance. At this stage, there is no reason to assume that cognitive agents are required to possess consciousness or that cognitive processing even by conscious agents needs always to be conscious.

We begin the account of relevance with what Hans Herzberger once called *primordial beliefs* [Herzberger, 1982, p. 133]. Primordial beliefs about something S are those held with such conviction that one is initially prepared to require of any theory of S that it formally sanction them. We say 'initially' because, as is sometimes the case, a theory of S evolves in such a way as to constitute a case for modifying the S-intuition that, so to speak, got the theory up and running in the first place. (A case in point — rather extremely so — is a theory of consciousness that ends up saying or being tempted to say that there is no such thing as consciousness. See e.g. [Dennett, 1988; Lewis, 1990].)

For us there are two primordial intuitions on which we are prepared to found a theory of relevance:

1. Cognition for beings like us is essentially and irreducibly a matter of making economical use of the requisite cognitive resources, which typically are in comparatively short supply.

2. A centrally important factor in the efficiency of cognitive processes is the comparative facility with which beings like us stay on point and evade irrelevance.

'What is wrong with irrelevance?', it might be asked. There is a twofold answer to this question: it impedes the realization of our cognitive goals, and it is *wasteful.*

Having pledged ourselves to the founding intuitions expressed by propositions (1) and (2), it is appropriate that we proceed as follows. We should first endeavour to say something about the cognitive economy in which individual human beings operate. We should then state the theory of relevance, and indicate the ways in which it facilitates the functioning of that economy.

2.2 Practical Reasoning

In one sense, all reasoning is practical.[1] All reasoning terminates in an answer to a question, a solution to a problem, a conclusion from some data, or a decision to postpone the quest until further facts are known; even aborted reasoning ('This is getting us nowhere!') produces a kind of termination.

Ordinary usage, even ordinary philosophical usage, gives little direct guidance for fixing the sense of practical reasoning. It is an expression layered with multiple meanings and suggestive of contrasts, among which are these:

ordinary, common *versus* esoteric, specialized
prudential *versus* alethic
moral *versus* factual
informal *versus* formal
precise *versus* fuzzy
conclusion is an action *versus* conclusion is a proposition
premiss is an action *versus* premiss is a proposition
goal-directed, purposive *versus* context-free
applied *versus* theoretical
concrete *versus* abstract
tolerant of incommensurabilities *versus* not

To these we add a further contrast, to which we think it prudent to take particular note of. It is the contrast of

practical *versus* strict

We illustrate with an example. In the game of (ice) hockey, a hat trick is achieved by a player scoring three consecutive goals against the opposition. (There is a counterpart achievement in cricket.) 'Consecutive' here means 'without any goal being scored between the first and the third of this triple by any of the hat-tricker's team-mates.' This is what a hat-trick is *strictly speaking*. But *in practice*, or for *all practical purposes* (including the triggering of bonus clauses in a player's contract), a hat-trick is just three goals in a game by one and the same player, never mind whether he scores them consecutively in our present sense of that term. So conceived of, practicality is resemblance enough to the real thing to be considered the

[1] There is a philosophical tradition in which a practical reason is reason for an action that involves bodily behaviour. Needless to say, not all reasoning is practical in this sense. We ourselves are disposed to think that practical reasoning in this sense hardly carves out a natural kind, so to speak. (See here, e.g., Velleman [2000]).

real thing. Thus, in one sense, 'practical' means 'approximate'. As we shall shortly see, this captures a part of our own conception of the practical.

2.3 Practical Agency

Ours is an agency view of logic. It betokens, as we said, a return to the Laws of Thought approach. On the agency view, logic is a theory of reasoning, a theory of what thinkers do and have happen to them. Correspondingly, a practical logic is a theory of what practical agents think and reflect upon, cogitate over and decide, and act. If the linguistic conception makes it necessary for the logician to say, with care, what sort of thing a language is, the agency view makes it necessary to say, with care, what sort of thing a practical agent is.

We think of practical agency as a *hierarchy* $\mathcal{H}$ of goal-directed, resource-bound entities A of various types. At the bottom of this hierarchy are individual human beings with minimal efficient access to institutionalized databases. Next up are individual human beings who operate in institutional environments — in colleges or government departments, for example, which themselves are kinds of agents. Then, too, there are teams of such people. Further up are disciplines and other corporate entities such as, again, the NASA or Italian physics in the 1930s. The hierarchy proceeds thus from the concrete to the comparatively abstract, with abstract structures being aggregations of entities lower down. Interesting as this metaphysical fact might be, it is not the dominant organizing principle of the hierarchy. The organizing principle is economic. Entities further up the hierarchy command resources, more and better, than those below are capable of.

So conceived, the hierarchy is a poset of objects partially ordered by the relation C of *commanding greater resources than.*[2]

Every agency in this hierarchy $\mathcal{H} = \langle C, A \rangle$ involves, whether by aggregation or supervenience or in some other way, the individual agent. Such agents are thus basic to any logic of agency, and it is to them that we shall concentrate our attention in the present section.

[2] We note in passing the difference of our hierarchical model from Harry Frankfurt's hierarchical model of autonomous action. On this latter conception, the behaviour that an agent makes happen in the fullest sense of that expression is that which is motivated by a desire which the agent desires to have. See Frankfurt [1988, 58–68]. But cf. Bratman [1999, 185–206].

We also note a resource-sensitive approach to cognitive agency in much of the psychological literature. See Simon [1957] and a, by now, large psychological literature ably reviewed in Stanovich [1999] and Gigerenzer and Selten [2001a].

Like all agents in the hierarchy, the individual is a performer of actions in real time. And nearly everything an individual is faced with doing, or is trying to do, can be done at the wrong time. It can be done at a time so wrong as to court equivalence with not doing it at all, or doing some opposite thing. It is not enough that an agent does the right thing, i.e., performs the right action-types. It is often essential that the right thing be done at the right time. As we look upwards at the agency-hierarchy, we see a diminishing susceptibility to exigent timeliness. No one doubts that NASA had a real deadline to meet in the 1960s, culminating in the moon shot. It might have been that the moon program would have been cancelled had that deadline not been met. Even so, individuals are exposed to myriad serious dangers, many of them mortal, that nothing 'up above' will hardly ever know on this scale; and essential to averting such dangers is doing what is required on time, directed by the right information in appropriate quantitites.

The dominant requirement of timeliness bears directly on a further constraint on individual agency. Individuals wholly fail the economist's conceit of perfect information. Agents such as these must deal with the nuisance not only of less than complete information, but with data-bases that are by turns inconsistent, uncertain, and loosely defined. To these are added the difficulties of real-time computation, limited storage capacity and less than optimal mechanisms for information-retrieval, as well as problems posed by bias and other kinds of psychological affect.

The two great scarcities that the individual must cope with are time and information. It is precisely these that institutional agents command more of, and very often vastly more of. With few (largely artificial) exceptions, the individual agent is a satisficer rather than an optimizer, a fact reflected in our distinction between the practical and the strict, and captured by the example of the hat-trick in hockey. It is also, and more centrally, on evidence in the individual's entrenched disposition to forgo truth-preservation or high levels of conditional probability in favour of rougher standards of what's plausible, which deliver the goods with requisite promptness and directness. For the most part, even seeking to be an optimizer would be tactically maladroit, if not actually harmful. The human agent is also highly sensitive to environmental cues, hence is drawn to adaptive strategies of the fast-and-frugal sort [Gigerenzer and Selten, 2001a]. The fact of the robust, continuing presence of human agents on this Earth amply attests to their effective and efficient command of scarce resources. It is a fact in which is evident the human capacity to compensate for scarcities of time and information.

We postulate that the individual agent embodies a **scare-resource compensation strategy**. Here, in rough outline and in no particular order, are the compensation-factors that strike us as particularly important. But, as a quick word of preface, we must lay some emphasis on the point that, as we use the terms 'scarce-resources' and 'scarcity', we intend only a quantitatively comparative rather than a qualitatively comparative notion of scarcity. When beings like us execute our cognitive agendas, the scarcity of the resources that we draw upon is in the general case simply a matter of their being fewer and less of them than in the general case is available to institutional or theoretical agents. Less and few are are not necessarily matters to regret. The individual agent is not placed at an intrinsic disadvantage under these ordinal and cardinal comparisons, although there are particular cases in which paucity of information or time or fire-power does indeed redound to the agent negatively. In such cases, the harm done by the scarcity is the difficulty it creates for executing the tasks in question against the requisite standards of satisfactory performance. This is an affliction that can apply to agents of all types, and is not a discouragement reserved for individual or practical agents, still less for practical agents *in the general case*. In the general case, the quantitatively comparative resource-scarcities with which the practical agent must deal with are compensated for by the degree of rigour imposed by performance standards appropriate to the kind of agent an individual is.

- Human beings are natural **hasty generalizers**. It was a wise J.S. Mill who observed [Mill, 1974] that the routines of induction are not within the grasp of individuals, but rather are better-suited to the resource capacities of institutions. The received wisdom has it that hasty generalization is a fallacy, a sampling error of one sort or another. The received wisdom may be right, but if it is, individual human agency is fallacy-ridden in degrees that would startle even the traditional fallacy-theorist.[3] Bearing on this question in ways that suggest an answer different from the traditional one is the fact that the individual's hasty generalizations seem not to have served his cognitive and practical agendas all that badly. Upon reflection, in the actual cases in which a disposition towards hasty generalization plays itself out, the generalizations are approximately accurate, rather than fallacious errors, and the decisions taken on their basis are approximately sound, rather than exercises in ineptitude. Not only is the individual agent a hasty generalizer, he is a hasty generalizer who tends to get things more or less right.

- How is it possible that there be a range of cases in which projections

[3]On what we are calling the traditional account of fallacies, hasty generalization is always an error. For a contrary view see Woods [2003].

from samples are so nearly right, while at the same time qualifying as travesties of what the logic of induction requires? The empirical record amply attests to a human being's capacity for pre-inductive generalization and projection. It would appear that exercise of this capacity involves at least these following factors, some of them structural, some of them contextual. The *pre-inductive* generalizer does not generalize to universally quantified conditional propositions. Rather he generalizes to **generic** propositions. There is a world of difference between 'For all x, if x is a tiger then x is four-legged" and "Tigers are four-legged.' The former is falsified by the truth of any negative instance, whereas the latter holds true even in the light of numerous negative instances of certain kinds. We could characterize this difference by saying that universally quantified conditional statements are highly *brittle*, whereas generic statements are *elastic*. Generic propositions are essential to what is sometimes called *stereotypical* reasoning. Clearly not all stereotyped reasoning is defective.

- The elasticity of what the pre-inductive generalizer generalizes to serves the generalizer's interests in other ways, two of which are particularly important. One is that the individual agent is a **fallibilist** in (virtually) everything he thinks and does. The other is that the individual agent has the superficially opposite trait of rather high levels of accuracy in what he thinks and does when operating at the level ordained for him by the hierarchy of agency. Generalizing to generic statements is a way of having your cake and eating it too. It is a way of being right even in the face of true exceptions. It is a way of being both right and mistaken concurrently.

Generalizing in this way also works a substantial economy into the individual's cognitive effort. It comes from the smallness of its samples and the elasticity of its generalizations. Generic inference is inference from small samples under conditions that would make it a fatally stricken induction. We see in this the idea of the affordable mistake. Generic inference is not truth-preserving. One can be wrong about whether Pussy the tiger is four-legged even though one is right in holding that tigers are four-legged. Affordable mistakes are like small infections that help train up the immune system. Just as an infant's summer sniffles is an affordable (in fact, necessary) infection, so too are the small errors of the cognitive agent which provide him evolving guidance as to the freedom and looseness with which to indulge his predilection for comparatively effortless generalizations. Baby's summer cold loops back benignly in the discouragement of more serious illness. Affordable mistakes loop back benignly in the discouragement of serious error. We can now see that the old saw of *learning from our mistakes* has a realistic motivation. We do not learn from mistakes that kill us.

- What is it about such samples that sets them up for successful generic inference? It would appear that the record of generic inference is at its best when samples, small as unit sets though they may be, are samples of **natural kinds**. There has been a good deal of philosophical controversy about whether natural kinds actually exist; about whether the putative difference between natural kinds and conventional kinds turns on a principled metaphysical distinction. Certainly there is nothing like a settled consensus as to how the distinction should be applied. Perhaps this tells against our here using the concept in any particular theory-laden way, but it leaves it open that we introduce it as a term from unanalysed common sense (but see here [Fodor, 1998, chapter 7]). Even so, we should not disdain this literature from psychology and computer science in which concepts resembling that of natural kinds seem to be doing useful work, concepts such as *frame* [Minsky, 1975], *prototype* [Smith and Medin, 1981], and *exemplar* [Rosch, 1978]. Then, too, there is a large literature from linguistics in which the semantics of natural kind noun phrases is intimately bound up with factors of genericity [Krifka *et al.*, 1995, pp. 63–94].

  Philosophical particularities aside, the empirical record testifies to our capacity for classifying sensory stimuli in ways that reflect similarities and differences that strike us as inhering things as they really are. There is ample evidence to suggest that our classifications originate with primitive devices of *type-recognition* together with the mechanisms of fight and flight. It is significant that some of our most successful and most primitive inferences involve the recognition of something as dangerous. Generic inference is part and parcel of such strategies. Just as our capacity for recognizing natural kinds exceeds the comparatively narrow range of immediately dangerous kinds, so too does our capacity for generic inference exceed the reach of fight–flight recognition triggers. But whether in fight–flight contexts or beyond, natural kinds and generic inference are a natural pair. It is an arrangement again favouring the economic — a compensation strategy for the scarcity of time and information — but not noticeably at the cost of error. If generic inferences from natural kind samples are not *quite* right, at least they don't kill us. They don't even keep us from prospering.

- The fallibilism of generic inference is also evident in its relation to **defaults**. A default is something taken as holding, taken to be true, in the absence of indications to the contrary [Reiter, 1980]. It is closely related to and may partially be characterized by a process known as 'negation-as-failure'. Most of what passes for common knowledge is stocked with defaults, and generic inferences in turn are inferences to defaults. Default reasoning is inherently conservative and inherently defeasible. Defeasibility is the cognitive price one pays for conservatism. And the great appeal of conservatism is also economic. Conservatism is populated with defaults in the form 'X is what people have thought up to now, and still do.' Conservatism is a method of default-collection. It bids us to avoid the cost of fresh thinking, and to make do with what others have thought before us (and, experienced and remembered, too).

- Conservatism places a premium on what is already well-received.[4] On the face of it, conservatism is the **ad populum** fallacy in endemic form. Here, too, we might grant the received wisdom (and note the large irony), and concede that individual agents are notorious fallacy-mongers on a scale not dreamed of even by the traditional fallacy theorist. But as we said in our examination of a similar indictment of hasty generalization, there are factors which seem to cut across so harsh a condemnation. One is that we are, by and large, enormously well-served by the trust we place in the testimony of others. This needs to be understood. The full account, even if we could furnish it, is beyond the scope of this chapter, but certain features stand out, and should be mentioned. Popular beliefs are what Aristotle called *endoxa*. They are 'reputable opinions', the opinions of everyone or of the many or of the wise. The mere fact of popular opinion triggers an abduction problem. What best explains that p is a proposition believed by everyone? An answer, which certainly can be criticized in respect of certain particular details, but which cannot convincingly be set up for general condemnation is that p's universal acceptance is best explained by supposing that p is true or that a belief in p is reliable. What is loosely called common knowledge is an individual's (or an institution's or a society's) inventory of endoxa. What is especially striking about common knowledge is that it is acquired by an individual with little or no demonstrative effort on his own part, and with attendant economies of proportional yield.

[4] Notwithstanding the joke in which 'a Conservative is one who is enamoured of existing perils, as distinguished from the Liberal, who wishes to replace them with others.' (Ambrose Bierce, *The Devil's Dictionary*).

- It is evident therefore that individual agents depend for what they think and how they act upon the sayso of others, on the more or less uncritical and unreflective testimony of people who by and large are strangers. Here is yet another respect in which the conduct of human agents would seem to fall foul of the received opinion of fallacy theorists (let us not forget that the *endoxa* of the wise are not guaranteed to be true!). For it would appear that individual agents are programmed to commit and implement the programme on a large scale, the **ad verecundiam** fallacy. But as before, the actual record of thoughts and actions produced by such dependencies is rather good; most of what we think in such ways is not especially inaccurate and, in any case, not inaccurate enough to have made a mess of the quotidian lives of human individuals. We may suppose, therefore, that the traditional fallacies of hasty generalization, *ad populum* and *ad verecundiam* are hardly fallacious as such (e.g., when considered as an individual's strategies or components of strategies for practical action), but are fallacies only under certain conditions. We shall return to this point below.

It has long been known that human life is dominantly social, and that individual agents find cooperation to be almost as natural as breathing. The routines of cooperation transmit to an individual nearly all of the community's common knowledge that he will ever possess. Even though the complete story has yet to be told, cooperation has received the attention of attractive and insightful theories (e.g. [Axelrod, 1984; Coady, 1992] and [Govier, 1988b]).

There is a natural and intuitive contrast between accepting something on the sayso of others and working it out for oneself. Cross-cutting this same distinction is the further contrast between accepting something without direct evidence, or any degree of verification or demonstrative effort on the accepter's part, and accepting something only after having made or considered a case for it. The two distinctions are not equivalent, but they come together overlappingly in ways that produce for individual agents substantial further economies.

Perhaps this is the point at which to emphasize that in our conception the individual is not the artefact of the same name championed by European thinkers of the seventeenth and eighteenth centuries. We demur from the notion (the decidedly odd notion, as we see it) that an individual's social relationships are merely contingent to his rationality. On the contrary, an individual's cognitive and decisional competence is in significant part constituted by his social relationships.

If this is right, it will matter for what we take a logic of individual cognitive and decisional agency to be. We will have more to say on this later, but will note in passing the prima facie attractions of a dialogue logic, as a formalized description of the individual agent.

Such additional economies are the output of two regularities evident in the social intercourse of agents. One has been dubbed the reason rule:

> *Reason Rule*: One party's expressed beliefs and wants are a *prima facie* reason for another party to come to have those beliefs and wants and, thereby, for those beliefs and wants to structure the range of appropriate utterances that party can contribute to the conversation. If a speaker expresses belief X, and the hearer neither believes nor disbelieves X, then the speaker's expressed belief in X is reason for the hearer to believe X and to make his or her contributions conform to that belief. [Jacobs and Jackson, 1983, 57], [1996, 103].

The reason rule reports an empirical regularity in communities of real-life discussants. Where the rule states that a person's acceptance of a proposition is reason for a second party to accept it, it is clear that 'reason' means 'is taken as reason' by the second party. Thus a descriptively adequate theory will observe the Jacobs–Jackson regularities as a matter of empirical fact. This leaves the question of whether anything good can be said for these regularities from a normative perspective. If normativity is understood as a matter of instrumental value, it would appear that the reason rule can claim some degree of normative legitimacy. Not only does it produce substantial economies of time and information, it seems in general not to overwhelm agents with massive error or inducements to do silly or destructive things. The reason rule describes a default. Like all defaults, it is defeasible. Like most defaults, it is a conserver of scare resources. And like many defaults, it seems to do comparatively little cognitive and decisional harm.

There is a corollary to the reason rule. We call it the *ad ignorantiam* rule:

> *Ad Ignorantiam Rule*: Human agents tend to accept without challenge the utterances and arguments of others except where they know or think they know or suspect that something is amiss, or when not challenging involves some cost to themselves.

Here, too, a good part of what motivates the *ad ignorantiam* rule in human affairs is economic. People don't have time to mount challenges every time someone says something or forwards a conclusion without reasons that are transparent to the addressee. Even when reasons are given, social psychologists have discovered that addressees tend not to scrutinize these reasons before accepting the conclusions they are said to endorse. Addressees tend to do one or other of two different things before weighing up proffered reasons. They tend to accept this other party's conclusions if it is something that strikes them as *plausible*. They also tend to accept the other party's conclusion if it seems to them that this is a conclusion which is within that party's competence to make — that is, if he is seen as being in a position to know what he is talking about, or if he is taken to possess the requisite expertise or authority. (See, e.g., [Petty and Cacioppo, 1986; Eagly and Chaiken, 1993; Petty *et al.*, 1981; Axsom *et al.*, 1987; O'Keefe, 1990], and the classic paper on the atmosphere effect, [Woodworth and Sells, 1935]. But see also [Jacobs *et al.*, 1985].) We see, once again, the sheer ubiquity of what traditionalists would call — overhastily in our view — the *ad verecundiam* fallacy.

- We see the individual agent as a processor of information on the basis of which, among other things, he thinks and acts. Researchers interested in the behaviour of information-processors tend to suppose that thinking and deliberate action are modes of **consciousness**. Studies in information theory suggest a different view. Consciousness has a narrow bandwidth. It processes information very slowly. The rate of processing from the five senses combined — the sensorsium, as the Mediaevals used to say — is in the neighbourhood of 11 million bits per second. For any of those seconds, something fewer than 40 bits make their way into consciousness. Consciousness therefore is highly entropic, a thermodynamically costly state for a human system to be in. At any given time there is an extraordinary quantity of information processed by the human system, which consciousness cannot gain access to. Equally, the bandwidth of language is far narrower than the bandwidth of sensation. A great deal of what we know — most in fact — we aren't able to tell one another. Our sociolinguistic intercourse is a series of exchanges whose bandwidth is 16 bits per second [Zimmermann, 1989].

  Conscious experience is dominantly linear. Human beings are notoriously ill-adept at being in multiples of conscious states at once. And time flows. Taken together these facts loosely amount to an operational definition of the linearity of consciousness. Linearity plays a role in the cognitive economy that tight money plays in the real economy. It slows things down and it simplifies them. Linearity is a suppressor of complexity; and reductions in complexity coincide with reductions in information.[5]

Psychological studies indicate that most of our waking actions are unattended by and unshaped by mental states.[6] This mindlessness of ordinary waking human behaviour is a kind of coping. Consider a case in which we are watching a short-order cook working at full blast at midday in New York. It is easy to see his behaviour as connectionist and mindless, as behaviour reflecting repertories of different skills which he draws upon concurrently and distributively, and without a jot of reflection when things are going well.

If these psychological studies are right, the received view is wrong. Conversation would just be linguistic coping. If so, the individual discussants are less often in a state of belief than many theorists suppose; and when someone is telling us, say, about the amenities of Amsterdam, though he tells us the truth, he is not transmitting any current mental state and he is not inducing new mental states in us, unless perhaps what he tells us is surprising. When we stop and think — when we put a temporary (and expensive) halt to coping — we find that in what we do in the world we are infrequently the owner of mental states, infrequently the possessor of beliefs. It is a respectable way of being mindless.

It is now evident that we must amend the claim that individual agents suffer from a scarcity of information. In so doing, however, we are able to lend appropriate emphasis to what remains true about that proposition. In pre- or subconscious states, human systems are awash in information. Consciousness serves as an aggressive suppressor of information, preserving radically small percentages of amounts available pre-consciously. To the extent that some of an individual's thinking and decision-making are subconscious, it is necessary to postulate devices that avoid the distortion, indeed the collapse, of information overload. Even at the conscious level, it is apparent that various

[5]We note in passing that the sheer paucity of information possessed by human consciousness at any given time contrasts with environments known to be fuzzy. Fuzziness, unlike probability, is unchanged by arbitrarily large increases in information.

[6]This is not a claim that everyone would endorse. Some would insist on the qualification 'conscious'. Advocates of Intentional Psychology (*IP*) tend to see such behaviour as caused by propositional attitudes, whose presence does not invariably require consciousness.

constraints are at work to inhibit or prevent informational surfeit. The conscious human thinker and actor cannot have, and could not handle if he did have, information that significantly exceeded the limitations we have been discussing. This makes the economic aspect of an agent's conscious thought and action an *ecosystemic* matter as well [Gigerenzer and Selten, 2001b, 9]. Human beings make do with slight information because this is all the information that a conscious individual can have.

Human agents make do with scarce information and scarce time. They do so in ways that make it apparent that in the general case they are disposed to settle for *comparative* accuracy and *comparative* sensibleness of action. These are not the ways of error-avoidance. They are the ways of fallibilism. Error-avoidance strategies cost time and information, except where they are trivial. The actual strategies of individual agents cannot afford the costs and, in consequence, are risky. As we now see, the propensity for risk-taking is a structural feature of consciousness itself. It might strike us initially that our fidelity to the reason rule convicts us of gullibility and that our fidelity to the *ad ignorantiam* rule shows us to be lazily irrational. These criticisms are misconceived. The reason rule and the *ad ignorantiam* rule are strategies for minimizing information overload, as is our disposition to generalize hastily.

Consciousness makes for informational niggardliness. This matters for computer simulations of human reasoning. That is, it matters that there is no way presently or foreseeably available of simulating or mechanizing consciousness. Institutional agencies do not possess consciousness in anything like the sense we have been discussing. This makes it explicable that computer simulations of human thinking fit institutional thinking better than that of an individual. This is not to say that nothing is known of how to proceed with the mechanization of an individual's conscious thinking. We know, for example, that the simulation cannot process information in quantities significantly larger than those we have been discussing here.

Consciousness is a controversial matter in contemporary cognitive science. It is widely accepted that information carries negative entropy. Against this is the claim that the concept of information is used in ways that confuse the technical and common sense meanings of that word, and that talk of information's negative entropy overlooks the fact that the systems to which thermodynamic principles apply with greatest sure-footedness are *closed*, and that human agents are not.

The complaint against the over-liberal use of the concept of information, in which even physics is an information system (Wolfram [1984]), is that it makes it impossible to explain the distinction between energy-to-energy transductions and energy-to-information transformations. Also singled out for criticism is the related view that consciousness arises from neural processes. We ourselves are not insensitive to such issues. They are in their various ways manifestations of the classical mind–body problem. We have no solution to the mind–body problem, but there is no disgrace in that. The mind–machine problem resembles the vexations of mind–body, both as to difficulty and to type. We have no solution to the mind–machine difficulty. There is no disgrace in that either.

For individual agents it is a default of central importance that most of what they experience, most of what is offered them for acceptance or action, stands in no need of scrutiny. Information-theoretic investigations take this point a step further in the suggestion that consciousness itself is a response to something disturbing or at least peculiar enough to be an interruption, a demand — so to speak — to pay attention.

Most of the information processed by an individual agent he will not attend to, and even if it is the object of his consciousness he will attend to in as little detail as the exigensies of his situation allow. Arguing is a statistically non-standard kind of practice for human agents, but even when engaged in it is characterized by incompletions and short-cuts that qualify for the name of enthymeme. The same is true of reasoning, of trying to get to the bottom of things. In the general case, the individual reasoner will deploy the fewest resources that produce a result which satisfies him. Here is further evidence that individuals display a form of rationality sometimes called 'minimal', [Cherniak, 1986],[7] or 'bounded' [Gigerenzer and Selten, 2001a]. In addition to features already discussed in this chapter, the minimal or bounded rationalist is, when he reasons at all, a non-monotonic reasoner and in ways that are mainly automatic, the successful manger of belief-sets and commitment-sets that are routinely inconsistent. Much of what makes for the inconsistency of belief-sets comes from the inconsistency of deep memory storage and further aspects of inconsistent belief-sets flow from the inefficiencies of memory retrieval.

The structure of minimal or bounded rationality shows the individual agent to be the organic realization of a non-monotonic, paraconsistent base

[7]In fact, it is better thought of as *minimalist* rationality, the rationality involved in making do with scarce resources.

logic, features which our logic must take care to embed. There is little to suggest that the strategies endorsed by classical logic and most going non-standard logics form more than a very small part of the individual agent's repertoire of cognitive and coping skills. If it is true that individuals are in matters of non-demonstrative import *pre*-inductive rather than inductive agents, the same would also appear to be the case as regards deduction. If so, human individuals are not the wet-wear for deductive logic, at least in the versions that have surfaced in serious ways in the sprawling research programmes of modern logic. There is a particularly interesting reason for this. If we ask what the value of deductive consequence is, the answer is that it is a guarantee of truth-preservation. Guaranteed truth-preservation is a guaranteed way of avoiding error.[8] But individual agents are not in the general case dedicated to error-avoidance. So for the most part the routines of deduction consequence do not serve the individual agent in the ways in which he is disposed (and programmed) to lead his cognitive and decisional life. This is not to say that agents do not perform deductive tasks even when performing on the ground level of our hierarchy. There is a huge psychological literature about such behaviour (accessibly summarized in Manktelow [1999]) and the point rather is that deductive thinking is so small a part of the individual's reasoning repertoire.

2.4 Practical Logics

In our description of it so far, we have left the theory of practical reasoning a fairly underdetermined affair. There is a desirable utility in such flexibility. We leave ourselves free to consider the pros and cons of extending or adapting our approach in many possible ways, and in so doing availing ourselves of the benefit of work already done and on the record. There is a lot of it, too, whether temporal logics (e.g., van Benthem [1991]), logics of action (e.g., Davidson [1980], Brand and Walton [1975], Brand [1984]), dynamic logic (e.g. van Benthem [1996], van Benthem *et al.* [2001] and Gochet [2002]), not to forget the huge literature on deontic logic, and the practical logics of the early pragmatic philosophers (e.g., Dewey [1938] and Schiller [1912]).

There are multiples of different ways of finishing a theoretical product from its relatively modest beginnings as a logic supplemented by designated resources for the treatment of action and time. This leaves the research community with multiples of chances of coming up with finished products

[8] That is, of avoiding errors not already in his database or his premiss-set or which follows from false prior information.

that receive and deserve consensus of a sort that we do not yet see much in evidence. Even so, it is an attraction of our approach that it serves the desirable end, and achieves the welcome economy, of a principled and modest shortening of the list of attributes on whose behalf the adjective 'practical' is invoked. If we return to the list developed in section 2.2 of the present chapter, it is clear that our logic sanctions some deletions.

A practical logic in our sense is not restricted to the study of reasoning about ordinary or commonplace matters. Nothing precludes the practical reasoner rushing to finish an arcane proof under press of his publisher's deadline.

A practical logic in our sense is no enemy of the alethic or truth-oriented. For example, there is a well-understood role in dialogue logic for parties to enhance their shared databases. In so doing they increase their resources for making more direct cases for various actions.

Practical logic pertains to moral reasoning but is not restricted to it. Nor does it exclude factual reasoning. (See above.)

Practical logic is no enemy of formality. Where appropriate it can involve express manipulation of logical forms; and even where reasoning is not formal in so sharply structural a way, practical logic is amenable to other grades of formal treatment. (Woods [1980], [1989], [2003, Chapter 15], van Eemeren et al. [1996]; cf. Johnson [1996, 120]).

Practical logic is not inherently about fuzzy reasoning, but can be extended to a fuzzy logic (e.g., Zadeh [1975], Chang and Lee [1975], Lee [1972], Przelecki [1976] and Hájek [1998]) or to a logic of vagueness (e.g. Tye [1990], Williamson [1994]) in those cases in which reasoning requires attending to in a more or less direct way the fuzziness of terms or, to fuzzy states of affairs. There are those who argue that practical reasoning is inherently fuzzy in just this sense. In our view this is an open question. (See, e.g., Woods [2000].)

Practical logic subsumes but is not restricted to what Aristotle calls practical syllogisms. The same is true for the adaptation of the same idea in Gabbay and Woods [1999]. In a practical logic of the kind under review, a move in a dialogue always occasions an action by the other party, even though his action needn't be the action, if any, implied or suggested by his *vis-à-vis* premisses. For example, one party may say to the other: 'So, you see, you ought to mow the lawn now.' One way for the second party to react to that move is to start mowing the lawn. This is an explicit action that will also serve as implicit acceptance of his interlocutor's claim. Or he might reply, 'Yes, I really should be mowing the lawn,' which is explicit acceptance and intimation of an action yet to be taken. A third answer is 'Like hell!' which is an explicit (and emphatic) rejection. A fourth is phoning a friend to arrange for a golf game, which is explicitly not mowing the lawn and implicit rejection of the argument that called for it.

Neither do we think that practical logic should be reserved for reasoning involving incommensurabilities. Incommensurability is ambiguous (Gray [2000]). In its most basic sense, reasoning from incommensurabilities is reasoning of a *pluralistic* kind. It is illustrated by the following schema.

1. Harry and Sarah value both friendship and patriotism.

2. Friendship and patriotism though different, and sometimes behaviourally non-co-satisfiable, are incomparable values.

3. In circumstances K, Harry opted for friendship and Sarah for patriotism.

4. Both acted rightly. Period.

It is true that normative reasoning is often occasion for judgements of incommensurability, but this is also sometimes true of scientific thinking. Pluralism abounds in logic, for example. And paraconsistent logics have been purpose-built to accommodate incommensurabilities (in the form of outright inconsistencies) whether in set theory or quantum mechanics (Priest [1998], and Brown [1993]). However, the incommensurability view of practicality intersects with our own conception, in the following way. Sometimes when faced with an incommensurability or an inconsistency, the practical (i.e., individual) agent has no realistic option but to let it be. He may lack the resources to adjust his database for consistency, which puts him in a situation in which he must think or act *in spite* of inconsistency. On the other hand, the very resources that an individual agent sometimes lacks are progressively available to agents of higher type.

The only interpretation that we ourselves are able to give the applied *versus* theoretical distinction in practical logic is one of the following inequivalent pair. First is the distinction between reasoning in a fully interpreted as opposed to a merely semi-interpreted vocabulary. To achieve its generality economically, a practical logic may operate with a semi-interpreted object language. But it will also have the means of giving its theorems full interpretations. (This is tricky. No such procedure will preserve formal invalidity. See here [Woods, 2003, chapter 15].) The second way of drawing our present distinction is to see it as an instance of a particular way of construing the descriptive-normative distinction. In a widely accepted view of this latter, the task of finding a descriptive application of a normative theory is a matter of (a) finding the discrepancies between them, and (b) accounting for the descriptive deviations as approximations to the ideal conditions, full compliance with which would qualify as normatively perfect performance.

Unless we are mistaken, the sense we have proposed to give our logic offers guidance on the applicability of other distinctions appropriated by those intent on giving 'practical' some principled meaning. The purported distinction between concrete and abstract is handled by what we have said about the applied-theoretic distinction. Also there covered is the distinction between unregimented language and canonical notation. The distinction between a natural logic and an artificial logic can be captured by the distinction just mentioned. Alternatively it is the distinction between the psychologically real and the psychologically ideal, which we have already discussed.

There is also an intuitive distinction between tasks whose performance requires little or no tutelage and those whose performance require specialized technical information. Cutting across this distinction, but in ways that produce some degree of overlap, is the contrast between ordinary and esoteric subject matters. If we wanted the distinction between practical and theoretical logics to be constrained by these contrasts, they would push in somewhat different directions; and formal logics such as first order quantification theory would elude classification altogether. We ourselves see little appeal in the first of these proposed criteria. A logic that attempted to give some insight into what goes on when an individual attempts to solve the Four Colour Problem is as much a practical logic as any that attempts to elucidate an agent's choice of breakfast cereal. Neither are we persuaded that, for our purposes here, there is any abiding value in the contrast between the ordinary and everyday and (say) the business of quantum non-locality in physics. A more fruitful way of drawing the contrast between a practical and theoretical logic is by piggy-backing on our distinction between a practical and a theoretical agent. The value of so doing (apart from the naturalness of the concurrence) is that it is very much less necessary to discredit a logic for its failure to model realistically actual human behaviour. Most mainstream logic since 1879, and most direct rivals of it, are subject to this failure. They fail for the most part because their strategies are too complex for the computational capacities of human individuals or, because their latitude in other respects (e.g., monotonicity) exceeds actual human reach. True, some mitigation of these misrepresentations can be found in the notion of idealization; but idealization is a more fraught device than is usually recognized (one cannot idealize at will). Even so, many of these logics, which fail as principled descriptions of what human individuals are capable of, succeed or come closer to succeeding as formalized accounts of what *institutional* agents are capable of. So a decision to regulate the distinction between practical and theoretical logics in this way has the virtue, even on an idealized agent approach to logic, of saving much of what fails as a practical logic as what succeeds as a theoretical logic.

We have already said that we find ourselves somewhat vexed by the descriptive–normative distinction in logic. As we bring this section to a close, it would be helpful if we could briefly shed some light on our reservation.

2.4.1 The Method of Intuitions

There is a considerable body of opinion in the century and a quarter since 1879 that a logician's job is axiomatization and that axioms are what the logician finds to be most intuitive. Much the same view can be found among logicians who favour natural deduction approaches. Here, too, one's choice of structural and operational rules is seen as a matter of what strikes the theorist as most intuitively correct. Much the same *modus operandi* is evident in other disciplines, especially abstract disciplines that lack — in any direct way anyhow — empirical checkpoints. In philosophy this approach is the heart and soul of conceptual analysis in the manner of G.E. Moore and an entire generation which fell under his influence.

The method of analytic intuitions raises a fundamental methodological question. Given that an intuition is what the theorist antecedently believes, and that a fundamental intuition is what he believes utterly, is there any good reason to suppose that intuitions are *epistemically privileged*? Is there any reason to suppose that what the theorist believes utterly qualifies as knowledge? If the answer is Yes, the essential methods of conceptual analysis are confirmed. If the answer is No, the methodology of the abstract sciences must take this into account.

One attraction of the method of analytic intuitions in logic is that it secures a comfortable purchase on the shelf of normativity. It allows for it to be the case that a human being *should* reason in such-and-such a way, if the logician-theorist's intuitions lend support to a rule or a theorem to the same effect. But shorne of the comforts of the method of analytic intuitions, the normatively minded logician will find less desired normativity a lot more difficult to get a sure grip on. It may be that such a theorist would be well-served in taking the following approach.

> First, he might try to make this account conform closely to how in the general case practical agents actually perform under the conditions the theory takes note of.
>
> Secondly, he might also try to take note of what in actual practice is regarded as mistakes or errors.

If he does both these things, we will say that his account is *descriptively adequate*. The sixty-four dollar question is whether:

> the theorist obtains a serviceable standard of normativity by putting it that a practical agent performs as he should if his performance conforms to what his fellows do and is not marred by mistakes in the sense of a paragraph ago. The answer is that we propose is strongly in the affirmative.

There is an ancient way of characterizing the practical. It is to be found in the contrast between Practical and Theoretical Reason, between *phronesis* and *epistēmē*. Perhaps we now have the wherewithal to characterize this contrast in ways that would be found credible by present-day readers. Accordingly, we repeat our proposal that Practical Reason be thought of as a repertoire of skills characteristic of the lower strata in the hierarchy of agency, that Theoretical Reason be thought of as sets of skills characteristic of higher up, and that the contrast be seen as a matter of degree — a matter of how low down and how high up the agent in question chances to be. Here is a suggestion which preserves the truth that *all* reasoning is goal-directed, that all reasoning portends *some* kind of action. But it allows us to cross-cut this universality with considerations of indigenous import, in which Practical Reason is characterized by features of the *agent* whose reasoning it is.

It is also well to emphasize that we are taking the agency view of logic, as opposed to the disembodied linguistic view. The distinctions we have been tracking and the exclusions we have been proposing, have been transacted within the tent of agency logic. Agency logic is the natural home of practical logic, and offers reasonable accommodation to one reasonable conception of theoretical logic. However, it is not our view that the linguistic conception of logic should be rejected. There is nothing good to be said for the idea that we should say no to recursion theory, model theory, proof theory and set theory. This is a book about the practical turn in logic. It obliges us to give sense to what is practical and to give some idea as to where the idea of the practical is best pursued by logical theory. In the end, it is this question which we bring to the distinction between the agency and linguistic conceptions of logic. And, with respect to the matters that concern us here, it is our view that an agency logic is a natural home for practical reasoning and that embodied linguistic logic is not. But saying so is a long way from pleading the exclusion of linguistic logic. We shall amply attest to this assurance when, in Part III of this book, we produce formal models of relevance. (So we aren't looking for a fight with champions of mainstream post-Frege logic!)

2.5 Allied Disciplines

In absorbing the dialogical approach to practical reasoning, we are free to engage — to appropriate or adapt — a large research literature. Dialogue logics come in a variety of stripes, some of the most interesting of which are Hamblin [1970], Lorenzen and Lorenz [1978], Barth and Krabbe [1982], Carlsen [1982], MacKenzie [1990], Walton and Krabbe [1995], Girle [1993], [1996], [1997], and Gabbay and Woods [2001] and [2001d]. A bounty of rich resources also arises from developments in cognitive science, AI and linguistics.

We take it as obvious that, irrespective of how we finally settle the question of the normative–descriptive distinction for theories of practical reasoning, it would be a mistake to ignore developments in these allied disciplines. For example, consider the impact of psychology. The psychological studies to date have concentrated on deductive, and probabilistic and inductive reasoning, with somewhat less attention given to decisional and causal reasoning. There is no simple dominant paradigm at present; in fact, there are at least four main approaches that are currently in contention. These are the *mental models* account (e.g., Johnson-Laird and Byrne [1991]), *mental logics* (e.g., Rips [1994]), *rational analysis and information gain* (e.g., Chater and Oaksford [1999], Oakford, Chater, Grainger and Larkin [1997]), and *domain specific reasoning schemas* (e.g., Evans and Over [1996]). Notwithstanding these theoretical and methodological differences, experimental evidence bears on the business of practical reasoning in two especially telling ways. One is that human beings do indeed seem disposed to commit fallacies, that is, errors of reasoning which are widely and cross-culturally made, easy to make and attractive, and difficult to correct. (Woods [1992]). A second point is that human reasoning performance seems to improve, that is, to commit fewer fallacies, when the reasoning in question is set in a deontic-context (Cheng and Holyoak [1985]). 'Deontic' here means directed to or productive of an action, which is the core sense of our notion of practicality. Since our *PLCS* is already moored in deontic and prudential contexts, a mature theory which is an extension of it must try to explain what is and what isn't a fallacy in a deontic environment or in a practical reasoning task, and why theoretical reasoning should be more prone to fallacies than practical reasoning. It is entirely possible that some of this difference lies in the fact that one and the same strategy might be a reasoning error in a non-practical context of reasoning, and yet be an error-free strategy deontically. (Gabbay and Woods [1999], [2004a].)

A practical logic should also incorporate important developments in the AI sector. It should exploit the fact that human reasoning is non-monotonic and that non-monotonic structures have been investigated by AI researchers (e.g., Geffner [1992] and Pereira [2002]). Human reasoners are also adept at recognizing and manipulating defaults. A default is something taken as true provisionally or, as is said, in default of information to the contrary (Reiter [1980]). Default reasoning introduces into the business of human inference some extraordinary economies, which a practical logic must take pains with. For reasoning is good not only when it produces the right answer, but when it produces it on time. As a related development from linguistics, generic inference discloses its thinking to default reasoning. Generic claims are generalizations of a particularly elastic kind. Like 'Tigers are four-legged,' they tolerate true negative-instances (Carlson and Pelletier [1995]). They also seem triggered by very small samples, as we have seen. The two features are linked. Somehow human beings are rigged for what classically would be seen as hasty generalization fallacies in precisely these cases in which the reasoner is not generalizing to a universally quantified conditional (which is as brittle as a generic generalization is elastic), but rather to a generalization certain negative instances of which happen not to matter.

It is easy to see how default reasoning and generic inference touch on the classical fallacy of hasty generalization, and necessitate a substantial reconsideration of its traditional analysis. Other forms of default reasoning pertain in the same way to the classical fallacy *argumentum ad ignorantiam*. The basic structure of the fallacy is the (invalid) argument form:

1. It is not known that P
2. Therefore not P.

On the standard analysis, *ad ignoratiam* arguments are not only deductively invalid, but wholly implausible as well. But as studies of autoepistemic reasoning show (e.g.,) there are non-deductive exceptions to so harsh a verdict, as witness:

1. If there were a Department meeting today, I would know about it.
2. But in fact I know nothing of any such meeting.
3. So, it can reasonably be supposed that there'll be no meeting.

Here is further occasion for a mature theory of practical reasoning to winnow out the mistakes in classical accounts of fallacious reasoning (concerning which see Gabbay and Woods [2005]).

2.6 Psychologism

In our conception of a practical, agent-oriented, resource-based logic, we have not honoured every stricture against psychologism. Critics of, for example, the logic of discovery, those who think it a misbegotten enterprise as such, are drawn to the idea that accounts of how people entertain and select hypotheses, form and deploy conjectures, and more generally how they think things up, are a matter for psychology. Underlying this view is something like the following argument. Let **K** be a class of cognitive actions. Then if **K** possesses an etiology (i.e., a causal ancestry), this precludes the question of the performing or disperforming the **K**-action for good or bad reasons. If there *were* a logic of **K**-action it would be an enquiry into when **K**-actions are performed rationally, that is, for the right reasons. Hence there can be no logic of **K**.

Against this Donald Davidson is widely taken as having shown that far from reasons for actions precluding their having causes, reasons *are* causes, or more carefully, *having a reason* for an action is construable as a cause of it. ([Davidson, 1963]. See also [Pietroski, 2000] to the same effect.)[9]

We ourselves are inclined to emphasize a substantial body of work in reliabilist and other forms of causal epistemology. In its most basic form, a subject performs a cognitive action rationally when his performance of it was induced by causal mechanisms that are functioning reliably, that are functioning as they should.

We would do well, even so, to take brief note of a possible objection. If the aspects of cognition in which a logician could be expected to take an interest are often a matter of being in the right psychological state, and if such states are sometimes the output of causal mechanisms unattended by either attention or effort on the agent's part, how can this be squared with our view of logic as a principled description of (aspects of) what a logical agent *does*? Our answer is that just as we deny that there is an inherent incompatibility between reasons and causes, neither do we find any essential incompatibility between being in a causally induced mental state in whose attainment the agent played no intentional role and being the subject of admissible answers to questions such as 'What is X *doing*?' (answer: 'He is thinking that P'), and 'What was X *doing* that he came to be in state S?' (answer: 'He was looking at Harry's Corot print'). In a quite general way, whenever there is something that an agent is doing, there are constituent happenings, not all of which qualify to be described as what X is doing,

[9]Another approach to the reasons–causes issue is that of *agent causation*, skillfully developed in [O'Connor, 2001]. While we do not adopt this view here, we recognize it as an attractive alternative.

which might nevertheless enter into the description of what *does* qualify for the designation 'what X is doing'.

The idea of logic as a theory of rational performance runs into a different, though related, objection. The trouble with such a view of logic, it is said, is that it commits us to *psychologism*, and psychologism is false.

Anti-psychologism is not a single, stable thesis. It is at least three pairwise inequivalent propositions.

1. In one sense, it is the case made by the argument we have just re-examined and rejected.

2. In another sense, it is the view that although logic deals with the canons of right reasoning, no law of logic is contradicted by any psychological law or psychological fact.

3. In a third and more emphatic sense, it is the view that logic has nothing whatever to do with how people do reason or should.[10]

Having dealt with anti-psychologism in the first sense, it remains to say something about the other two. Sense number two need not detain us long. It is a view of anti-psychologism which is accepted by logicians who take a traditionally normative view of logic. On this view, psychology is purely descriptive, and logic is purely prescriptive. Hence the laws of logic remain true even in the face of massive misperformance on the ground. On the other hand, those who plump for reliabilist theories of rational performance will reject anti-psychologism in its present sense, just as they reject it in sense number one.

This leaves the third conception, the idea that logic has nothing to do, normatively or descriptively, with how human beings — or other kinds of cognitive agents, if any — think and reason. It is a view with an oddly old-fashioned ring to it, suggesting a position which simply has been overtaken by events of the past quarter century, referred to collectively by the

[10]It is interesting that the case which Frege actually pressed against psychological methods in logic are not transparently present in the trio of interpretations currently in review. In Frege [1884] and subsequent works, Frege's resistance was twofold, as was mentioned in the Preface of this book. First, if psychological methods were engaged in such a way as to make mathematics an experimental science, then those methods should be eschewed or anyhow not deployed in such ways. Second, if psychological methods were engaged in such a way that mathematics lost its intersubjective character, then psychological methods should be either abandoned or not employed in such ways. It bears on the present point that whereas Boole was a psychologicist about logic, and whereas Frege was a critic of Boole, Frege never criticized Boole for his psychologism. Logic for Boole is not a matter of how people *actually* think but rather is a normative account of the correct use of reasoning [Boole, 1854, pp. 4 and 32].

founding editor of the *Journal of Logic and Computation* as 'the new logic'. He writes:

> Let me conclude by explaining our perception of the meaning of the word 'Logic' in the title of this Journal. We do not mean 'Logic' as it is now. We mean 'Logic', as it will be, as a result of the interaction with computing. It covers the new stage of the evolution in logic. It is the new logic we are thinking of.
>
> [Gabbay, 1990]

Twelve years on, the editor's prediction has been met with considerable confirmation, and then some. The buds of the early 1980s have in numerous instances achieved full flower. Non-monotonic logics, default logics, labelled deductive systems, fibring logics, multidimensional, multimodal and substructural logics are now better established and methodologically more self-aware than they were even a decade ago. Intensive re-examinations of fragments of classical logic have produced fresh insights, including at times, decision procedures for and equivalency with non-classical systems. Perhaps the most impressive achievement of the new logic as arising in the past decade or so has been the effective negotiation of research partnerships with fallacy theory, the logic of natural language reasoning and argumentation theory.[11]

The new logic, the logic born of the application of the procedural sophistication of mathematical logic to the project of informal logic, has triggered the very rapprochement that mathematical logic was not structured to deliver or to seek. The new logic, whatever its multifarious differences of mission and detail, has sought for mathematically describable models of what human agents actually do in real-life situations when they cogitated, reflected, calculated and decided. Here was an approach that would in an essential way take what mathematical logic would see as inert context into the theory itself, where it would be directly engaged by the ensuing formalisms.

If psychologism is the view that logic has something to do with how beings like us think and reason, then we are psychologicists. But we are psychologicists of an ecumenical bent which counsels the theoretical rapprochement of logic more narrowly conceived with cognitive science and computer science. It is an approach to logic which leaves it an open research programme as to whether there might be a satisfactory logic of discovery.

In so saying, we do not place ourselves squarely in or squarely out of the ambit of our interpretations of psychologism (save the first). In particular,

[11]Attested to, for example, by the Netherlands Royal Academy Conference in Logic and Argumentation in 1995, and the two Bonn Conferences in Practical Reasoning in 1996 and 1997, and the De Morgan Conference on Logic, held in London annually since 1999.

we have not expressly declared ourselves on what might be called *Boole's question*. Is our approach one in which how people do reason is ignored in favour of how they should reason? Our answer at this stage is somewhat equivocal, but it is the best we can do for now: *we have doubts about the purported exclusiveness of this very distinction.*

2.6.1 Issues in Cognitive Science

The psychologism of our approach to logic places us in a nettle of contentious and unresolved issues in the philosophy of psychology and cognitive science. Exposure to these issues would be nothing if not tactically maladroit except for the various psychological indispensabilities to the laws of thought approach to logic. We do not have the wherewithal to settle the contentions that such a conception lands us in. But we would do well, even so, to try to situate ourselves in the midst of these entanglements. Like it or not, psychology, especially cognitive psychology, is a part of our project, and we meet with psychology as we find it, warts and all.

Cognitive science has taken on two principal tasks. One is to give a mentalistic description of the laws under which cognition occurs (and is largely successful). The other is to give an account of the mechanisms by which these laws function without drawing upon the lexicon of mental terms and expressions.

For the better part of a generation, it has been widely assumed by cognitive scientists that this latter account will prove to be a computational one. The still dominant view is that the cognizer's mind operates as a linear symbol processor, by which mental symbols are transformed by virtue of the syntactic character of those symbols. Against this, is the view that the practical agent is a parallel distributed processor, many whose operations are parallel rather than linearly connected, and non-symbolic or pre-linguistic. Their difference of opinion has yet to be resolved. We ourselves lean to a PDP approach if only because of its clear affinity to our fast and frugal conception of individual agency.

Either way, however, further assumptions are granted and further problems are met with. Whether on the standard computational or the PDP approach there is general agreement about the modularity of mind (see, e.g., Fodor [1975]) and disagreement as to whether the mind is comprehensively modular or whether central cognition (hypothesis formation, belief revision and the various other routines of practical reasoning) can be satisfactorily modelled in computationally symbol-processing terms. We see in this a natural concurrence between the modular and standard computational approaches. Part of the promise of PDP theories is that it disrupts this rough equivalence and frees up the question of the modularity of central cognition from strictly symbolic assumptions.

Another matter on which virtually all are agreed is the importance of a distinction between automaticity and control in matters of cognitive attention. Here, too, there are disagreements. There are those who hold that automatic processing does not require attention, whereas central processing is effortful and subject to voluntary control (Schneider *et al.* [1984]). Others (e.g., Kahneman and Treisman [1984]) distinguish between early-selection (or filtering) models of attention and late-selective models, both of which appear to be automatic and yet the second of which requires attention. Bearing on this question is the further issue of at what stage does information processing take on a semantic character. A good many cognitive scientists are of the view that semantic processing and control go hand in hand, leaving no room for automatic-belief revision. But here too the evidence of semantic processing of information lodged in unattended channels. (See Treisman [1960] for the classic paper; also Treisman [1964], Corteen and Wood [1972] and von Wright *et al.* [1975]. For doubts see Dawson and Schell [1982] and Treisman *et al.* [1974].)

Among philosphers of mind, Fodor is perhaps best known for his insistence on a limitedly modular analysis of cognitive systems (Fodor [1975] and [1983]). Central cognition, he says, is holistic in design and operation, and, as such, slips entirely out of the ambit of cognitive psychology (see also Fodor [2000]). Fodor argues for the holism of central processing from the holism of science. Since holism requires comprehensive surveys of knowledge-bases (or belief-sets), and such surveys are computationally intractable, Fodor infers the computational intractability of central cognition if it *had* a requisitely computational structure. But central cognition actually occurs, so it cannot, he concludes, be computationally structured.

Our own view is that the holism of central cognition does not follow from the fact (if it is a fact) that science is holistic. There is room therefore for a non-holistic orientation in investigations of central cognition. Two such enquiries stand out. In the one, an attempt is made to link central cognition to local problem-solving heuristics that are cued automatically. In the other, evolutionary psychologists are drawn to modularist explanations on the basis of the highly structured complexity of the cognitive agent's brain. Since an entirely holistic central cognitive system, while highly complex, couldn't have anything like this same degree of structure, evolutionists conclude that it is more plausible to model the actual complexity of central cognition on the structured complexity of the cognizer's brain.

We find ourselves floating on the choppy seas of these interesting and interconnected disagreements. (These are nicely reviewed in Botterill and

Carruthers [1999].) If they have not yet been brought to successful resolution by psychologists, how much less the imperative of definitive pronouncement by logicians. Still, the practical logic of cognitive systems carries some expressly psychological assumptions, which are caught in the cross-hairs of these rivalries. To some extent, therefore, we find ourselves pitched on one or other side of these issues. Like any psychologically real account of cognition, the computational aspects must be made compatible with the plain fact of computational tractability (indeed of low-time, high pay-off set-ups quite generally). Both PDP and comprehensively modular approaches show promise here. A psychologically realistic account of cognition must also leave room for subconscious (and possibly pre-linguistic) and largely automatic cognitive operations. Here, too, the psychological literature on attention (e.g., Parasuraman and Davies [1984]) is, even though equivocal, helpful in setting the relevant parameters. If, for example, automatic processing is not always completely non-attentional, and yet if some even non-attentional processing can be said to have a semantic character, there is room for the idea that the avoidance of irrelevance is a centrally important component of cognitive success which is achieved automatically.

Consciousness is tied to a family of cognitively significant issues. This is reflected in the less than perfect concurrence among the following pairs of contrasts.

1. conscious *versus* unconscious processing
2. controlled *versus* automatic processing
3. attentive *versus* inattentive processing
4. voluntary *versus* involuntary processing
5. linguistic *versus* non-linguistic processing
6. semantic *versus* non-semantic processing
7. surface *versus* depth processing

What is striking about this septet of contrasts is not that they admit of large intersections on each side, but rather that their concurrence is approximate at best. For one thing, 'tasks are never wholly automatic or attentive, and are always accomplished by mixtures of automatic and attentive processes' [Shiffrin, 1997, p. 50]. For another, 'depth of processing does not provide a promising vehicle for distinguishing consciousness from unconsciousness (just as depth of processing should not be used as a criterial attribute for distinguishing automatic processes ...' [Shiffrin, 1997, p. 58]. Indeed '[s]ometimes parallel processing produces an advantage for automatic processing, but not always .... Thoughts high in consciousness often seem serial, probably because they are associated with language, but at other times consciousness seems parallel ...' [Shiffrin, 1997, p. 62].

In what follows, these and other such matters will arise from time to time. If, when this happens, we judge ourselves to have something useful to say, we shall propose it. Otherwise we shall attempt to negotiate our way past.

Chapter 3

Logic as a Description of a Logical Agent

> A great deal of modern economics is based on the accommodation of the discipline to the demand of mathematics. Models based on dynamic disequilibrium or nonlinearity ... are intractable to mathematical formulation. Without the postulate of general equilibrium there is no solution to the system of simultaneous equations which economics needs to prove that markets allocate resources efficiently. That is why economics has been uncomfortable with attempts to model economies as sequences of events occurring in historical time — which is what they are. There is a nice irony here. The more 'formal' economics becomes, the more it has to treat reality as a purely logical construction. When it looks on the market system and finds it good, its admiring gaze is actually directed at its own handiwork.
>
> Robert Skidelsky, *New York Review*, 8 March, 2001

The structure of bounded rationality shows the individual agent to be the organic realization of a paraconsistent base logic. There is little to suggest that the strategies endorsed by classical logic and most going non-standard logics form more than a very small part of the individual agent's repertoire of cognitive and conative (decision-making) skills. 'Putting this more generally, deductive logic so far has little to say about the meso- and macro-levels of reasoning, which is where most of our strategic thinking takes place.' [van Benthem, 1999, p. 33]. If it is true, as suggested above, that individuals are, in matters of non-demonstrative import, pre-inductive rather than inductive agents, the same would also appear to be the case as regards deduction. If so, human individuals are not the wet-wear for deductive logic, at least in the versions that have surfaced in serious ways in the sprawling research programmes of modern logic. There is a particularly interesting reason for this, touched on briefly in the previous chapter. If we ask what the value of deductive consequence is, the answer is that it is a guarantee of truth-preservation. Guaranteed truth-preservation is a good way of avoiding error. But individual agents are not in the general case dedicated to error-avoidance. For the most part, the routines of deductive consequence do not serve the individual agent in the ways in which he is disposed (and programmed) to lead his cognitive and decisional life.

Let us briefly take our bearings: Complexity is a relatively recent item on the agendas of logicians. It is known that the most extreme complexity embedded in any formal or logical apparatus utterly pales in comparison to the speed with which individual agents perform their cognitive tasks in real time. We have been suggesting a certain explanation of this. The basic idea is that speed is a trade-off for strict soundness and completeness. While cognitive strategies employed by individuals cannot pretend to ensure complete accuracy, still less absolute certainty, they serve us well when things go awry and start to degrade. The kind of cognitive competence which such procedures serve rather well has nothing to do with the hell-bent accumulation of logical truths or with the output of some well-constructed and well-programmed theorem-prover, but with timely, composed, and sensible reactions to difficulty and challenge. On this view, 'rationality is repair' [van Benthem, 1999, p. 42]. The rationality-is-repair approach does not however preclude the possibility of building formal systems with greater real-time fidelity. It is more easily said then done. Van Benthem points out that the logic of refutations and first-order logic has been adjusted for arrow logic and modal first-order logic ([Venema, 1996] and [van Benthem, 1996]). This raises the possibility that decidable systems might in turn be reduced to less complex systems, which might better model real-time cognitive performance. But, a warning: such systems will nevertheless be highly complex.

A third option bears rather directly on the question of how could we write rules for what is largely instinctual behaviour. The present option suggests an answer. It is to construct architectures which represent automatic, subconscious, sublinguistic and (probably) highly connectionist delivery systems for much of what passes for execution of the rationality-is-repair model of cognitive competence. One virtue of this, the 'phantom-algorithms'approach, is that the theory has principled occasion to explain why our overt cognitive output, while often wrong in detail, is basically right.

Information-theoretic studies of consciousness suggest the phantom algorithms approach, that the basic structure of consciousness is such as to exclude from his attention most of the information that an individual is processing at any given moment. This in turn suggests a certain approach to what we might call the Cut Down Problem. It appears that discounted information is irrelevant to whatever a conscious agent is currently attending to, that consciousness *itself* is a relevance-filter. Even within consciousness, individuals have the uncanny ability to distinguish the irrelevant from the relevant. Consider an event that has penetrated an agent's consciousness. Already an economically and informationally aberrant occurrence, it stands out in ways that call for attention. In many cases such occurrences call for explanation. For any such occurrence the number of possible explanations is indefinitely large. The number of possible explanations which the individual will actually attend to is correspondingly very small. Thus the *candidate space* of (say) an abduction problem is a small proper subset of an indefinitely large set of possible explainers (or, more generally, possible resolvers). This suggests an operational characterization of relevance. A possible resolver is relevant to an agent's abduction task if and only if it is a member of his candidate space, if and only if it is a possible resolver that he actually considers.

On this account, relevance is indeed a largely automatic affair, which is where the principal economies lie. It is a concomitant of the consideration of possibilities. Relevance marks the boundary between possible resolvers and *candidate-resolvers*. It also marks the boundary between the more general distinction between *mere* and *real* possibilities. Something is a mere possibility for an individual agent when it does not intrude itself into the agent's action plan. Mere possibilities are those that give the agent no grounds, proactively or retroactively, for action or for deliberation. Something is a *real* possibility for an agent when and to the extent that he is prepared to give it standing (even counterfactual standing) in his deliberations. An agent might be got to concede that there *might* be a massive earthquake in London later this afternoon. It is a mere possibility for him if the agent gives it no standing in his action-plans for today. It is a real possibility if it is something he is prepared to reflect upon in organizing his day, to reflect upon even if it subsequently meets with his dismissal upon reflection. Like sets of possible explainers, an agent's totality of mere possibilities is a large set at any given time. Like an agent's candidate spaces, his real possibilities constitute a (comparatively) small set at any given time. Just as *relevance* is defined over sets of possible resolvers as that which screens possible explainers into candidate spaces, relevance is likewise the filter that takes possibilities into real possibilities.

It is well to note that an agent's place in the hierarchy is not a one-off matter. Within limits, the sort of agent he is is the sort of agent he can afford to be, which in turn depends on what is currently or prospectively on his agenda. If he is writing a book on relevance, he should take pains and he should take time. He should even be prepared to give up if there is a notable lack of progress. But if the same person notices the open back-door of his presumedly locked-up house, he has options to consider and actions to take right then and there.

3.1 Heuristics and Limitations

In the sequel to this book, we attempt to make something of the contrast between abduction as a practical matter and abduction in science. The contrast we propose is reflected in the distinction between practical and theoretical agents, a distinction which makes positions in a hierarchy $\mathcal{H}$ of agent-types partially ordered by the resources that agents command. Conceived of in this way, there is little short of teamwork and access to a big computer that a practical agent can do to enlarge his command of resources and thereby advance his place in $\mathcal{H}$. We say that there is little he can do, but not nothing. Here is an example, which flows from the creative power of individual agents. Despite the scarcity of time, information and computational capacity, practical agents are capable of highly significant theoretical achievements. Practical agents are adept at thinking up theories. This has something to do with heuristics. Heuristics we understand in Quine's way [1995]. They are aids to the imagination. They help the theorist in thinking up his theories. It cannot be put in serious doubt that in the business of thinking up his theories, there are some things the theorist cannot do without, including his most confident and enduring convictions about principles he thinks the theory must honour. Even so, not every belief required by the theorist to conceptualize and organize his theory need itself be a theorem of the theory. A case in point is any scientific theory eligible as input to the Löwenheim–Skolem theorems. All such theories must be extensional. Yet for all kinds of purely extensional theories, there isn't the slightest chance of our being able to think them up in a purely extensional language. In such cases, the intensionality of the thinking-up language is indispensable; but it would be a mistake to import those indispensable intensionalities into any theory governed by the Löwenheim-Skolem theorems. The mistake is bad enough to qualify for a name. We call it the

> *Heuristic Fallacy*: Let **H** be a body of heuristics with respect to the construction of some theory T. Then if P is a belief from **H** which is indispensable to the construction of T, then the unqualified inference that T is incomplete unless it sanctions the derivation of P, is a fallacy.

If, then, the theorist bides the Heuristic Fallacy, he will be reluctant to enshrine in his theory those things that restrained him in thinking the theory up. If, for example, his theory is a logic or formal semantics or an exercise in econometrics, it is completely open — indeed likely — that the theorist will sanction procedures or algorithms which are canonical in the theory, but which he, their inventor, could never run.

In this, the theorist is met with the ticklish problem of simultaneous avoidance of the Heuristic Fallacy and fidelity to the project of constructing ideal models of *appropriate* (that is to say, approximate) concurrence with actual human performance. It is a task more easily prescribed than executed.

Given the striking and essential differences exhibited by agents at different ranks in the hierarchy of agency, it is easy to see that a logic which does well for a given type of agent does badly for agents of a different type. There is a standing invitation to logicians to commit this mistake, and the history of logic is liberally dotted with its commission. The propensity to make this mistake in an essential structural feature of what constitutes a logic. A logic is an idealization of certain sorts of real-life phenomena. By their very natures, idealizations misdescribe the behaviour of actual agents. This is to be tolerated when two conditions are met. One is that the actual behaviour of actual agents can defensibly be made out to *approximate* to the behaviour of the ideal agents of the logician's idealization. The other is the idealization's *facilitation* of the logician's discovery and demonstration of deep laws.

There are limits to how far the theorist's idealization can go. It is by now widely agreed that classical first-order logic is an excessive idealization of the behaviour of individuals, of agents at the bottom of the hierarchy of agency. Of course from the point of view of descriptive adequacy, *all* logics go too far, because all idealizations are descriptively inadequate. This is not to say that anything goes, or that nothing does. We propose the following limitation rule.

> *Logic Limitation Rule*: A logic is inappropriate for actual agents of type τ (or actual agents of type τ in relation to a given agenda) to the extent to which factors which make for agency of type τ are indiscernible in the behaviour of the logic's ideal agents.

It is well to note in passing the availability of machine modelling to serve—or try to—the requirements of a theory of individual cognitive agency. The great success of Turing's models in AI notwithstanding, it is unlikely that this is the way to go. For one thing, 'Turing machine programming is about the least perspicuous style of defining algorithms that has ever been invented' [van Benthem, 1999, 37]. An alternative kind of approach suggests itself. The game-theoretic approach has already achieved something of a beachhead in logical theory. There are logical games for semantic interpretation (e.g. [Hintikka, 1973; Lorenzen, 1965; Lorenzen and Lorenz, 1978]); for dialogue logic (e.g., [Barth and Krabbe, 1982; Carlsen, 1982; Walton and Krabbe, 1995; MacKenzie, 1990; Girle, 1993; Woods and Walton, 1989; Hintikka and Bachman, 1991], and [Gabbay and Woods, 2001], among others); and for the comparison of models ([Ehrenfeucht, 1961] and [Fraissée, 1954]).[1]

Notwithstanding the prominence of the game-theoretic orientation, it too is met with nasty intractability problems, especially in dialogue logic. Nor does the game-theoretic approach exclude any notion of computability, never mind the difficulties to date (see here [Moore and Hobbs, 1996]).

3.2 Three Problems

Before bringing this chapter to an end, we take note of three particular challenges which the theorist of practical reasoning must try to subdue. This is not the place for solutions. It suffices that the problems be clearly set out and well-motivated. They are what we shall call the Complexity Problem, the Consequence Problem, and the Approximation Problem.

3.2.1 The Complexity Problem

In a purely commonsense way, individual agents are unable to deal with matters when doing so exceeds the time that can be afforded and the agent's computational power. This last is a constraint on complexity, and complexity here is a *first-level operational* matter. It should not be confused with *metamathematical* complexity. A case in point is the intractability of the decision problem for systems of relevant arithmetic. It is a problem no less hard than ESPACE-hard — a computational horror. If anything is obvious about individual agency, it is how adept human beings are at evading irrelevant information. This is done massively by the structure of consciousness itself, as we have said. But even within consciousness, most of what an agent

[1]A good survey of logic games is [van Benthem, 1988] and [1993].

is aware of is irrelevant to the given task at hand. The obviousness of this fact carries over to one of its most interesting consequences: Efficient and timely management of the relevant–irrelevant distinction is *not* too complex for the individual agent to provide. So, in particular, we must avoid the mistake of uncritically endowing metamathematical complexity with operational significance. This we take to be the moral of the reason-is-repair slogan, and the several canons of minimal rationality that trail along in its wash.

Relevant logic aside, we join with Harman and others in saying that classical first-order logic, and the probability calculus, too, are too complex for the likes of us. That is to say, if *our* rules of inference included *its* 'rules of inference', and if we ran those rules in the way that they were run in first-order structures, then, apart from some trivial exceptions, we would lack the time and the computational heft to make inferences at all. We are also minded to agree with those who claim that non-monotonic reasoning (to take just one example) is more efficient, more psychologically real than its monotonic vis-à-vis. In one sense, non-monotonic reasoning is less complex. But as studies in AI make clear, non-monotonic reasoning is also more complex. In fact, any logic that deviates from the standard extensional logics involves an increase in complexity. It is not just that such systems are metamathematically complex; running their programs also represents a jump in complexity. So a question presses. How can, e.g., non-monotonic logic be simpler to use for practical agents and yet more metamathematically complex than first-order structures which are difficult (to say the least) for practical agents to use? A case in point is consistency-checking. Consider the default rule:

$$\alpha : \quad \frac{\beta}{\beta}$$

which we can read as 'deduce β if in context, α, β is consistent'. The requirement is computationally complex for a machine. But typically a practical agent just 'intuitively' checks at little or no cost.

The problem, then, is this: how can it be the case that in everyday operational terms, individual agents are more or less good at ranges of tasks for which complexity is no particular problem, and yet, as studied by logicians and computer scientists, it is precisely those tasks that carry a degree of complexity which, if it actually obtained, would paralyse the individual's thought and action?

We have already noted that consciousness is a radical suppressor of complexity, and that computer simulation to date of individual agency have been unable to operationalize the distinction between conscious and non-conscious systems. The result of this is that in all simulations of cognitive performance, there is vastly more information involved than any individual can consciously take in. Correspondingly, the simulating mechanizations exhibit (and handle) levels of complexity which are provably beyond the reach, often by several powers, of any conscious agent.

This appears to leave us with two options, both of which are underdetermined by any available evidence. One is to retain these over-complex systems, these aggregations of informational glut, and to postulate that they apply to agents *pre-consciously*. Below the threshold of consciousness, human systems are devourers of information, which enables them to handle substantial levels of complexity. We might judge it reasonable to think of the human neurological system as organic realization of PDP architecture, i.e., as computer analogues of the brain's own neurological network structure, the computer descriptions of which would then be of approximately the right type.

The second option is more radical, but it is no more foreclosed by the available evidence than the first alternative. In exercising it we would simply refuse to accept that any going logic or any going computer simulation stands a chance of elucidating individual agency in a realistic way.

Either way, we see it as a matter of urgency that logicians and computer scientists forge serious, substantial, and long-term partnerships with the brain sciences.

Before leaving this matter, it is well to emphasize that intractable, and otherwise unrealistic, theories T of agency are devised by practical agents using cognitive and creative resources which do not find their way into T, either at all or in a descriptively adequate way. To some extent, their exclusion is justified by the necessity to avoid the Heuristic Fallacy. Beyond that, the exclusions constitute an abduction problem for the theorist. What best explains the exclusion from a theory of cognitive competence of those very cognitive skills which the theorist draws upon in constructing his theory? Various conjectures can be considered. One is that the theorist has a general idea of, but lacks a sufficiently detailed and descriptively adequate command of, how those resources are deployed in real life. So, he activates the general idea in his theoretical model. Another is that the theorist's agenda is in part normative. If so, then his task must include the specification of norms which real life agents may and do deviate from in practice. The theorist will also be aware that in the very idea of a performance-norm is the requirement that actual behaviour counts as disconforming only if it is made out to bear a certain resemblance to the norms it violates. Another way of saying this is that only behaviour that approximates to a norm can be characterized as violating it. Why, then, is there often such a huge gap between what the ideal model prescribes and what practical agents are actually capable of? Our answer is that theorists have not yet succeeded, even where the need to do so has been recognized, in formalizing an approximation relation adequate for this theoretical task.

Examination of the historical record of theory formation in the areas of human performance suggests that idealized models fail to capture the actual — performable or near-performable — behaviour of practical agents. If this historical observation is correct, it must quickly be supplemented by recognition of the fact that theories that fail in this way may be seen as more faithful models of non-practical agency, of agencies of types that occur higher up in the hierarchy of agents. Agents so positioned we have dubbed theoretical. Theoreticality, like practicality, is a matter of the agent's command of the requisite cognitive and other resources required for cognitive performance; hence, twice-over, a matter of degree. Computational complexity is a case in point. Individuals, i.e., practical agents, have comparatively little of it, and collectivities, i.e., theoretical agents, have comparatively lots of it. A theory of human performance whose ideal models embed a lot of computational fire-power may fail as a model of practical agency and yet succeed as a model of theoretical agency.

This allows us to re-frame an important question. Why is it that theorists who seek to formalize practical or individual agency so often end up building models that fail for such agents and yet succeed, or come closer to succeeding, as models of theoretical agency? Our abduction is that this is the best that such theorists know how to do, that in questing for models appropriate to one type of agency they succeed in finding models that do well (or better) for other types of agency, which in their turn only approximate to the originally targeted agency-type. Here we meet with a methodological principle of substantial provenance. We call it the *Can Do Principle.* In its most basic form, the

> *Can Do Principle* bids an investigator of a question Q in a domain D to invest his resources in answering questions $Q_1^*, \ldots, Q_n^*$ from domain D^* when the following conditions appear to have been met. First, the investigator is adept at answering the Q_i^*; and second, he is prepared to attest that answering the Q_i^* facilitates the answering of the initial question Q.

There is nothing to dislike in investigative practice governed by the *Can Do Principle*, provided there is reason to believe that what the theorist attests to is actually the case. But as the present situation in, for example, rational choice theory, probability theory and mathematical logic itself clearly indicates, the attendant attestations sometimes stand little serious chance of being true. So the theorist plugs away at what he is able to do rather than what he himself has set out as his primary task.

Neo-classical economics is an instructive case. As is widely known, the neoclassical theory replaced the law of diminishing marginal utilities with the law of diminishing marginal rates of substitution. With the additional 'simplification' that goods are infinitely divisible, the theory had direct access to the firepower of calculus and could be formulated mathematically. Thus, for significant ranges of problems, it is easier to do the mathematics than the economics, with an attendant skew as to what *counts* as economics.

In its justified forms the *Can Do Principle* represents a sensible diversion of investigative labour, together with an implied (and usually rough) rank ordering. The Principle is justified when the enquirer has adequate reason to think that his investment in 'off-topic' work will eventually conduce toward progress in his 'on-topic' programme. It matters that whether the Principle is indeed justified is often indiscernible before the fact. In the natural history of the use of the Principle, its subscription is often tentative and conjectural, turning on features which give to the methodology of the investigation underway an abductive character.

3.2.2 The Approximation Problem

It remains our view that a logic is a formal idealization of a logical agent. The Logic Limitation Rule bids the theorist not to make too free with his idealizations. If the logician's or the computer scientist's ideal model is to be seen as modelling what actual agents actually do, what happens in the ideal model must be recognizable as the sort of thing an actual agent could or might do, or actually does. This factor of recognizability we have tried to capture by the relation of approximation, which bears on our problem in two ways. In the first place, an ideal agent's behaviour, *IB*, is recognizable as the sort of thing, *RB*, an actual agent really does, or could or might do, just in case, or the degree to which, *RB*ing is an approximation of *IB*ing. But secondly, a theory T which fails to model with appropriate approximation the behaviour of agents of type k, may succeed in modeling the behaviour of agents of higher or lower type k^*. Even though T fails the approximation requirement in relation to the actual — or performable — behaviour of k-agents, T may still provide valuable insights into the workings of k-behaviour if the agency-type k^*, which fits T's norms more comfortably, is itself an approximation of requisite closeness of k-agency. We take it as a condition on a satisfactory theory of approximation that it preserves the intuitive inequivalence of these two notions of approximation.

The concept of approximation is borrowed from the natural sciences. The physics of frictionless surfaces is a case in point, as we saw. Frictionless surfaces are mathematically describable idealizations of the slipperiness of real life, of the pre-game ice of the rink at the local hockey arena. Though the surface of the ice is not frictionless, it approximates to that state. There are limits on what to count as an approximation. After three periods of play, the surface of the ice is a less good approximation of frictionlessness than in its pristine pre-game condition. But no one will seriously suppose that #04 sandpaper is also an approximation of frictionlessness, only less good still.

The approximation problem for logicians and computer scientists is the problem of specifying the mix of similarities and differences admissible by what they are prepared to call approximations of ideal performance. It is a difficult question. We may say with some confidence that no ESPACE-hard regime can be considered to be in the counterdomain of any approximation relation on conscious individual agents. But we don't want to restrict approximations to things which such a being could do if he went into training and tried really hard.

When recently the present authors were expounding the material of the present chapter to a meeting of computer scientists and electrical engineers, a member of the group said something along the following lines: 'I like your characterization of individual agency. And I too see a logic as a formal idealization of a type of agent. But are you sure that you're going to be able to write rules for this sort of case? I really need to see your rules!' It is a good question, and a hard one. It brings into apposition both the approximation problem and the complexity problem. The complexity problem is in part the problem of how much complexity in an ideal performance qualifies as that to which an actual agent's behaviour bears the approximation relation. And the question, 'Can you write rules for individual agency?' subsumes the question — or a question tantamount to the question — whether it is possible to make computer models of what is information-theoretically and complexity-theoretically *distinctive of* individual conscious agency.

3.2.3 The Consequence Problem

In its more purely classical state, a logical system can be seen as giving an account of the consequence relation. Non-classical variations can be understood in turn as principled descriptions of alternatives or rival consequence relations. We have already remarked on the difficulty such an approach presents the agency view of logic, that is, any view of logic in which a logical system is a formal idealization of a type of agent. The problem is that consequence relations are specifiable by truth conditions, or by proof-theoretic constraints, independently of anything that might be true of any actual agent.

It is possible to improve upon this austerely truth conditional approach to logic, that is, to a logic of agency, by taking a logical system to be an ordered pair $\langle S, \mid\!\sim \rangle$ of a designated consequence relation $\mid\!\sim$ and a set of instructions for proving when the consequence relation obtains in a context. In the example at hand (derived from [Gabbay, 1994]), $\mid\!\sim$ is non-monotonic consequence and S is a proof theory purpose-built for its peculiarities. In commonsense terms, a logical system of this sort is a principled description of the conditions under which an agent can declare (or recognize) a logical consequence of a database. The condition of S clearly enough adumbrates the idea of agency, and we can see in S an attempt of sorts to inferentialize the consequence relation. This is something Aristotle attempted 2500 years ago. Syllogistic consequence is just classical consequence constrained in rather dramatic ways, in ways that make the theory of syllogisms the first ever linear, relevant, intuitionistic, non-monotonic, paraconsistent logic, or some near thing. Aristotle's question was in effect this: Can we get a plausible theory of inference from constraints imposed on the consequence relation? This is also a question for proponents of $\langle S, \mid\!\sim \rangle$. Can we get a plausible formal idealization of an actual agent by softening the consequence relation and harnessing it to a purpose-built proof theory? Our answer is that it depends on the type of agent, and his (or its) rank in the hierarchy. But it also seems correct to say that the lower down we go the less plausible the $\langle S, \mid\!\sim \rangle$ approach becomes. But we note in passing that the more a logic of agency imposes constraints on the consequence relation, or the more it supplements it with additional structure, the more we remove from centre stage what we have been calling the purely classical view, in which logic is dominantly a bunch of truth conditions on the consequence relation.

3.2.4 Truth Conditions, Rules and State Conditions

The mathematical turn in logic changed (for a while) the conception of what a logic could and needed to be. In Frege's hands, logic needed to be re-jigged and retrofitted in order to accommodate the burdens of a particular thesis in the epistemology of arithmetic. In Frege's conception of it (but not Russell's) logicism was the view that since arithmetic is reducible to logic and logic is analytic, so too is arithmetic analytic, *pace* Kant.[2] Nothing in Frege's logicist ambitions for the new logic required it to address,

[2]There are reasons simple and complex as to why Frege's logicism can't have been the same as Russell's. The simplest of of these is that Frege wanted logicism to prove the analyticity of arithmetic, whereas for Russell the truths of arithmetic were synthetic.

still less to elucidate, the strict deductive canons of human reasoning and argument. When logicism expired (it could not survive the Gödel incompleteness result), the new logic was dispossessed of its historic *rasion d'etre.* It is open to wonder why the new logic didn't likewise lapse. That it didn't is a striking feature of the intellectual history of the twentieth century, and it is explained in part at least by the *Can Do Principle.* In the span of time from 1879 to 1931, logic had become a dazzlingly successful intellectual enterprise — a growth industry, so to speak. In historically unrigorous hands, the logic of Frege and his successors reverted to its ancient status as a theory of strict reasoning, with evidence perforce of the *Can Do Principle* liberally at work. The boom times in recursion theory, proof theory, model theory and set theory are explainable by the fact that this was work that people were able to do, and to do extremely well; and it was seen as work that facilitated the overarching goal of producing a comprehensive logic of deductive thinking. Among those who knew better, the new logic was permitted at least as much because it was found to be intrinsically interesting as that it was possible to do it well; and the *Can Do Principle* delivered the goods for that intrinsic interest.

As it has developed, mathematical logic, in both classical and non-standard variations, examines the properties of structures. Such structures were not of a type that could pass for models of cognitive systems, except at levels of abstraction that made them unconvincing simulations of the actual practice of individual cognitive agents. For the most part, investigators of those structures hadn't the slightest inclination to think of them as models of human cognitive processes. They were studied because they *could* be studied, and because they were thought to be intrinsically interesting — as is virtually any enterprise that offers promise of well-regarded, long-term employment, which was the state of play in mathematical logic for virtually all of the past century.

Against this background, two historically important developments stand out. One involved the rising fortunes of non-standard systems within logic itself. The other was the brisk evolution of AI. The two developments converged on an ancient idea; indeed it is the original *raison d'etre* of logic itself. Thus some, (though not all) of the non-standard systems and most of the approaches to computer logic were motivated by the desire that logic be a seriously deliberate account, or part of an account, of how thinking can and should be done. In the hands of logicians, this *was* an attempt to convert mathematical structures into cognitive systems; and, as was the case with relevant logicians, this was done by imposing non-classical constraints on classical rules and operations. In the hands of computer science this was

The more complex story is well told in [Irvine, 1989].

done by writing programs that simulated actual human performance. And, here, too, this was largely a matter of constraining the classical algorithms.

As we have seen, both these attempts to recur to logic's original motivation have met with various difficulties. Chief among them has been the high computational costs, higher than in classical systems, of running their algorithms, executing their protocols and deploying their rules. The results we have cited on the play of information on consciousness suggests an unattractive dilemma for the new, user-friendly logics. Either the new logics cannot be run by beings like us, or they can be and perhaps are run, but not consciously.

Logic's historic connection with thinking has always been with conscious thinking. If our present dilemma is well-grounded, then we would seem to have it that logic cannot discharge its historic mission (which would be another explanation of why mathematical logic doesn't even try).

One dilemma leads to another. Either what we are calling the new logics are bad theories of human thinking, or they are possibly good theories of human *unconscious* thinking. Apart from the difficulty of determining which of these is likely to be true, there is the further difficulty that — historical anti-psychologism aside — theories of subconscious cognition have never been thought of as *logic*. We are now in the precincts of tacit knowledge, in which psychology has had what seems to have been a near thing to a monopoly. The further dilemma to which this gives rise, is a dilemma about logical rules. If rules of logic are thought of as having something to do with how human beings actually think, then by and large they are too complex for conscious deployment. On the other hand, unconscious performance or tacit knowledge is a matter of certain things happening under the appropriate conditions and in the right order, but it is unsupportably personificationist to suppose that this is a matter of following rules (an inclination which seems unshakably embedded in contemporary computer science.) *Façons de parler* being what they are, we can readily enough reconceptualize such 'rules' as causally enabling regularities; but then all semblance of logic as a prescriptive discipline is lost. A further dilemma, then, has it that logic has rules which humans can't conform their (conscious) thinking to or except for some fairly trivial conscious exceptions, logicality cannot be a matter of following rules.

Recent work on analogical thinking, emphasizes that '... thinking by analogy is an implicit procedure applied to explicit representations' [Holyoak and Thagard, 1995, p. 21]. Accordingly the goal of analogic is 'to make explicit how that implicit procedure operates.' (idem.). Plainly this cannot mean that the goal of analogic is to make explicit the rules which the subject explicitly runs to make the procedure work. It means rather that the goal of analogic is to make those rules or procedures explicit to the theorist. Even this is a trifle tendentious. The theorist will explicitly conjecture a procedure of a *type* that he thinks plausibly applied to analogical thinking. He will say, for example, that the analogizer is adept at seeing relevant connections. In so saying the theorist is nothing but right that the correctness of his observation needn't involve his giving an account of relevance or specifying the conditions under which analogizers are good at detecting it; to say nothing of rules which the analogizer expressly deploys.

Explicit knowledge tends to be accessible to consciousness, and is therefore readily verbalizable by beings who have acquired the ability to speak. 'Using explicit knowledge often requires noticeable mental effort, whereas using implicit knowledge is generally unconscious and relatively effortless' [Holyoak and Thagard, 1995, p. 22]. Here, then, is a mistake to avoid. Thinking is often conscious. When it is, it often involves propositional representations. It is entirely helpful to have good theoretical accounts of propositions — of how they are represented, of their grammatical structures, of their intentionality, and of those various properties and relations, possession of which bears on issues such as these. But it is a mistake to suppose that all our interactions with things we're conscious of are likewise objects of our consciousness. In particular, even if it is true that propositional representations require consciousness, it does not follow, and is not the case, that manipulating such representations is necessarily conscious. Still less does it follow that the cognitive manipulation of items of which we are conscious is a matter of following rules.

Logic is a model of a logical agent. Agency operates at various levels, central to which is the distinction between

- the conscious and propositional
- the subconscious and prelinguistic.

Logic accordingly involves

- a description of propositional structures, emphasizing properties deemed relevant to the description and/or evaluation of cognitive tasks

and

- a body of inferences about what goes on 'down below', and how it might influence or be influenced by conditions that obtain 'up above', i.e. propositionally
- conceptual analyses or definitions of the key ideas involved in the above two accounts.

Here is a conception in which logic is an enterprise with significant limits. Beyond the ingenuity of the theorist, chief among these limitations is the theorist's inability to inspect what goes on down below, on how propositional structures are actually handled, even consciously so. Recurring to the example of relevance, beings like us are adept at discounting and otherwise disengaging from irrelevant information. Some of the time, therefore, the propositional structure that has popped into a human head will be the output of his irrelevance evading devices. But it cannot simply be assumed that there are linguistically representable properties of his propositional structures that answer directly to the fact that it is a *relevant* propositional structure; which is a lesson lost on certain self-styled relevant logicians. The difficulty of determining the interconnections between what goes on up above and what goes on down below is noticeably less so in the negative cases. Thus, if the theorist-logician conjectures that the irrelevance-evading cognitive agent is someone who runs the algorithms that solve the decision problem for the standard Anderson and Belnap system minus the distributivity law, then he attributes to the agent computational capacities which it is known that he cannot begin to approximate. This leaves a good question. What, on the agent's behalf, are we to make of the 'rules of inference' preferred by the theorist of propositional relevance?

It should not be forgotten that those who conceive of logic as exclusively the examination of propositional structures, with an emphasis on selectively important properties and on operations under which those properties are closed, are well-positioned to save themselves all the grief presently under review, and then some. All the more so, once the move is made from linguistic structures to mathematical structures of higher abstraction. To restrict logic thus makes more of a claim on prudence than is strictly justified perhaps, but there can scarcely be a logician alive who is unaware of such temptations.

There remains the fact that not all logicians are so methodologically circumspect, or ruthless. The new logic is awash in claims that go too far, in conjectures that are too much to bear by any fair measure. A good part of their problem flows from the very conception of logic that their work reflects. It is a conception that originates with Aristotle. Aristotle wanted a comprehensive theory of argument. Owing no doubt to the ambiguity of the Greek word *syllogismos*, which our own word 'deduction' also inherits, Aristotle thought that a theory of syllogistic argument would also be a theory of deductive thinking. Indispensable to both projects is a theory of propositional structures which Aristotle called syllogisms. Syllogisms in this core sense are neither psychological nor dialectical entities. A syllogism is simply a triple of propositions answering to certain truth conditions. On the other hand, arguments in the sense for which he wanted a comprehensive theory are dialectical structures held to certain standards which are representable as sets of rules. Inference, or deductive thinking, is a kind of psychological modality subject at the descriptive level to certain psychobiological state conditions.

Two things of importance require attention. One is that truth conditions, dialectical rules and psychobiological state conditions are three different things (see [Woods, 2002b]). What is plausibly supposed of a propositional relation such as implication (for example, that it answers to truth conditions in virtue of which it is monotonic), cannot be plausibly said either of the dialectical rules of real-life argument or of the psychobiological state conditions of real-life belief-revision. No rule of argument will put up with the limitless supplementation of a valid argument's premiss-set, and no conditions under which an agent deduces a belief from a database will induce him arbitrarily and repeatedly to augment that database in ways that leave him wholly uninterested in whether his belief in the conclusion would (or need) change. It is true that Aristotle thought that the truth conditions of his purely propositional logic could be modified in ways that enabled them to be more plausible simulators of dialectical rules of dispute and argumentation and the psychobiological constraints on belief revision. Even so — and here is a second point that calls for attention — a problem arises that Aristotle could not have been aware of. It is the vexation that flows from the fact that imposing constraints on truth conditions with a view to their serving as dialectical *rules* makes for computational complexity on a scale that is hardly less than daunting.

Something of this difficulty is reflected in the entrenched affection of logicians and, especially, computer scientists, for anthropomorphizing the causal modalities of electric circuitry, or pretending that algorithms are actually instructions to an entity capable of reading and complying with them, when in fact they are causal triggers and regulators of digitalizable electronic flows (phantom algorithms, as we said earlier). Such processes bear a resemblance to what we are calling psychobiological state conditions, but even here there is a danger of a considerable misconception. There is reason to believe that under certain circumstances, psychobiological states are regulators of conscious states in beings like us. There is not yet reason to believe that the electronic etiologies which drive computer simulations of human cognitive effort succeed in producing anything that might pass for consciousness.

If we allow that a logic is a description of a logical agent and that human logical agency plays itself out both consciously and unconsciously, we leave it comfortably open in principle that the algorithms of an electrical engineer's making might enjoy literal application in matters of subconscious logical agency, and that the complexity discouragements that would bedevil the conscious running of such algorithms well might evaporate when run unconsciously in suitably layered architectures of the PDP kind. Talk of rules, on the other hand, is best reserved for the conscious domain, where it must be responsive to its very high levels of informational entropy.

The various issues make it desirable to revisit the Heuristic Fallacy, which is the mistake of supposing that every proposition necessary for the theorist to believe in order to think his theory up is a proposition which the theory itself must formally endorse. The sheer attractiveness of the fallacy is hard to overestimate. There is an entrenched methodology in philosophy and the abstract sciences generally according to which the theorist's core 'intuitions' must be preserved by any subsequent theory. The general inadequacy of this assumption need not detain us here (but see again [Woods, 2002a, Ch. 8]). Even so, if the theorist is not permitted to lodge in his theory any of his pre-theoretical beliefs, it is difficult to see how theories are possible. So some propositions, whose omission to believe would cause the theorist to fail to think up his theory, must be admitted. But which?

The Heuristic Fallacy (or the prospect of it) is important in another way. It is a way that offers encouragement to the logician concerned with matters down below. Logic, we say, is intrinsically abductive. It is a theory of how logical agents behave. Some aspects of that behaviour are attended by consciousness and are open to propositional representation and the discipline of rules. In other respects, the agent is a stranger to his own cognitive endeavours. He has no more access to the operations of his subconscious structures than his next-door neighbour or the cognitive psychologist down the street. The encouragement offered the logician of matters down below is in strictness offered not so much by the converse of the Heuristic Fallacy but rather a variation of it, according to which it is a fallacy to suppose that the mechanisms at work down below are nothing but the devices that constitute the cognitive agent's bag of heuristic aids. If it is supposed that only what is propositionally representable and consciously accessible is subject for a logician's theory, then all else that facilitates cognition would find itself relegated to the category of heuristics. But the supposition in question is unreasonable. It suggests uncritical affection for propositional structures and over-ready susceptibility to the *Can Do Principle*.

Logic is a theoretical description of a logical agent. We may take it as given that in his various undertakings, the cognitive agent sometimes operates consciously and propositionally, and sometimes not. We may also take it that in its various undertakings, cognitive agency sometimes involves the manipulation of propositional relations — or at least is constrained by them; that sometimes it involves what Harman calls changes in view; and that sometimes it involves reacting to proposals in argumentatively appropriate ways. All in, the cognitive agent operates at two levels, conscious and tacit, and engages or is influenced by truth conditions on propositional structures, state conditions on belief structures, and sets of rules defined for various argumentative structures. The story of the cognitive agent will vary with the propositional relations he is contextually placed — and able — to take into account, with cognitive inducements to change his mind or to think in some sort of different way, and with dialectical provocations to deploy various strategies of argument. If our agent is an individual, he will face these various conditions and incitements with scarce resources, implicit in which are limits on what counts as smart, or rational even. If the agent is a theoretical agent, then its command of problem-solving resources enlarges in ways that match the degree to which the agency qualifies as theoretical, and criteria of success and failure change accordingly.

3.2.5 Rules Redux

The logic of an individual's cognitive agency is an account of various practices — for example, the processing, storing and analysis of information, and drawing inferences therefrom. Since these are practices which cut across the distinction between conscious and unconscious processes, they are taken as flowing from capacities an agent possesses either tacitly or expressly or in combination. Three things are involved in the execution of these capacities. One is the agent's manipulation of truth conditions on propositional structures; another is the deployment of and reaction to rules for making and for evaluating arguments — rules attending the agent's case-making proclivities; and the third is responsiveness to the causal inducements at play in the fixation of belief and the further aspects of changes in view. Since this trio of capacities cuts across the divide between the tacit and express, they will play with differential force depending on the particular theatre of operation. So, for example, an individual may have a change of mind in one of two ways, and at either of two levels. His new state of mind may be something his psychobiological conditions — his state conditions — put him in; or he may have changed his own mind in consequence of a case-making encounter with an interlocutor (and it is necessary to note that ultimately this present 'or' is not that of exclusive alternation). It may be a likelier thing than not that changes of the first sort are more frequently tacit than changes of the second, but there is no question here of perfect concurrence. Whether his mind was changed for him or he changed his own mind, recognition of propositional properties (e.g., consequence or consistency) may have been in play; but it is not invariable that this is so, and here, too, such recognitions can be tacit as well as express.

Notwithstanding the critical differences between and among truth conditions, rules and state conditions, the rules approach is an entrenched habit among logicians. It is one thing to rail against bad habits. It is another, and better, thing to try to make them not matter, that is, to accommodate them in ways that minimize their sting. We may take it, then, that the postulation of rules and the attribution of rules-behaviour to logical agents is something to tolerate when the following condition is met.

> It is reasonable to attribute to the agent in question the wherewithal (possibly tacit) to be situated *as if* he had consciously followed the 'rule' in question.

When this condition is met, we are free to attribute to real-life individuals what might be called *virtual rules*. In the spirit of the first condition, we might attribute to an agent conformity to the rule, 'Be relevant', when it is reasonable to suppose that the agent has resources, whatever they are, which place him in a situation that he would have been in, or that closely approximate to such a situation, had he had the means to follow the rule literally and had he done so in fact. The second condition secures a purchase in, e.g., the conjecture that since real-life individuals tend to transact their quotidian affairs in timely ways, such agents possess the wherewithal to evade or otherwise discount masses of information irrelevant to the task at hand. Thus 'Be relevant' could be a rule which the logical theorist sees fit to impose as a rational norm on the cognitive effort of real-life individuals without it being the case that, except in the attenuated sense presently in view, there is any reason to postulate that any agent's irrelevance evading behaviour is the result of following the rule to be relevant. Rule-talk in logic, therefore, is largely a *façon de parler*. Once the *façon* is properly understood, there is no harm in the *parler*, for most of the rules cited by a logician — even a *nouvelle vague* logician — are virtual rules.

3.2.6 Logics for Down Below

In the past pages we have flirted with the idea that a *PLCS* might extend or have an adaptable component that extends to cognitive processes that are pre-linguistic and subconscious. Some people will simply abhor the idea, needless to say. We ourselves are not so sure. For consider the following cases.

Connectionist Logic

There is a large literature — if not a large consensus — on various aspects of subconscious, pre-linguistic cognition. If there is anything odd about our approach, it can only be the proposal to include such matters in the ambit of logic. Most, if not all, of what people don't like about so liberal a conception of logic is already present in the standard objections to psychologism, which we have already discussed. Strictly speaking, there is room for the view that, while psychologism is not intrinsically hostile to logic, psychologism about the unconscious and the pre-linguistic simply stretches logic further than it can go, and should therefore be resisted.

This is an admonition that we respect but do not intend to honour. In this we draw encouragement from work by Churchland and others ([Churchland, 1989] and [1995]) on subconscious abductive processes. As Churchland observes, '... one understands at a glance why one end of the kitchen is filled with smoke: the toast is burning!' [1989, p. 199]. Churchland proposes that in matters of perceptional understanding, we possess '... an organized library of internal representations of various perceptual situations, situations to which prototypical *behaviours* are the computed output of the well-trained network' [1989, p. 207]. Like Peirce [1931–1958, p. 5.181], Churchland sees perception as a limit of explanation, and he suggests that all types of explanation can be modelled as prototype activation by way of '... vector coding and vector-to-vector transformation" rather than linguistic representation and standardly logical reasoning. On this approach the knowledge that comes from experience is modelled in the patterning of weights in the subject's neural network, where it is seen as a disposition of the system to assume various activation configurations in the face of various inputs. Thus, as Robert Burton nicely puts it, Churchland is drawn to the view that "inference to the best explanation is simply activation of the most appropriate available prototype vector' [Burton, 1999, p. 261].

The suggestion that abduction has (or has in part) a *connectionist* logic is attractive in two particular ways. One is that, unlike every other logic of explanation, connectionist explanation has a stab at being psychologically real. The other, relatedly, is that a connectionist logic is no enemy of the subconscious and pre-linguistic sectors of cognitive practice. It is no panacea, either. (See the section just above.) There is nothing in the connectionist's prototype-library that solves the problem of the deployment of wholly new hypotheses, as in the case of Planck's postulation of quanta. On the other hand, the same is true of computer systems such as PI [Thagard, 1988], which mimic simple, existential, rule-forming and analogical genres of abduction. (See here [Burton, 1999, p. 264].) We return to systems such as PI in chapter 5 below.

Beyond that, we should not want to say that serial processing *requires* consciousness:

> Thoughts high in consciousness often seem serial, probably because they are associated with language, but at other times consciousness seems parallel, as when we attend to the visual scene before us. So the distinction between parallel and serial processing does not seem to map well onto the distinction between the conscious and the unconscious. [Shiffrin, 1997, p. 62].

RWR Models

Another possibility is the *RWR* (representation without rules) approach to cognitive modelling. On this approach cognitive systems employ representational structures that admit of semantic interpretation, and yet there are no representation-level rules that govern the processing of these semantically interpretable representations [Horgan and Tienson, 1988; Horgan and Tienson, 1989; Horgan and Tienson, 1990; Horgan and Tienson, 1992; Horgan and Tienson, 1996; Horgan and Tienson, 1999b; Horgan and Tienson, 1999a]. Critics of *RWR* argue that it can't hold of connectionist systems [Aizawa, 1994; Aizawa, 2000]. Since we want to leave it open that some at least of the cognitive processing of practical agents occurs 'down below', it matters whether this criterion is justified. We think not, although we lack the space to lay out our reservations completely. The nub of our answer to critics of the *RWR* approach is as follows.

1. Critics such as Aizawa point out that connectionist nets are describable by programmable representation level rules. They conclude from this that connectionist nets execute these rules. [Aizawa, 1994, p. 468]
2. We accept that connectionist nets are describable by programmable representation-level rules. But we don't accept that it follows from this that connectionist nets should be seen as executing such rules.

There is an apt analogy from Marcello Guarini:

> The orbits of the planets are rule describable, but the planets do not make use of or consult rules in determining how they will move. In other words, planetary motion may *conform* to rules even if no rules are *executed* by the planets.
> [Guarini, 2001, p. 291]

A full development of this defence can be found in this same work [Guarini, 2001].

What, we were wondering, could a virtual logic be? We propose that a reasonable candidate is the requisite description of a cognitive system seen as a connectionist net that satisfies the condition of the *RWR* approach. It could be a logic of semantic processing without rules.

Questions about Representationalism

Here would be a good place to raise a question about representationalism *as such*. For a long time, 'the dominant position in cognitive science was not merely that the concept of representation might often play an important part in good scientific explanation of intelligent behaviour, but that explanatory strategies which appealed to representations offered our only hope for a scientific understanding of such behaviour.' [Wheeler, 2001, 211]; see also [Sterelny, 1990]. However, as Wheeler and others[3] have recently proposed, this dominant idea lies open to question. In the interests of space, we shall confine our remarks to a line of criticism developed in [Wheeler, 2001].

Part of what makes representationalism so interesting is that it is a claim about the central nervous system in beings like us. It proposes that neural structures play a distinctive role in explaining intelligent behaviour and that part of that distinctive role is discharged representationally. If, then, something is to be found wanting in this picture as it relates to its representational presumptions, it must consist in some difficulty with the view that wherever there is intelligent behaviour going on, there must be some representation going on in strictly neural terms.

The key test for representationalism is *on-line* intelligent behaviour, i.e., 'the sort of behaviour that reveals itself as a suite of fluid and flexible real-time adaptive responses to ongoing sensory stimuli.' [Wheeler, 2001, 213]. Off-line intelligence, on the other hand, is embodied in tasks such as wondering whether to have soup for lunch or reflecting on the advantages of daily exercise.

Here is a standard example of the orthodox representational approach as developed in AI. Consider a robot whose task it is to navigate around obstacles in getting to a light source. Given sensory inputs from a video camera, the robot executes perceptual inferences that enable it to build an internal model of the external environment. By consulting the model the robot is able to distinguish and coordinate between light source and obstacle,

[3]E.g., [Shannon, 1993; Thelen and Smith, 1993; Globus, 1992; Hendriks-Jansen, 1996; Wheeler, 1994; Beer, 1995; Brooks, 1991; Webb, 1994]. The span of these works is significant; they range over cognitive psychology, developmental psychology, neuroscience, cognitive philosophy and robotics.

and plan accordingly, encoding the route to a satisfactory outcome as a set of movement instructions. We see in this example that 'the bona fide well-springs of intelligence are fundamentally neural (e.g., inner mechanisms of inference, discrimination, estimation and route-planning)'. [Wheeler, 2001, 214]. Furthermore,

> within this heavily neuro-centric picture, representations are conceived as essentially context-dependent, stored descriptions of the environment, built during perception and then later accessed and manipulated by cognitively downstream reasoning algorithms that decide on the best thing to do, in order to achieve certain current goals. [Wheeler, 2001, 214]

Recent work in behaviour-based robotics (e.g., [Brooks, 1991]) and evolutionary robotics (e.g., [Husbands and Meyer, 1998]) has had some success in constructing control systems of a sort whose success casts doubt on representational presumptions. Such systems are especially good in dealing with a phenomenon that Wheeler and Clark [1999] call 'causal spread'.

> *Causal Spread*
> Causal spread obtains when some phenomenon of interest turns out to depend, in unexpected ways, upon causal factors external to the system previously/intuitively thought responsible.
> [Wheeler, 2001, 216]

In the standard representational approach, what makes a robot behave cleverly in the presence of such factors are interactions between neurally sited representations and computational events. However, on the evolutionary approach, this robotic cleverness — its adaptive richness and flexibility — flows not only from its neurological wherewithal but also from features built into the robot's body and to aspects of the robot's environment. In this newer picture the notion of representations as descriptions of the environment is replaced with the idea of extra-neural 'context-dependent codings for action' [Wheeler, 2001, 218]. For this to matter, it must be true that part of the explanation of the 'adaptive richness and complexity' of the robot's behaviour *not* be supplied by the functioning of its nervous system, but rather by appeal to various of its non-neural capabilities; and the point about causal spread is that, in dealing with it, the robot is able to code up for action in ways that do not involve the creation of an inner model of the external environment. These later Wheeler sees as part of the *normal ecological backdrop* of representational states and processes, which is not itself representational [Wheeler, 2001, 219].

Wheeler considers conditions under which it might be argued that the coding for action that it seems appropriate to attribute to a representation system's normal ecological backdrop can, after all, be attributed to the system's representational functions. Such might plausibly be supposed, Wheeler allows, provided that representational structures are both *arbitrary* and *homuncular*. A representation system is arbitrary when its representation functions turn not on any particular non-information properties of the system, but rather in the ways in which such components are organized and used. Right use, in turn, requires a homuncular mode of organization, typically a hierarchical arrangement of task-specific communicating subsystems, whose collective contribution constitutes performance of the main business of the overall system itself.

There is reason to think, however, that there are conditions in which a system behaves intelligently and yet the homuncularity assumption fails. As standardly understood in the literature, a homuncular system is a kind of modular system. If homuncularism is true of beings like us when engaged in intelligent behaviour, then it must also be true that our neural activity embodies a recognizable neural modularity that involves the intercommunication of (at least somewhat) hierarchically organized modules.[4] But, as Wheeler observes, there are conditions under which intelligent behaviour belies these assumptions.

Continuous Reciprocal Causation

Typical of a modular system is what Wimsatt [1986] calls an *aggregate system*. An aggregate system is one in which various parts are identifiable by their explanatory function independently of taking note of the other parts, and non-trivial cases of system-wide behaviour can be explained by reference to the operation of comparatively few parts. Consider now what Clark [1997] calls *continuous reciprocal causation*.

> This is causation that involves multiple simultaneous interactions and complex dynamic feedback loops, such that (i) the causal contributions of each component in the system partially determines, and is partially determined by, the causal contributions of *large* numbers of other components in the system, and, moreover, (ii) those contributions may change *radically* over time.
>
> [Wheeler, 2001, 224] (emphases added)

Faced with causation of this character, a system's aggregativity begins to break down. In such circumstances, the system's behaviour is more and

[4]Not everyone would see it this way; e.g., those who endorse a non-reductive supervenience of the intentional on the neural.

more irreducibly *holistic* or *higher-level*. To the extent that this is so, the modularity assumption is compromised, and with it the view that the system in question is homuncular.

The standard view that intelligent behaviour requires a thoroughgoing representationalism is challenged by the existence of causal spread. This challenge would be met if it could be shown that systems for intelligent behaviour were both arbitrary and homuncular and that the capacity for the appropriate exploitation of informational organization, required by the assumption of arbitrariness, is not itself supplied by the system's homuncularity. There is no homuncularity without modularity, and if modularity is typified by aggregate systems, then there is reason to suppose that in the presence of continuous reciprocal causation, intelligent systems cannot be aggregative; hence are not modular in ways that aggregate systems typify; hence cannot easily be seen as homuncular; hence cannot easily be seen as having the wherewithal for appropriateness of response to the information-organization arrangements required by the arbitrariness assumption. So it would appear that representationalism's defence against the phenomenon of causal spread does not succeed and, finally, that it cannot be said, with confidence at least, that on-line intelligent behaviour (the production of fluid and adaptable responses to ongoing sensory input) must or should be explained by appeal to neurally located representations.

An Example from Decision Theory

According to classical decision theory, to the extent that he is rational an agent will decide for courses of action that have the highest subjective expected utility (Raiffa [1968]). Such decisions are said to satisfy Bayes' Decision Rule. Solutions of decision problems can be represented as decision trees. A decision tree is a mathematically describable structure in which an agent's subjective probabilities and his utility functions are computed in ways that produce his subjective utilities averaged over various possible outcomes of alternative actions. This methodology is laid out in every textbook on the subject and will not detain us here.

A decision tree can be said to be *bushy* (Cooper [2001]) when it exhibits a high degree of complexity. This is the complexity concomitant with large numbers of decisive situations flowing from the branches of a decision tree, of which, in turn, the branches may also be bushy. As Cooper points out,

> there is no limit to how many variations a complex decision situation might have, and the variations need not be trivial ... It is mathematically obvious that when a great many mutually exclusive outcomes of a chance event are possible, with probabilities

> summing to one, most of these probabilities must be extremely small. [Cooper, 2001, pp. 54–55]

Bushy problems, as we may now call them, require that the decisional agent not merely hit upon the same expected subjective utility as would be determined by an explicitly constructed decision tree. Rather the decisional agent must become his own decision theorist and do something that is similar to expressly constructing the requisite tree. Another way of saying this is that bushy problems require the deciding agent to do something fairly describable as similar to making an explicit decision theoretic analysis of his own decisional situation. As Cooper sees it,

> Of course, the organism's processing needed to accomplish all this might not proceed in ways exactly analogous to [the production of right-to-left computational tree algorithms]. No one supposes that an organism will literally draw trees in its brain. It has only to execute some black-box approximations of that, with the processing giving rise to behaviour that looks *as if* a tree analysis had taken place. It isn't even clear that it must depend on the same general distinctions between choices, events, probabilities, consequences, and so on. The process need only result in behaviour that is so interpretable to us as analysts accustomed to these concepts. [Cooper, 2001, p. 58]

Let us reprise. Bushy problems can't be solved by just any process that produces the same answer as a decision tree. While the real-life practical agent needn't actually construct the very edifice that the mathematics of decision theory does construct, he must do something approximating to it. While he must do something that approximates to the construction of a decision tree, it is not required that he even have the concepts necessary for knowing what a decision tree is. And although he needn't be able to conceptualize a decision tree, whatever the practical agent does do in that black box of his, it must be interpretable by those who do have the concept of a decision tree as the construction of a decision tree.

The decision theory of 'down below' might now be identified with the task of determining whether, and upon what basis, what goes on in the decider's black box *is* interpretable as approximating to the construction of a decision tree. Making this determination depends on whether we are able to say, and upon what basis, that the agent's decisional behaviour is construable *as if* such a tree had been constructed. This much seems clear: that classical decision theorists take the view that whenever a practical agent takes a decision that comports (or comes close to comporting) with the winning answer produced by the requisite decision tree, then there exists a mathematical structure *MS* described by that tree, and further that the tree description of *MS* invokes concepts (choices, events, probabilities, utilities, consequences, etc.) which according to the decision theorist are necessary for an adequate conceptual analysis of decision. This, too, is the view of the present authors.

The existence of *MS* gives rise to two possible inferences, one strong and one weak. The strong inference is that *MS* fits the circumstances of actual decision-making. The weak inference is that those actual circumstances can be interpreted as if *MS* fits them. (We note in passing that though they are exclusive, Cooper runs both inferences). The decision theory of down below tries to sort out which if either of these two inferences to draw. We ourselves are of the view that nothing stronger than the weak inference is plausible, and that even in its weak form, it may be too strong for its own good.

This suggests a third possibility, both for the decision theorist and the logician. Grant that for every more or less correctly taken decision of a practical agent, there exists an *MS*. Similarly, grant that for every successfully made logical operation by an actual agent there also exists an *LS*, i.e., a logical structure describable in some requisite logical theory in a language that invokes concepts (e.g., consequence, consistency, revision, plausibility, and so on) necessary for an adequate conceptual analysis of the kind of reasoning in question. Now the third option says, in effect, that not even the weak inference should be drawn, but rather that the task of determining *whether* to draw it (or some other) should be sent over to the research programme of cognitive psychology. Thus the logician's contribution or the decision theorist's contribution is to construct the requisite structure, *MS* and *LS*. A further contribution is whenever possible to provide reasons (such as complexity-overload) that count against at least the strong inference. The psychologist's contribution is, whether by experiment or abduction, to get inside the reasoner's black box to search out further details of the fit or lack of it with *MS* and *LS*.

Chapter 4

Formal Pragmatics

> The topic of relevance has suffered much from those who have taken a part of the topic as the whole.
>
> [Cohen, 1994, p. 171]

4.1 Pragmatics

In his William James Lectures at Harvard in 1967, Paul Grice sketched a theory of conversation and forwarded some celebrated advice:

> Under the category of RELATION I place a single maxim, namely, 'Be relevant'. Though the maxim is terse, its formulation conceals a number of problems that exercise me a good deal ... I find the treatment of such [problems] exceedingly difficult, and I hope to revert to it in later work. [Grice, 1991, p. 308]

Regrettably, he wasn't able to do so before his death in 1988.[1]

What is it, then, that Grice bids us to be? If we were to consult virtually any library of works in philosophy or the social sciences, arbitrary selection would produce a volume which, page after page after page, employed the idioms of relevance in its critical and descriptive passages. Yet consult its index and we would be surprised to find a listing for 'relevance'. In the eight volumes of *The Encyclopedia of Philosophy* there is no entry for relevance, and it is given desultory recognition in the index only twice.[2] Nor,

[1]Although there is a huge Gricean literature; e.g., [Atlas, 1989; Horn, 1989; Hirshberg, 1991] and [Levinson, 2001].

[2]Richard Taylor [1967, vol. 2, p. 60] speaks of relevant similarity in the analysis of causality. He cites 'the great difficulty of defining "relevance" in this context without

apart from relevance *logic*, do we find entries in *The Oxford Dictionary of Philosophy* [Blackburn, 1994], *The Oxford Companion to Philosophy* [Honderich, 1995], *The Cambridge Dictionary of Philosophy* [Audi, 1999] and the *Routledge Concise Encyclopedia of Philosophy* [2002]. An exception is the *Penguin Dictionary of Philosophy* [Mautner, 1999], which has entries for 'relevant' as well as 'relevance logic'.

The logical canon has recorded some impressive accomplishments these past two millennia. Some things have done better than others. Validity has prospered. Inductive strength can claim some lesser, though substantial, achievements. Implication has made strides that inference cannot pretend to match. In comparison, relevance has not done very well.[3]

Theories that have most interested logicians have been those in which relevance is a kind of logical relation,[4] anyhow a relation defined over propositions or proposition-sets. This correlation is a clear reflection in turn of what these theorists take a logic to be. In some accounts, relevance is a semantic relation [Govier, 1988a, pp. 122–23], affecting truth or falsehood; in others, it is a probabilistic relation ([Johnson and Blair, 1983, 15–16]; [Bowles, 1990, pp. 65–78]), affecting likelihood; in still others, relevance is a condition on implication, and so is a matter of topical overlap [Walton, 1982, p. 83], and [Epstein, 1979, pp. 137–173]) or the sharing of propositional variables [Anderson and Belnap, 1975] or the full use of hypotheses in a proof [Anderson and Belnap, 1975].

Given our own propensity to see logic as a pragmatic theory of cognitive agency, it will come as no surprise that we take the propositional approach to relevance to be too narrowly focused for our needs. Apart from that, the intuitive idea of relevance as primarily a propositional relation seems not, in detail, to have attracted much consensus among like-minded theorists.

---

spoiling the whole analysis'. And A.N. Prior [1967, vol. 5, p. 6] makes glancing mention of early work on relevant logic. 'Relevance' is not the only shrinking violet, of course. See, for example [Toulmin, 1972, p. 8]: 'The term *concept* is one that everybody uses and nobody explains—still less defines'. (An exception is [McGinn, 1989; McGinn, 1999]) [Putnam, 1988, p. 1]: 'Yet few [thinkers] ever say what the word [=intentionality, in this case] means ... [I]t has become a chapter-heading word: a word which stands for a whole range of topics and issues rather than for one subject'; and [Dretske, 1981, p. ix]: 'A surprising number of books, and this includes textbooks, have the word *information* in their title without bothering to include it in their index'.

[3]The present state of relevance theory puts us in mind of Hamblin's 1970 *cri de coeur* about the fallacies. 'The truth is that nobody, these days, is particularly satisfied with this corner of logic ... We have no *theory* of fallacy at all.... In some respects... we are in the position of medieval logicians before the 12th century: we have lost the doctrine of fallacy, and we need to rediscover it.' Even so, relevance is different. There never was a 'doctrine of relevance' to lose. See [Hamblin, 1970, p. 11].

[4]A 'timeless quasi-logical relation', according to Cohen. See [Cohen, 1989, p. 150; cf. 11–12].

Perhaps, as Isaiah Berlin has it, ' "relevance" is not a precise logical category ... the word is used to convey an essentially vague idea' [Berlin, 1939, p. 21]. In any event, semantic, probabilistic and topical theories abound in construals that are both half-baked and excessive. Commonly relevance is only partially defined (either as a merely sufficient condition of something or a merely necessary condition of something) — thus the problem of half-bakedness;[5] and often a theoretical reconstruction produces embarrassing consequences, such as that everything is relevant to everything or that nothing is relevant to anything—thus the charge of excessiveness.

Some logical accounts do better than others. One of the most interesting of these represents relevance as conditional probability constrained in ways to avert counterexamples [Schlesinger, 1986, pp. 57–67], and [Bowles, 1990, pp. 65–78]. Hardly half-baked or excessive, such treatments, even so, fall into the camp of the attractive but troubled.

> I do not want to say that [my explication] is fully adequate; in fact it is quite obvious that it needs to be qualified in a number of ways, for as it stands it is subject to objections.
>
> [Schlesinger, 1986, p. 66]

The received ideas about relevance reflect a twofold pre-supposition: that relevance is a semantico-probabilistic relation, and that relevance is dyadic. It might be thought that the two traits are linked. For take any purported semantic relation beyond the two-place, and there is some chance that you will have recast it pragmatically, finding at place three a role for speakers or purveyors and takers-in of information. The generally bad history of relevance as a two-place semantic (or probabilistic) relation suggests that we might do better to cast our nets more widely, to the third place at least, and that in doing so we position relevance for pragmatic attention.[6]

[5] Half-bakedness is not by any means confined to semantic and probabilistic accounts. For an example from conversation analysis, Jacobs and Jackson distinguish informational from pragmatic relevance. It is not clear whether 'having a bearing on deciding on the acceptability of a proposition' is intended as giving a necessary and sufficient condition for informational relevance (circularity aside), but it does seem apparent that pragmatic relevance is, at best, attended by sufficient conditions only. See [Jacobs and Jackson, 1992, 161–172; 162 passim]. A clearer case is afforded by the pragma-dialectical treatment of van Eemeren and Grootendorst. They offer 'a general definition of relevance: An element of discourse is relevant to another element of discourse if an interactional relation can be envisaged between these elements that is functional in the light of a certain objective'. Here again we have sufficiency only. See [van Eemeren and Grootendorst, 1992, 141–159; 141].

[6] We should not, however, take the suggestion too inflexibly. William Lycan has a truth predicate that is *pentadic*, but which assigns no express role to language-users or processors of information [Lycan, 1984, chapter 3].

'Pragmatic' is also something of a chapter-heading word. According to the coiner of the term pragmatics is the study of 'the biotic aspects of semiosis, that is, ... [of] all the psychological, biological and sociological phenomena which occur in the functioning of signs.'[7] Some writers are chary of so untidy and heterogeneous a domain for pragmatics. They propose something more circumscribed:

> Pragmatics will have as its domain speakers' communicative intentions, the users of language that require such intentions, and the strategies that hearers employ to determine what these intentions and acts are, so that they can understand what the speaker intends to communicate.[8]

We shall propose something broader. Pragmatics is a psychologically realizable theory of certain kinds of informational competence. It is the kind of competence that we associate with operation of cognitive systems. We propose this in the spirit of [Sperber and Wilson, 1986], which has rightly been said to be 'the first account of pragmatics which is grounded in psychology' [Carston, 1987, 713]. In the broadest possible way, the kinds of information-processing that we have it in mind to consider covers all aspects of what we we are calling *cognitive agency.* Since we take this to include the firing of devices at subconscious and pre-linguistic levels, we must propose that our notion of pragmatics be understood accordingly. On our view, pragmatics also includes but cannot be restricted to a speaker's intentions. And since we shall be taking a pragmatics approach to relevance, the same latitude needs to be accorded to relevance. Accordingly, we shall say relevance can be in play in an agent's cognitive life independently of his intentions and without his awareness.

In this, we find ourselves in sympathy with Diane Blakemore:

> The fact that some aspects of linguistic form do not contribute to the truth-conditional content of utterances is frequently acknowledged but very rarely explained. This is not, perhaps, surprising, given the range of expressions and constructions that convey nontruth-conditional meaning and the variety of effects to which they give rise. Moreover, until very recently one could camouflage the lack of progress by designating all such phenomena as 'pragmatic', the assumption being that someone would eventually provide a pragmatic theory. [Blakemore, 1987, 712]

[7]See 'Foundations of the Theory of Signs', in [Morris, 1971, pp. 17–74; p. 43]. Cf., '... pragmatics, ... as Bar-Hillel once said, functions as the waste paper basket of linguistics, a place where recalcitrant phenomena can be deposited after they have been declared irrelevant.' Quoted from [Gamut, 1991, p. 196].

[8][Davis, 1991, Introduction, p.11].

It is Richard Montague's view that pragmatics is a branch of mathematics [Thomason, 1974, p. 2]. We mention this only to say that it is not pragmatics in our sense. Pragmatics is a psychologically realizable theory of a certain kind of informational competence. Boldly stated, it is the ability to process or to react to information in ways that give rise to successful communication or reasoning. As such it stands somewhere between a theory of interpretation of the communicational intentions of speakers and the wide-open spaces encompassed by Morris' latitudinarian conception. Whatever the details of its mandate, pragmatics will include a theory of inference, that is, a theory of belief-adjustment under certain constraints, or of what Harman calls *changes in view* [Harman, 1986]. This may seem an odd inclusion, perplexing to those for whom it is a settled question that logic is at least a large part of the theory of inference. Our own view is that the theory of inference is indeed a large part of logic, but that this is nothing to be startled about. For we also think that, in its fullest sense, logic is also pragmatic. (See the preceding chapter.)

We do not venture lightly into the pragmatics of relevance. We are mindful of those who say that 'no attempt to apply semantic theory to this notion has been successful enough to provide a model that would be usable in pragmatics' [Thomason, 1990]. And yet we are also aware that left to its own devices, 'current accounts of conversational interaction depend crucially upon the *undefined* notion of "relevance".' [Werth, 1981, p. 30] (emphasis added).

In the chapter to follow, relevance appears as a two-place semantic or probabilistic relation. So taken, it doesn't fare especially well, as we shall see. That chapter tells a cautionary tale. It cautions against the deployment of analytical lexicons which may prove too coarse-grained for relevance. The principle task is motivational rather than demonstrative. There is no thought of proving that semantico-probabilistic accounts are an intrinsic failure for relevance, only that many are in fact. Thus, again, the rhetorical motifs of excessiveness and half-bakedness. The burden of the chapter, as we say, is motivational. It furnishes the occasion to look elsewhere for an account of relevance, in an analytical lexicon admitting conceptual nuances that the more austere propositional vocabularies ignore or suppress.

Chapter 6 is reserved for consideration of some important issues raised by Sperber and Wilson in their book, *Relevance* [Sperber and Wilson, 1986]. In certain ways, *Relevance* is the best thing produced to date, and in certain respects it will be difficult to improve upon it (which is not to overlook some stern and effective critics; e.g., [Levinson, 1989]). This book bears the ambitious subtitle, *Communication and Cognition*; it promises a good deal more than one would look for in an analysis or explication of the relevance relation. Some of what is said about those further things will be of interest for the evolving argument on behalf of agenda relevance, which is the principal business of this book to develop. For the most part, however, we concentrate on their explication of the relevance relation itself.

The positive conceptual account of agenda relevance is the business of chapters 7–10. We shall present a pragmatic treatment in which relevance is a causal relation defined over triples $\langle \mathbf{I}, \mathbf{X}, \mathbf{A} \rangle$ of *information*, *cognitive agents* and *agendas*. Distinctions are tentatively invoked between *de facto* and objective senses of relevance and, as a loose counterpart, between descriptive and normative accounts, respectively, of the prior two. As we employ the notion, a descriptive theory includes an explication of the notion of *de facto* relevance, followed by a psychological account which specifies conditions under which *de facto* relevance actually obtains. And, initially at least, a normative theory comprehends an explication of the notion of objective relevance, followed by a normative theory specifying conditions under which objective relevance actually or counterfactually obtains. The idea of relevance as a causal relation has been put forward (and later abandoned) by Blair [1992, pp. 67–83; 68]. Relevance is defined for triples in [Hitchcock, 1992, pp. 252 and 265], but Hitchcock and we specify our triples differently, as we shall see in due course.

As a slack convenience, we sometimes describe what we are doing in these pages as providing descriptive and normative accounts of relevance. It is a convenience that borders on indulgence. If we bear in mind that the descriptive theory comes in two parts — an explication or analysis of *de facto* relevance and a psychological theory about it — then, as will become clear as we proceed, our remarks are directed almost exclusively to the first, or explicational, task. Our philosophical forbears might have spoken of this as a prolegomenon.

As for a normative theory, it too would come in two parts — an explication of objective relevance, followed by a philosophical theory about it. But we fear that we have little to say that lays even indulgent claim on the name of normative theory. For one thing, we are not sure about how to proceed with the explication of objective relevance. This and other vexatious matters are reserved for chapter 10. In chapters 11–15, we shall construct some elementary formal models of results proposed in the prior seven. A principal function of the formal models methodology is to find abstractions that enable otherwise inapparent connections to be made, thus bringing to the conceptual account a certain degree of finish. Whether it is also possible that formalization will stabilize the linked questions of objectivity and normativity is something we shall take up as we proceed.

The putative distinction between *de facto* and objective relevance may strike the reader as a trifle odd. Wouldn't something more obviously antonymous be a more natural choice? We have nothing against subjective relevance. We might say that something is subjectively relevant for a person when he thinks it is, or judges it to be, relevant for him. This is not, in any case, the target of what we are calling a descriptive theory. A descriptive theory is a theory about things that are *in fact* relevant for someone (Sarah, say) independently of whether she knows this or entertains any views about the matter. A normative theory has objective relevance as its target. Objective relevance is *de facto* relevance that obtains, actually or counterfactually, in fulfillment of a condition. The condition answers roughly to the idea of 'things happening as they should'. Here, too, something might be objectively relevant for someone without one having the slightest idea that this is so. The distinction we are after, and shall eventually get to, is a distinction between what a descriptive and a normative theory of relevance are theories of. 'Subjective' won't deliver the goods for these.

The idioms of relevance bespeak a rather sprawling notion. Ambiguous, vague and often redundant, 'relevant' is a conversational commonplace. The magnitude of the sprawl may be standing and effective discouragement of a theoretical treatment that answers to it all. In that respect 'relevant' is like 'thing'. Relevance has an interesting etymology. It originates in the mediaeval Latin *relevantem*, present participle of *relēvare*: to raise (up; against); to assist, to relieve. The Italian *rilevento* brings us closer to home: of importance, worth, consequence. The Compact Edition of the *Oxford English Dictionary* 1971, gives pride of place to *bearing upon*, *connected with*, *pertinent to* (some matter at hand). These are surprisingly modern uses, rare before 1800, and the prior uses, reflective of the etymology, *relieving*, *remedial* are long since obsolete.

The lead-entry of the *OED* is instructive. It presents us with a nice little knot. Something is relevant when it is pertinent to some matter at hand. 'At hand' suggests come contextually relevant matter. So something is relevant when it is pertinent to some relevant matter, to some matter to which it is pertinent. The circularity is unattractive. It suggests that we drop 'at hand' or else reinterpret. Something is relevant to a matter when it is pertinent to it; or something is relevant when there is some contextually specified matter to which it is pertinent. 'At hand' now suggests 'at hand for someone or something', and that would seem to make of relevance a three-place relation. Something is relevant for someone or something with regard to a matter at hand.

Something of the sprawl of 'relevance' is indicated by the generosity of its lexical affiliations. Something is relevant when it is pertinent, has to do with, has a bearing on, is important for, is involved with, is evidence for, is on-topic, consequential, confirming, potentially falsifying, significant, helpful (shades of the antique 'remedial'), and interesting. One could go on. Ambiguity and vagueness speak for themselves. Redundancy requires a brief aside. We sometimes speak of 'relevant evidence' when 'evidence' alone would do. In a court of law evidence is relevant testimony, and relevant testimony is what is admitted as evidence. In a similar vein, relevant factors are hardly more than factors, relevant answers are replies that *are* answers, and irrelevant considerations aren't considerations after all. Issues that pertain relevantly are issues that pertain, and having a relevant bearing on something is having a bearing on it. Having a more relevant bearing on something is having more of a bearing on it than others things that bear.

Redundancy, as we see, is an attractive device of emphasis and of lexical relief and, often enough, occasion of a kind of discursive pomposity. The relevance idiom is a lazy convenience, like that of 'appropriate' and 'significant'. We issue promissory notes with them, routinely left unredeemed.

It is notable, in any event, that 'relevance' is a word whose currency varies inversely with the availability of theories to account for it. To repeat an earlier point, even in regimented, self-consciously scientific discourse, pick any of your favourite volumes on cognitive science, artificial intelligence, or argumentation theory. Although relevance is always relevant to these works, its theoretical treatment is notable by its absence.[9] This is surprising on the face of it. It would seem that relevance recognition and irrelevance avoidance are two of our most primitive skills, essential to survival and prosperity alike, and efficiently up and running well ahead of the mastery of speech. And yet attempts to get at good theories of relevance have not met with much success.

4.2 Theoretical Recalcitrance

Lexical sprawl, ambiguity, vagueness, redundancy; the primitiveness of relevance detection skills; the bad record of theory. These facts may suggest that relevance is not a theoretically tractable notion, that it is, so to speak, analytically or conceptually primitive. As we will see, attempt upon attempt

[9]The list goes on. See, for example [Nisbett and Ross, 1980; Dretske, 1981; Pylyshyn, 1984; Holland *et al.*, 1986; Rumelhart *et al.*, 1986; Stillings *et al.*, 1987; Boden, 1987; Kanerva, 1987; Gabbay, 1994; Josephson and Josephson, 1994; Brandom, 2000; Barringer *et al.*, 1996; Glymour and Cooper, 1999; Stanovich, 1999; Flach and Kakas, 2000; Walton and Krabbe, 1995; Von Eckard, 1993; Huhns and Singh, editors, 1998; Rey, 1997; Antoniou, 1995; Thagard, 1992; Stein, 1996; Adler, 2002; Grice, 2001].

at theory lands us in triviality or vacuity. Some people propose that we take as a serious possibility the conceptual primitiveness of relevance. As Michael Scriven points out (following Frege, and before him Kant),[10] truth has done well as a primitive in Tarski semantics. (It is not a *Tarskian* primitive, but let that pass.)[11] Perhaps the bad record of relevance theory suggests a degenerating research programme in the sense of Lakatos, except that it seems not to have been preceded by anything like a robust research programme, so to speak [Lakatos, 1970, pp. 91–96]. If so, this would indicate well enough the recalcitrance of relevance. But recalcitrance is one thing. Primitiveness is another thing altogether. If relevance theory is a degenerating research programme it could not be on account of primitiveness that this is so.[12]

Why then introduce it? The answer is that a discussion of primitiveness helps us set our targets. If relevance were primitive, that alone would not make the case for theoretical recalcitrance. But it would matter in other more constructive ways. Zero is primitive in Peano arithmetic. Here a primitive notion is used to define a further one — natural numberhood in arithmetic. The definition is recursive rather than lexical. It has also been said that although undefined either recursively or lexically, zero is defined implicitly, defined by its systematic contributions to theories which invoke it. In another example, the concept of *problem* is primitive in computational complexity theory (e.g., [Kolmogorov, 1965]). The problem of what it is to be a problem has not yet attracted the attention of analytical theories. Here, too, one searches in vain the indexes of works that deal with problems and problem-solving for an entry for 'problem.' Other examples are the primitiveness of the concept of intention in the planning theory of [Allen *et*

[10]Intervening at the Third International Symposium on Informal Logic, University of Windsor, June 1989. We had thought of adding J. Anthony Blair to this list. Blair speaks of 'premissary relevance', and 'doubt[s] that such relevance can be analyzed — shown to be derived from or reducible to other concepts...' Even so, he quickly goes on to give a provisional definition of it. See [Blair, 1992, pp. 204–205].

[11]In some versions denotation is explicitly definable, in first-order arithmetic for example, but let that pass. See [McGee, 1991, p. 69].

[12]In some respects, the present suggestion resembles one set out in [Fodor, 1983]. Fodor there develops a tripartite account of cognition. At one level, cognition involves the operation of central processes, which Fodor characterizes as *Quinean* and *isotropic*. They are Quinean because they cannot be atomically decomposed, and they are isotropic because they receive no guidance from domain-specificity. Fodor takes it to follow from these characteristics that general processes are slow and virtually impossible to understand. Always good for a joke, Fodor proposes 'Fodor's First Law of the Nonexistence of Cognitive Science': the more a cognitive process has these characteristics the less it can be understood. Such processes are also called global. Fodor's Law implies that highly global processes are not presently understood; 'nor is there much hope that they ever will be'. [Fodor, 1983, p. 107] and [Fodor, 1998] *passim*.

al., 1991] and the concepts of time, period and meet in the interval-based temporal logic of [Allen and Hayes, 1989].

We see that terms are subject to different kinds of analytical working up. Lexical definitions come by way of the specification of truth conditions that license the substitution of a defining term for a defined term. Sometimes it is said that substitutivity is sanctioned by lexical synonymy, as with 'bachelor' and 'unmarried man'. We shall not say so here. We shall say instead that lexical substitutions of term τ for term τ^* in a context C are those sanctioned by an appropriate translation manual (here a dictionary, approximately). A translation manual counts as appropriate when it fulfils what could be called 'Quine's pragmatic test'. That is, appropriateness is a matter of the extent to which a manual abets smoothness of linguistic negotiation and general conversational fluency [Quine, 1990]. It is worth noting that appropriateness here is an attribute of manuals. An appropriate manual can sometimes sanction lexical substitutions that would not be likely to abet the easy flow of conversation. Our manual tells us that 'yclept' substitutes for 'known as'; but we wouldn't want to say that police station poster which read, 'Wanted for bank robbery: Spike McGurk, yclept Mike Jones', would be an efficient communication for its target audience.

Lexical definitions are sometimes stipulative. They count as stipulative in a language L just to the extent that no appropriate translation manual for L sanctions the associated lexical substitution. In such cases, substitutivity is underwritten, not by a translation manual that is up and running, but by a theory. Sooner or later, some theories catch on in ways that influence translation manuals; and stipulativeness then trails away.[13]

Recursive definitions make use of truth conditions in a different way. The formation rules for 'sentence' in first-order theories of quantification recursively enumerate the sentences of quantification theory, but not in a manner that permits lexical substitutivity. Contextual elimination is a third case. Russell's treatment of definite descriptions is a classical example. Terms of the form $\ulcorner$the $\Phi\urcorner$ prove to be incomplete symbols. For any sentence in which such a term occurs there is, equivalently, another in which it doesn't and in which no term is substitutable for the definite description in the first. Lexical substitutivity defers to sentential equivalence.

Lexical, recursive and contextual definitions all turn on the specification of truth conditions necessary and sufficient for their definienda. These may be thought of more broadly as biconditional definitions, and we shall speak of them this way here.

Implicit definitions stand apart. They are not everyone's cup of tea. They fare best in theories that are the deductive closure of categorical ax-

[13]For more on stipulation, see [Woods, 2002b, Ch. 6].

ioms — zero, again, in second-order Peano arithmetic, in which all models are isomorphic. In less determinate environments, implicit definition is a matter of degree. Partial definitions now, they do better with sufficiency than with necessity. Even so, we don't doubt the utility of implicit definitions. A theory implicitly defines a term to the extent that it fixes its extension beyond the provisions for it already made by biconditional definitions (if any). Seen this way, theories containing biconditional definitions of their target terms also routinely afford implicit definitions of them.

In these cases, implicit definitions convey information about target notions that could not be derived from their biconditional definitions alone. Some writers dislike this way of talking. They regret the absence of a sharp distinction between the conceptual and the empirical, with which to constrain the reach of implicit definitions. Thus implicit definitions of a term τ are the contributions of a purely conceptual kind, underivable from biconditional definitions alone if any, that a theory of τ-hood generates. For those who are easy with a sharp divide between the conceptual and the empirical, there is no harm in the constraint. We are not so minded, however. We are content to let any theory worth its salt to count as a (partial) implicit definition of its target concepts τ exactly when it sanctions claims about τ-things underivable from biconditional definitions alone.

Implicit definitions are interesting. They help us get clear about primitiveness. Suppose that a term occurs in the language of a theory T. If T furnishes τ with a biconditional definition then we will say that τ is complex in T; alternatively, that τ is explicitly definable in T.[14] When T itself qualifies as an implicit definition of τ, and yet τ is not, in our present sense, complex, we will say that it is primitive in T. Moreover, τ is absolutely primitive if and only if there exists no theory T^* in which it is explicitly definable. Primitiveness is not a natural kind. Whether a term is primitive in a theory is a matter of the theorists' decision to make it so. A rearrangement of axiomatic arithmetic is possible in which zero comes out complex, but it would not seem a 'natural' arrangement. Often, of course, a decision for primitiveness is a matter of the theorist not being able to contrive a complex role for it, a failure of the theorist's imagination. The means are now at hand to say something about explication. We reserve the name of explication, and of analysis too, for any definition that makes an explicated term complex in the theory that defines it. Thus T explicates τ if for some $T' \subseteq T$ not containing τ and ϕ we have $T' \vdash \exists x \phi x$ and $T \vdash \tau = (\iota x)\phi(x)$. If $T = \{(\tau = c) \wedge \exists! x(x = c)\}$, then τ is explicitly definable.

[14]Formally, τ is complex iff there is a wff $\varphi(x)$ not containing τ such that $T \vdash \exists! x\varphi(x)$ and, provided that $t \notin T$, we define $\tau =$ the x such that $\varphi(x)$, i.e., $\tau = ((ix)\varphi(x))$. τ is primitive iff τ is in the language and $T \vdash \varphi(\tau)$ for some φ, and $T \vdash \exists! x\phi(x)$.

Primitiveness calls to mind Russell's notion of a minimum vocabulary. M is a minimum vocabulary if and only if M is a set of expressions such that no expression of M is definable in M. (Implicit definability is not at issue here.) M is a minimum vocabulary for a theory T if and only if M is a minimum vocabulary and every expression in T's vocabulary that is not in M is definable in M.[15] A term τ is primitive in a theory T just in case T possesses a minimum vocabulary and τ is a member of it. A term τ^* is complex in a theory T just in case it does not occur in M and yet is definable there, where M is a minimum vocabulary for T. Attempting an explication of a complex term τ^* involves finding a theoretical language in which τ^* is complex and in which the definition of it in some M is brought off in a satisfactory way.

Recalcitrant terms are terms that have not won their way into the vocabularies of decent theories. So, decisions on recalcitrance are a function of what counts as decent. At times, theorists such as Quine are prepared to recognize the complexity of a term such as 'synonymous', by way of identity of meanings, but for them synonymy is recalcitrant. At other times synonymy is seen as primitive, with meanings defined as its equivalence classes. Either way, synonymy is held to be recalcitrant and, each time, it has nothing essentially to do with primitiveness or complexity. Any theory admitting synonymy is said to fail conditions on a good semantic theory. This may or may not be so. Quine's judgement on synonymy is for illustration only.

Judging for recalcitrance is just a way of judging for the unavailability of decent theories. In the case of relevance, a finding of intractability would require two things. One is the identification of theories whose working vocabularies contain the word 'relevant'. The other involves the specification of conditions under which the theory qualifies as a good theory. So seen, it is immediate that relevance is not recalcitrant. 'Relevant' occurs in the working vocabulary of relevant logic, various versions of which are sound and complete and conform to the intuitions of lots of theorists. If it strikes us as queer that the charge of recalcitrance should prove to have been so easily stilled, it may be that our first requirement should be amended. Bearing in mind that no theory is a theory of relevance just because 'relevant' occurs in its working vocabulary (and so no one seriously thinks that relevant logic is a *theory of relevance*), we might better say that 'relevant' is recalcitrant just in case, for anything counting as a theory of relevance, adequacy conditions will go unmet. By these lights, a positive finding is just a claim that there is no such thing as a good theory of relevance. Recalcitrance makes the claim; it does not explain it. In so saying, the intractabilist about relevance

[15]This leaves it open that a minimum vocabulary for a theory not be part of the theory's language.

take on a burden assumed by the intractabilist about synonymy. Each must independently show the impossibility of good theories. Quine and others have made a stab at discharging the onus in regard to synonymy. Nobody, so far, seems even to have acknowledged the onus — never mind discharged it — in the case of relevance. We ourselves have no workable idea of how to proceed with a claim to the effect that there could be no such thing as a good theory of relevance. The onus is not ours in any event, and we shall not trouble further with recalcitrance. That is, we shall not trouble with it further until chapter 10 where we revive the issue by way of skeptical remarks about objective relevance and about putatively normative theories to account for it.

We have said that terms do not stand forth as candidates for recalcitrance in the absence of independent reasons for thinking that they are or are not susceptible of decent theories. There is, of course, an exception to this. Our intuitions about the use of terms such as 'true' and 'set' are inconsistent. The Liar paradox and the Russell paradox show them to be so. This anyhow is the received wisdom.[16] They are, thus, recalcitrant; and finding them so does not await an independent verdict on whether there could be decent theories about them. Of course, dialethic logicians aside, there could not be good theories about them. But this is a finding implied by recalcitrance, not independent of it. The conception of truth, or of set, must change and with it the idea of what a good theory would be.

Theoretically recalcitrant terms should not, just as they stand, be dismissed. Their recalcitrance is not intrinsically inimical to their efficient and indispensable use. Ziff once said, in effect, that 'to' in its first occurrence in 'I want to go to Istanbul' is recalcitrant in any theory of meaning. But he did not intend that such uses of 'to' should be expunged from English or that grammar should take no notice of it [Ziff, 1960, pp. 42–43].

'Relevance' occurs conspicuously in the vocabularies of a great many theories which don't (or shouldn't) call themselves theories of relevance. They occur there primitively, as in Grice's theory of conversation. In accounts that qualify as theories of relevance, 'relevant' is often accorded complexity of high grade, or at least the promise of it, for there are many accounts in which biconditional definitions are ventured, though often enough they are only half-provided. Let us say that, taken so, relevance is thought of as biconditionally complex. Such theories have not flourished. This alone calls into doubt assumptions of biconditional complexity. The question arises as to whether it is possible to attribute biconditional complexity to relevance

[16]But for a heterodox approach to these matters, see [Woods, 2002b, Ch. 7], Slater [2002] and Irvine [1992].

in any theory that qualifies as interesting and deep. It is a matter of how far we want to press the idea of necessary and sufficient conditions.

4.3 Analysis

Conceived as an effort to recognize the biconditional complexity of relevance, a theory of relevance can expect to meet with a certain amount of skepticism. There are those who think that no common sense term is definable by way of necessary and sufficient conditions. It is certainly true that if we mean by a biconditional definition of a common sense term τ something that gives its meaning(s) in the speech community S in which τ occurs and that it does this in a way that makes the extension of τ effectively recognizable in S, then there will be many fewer successful biconditional definitions than we might have supposed. And if we mean by the explication or analysis of a term that which is afforded by a biconditional definition of it in fulfilment of these same two conditions, then there will be many fewer explications or analyses than we might have supposed. It could be that nothing would qualify as an explication or analysis of relevance in this sense.

Analyses of the sort in question we could dub 'algorithmic'. Algorithmic analyses are not easy to come by as a general rule. In standard first-order theories in which quantification is monadic (only)[17] an algorithmic analysis of 'valid argument form' is possible. It is one for which there is no admissible valuation on its atoms that simultaneously verifies the premisses and falsifies the conclusion. Validity, as defined, is also decidable. Decidability is lost, and algorithmic analysability too, once quantification ventures beyond the monadic. Yet the definition of validity stays the same. It suggests that analysability is an unrealistic ideal. For this reason, among others, we do not have it in mind to produce an algorithmic analysis of relevance. We are after an analysis of relevance which could be called 'theoretical'. Necessary and sufficient conditions are proposed as carving out a target concept of relevance. The target concept is presumed to be reflected in a range of uses of the word 'relevant' and cognates and antonyms of it by speakers of English. It is not supposed that the target concept discloses what those speakers mean when they speak in such ways, though neither is it foreclosed that some do mean this on some occasions of speaking in these ways. The concept in question is a set of truth conditions. Sentences attributing relevance are thought to fulfil the conditions outright or after

[17]By a fragment of classical logic in which 'quantification is monadic' we mean either the usual monadic predicate logic or the newly identified 'guarded fragments' of classical logic, where each quantifier is guarded by an atomic predicate (e.g., $\ulcorner\forall x(G(x) \rightarrow \psi(x, y))\urcorner$).

some paraphrasing. Necessary and sufficient conditions can be thought of as specifying a sense of the world 'relevant'.

Whether a proposed sense of the word is worth bothering with will depend on two things. One is the interest that antecedently attaches to uses of 'relevant' with respect to which that sense is specified. In particular, we don't propose that uses in which 'relevant' in redundant — as in 'relevant option' — are interesting for an analysis of relevance. In fact, we should expect that such uses will not be captured by any definition purporting to give an analysis of relevance. It is common to try to protect one's definition against the counterexamples portended by recalcitrant uses, by invoking the strategic device of ambiguation. Uses of 'relevant' that are redundant in this way are not the same sense of 'relevant' as ours. In fact, they do not constitute any sense of the word 'relevant'. Ambiguation, here, is the extremity of attaching the null sense to redundant uses of 'relevant'. Ambiguation should not be a strategy available just for the asking. There is a semantic version of Occam's Razor. It bids us not to postulate senses, beyond necessity.[18] It is hard to be specific about this. Presumably one should not postulate senses that would disarm counterexamples that should not be disarmed. But we have no general recipe for this.

Necessary and sufficient conditions are sometimes regretted on account of fuzziness of the world. At best, people will say, the world approximates to the satisfaction of necessary and sufficient conditions; and this makes them not be necessary or sufficient. In this spirit, enthusiasm for truth gives way to a reconciliation to truth-likeness and so on. We are not so discouraged by fuzziness. We take it that some uses will fulfil outright the truth conditions on relevance in the theoretically intended sense. If those uses are interesting and if the analysis of the relevance concept that they reflect proves theoretically fruitful in the sense just touched upon, we would nevertheless expect that there would be interesting uses of 'relevant' that do not satisfy the analysis and yet for which we would be loath to press either for a verdict of counterexample or for recognition of a different sense of 'relevant'. Such uses inhabit a twilight zone; they can be thought of as approximating to the satisfaction of a theory's truth conditions. In this we agree with van Fraassen: 'a vague predicate is usable provided it has clear cases and clear counter-cases' [van Fraassen, 1980, 16].

Our provisional and somewhat hopeful assumption is that relevance is susceptible to what we can now call a *theoretical analysis*. A theoretical analysis sets the stage for a descriptive theory. It specifies what the descriptive theory is about and it imposes partial and provisional constraints upon what theory can go on to say about relevance so conceived of. Perhaps

[18]Among hard-hearted extensionalists it is proposed that we not postulate them at all.

the most justly celebrated theoretical analysis is the one Tarski produced for truth in a language L. Tarski recursively characterized a set of sentences giving the truth conditions for all declarative sentences of L. In so doing Tarski specified the extensions of the predicate 'true(-in-L)', but this was not done in ways that made 'true(-in-L)' decidable. This was, in our present sense, a theoretical analysis rather than an algorithmic one. Tarski also held his theoretical analysis of truth to the requirement that, as much as possible, it account for uses of 'true sentence' that are 'in harmony with the laws of logic and the spirit of everyday language' [Tarski, 1956, p. 164]. Notoriously, Tarski thought that Liar-sentences precluded the fulfilment of the requirement in the case of natural languages. Accordingly, he re-tooled the analysis, applying it to formalizable object languages, and holding 'true' to rigid stratification. All the same, he inspired condition T. His account of 'true' would be required to generate every sentence of the form $\ulcorner\Phi$ is true iff $\Phi\urcorner$. This, among other things, was Tarski's way of being faithful to everyday uses.

It is important to emphasize the provisional character of the constraints that an analysis places on a theory. The analysis of relevance might make it plausible to say that relevance is comparative and the theory might go on to say that it is. Future developments might persuade us of the contrary view. We would not want such a discovery to constitute what, in effect, would be the discovery of a different sense of relevance. We should leave it open that the analysis should be changed.

Semantic Occam's Razor bids us to minimize the ambiguity of relevance, but to do so in a principled way. It may seem to some an ill-considered prescription for any theorist who aims to produce an account of relevance that honours the syntactically abundant diversity of its uses. Studies in cognitive psychology recommend a certain caution. Studies of conceptualization and categorization suggest that simple, one-word common sense terms do not answer well to unitary sets of necessary and sufficient conditions. Smith and Medin write attractively in support of the exemplar theory of concepts [Smith and Medin, 1981]. Simple common sense concepts lack summary representations, that is, unitary representations that fix a concept's extension either by way of necessary and sufficient conditions or by way of conditions exceeding an assumed threshold of probability. Smith and Medin propose that common concepts-in-use are represented by different exemplars, including possible concrete instantiations, concerning which there is no pretense of exhaustiveness [Smith and Medin, 1981, ch, 7]. If this is right, it would seem to be bad news on two fronts. It would seem that ordinary concepts are, just as they come, 'half-baked'. If so, this empties the complaint of half-bakedness of weight. And, if different exemplar representations of a concept were to qualify as different senses of it, it would appear that ordinary concepts are ambiguous just as they come. If so, our invocation of Semantic Occam's Razor is either an empty gesture or a mistake. It is an empty gesture if it means that we should not make relevance more ambiguous than it already is. It is a mistake if it means that we should suppress the ambiguities already in it.

A theoretical analysis of the biconditional kind that we will propose has something to answer for. It must strike a balance between fidelity to a common sense concept and a stipulativeness that fills a theory in. It must try to displace half-bakedness with something more fully realized in ways that do not derange the likelihood of its being able to assimilate relevance's diversity of uses. It must acknowledge, and say something about, the twilight zone of uses concerning which a judgement of ambiguity or of counterexample would seem ill-advised. And it must look for truth conditions which, in doing these various things, also conspire to mitigate the presumption of relevance's multiple ambiguity. Promise of this is encouraged by recognition of the fact that the truth conditions proposed for a theory's target concept need not constitute an exemplar of that concept-in-use, and need not be semantically incompatible with any exemplar of it.

It is evident from its diversity of common uses that relevance is not just a semantic notion or a probabilistic notion. If we hold a theory of relevance to fidelity to common use, it is foreclosed that a semantic analysis of relevance or a probabilistic analysis of it will qualify as good theories under providence of Semantic Occam's Razor. In chapters to follow, semantic and probabilistic accounts are critically reviewed. Why not dismiss them outright? Why should they not be cashiered wholesale for their failure to conform to the present conception of what a theory of relevance should be? The answer is that we have not yet demonstrated the adequacy of such a conception; we have only pleaded it. What is needed is a scrutiny that does damage to semantic and probabilistic rivals apart from our current presumptions about what makes for a theory of relevance.

In building a conceptual model for relevance (a task to which we turn in the chapter to follow), we represent ourselves as in the tradition of philosophical analysis or analytic philosophy. But we should quickly add that what passes today for philosophical analysis has distanced itself considerably from the original conception forwarded by G. E. Moore and others early in the century just past. On that older view, philosophy is literally the decomposition of complex concepts into analytically inert conceptual atoms. Now it is an altogther striking thing that, when one visits the great achievements of analytic philosophy over the past hundred years, whether Russell's theory of definite descriptiuons, Carnap's *Aufbau*, Popper's falsificationism, Austin's speech acts, Quine's extensional pragmatics, there are but two places in which on can see the slightest evidence of conceputal decomposition literally at work: Wittgenstein's *Tractatus* and Russell's *Lectures on Logical Atomism.*

By the lights of one present-day philosopher, there is an explanation of this dearth; it is that conceptual decomposition is impossible, since *all* concpets are atomic, hence decomposable ([Fodor, 1998, pp. 162–163] *et passim*). We won't take the time to take the critical measure of Fodor's radical (and very interesting) diagnosis. But we *are* minded to agree with something else that Fodor proposes.

> I guess what I really think is that philosophy is just: whatever strikes minds like ours as being of the same kind as the prototypical examples. But maybe that's wrong; and, if it is, then maybe we were to stop saying that philosophy is conceptual analysis that would leave philosophy without a defensible metatheory, well, so be it. We wouldn't be worse off in that respect than doctors, lawyers, dentists, artists, physicists, chicken sexers, psychologists, driving instructors, or practioners of any other respectable discipline that I can think of.
>
> [Fodor, 1998, 163]

Here we find ourselves at one with Fodor. We are analytic philosophers who seriously doubt that good philosophy is usually or even typically in any literal way the result of the decomposition of everyday concepts. In this we stand as weak AI stands to strong AI, who don't believe in strong AI even though their *practice* embeds the contrary assumption. The analogy is apt. We are *weak* conceptual analysts. We proceed as if strong conceptual analysis were the way to go in philosophy. It isn't the way to go; *pretending* that it is is the way to go. In making the effort to make a conceptual analysis of a given idea — say the common notion of justice, or of truth or of relevance — one succeeds not by decomposing it into its primitive notions but rather by the accumulated clarity that attends the drawing of semantical distinctions and the teasing out of hidden nuances. The net effect is a better understanding of what, in a sense, we have already known.

We could say, if we wished, that what this net result gives is an improved philosophical understanding of the notion at hand. For the theorist, there is *always* a gap. But somebody should ask what work is the word 'philosophical' here performing. If the net result of our analytical labour is an improved philosophical understanding of a given concept, is this different from, or better than, an improved understanding of this notion?

We belong to that group of philosophers that takes the philosophical enterprise to be *theory-construction.* A theory of something takes off from what is currently understood about it in the direction of systematic re-description and linkage with other (not always apparently connected) issues. In taking the theoretical stance — as we do most aggresively in Part III of the present work — we place ourselves in the position of all theorists. It is the position in which the available data underdetermines theory. In constructing a logical theory of practical reasoning or of relevance, or indeed of anything at all, the gap between data and theory must be traversed in a principled way. One way in which it cannot be traversed is simply by having more data or an improved understanding of the data ready to hand. Good data are indispensble, of course. In the approach we take to relevance these data are the best understanding that we can achieve of the common concept of relevance. This we seek to accomplish by attempting to decompose the concept of relevance into its primitive notional elements; in other words, by applying to relevance the methods of weak conceptual analysis.

Proceeding in this way has the virtue of underlining an important pair of methodological principles. One is that in constructing a thing of X we must begin with what we already think we (and our readers) know of X, the more the better. The other is that as the theory develops one must be prepared to *de-privilege* some of what was originally said of X when there are good theoretical reasons to do so.

Part II

Conceptual Models for Relevance

Chapter 5

Propositional Relevance

It is a capital mistake to theorize before one has data.

Conan Doyle, *Scandal in Bohemia*

Relevance is our subject here. How are we to think of it? How should we go about conceptualizing it? To what considerations, or type of considerations, might we turn for guidance? We said at the beginning that, in its most basic informal sense, relevant information is *helpful* information. This is a fundamental dataum for our machinery of (weak) conceptual analysis. But helpful how, and to whom, and under what circumstances?

5.1 Introductory Remark

We begin with a small bit of technical machinery, with which we explore the option of defining relevance as a binary metapredicate $\mathbb{F}(P, Q)$ in a possibly non-classical logic $\vdash$ together with other means (e.g., probability on $\vdash$). Let $\vdash$ be a consequence relation on formulas $A, B, \ldots$ of the form $A \vdash B$. Let $\mathbb{M}_1, \mathbb{M}_2 \ldots$ be some additional metapredicates which we consider as coming with the system $\vdash$. For example, we might have a probability set-up and a predicate $Pr(Q|P)$, or a labelling discipline with a label (t, A), written $t : A$. These predicates along with $\vdash$ allow us to define the relevance metapredicate $\mathbb{R}(P, Q)$, read as 'P is relevant to Q'.

For example

1. Condition IR on page 92 below.

2. Condition CP on page 95 below.

3. Condition TR* on page 105 below.

4. Relevance of Sperber and Wilson on page 124 below, etc.

The success or failure of essentially reducing $\mathbb{R}$ to $\vdash$ and $\mathbb{M}_1, \mathbb{M}_2, \ldots$ depends heavily on $\vdash$ (e.g., it might be a very bad idea if $\vdash$ is classical logic and not so bad if $\vdash$ is a weaker logic) and on the success and intuitiveness of the auxiliary metapredicates $\mathbb{M}_1, \mathbb{M}_2$, etc.

We call such attempts *propositional relevance* because they are basically based on a consequence-relation $\vdash$, (with no consideration of time–action agendas, as we shall see later).

5.2 Propositional Relevance

What should we take relevance to be? Propositionalists answer as follows. 'If R is relevant to Q, ... then R's being true would increase the likelihood that Q is true, while R's being false would increase the likelihood that Q is false. ... If there is no effect one way or the other, then you have ample grounds for your claim that R is irrelevant to the acceptability of Q' [Johnson and Blair, 1983, pp. 15–16]. A similar theme is sounded by Govier:

> (PR) P is *positively relevant* to Q if P's truth counts in favour of Q's truth.
>
> (NR) P is *negatively relevant* to Q if P's truth counts in favour of Q's falsity.
>
> (IR) P is *irrelevant* to Q if neither the truth nor falsity of P counts toward the truth or falsity of Q. [Govier, 1988a, pp. 122–123]

Consider, too, the definition of relevancy in English law and successive traditions.

> One fact (conveniently called an evidentiary fact) is relevant to another when it renders the existence of the other fact probable or improbable. Relevancy is therefore a matter of common sense and experience rather than law. [Cross and Wilkins, 1964, 148]

If we assume the interchangeability of 'counting towards truth (or falsity)' and 'increasing the likelihood of truth (or falsity)', the accounts of

Johnson and Blair and of Govier come to the same thing and may be dealt with as a single position. Neither Johnson and Blair nor Govier specify the base system in which their intuitions are embedded. But it is clear from context that it is classical probability theory. We also take it that these authors assume a classical background logic.

It is well to notice that in their respective characterizations of relevance, Johnson and Blair offer only necessary conditions, and Govier and Cross and Wilkins only sufficient conditions. For example, in PR and NR we have sufficient conditions which are, moreover, defined only for the truth of P. But at IR irrelevance is defined for the truth and falsity of P, though here, too, we have only a sufficient condition.

This won't do as it stands. It is possible to specify Ps and Qs in such a way that neither PR nor NR gives the relevance of P for Q nor yet does IR give their irrelevance. To see this, put '$2 + 2 = 4$' for P and 'The cat is on the mat' for Q. Then the truth of P counts towards neither the truth nor falsity of Q and so P fulfils neither PR nor NR. However, since the denial of P is a logical falsehood, then P's falsehood entails that the cat is on the mat, and P is not after all irrelevant to Q. This is an odd and uncongenial result and getting it turns on the assumption that entailment delivers some of the goods for the concept of 'counting toward the truth of'. It may be that reasons will emerge to abandon this assumption, but we shall let it stand for the present. The assumption afflicts the Johnson and Blair account as well. We take it that when they characterize P's irrelevance to Q as P's having no effect one way or the other on whether Q is true or false, this is tantamount to Govier's notion of irrelevance: neither the truth nor falsity of P would count toward the truth or falsity of Q.

Unless one had a principled reason for thinking that the concept of relevance really is half-baked, one could repair the deficiency of the paragraph above by tightening IR and reissuing it as a biconditional. Thus

> (IR*) P is irrelevant to Q iff neither P's truth counts towards Q's truth, nor P's falsehood towards Q's truth, nor P's truth toward Q's falsehood, nor P's falsehood toward Q's falsehood.

IR* has the virtue of forwarding both necessary and sufficient conditions, and it also goes some way toward cashing the idea in which irrelevance 'has nothing whatever to do' with whether something is the case. If IR* is accepted over IR, then a biconditional for relevance easily drops out which allows us to avoid the cumbersomeness of positive and negative relevance. Thus

> (R) P is relevant to Q iff P is not irrelevant to Q.[1]

[1]Similarly for Johnson and Blair. If IR captures their notion of irrelevance, it is

By these lights, relevance and irrelevance are biconditionally complex relations. Promising though R is, it is not by any means trouble-free. For consider that R provides that P is relevant to Q when, for example, $P \rightarrow Q. \vee .\neg P \rightarrow Q$, where '$\rightarrow$' is intended to symbolize the 'counting toward' conditional, whatever that is precisely. If '$\rightarrow$' is at least as strong a conditional as the material conditional, then we have it from

$$(1) \quad P \rightarrow Q. \vee .\neg P \rightarrow Q$$

that

$$(2) \quad \neg P \vee Q \vee P \vee Q$$

which, for arbitrary P and Q, is a logical truth. And so every proposition is relevant to every proposition, an excessive result.

Two courses are open to us. We could abandon R, which would run uncomfortably against the nap of intuitiveness; or we could give up on the assumption that '$\rightarrow$' gives a conditional at least as strong as the material conditional. 'Counting for', in this second case, must not only be weaker than the material 'if ... then', it must also derivatively disconform to the classical deductive schema

from $\ulcorner P \rightarrow Q \urcorner$ to derive $\ulcorner \neg P \vee Q \urcorner$

So, the $\rightarrow$-relation cannot be a classical truth-function. The terminology of the Johnson and Blair account suggests this very thing: Relevance is not truth-functional but probabilistic; it is a matter of influencing likelihood.

The obvious question now is whether the '$\rightarrow$' embedded in the biconditionals R and IR* will bear construal by way of the standard probability calculus. If it did, then, among other things, (1) would go over to the probabilistic

$$(1^*) \quad Pr(Q/P) > Pr(Q). \vee .Pr(Q/\neg P) > Pr(Q)$$

from which there would be no probabilistic analogue of (2). It is clear, however, that the probability calculus is a thorny thicket for relevance theory. We shall mention just two difficulties, both of which are serious.

One difficulty is that conditional probability is not defined for contradictions. This means that where P is a contradiction $Pr(Q, P)$ is undefined, and the first disjunct of (1*) does not compute. On the other hand, if P is a contradiction, then $\neg P$ is a tautology. Since for any Ψ, the probability

clear that they understate their condition on relevance. Better, too, in their case to take irrelevance up to a biconditional like IR* and redefine relevance as the absence of irrelevance so construed.

of Ψ given a tautology is precisely the same as the probability of Ψ alone, then the second disjunction of (1*) is false for every interpretation of Q and every interpretation of P for which $\ulcorner \neg P \urcorner$ is a tautology.

It might seem the safer course would be to banish from relevance theory contradictions and tautologies altogether. This would release (1*) from the embarrassment that probability theory produces for it, but there is reason not to do it. Contradictions and tautologies should not be expunged from relevance theory. Let P be the tautology that the Russell set is either a member of itself or not. And let Q be the proposition that the Russell set is a member of itself if and only if it is not a member of itself. Notoriously, P entails Q. Should we be made to say that, on account of their respective tautologousness and self-contradictoriness, P is of no relevance to Q? But if one is going to do one's business in probability theory, these intuitions must be overridden, since in each case the putative relata fail the independence condition.

A second difficulty is that conditional probability requires that, where $Pr(Q/P)$ is the probability of Q given P, there is definable a probability value for Q alone. Where Q describes a state of a playing card or the side of a die, probabilities are intuitively definable for it. But for most interpretations of Q, such is not the case.

This is the notorious problem of the indeterminacy of priors and a standing difficulty for Bayesianism. This leaves us oddly positioned. For although it remains perfectly true that in some indeterminate way judgements in the form 'The probability of this given that is greater than the probability of this alone', can strike us as intuitively right or wrong, such judgements don't make for any kind of theoretical gain over judgements in the form 'This is relevant to that' in *their* indeterminate and unanalysed states.

All the same, the conditional probability approach retains a certain appeal. We might as well grant that contradictions spoil its generality and that the matter of prior probability assignments is decisionally troubling. But surely, it might be argued, the conditional probability construal of relevance makes a substantial conceptual advance, and should not be altogether given up on. Why not, then, make do as we can with the following rather intuitive definition:[2]

$$\text{(CP): } P \text{ is relevant to } Q \text{ iff } Pr(Q, P) \neq 0.5$$

[2] Here and in the several paragraphs that follow we draw upon George Bowles' paper [Bowles, 1990]; cf. what Peter Gärdenfors calls the 'traditional' definition:

(D1) (a) P is relevant to Q on evidence E iff $Pr(Q/P \wedge E) \neq Pr(Q/E)$

(b) P is irrelevant to Q on E iff $Pr(Q/P \wedge E) = Pr(Q/E)$

The definition is cited in [Schlesinger, 1986, p. 58].

Given that relevance and irrelevance are contradictories, we also have it by CP, that P is irrelevant to Q iff $Pr(Q, P) = 0.5$. By these lights, the minimal vocabulary for the theory of relevance is the minimal vocabulary, M, of the calculus of probability; and 'relevant', not occurring in M, is definable there.

CP resembles the Principle of Indifference of the classical interpretation of probability. It is not that principle exactly, for it has nothing to say about the fixing of prior probabilities. But it sufficiently resembles the Indifference Principle to lie open to two criticisms which resemble complaints that Keynes directed against it.

Here is the first argument contra CP (see [Keynes, 1971, pp. 45–46]; cf. [Schlesinger, 1986, p. 58].) Consider the three statements, 'This book is red', 'This book is black' and 'This book is blue.' To each of these a fourth statement, 'This book weighs a pound', is irrelevant. Thus the probability of each conditional upon 'This book weighs a pound' is 0.5.

Now we have it quite generally that whenever Q, R, S are mutually exclusive, then

$$(D) \quad Pr(Q \vee R \vee S, P) = Pr(Q, P) + Pr(R, P) + Pr(S, P)$$

But substituting 'This book is red' for Q, 'This book is black' for R, 'This book is blue' for S and 'This book weighs a pound' for P, we have as an instance of $D*$

$$(D*) \qquad 0.5 + 0.5 + 0.5 = 1.5$$

Which is impossible.

The second criticism is also inspired by Keynes [1971, p. 47]. A book's weight is irrelevant to its colour. Likewise a thing's weighing a pound is irrelevant to its being a red book. Thus CP provides both that

$$\text{(a) } Pr \text{ (} x \text{ is red, } x \text{ weighs a pound)} = 0.5$$

and that

$$\text{(b) } Pr \text{ (} x \text{ is red} \wedge x \text{ is a book, } x \text{ weighs a pound)} = 0.5$$

whenever Pr (x is red, x weighs a pound) $=$ Pr (x is red $\wedge$ x is a book, x weighs a pound). But it is a theorem of the calculus of probability that if $Pr(B, A) = Pr(B \wedge C, A)$, then B *entails* C given A. Interpreting with the statements of the case at hand, this requires that 'x is red' entail 'x is a book given that x weighs a pound', another absurdity.

Earlier we saw that the probabilistic treatment of relevance was troubled in two ways. It cannot allow relevance to be defined for contradictions, and it merely assumes the satisfactory distribution of prior probabilities. But, we said, let us consider these difficulties as peripheral and establish a proper and welcome recognition to the fact that conditional probabilities seem to give powerful and intuitive (though not perfect) linkage with relevance. That, anyhow, could turn out to be a large part of the story: that is, relevance is *largely* a matter of conditional probabilities.

As we now see, our two Keynesian objections appear to put paid to any such option. Against this George Bowles has attempted a reformulation of CP that retains much of its intuitive plausibility and yet resists the Keynesian objections. He suggests 'that we modify CP by adding a restriction ...: when we say something like 'P' is relevant or irrelevant to 'Q' if and only if the probability of 'Q' is some value, n, conditional on 'P', our determination of 'n' [be] based on a consideration of 'P' and 'Q' alone' [Bowles, 1990, p. 69].

The proposed restriction works this way. Consider objection one. We comply with the restriction when we withhold the analytical apparatus of conditional probability from truth-functional compounds of propositions on whose conditional probability CP has already pronounced. Thus the conditional probability, given that this book weighs a pound, for each of 'This book is red', 'This book is black' and 'This book is blue' is 0.5. If we seek to compute the probability, on the same condition, of their alternation we violate the restriction, since that computation turns not on the consideration of the alternation and the condition alone, but also on consideration of the three disjuncts. This blocks objection one. The second criticism is similarly disarmed.

The blockage is *ad hoc*, of course, but this will not cut much ice with those for whom a constraint is justified by the goodness of the results that its employment facilitates. The more important question that Bowles' constraint seizes upon is whether relevance answers *at all* to closure conditions under basic logical operations. Intuitively, the compound statement, 'The book is red or the book is black' is irrelevant to the proposition that the book weighs a pound. And that fact turns on semantic relations with the disjuncts of our disjunctions. The irrelevance of the book's weight to the disjuncts must bear on its irrelevance to the disjunction. So relevance is at least somewhat responsive to (some) closure conditions on (some) logical operations.

It would appear that Bowles is snagged by a dilemma. Either the theory of relevance acknowledges relevance's closure-sensitivity, but then in representing it in the theory of conditional probability, one seriously misrepresents it. Or one constrains the theory of conditional probability, in which case, one leaves the account of relevance substantially understated. Probability theory with Bowles' restriction underdetermines relevance; without it, it overdetermines it. Under press of the restriction, intuitively compelling cases of relevance and irrelevance are rejected. Free of the restriction, mathematical absurdities qualify as the genuine article. The theory at hand averts the overdetermination problem only at the cost of underdetermination. Of the two, underdetermination is the lesser cost. Bowles' account could in these respects be likened to formal theories for which consistency is provable only at the price of incompleteness. We prefer our theories to be complete, but for most people inconsistency is too much to ask for completeness.[3]

Even so, incompleteness or, more casually, underdetermination is a sufficiently disappointing result to require some crisis management. In the case of theories capable of expressing arithmetic in a certain way, incompleteness is acquiesced in by way of the Gödel theorems, as a provability-limitation inherent in theories of a kind that, for various reasons, we find that we are not prepared to do without. In the less dramatic cases, a crisis manager might attempt to show that the theory's findings are the core findings and that the excluded cases, intuitively appealing as they assuredly are, are of lesser moment; or perhaps that they illustrate a different sense of the notion captured by the theory's findings. A further and more hopeful response would be to argue that the theory in question, underdetermining though it is, is the best theory that we have, and it will have to do until a better one presents itself.[4]

There is reason to think that Bowles' might be drawn to these last two responses. For one thing, excluded from the outset are numberless cases of relevance on which the idiom of conditional probability, whether Pascal's or Bowles' own, lays no glove.

Lost at the outset are such as these:

1. That it will rain today is relevant to the fact that the picnic was scheduled for today.

2. A patient's wishes are relevant to a surgeon's entitlement to operate.

3. That Harry decided to go to the movies was relevant to the question of whether he favours light entertainment over theatre of the absurd.

4. Recent findings in archeominerology are relevant to Sarah's interest in pre-Columbian civilization.

[3]There is also the point that in making the conditional probability of Q on P dependent only on P and Q, the resulting account is basically a 'laundry list" of what is relevant to what.

[4]In particular, we haven't ruled out the option of relevance defined for, e.g., resource- or non-monotonic logics together with a Pr function.

5. Be relevant!

6. An arts & science degree is irrelevant in today's world.

7. Harry always peppers his stories with mindless irrelevancies.

8. Harry is the most irrelevant guy we know.

It may be that Bowles' interest in relevance is a conceptually circumscribed one, much as is Schlesinger's own, for which relevance is a notion more basic than confirmation and a conceptual underpinning of it.[5] Within limits, a theorist is free to set his own analytical targets. Within limits, he is also free to set conditions on what counts as a satisfactory treatment of them. For all this latitude, care needs to be taken, lest we allow the theorist the freedom to fix a target concept as precisely that which his theory chances to provide and to judge his theory adequate just because it specifies that concept in the way that it does. This has to do with the antecedent coherence of a target notion prior to a theory's detailed treatment of it. The attraction of Keynes' approach was that it answered well to this idea of the prior or pre-theoretic coherence of a target concept. Keynes' target was a sense of relevance in which relevance was a matter of increasing or decreasing the likelihood of propositions to which relevant information is relevant.

The machinery of conditional probability was invoked to regulate the increasing or decreasing of probabilities in ways that elucidate relevance. It didn't work. It overdetermined the extension of the target notion. Bowles leans to the same prior notion. He wants a sense of relevance which is cashable in the idiom of mattering for likelihood. Keynesian excesses are averted by constraining conditional probability. The constraint is too severe. It leaves the extension and anti-extension of 'relevant' noticeably underdetermined. It is important to be clear about the underdetermination complaint. The objection is not that Bowles' account forbids recognition of relevance phenomena such as may be found in our eight cases listed above — for example, Harry's being the most irrelevant guy we know. Of these it could be said that there was no prospect of capturing them by way of a prior notion of mattering for likelihood. They could be given principled exclusion on grounds that they didn't exemplify the theory's target conception of relevance. On the other hand, the fact that 'This is black or this is blue or this is red' is irrelevant to 'The book weights a pound' is fully compliant with the target idea of irrelevance as not mattering for likelihood. There is a difference between this case and the prior eight. The prior eight are not

[5][Schlesinger, 1986, p. 57]; 'It may ... be said that "relevance" is a simpler concept than "confirmation".' Relevance may prove useful 'for adjudicating among completing hypotheses...'.

target-compliant in the theory of Bowles, whereas the present case certainly is. The trouble is that the theory excludes *it*. The apparatus of constrained conditional probability proves too coarse-grained. It refuses cases which, by the theory's own target notion, it should admit.

Bowles' account may also strike one as excessively promissory. It offers a conception of conditional probability made interesting mainly by its failure to fulfil the axioms on conditional probability. Pascalian resentments aside, grumpy critics are bound to say that if Bowles won't tell them what conditional probability *is*, they can hardly be expected to think that he has told them what relevance is.

The grumps are overdoing it. There is no particular reason why conditional probability can't be primitive in Bowles' account. Bowles is right to suggest, in effect, that the justification of the use of a primitive term in a theory depends on the work that it does there. Zero serves well in the definition of the natural numbers, so well in fact that Peano arithmetic might be said to constitute a good implicit definition of that primitive notion, owing to the categoricity of its axioms. Perhaps there is insufficient cause to be quite so relaxed about Bowles' relevance theory, but it is unjustified to dismiss it for its failure to define its non-standard relation of conditional probability. We find ourselves in guarded disagreement on this point with, e.g., Lycan for whom unexplicated notions are to be resisted on grounds of a disguised potential for circularity. The disagreement is guarded because it is not clear to us what the likelihood is that lurking in Bowles' unanalysed conditional probability is a furtive analytical engagement of relevance considerations. Lycan's reservations pertain to the use of probabilities short of unity in the analysis of doxastic justification. 'What', he asks, 'is the difference between unanalysed conditional probability [e.g. 'the likelihood that one's belief is true given its existence and/or its provenance...'] and an unanalysed relation of doxastic warrant?' It is quite true that analysing doxastic justification via doxastic warrant might be circular. And it may be that crimping the closure conditions on putative relata of a relevance relation offends in the same way. Where P is relevant, in Bowles' target sense, to Q, we have it that with regard to P and Q alone the conditional probability of Q on P is greater than some n. The restriction is imposed to avert computational derangement; for example, certain conditional probabilities not so constrained would compute to a number exceeding one. This alone is reason to abandon unrestricted conditional probability, and it seems to have nothing inherently to do with lurking linkages with the concept of relevance prior to the proposed explication of relevance itself (see [Lycan, 1988, p. 106].)

Readers will be troubled by other factors, no doubt. One is that on the present account every proposition is relevant to every logical truth. This is not wholly excessive but it is close enough to be disturbing. Here, too, we have a situation in which by the theory's own target notion, an arbitrary proposition shouldn't matter for the likelihood of an arbitrary logical truth. But the theory provides otherwise, and in so saying our complaint is reissued: Bowles' conditional probability is too coarse-grained for his own target concept of relevance.

Bowles sees the problem coming and tries to be ready for it. It is possible, he says, that such a result is acceptable since it is possible that no treatment of relevance could avoid it [Bowles, 1990, p. 73]. The response is rather more hopeful than disarming, but it does have some point. It challenges those for whom the 'paradoxical' result is disagreeable to do better. It presses the question: Can there be a good theory of relevance in which the 'paradoxical' result is avertible? A fair challenge and a good question. See below, and chapters 6–10.

We might, however, have a space of 2^k events, and we might try defining the relevance of P to Q as $Pr(Q|P) > f(k)$, where the cut-off number depends on the overall number of events. In that case the D^* of p. 96 would be $Pr(Q \vee R \vee S/P) = f(3) + f(3) + f(3)$, where the more we add, the more f changes (i.e., $Pr(\bigvee_{i=1}^{k} X_i|P = kf(k))$). (See Paris [1991].)

Consider the propositional variables $p_1, \ldots, p_k$. Fixing n, there are 2^n basic propositions in this universe, namely, all conjunctive normal forms $x = \bigwedge_{i=1}^{k} P_i^{\varepsilon_i}$, where $\varepsilon_i \in \{0, 1\}$. If we give basic probability weights $Pr(x) = \omega(x)$ (usually one gives them equal probability $\omega(x) = \frac{1}{2}k$) then for any wff A, $Pr(A) = \sum_{x \vdash A} \omega(x)$, where, i.e., $\sum_x$ goes over all x in the normal form of A, $A \equiv \bigvee_{x \vdash A} x$.

In case the basic weights are not equal, we put it that $\sum_x \omega(x) = 1$.

We can also assume $\omega(x) > 0$ for all x. We could now define $f(\ ) = \min\{\omega(x)\}$ and modify CP accordingly.

P is relevant to Q iff $Pr(Q|P) > f(k)$. This however makes $\ulcorner \neg P \urcorner$ relevant to Q if P is not relevant to Q. So further considerations would be needed to supplement CP. The appeal of this approach is that it can be worked up in other logics as well, such as intuitionistic logic. (See here Williams [1982].)

Promising as such a development might be, it leaves it true that there is more to relevance than probabilistic relevance (which is the burden of this book to show). Our interest lies not in discussing alternative views, but rather in discussing their limitations as well as their strengths. Our approach is ecumenical. To the extent possible we want an account of relevance that absorbs the virtues of alternative views.

5.3 Legal Relevance

Before leaving our discussion of probabilistic relevance, it would be well to re-visit the definition of relevance developed by English jurisprudence. As we saw earlier in this chapter, the relevance of a claim is [half-] defined as one that increases or decreases the probability of some other claim [Cross and Wilkins, 1964, 148]. However, when one examines the standard textbooks on the law of evidence — *An Outline of the Law of Evidence* [Cross and Wilkins, 1964] and *Murphy on Evidence* [Murphy, 2000], for example — one sees that the utterly dominant approach to relevance has to do with grounds for the admittance or exclusion of testimony — especially testimony as to the accused's character — on grounds of its relevancy or lack of it. What is especially interesting is that these juridical determinations are almost never determination as to whether proposition P enhances or reduces the probability of proposition Q. Another way of saying this is that the juridical interest in the relevance or irrelevance of a piece of character evidence P is hardly ever whether, in relation to Q the charge against the accused, P satisfies the legal *definition* of relevancy. Instead what a judge is required to do is to determine whether such evidence would, if submitted, prejudice the jury, or induce it to give it more weight than it should. Think here of a case in which the accused is charged with paedophilia and evidence on which the judge must rule is a prior history of violent sexual predation (but not paedophilia). What the law of evidence requires of the judge is that he refuse to admit it if he determines that the jury will make more of it than it should in the following sense: He is not in general required to determine whether this evidence would increase the likelihood of the accused's guilt; rather he is required to find that this evidence — even though it *did* increase the probability of guilt — would violate the very special protections which the criminal law has evolved for person's indicted for serious offences. One such protection is jury impartiality. An other is a high standard of proof for conviction, underwritten by the law's *strategic* skepticism concerning what would suffice to demonstrate guilt subject to that artificially high standard. When a judge finds that such protections would likely be compromised, he enters a finding of *irrelevance*, and he does so irrespective of whether that evidence would, in contexts other than those of judicial skepticism, fail to increase the probability of the correctness of the charge in question.

What we learn from this is that, in operational terms, the law of evidence embodies a notion of relevance which is different from the relevance it formally defines. The embodied notion of relevance is a matter of what bears on the court's chief obligation, which is to try the accused in ways that conform to the law's artificially high standards for what constitutes winning a case in a criminal trial. We shall see in good time that *this* conception of relevance is a case of what we call *agenda relevance* (cf. Cross and Wilkins [1964, 148–149, 153–156], and Murphy [2000, 8–9, 132–149, 162–167, 178–179, 216–219, 360–365]).

5.4 Topical Relevance

The concept of relevance that we have been addressing in the preceding pages resembles what Douglas Walton calls probative relevance. Thus

> (PR): a proposition P is probatively relevant to a proposition Q if either P logically follows from Q or Q from P, or P is logically inconsistent with Q. [Walton, 1982, p. 83]

Probative relevance is a much stronger (and correspondingly less intuitive) notion than that of our biconditional R. Probative relevance gives rise to problematic consequences. One involves the numerous examples of intuitively correct judgements of relevance which PR leaves undetermined. (Note that PR also gives only a sufficient condition.) Statements such as 'Spike's fingerprints are on the murder weapon' are obviously enough relevant to the investigator's interest in whether Spike did it or not. But PR leaves these cases unpronounced upon. On the other hand, if PR were to go over into PR* a biconditional, things would be even worse; intuitively correct examples, such as that of Spike, would now be false. That is, would be false in the theory of probative relevance. Their falsehood there would not be a refutation, of course. Relevance of the Spike kind is not a target notion for the theory of probative relevance. Still, the consequence might be unwelcome for some people. They might judge that it offends against *SOR*, the semantic version of Occam's Razor. One might have hoped for broader targets.

Probative relevance runs straight into the intuition that an arbitrary contradiction cannot be held to be relevant to an arbitrary proposition,[6]

[6]This is also a consequence of Bowles' account. See [Bowles, 1990, p. 73]. It afflicts James Freeman's treatment as well. Freeman defines immediate descriptive relevance as follows:

> A is immediately [descriptively] relevant to B with respect to a system of rules $\mathbb{I}$ if and only if there is an $I \in \mathbb{I}$ which licenses the inference from A to B.

Normative relevance is got by constraining the set I. The rules of $\mathbb{I}$ must be authoritatively warranted rules. Formal validity is a sufficient condition of authoritative warrantedness. Thus if A is a contradiction it is relevant to any B, assuming $\bot \vdash B$ for any B. One could have $\bot_x$ for each x which is inconsistent. Thus $\bot_x \vdash B$ only if B is relevant to x or, more strongly, Relevant(x, B) iff $\bot_x \vdash B$. See [Freeman, 1992, pp. 223–225].

that their (joint) arbitrariness precludes relevance. To be sure, Walton could again emphasize the adjective 'probative', and in so doing remind us that the relevance that his account seeks to capture it does capture; for it sees relevance only as a matter of mattering for truth (or falsehood). Arbitrariness is no discouragement of relevance in this sense.

All the same, two further objections might be considered. One is that the relevance imputed is uninteresting, and the other is that, in the absence of the relevance that probative relevance doesn't capture, the *entailment* is wrecked; and so we don't even have probative relevance. This latter complaint, routinely heard in Pittsburgh and Canberra, may not strike everyone as decisive. Walton himself shows some sympathy for it when he decides to undertake the deeper analysis of probative relevance in a non-classical relatedness logic. We mention in passing the Anderson and Belnap condition or content-overlap relevance:

(AB) Φ is not relevant to Ψ if Φ and Ψ do not share a propositional variable.

AB is not to our present purpose, however. It is a necessary condition on a necessary condition on *entailments* expressible in propositional systems. The closest it comes to adumbrating a serviceable idea of relevance for natural-language contexts, though it doesn't even do that, is variable sharing, which suggests topical relevance to which we turn just below. (Relevance logic is also taken up in chapter 9 and, more hopefully, in chapter 14 where we prove an interpolation theorem for certain of our systems: if $A \vdash B$ then there is a C in the common language of A and B such that $A \vdash C$ and $C \vdash B$.)

We suggested that there are reasons to think that relevance requires interpretation via an implication relation weaker than material implication. But it is Walton's proposal, in effect, that what is really wanted for relevance is an analysing relation that is stronger than classical (i.e., for present purposes, material) implication. Suppose then that we define probative relevance in terms of *relatedness* implication and *relatedness* inconsistency. Since relatedness inconsistency is typically taken to coincide with classical inconsistency, relatedness implication is the central idea for present purposes, since relatedness implication and classical implication do not coincide. (Cf. [Woods and Walton, 1982, pp. 196–197], and [Woods *et al.*, 2000, pp. 141–150].)

A proposition is said to imply another proposition relatedly just in case the first classically implies the second and the two share a topic. So unless P and $\ulcorner Q \wedge \neg Q \urcorner$, for arbitrary Q, share a topic, P does not (relatedly) imply $\ulcorner Q \wedge \neg Q \urcorner$ and arbitrariness is allowed to defeat relevance.

It is plain that implication so construed is just classical implication constrained by a relevance condition, by what Walton calls *topical relevance.*[7] Topical relevance is a matter of shared subject matter. Thus

(TR) P is topically relevant to Q if P and Q have at least one subject matter in common.

Though TR gives only a sufficient condition, we see no reason not to strengthen it. Thus

(TR*) P is topically relevant to Q iff P and Q share a topic or subject matter.

Relatedness logic seeks to impose a relevance condition upon certain of the classical operations. It introduces a propositional relation, r, definable in the first instance over atomic sentences but easily generalizable to molecular ones as well. We have it, then, that $\ulcorner r(P,Q)\urcorner$ obtains just in case P and Q share at least one subject matter. The idea of a subject matter is handled set theoretically. Let $\mathbf{T}$ be a set of topics — roughly all of the things that the totality of the sentences of our given language L are *about.* The idea of $\mathbf{T}$ is not far off the idea of a non-empty universe of discourse for L or L's domain of interpretation. Now let $\mathbf{P}$ be the subject matter of P and $\mathbf{Q}$ of Q. Both $\mathbf{P}$ and $\mathbf{Q}$ are subsets of $\mathbf{T}$. $\mathbf{P}$ and $\mathbf{Q}$ share a subject matter just in case $\mathbf{P} \cap \mathbf{Q} \neq \emptyset$, that is, just in case there exists a non-empty intersection of $\mathbf{P}$ and $\mathbf{Q}$. Equivalently, $\ulcorner r(P,Q)\urcorner$ holds just in case $\mathbf{P} \cap \mathbf{Q} \neq \emptyset$. (See for example, [Epstein, 1979] and [Walton, 2003].)

The topical account also provides a rather coarse-grained treatment of relevance. Like the relevant logics of Pittsburgh and beyond, relevance is offered as a constraint on implication. Relevance is needed to filter out impurities that afflict classical implication. It is quite true that Walton also puts topical relevance to other uses. He proposes that topical relevance will assist in the construction of expert systems devoted principally to classification. But topical relevance is too crude to serve the interests of propositional relevance. For example, given that Sarah, Harry and Peter are members of the set of humans then we will have it that

(*) 'Sarah hit Harry' is relevant to 'Peter plays the cello'.

Similar cases abound.

It may seem that topical relevance begets much too much relevance for the idea of propositional relevance to bear. Topical relevance is not heavy handed to the point of excessiveness — for not everything is relevant to

[7] [Woods *et al.*, 2000, p. 61].

everything in Walton's system. But it may strike us that it is still too promiscuous by half.

It is perhaps unsurprising that the theory of topical relevance should lapse into such promiscuity. It employs a set theoretic apparatus which is too undiscriminating for relevance.

The charge of promiscuity is, in logic as in life, a good deal harder to justify than to lay. Walton [1982] is not seriously involved in providing an analysis of a concept of relevance as might be embedded in a rich variety of uses in the manner of our eight cases at pages 98 and 99. We may recall that a theoretical analysis of a common sense term is one that specifies truth conditions for a syntactically abundant range of uses of it. It is sometimes said to be one of which it can plausibly be asserted that the truth conditions give what is meant by competent speakers when such uses are spoken by them. A theoretical analysis of this sort could be thought of as a common analysis, 'common' here evoking the idea of common usage associated with a common sense concept. Tarski, in imposing convention T, was trying to keep his analysis of 'true' as common as the technicalities would allow. Often however a theoretical analysis preserves the truth conditions and lightens up on what speakers mean. In so doing, it sanctions a departure from commonness. There is no *a priori* limit, except *en gros*, as to how far an analysis can move along the continuum from common analysis in the direction of sheer exoticism. If we bear in mind that truth conditions are sometimes abstracted from what Ziff had in mind when he spoke of semantic regularities[8] and that at other times truth conditions are proposed in the absence of semantic regularities, then we see that truth conditions, too, move along a continuum from clarification to stipulation, as Quine has said. By these lights, common analyses give truth conditions that clarify antecedent usage, and uncommon analyses stipulate conditions for new or reformed usage. Quine thinks that in virtually any theory worth its salt the distinction between clarification and stipulation will come close to collapsing, and with it, therefore, our distinction between common and uncommon analyses. Still, the principle of the distinction is clear enough to enable us to say that with stipulation a theory takes on its heaviest pragmatic debt — the debt of fruitfulness of the stipulation for theoretical pronouncements of greatest attractiveness.[9] Uncommon analyses are less attractive on their face when they are analyses of common sense notions. But this is not to say — far from it — that they cannot be amply supported by their overall contribution to mature theory. Witness 'set' as an analysis of the common sense notion of collection.

[8]See [Ziff, 1960, pp. 26–34].

[9]Again, stipulation is discussed in detail in [Woods, 2002b, Ch. 6].

It is, we think, fair to see Walton's account as standing on the continuum a fair distance from commonness. Here is a notion of relevance, Walton is saying, that we can work up in a relatedness logic. The relevance that relatedness logic contrives will be helpful for the specification of expert systems in which documentary classification is a principal task.

This gives a certain shape to our interest in promiscuity. Whether it is possible to judge 'Sarah hit Harry' as relevant to 'Peter plays the cello' turns on whether it is promiscuous to judge that the two sentences share a subject matter. This judgement can't be made independently of knowing whether a classification program for an expert system is abetted by having it so. We might discover that the cataloguing devices of an expert system need to be contrived so as to recognize a common subject matter here. If so, the charge of promiscuity would be blunted. It would succeed luxuriantly had *Topical Relevance* been oriented towards a common analysis of relevance. But Walton says that it is not so, and we believe him. So we will say what, in effect, Walton himself says. Topical relevance will not do as a common analysis of relevance.

Deep in the heart of topical relevance is the idea of 'aboutness'. Aboutness is contextually sensitive.[10] Whether 'The Pope has two wives' and 'There are just two states in the U.S.A.' are about some same thing *for example, about the number two*, is fixed only by context. It turns out that in the theory of topical relevance they are relevant, *context be hanged* (see [Iseminger, 1986, p. 7]). This is embarrassing on its face. It lumbers us, as Gary Iseminger points out, with the true relatedness conditional, 'If the Pope has two wives then there are just two states in the U.S.A.' Its constituent sentences both false, the theory declares them to be topically relevant.

Not all accounts are subject to such an objection. Consider, for instance, the following two sentences: 'Sarah is married to Harry', 'Sarah is married to Lou'. Considered separately, and in the absence of any specific presuppositions to the contrary, neither of these two sentences is about the topic of bigamy, although their conjunction almost certainly is. So the conjunctive mode of combining the two sentences may itself alter the class of topics concerned [Demolombe and Jones, 1999, p. 116].

Compared with Walton [1982], Demolombe and Jones [1999] is an approach of considerable technical sophistication. Like Walton [1982], the latter work seeks to analyse sentences in the form 'p is about t', where 'p' is a sentence and 't' is a topic. To this end, Demolombe and Jones provide

[10]Concerning his own probabilistic definition, Schlesinger allows that it may be necessary to contextualize it by talking 'about the relevance of p to r on evidence e *in the context of* q_1 and so on'. [Schlesinger, 1986, p. 65], emphasis in the original.

a syntax, a 3-valued semantics and an axiomatization. We here sketch the model theory.

A model $M = \langle W, I, J, T, S, N, F \rangle$ where

1. W is a set of worlds;
2. I is a function that assigns to each topic name a topic;
3. J is a function that assigns to each sentence name a sentence;
4. T is a set of topics;
5. S is the set of sentences of the classical propositional calculus (CPC);
6. N is a function that assigns sets of topics to pairs of sets of worlds (i.e., $2^W \times 2^W \rightarrow 2^T$);
7. T is a function that assigns to each atom in CPC a set of worlds;
8. F is a function that assigns to each atom in CPC a set of worlds.

M also provides that $T(p) \cap F(p) = \varnothing$. The further rules for T and F are

9. $T(\neg p) = F(p)$;
10. $F(\neg p) = T(p)$;
11. $T(p \vee q) = (T(p) \cap D(q)) \cup (T(q) \cap D(p))$ (where $D(p)$ abbreviates $T(p) \cup F(p)$);
12. $F(p \vee q) = F(p) \cap F(q)$.

Truth conditions are:

13. $M, w \Vdash p$ iff $w \in T(p)$, if p is an atom of CPC;
14. $M, w \Vdash \neg p$ iff $M, w \nVdash p$;
15. $M, w \Vdash p \vee q$ iff $M, w \Vdash p$ or $M, w \Vdash q$;
16. $M, w \Vdash A(t, `p\text{'})$ iff $I(t) \in N(T(J(`p\text{'})), F(J(`p\text{'})))$. (It is permitted to abbreviate $J(`p\text{'})$ to p.)

Thus '$A(t, `p\text{'})$' is true iff the topic t is a topic assigned by N to the proposition expressed by the sentence 'p'.

A sentence scheme is valid iff it is true in all worlds in all models

i) $(A(t, `p\text{'}) \wedge A(t, `q\text{'})) \rightarrow A(t, `p \wedge q\text{'})$ is a valid sentence; but

ii) $A(t, `p \wedge q') \rightarrow (A(t, `p') \vee A(t, `q'))$ is invalid.

Topicality is closed under negation, i.e.,

iii) $A(t, `p') \rightarrow A(t, `\neg p')$ is valid.

The full biconditional is got from (iii) and the assumption of

iv) If $\Vdash p \leftrightarrow q$ and p and q contain just the same atoms, then $A(t, `p' \leftrightarrow A(t, `q')$.

The ensuing system, which we dub *TopCPC*, has several attractive applications. In Cuppens and Demolombe [1988] and [1989], a system of *cooperative answering* is developed. The basic idea is that a cooperative answer responds to an interlocuter's questions with sentences that are about the questioner's topics of interest. This is nearly enough equivalent to the claim that a cooperative respondent is one who gives topically relevant answers. If we put it then that if a discussant is interested in topic t, he is interested in all sentences about this topic, we can catch this axiomatically in the language of *TopCPC*:

$$IT_a(t) \wedge A(t, `p') \rightarrow Ia(p)$$

where IT_a means that a is interested in all sentences about t and $I_a(p)$ means that a is interested in 'p'.

Alternatively, a sentence that answers an interlocuter's question is one that is topically relevant for him. More generally, a sentence or piece of information is topically relevant for an agent if it answers to his interests. We note here an affinity to the account of relevance — the agenda-relevance theory — that we shall develop in subsequent chapters. On this account, a piece of information is relevant for a cognitive agent if it plays on him (or it) in such a way as advances or closes one (or more) of his *agendas*. (But we are getting ahead of ourselves.)

5.5 Topical Relevance and Computation

A computer is a universal symbol system, also known as a general-purpose stored-program computer. Any such system is subject to three classes of operation: **general operations**, such as *identify* (by which the system's symbols can be identified at any given location); **specific**, such as the *delete* or *erasure*-operation; and **control**, such as *halt*. Any general-purpose stored-program computer requires the storage of large quantities of factual information, or knowledge. This generates the knowledge-problem, which encompasses three subproblems. One is the *knowledge-organization problem.* It is the problem of deciding on the various patterns in which knowledge should be stored. A second difficulty is the *frame problem.* It is the problem of determining precisely where in the system's knowledge base to make updates or revisions when new information is made to flow through the system. The third problem is the *relevance problem.* It is the problem of determining what information in the knowledge base would or might be of assistance in handling a given problem that has been presented to the computer.[11]

The knowledge problem is an extremely difficult one, and is taken by lots of AI researchers as the fundamental problem of computer science. One way in which to make the problem manageable is to constrain the knowledge base by a 'microworlds' assumption. This is common practice in computer diagnostics — MYCIN, for example — in which the knowledge base is stocked with very little information, which is also comparatively easy to organize (e.g., 'symptom' and 'disorder') and retrieve. In such highly restricted contexts, the relevance problem is often satisfactorily handled by way of measures for the determination of topical relevance. In a wholly general way, this means that in its search for relevant information, for information that might help solve some problem at hand, the computer would search for information that was 'about' what the problem was about.

For problems of any degree of real-life complexity, measures for topical relevance don't solve the relevance problem; topical relevance greatly underdetermines the relevance required for specific problem-solving,[12] as computer scientists become increasingly aware of the necessity of realistic problem-solvers to have very large knowledge bases. In [Lenat and Guha, 1990], and other works by Lenat's CYC team, the central problem of relevant search became increasingly ill-handled by way of topic-matching (the letters CYC compact the word 'encyclopedia'). We propose to take this lesson to heart. Topical relevance is something that a theory of relevance should attempt to elucidate, but doing so is a small part of a solution to the general problem of relevance.

We note in passing the inadequacy of CYC's efforts to bring the more general notion to heel,

---

[11]Cf. Minsky: 'The problem of selecting relevance from excessive variety is a key issue... For each 'fact' one needs meta-facts about how it is to be used and when it should not be used.' [Minsky, 1981, p. 124].

[12]Again, this is not to minimize the difficulty of producing fruitful measures for tracking topical or aboutness-relevance, as witness [Demolombe and Jones, 1999] and [Bruza *et al.*, 2000].

> It is well known that the performance of most inference mechanisms (especially those that operate on declaratively represented bodies of knowledge) degrades drastically as the size of the knowledge base ... increases. A solution of this problem needs to be found for the declarative paradigm to yield usable systems. The main observation that suggests a solution is that while the KB might have a large body of knowledge, only some small portion of it is used for any given task. If this relevant portion can be *a priori identified*, the size of the search space can be drastically reduced thereby speeding up the inference.
> [Guha and Levy, 1990, p. 1] (emphasis added)

For the *à priori* specification of relevant portions of the KB for any given problem, the CYC team proposed specific and general axioms for relevance. Specific axioms specify different sectors of the knowledge base 'according to their relevance to the problem-solving task at hand.' [Blair *et al.*, 1992, p. 15]. If the problem is one in aircraft wing design, the KB will be subject to an axiom that tells it that it is better to look in the aeronautical engineering section rather than the biochemistry section. But the relevance afforded by this axiom is little more than topical relevance at best.

Among the general axioms is the axiom of

> *Temporal proximity*: It is necessary to consider only events that are temporally close to the time of the event or proposition at issue. [Guha and Levy, 1990, p.7]

There are also general axioms of *spatial* and *informational proximity* [Guha and Levy, 1990, pp. 8–11], and a *level of grain* axiom. (In determining whether Harry is qualified to be County Treasurer, it is unnecessary to consider the molecular make-up of his thumb). It is easy to see, however, that the axioms often give the wrong guidance and that, even when it is not wrong, it leaves the search space horrifically large. This prompts a sobering thought from Jack Copeland:

> Perhaps CYC will teach us that the relevance problem is intractable for a KB organized in accordance with the data [i.e., symbol processing or linguistic] model of knowledge.
> [Copeland, 1993, p. 116]

We will return to this point in due course.

5.6 Targets for a Theory of Relevance

Throughout its lengthy history, logic has been a *service* discipline. For all its intrinsic interest, the great logicians saw logic's principal value as the contribution it would make to some or other enterprise that could not be considered as wholly logical, if logical at all. For Aristotle, logic, or the theory of syllogisms, was contrived to serve as the indispensable theoretical core of a wholly general theory of argument. For Frege, logic would serve as the host system of logicism, which in Frege's version it was a central plank in his epistemology of arithmetic. In the approach that we are taking here, a theory of relevance is part of logic, which in turn is a formal idealized description of a logical agent, i.e., as a certain type of information-processor.

Hardly anyone thinks that the idea of relevance possesses no theoretical or analytical interest just as it stands. But it is easy to see that most theories of relevance are intended, whatever else their objectives might be, as contributions to something else, to some larger intellectual project. We ourselves are unaware of any account of relevance that fails to have a service objective, beyond any interest it may also have in relevance *as such*. With certain exceptions, all the accounts we have considered so far, as well as others to come, look upon their respective approaches to relevance as contributions to the more comprehensive task of a theory of argument. In this, they resemble Aristotle who, though he did not have a developed account of relevance, nevertheless imposed a relevance condition (viz., premiss-irredundancy) on syllogisms. The relevance theory of Sperber and Wilson, which we take up in the chapter to follow, is intended to facilitate the larger designs of a theory of communication. Relevant logicians in the tradition of Anderson and Belnap have no developed theory of relevance, but like Aristotle, they too impose relevance conditions both on the entailment relation and on proofs of formulas from sets of hypotheses. In each case, the larger objective is to facilitate the ensuing logics contributions to a theory of deductive inference. (As we say, relevance logics are discussed in later chapters.)

Our own approach to relevance is similarly motivated. Like the others, there is a larger canvas on which relevance is drawn. For those who see logic our way, logic is the intended target. For those who understand logic more narrowly, it remains true that our interests extend to theories of information-processing competence, never mind what else they might also be called. But, unlike some of the alternative approaches, our account of relevance also aims at analytical adequacy. We want as much as possible to honour the common concept of relevance. In this, the theory of agenda relevance resembles a Tarskian theory of truth. It, too, has both an instrumental and an analytical objective. The instrumental objective is to facilitate production of a theory of meaning for artificial languages (or, in Davidsonian extensions, a truth conditional semantics for natural languages). Its analytical objective is to honour the colloquial meaning of 'true' as much as the instrumentally motivated technicalities allow.

On the face of it, the various accounts of relevance discussed here are rivals; that is, they can't all be true. Undoubtedly this is the appearance of things; the reality may be somewhat different. This we can see by considering the evaluation criteria appropriate to a theory of relevance. These, we think, are indicated in questions of the following sort. Let R be a theory of relevance. Then,

1. Does R succeed instrumentally? Does R adequately serve its extrinsic ends?
2. Does R succeed intrinsically, viz., as an analysis of the (or a given) concept of relevance?
3. Are R's extrinsic goals reasonable or appropriate?

One way in which a theory fails instrumentally is by way of internal defects, such as inconsistency. A common way for the analytical adequacy requirement to fail is by way of counterexample. It is harder to show that a theory's instrumental goals are inappropriate. Even so, a case comes to mind. It is a celebrated and important case. It has been part of the logical scene since Aristotle, and it serves in the work of modern-day relevant logicians. Let E be a theory of entailment. Let us now ask whether any set of qualifications on E's entailment relation will serve as normatively sound and psychologically recognizable strategies in a theory In of inference or belief-modification. If you see things Harman's way [Harman, 1986]), the answer is in the negative. If this is the correct answer, then In would not be an appropriate service target for E. (We will return to this issue.)

As we will see, the theory of agenda relevance differs in certain respects from, e.g., the theory of Sperber and Wilson. The account of agenda relevance seeks to produce conceptual analysis of the common notion of relevance. SW-relevance is a theoretical construct, whose fit, partial or more substantial, with intuitive meanings is wholly adventitious. The theory of Sperber and Wilson is aimed at facilitating a theory of communication. This, in turn, is realized by a general theory of cognition in which a relevance principle is the driving theoretical factor. The theory of agenda relevance has a different service-target. It would not be appropriate to fault either theory for either of the differences. These are differences that make the respective accounts different, not necessarily better or less good. Even so, it would be wholly legitimate to criticize these different accounts for a failure to hit intended targets, never mind that they are different targets.

This will be one of the criticisms we make of the Sperber–Wilson account of relevance. We will say that it suffers from internal difficulties that preclude its hitting its own service-targets, not ours. (But we will also suggest analytical violence to anything deserving even the technical name of relevance.) This is also the line we take with other theories, with, e.g., Walton's account of dialectical relevance (chapter 9) and the probability approach to relevance.

We take very seriously the possibility that a given theoretical insight into relevance might sound right even though a given articulation of that insight is defective. Where this is so, we judge it to be a desideratum of any theory of the sort we propose to try to accommodate the insight while keeping the articulation difficulties at bay. In our view, getting relevance deeply right is a difficult task. The ecumenism we espouse is not only an intellectual virtue; it is also the practical virtue of a readiness to accept all the help that might be available to us.

5.7 Freeman and Cohen

5.7.1 Freeman

For Freeman, as for Blair ([Freeman, 1992] and [Blair, 1992]), relevance is defined over triples $\langle Pa, W, Ca \rangle$ in which the first and third are propositions and W is a warrant. $\ulcorner Pa \urcorner$ is relevant to $\ulcorner Ca \urcorner$ with respect to W just in case W is authoritative. Freeman's relevance is thus 'normative' relevance. W is authoritative just in case its associated generalization $AG(W)$ here, $\ulcorner \forall x(Px \rightarrow Cx) \urcorner$ is supported. In the case in which $AG(W)$ is an empirical generalization, its support is a matter of its surviving structured series of trials. The basic apparatus for this is L.J. Cohen's theory of inductive support [Cohen, 1977]. An $AG(W)$ is supported by evidence E at trial stage i just in case $AG(W)$ on E gives a support value appropriately greater than zero. In case $I > i > n$, and E supports $AG(W)$ at all $k < i$, $AG(W)$ will be rather strongly supported by E, certainly more than would be the case in a single successful trial. Where $AG(W)$ fails the test at the next trial or at a subsequent trial $j > i$, then $AG(W)$ is falsified at j but, according to Cohen, does not lose all support at j [Cohen, 1977, p. 135]. Freeman is disturbed by this. If the $AG(W)$ test did fail at j, 'wouldn't [a critic] be right in saying that in these circumstances ... the premise [i.e. $\ulcorner Pa \urcorner$] is not relevant to the conclusion [i.e., $\ulcorner Ca \urcorner$], at least in a normative sense?' [Freeman, 1992, p. 232]. Accordingly, Freeman extends the notion of inductive support in the following way. $AG(W)$ is supported at i if it is supported at all $k < i$ and for any $j > i$ there is a presumption that it will be supported at j.

Presumption, here, is a dialogical notion. There is a presumption in favour of a proposition Φ in a dialogue or dialectical inquiry D just to the extent that parties to the enquiry have no good reason to query Φ and no evidence that Φ is untrue. With that said, normative relevance is presumed to drop out.

> Pa is normatively relevant to Ca with respect to W if and only if W licenses the inference from Pa to Ca, $s[AG(W), E] = i/n$, $i > 0$, and for all j, $i < j < n$, there is a presumption that the value of vj is non-rebutting. [Freeman, 1992, p. 234]

That is, the support of the associated generalization of $W, AG(W)$ on evidence E is appropriately non-zero on the ith trial (and preceding ones), and there is a presumption that the considerations that bear on the jth trial ('the value of vj") will not rebut $AG(W)$.

It is apparent that Freeman's account promises little more than lexical relief. Relevance 'just is' the warrantedness of inferences drawn from premisses. Support for warrants is sketched in Cohen's approach of inductive support supplemented by a dialogical notion of presumption. In embedding relevance thus, no new insights are offered about the apparatus of inductive support, nor is the idea of presumptiveness deepened in any noticeable way (whatever else one might think of it). Freeman writes that he is confident that the above definition marks a significant point of departure. 'Due to the centrality of inductive generalizations and so of inductive warrants, it should constitute a significant component in any explication of relevance' [Freeman, 1992, p. 234]. We ourselves aren't so sure.

It bears on the point at hand that Cohen himself does not regard his theory of inductive support as a theory of relevance or as one which would yield a theory of relevance under some modest extension of its vocabulary and a modest sprinkling of definitions. True, Cohen's theory makes principled use of the notion of relevant variable, as does Freeman's, but it is clear that the theory of inductive support is not a theory of the relevance that characterize variables when they are relevant variables. Freeman doesn't discuss whether his account of relevance is also meant to elucidate the relevance of relevant variables, but here too, it would seem not. We shall say in a moment how the notion of relevant variable can be incorporated into Cohen's relevance theory as special cases of more general notions.

The inductive support aspects of Freeman's account strikes us as problematic in a second way. As we have been saying, a decent theory of relevance is part of what would count as a *PLCS*, a practical logic of cognitive systems. When the logic is practical, our convention is to restrict the investigation of cognitive systems to those possessed or instantitiated by individuals. But individuals occupy the lower regions of our postulated hierarchy $\mathcal{H} = \langle C, A \rangle$ of goal-directed, resource-bound cognitive agents C, operating with scarce resource R. Agents such as these are practical agents, beings like you and me. Practical agents are cognitive systems so situated that it is rationally required of them to proceed with cognitive tasks economically — to make do with less, so to speak. This rational imperative takes a number of forms, but three examples are especially important. Individual agents have a vital stake in sorting out helpful from unelpful information; i.e., they are well-served by relevant information. Individual agents do not in the general case aim at truth-preservation in their reasonings. Nor does it serve them well to make high conditional probability a common cognitive target. Taking the first and third of these together, we can simplify the point at hand as follows. Freeman says, in effect, that beings like us honour the requirement of relevance by hitting the requisite inductive targets of inductive strength, at the core of which is conditional probability. By our own lights, this is a recipe for failure. If relevance were the inductive notion that Freeman takes it to be, relevance in the general case would be neither an easy or a desirable target for the rational individual to attempt to hit. This seems to us an acceptable consequence.

5.7.2 Cohen

'The topic of relevance has suffered much from those who have taken a part of the topic as the whole.' [Cohen, 1994, p. 171]. Even so, Cohen proposes that there is a general conception of relevance that has an underlying structure that 'unifies it, despite the variety of criteria for applying the concept.' [Cohen, 1994, p. 172]. A theory of relevance must honour a rich diversity of usages. They can be taken as pre-theoretical data which the theory must try to accommodate. There 'is a wide variety of types of entity that in suitable contexts can be said to be relevant ... to something. These include objects, actions, states, events, processes, facts, rules, principles, assertions, commands, questions, attitudes, and many other things.' [Cohen, 1994, p. 176].

Cohen distinguishes between the non-conversational relevance and the conversational. If we came upon the unwarranted claim

> The presence of footprints outside the window is relevant to resolving whether the butler was the murderer

we would encounter a claim that bears two interpretations. On one of them, the presence of footprints outside the widow is evidence about the butler's possible complicity. In the other, discourse about the presence of footprints would not be out of place when considering whether the butler was involved. Notwithstanding the syntactic complexity of relevance-talk, 'a standard, normal form is discernible ... Specifically, a statement about relevance to actions, states, events, processes, properties, facts, rules, principles, assertions, commands, attitudes, etc., can always be reformulated as a roughly equivalent statement about relevance to a corresponding question or to consideration of a corresponding question (where 'question' means 'issue' or 'problem' ...)" [Cohen, 1994, pp. 176–177]. Relevance is then defined:

> (DR) A true proposition R is non-conversationally relevant to an askable question Q if and only if there is a proposition a such that the truth of R is a reason, though not necessarily a conclusive reason, for accepting or rejecting a as an answer to Q. [Cohen, 1994, p. 178]

And

> (DD) Consideration of a proposition R is conversationally relevant to consideration of a question Q if and only if consideration of Q raises a question Q^* that is answered by a proposition for the acceptance or rejection of which R would be a reason. [Cohen, 1994, p. 178][13]

As DR and DD make clear, Cohen's is not a strict propositional account of relevance. Relevance is a dyadic relation over propositions and questions (non-conversational) and over consideration of propositions and consideration of questions (conversational). The theory gives no account of whose questions or whose considerings they might be, and so it is not a pragmatic theory. Though not an exclusively pragmatic relation, Cohen's relevance deserves the name of logical. In a pre-publication version of the paper under discussion, Cohen says that the fine print of the theory of relevance could be found in details about the logic of questions. This suggests that the account of relevance is essentially complete. It isn't.

Let Q be the question of whether to go to the movies tonight and R the true proposition that 'Hotel Paradiso', the winner at Cannes some years

[13] We said that we would show that the idea of relevant variables assimilates to this more general conception of relevance. A relevant variable is a potentially falsifying variable v in the context of a set of trials of the inductive support a body of evidence E affords an hypothesis H. Let v be such a variable. Then v is *de re* relevant to the question of whether H on E when v gives some reason in support of an answer to that question. It does so when v actually obtains. Similarly, consideration of v is *de dicto* relevant to consideration of whether H on E when consideration of that gives rise to a question, e.g., 'Would v if it obtained damage the case for H on E?', to which v itself is an answer. (For recall that v is a potentially falsifying variable.)

back, is playing. If R is reason, though not necessarily conclusive reason, for a, 'It would be good to see that movie again' or 'It's a must-see, a classic', then if a answers Q, R is relevant to Q. But what if the questioner is left wholly undecided about whether to go to the movies? 'I just can't make up my mind', he says. Intuitions tug in opposite directions. Of course, what's playing and the reputation of what's playing is relevant to the question whether to see it. But if that information didn't in any way help to reach a decision, it would seem that on Cohen's account, it isn't relevant to the question at hand. Which it is, relevant or not, awaits elucidation of 'reason for' and 'answer to', neither of which is provided here. So the theory fails to instruct us in a simple and common kind of case.

It is the same way with conversational relevance. Let Q be the problem of how to go about proving Fermat's theorem. In considering Q our mathematician also considers whether he should sharpen his pencil. This is Q^*. Considering Q gives rise to considering Q^*. Now, as it happens, our mathematician sees by looking that his pencil is fine (no pun). This is R. R is a reason, probably a conclusive reason, for a, 'The pencil doesn't need sharpening'. R then is a reason for a which answers Q^* which arose from consideration of Q. So 'The pencil is fine' is relevant to considering 'How is Fermat's theorem to be proved?'. No. It all depends, of course, on 'arising'. But 'arising' isn't elucidated. Perhaps this is not quite true of 'reason for'. Cohen says that Φ is a reason for Ψ when there is a covering law, or a counterfactualizable correlation, K that licenses the inference of Ψ from Φ. K might be a law of nature, or a principle of jurisprudence, or a provision of the Medical Society's statement of ethics. It will also be a law of logic, presumably? Sometimes. *Ex falso quodlibet* is such a law: from a contradiction everything follows; and its contrapositive, a logical truth follows from everything. But, says Cohen, neither *ex falso* nor its contrapositive licenses the inference of consequent from antecedent. Why not? Because they are not laws whose antecedents are reasons for their consequents.

This is quite right, but it is problematic all the same. Being a reason for was to have been elucidated by way of true covering laws. *Ex falso* is a true covering law, but it fails to provide that its antecedent is a reason for its consequent. Only those covering laws that ground the reason-for relation are those whose antecedents are reasons for their consequents.

It is a condition on the non-conversational relevance of a proposition R to a question Q that R be true. Harry is in the stands. It has been a long day. He wonders whether to stay for the next event, the women's javelin-throw. This is Q. A nearby spectator exclaims, 'Oh, your wife has fainted!'. This is R. 'We must leave at once', Harry says. This answers Q. But R is false. It isn't Harry's wife who has fainted; it is his sister. So R isn't relevant to the question of whether to take in the javelin-throw. Perhaps we can fix this. Instead of requiring R to be true, we might require that it imply or presuppose some R^* that is true. If R^* is relevant to Q, so is R. No. Let R now be 'The set exists of all those sets that are not members of themselves'. R implies R^*, 'Your companion has fainted', and this is true and relevant to Q. So any contradiction is relevant to any question, if anything is relevant to it. Suppose now that Harry's sister, who desperately hates the javelin-throw, has faked her fainting spell. No one has fainted, and so no one with whom Harry is relevantly associated. Is 'Oh, your wife has fainted!' now relevant to Harry's decision about whether to leave, or is it not?

Before quitting the present chapter, we should like to emphasize three points:

1. We do not deny that there is a serviceable notion of propositional relevance, whose logic it would be worth our while to try to get right.

2. We persist in the view that propositional relevance is not all there is to relevance.

3. We also retain our view that the approaches to propositional relevance lately reviewed are unsatisfactory (repairs are essayed in chapters 13 and 14).

That a theory of relevance should know the nuisance of internal difficulties is no rare thing. All the relevance theories we have examined so far are affected by such difficulties. It may be that revisions to the present theory will eliminate the snags. We want to press a different point. In general, says Cohen, 'we must expect that intuitive judgements of deductive-logical relevance and irrelevance will reflect intuitive judgements about what is a deductive-logical reason for what, ... [and that] projects for the formal reconstruction of the former type of judgement will face all the difficulties encountered by projects for the formal reconstruction of the latter type' [Cohen, 1994, p. 183].

Readers familiar with their work may have even higher hopes for the efforts of Sperber and Wilson. The heart of relevance, their way, is the idea of contextual effects.

Chapter 6

Contextual Effects

> He doth like the ape, that the higher he climbs the more he shows his ars.
>
> Francis Bacon

6.1 Introductory Remarks

We said in section 5.6 that a theory R is judgeable against the background of three questions.

1. Does R succeed instrumentally, i.e., does it adequately serve its extrinsic ends?

2. Does R succeed intrinsically, namely, as an analysis of R's target concept(s)?

3. Are R's extrinsic goals reasonable or appropriate?

Let us say at once how we take Sperber and Wilson's account of relevence to fare with respect to these questions, omitting at present most of the pertinent details.

Concerning question (1), Sperber and Wilson require a theory of relevance to facilitate the broader objective of producing a theory of cognition, which in its turn would assist in reaching their ultimate objective, which is to produce a (non-Gricean) pragmatic theory of communication. In the years following publication of *Relevance*, there has been considerable debate about Sperber and Wilson's proposals. Perhaps the debate is most intense between Griceans and non-Griceans about communication. Whatever the merits of these contending positions, our own view is that (aside from some internal difficulties), given the theory of communication that Sperber and Wilson aimed to produce, their account of relevance does facilitate the articulation of that theory.

We should say a word about 'internal difficulties'. We say that a theory encounters an internal difficulty when it carries unintended consequences that damage the theory (certain kinds of inconsistency are a case in point). It should be noted that a theory about a certain matter K can succeed in getting the basic idea of K right and yet be defaced by internal difficulties. Question (2) should be understood in this light. It asks not only whether a theory has a decent analogue of K but also whether it is free of these internal difficulties.

Concerning question (2), the answer is a qualified No. Sperber and Wilson have not undertaken to produce an analysis of the common conception of relevance, and so have not set themselves the task of achieving the intrinsic adequacy that question (2) speaks of. However, such a task *is* one of the tasks that the writers of this book have set for themselves. So it is perfectly in order to ask whether the theoretical construct that Sperber and Wilson have produced would satisfy our quest for successful analysis of the common conception of relevance. Our answer is equivocal. Theirs, we think, is the right kind of way to be thinking of relevance, but we think that it does not go far enough.

Question (3) asks whether the extrinsic goal, namely, a theory of communication, is reasonable or appropriate. If this is to ask whether the phenomena are amenable to scientific enquiry, our answer is Yes. If it asks whether the target theory is a correct theory of communication, we confess to some Gricean leanings and will let it go at that. (We are, after all, interested in relevance for its own sake.)

Finally, question (4), which asks whether the Sperber–Wilson account of relevance is free from internal difficulties. Our answer is No, but that in the main these are difficulties admitting of repair, or at lest of a degree of mitigation.

More of this anon.

6.2 Contextual Effects

The most damaging internal difficulty that a theory of relevance can run into is excessiveness, in which it is derivable that nothing is relevant to anything or that everything is relevant to everything or, twice-over, some dangerous approximation thereto. Excessiveness is so undesirable a consequence that it is necessary to impose as an adequacy condition on any would-be theory of relevance the requirement that:

AC1: A theory of relevance should not be excessive.

But we must not think that AC1 is itself free of conditions. AC1 applies to a theory to the extent that it offers a common analysis of relevance. A theory that provides a purely stipulative analysis of relevance could turn out to violate AC1. There may be reason to like such theories. They may turn out to be good theories of this, that, or the other thing, whose goodness is facilitated by, among other things, stipulations about relevance. But what such a theory cannot be is an interesting theory of relevance on the hoof. A theory will be a good theory of relevance only if it makes substantial headway with a common analysis of it.

The Sperber–Wilson account of relevance is a case in point. What Sperber and Wilson are after is something close to our notion of common analysis of communication and cognition (as common as scientific accuracy will allow). What they are not interested in is a common analysis of *relevance*. They are ready to judge their account of relevance on the strength of its contributions to the common analysis of communication and cognition. So, while Sperber and Wilson can't be faulted for not producing what they had no intention to produce, the account of relevance would fail in its service role if it dishonoured AC1. Sperber and Wilson are interested in a psychologically realistic account of communication. To this end, the following questions must be answered: 'What shared information is exploited in communication? What forms of inference are used? What is relevance and how is it achieved? What role does the search for relevance play in communication?' [Sperber and Wilson, 1987, 699].

Sperber and Wilson base their account of communication on a general view of cognition. 'Human cognition', they say, 'is relevance-oriented' [Sperber and Wilson, 1987, 700]. In this connection, Sperber and Wilson postulate what they call the *deductive device*. The deductive device mimics the deductive abilities of actual communicators. The deductive device is an abstraction from these abilities. It is a model of the actual thing, rather than the actual thing itself. Sperber and Wilson 'see it as a central function of the deductive device to derive, spontaneously, automatically and unconsciously, the contextual implication of any newly presented information in a context of old information' [Sperber and Wilson, 1987, 702].

Sperber and Wilson define relevance for ordered pairs, $\langle P, C\rangle$, where P is an assumption or belief and C a context, itself a conjunction of beliefs.[1] This

[1]'Assumption' is their preferred term, but it is clear that it is sufficiently interchangeable with 'belief' for our purposes here. The same holds for their 'thesis' which sometimes

leaves the adicity of 'relevant' at two. But bearing in mind that contexts are contexts for information-processors, this way of proceeding adumbrates the three-place. So defined, theirs is another basically propositional approach. The principal claim of their account of relevance is:

> *Relevance.* An assumption is relevant in a context if and only if it has some contextual effect in that context.
> [Sperber and Wilson, 1986, p. 122]

We must say again that these authors

> are *not* trying to define the ordinary and fuzzy English word *relevance.* We believe, though, that there is an important psychological property — a property involved in mental processes — which the ordinary notion of *relevance* roughly approximates, and which it is therefore appropriate to call by that name, using it in a *technical sense.* [Sperber and Wilson, 1987, 702], emphasis added in the fourth instance

The notion of a contextual effect is essential to a characterization of relevance [Sperber and Wilson, 1987, 702]. An assumption or belief has a contextual effect in a context when it strengthens or reinforces a belief contained in that context, when it contradicts a belief contained in that context and thus forces an 'erasure', or when it licenses implications. Contextual effects can in each case be likened to changes of mind. Degrees of confidence are raised or lowered, beliefs are contradicted and erased, or new beliefs are derived.

Contextual implication is defined in the following way. Where P is a belief and C a context and Q a further belief, then:

> *Contextual implication.* P contextually implies Q in context C iff (i) $\ulcorner P \wedge C \urcorner$ non-trivially implies Q; (ii) P does not non-trivially imply Q; and (iii) C does not non-trivially imply Q.

Here, then, the central idea is that, upon placing new information P into a given inventory of beliefs C, an implication is sanctioned of some further assumption Q, where Q couldn't be got either from C alone or from $\{P\}$ alone.

It is necessary to say something about the idea of non-trivial implication, which drives the definition of contextual implication.

---

does duty for 'assumption'.

> *Non-trivial implication.* P logically and non-trivially implies Q iff when P is the set of initial theses in a derivation involving only elimination rules, Q belongs to the set of final theses.
> [Sperber and Wilson, 1986, p. 97]

Requiring the deductive device to run only elimination rules, is supposed to spare the deduction device from producing infinite outputs. This it would surely do according to Sperber and Wilson if it executed introduction rules and obeyed the constraints of relevance, which require it to produce the largest possible non-trivial output at least possible cost.[2] 'Elimination rules ... are genuinely interpretative: the output assumptions explicate or analyse the content of the input assumptions.' [Sperber and Wilson, 1986, p. 97]. Further, '[o]ur hypothesis is that the human deductive device has access only to elimination rules, and yields only non-trivial conclusions ... .' [Sperber and Wilson, 1986, p. 97].[3]

Contextual implications also involve synthetic implications [Sperber and Wilson, 1986, p. 109]. A synthetic implication is one using at least one synthetic rule of derivation [Sperber and Wilson, 1986, p. 104], where a synthetic rule takes not one but 'two separate assumptions as input'. So, for example, the rule of $\wedge$-elimination 'which takes a single conjoined assumption as input, is an analytic rule, and *modus ponendo ponens*, which takes a conditional assumption and its antecedent as input, is a synthetic rule.' [Sperber and Wilson, 1986, p. 104].

6.3 In The Head

Relevance, and contextual implication too, is defined over propositions.

> Treating relevance as a property of propositions or assumptions (as is often done in the pragmatic literature) involves a considerable abstraction.
> [Sperber and Wilson, 1987, 703]

The definitions involve no parameters about what goes on in an inferrer's head or in his 'inference organ', wherever that might be.[4] Although the canonical form of a synthetic implication might be said to, and sometimes does, simulate what goes on in the inference organ of an efficient inferrer,

---

[2] One wonders, however, about the infinity let loose by the commutatitivity rule.

[3] In Gabbay [1996], introduction rules are definable from elimination rules. So any logic can be presented via elimination rules only. See Remark 13.20 below and its follow up.

[4] Perhaps strengthening is an exception. See below.

none of this is given formal definitive admittance into the theory itself. Relevance is not there a property of inference strategies; it is a property of propositional relations. It is defined over the propositional elements that are abstracted from the din and swirl of inferential practice.

In confirmation of head-independence, Sperber and Wilson emphasize not only the automaticity of the operation of relevance in human cognition and communication, but also the extrinsicness of its operation on the processing system, i.e., relevance itself is neither mentally represented or the subject of the cognizer's computation (Sperber and Wilson [1986, 132]; [1987, 697]).

Even so, the definition of relevance, they say,

> is insufficient for at least two reasons: The first is that relevance is a matter of degree and the definition says nothing about how degrees of relevance are determined; the second reasoning is that it defines relevance as a relation between an assumption and a context, whereas we might want to be able to describe the relevance of any kind of information to any kind of information-processing device, and more particularly to an individual. At the moment, then, we simply defined a formal property, leaving its relation to psychological reality undescribed.
>
> [Sperber and Wilson, 1987, pp. 702–703]

Relevance is treated at two removes from the actual thing. It is offered as a technical notion which only approximates to the ordinary notion of relevance, whatever that might actually be; and although in its technical use it denotes an actual psychological property of human mental states, it is here abstractly defined as a formal property of propositions, which leaves the underlying psychological reality underspecified.

So, whereas the definition of relevance is independent of what goes on in the head, what relevance is defined *for* is contrarily a matter of how heads work when cognition is in process. The larger purpose of this work on relevance and occasion of much agitation among critics, is to reposition pragmatics in the deep centre of a general account of cognition.

Even so, contextual implication is troublesome. Syntheticity assumptions are insufficient to make it behave. To take just one example, syntheticity fails for the competent management of inconsistency.

6.4 Inconsistency Management

Why not say that erasure dominates over inconsistency? By all means, say it when it does. There was a time when ordinary human reasoners with enough education to be at home with naive versions of the calculus knowingly held inconsistent beliefs and hadn't the grace to be troubled by it. The infinitesimal both was and was not equal to zero. When relief was supplied first by Weierstrass in the 1830s, and a hundred and twenty years later by Robinson's invention of non standard analysis, the theory of the hyperreals [Robinson, 1966], most of the mathematically educated ignored it and have ignored it since. (Likewise, most people who work with sets continue to use the old comprehension axiom, which sometimes — but not always — comes equipped with a warning. ZF and ZFC are set theories for the comparatively sophisticated.) We can imagine Harry as a fledgling who already knows that division by α requires that $\alpha \neq 0$, where α is an infinitesimal. Today he learns that by the requirement that infinitesimals and their products be discounted in the final value of the derivative, $\alpha=0$. No eraser he, Harry adds the new information to his prior inventory.

Should he also chance to be a budding proof theorist, Harry will believe that negation-inconsistency implies absolute inconsistency. Harry's calculus teacher might happen to be commendably candid. He might point out the negation inconsistency of what Harry now holds about infinitesimals. We need both halves of the inconsistency, so do not erase, he tells Harry (in effect). And Harry doesn't. Harry's new information engages his prior knowledge in a striking way. That $\alpha \neq 0$ and $\alpha = 0$, together with ⌜For any pair Φ, $\neg\Phi$, arbitrary Ψ follows⌝, the contextual implication of Ψ goes through, undeterred by the syntheticity of the implication. Since Ψ is arbitrary, what Harry now knows contextually implies everything, that is, everything representable as a declarative sentence in any extension of the language of the calculus. That would seem to be all of any natural language that Harry speaks or understands, and implied will be every declarative sentence that he understands, and more besides. The information that $\alpha = 0$ is not just relevant in the context of what Harry already knew, it is lavishly relevant. For if a proposition is relevant in a context, the greater the number of its contextual implications and the less the effort required to process the new information. It is a commonplace of information theory that a contradiction contains maximal information. This is now inadvertently mimicked by relevance. Information triggering the implication of all consequences is maximally relevant.

Let $K(C)$ be the deductive closure of a context C. Then in Harry's case the absence of particular anti-triviality provisions, $K(C)$ contains (the propositional content of) every declarative sentence that he understands, and more besides. Given the conditions of the case, we might think of $K(C)$ as Harry's successor context with respect to the addition to C of the new information that $\alpha = 0$. $K(C)$ then would be a maximal context for

Harry. There is the empirical question of whether beings like us are capable of having maximal contexts. Since we assume not, perhaps maximal contexts should be admitted, if at all, only as artifacts of theory. Even so, they are a liability. Syntheticity was invoked to block indiscriminate, trivial and potentially infinite outputs of the deductive device. If $K(C)$ doesn't qualify as indiscriminate, trivial and infinite, nothing does. Synthetically generated, $K(C)$ discredits syntheticity as a constraint. It was offered us for the theoretical good that it would do, never mind that it overrode empirical facts about human reasoning, the empirical fact, for example, that sometimes we make commutativity inferences that are far from trivial, or that sometimes we make distributivity inferences, the (apparent) transgressions of which by quantum mechanics was, at least initially, a nasty shock.

$K(C)$ is devastating news for relevance. Contextual implication, strengthening and contradiction/erasure alike are thrown into disarray. Since $K(C)$ is maximal for Harry, the unit set of every proposition is a subset of it. If C was a context in which every proposition is contextually implied, $K(C)$ is a context in which no proposition is contextually implied. Let P be any proposition and Q any proposition considered as a candidate for contextual implication by P in $K(C)$. Since $K(C)$ is maximal, it contains both P and Q, each is implied by it. No Q is contextually implied by P in $K(C)$. C was troublesome on the ground that every proposition is relevant there; $K(C)$ is troublesome on the ground that no proposition is relevant there by way of contextual implication. Every Q is non-trivially implied by $K(C)$, owing to the presence of R, "$\neg R$" for every proposition R, together with $\ulcorner$For all Φ, if $\Phi \wedge \neg\Phi$, arbitrary Ψ follows$\urcorner$. So, for no P (alone) will there be a contextual implication in $K(C)$ of any Q from it.

$K(C)$ deranges strengthening. We have it in general that whenever a proposition Q strengthens a proposition P in a context, then for every deductive consequence R of P (in C), Q enhances to some non-zero degree the confirmation of R at least to the extent that Q itself enhances the confirmation of P (by virtue of which it strengthens P). Since every proposition is a deductive consequence of any P in $K(C)$, there are two cases to consider.

Case one: R is a deductive consequence of P in $K(C)$, Q strengthens P and so is confirmatory for R. But given the specification of $K(C)$, Q is also confirmatory to the same non-zero degree for "$\neg R$". This is implausible.

Case two: R is a deductive consequence of P in $K(C)$, and Q strengthens P. Further let it be the case that 'Q confirms R to some non-zero degree' is false in any known theory of confirmation (by way, for example, of the irrelevance of Q to R). But 'Q confirms R to some non-zero degree' is evaluated here as true. There is no reason to believe the valuation.

If our prior argument managed to show that the concept of contextual implication is empty in $K(C)$, the present cases make the same argument for strengthening. Contradiction fares no better.

Every P contradicts some Q in $K(C)$. When this happens, the strategy of erasure is involved. It requires the erasure, without the requisite postulates for revision, of the least strengthened proposition that will eliminate the contradiction. But there is in $K(C)$ no proposition distinguished from the others as a candidate for erasure. All propositions in $K(C)$ possess sufficient degrees of strength to resist erasure if contextual implication is sufficient for relevance. This presents us with two options.

Option one: A proposition P is relevant in a context when it there contradicts some proposition Q, never mind that for structural reasons erasure is now a null strategy.

Option two: If a proposition P contradicts a proposition Q in a context and erasure is a null strategy in that context, then P is not there relevant to Q.

By option one everything is relevant in $K(C)$. By option two nothing is.

The surveyed results disclose that contextual implication is empty in $K(C)$, that strengthening is empty in $K(C)$, and that contradiction/erasure is either empty in $K(C)$ or maximally non-empty in $K(C)$. Since $K(C)$ itself is maximal, every proposition is irrelevant in $K(C)$, or irrelevant in $K(C)$ and also relevant in $K(C)$. $K(C)$ makes the theory of relevance excessive several times over.

We have been assuming without argument that the deductive closure of a context under contextual implication is itself a context. Without that assumption $K(C)$ will probably fail to qualify as one. This is both good and bad. It is good in as much as it allows deductive closures of contexts to float about in logical space free of the necessity of supposing that they are contexts *for* actual human reasoners. This would answer to the intuition that no human could ever process all that his processed beliefs committed him to. The denial that contexthood is closed under contextual effects also spares the theory of relevance the nuisance of excessiveness. If we insisted that relevance is defined only for ordered pairs of propositions and *bona fide* contexts, this consequence would be averted if we knew in what the *bona fides* consisted.

With the good comes some bad. It is very bad if a version of Gresham's Law obtains: bad drives out good. The problem is that if a context is just a set of propositions, there is no way of keeping the deductive closure of such a set under contextual implication from being a set of propositions, hence a context. We cannot permit this. Given the resources that Sperber and

Wilson have provided us, we cannot allow contexthood to be closed under contextual consequence. This is the lesson of our story about Harry.

Contexts then are sets of propositions to which certain relations are borne. It would be nice to know what these relations are. The deductive device was contrived by theory to perform the task of replacing contexts with successor contexts. There is no doubt that humans have considerable facility when it comes to forming successor contexts. A good deal of what goes on involves inference and, in turn, deductive inference. The deductive device was meant to tell this part of the story. It doesn't. It doesn't produce a *bona fide* successor context for Harry. So it doesn't specify a way of avoiding excessiveness. The problem is not that Sperber and Wilson have the wrong *idea* about relevance. The problem rather is that the structural machinery of contextual effects is too crude for its articulation, even at the level of abstraction at which they present it.

Ex falso quodlibet is the name given to the theorem that an inconsistency implies everything whatever. *Ex falso* causes great trouble at this juncture of the Sperber and Wilson approach to relevance. And *ex falso* is provably true of classical implication. This suggests a remedy. Why not *declassify* implication? Of course, contextual implication is not classical implication. It is classical implication under the syntheticity constraint. But the syntheticity constraint won't block what classical implication already delivers, namely, that any formula whatever follows from any inconsistent set of formulas. Even so constrained, contextual implication does not sufficiently mimic our belief-revision procedures to evade the trouble presently in view. No one thinks that a human inferer would or could infer everything whatever from an inconsistency; which means (importantly) that the story about *reasoning* from inconsistencies is different from the story of what those inconsistencies *imply*. Contextual implication seeks to close this gap, to have its cake and eat it, too. In this it fails,[5] which leaves us with two options. One is to constrain implication even further, to declassify it to the point at which it cannot deliver *ex falso quodlibet* (an option exercised by paraconsistent logicians).[6] The other is to leave implications be and to continue with a purpose-built reasoning strategy which inhibits *ex falso* inferentially (as it should). The first way, we pretend that, properly understood, implications are actually inference-protocols. The second way, we abandon the pretence; we acknowledge from the outset that implication statements and inference-routines are different animals, and that no non-classical logic of implication can do equal justice to both.

[5]As did the founder of logic, who sought for plausible principles of reasoning by imposing syllogistic constraints on ordinary (i.e., classical) validity. See [Woods, 2001].

[6]For detailed discussion, see [Woods, 2002b].

What are the gross empirical data about the management of inconsistent contexts for which erasure is not invoked? The data of common experience suggests at least four strategies. Faced with a noticed inconsistency in a context, the human reasoner may

A. Ignore the inconsistency and quickly forget that it is there if it seems harmless and inessential to any of his cognitive tasks at hand. (The strategy recalls Emerson's couplet that 'a Foolish consistency is the hobgoblin of minds, adored by little statesmen and philosophers and divines'.)[7]

B. If he recognizes that it may be important for his cognitive agenda to resolve the inconsistency and if he lacks the means of doing it now, he may quarantine the inconsistency and keep it out of premissary action for the time being. (This evokes Wittgenstein's supposition that an inconsistency which we don't know how to dissolve can be 'sealed off' and allowed to stand.)

C. If his cognitive agenda presses for resolution then and there, he may attempt to eliminate the inconsistency, short of erasure, by searching for an ambiguity, and so to discover the sense in which the offending proposition is true is not the same sense as the sense in which it is untrue. (But let us not forget Semantic Occam's Razor.)

D. Depending again on the urgency of the cognitive work at hand, he may 'split' the inconsistency and put each part to disjoint premissary work, this too on sufferance, until more stable remedies suggest themselves.

There is a fifth possibility, which is Sperber's and Wilson's own:

E. If $\{P, Q\}$ is an inconsistent set of assumptions, compute a confirmation value for each, and expunge the assumption with the lower value. [Sperber and Wilson, 1986, 111]

For big knowledge-base computer systems such as CYC, inconsistency is handled in the first instance by a procedure called *truth maintenance*. CYC backward chains to the respective premisses of the two sentences that are jointly inconsistent and rejects one of them if it can. This is done when the knowledge base of the system makes it possible to discern which premisses are least likely to be true or which admit of exceptions, and so on. (The

[7] Cf. Donald Davidson on the Liar-induced inconsistency of natural languages: '... I think that we are justified in carrying on without having disinfected this particular source of conceptual anxiety' [Davidson, 1967, p. 314].

recovery of premisses is made possible by the unique address possessed by each member of the knowledge base. The address is a kind of label, and is anticipation of the labelled deductive systems approach to logic, in the manner of [Gabbay, 1996] and chapter 13, below.)

Needless to say a system's truth maintenance procedures will often fail to produce a resolution, since it won't be possible to provide a principled basis on which to reject any given premiss over any other. In that case, as Copeland observes,

> CYC can do one of three things. (1) Shut down and await human intervention. (2) Quarantine all assertions implicated in the inconsistency and try to do without them ... (3) Brazen it out. Carry on and hope the malign effects of the inconsistency won't spread too far. [Copeland, 1993, p. 119]

We note that Copeland's (1) is akin to allowing *ex falso* to operate with the resultant paralysis of the system. His (2) is essentially our (B), and his (3) is a general resolution strategy of which our (A) and Davidson's 'carrying on' (see footnote 7) are instances. It is also what CYC's originators propose.

> There is no need — and probably not even any possibility — of achieving a global consistent unification of ... [a] very large KB ... We expect ... that ... [the position that] inconsistencies may exist for a short period but ... are errors and must be tracked down and corrected ... is just an idealized, simplified view of what will be required for intelligent systems ... How should the system cope with inconsistency? View the knowledge space, and hence the KB, not as one rigid body, but rather as a set of independently supported buttes ... [A]s with large office buildings, independent supports should make it easier for the whole structure to weather tremors such as local anomalies ... [I]nferring an inconsistency is only slightly more serious than the usual sort of 'dead end' a searcher runs into ... [Lenat and Feigenbaum, 1991, p. 217].

With the exception of strategy three, none of these routines of inconsistency management is the Sperber–Wilson deductive device equipped to perform. It cannot even discharge the requirements of their own option E. Having declined to furnish the deductive device with the wherewithall of the calculus of probabilities (no mean thing in itself), Sperber and Wilson don't get around to indicating how the requisite confirmation values are determined. Provided we are prepared to say that the rational management of unresolved inconsistency is something that the deductive device *should* do, then we can conclude that the deductive device is too crude for the purposes for which it was contrived. And given that drawing implications constrained by the syntheticity requirement is a core operation of the device, we have reason again to think that, like conditional probability, implication (syntheticity constraint and all) is too coarse-grained for relevance. Lost, too, as we say, is the motivation for the syntheticity constraint. Lacking for a rationale in the actual behaviour of human thinkers, it forwarded itself pragmatically, on the strength of the contributions it promised to theory. But the promise is unredeemed.

It needs to be emphasized that the deductive device stands convicted of the failure to mimic our four strategies of inconsistency management only if this is the sort of thing that we should expect of it. But surely requiring it of the device is too much. It is tantamount to obliging it to behave irrationally. For isn't the holding of beliefs known to be inconsistent an irrational thing to do? Why in the world would we hold the device to such debased a standard of performance? Complaining that the device doesn't reproduce three of our strategies of inconsistency management is like complaining of plane geometry (the 'geometrical device') that it doesn't square the circle. So hasn't the deductive device and, with it, synthetic implication been unfairly knocked?

6.4.1 Bounded Rationality

Awash in cognitive finitude, it is interesting to speculate about what the possession of a cognitive system would consist in. How is one to be rational in such circumstances? Rationality is the effective negotiation of a bad hand. It is the facilitation of pay-off in low-finite time drawing on low-finite subsets of cognitive resources, against the persisting prospect of error. To infer too much, to reflect too long, to recall over-abundantly — these are the ways of cognitive paralysis. The cognitive agent is one who knows how to manage effectively and in a timely way his own intractable finitude. He (or it) knows the ways of the fast and the frugal [Gigerenzer and Selten, 2001a].

'Yes, yes,' we can hear people saying. 'Life is difficult, and to err is human and all that. But surely someone is rational to the extent that he rises above his limitations.' Such people are speaking of rationality as a kind of ideal and of consistency as its centre-piece.

How then would we have humans be consistent? What is the ideal that we would have them approximate to? Perhaps as a sort of minimal approximation, we could postulate for humans an internalized propositional logic, sound and complete, which assists the naive logician in drawing all and only the inferences appropriate to his interests. Fortunately for our logician, the concept of a tautological consequence from a set of assumptions is decidable in his internalized logic. So we could expect him to monitor his inferences for consistency with respect to what he already believes or accepts.

It is an attractive idea. The trouble is that it is too much for a human being to follow through within polynomial time. Consistency with respect to a context C or a belief inventory is a theoretically computable thing. The consistency problem, as it is called in complexity theory, has a positive theoretical solution. It is also true that the consistency problem belongs to a set of problems known as non-deterministic polynomial time problems — problems that are solvable in polynomial time by a non-deterministic Turing machine. They are also solvable for decidable logics by a deterministic computer in exponential time.

Such problems are human-computation impossible. (See [Cook, 1971; Cook, 1983; Karp, 1972]; [Cherniak, 1986, esp. p. 78–81], and [Hájek, 1998, Ch 5].) We conclude, then, that rationality is a matter of how well we manage inconsistency, at least as much as it is a matter of how well we manage to avoid it. If this is so, it is unrealistically severe to oblige the deductive device to avoid inconsistency no matter what. The device might be able to do this, but we cannot.

Monitoring for consistency, even for truth functional inconsistency, is too complex a task for beings like us. This shows that we can't realistically be held to a rationality requirement that binds us to tasks we cannot perform. But this is a far cry from what we earlier claimed — that it is not a requirement of rationality that we do everything in our power to disarm any inconsistency that we have succeeded in monitoring.

What is to be said? Suppose it were a requirement of rationality that inconsistent beliefs be withdrawn from service pending resolution. This would have obliged the rational among us to have suppressed the calculus for two hundred years. It would oblige contemporary rational animals to forgo the calculus in favour of the hyperreals. But non-standard analysis is daunting in comparison with calculus. It is harder to learn and takes longer to master. Perhaps it would be better if we all learned it, but it is unconvincing to call those who don't irrational. Say what we will about this case, thinking that pre-Robinsonian mathematicians were irrational to persist with the calculus is just silly. So we cast our lot with those who say that 'even perfect rationality does not entail... consistency; ... in fact, rationality entails a failure of consistency' [Kyburg, 1987, p. 141].

Rationality is the efficient and timely management of our intractable finitude, including the inconsistencies that we are somehow stuck with.

6.5 Is Inconsistency Pervasive?

We are aware of having left room enough for people to complain that, although there may be a good deal more of it that is generally supposed, inconsistency is still comparatively rare; and since this is so, it is a mistake — a misplaced effort — for us to go on so about it. We want to consider this further.

We imagine that at any given time we possess belief-sets. Talk of belief-*sets* is an informal convenience. We don't think of belief-inventories in strictly set theoretic terms, lucidly and constructively individuated by exhaustive retrieval of their members, individuable in turn by their possessors. All that we require is that at times we have some degree of efficient and reliable congress with some of what, *au pluriel*, we then believe or accept and that, this being so, we are at such times t in a position to deal with the matter of what adjustments to make to my belief-inventory as we endure life's dynamic passage from t to $t+1$.

In some such terms as these it is possible to make sense of inference. Inference, we might say, is a subspecies of the adjustment of our belief-sets under the stimulus of new information. Following Harman, we could liken inference to a function, f, from belief-sets Γ to belief-sets Δ, where Δ arises from Γ by adding or deleting one or more beliefs, or both [Harman, 1986, Chapter 1]. There is little doubt that f conspires to keep its values (its outputs) as doxastically stable as possible, short of inordinate cost, and that quite often this will involve attempts to preserve or reacquire consistency. Perceptual adjustments share in this feature, too. We see a man walking his dog. They are at the corner of 16th Street and 10th Avenue 'A'. Now they are in the middle of the intersection. Now they are at the northeast corner of 10th Avenue 'A' and 16th Street, now on 10th Avenue 'A' heading west, now passing 14th Street, now west of 14th Street, now out of sight. Even in so commonplace a situation we see that new perceptual beliefs displace prior ones on pain of inconsistency. This is not inference, vulgarly conceived, but it resembles it in a salient way. For we must now ask, if we suppose our belief-adjustment device f is so hell-bent on preserving and reacquiring consistency, why not suppose that it is rather good at what it sets itself to do? Why not, in short, suppose that inconsistency is a comparative rarity?

Let us look at f more closely. It is our belief-adjuster. A principal function is to negotiate the passage from Γ to Δ consistently. This doesn't mean that f will try to make $\Gamma \cup \Delta$ consistent, for in the dynamically general case that cannot be so. It means that f will try to make Δ itself as consistent as it practicably can. A lurking and large difficulty for f is that it won't be able to edit Γ in ways that make suitable provision for

Δ. The f-device operates dynamically. Bombarded by new information at every turn, editing is a constant necessity. We know that at certain levels of description of f, one can claim a rather good track record, for we are doxastically stable at those levels of description much of the time. The f device can be seen as part of a larger conception of information-processing creatures. Lycan calls it the Homuncular Functionalist (HF) conception. Though seriously intended, it can be abstractly characterized: A human being

> is a kind of corporate entity — ... an integrated system of intercommunicating 'departments' that corporately go about the business of interpreting the stimuli that impinge on the corporate organism and of producing appropriate behavioral responses. [Lycan, 1988, p. 5]

Each subsystem breaks down into its own component sub-subsystems ... and so forth [Lycan, 1988, p. 5]. Under further deconstruction 'their characterization will become more recognizably biological, though still job-descriptive — and, finally, neuroanatomical.' [Lycan, 1988, p. 5] The f-device might be thought of as the department head of the belief-box subsystem of the human organism. We shall think of it this way until further notice, and in so doing show a leaning toward a modular approach to central cognition. (But neither must we ignore the likely fate of modularity assumptions under conditions of continuous reciprocal causation, discussed above in section 2.6.1.)

How is f able to perform so vital a task? Two stories press for a telling, though we say with emphasis that they are 'only stories'. They are, in Sober's phrase, a kind of epistemological fairy tale [Sober, 1988, p. 27]. Why then do we bother to tell them? They are told under sway of a powerful assumption. The assumption is that human rationality is largely a matter of upgrading beliefs consistently. We want to tell these stories in order to call into question the assumption that motivates them. In story one, f is a Seer of Trouble Coming; in the other, f is a Putter of Things Right.

Seen the first way, f notices inconsistency coming and does its best to avert it, editing old information before the admittance of the new, or editing new information prior to arrival, or both. In the other story, f edits only after inconsistency has visited the scene. These are greatly differing stories. If f is a Seer of Trouble Coming, it is reasonable to expect f to produce quite a lot of consistency quite a lot of the time. If f is a Putter of Things Right, we can expect there to be quite a lot of inconsistency, that is, some inconsistency nearly all of the time (though not the same inconsistencies at all times; far from it). In both stories we imagine f to be performing in real time. Most of the time this is real time sliced vanishingly thin. The complexity of the task that f must execute is a salient consideration, the more so the more thinly is time sliced. It seems not unreasonable to suppose that f will perform efficiently. If f is a Seer of Trouble Coming, it must check candidates for admittance to Δ with everything in Γ with which it might be inconsistent and compose Δ accordingly. It is quite clear that f cannot do this by examining all combinations of beliefs in Γ. As we have seen, such a task is polynomial-time unperformable. So, then, if our present story is to be persisted with, f must check manageable subsets of Γ for consistency against incoming information. The question is, how does f know which subsets to inspect? Where f is a Putter of Things Right, we must postulate that the passage from Γ to Δ is mediated by $\Gamma \cup \Sigma$ which is very often inconsistent, where Σ contains the new information seeking for admittance. For such cases, Δ then represents a belief-set restored to the (momentary) consistency from the (momentary) inconsistency represented by $\Gamma \cup \Sigma$.

Is there a principled reason to think that f will do better as a recognizer and remediator of information present than as a predictor of inconsistency that threatens to come? Perhaps there is. We asked, moments ago, how would f, it it were a Seer of Trouble Coming, know which subsets of Γ to test for inconsistency against incoming new information. We might ask the counterpart question where f is a Putter of Things Right. How does f know which beliefs to examine as candidates for erasure in the cause of reclaimed consistency? If negation inconsistency implies absolute inconsistency, then every belief in Δ will have to be examined for possible erasure. Such an assumption places f in the same kind of polynomial time intractability in which we have already seen the rival story to have placed it. So it could be conjectured that for belief sets β negation inconsistency does not produce absolute inconsistency. If this were right, perhaps inconsistency would be a localized phenomenon identifiable by its semantic structure. That is, perhaps negation inconsistency will be a localized and structurally and/or semantically recognizable trait of inconsistent belief-sets. Typically inconsistency in β would be contained in small subsets of it; so typically there would be a small number of candidates to consider for erasure. One could conclude from this that it is intelligible that f is a Putter of Things Right and that it is not intelligible in the general case that it is a Seer of Trouble Coming. It might even be said that, as a Putter of Things Right, f manages the tactical/strategic distinction in a way that does it credit. It routinely loses small battles against inconsistency in order that the war against inconsistency be prosecuted with reasonable success and affordable cost. In this way, the underlying dynamic of belief-adjustment is the momentary but utterly routine inconsistency of our belief states. Belief-adjustment is deeply a matter of eliminating inconsistencies and tangentially, by comparison, a matter of avoiding them.

If the story of f as a Putter of Things Right were a true story, there would be reason to suppose that inconsistency is evermore pervasive and recurring in our doxastic lives than we were saying earlier. If this were right, no theory of cognitive virtue could ignore it; and any theory that made of it a catastrophe or lesser kinds of big trouble would be revealed as deeply inadequate.

Truth to tell, these are not wholly impressive stories. They reflect the bad habits of their imaginary tellers. One of these bad habits is an affection for quasi-empirical make-believe. Regarding the story of f as a Seer of Trouble Coming, we asked 'how does f know which subsets to inspect?', suggesting that the story couldn't supply an answer. This was supposed to be bad news for f. But is it? Let m be a function that retrieves memories. Both functions m and f alike must somehow know where to look for specific information. In the case of m, talk of spreading activation and networks of nodes looks promising. There is no reason that a similar approach couldn't be tried for a Seer of Trouble Coming function.

Even so, we said that f will do this sort of thing better in its role as the Putter of Things Right. For negation inconsistency will be localized and structurally and/or semantically recognizable as traits of inconsistent belief-sets. This makes it significantly more efficient for f to deal with inconsistency.

But what was meant by a 'structurally recognizable trait'? Is it something in neurophysical structure or in semantic network structure? The former is an empirical guess for which there is an impressive dearth of evidence. For example, no one, as yet, has been able to read a brain in ways that enable the specification of a structure exemplifying contradiction. As for the latter, it has much of the attraction of Molière's dormitive virtue. It is scarcely more than that which enables f to recognize inconsistency. It also bears on this question that, to the extent to which the P-device *attends* to the inconsistency involved in adding new information to the old set of beliefs, there are various kinds of information-processing in which attention occurs not at the point of receipt of new information, but later in the process at various sites of memory (Schiffrin [1977]). In as much as an attended-to inconsistency involves an inconsistency already present, the issue of how the cognizer best manages attracts the hypothesis of the Putter of Things Right in a rather direct way.

And why suppose that inconsistency is localized? (cf. [Lenat and Feigenbaum, 1991, fn. 21]). Neurophysically we know of nothing that suggests it. At the level of semantic networks there is nothing to require that P and $\ulcorner\neg P\urcorner$ be close or highly linked or in any other way propinquitous. If by a 'semantically recognizable trait' we mean a flag or marker, where is it? Or does it reside in the simple fact that belief$_1$ is 'P' and belief$_2$ is 'not P'? If we mean the first thing, how would the marker be created? By a function, f_2, that identifies but not rectifies inconsistencies? In that case f_2 appears to have a job that it cannot complete in polynomial time, since it must look all over for inconsistencies. If the latter is meant, what makes the presence of P along with $\ulcorner\neg P\urcorner$ in a belief-set a more recognizable trait, more recognizable than P along with any Q?

Our critic seems to be plumping for f as a Seer of Trouble Coming. That alone would be interesting, for it would deny us a reason for saying that our beliefs-sets are inconsistent all the time and recurringly. That may be so (but see just below). But it still leaves us with quite a lot of inconsistency quite a lot of the time.[8]

6.5.1 A Case in Point: Mechanizing Cognition

It is often rational for an agent to invoke an hypothesis on the basis of its contribution to some cognitive end that the agent desires to attain. This is abduction, broadly speaking, an important part of our cognitive practice. Abduction is a fallible enterprise, something that even the modestly reflective abducer is bound to have some awareness of. He will thus call down his hypotheses even in the teeth of the possibility that they are false. In general, the falsity of the hypothesis does not wreck the implication which the abducer seizes upon as warranting the inference to its truth or its likelihood. In many accounts of implication, the falsity of the hypothesis strengthens the implication to the object of the abducer's desired outcome. The fallibility of abduction provides for the possibility that the implication that the abducer seeks to exploit will have the form of a counterfactual conditional:

If H were the case, E would also be the case.

Counterfactuals also crop up in another way. Whether he does so consciously or not, the abducer is faced with the task of hypothesis selection.

[8]It also leaves us with a puzzle. Why have mathematicians been so *blasé* about inconsistency in the theory of infinitesimals and so alarmed by inconsistency in the theory of sets? Someone like G.H. Hardy might conjecture that the calculus was brought forth in the heyday of seventeenth century English mathematics (no offence to Leibniz) when mathematics was cheerfully sloppy. And the calculus has prospered ever since, e.g., in engineering, which can tolerate sloppiness as long as bridges don't fall down. Set theory issued in the late nineteenth century when mathematics was surrendering to metamathematical rigours championed in Germany.

Essential to that process is the cutdown of sets of possibilities to sets of real possibilities; thence to sets of relevant possibilities; thence to sets of plausible alternatives; and finally, if possible, to unit sets of these. At each juncture there is an elimination strategy to consider: Does the candidate H in question imply a falsehood F, never mind that it genuinely gives us E? If so, then, provided the implication holds, the agent will have reasoned conditionally in this form:

> Even though H is false, it remains the case that were H true then E would be true.

We may take it, then, that real-life abducers routinely deploy counterfactual conditionals. A psychologically real account of cognition and communication must take this fact into account.

Computer simulations of what cognitive agents do are attempts at producing mechanical models that mimic abductive behaviour. A model gives a good account of itself to the extent that is mimicry approximates to what actually happens in real life. In particular, therefore, such a model works to the extent that it succeeds in mechanizing counterfactual reasoning. Can it do this? People who are disposed to give a negative answer to this question are also drawn to the following question: What is involved in expressly counterfactual thinking when it is done by real-life human agents? It appears that the human agent is capable of producing some important *concurrences*. For one, he is able to realize that P is true and yet to entertain the assumption that P is not true, without lapsing into inconsistency. Moreover, the human agent seems capable of keeping the recognition that P and the assumption that not-P in mind at the same actual time. That is, he is able to be aware of both states concurrently. Thirdly, the human agent is capable of deducing from the assumption of not-P that not-Q without in doing so contradicting the (acknowledged) fact that Q might well be true.

When the AI theorist sets out to simulate cognitive behaviour of this sort, he undertakes to model these three concurrences by invoking the operations of a finite state Turing machine. Turing machines manipulate syntax algorithmically; their operations are strictly recursive. The critic of AI's claim to mechanize counterfactual reasoning will argue that no single information processing program can capture all three concurrences. It may succeed in mimicking the first, in which the agent assents to P and assumes its negation, by storing these bits of information in such a way that no subroutine of the program engages them both at the same time. But the cost of this is that the second concurrence is dishonoured. The human agent is able consciously to access both bits of information at the same time, which is precisely what the Tuning machine cannot do in the present case.

It is possible to devise a program that will enable the simulation of the first and second concurrence. The program is capable of distinguishing syntactically between the fact that P and the counterfactual assumption that not-P by flagging counterfactual conditionals with a distinguished marker, for example $\otimes$. Then the program could have subroutines which have concurrent access to 'P' and '$\otimes$not-$P\otimes$', without there being any danger of falling into inconsistency. Here, too, there is a cost. It is the failure of the program to honour the third concurrence, in which it is possible correctly to deduce '$\otimes$not-$Q\otimes$' from 'P', '$\otimes$not-$P\otimes$' and 'if not-P then not-Q'.

Of course, the program could rewrite 'If not-P then not-Q' as 'If $\otimes$not-$P\otimes$ then $\otimes$not-$Q\otimes$'. From the counterfactual assumption '$\otimes$not-$P\otimes$', the deduction of '$\otimes$not-$Q\otimes$' now goes through, and does so without there being any question of an inconsistency on the deducer's part.

Still, there is a problem. It is that $\otimes$-contexts are intensional. There are interpretations of P and Q for which the deduction of '$\otimes Q \otimes$' from 'not-P', 'counterfactually if P then Q' and '$\otimes P \otimes$' fails. Thus it is possible to assume counterfactually that Cicero was a Phoenician fisherman, and that if Cicero was a Phoenician fisherman, then Tully was a Phoenician fisherman, without its following that I *assume* that Tully was a Phoenician fisherman. The notation '$\otimes Q$' expresses that Q is assumed. Assumption is an opaque context [Quine, 1960], hence a context that does not sanction the intersubstitution of co-referential terms or logically equivalent sentences. (See here [Jacquette, 1986].) Thus $\otimes$-inference-routines are invalid. Their implementability by any information-processing program that, as a finite state Turing machine must be, is strictly extensional dooms the simulation of counterfactual reasoning to inconsistency.

We should hasten to say that there are highly regarded efforts to mechanize reasoning involving counterfactual or belief-convening assumptions. Truth-maintenance systems (TMS) are a notable case in point. ([Rescher, 1964; Doyle, 1979]; see also [de Kleer, 1986; Gabbay *et al.*, 2003] and [Gabbay *et al.*, 2002b].) The main thrust of TMSs is to restore (or acquire) consistency by deletion. These are not programs designed to simulate the retention of information that embeds belief-contravening assumptions and their presentation to a uniformly embracing awareness. The belief that P is not inconsistent with the concurrent assumption that not-P. There is in this no occasion for the consistency-restoration routines of TMS. Thus $\otimes$-contexts resemble contexts of direct quotation. Such are contexts that admit of no formally sound extensional logic (Quine [1960; 1975]). No strictly extensional, recursive or algorithmic operations on syntax can capture the logic of counterfactual reasoning. Whereupon goodbye to a finite state Turing machine's capacity to model this aspect of abductive reasoning.

Named after the German word for assumption, ANNAHMEN is a computer program adapted from Shagrin, Rapaport and Dipert [Shagrin *et al.*, 1985]. It is designed to accommodate hypothetical and counterfactual reasoning without having to endure the costs of either inconsistency or the impossibility of the subject's access to belief-contravening assumptions and the beliefs that they contravene. ANNAHMEN takes facts and counterfactual assumptions and conditionals as input. The latter two are syntactically marked in ways that avoid syntactic inconsistency.

This input is then copied and transmitted to a second memory site at which it is subject to deduction. The previous syntactic markers are renamed or otherwise treated in ways that give a syntactically inconsistent set of sentences. The next step is to apply TMS procedures in order to recover a consistent subset in accordance with an epistemic preference-heuristic with which the program has been endowed. In the case before us, the TMS is Rescher's logic of hypothetical reasoning, or as we shall say, the 'Rescher reduction'. From this consistent subset the counterfactual conclusion is deduced by a Lewis logic for counterfactuals and syntactic markers are re-applied. Then all this is sent back to the original memory site. It mixes there with the initial input of beliefs and belief-contravening assumptions. ANNAHMEN can now perform competent diagnostic tasks and can perform well in a Turing test [Turing, 1950]. As Jacquette [2001] observes,

> the functions RESCHER REDUCTION and LEWIS LOGIC call procedures for the Rescher-style reduction of an inconsistent input set to a logically consistent subset according to any desired extensionally definable set of recursive or partially recursive heuristic, and for any desired logically valid deductive procedure for detaching counterfactual conditionals, such as David Lewis' formal system in *Counterfactuals.*

The problem posed by the mechanization of counterfactual reasoning is that there appeared to be no set of intensional procedures for modelling such reasoning which evades syntactic inconsistency and which allows for what Jacquette calls the 'nity of consciousness' of what is concurrently believed and contraveningly assumed. ANNAHMEN is designed to show that this problem is merely apparent. The solution provided by this approach is one in which the inconsistency that occurs at memory site number two exists for nanoseconds at most and occurs, as it were, subconsciously. Thus counterfactual reasoning does involve inconsistency. But it is a quickly eliminable inconsistency; and it does not occur in the memory site at which counterfactual deductions are drawn. Inconsistency is logically troublesome only when harnessed to deduction. It is precisely this that the ANNAHMEN program precludes. It may also be said that the program is phenomenologically real. When human beings infer counterfactually, they are aware of the concurrence of their beliefs and their belief-contravening assumptions, but they are not aware of the presence of any inconsistency. (Rightly, since the counterfactual inference is performed 'at a site' in which there is no inconsistency.)

The ANNAHMEN solution posits for the reasoning subject the brief presence of an inconsistency that is removed subconsciously. It is therefore of interest that the program implements the operation Putter-of-Things-Right. This is a device postulated for the human information processor. What makes the ANNAHMEN proposal especially interesting in this context is that, in effect, it purports to show that Putter-of-Things-Right is mechanizable.

Whether it is or not, we find ourselves in agreement with Jacquette in the case of an ANNAHMEN approach to *counterfactual* reasoning. Jacquette shows that while ANNAHMEN handles certain types of counterfactual reasoning, it fails for other types. Furthermore, even though certain refinements to the ANNAHMEN protocols — in the manner of Lindenbaum's Lemma for Henkin-style consistency and completeness proofs or in the manner of the Lemma for consistent finite extensions of logically consistent sets — resolve some of these difficulties, they cannot prevent others [Tarski, 1956; Henkin, 1950]. We agree that there 'is no satisfactory extensional substitute for the mind's intentional adoption of distinct propositional attitudes toward beliefs and mere assumptions or hypothesis.' We shall not here reproduce details of these criticisms; they can be found in [Jacquette, 2001].

Cognition sometimes involves consciousness, what in Block [1995] is called P-consciousness, or phenomenal consciousness. 'P-conscious properties', says Block, 'include the experiential properties of sensations, feelings and perceptions, but I would also include thoughts, wants and emotions.' (230). Computational artefacts can also, quite properly, be described as conscious. But it is not P-consciousness that they have when conscious, but rather what Block calls A-consciousness or *access*-conscious. A-consciousness is the sort of consciousness that can be ascribed to, e.g., theorem provers that have the means to generate natural language constructions. They are in a condition that can be described as follows:

> A state is access-conscious (A-conscious) if, in virtue of one's having the state, a representation of its condition is (1) informationally promiscuous, i.e., poised to be used as a premise in reasoning, and (2) poised for control of action and (3) poised for rational control of speech. [Block, 1995, p. 231]

It has long been known that computation is reversible, not always in trivial ways [Bennett, 1973]. In its most primitive sense, a computational process is reversible when there is a programmable command under which the process 'runs backwards'. Computational devices that possess A-consciousness are reversible in principle. But it would seem that P-conscious processes are irreversible in principle. That anyhow is our view; it is nicely developed in Bringsjord and Zensen [1997].

In an important sense, then, cognition is uncomputable. It is uncomputable when it is intrinsically P-conscious, and it owes its incomputability to the fact that computational processes are reversible and P-conscious process are not. In plumping for the uncomputability of (phenomenally conscious) cognition, we find ourselves supporting Jacquette's finding. Cognition is computable, he says, only at the cost of the *unity of consciousness* of the computing agent. Consciousness disunified cannot be P-consciousness; so Jacquette's finding is, in effect, that P-conscious cognition is uncomputable.

In rejecting the thesis of the computability of cognition, we have no interest in giving up on cognitive science as a genuine science of the mental and other processes that constitute cognition. We part company rather with the proposition that an account of something is genuinely scientific only if it is implementable. Quantum states have long enjoyed the deep predicative control of a good scientific theory, but no one has yet produced its implementation.

6.6 Further Difficulties

We have strayed a little from the SW-account of relevance, never mind that it was our interest in it that got us to wonder about inconsistency management and, thereupon, the SW-claim that the relevance principle works automatically without being cognitively processed or represented. But it is time to get back to business.

On the Sperber–Wilson approach an assumption is relevant in a context C if and only if there is some wff that it together with C contextually implies, or which contradicts or strengthens an assumption in C. Relevance is indispensible for cognition and communication. We could liken a cognitive agent's set of beliefs at a time, or the hypothesis that he may be assuming at that time, to a context C indexed to indicate the time in question. What Harman calls changes in view can then be represented by the successor context with a suitably adjusted index. Let the first context be C_i and its successor C_{i+1}. Then the role of relevance is to guide the cognitive agent in the passage from C_i to C_{i+1}. If, for example, C_i is a set of beliefs,

C_{i+1} might be a set of those same beliefs together with a set of hypotheses explaining some subset of C_i. Intuitively, the agent is usually better off to consider relevant hypotheses rather than irrelevant.

For every C there is a set R of wffs relevant in it. On our present intuition, it often helps in forming the successor context to be guided by R. Thus we might say in a quite general way that in constructing a successor C_{i+n} to a C_i that one is usually better off to consider making only relevant adjustments to C_i. The question is: If R is made up of Sperber–Wilson relevancies does it serve this purpose in any very realistic way? We doubt it.

Here is a related difficulty. Let C be a set of wffs $\{A_1, \ldots, A_n\}$. Then R will contain every wff incompatible with any wff in C. This is getting to be quite a lot of wffs; an infinity of them in fact. We might subdue this hefty cardinality by imposing a further condition on adjustment. We might restrict consideration of R to those subsets that are *true*. Leaving aside the point that often our agent will be unable to determine whether this further condition is met until (at best) after C_{i+1} has been constructed and then tested, even in these cases in which the agent is able to discuss its fulfilment, the relevance of the relevant adjustment now gives over entirely to its truth. It is a truth $\top$ that contradicts an old wff; and this makes it relevant consideration on the Sperber–Wilson account. Apart from its truth, the relevance of $\top$ has no explanatory role to play here.

Here is a fact of some importance about contextual implication. Let C be a context and Q any wff, in C or not in C, it doesn't matter. Then it follows from the definition of context and implication that for no part C' of C, does C' contextually imply Q in C.

Let C^* be C's successor, and suppose that, as we have been assuming, C^* arises from C by relevant adjustment. Suppose, too, that P contextually implies Q in C, hence that P is relevant in C. Suppose finally that Q is also in C. It might then occur to us that since P implies something already believed (and recorded in C), a plausible candidate for adjustment would be to add P to C, giving $C^* = C \cup \{P\}$. But by the theorem just noted, P is relevant to nothing in C^*.

There is no doubt that this is precisely what the Sperber–Wilson account of relevance provides for. Adding a relevant new wff to a set of beliefs or hypotheses kills its relevance. Affirmation of a relevant assumption guarantees the irrelevence to the new context of that which is affirmed. It would be quite wrong to make too much of this point. We are not here in the company of the paradox of sets or of semantic self-reference. In fact, there are some accounts of relevance in which this transition from relevance to irrelevance is wholly explicable. Agenda-relevance is a case in point, as we shall see. On that account, information is relevant when it closes or helps close an agent's agenda. Consider a case. Harry wants to know whether it snowed overnight. (This is his cognitive agenda.) He looks out of the bedroom window. The streets below are clogged with huge drifts. The information that Harry's observation provided was relevant. It closed Harry's agenda. But since the agenda is now closed, that information can no longer close it. It is, as regards *that* agenda, no longer relevant. (Though it might, of course be relevant with regard to another of Harry's agendas, e.g., to decide whether to go skiing.)

There is no such story discernible in the Sperber–Wilson account of relevance. Relevance for them is a technical notion subject to the fate that its technical conditions provide for it. But the technical account also serves as an approximation to the real thing. If the real thing is taken in the agenda-relevance sense, this sense can be made of the otherwise surprising technical result that set-theoretic union extinguishes prior relevance. But Sperber and Wilson give the real thing no characterization that subdues the oddity of this technical result. So it is a result that damages the intuition that successor contexts are constructed under the guidance of sets of relevant considerations, when relevance is taken this way. This requires that we repeat two related objections. One is that the technical account is too coarsely grained, and is made so by the limitations that flow from the strictly propositional operations of negation and implication (strengthening is trickier, as we shall see). The other is that the technical account is developed at too far a removal from psychological reality to serve its intended explanatory functions in the theory of cognition and communication.

We close this section with a further illustration of these points.

Let $C = \{A_1, \ldots, A_n\}$. Let P = 'Marilyn Monroe is a man' and Q = 'Marilyn Monroe is a bachelor'. Let A_i = 'Marilyn Monroe is unmarried'. We have it then that:

1. P contextually implies Q in C
2. P is relevant in C
3. $\neg Q$ contextually implies $\neg P$ in C
4. $\neg Q$ is relevant in C.

It is also apparent that

5. Q non-trivially implies A_i
6. Q non-trivially implies P
7. Q doesn't contextually imply A_i in C

8. Q doesn't contextually imply P in C

9. Q isn't relevant in C.

The range of cases for which this is an apt illustration is large. It is made up of every triple of propositions, $\langle X, Y, Z \rangle$ such that the first two give the genus-species implication of the third. In each such case we have it that a proposition that implies the falsehood of a proposition relevant in C is nevertheless not itself a proposition relevant in C. Propositions that negate propositions relevant in C are not relevant in C. More carefully, they are not relevant in C unless the propositions that they negate and are relevant in C are also members of C. Suppose that a cognitive agent whose belief-set is represented by C wanted to upgrade his beliefs on the strength of the discovery that $\ulcorner \neg Q \urcorner$ is true. C^* then is $C \cup \{\neg Q\}$. By our previous theorem, although $\ulcorner \neg Q \urcorner$ is relevant in C, it is not relevant in C^*. Further, although Q is not relevant in C, it is relevant in Q^*, since Q contradicts $\ulcorner \neg Q \urcorner$ and $\ulcorner \neg Q \urcorner \varepsilon C$.

There is, again, no doubting that these intuitively surprising flip-flops are catered for by the technicalities of the Sperber and Wilson relevance relation. There is in these flip-flops nothing approaching a *reductio* of the technical account. But its distance from psychological and intuitive normalcy again is wholly apparent.

6.7 Reclaiming *SW*-Relevance?

If $C \vdash P$ then P is not relevant, as it has no contextual effects in C. If $C \nvdash P$, then perhaps we can in the *spirit* of Sperber and Wilson define contextual effects as all possible abductive candidates α such that $C + \alpha \vdash P$ (=Abduce). It suffices here to approach abduction intuitively, as the process of finding those α and that together with C deliver the goods for P. (C, P) is *SW* relevant falls under our characterization above of propositional relevance. But we can involve it in a process of abductive revision, as follows:

1. If $C \vdash P$, do nothing.

2. If $C \nvdash P$ and C is consistent with P, then abduce all candidates α such that $C + \alpha \vdash P$.[9] Some of these α will be chosen as best from a contextual effects point of view. So the new theory is $C + \alpha^{\text{best}}$.

3. If $C \nvdash P$ but $C + P$ is inconsistent, then we use *abductive revision* and revise $C + P$ to $C \circ P$, and then the best revision incontextual effect is the one to be chosen.

[9]This is discussed in detail in our abduction volume [Gabbay and Woods, 2004a].

We can define P's relevance to C if the best contextual effect to be chosen is considered *Rich* according to some measure. So 'Relevance' would be reduced to 'Abductive Revision', '$\vdash$' and 'Rich'.

It may well be that this is fine as far as it goes. Perhaps it has attractions, however modest, for the many proponents of SW-relevance. But they will have to pay a price. They will have to endow the inference engine with abductive powers, over and above its deductive wherewithall (see here [Sperber and Wilson, 1986, 121–122]).

6.8 The Grice Condition

'Relevance' is a common sense term enjoying a diverse abundance of common uses. In the absence of good reasons to the contrary, one should try to contrive one's account of relevance so as to honour this abundance as much as possible. We take it that steps would be taken in this direction if we were to impose a further condition of adequacy. [10]

> **Grice**: For any response fulfilling Grice's maxim, 'Be relevant', the truth of the assertion, 'That response was relevant' is preserved under the translation of the word 'relevant' via the theory's semantic provisions. That is, 'That response was relevant' will remain true under the theory's interpretation of 'relevant'.

Sperber and Wilson might protest (see footnote 11). What justifies the decision to hold the theory of relevance to Grice's account of it? In Grice's work, '[E]ssential concepts are left entirely undefined. This is true of *relevance* for instance: hence appeals to the 'maxim of relevance' are no more than dressed-up appeals to intuition' [Grice, 1991, p. 36]. Except for the 'dressed up' part, we agree with this entirely, and so does Grice. In no sense does what Grice produced in 'Logic and Conversation' qualify as an account, an analysis or a theory of relevance. So there can't be any question of Sperber and Wilson having to conform their theory to Grice's. The object of *Grice* is not to get people to make Grice happy.

It is true that *Grice* turns on intuitions in a modest way. *Grice* is, as we say, little more than a device that tests an analysis of relevance for commonness. It invites judgements about what we would find it natural to characterize as relevant responses in certain contexts. (*Not*, 'Responses relevant according the relevance theory of H.P. Grice'; rather responses relevant according to the intuitions of Dan Sperber and Deirdre Wilson,

[10]Let us be clear. We are speaking of adequacy conditions on our theory, not the SW-account. SW-theory was designed to put Gricean theories out of business!

John Woods, Dov Gabbay and Joe Blow — and these are intuitions about the relevance of responses, not about the meaning or analysis of the word 'relevant'.) Whatever we might think of it, every theory of relevance that we know of fails this condition. That alone should give us pause, since it is some evidence that the condition may be unrealistic.[11] We might lower our sights and proclaim *Grice* a desideratum. In any event, we now want to show there are interesting issues raised by the question of whether the Sperber and Wilson account satisfies it.

Here is a case. Harry stops Peter in the hallway of a building and asks, 'Where is the office of the Rector, please?' and Peter replies, 'You're standing in front of the office of the Rector'. Did Peter fulfil the maxim, 'Be relevant'? We cannot easily imagine that he did not. But it may seem that 'You're standing in front of the office of the Rector' doesn't qualify as relevant in the sense of Sperber and Wilson. It carries the needed information all by itself, and so we have no contextual implication here. Neither do we have strengthening if Harry had no prior idea about where the Rector was to be found. But don't we have contradiction/erasure? Can't we assume, at a minimum, that prior to Peter's reply Harry's belief-set contained something like 'I don't know what his answer will be'? With the reply made, Harry erases that belief and replaces it with something like 'Ah, that was his answer'. So it is a mistake to say that the relevance of Peter's response can't be accommodated by Sperber and Wilson. Yes. But admitting it is cold comfort for their account. Every context C that someone might be supposed to have either contains P or it does not. Where it does, any proposition that co-opts P for contextual implication or which strengthens it or contradicts it in ways that allow for erasure will be relevant in that context. So far so good.

But what of the contrary case, in which $P \notin C$? If C is meant to mimic belief-sets of us ordinary mortals, there can be no question of its being the case generally that C will include the negation of P or even any belief in the form 'I don't know whether P' or 'I recognize that I don't believe not-P'. This is entirely as it should be. Human beings will be non-committal with regard to all sorts of propositions and they will manage only fragmentary doxastic transparency. There will be only so many beliefs in the form 'I don't know whether P'. What this guarantees is the irrelevance of a large class of propositions which impart new and absolutely unexpected information and yet which do not trigger contextual implication or strengthening or contradiction/erasure. 'Unexpected' here means 'un-entertained' rather than 'surprising'. The phone rings and Harry answers it. 'This is Paul

[11]We certainly do not want to claim for pre-theoretical intuitions the sort of epistemic privilege presumed in the heyday of analytic philosophy. See [Woods, 2002b, Ch. 8].

Wolsey of the National Trust', he hears the caller say. Harry has never heard of Paul Wolsey. Do we want to deny that that information was relevant for him, that its relevance consisted in its telling Harry the name of his caller? That must be the verdict of the theory of acontextual effects. 'What Harry's caller said was relevant' is false in the theory of contextual effects. We need not take this as refuting the theory (ambiguation strategies lurk nearby), but we might find the exclusion regrettable even so.

Again, the culprit is not so much the *SW-conception* of relevance as it is the logic that underlies their account. 'What Harry's caller said was relevant' is false in the theory of contextual effects because the underlying logic is static. (It is a fragment of classical logic.) A time and action logic might well change our verdict on 'What Harry's caller said was relevant' without necessitating the abandonment of the *SW*-notion of relevance. Our own intuitions incline us to a logic with some dynamic features; and so we shall shortly begin developing our notion of *agenda* relevance.

The deductive device performs some of the functions of our belief-adjusting device f. There are three options to consider. If f is a Seer of Trouble Coming, it will have to know whether it contains any belief incompatible with any incoming P that it doesn't yet contain. If f sees that C does contain not-P or some belief implying it, then the contradiction/erasure routine is run. If C contains some proposition that P's admittance would strengthen, presumably f will admit it. If P is consistent with every belief of C, f will detect this and will admit it in conjunction with the belief 'P is consistent with every belief in C'. Of the admittance options that f has under present assumptions, the first two qualify P as relevant in C and a large set of instances of a suboption of option three also do. The suboption is the admittance of P to C when it conspires toward a consistently premissed contextual implication in C. This leaves us with the question: Why not allow all the suboptions of option three to make P relevant to C? Not doing so would require us to divine differences between those suboptions of option three that would seem to matter for relevance in an essential way, that is, to the point of recognizing a relevance-significance in the one suboption but not the other. It is doubtful that such a difference can be found non-*ad hoc*ly. This matters. What makes it matter is that every proposition that f considers for admittance and either rejects or admits is relevant in the context of the beliefs it regulates. Every proposition that f believes is relevant in f's inventory of beliefs. It is not that this is obviously wrong; it is rather that it needs to be accounted for by any theory seriously proposing itself as a theory of relevance.

It is also necessary to consider f's contribution in its role as a Putter of Things Right. Presumably it will perform options two and three in the same manner as does Seer of Trouble Coming. Option one — contradiction/erasure — it will perform differently. It will wait for the inconsistency, if any, to present itself. Then it will erase. Here, too, this is but a suboption of a more general one: Check for consistency and (i) in conjunction with the belief that new P is inconsistent with some old Q, erase P or Q; and (ii) in conjunction with the belief that P's admittance has produced no (new) inconsistency, withhold erasure routines. Differences there are between (i) and (ii), but we are hard pressed to see that (i) makes P relevant in C and yet (ii) does not. If this is right, once again we are met with a substantial finding. And we see that the present theory fails to account for the fact that it does not endorse it. The finding is that every new belief is relevant for him who believes it. As we say, this is not obviously wrong; if anything it is obvious that it is more nearly right than wrong after some tinkering.

6.8.1 Relevance To and For

This looks mistaken somehow. How can we pretend to have shown that everything that is input for f or could be is relevant in the context C of f's beliefs and yet that this might not be something to worry about? Doesn't this at once convict the account of excessiveness and overturn the conviction on grounds that no real offence was committed? We do want to say both things, with due care for taking the sting out of 'convict'. At one level of description, everything that f processes or could should count as relevant for it. At another level of description we should not want such a result. The level at which we should not want it is at the level we talk about Harry. We want an account of relevance in which the following *is not* necessarily true: If f is Harry's belief-adjuster, then anything relevant to f is relevant *for Harry*.

How could we get it to come out true that not everything that is relevant *to* f is relevant *for* Harry, when f is Harry's own? After all, the beliefs that f is supposed to regulate are Harry's beliefs. f inhabits a luxuriant and dark underworld of doxastic sophistication in which f outperforms by far what Harry does on his own turf. This makes for a 'teeming prosperity' of relevance[12] for f and much less for Harry, as if relevance for Harry were a contingency of his sluggishness, and a good thing too in light of the injunction against excessiveness.

[12] In a lovely phrase about another thing. See [Quine and Ullian, 1970, p. 26].

We might conjecture that the connection between f and Harry is this: that most of f's occurrent beliefs will be tacit beliefs for Harry and that most of f's overt semantic discriminations will be tacit discriminations for Harry. This is how it gets to be true that not everything relevant to f is relevant for Harry. What is it for Harry to have tacitly a belief that his own belief-adjuster has occurrently? Perhaps it is a matter of how Harry behaves or is disposed to behave, and of this behaviour's somehow conforming to that belief. This has it that Harry believes something tacitly when his behaviour conforms to f's beliefs, not his own. Thinking of it this way may be all right for certain cases. It may be all right for those tacit beliefs and tacit semantic discriminations that stand efficiently open to Harry's occurrent accommodation. So a belief will be tacit to the extent that it can (without too much effort) be got to be occurrent. Harry believes occurrently that Sarah's shoes are heliotrope. He does not believe occurrently that they are a shade of purple. This he believes tacitly to the extent that he can be got to believe it occurrently, supplemented perhaps by the thought 'I believed it all along'. As long as we think of f as regulating perceptual and reminiscential flows of information, it is clear that most of what f believes can never be tacit belief for Harry. Thinking of f in such terms, either as a Seer of Trouble Coming or as a Putter of Things Right will leave it largely unexplained how f manages to regulate Harry's belief-set. So we conjecture that thinking of f in these terms is a theoretical encumbrance rather than a theoretical aid. That is, the device that regulates for inconsistency (however this is managed) is not usefully thought of, as such, as a manipulator of *beliefs*. This is the assumption, common to both of our stories about f, which we now think that we should abandon.

The regulation of belief and the promotion of consistency-equilibrium bears a certain resemblance to what certain philosophers call the frame problem in AI.

> The depiction of one's knowledge as an immense set of individually stored 'sentences' raises a severe problem concerning the relevant retrieval or application of ... internal representations. How is it one is able to retrieve, from the millions of sentences stored, exactly the handful that is relevant to one's predictive or explanatory problem, and how is it one is generally able to do this in a few tenths of a second? This is known as the 'frame problem' in AI, and it arises because, from the point of view of fast and relevant retrieval, a long list of sentences is an appallingly inefficient way to store information. [Churchland, 1989, pp. 155–156][13]

[13]Cf. [Haugeland, 1987, p. 204]: '... the so-called frame problem is how to 'notice'

(We note again that what philosophers call the frame problem, AI theorists call the *relevance problem* (see section 6.4 above). As characterized by AI researchers, the frame problem is that of knowing how in detail to adjust the knowledge base to accommodate the flow through of new information.)

PDP (parallel distributed processing) models of cognition are a peculiar response to the (philosopher's) frame problem. Rather than undertaking a solution to the problem, PDP theorists tend to the view that there is no problem to be solved. They reject a presupposition of it.

> The old problem of how to retrieve relevant information is *transformed* by the realization that it does not need to be 'retrieved'. Information is stored in brainlike networks in the global pattern of their synaptic weights. An incoming vector activates the relevant portions, dimensions, and subspaces of the trained network by virtue of its own vectorial make up. [Churchland, 1989, p. 195]

Where does this leave us in regard to f? It is assumed that information flow and information storage are governed by mechanisms that abet consistency equilibrium. And it is known that beliefs are somehow routinely upgraded in ways that conspire to that same equilibrium. If consistency management and belief adjustment were essentially matters of sentential manipulation, it would be not at all far-fetched to think of these routines as involving essentially the survey and retrieval of masses of sentences. Thinking in these ways bequeaths us the frame problem. In the next chapter, we tentatively cast our lot with parallel distributed processing models of cognition. This enables the frame problem to be side-stepped (or rather, there is promise of side-stepping it). Concurrently lost is the idea of sentential manipulation as the critical mass of cognitive virtue, and with it the idea that the routines of consistency equilibrium are sententially manipulative. It was an assumption of the stories of the Seer of Trouble Coming and the Putter of Things Right, that the Seer and the Putter were manipulators of sentential objects. It has likewise assumed that f, our belief adjustment function, stores and edits sentences (themselves representing the propositional contents of beliefs). This is a troublesome assumption for any PDP theorist who wants to retain the notion of belief as an artifact of theory. In each case, consistency equilibrium and belief adjustment would have to be made out as largely subsentential affairs. For that to be so, consistency and belief

---

salient side effects without having to eliminate all other possibilities that might conceivably have occurred...' And: 'The frame problem is superficially analogous to the knowledge-access problem. But the frame problem arises with knowledge of the current situation, here and now — especially with keeping such knowledge up to date as events happen and the situation evolves'.

would somehow have to be definable subsententially. We shall return to this issue.

Sperber and Wilson have broken new ground in important and lasting ways; they stepped forward when others wouldn't or couldn't. The failure to make relevance a high priority for theory has been a disgrace, especially in philosophy. Sperber and Wilson are fundamentally right in their primary insight: information is relevant when it invades a context and matters there or, to subdue the circularity of 'mattering', does some work there or is helpful there. We say again that the theory of contextual effects, though conceptually right-headed, is too thickly grained a structure to deliver a consistent and suitably nuanced articulation of the main idea, even taking into account its abstract and technical character. What is problematic about their account is, therefore, how the insight should best be elaborated theoretically.

Contextual effects reappear in the formal model in section 13.2.5.

Chapter 7

Agenda Relevance

> The relevance problem is ... similar to the problem of alienation for Marxists ... It is too fundamental and too general to be dealt with in one stroke.
>
> [van Eemeren and Grootendorst, 1992, p. 141]

7.1 Adequacy Conditions

As we propose to develop it here, *AR*, the theory of agenda relevance, has three principal objectives. One is that it attempts to integrate with *PLCS*, a practical logic of cognitive systems. Another target of *AR* is to give an adequate analysis of relevance as common concept. To this end we shall propose, in this chapter, further adequacy conditions that *AR* should attempt to satisfy. Ecumenism is a third objective. To the extent possible *AR* should preserve what it can of alternative approaches to relevance. This is a matter that we revisit in chapters 12 and 13. For now our concern is to state some adequacy condition for a conceptual analysis of relevance.

AC1. The theory should not make excessive provision for relevance. That is, it should block the derivation of 'Nothing is relevant to anything' and of 'Everything is relevant to everything'.

AC2. It should acknowledge that relevance is context-sensitive. Things relevant in some circumstances aren't relevant in others.

AC3. It should honour the comparative nature of relevance. That is, it should provide that some things are more (or less) relevant than others.

AC4. It should provide for a relation of negative relevance, distinct from the idea of mere irrelevance.

AC5. The theory should help elucidate the fallacies of relevance.

AC6. The theory should make a contribution to territorial disputes between classical and relevant logic.

AC7. It should make a contribution to a satisfactory account of belief-revision.

AC8. The account should investigate the suggestion that relevance is intrinsically a dialogical notion.

AC9. It should satisfy the condition of semantic distribution, i.e., it should provide a common analysis of relevance.[1]

AC10. It should be able to absorb insights from alternative approaches to relevance.

Most of these conditions are intuitive just as they stand; the others will be motivated and clarified as we proceed.

The notion of adequacy conditions is rather loosely intended. Some will weigh more heavily than others. Some, such as AC1, would seem to have the full force of necessary conditions. Others, for example AC5 weigh less heavily. AC5 says that a theory of relevance should try to elucidate the fallacies of relevance, so called. A theory of relevance that failed it could be regretted on the score of incompleteness, or some such thing, but it would be over -doing it to give it up as a thoroughly bad job. So our adequacy conditions include both necessary conditions and what we might think of as desiderata.

We want to say something further about pre-analytic data about relevance. We admit to a hankering for some appropriate generalization of *Grice*. As our list, found in chapter 4, quickly demonstrates, the relevance idiom has a varied provenance in English. It is desirable that attributions of 'relevant' will brook interchange with idioms linked by lexical definitions or

[1]It should be remarked that AC9 makes it unnecessary to qualify AC1 in some such fashion as, 'to the extent to which a theory of relevance offers a common analysis of it'. AC9 guarantees that this should be the case. (It is easy, by the way, to see that AC7 and AC8 are special cases of AC9 , but we will let the redundancy stand.)

will yield to contextual elimination by way of definitions in use, without too much damage to the naturalness and accuracy of the paraphrase. A theory of relevance that does this more or less well will be said to produce paraphrases that mimic more or less well the semantic distribution in English of the word 'relevant' and its cognates. So we propose as a desideratum the condition of semantic distribution, as we will call it. In other words, unlike Sperber and Wilson, we are proposing that the account of relevance should aspire to the status of a common analysis.

Results fulfilling adequacy conditions subdivide into the substantive and the programmatic, although the distinction is not exact. Adequacy condition AC3 calls for a result that is rather more in the substantive camp. The condition is fulfilled just in case the theory underwrites a claim in the form

(*) Relevance is a comparative relation

and, that done, gives to (*) a role in influencing some of the details of the theory's description of relevance.

It would be helpful to have a word for disclosures of theory that do not answer in any direct or tight way to these *substantive* adequacy conditions. These are the results that make a theory interesting. They are its surprises and natural occasion of its authority. Suppose, for example, that theory recognized a distinction between being of no particular relevance and being utterly irrelevant. Or imagine that theory provided occasion to suggest that sometimes information could be said to be relevance-*creating*. Such results can be seen as largely independent of what is achieved by the fulfilment of adequacy conditions. We would take it as striking if all of what an interesting theory could aspire to could be encompassed at the outset by its adequacy conditions. One should look for results that exceed their reach in a fairly obvious way. It is with them that the theorist indulges his conceptual sovereignty, as Quine has called it; they are results free for the thinking up.

A theory's pronouncements thus trip along a continuum from those that answer tightly to adequacy conditions, to those that are rather freer for the thinking up. Whatever their grade of depending on or independence of adequacy conditions, these are the theory's *propositions*. Propositions here are not the abstract entities that nominalistically minded ontologists are so leery of. They are what the theory proposes. Seventeenth century philosophers employed the word in that same sense, and they sometimes numbered their propositions. We shall do likewise.

Some propositions will be flagged under that name. Others will be forwarded as definitions. Propositions preceded by a '♡' are first approximations and will meet with subsequent refinement where possible.

Propositions fulfilling adequacy conditions may be thought of as constituting 'pre-analytic intuitions', as they are sometimes called. The more substantive the condition of adequacy that a result satisfies the more determinate and commanding its role as a pre-analytic intuition of theory. Other results would then be thought of as more strictly theoretical. We don't mind these equations so long as the distinction on which they hinge is not pressed too far. The intuitive-theoretical distinction here intended is little more than that between what we would be prepared to say about relevance prior to theory and what we would be prepared to accept (though perhaps only tentatively) afterwards on the strength of the case for it that theory makes. The personal pronoun 'we' is unavoidable, for obvious reasons. No eccentricity is intended. Readers are assumed to share our intuitions and they are invited to give the nod to our propositions.

A good part of the basic idea is that relevance matters for reasoning. It is not the whole idea, as we will see, but it is of central importance all the same. Reasoning we take in Harman's way [1986, Ch. 1]. Reasoning is the adjustment or updating of one's inventory of beliefs under the dynamic press of new (cognitive and conative or decisional) stimuli. Thus under life's inexorable turnings, information presents itself and requires either consequences to be drawn, new beliefs added, old beliefs suspended or displaced, degrees of confidence altered, plans revised or scrapped, and so on. Information is relevant when it prompts such things to happen.[2]

7.2 The Basic Idea

As a first approximation, relevance is defined over ordered triples $\langle \mathbf{I}, \mathbf{X}, \mathbf{A} \rangle$ of items of information **I**, cognitive agents **X**, and agendas **A**. This alone constitutes satisfaction of AC2, which calls for recognition of relevance's contextual variability. The basic task of the theory is to specify truth conditions; or, pending the actual semantics for this,[3] an algorithm for deciding when to adopt such a sentence for open sentences, $\ulcorner$**I** is relevant for **X** with regard to **A**$\urcorner$.[4] We shall propose that **I** is relevant for **X** with regard to his or her agenda **A** if and only if in processing **I**, **X** is affected in ways that advance or close **A**. For now, and until further notice, our 'information' is a

[2]A similar-seeming view can also be found in [Sperber and Wilson, 1986, pp. 103–104]: '... the relevance of new information to an individual is to be assessed in terms of the improvements it brings to his representation of the world. A representation of the world is a stock of factual assumptions with some internal organization.'

[3]A semantics, while not easy, is probably not impossible. See [Gabbay, 1998b].

[4]Readers interested in having a quick glimpse of a formal model can jump ahead to section 11.3.

descendent of a word of the same name introduced in a scientifically serious way in early writings on information theory. A *locus classicus* is [Shannon, 1948]. Shannon's treatment ensued upon Hartley [1928]. The basic idea in these writings is not that of information but rather quantities of it. Information itself secured a place in semantic theory only somewhat gradually. Bar-Hillel and Carnap attempted to adapt statistical information theory to the purposes of semantics in their [1952]. Hintikka's 'On Semantic Information' represents a further development. It may be found in [Hintikka and Suppes, editors, 1970]. We follow Hintikka [1970] in distinguishing the concept of information elucidated in the work of Shannon and Weaver and the concept of information in its more common meaning as that which is grasped when a meaningful sentence or transmission is understood. The former is *statistical information* and the latter is *semantic information*. We have already mentioned the pioneering developments in the area of semantic information by Bar Hillel and Carnap in the 1950s. In this they were anticipated by Popper [1934] nearly twenty years earlier.

Hintikka rightly observes that 'the relation of this theory of semantic information to statistical information theory is not very clear' [Hintikka, 1970, p. 6]. Even so, there is enough clarity about semantic information to justify Jamison's assertion that the concept of information subsumes two subconceptions, *reduction in uncertainty* and *change in belief* [Jamison, 1970, p. 28]. Either way, semantic information is defined probabilistically. Assuming the requisite differences between the relative frequency, logical and subjective conceptions of probability, these three interact with the prior two to give six alternative ways of constructing a theory of information. We here follow [Jamison, 1970, p. 29]. Let R, L and S denote respectively, relative frequency, logical and subjective conceptions of probability and let C and U denote the change in belief and reduction of uncertainty conceptions of information. Then there are in principle the following six *theories* of information:

$$CR$$
$$UR$$
$$CL$$
$$UL$$
$$CS$$
$$US$$

As Jamison points out, UR was developed by Shannon and Weaver, whereas Carnap and Bar-Hillel [1952] jointly produced UL. Bar-Hillel [1964; 1955] anticipated something like US or CS. Smokler [1966] and Hintikka and Pietarinen [1966] extended developments in UL.

A drawback of US is that it denies information to the logical truths, although Wells [1961] has made inroads in showing how this consequence might be averted for *a priori* truths. Howard [1966] has extended US to decision theory, as has McCarthy [1956] to value theory.

We join with Jamison in holding that the most intuitive conception of semantic information (of these six alternatives) is CS, change in belief as manifested by change in subjective probabilities. The betterness of CS consists in the fact that change of belief subsumes the idea of uncertainty reduction, and in the further fact 'that reality is far too rich and varied to be adequately reflected in a logical or relative frequency theory of probability'. [Jamison, 1970, p. 30]

Let Δ be an agent's belief states prior to the reception of some information I and Δ^* his belief afterwards. Then it is possible to define the amount of information furnished by I, or contained in I, as a strictly increasing function of the distance between Δ and Δ^*, i.e.,

$$\inf(I) = \frac{m\sqrt{m(m-1)}}{2(m-1)}|\Delta - \Delta^*|$$

where m is the number of mutually exclusive and collectively exhaustive possible states of affairs. The rest of [Jamison, 1970] concentrates on the provision of a subjectivist theory of induction in which the logical theories of Carnap and Hintikka appear as special cases. So, beyond the introduction of basic concepts, Jamison [1970] is not directly to our purposes here.

An extremely influential semantic treatment of information is [Dretske, 1981]. Dretske gives a fuller account of the theoretical transition from quantities of information to semantic information at pages 237 and 241 of that work. Important recent development include the situational semantics of [Barwise and Perry, 1983; Barwise, 1989a].

In situational approaches to semantics, the concept of information is handled in ways that we find attractive and helpful. Let P be an n-place relation and let $a_1, \ldots, a_n$ be admissible arguments to P. Then

$$\langle\langle P, a_1, \ldots, a_n, 1\rangle\rangle$$

is the item of information, or *infon*, that the a_i stand in the relation P, and

$$\langle\langle P, a_1, \ldots, a_n, O\rangle\rangle$$

is the infon that the a_i do not stand in the relation P. Infons are digitizations of information ([Devlin, 1991, pp. 22–23] and [Barwise, 1989a]).

Part of what is distinctive about situation semantics is that it sees inference as the extraction of information. A sound inference 'is one that has the logical structure necessary to serve as a link in an informational chain but that need not use language at all' [Barwise, 1989b, 39]. Similarly,

> Sound inferences are those that meet the conditions necessary to ensure that the resulting mental states contain information concerning the external situations they are about.
> [Barwise, 1989b, 53]

Ours is a conception that bears a clear affinity to the notion of information developed in systems of *dynamic logic*, such as Groenendijk and Stokhof [1991] and Groendendijk *et al.* [1996]. It gives rise in turn to a conception of meaning, of which our own notion of agenda relevance can be seen as an adaptation. Suppose we grant that

> you know the meaning of a sentence if you know the change it brings about in the information state of anyone who accepts the news conveyed by it. [Veltman, 1996, p. 221]

Then the adaptation to relevance is comparatively straightforward, even in advance of the detailed analysis to follow. We have already said that the basic idea about relevance is that it is *helpful information*. Helpfulness, of course, is helpfulness *to or for something in certain respects*. We conceptualize this raw intuition in the way already noted. Information **I** is relevant for a cognitive agent **X** when in processing it **X** is affected in ways that advance or close one or more of his agendas.

The snow example again: Upon arising, Harry wishes to know whether it has snowed overnight. This is his agenda. He looks down into the street and sees that it is piled high with drifts. The information contained in this observation was processed by Harry in ways that produced the belief that it snowed overnight. This closes Harry's agenda.

Although the notion of meaning found in dynamic logic is defined for sentences, it is adaptable to items of information, irrespective whether they are in sentential form. The information contained in Harry's observation was processesd in such a way that it changed Harry's information state; it produced the belief that it snowed overnight. Strictly speaking, Veltman's is not a definition of meaning of an item of information, but rather of what it is to know its meaning. We may take it as given that we ourselves — and, in this simple kind of case, Harry too — do know the meaning of the information contained in Harry's observation of all that snow; for we could certainly be expected to think that it would 'tell' Harry that it snowed overnight and that, in having been told it, Harry's wish to determine whether it snowed overnight would have been satisfied. Thus we know two things about the information conveyed. We know its meaning and we know its relevance.

In knowing these things, it is natural to raise a pair of related questions:

1. Does the relevance of a piece of information require it to have meaning?

2. In knowing what the relevance of a piece of information is, is it necessary to know its meaning?

Our answer to question (1) is No. Although we acknowledge that, for large ranges of cases, information that closes agendas will be information that carries meaning, we want also to recognize cases in which information is efficacious short of having been processed semantically.

When considering (2), it is important that this question not be confused with its look-alike,

2* In knowing that a piece of information is relevant, is it necessary to know its meaning?

The answer to (2*) is also No. Sarah overhears Lou saying someting in Hungarian to Harry and hears Harry's reply (in English): 'Ah, that tells me what I wanted to know'. Even though Sarah speaks no Hungarian, she could nevertheless see that the information contained in Lou's utterance closed (or advanced) some agenda of Harry's. Question (2) is different. It asks whether it is possible to know why, with repsect to a piece of information processed by Harry, it was such as to have affected Harry in ways that advanced one or more of his agendas. For us to know that, we would need to know the changes brought about in Harry's information state. So knowing what it was about that information that got it to be the case that it satisfies the definition of agenda relevance does require that we grasp its meaning.

We bring this brief digression to a close by noting that, as conceived of by dynamic logicians, information changes a subject's information state only if he 'accepts the news conveyed by it'. We have already registered the claim that such changes can be made short of semantic processing (so the information that runs the trick needn't always contain 'news'). A similar latitude might be extended to acceptance. So we shall leave room for the idea of tacit acceptance, and will retun to it in due course.

Our basic idea about relevance resembles an extension of Sperber's and Wilson's basic idea. They write '[t]o convert our definition of the relevance of an assumption in a context into a definition of the relevance of a phenomenon to an individual', it suffices to impose two further conditions.

Extent Condition 1: A phenomenon is relevant to an individual to the extent that the contextual effects achieved in processing it are large.

Extent Condition 2: A phenomenon is relevant to an individual to the extent that the effort required to process it is small [Sperber and Wilson, 1987, 703].

Still, there are problems. Suppose we combine these two conditions in the formula

$$R = \frac{E \text{ (number of contextual effects)}}{C (\text{cost of effort in getting } E)}$$

If as Sperber and Wilson aver on p. 142, R's value is fixed, E has to be increased until that value is reached. But many different ways of expanding E will do the trick. So which is the right way?

At times R is a comparative measure by which the best expansion of E is achieved. But computing the measure requires that all alternative expressions be reckoned. This so drives up the cost that the formula requires that the cheapest thing is to pick any expansion at random. (It gets worse; see [Levinson, 1989, 463] for details.)

7.2.1 Causality

Relevance is a causal relation. Among other things, it causes or helps cause changes of mind. If Harry's agenda is to determine whether there is a flight from London to Saarbrucken on Sunday mornings, then the information that no such flight is posted is relevant for Harry with regard to that agenda. It was information that brought about the requisite change of mind, from not having to know whether such a flight exists. Treating relevance in this way puts us in the embrace of a difficult notion. This may strike the reader as imprudent. For can it really be said that causality is a clearer idea than relevance? Clarity is not the point. Theoretical command is the point. Quantum non-locality is the subject of impressive theoretical command, but we would not say that the idea of non-locality is all that clear. Perhaps causality is not all that clear either, though for most people it is a good deal clearer than quantum non-locality. What signifies here is that causality is the subject of theories more substantial, detailed and subtle than anything as yet dreamt up for relevance, and it is for this reason that we do not scruple to put causality in the service of relevance. So, on the principle that the proof of the pudding is in the eating, we shall press on and presuppose for relevance a non-deterministic probabilistic account of causality, such as that propounded by Suppes [1984, esp. Ch. 3].[5]

The causal theory of relevance is embedded in a certain picture of the practical agent. We will assume for now that it is a picture that resembles a parallel distributed processor,[6] perhaps even of a processing activation vector through appropriately weighted neural networks [Churchland, 1989, p. 195]. The assumption is made undogmatically and with ecumenical intent. How human agents make relevance determinations will depend on how they in fact are, on what they are like and what they can and cannot do. How they are involves the physical realization of programmes by virtue of which they are efficient and finite consumers of boundless information. PDP models of human cognition are different from conventional AI models. But they need not be hostile to them. We make the PDP assumption in this spirit. It is the spirit of Smolensky who has described a device called 'the conscious rule interpreter' (CRI). CRI is a PDP system adapted to computational simulations of a device running a standard AI program (see [Smolensky, 1988] see also [Hogan and Tienson, 1996]).

It is fair to ask whether our decision to adopt a probabilistic conception of causality or, albeit tentatively, a PDP approach to cognitive agency tilts the scales for or against any given type of account of relevance. The answer is that it does not tilt for any type of account that we have already decided not to adopt, and that it leaves open any approach in which relevance is a matter of a cognitive agent being affected in ways that conduce to some contextually indicatable end. What our account of agenda relevance does not require is strict and absolute adherence to Suppes' treatment of causality or the PDP notion of the human information processor. It is so, in any event, that the human agent is equipped with various evolutionary endowments, and ecologically induced skills arising therefrom, which serve in the quest for survival and for a more or less integrated and coherent life, with various prospects for satisfaction and delight. A person's genetic and ecological endowments include his or her cognitive devices, the mechanisms whereby appropriate inputs bring about the appropriate perceptions, memories, and beliefs. It is understood that the cognitive devices aren't perfect and that

[5] A more technical approach by the same author is [Suppes, 1970a]. For a critical reaction to Suppes, see, for example [Otte, 1981].

[6] The standard texts are [Rumelhart *et al.*, 1986] and [McClelland *et al.*, 1988]. In seeking a theoretical alliance between informational semantics and an underlying PDP model of cognition, there is a certain tension over probability. PDP models retain the probabilistic approach of [Shannon, 1948]. Dretske deviates (and Barwise and Perry too). Dretske identifies the information carried by signals with conditional probabilities of 1. For our purposes here, it is unnecessary to resolve this tension. There is no bar in principle to a PDP theory's absorbing a Dretskean notion of information. See [Smolensky, 1986, p. 195, note 1].

when they misfire or when they operate inefficiently the human agent is liable to error. Similarly, a human being possesses conative (i.e., decision-making) devices which process appropriate optative inputs, with resultant determination of decisions to act. It is sometimes held that beings driven by such conative mechanisms cannot be thought to act freely.

We are compatibilists about such things. One does not discredit or diminish the human achievement of seeing what's there,[7] of remembering that May 24th is the anniversary of Queen Victoria's birth, or of realizing that $2+2 \neq 88$, just because they are causal outputs of more or less efficient cognitive mechanisms, of a central nervous system that works properly. One does not withhold the verdict of 'rational' from such accomplishments. A being is rational to the extent that the causal mechanisms are cognitively in order. It can scarcely be different for freedom of action. A person's actions are free to the extent that they are caused by optative factors, these in turn processed by the conative devices. True, radical misperformance of the conative apparatus can take on pathological significance and deprive the output the status of free action, just as cognitive misperformance can deny the output the status of knowledge, or (veridical) perception or (veridical) memory. But the prospects of performance disorder don't discredit the causal idiom; they reinforce it. And so we have it: freedom is to free action as cognitive rationality is to cognitively rational performance. We don't wish to be over-sanguine about the relationship between one's rationality and the functioning of one's cognitive devices. Although we ourselves doubt it, it is possible that our causal mechanisms have evolved in such a way as makes us extremely conservative and prone to an abundance of false positives. If so, might we not wish to improve our rationality, assuming that the original selective processes are now abated, by tinkering with the output of our cognitive devices? The short answer is, 'Of course'. Self-reflective criticizability is not ruled-out on the present account. On the contrary, critical self-reflection is essential to human rationality, and nothing we know of precludes its being in the control of (largely) causal mechanisms. We assume without argument that humans are much less conservative than (say) rats. This suggests, but certainly doesn't guarantee, that we have a better record of false positives. Part of this superiority is a function of devices naturally selected for, but it is also in part a function of broadly cultural endowments (and of the learning that arises from each). But, again, nothing we know of precludes a broadly causal analysis of it all.

[7]'Seeing what's there.' Though there is more to perception than vision, it is appropriate to note the causally probabilistic character of 'our highly sensitive sense of vision-sensitivity down to a level of a single photon'. [Suppes, 1984, pp. 13–14]. Biochemical theories of smell likewise draw down probabilistic notions of causality. Cf. [Semb, 1968].

We said earlier that the extension of the basic Sperber and Wilson account of relevance in a context to relevance for an individual runs into the same kind of difficulties that crop up in the basic account. We bring this section to a close by revisiting this point. Let C be a set of beliefs (a context) of some individual **X**. Let C contain the belief that a logical falsehood entails the truth of every proposition whatever. Let P be new information for **X** to the effect that, for some $Q \in C$, Q is a logical falsehood. For concreteness, let Q be the proposition that the Russell set exists, and let P be the proposition that the proposition that Russell set exists is a logical falsehood. So by *modus ponens*, we have the proposition that every proposition is true. But the sentence 'Every proposition is true' contextually implies for each proposition Z, the proposition that Z is true. The contextual effects of the conjunction of the new belief with the old have a cardinality of not less than the countably infinite, and the processing of the information that puts these consequences in place requires very little effort. To see that this is so, it is not necessary for the processing of information that *produce* contextual effects involves *processing* those conceptual effects. In our example, it is not necessary for the fact that the truth of every Z is contextually implied by information that **X** processes (together with beliefs he already has) that **X** *draw* those consequences.

This is tantamount to a demonstration that Russell's fateful letter of 1902, which communicated to Frege the inconsistency of (in effect) the proposition that the Russell set exists, was relevant to a degree than which the greater does not exist. No one doubts the momentousness of the disclosure or the sick panic that it struck in Frege's heart. But there isn't the slightest reason for thinking that this story gets *relevance* right.

The moral, as we have had occasion to say before, is that whereas the idea of relevance of something for an individual as something he can get from it without unreasonable effort is an attractive one, the machinery of contextual effects is too crude for its articulation. This, in effect, is also the view of Sperber and Wilson. They 'see it as a central function of the deductive device to derive, spontaneously, automatically and unconsciously, the contextual implications of any newly presented information in a context of old information' [Sperber and Wilson, 1987, 702]. Since contextual implications are generated by elimination rules attached to concepts, it is demonstrable, they say, that 'from a finite set of premisses, [to] automatically deduce a finite set of nontrivial conclusions' [Sperber and Wilson, 1987, 702]. But as we see, it is not possible to demonstrate this; indeed it is false.[8] Finally, it is easily seen that the present problem does not turn

[8] It is false, that is to say, given what we take to be the SW-background logic. However, in a relevance logic with $\wedge, \rightarrow$ and $\perp$, a finite set of atoms does generate a finite set of

essentially on having extended the original account of relevance (which is 'simply a formal property' [Sperber and Wilson, 1987, 703] to a concept of relevance *for* an individual.

Here, too, is another point that repays repeating. Sperber and Wilson's project is to construct a theory of communication which is based on a certain account of cognition. 'Attention and thought processes, we argue, automatically turn toward information that seems relevant: that is, capable of yielding cognitive effects — the more, and the more economically, the greater the relevance' [Sperber and Wilson, 1987, 697]. To achieve the goal of a theory of communication, it is necessary therefore to give an account of how relevance plays in human cognitive practice; and to do this requires an account of relevance. Our own objective is in a certain respect more circumscribed, much as we like the general outlines of the larger project of Sperber and Wilson. Part of our project is to give an adequate common analysis of relevance. What we object to in the Sperber and Wilson approach is the account they give of *relevance*, not the account they give of communication or cognition, on which, aside from some Gricean leanings, we are mute. This matters. It allows for the possibility that Sperber and Wilson could by and large be correct in what they say of the *role* of relevance in communication and cognition, even if they are less right in their analysis of what relevance is. On this our condition of ecumension has a tangential bearing. It requires that to the extent possible we absorb alternative accounts of relevance into the theory of agenda relevance. Even where that might not be wholly possible, it lies in the spirit of this condition to fashion our account of relevance in such a way that it might play the role intended for an account of relevance in a theory of communication and cognition in the manner of Sperber and Wilson. If we are not mistaken, precisely this kind of role can be claimed for the theory of agenda relevance.

7.3 Belief

We have already made abundant use of the idea of belief. Most of the issues discussed in the previous chapter would have taken a very different turn, assuming that they could have been discussed at all, had the doxastic idiom been unavailable to us. It will seem to some readers that, having thrown our hat into the PDP-ring, consistency requires that we give up belief as a bad job. There is more than one way in which a PDPist could be troubled by belief. If he is an eliminative materialist in the manner of Churchland his principal reservations will be methodological. For over two

non-equivalent wffs.

millennia we have tried to account for human psychological processes by way of accounts in which belief is a deep and pivotal artifact of theory. But psychology is an unrelieved mess, Churchland says. It should be abandoned for approximately the same reasons that alchemy was abandoned. And its central concepts should be retired much in the way that the central concepts of alchemy were retired. Care needs to be taken lest the rejection of belief turn on the ancient fallacy of division. Even if psychology is no good at all it doesn't follow that none of its concepts is (this would be the division fallacy). Supplementary argument would be needed to show that in psychology's successor theory (e.g. neuroscience) there is no room for or anyhow no need of belief. This is what eliminationists do in fact think, though it makes the rejection of belief somewhat programmatic (and is what might prompt us to characterize eliminationism as 'promissory note materialism'). See [Churchland, 1989, Ch. 1].

Another reason for disliking belief and the other propositional attitudes, we associate with the name of Quine. The propositional attitudes will not go over into canonical notation. Sentences ascribing beliefs, desires and the like resist paraphrase in first-order extensional languages. Theories in which such construction are indispensable cannot be regarded as scientific, either at all or in some preferred sense.[9]

A third reason for distrusting belief arises from a basic claim of the PDP approach to human cognition. It is the view that cognitive processes are not, exclusively or basically, language-manipulating processes. Any physical system — including us — can be described information-theoretically. A cognitive agent is then an information processing system. Sometimes the information an agent processes will be linguistic information, but the processing of linguistic information does not constitute the essence of his cognitive processes, not even of his 'higher' processes such as inference.

[9]Quine shifted his position over the years. In [Quine, 1960, p. 221] Quine spoke of the baselessness of intentional idioms and the emptiness of a science of intention. In [Quine, 1990, p. 71] Quine writes that 'the keynote of the mental is not the mind; it is the content-clause syntax, the idiom 'that p'. Brentano was right about the irreducibility of intensional discourse'. All the same, there is

> no discussing it. It implements vital communication and harbors indispensable lore about human activity and motivation, past and expected. Its irreducibility is all the more reason for treasuring it: we have no substitute [Quine, 1990, p. 71].

But Quine would not allow the psychology of propositional attitudes to count as preferred science; it could not be 'extensional science' [p. 72] since it is of doubtful 'existential intelligibility' [p. 72].

He commends the efforts of Churchland and others 'to reclaim territory from the intensional side, by dint of discoveries and reconceptualization on the extensional side....' [Quine, 1990, p. 72]. See [Quine, 1960; Quine, 1990].

Whatever goes on in the mind of a human subject under conditions that make it true that he is in a cognitive state, it seems not to be true that being in that state is constituted without exception by his manipulating a language, even a language of thought.

This might not be a correct view; certainly it is a long way from having been firmly established as correct. But, if true, it is a position that carries significant consequences. In everyday speech, 'belief' is ambiguous as between a psychological state and that which is believed when one is in that state. There are substantial theoretical economies if we take this latter to be a sentence, i.e., a sentence of a kind that might be said to express propositions. This makes it easy to simulate the intentionality of belief — its 'aboutness'. A standard semantics for sentences trades deeply in designation- and assignment-functions which prescribe what a sentence could be said to be about. A related virtue of taking beliefs as sentences is that sentences have truth conditions. Beliefs can be said to be true when their truth conditions are satisfied.

PDP theories are a departure from all this theoretical tidiness. They are a risky business. If PDP approaches are right, cognitive competence is not a matter of relating in appropriate ways to entities that satisfy truth conditions as standardly conceived of. Truth conditions are conditions on sentences, and cognition is not as such a matter of one's standing in sentential relationships. If Sarah is a PDP theorist, she is a neoconnectionist about cognition.[10] She holds that cognitive success or failure is fundamentally a matter of the configuration and distribution of neural nets. It is easy to see that she would have little sympathy with our stories of the belief-adjustment function *f* in chapter 6. Whether as a Seer of Trouble Coming or a Putter of Things Right, *f* is a scrutinizer of entities bearing semantic properties such as consistency and inconsistency, never mind that proper subsets of these are syntactically recognizable. Even if we allow that the device sometimes tracks such properties syntactically, either way these are

[10]Let us be clear about truth conditions. Truth conditions originated in the truth conditional semantics for uninterpreted languages such as that of classical logic. Such meaning as such a sentence S can have is taken as the disjunction of all conjunctions of literals in any row of its truth table in which S comes out true.

A more relaxed notion of truth conditions is taken as the 'other half' of a true bi-conditional. Thus a truth condition on bachelors is that they be unmarried. The shift from meta- to object-level disguises an ambiguity. Consider beliefs. There are conditions which render a mental (or psychological) state as a belief, rather than, say, a desire or a pain. These might be called its truth conditions in the sense of defining conditions. But there are also conditions under which a belief is true. These are its truth conditions properly speaking. More generally, the truth condition, properly speaking, of *anything* are the conditions under which it is true and false. Alternatively, anything that has truth conditions is something that has conditions in virtue of which it is *truth-valuable*.

properties of linguistic entities. Since f is presumed to do the job of the upgrading of an agent's cognitive state in general, the PDP theorist would disdain this characterization of f. She should disdain it as a characterization of Harry, too, since in each case cognitive state-upgrading would be a matter of reconciling with linguistic properties.

The PDP theorist is faced with an interesting option. Either she must, like the eliminationist, get rid of belief altogether as a deep artifact of theory. Or she must reconfigure belief in ways that sever its essential tie to language. The same options are pressed on her with regard to truth and truth conditions. If she wants to represent an agent's cognitive career as involving his sometimes having beliefs, and if she wishes to make theoretical provision for some of his beliefs being true, and if she wishes to construe true belief as belief which satisfies truth conditions, she must pledge to a renegotiation of these ideas in which they become definable over non-linguistic — perhaps purely neurological — entities or states of affairs. This latter produces a nastier shock than the wrench of trying to theorize about human cognition without the comforts of folk psychology. After all, folk psychology may be bad science, like alchemy, but Tarski's theory of truth is widely accepted as a paradigm of what theory should be.[11] If truth is defined for non-linguistic entities, Tarski's semantics fails for it and there is nothing presently in sight to take its place.[12] This is also a problem for the eliminationist. Belief he may be prepared to do without altogether, but he has not usually been as forthcoming about truth. Putnam recounts a conversation about this. 'I once put this question [of why the eliminationists don't speak of 'folk logic' as well as of 'folk psychology'] to Paul Churchland and he replied 'I don't know what the successor concept [to the notion of truth] will be' [Putnam, 1988, p. 60].[13]

Either way, whether eliminationist or reconfigurationist, the sciences of cognition would need to be done with successor concepts. For the reconfigurist, 'true' and 'belief' would be retained and would, in their successor

[11]Perhaps this is a trifle lavish. There are reasons not to like Tarski's solution of the Liar paradox. Thus McGee, [1991, p. 147]: 'The most common misfortunes to befall philosophical misfortune has befallen Tarski's doctrine about how to cope with the antinomies. It has been accepted too well.... Like the proverbial eye-glasses that we cannot see because they are on our face, Tarski's doctrine has been accepted so thoroughly that it has been invisible.' For more of this kind of heterodoxy, again see [Woods, 2002b, Ch. 7], Slater [2002] and Irvine [1992].

[12]This is especially tricky for Quine. About belief Quine is a reluctant intensionalist; he yearns for headway on the eliminationist side. But, 'I want to keep the truth predicate [as is]. I need it for semantic ascent'. [Quine, 1990, p. 347].

[13]The conversation is printed, together with supplementary remarks from Churchland, in [Pylyshyn and Demopoulos, 1986].

roles, be assigned extensions having a substantial non-linguistic membership. For the eliminationist, the extensions will be empty.

It is a fair question as to what we should be doing until the brain sciences grow up. We propose the following: To retain the idioms of belief and truth conditions under the reconfiguration option, because, like everyone else, we don't know how else to get on with the business at hand. We need it to be true that belief and truth conditions are specifiable in principle for a cognizer's states on occasions when nothing linguistic is being manipulated. We don't need it to be true that on such occasions belief and truth conditions are construable as properties of neural nets — although perhaps this is what they are. By these lights, it becomes desirable that information states of an agent should sometimes be subject to transformations to informational states of which belief and truth conditions are admissible characterizations. (It is not foreclosed that sometimes the transformation in question will be the identity transformation, taking an information state into itself.) When this happens we will say that information states have been doxastically coded up and truth conditionally primed. But it will not in general be true that a doxastic code describes a linguistic operation.

On the face of it, we have ventured far from shore onto some alarmingly thin ice. It seems that we want to have it every which way, to the extent that continuous reciprocal causation, allows we want to think of sentient organisms in Homuncular Functionalist terms. We want to think of cognition in PDP or connectionist terms. And we want to retain what we can of folk psychology. We might just as well have wanted to square the circle or prove the consistency of the Russell set. For isn't Homuncular Functionalism inconsistent with connectionism, and isn't connectionism inconsistent with folk psychology? We think not, both times, though we concede that there is room for argument.

Part of the problem is explaining how, if it is not strictly speaking a function of connectionist architecture that they carry 'algorithmically constructed content', that is, symbolic propositional representations, how is it that they do carry them, if they do? They do so, says Lycan, for a suitably weakened notion of function. Their 'contents could be thought of as a kind of pleiotropism', and so '...there is no principled opposition between HF and connectionism per se...' [Lycan, 1991, p. 270]. Moreover, where an HF theorist imagines that an organism 'has a 'belief box' whose function [sic] is to store information and to map the external world, plus an inference-machine and other sorts of information manipulators, all with appropriate connections to perception and memory' [Lycan, 1991, p. 272], he is thinking of a particular kind of functionalism which we might call Representational Homuncular Functionalism (RHF).

Some theorists — Smolensky is one [Smolensky, 1988] — distinguish within AI between symbolic and subsymbolic paradigms of cognition, arguing that honest-to-goodness cognition is subsymbolic, and that folk psychology is a murky epiphenomenon at best. But if we allow for different levels of attribution, folk psychological descriptions may do genuinely explanatory work, and may reasonably be allowed by way of inference to the best explanation. Perhaps the connectionist hardware *is* absolutely rock bottom.

But that should no more require the abandonment of folk psychological explanations than the fact that chemical reactions have atomic structures must vitiate the legitimacy of chemical explanations of them. 'Connectionism is compatible not only with RHF but, so far as has been shown, with all of folk psychology as well' [Lycan, 1991, p. 274]. At any rate, that is what we will be assuming here.

We don't want to appear over-casual about taking the present course. For one thing, we lose (or appear to) what Quine was not prepared to lose, the semantic theory of truth for reconfigured truth. Then, too, in putting belief back into harness, we reinstate a number of thorny problems. One is that of deciding whether the myriad differentials between belief, acceptance and commitment would eventually be needed to be worked out in ways that are made to matter for theory. For example, beliefs cannot be summoned by the will; acceptance can. We can decide to accept Big Bang, but we can't decide to believe it. In fact, how could we believe Big Bang, knowing so little of the ins and outs of cosmology? But, that said, we don't want our cognitive lives dispossessed of Big Bang or the other exotica of an interesting intellectual life.

More generally, as van Fraassen has observed, one way of not being a scientific realist is to accept or commit to a scientific theory yet not believe it. It is methodologically desirable that we not inadvertently deny to the epistemologist of science van Fraassen's way of being an anti-realist. See [van Fraassen, 1980, p. 8].

Belief is more hostile to logical closure conditions than commitment. It is hopeless to set out to believe all the consequences of what I believe. It couldn't be done. But being committed to the consequences of what I am committed to is, by contrast, a trifling matter. See [Harman, 1986; Dennett, 1984; Bach, 1984]. See also [Woods, 2002c, Ch. 3].

We can't, without some modal fiddling, believe what we don't understand. It is a commonplace to accept and so to be committed to what one doesn't understand. Most people committed to '$E = mc^2$' don't understand it (really), but it would be skeptically over-severe to insist that they eliminate it from their cognitive repertoires.

Belief is held to some sort of low-level transparency condition, expressible by low-finite iterations of a belief-operator. Thus if we believe that the cat is on the mat, it is widely assumed that we can be expected to believe that we believe that the cat is on the mat, and even to believe that we believe that we believe that the cat is on the mat.[14] Longer iterations are unmanageable; no human being can process, e.g., $\ulcorner$BBBBBBBBBBBBBBBBBBBBBB$\phi\urcorner$. So there is the question of at what point in such iterations to suspend the transparency expectation, and why. Commitment fares better, though not perfectly, with transparency issues. True, much of what we are committed to we will be expected to realize that we are committed to. For much else there is no such expectation, e.g., most of all the uncounted and unexpressed consequences of anything to which I realize that we are committed.[15]

If this weren't enough, Stephen Stich has produced an argument designed to show two things. One is that the notion of belief is theoretically intelligible in PDP models of cognition only if a crucial assumption is true. The second is that the crucial assumption is not true. The assumption in question is that cognitive structures are sufficiently modular as to give open sentences of the form '... is a belief' a denotation. A belief system is modular '... to the extent that there is some more or less isolatable part of the system which plays (or would play) the central role in a typical causal history leading to the utterance of a sentence'. Although the empirical evidence is thin, Stich cites several investigators who suggest that, just as some computer programs exhibit 'behaviours' that are not clearly coded for in any particular part of the program, so people's beliefs might be properties which do not originate in any localized structure [Stich, 1983, p. 237].

PDP theorists, again, have an answer for Stich, and it seems to us that it disarms the objection satisfactorily. A typical expression of it is given by Bechtel and Abrahamsen, who maintain that even if beliefs are not localized phenomena, belief could still be an intelligible and load-bearing notion in PDP theory. This would be because theories of belief are not about brain states but about whole people. At the level of description of the whole person, belief-talk may turn out to be useful and defensible even if it is not adequate to describe PDP processes [Bechtel and Abrahamsen, 1991, pp. 287–289]. This is welcome reassurance for the reconfigurationist about

[14]Even so, the move from believing that the cat is on the mat to believing that one believes that the cat is on the mat is certainly not trivial. The former requires the concepts of cat and mat. The latter requires something more, the concept of belief.

[15]True, some of the pressure could be taken from belief were we to speak of tacit or implicit belief. For reasons to prefer talk of commitment to talk of belief, see [Hamblin, 1970, Ch. 8]. For problems with tacit belief see [Lycan, 1988, Ch. 3]. For example, 'not even tacit belief is closed under deduction' [Lycan, 1988, p. 60]. For an interesting account of differences between belief and acceptance, see [Cohen, 1989].

belief. She doesn't need to retain all of the common sense features of belief. She will want to keep certain key features, e.g., that beliefs can have truth values, and that they are entities for which truth conditions are an intelligible notion. We said before that we wanted a concept of information transformation such that information transformed by it qualified for belief and truth conditions and that in general transformations need not depend upon or eventuate in concurrent or consequent linguistic manipulation. Now we are prepared to say that when an agent doxastically codes up in this way, the belief that becomes intelligibly ascribable is ascribed to the agent and in ways that don't *entail* its ascribability to her subagents, if any, and certainly not to her neural states.[16] Hereafter when we speak of processing information in ways that qualify for belief, belief is understood to be attributed at appropriate levels of description.

Even if she is a *PDP*-structure with beliefs, our connectionist, Sarah, has another string to her bow, of course. She may have access to a connectionist logic in which there is no required role for belief [Churchland, 1989].

7.4 Corroboration

A form of the notion of relevance that we are after was suggested by Sperber and Wilson:

> *Relevance*: A belief is relevant in a context if and only if it has some contextual effect in that context.
>
> [Sperber and Wilson, 1986, p. 122]

A belief or assumption has a contextual effect in a context when it strengthens or reinforces a belief contained in that context, when it contradicts a belief contained in that context and thus forces an 'erasure', or when it licenses implications. Contextual effects can in each case be likened to changes of mind. Degrees of confidence are raised or lowered, beliefs are contradicted and erased, and new beliefs are derived. We saw in chapter 6 that the *SW*-account of relevance meets with some difficulties. But we wish here to emphasize the rough conceptual kinship that their account and the present one share. A case in point is strengthening.

[16]Stich forwards another assumption as crucial for the retention of beliefs in PDP models, and this too he thinks is false. The assumption is that if people have beliefs, the beliefs they have will influence behaviour, linguistic and non-linguistic. If that weren't so, belief-talk would lose its explanatory force. But there is abundant empirical evidence that people's actions belie what they (say they) believe. So belief doesn't play a role in non-verbal behaviour. The objection evidently pivots on the further assumption that beliefs, if there are any, are transparent. This is an assumption that we don't grant. So we aren't much moved by the present objection.

Strengthening stands as an intuitively appealing condition on relevance. Imagine that Harry bumps into Lou at the club and Lou says, 'Guess what, Sue has left Arnold.' Harry says to himself, 'I wonder if that can be? Mmm, perhaps she *has* left him.' Harry now has a context which includes a weak belief, expressed as 'Perhaps Sue has left Arnold.' Later Harry goes home and is met at the door by his wife, who says, 'You'll never believe this, but Sue and Arnold are quits.' Harry now replaces the former weak belief with the more confident, 'Well, well, she *has* left him.' This, or something like it, is strengthening, and it is obvious that given what he had already accepted, Harry's wife's news is relevant, for it corroborates what he had heard earlier.

Intuitively fine, the idea that corroborating information is sometimes relevant (because strengthening) is nevertheless an extremely unruly one. We wish at this point to offer a conjecture. Corroboration is a difficult notion to make behave when construed probabilistically. We have, by now, given sufficient attention to probabilistic analysis of relevance to have some basis for suggesting that probability theory is not likely to do much better for corroboration than it has for relevance. Perhaps this has something to do with the fact the corroboration relations also seem to be relevance relations. The question of what justifies our confidence in the reinforcement afforded by corroboration has been, as we say, a problem of celebrated difficulty for some years, thanks especially to work by Jonathan Cohen [1980; 1982; 1986]. Along-side is the question of what *gets* us to think (when we do) that corroboration is strengthening, and the still further question of when corroboration makes for strengthened belief, whether or not the believer is aware of it. We mention this here, not to provoke a detour from our main purpose, but to raise the methodological question of where it would be more appropriate to deal with the justification of corroboration as a strengthening factor, in the descriptive account of relevance, or in the normative account. This will also give us occasion for a further word about imputations of causalness to relevance.

The corroboration difficulty is well-expressed by George Schlesinger: [1988, p. 141].

> In fact, however, from the assumption that a story is confirmed to a certain degree through being affirmed solely by A or by B, it is impossible to derive logically that their joint affirmation confirms it to a higher degree.[17]

[17] It is important to emphasize that in the general case this is the rule and not the exception, and as it stands it should not be complained of or regretted. However, since it is sometimes true that corroboration *is* strengthening, some representation of the fact is needed.

If strengthening-via-corroboration is a legitimate or useful notion, further assumptions are required. What might they be? If, following Schlesinger, we put it that $S =$ Sue has left Arnold, $R_1 = A$ reports that S and $R_2 = B$ reports that S, then according to Cohen the conclusion which cannot be derived from the above assumption alone is:

$$(7) Pr(S/R_2 \wedge R_1) > Pr(S/R_1)$$

Cohen has shown that (7) can be derived from the following assumptions:

$$\begin{array}{ll} (1) & Pr(S/R_1) > Pr(S) \\ (2) & Pr(S/R_2) > Pr(S) \\ (3) & Pr(R_1 \wedge R_2) > 0 \\ (4) & Pr(R_2/S) < Pr(R_2/R_1 \wedge S) \\ (5) & Pr(R_2/\neg S) < Pr(R_2/R_1 \wedge \neg S) \\ (6) & 1 > Pr(S/R_1) \end{array}$$

Schlesinger proposes that it is possible to weaken these conditions, replacing Cohen's (3), (4) and (5) with the single assumption Φ and Cohen's (1) and (2) with the weaker premises (1′) and (2′). Thus

$$\begin{array}{ll} (\Phi) & Pr(R_2/R_1 \wedge S) > Pr(R_2/R_1) \\ (1') & Pr(S/R_1) > 0 \\ (2') & Pr(S/R_2) > 0 \end{array}$$

If it were agreed that Schlesinger's simplification secures the desired conclusion (7), we could take it without further ado that (1′), (2′), (Φ) and (6) constitute some kind of justification of our confidence in corroboration-strengthening.[18]

Let us call this justification *Just*. What is the place of *Just* in the life of a cognitive agent **X** for whom corroboration is strengthening? Is **X** obliged to know *Just* before corroboration actually does strengthen any of his beliefs? Must **X** know why corroboration is strengthening before it *is*? **X**'s actual and knowing use of *Just* in his belief strengthening moments is clearly out of the question. He does not in fact resort to *Just* as a condition of his belief's strengthening, and it isn't at all clear that even a normatively ideal reasoner would do so either. If the ideal reasoner were expected to do so, then actual reasoners would fail the rationality ideal dismally. We may think that our actual reasoner is rational just when his beliefs do in fact strengthen under

[18]As it happens, Cohen doesn't think that Schlesinger's simplification works (personal communication and [Cohen, 1991]). See also [Cohen, 1994]. Even so, since settlement of this matter between Cohen and Schlesinger doesn't affect the points at hand, we will stick with Schlesinger's purported simplification.

press of the relevantly appropriate reinforcement. If, as we are assuming, *Just* legitimizes what he is doing, yet **X** is unaware of *Just* and gives it no sway in actual practice, it is left open to wonder whether *Just* has a role in rational life and what it could be. If *Just* is not resorted to either in everyday practice or in normatively streamlined practice, are we to say that *Just* is dispossessed of any place in the human ratiocinative agenda?

Consider the case in which a competent reasoner, **X**, on having "$\neg Q$" added to his context C, in which there occurs the conditional "$P \rightarrow Q$", derives "$\neg P$". ('I'll go to this party only if Sarah comes; but I hear now that Sarah isn't coming, so I'm going to the movies instead.') **X**'s adjustment of his belief-stock reflects the structure of *modus tollens*. **X** may or may not be able to identify this or to establish its legitimacy, by truth tables, for example. By and large, most competent reasoners seem not to do this, even when they reason entirely satisfactorily in accordance with the justifying *modus tollens*.[19]

How do such people manage to do the right thing without, so to speak, knowing what they are doing? It may be that they have internalized something like *modus tollens* and that that fact, the fact that they have internalized something like {"$\neg Q$", "$P \rightarrow Q$" $\therefore$ "$\neg P$"}, rather than something like {"$\neg P$", "$P \rightarrow Q$" $\therefore$ "$\neg Q$"},[20] has to do with the former's being a legitimate strategy and the latter not. The human reasoner is competent to the extent that he has internalized strategies that are right, not wrong. So the legitimacy of *modus tollens* does have a role to play in actual rational practice, after all. The cognitive mechanism somehow vets its possible strategies for legitimacy. It is perhaps a trifle far-fetched to suppose that the justification of *modus tollens* is hard-wired or that justification *Just* for belief-strengthening is hard-wired, but if our cognitive processes are entirely blind to the legitimacy of the strategies that it is willing to internalize, then that we possess good strategies rather than awful ones is something that merely happens. This is too much serendipity for our tastes; and so we might hypothesize, tentatively and for now, that our cognitive mechanisms are structured as if they had taken something like *Just* into account. *Just* or something like it gives (part of) the blueprint for the cognitive engineering that gets us to adopt corroboration as a belief-strengthening strategy. So if *Just* or something like it does have a role in human cognitive practice, it will be, if anything, a causal role.

---

[19]Reported by Richard E. Nisbett, [1989]. Actually Nisbett's results hold when sentences are interpreted. Lance Rips (among others) has demonstrated a quite good and basic competence with simple conditional reasoning, of the *modus tollens* sort, where there is no interpretation. Rips takes such competence to be hard-wired. See [Rips, 1983].

[20]Though, notoriously, in actual practice such a 'rule' does show some evidence of having been acquired to some extent.

It may be, as we say, that *Just* justifies our confidence in corroboration as strengthening. But here, of course, we are rather more interested in how an agent gets to treat corroboration as strengthening, or more primitively how his belief gets to be strengthened by way of corroboration. We conjectured that he has internalized *Just* or something like it. That *Just* is also a justification, if it is, is a welcome bonus and occasion of a further conjecture. The further speculation is that our cognitive devices are so designed as to make of us in the general case cognitive successes rather than cognitive misfits. The prospect provokes hard questions of its own. One queries the relationship between cognitive success and the attainment of truth. Another asks whether we have, or could have, adequate reasons for supposing that human rationality is in-built or ecologically supplied. We do not pursue such questions here. It will suffice to declare without benefit of argument, that to some considerable extent the factual-normative distinction implodes in the faithful description of human cognitive performance. We come back to this idea in chapter 10.

7.5 Probability

The probability idiom enters our account in a number of ways. We must take care not to overdo it. Probability is needed for causality and information, and probability is needed for the present treatment of corroboration. Causality is also needed for relevance. But the account of relevance does not proceed by way of theorems of the probability calculus. Relevance is not defined, not in any direct way, via probabilities. Though probability enters into the explication of causality and of information, and causality and information figure in the explication of relevance, probability enters the picture only because causality and information do. Provided we bear this qualification in mind, it is perfectly all right to allow that ours is a probabilistic account of relevance.[21]

There is another way of saying this. Agenda relevance is not analysable in the minimum vocabulary of probability theory. It is analysed in an alliance of semantic information theory, cognitive science, a theory of probabilistic causality and a theory of agendas. We assume the alliance to possess

[21]There is, of course, a well-established direct usage of 'relevance' in probability theory. In personalist accounts of probability, of the Ramsey and de Finetti sorts, there are good technical reasons to constrain conditional probability in the following way. We put it that $Pr(A/B)$ is the probability given to A where B expresses the sole relevant additional fact to come to light. This is all right as far as it goes, but saying so makes for circularity as long as one wishes to define relevance via conditional probabilities. Thus a fact B conveys all evidence relevant to a proposition A only if there is no fact C such that it is not the case that C entails A and $Pr(A/B) \neq Pr(A/B \wedge C)$.

a minimum vocabulary M. We also assume that M properly includes M^*, a minimum vocabulary of probability theory. Those who think that probabilistic accounts of relevance are unpromising will be disposed to rule out M^* (or restrictions of it) as an analysing notation for relevance. But there is no reason why the anti-probabilistic relevance theorist couldn't very seriously look for his analysis in M.

Relevance has a causal role in the changing of beliefs and thus has a role in reasoning. Following Harman, it is necessary to caution against supposing that the axioms of the probability calculus have been internalized by human cognitive agents as rules of reasoning, as, in particular, rules of inference. The trouble with such a supposition is that inference, so taken, lands the inferrer in an exponential explosion vastly beyond his capacity to manage. Suppose, for example, that we took conditionalization to be a rule of inference. Let P be a belief and E^1, E^2, $\ldots E^n$ atomic evidence propositions. If conditionalization were a rule for increasing the degree of beliefs, the rule would look basically like this:

$$\textit{updated } Pr(P) = \frac{\textit{old } Pr(P \wedge E)}{\textit{old } Pr(E)}$$

However,

> for every proposition P one wants to update, one must already have assigned probabilities to various conjunctions of P together with one or more of the possible evidence propositions and/or their denials. Unhappily, this leads to a combinatorial explosion, since the number of such conjunctions is an exponential function of the number of ... evidence propositions. To be prepared for twenty evidence propositions, one must record a million probabilities. [Harman, 1986, pp. 25–26]

So conditionalization is not a virtual rule of belief-revision.[22]

There is another thing that we might find it plausible to think about *Just* (and about *modus tollens*, too). If conditionalization is not a rule of belief revision, not, that is to say, a rule of inference, what chance is there of *Just*'s being one? And if the rules of probability theory are not rules of inference why should we think that the rules of classical logic are? Harman thinks that they are not [Harman, 1986, Ch. 2]. We think so, too. We shall revisit this point in chapter 8. But we also want to make a further point about *Just*. The single best reason that we could have for supposing that *Just* has in some sense been internalized by human agents is that our competent

[22]For a stab at a more psychologically realistic approach to probability, see [Cohen, 1972].

coroborational inferences are legitimized by *Just* and that the reason for thinking so is that *Just* is a correct rule of inference. But it seems all but certain that *Just* is not a good rule of inference. So although it is quite true that our competent corroborations are what they are in virtue of something about us that makes them so, we have no reason to think that it is, or is described by, *Just*.

Probabilistic causality is not by any means trouble-free. For one thing, there are worries about the explanatory potential of probabilistic statements.

> A primary reason for believing that causal laws cannot be reduced to probabilistic laws is broadly inductive: no attempts so far have been successful. The most notable attempts recently are by the philosophers Patrick Suppes and Wesley Salmon, and in the social sciences by a group of sociologists and econometricians working on causal models, of whom Herbert Simon and Hubert Blalock are good examples.
>
> [Cartwright, 1983a, p. 23][23]

The trouble is that a cause seems not always to increase the probability of its effect. There is a celebrated Norwegian study on smoking and heart disease [Belke, 1975]. We say with some confidence that smoking causes heart disease. It is reasonable to expect that the probability of heart disease is greater among smokers than otherwise. Granting the truth of the causal link between smoking and cardiac trouble, the dominance of the conditional probability over the unconditional probability will be overridden if smoking is correlated with intake of dietary vitamin A or with exercising. Preventative factors tend to suppress the expected probabilities. This is explained to some extent by Simpson's paradox [Simpson, 1951].[24]

Nancy Cartwright proposes to recover the link between causality and enlarged probabilities by qualifying the increase in probability in the following way:

> C causes E if and only if C increase the probability of E in every situation which is otherwise causally homogenous with respect to E. [Cartwright, 1983a, p. 25]

This is not offered 'as an analysis; as such it would be circular but it might nevertheless succeed as a constraint relating causation to probabilities' [Lewis, 1986, p. 177, fn. 4].

[23]Cartwright's references to Suppes and Salmon are: [Suppes, 1970a, fn. 31] and [Salmon, 1971].

[24]A good discussion of a forbear of Simpson's Paradox can be found in [Cohen and Nagel, 1934].

Probabilistic causality need not be tied to conditional probability. In some accounts, causality is counterfactual probability. David Lewis proposes this:

> c occurs, e has some chance x of occurring, and as it happens e does occur; if c had not occurred, e would still have had some chance y of occurring, but only a very slight chance since y would have been very much less than x. We cannot quite say that without the cause, the effect would not have occurred; but we can say that without the cause, the effect would have been much less probable than it was.

And yet,

> 'I think we should say that e depends causally on c and that c is a cause of e'. [Lewis, 1986, p. 176]

Whatever their rough spots, probabilistic accounts of causality are attractive for anyone who finds the world chancy; and 'chancy enough so that most things that happen had some chance, immediately before hand, of not happening'. (See also [Hacking, 1990].) It is nothing but right to think of the world in this way. Better, then, to equip ourselves with an account of causation under indeterministic assumptions, 'causation of events for which prior conditions were not lawfully sufficient' [Hacking, 1990]. Of course, it could be that the world is not chancy. In that case we would have overprepared ourselves in producing probabilistic accounts of causality. But doing so would have been no disaster, since such accounts also provide for causation under assumptions of determinism. Moreover, under deterministic assumptions it can be seen that regularity analyses of causality all but give the same conditions for causal dependence as the counterfactual account does. So we concede that it might be said that it is the assumption of indeterminism that shows non-regularity accounts to better advantage. See [Lewis, 1986, pp. 162,169, fn. 11]. We propose, therefore, to stay with probabilistic causality.[25]

[25]For an important development, see [Eells, 1991], which builds on the work of Suppes and Salmon and others and is in several ways a significant advance upon it. Still, for our purposes Eells' treatment is a liability. Relevance is embedded in the analytical account of probabilistic causality. Suppes' theory is free of such encumbrance. Another attempt to capture causality probabilistically is [Pearl, 2000]

7.6 Agendas: A First Pass

Definition 7.1 (Relevance) *Information* **I** *is relevant for* **X** *with respect to agenda* **A** *iff in processing* **I**, **X** *is affected in ways that advance or close* **A**.

An agenda may involve things an agent desires to know or would find it useful to know for the transaction of certain tasks, or the making of certain decisions in some contextually circumscribed circumstances or states of affairs he is disposed to realize. An agenda is something like a network of tasks or programmes to be discharged. Agendas are more or less global or comprehensive. Taking it upon oneself to obtain a good arts degree is both a more global agenda than discovering the whereabouts of Central Station and less global than undertaking to live an honourable and productive life.

We note here that one of the criticisms pressed against SW-relevance is that it does a bad job of capturing 'pre-theoretic' relevance [Levinson, 1989, 467]. In many ways this is right; but the criticism is blunted by Sperber and Wilson's disavowal of any intention to preserve the pre-theoretic meaning of relevance. Still it does not preserve it (very well), whereas by the lights of agenda relevance Levinson's own account does much better. Levinson analyses relevance in the context of communicative interaction; he proposes that 'pre-theoretical relevance is largely about the satisfaction of others' goals in interaction, and the satisfaction of topical and sequencing constraints in discourse, as in the expectation that an answer will follow a question ... ' [Levinson, 1989, 467]. The affinity to agenda relevance is unmistakable. This same conception is clearly at work in Levinson's attempt to secure the post-*SW* fortunes of neo-Gricean pragmatics [Levinson, 2001, 17, 46, 51–52, 163–164, 380 n.4].

Some agendas never close, for example, the living of an honourable and productive life. Agendas such as these can be terminated, of course. Death terminates them. But termination is not what we meant by closure. To close an agenda one completes its various constituent tasks or the subagendas which are linked to it. In simple situations in which we have an agenda of low complexity, it is sometimes possible to induce gross performance-orderings. If the agenda were to produce some stiffened egg whites, then some idea of order of procedure is available to us: separate some eggs, collect the whites into an appropriate vessel, apply a wire whisk in the appropriate ways, do this for a certain length of time, then stop. Tasks are not in general so procedurally lucid and, in any event, vanishingly few tasks of whatever procedural transparency lie open to the guidance of algorithms. Even for the simplest constituent programmes the route from intention to action is deeply probabilistic, involving gross averages of possible stochastic sample paths. 'There is more than one way to skin a cat' is a huge understatement at the right levels of description.

This is significant. In an important sense we often don't know what we are doing until we've done it, and once done it is rare that we know, except *en gros*, how it got done. On one view of such things, we would do well to surrender to a notion of practical spontaneity. Better, we think, to postulate for our stochastic sample paths a loosely causal import. For one thing, the causalness of relevance takes on a renewed appeal. For how could information relevant to the closure of agendas not have a casual role?

People carry around with them numerous agendas. On awakening, Harry might call down to Sarah, 'Did it rain last night?', 'Did you find my polka-dot tie?', 'Did the dentist phone?', and 'Where is Harry Jr.?' (Harry is a bit of a pest). In so doing he might be understood to be seeking information of service to the following interests:

- Whether to water the lawn.
- Whether to wear his grey suit.
- Whether to arrange to leave the office early.
- Whether to scold Harry Jr. before leaving for the office or sometime later.

Grudging ontologists might complain. What, they might ask, are the identity conditions for agendas? Have we here Many or One? We will not here press such questions. Suffice it to say that several agendas (whether ultimately reckonable as One or Many) can be carried into the cognitive fray more or less concurrently and with varying degrees of urgency and dormancy. (Dormancy: In 1990, Harry asked an art dealer to let him know when a minor Corot lithograph could be had reasonably. Then he forgot about it. Now, he receives a letter from the dealer. 'I can get you a Corot print for under $4,000.' 'Super,' cries Harry, as he reaches for the phone to contact his bank manager. Lucky Harry.)

Agendas sometimes call for information of a type that **X** more or less expressly desires to have, and also for information which he would desire to have if only he knew about it, so to speak. There is in this the difference between recruitment and happenstance. Harry asks, 'Did you find my polka-dot tie?' recruiting a Yes or No answer. Sarah replies, 'Your grey suit isn't back from the cleaners' (happenstance). Harry didn't get what he recruited for, but Sarah's reply was completely relevant for his agenda, for he decides to wear his blue suit. His agenda has closed.

In section 13.2.5, we make a proposal regarding what we call Sperber–Wilson abduction revision. On that proposal, it could be abduced from Sarah's answer that Harry wanted to wear his grey suit, under the assumption of maximizing contextual effects.

Suppose that another of Harry's agendas is to determine whether to drive his car to the office today. He gets out of bed, looks down at the street and checks for snow (recruitment). The snow is piled high. But he also notices that his windshield is smashed (happenstance). He decides to take the bus.

It is also necessary to make a distinction between taking information in and integrating information with beliefs that service an agenda. Human beings take in and file all sorts of information with which they do nothing (else). Such information is understood, accepted (for a while), remembered (for a while); it may be more or less interesting in its own right, but it is not acted on. Information of this sort obviously changes minds, for it is understood, remembered, stored up in belief-inventories and so on. It is best to think of such information not as having no relevance whatever, but rather as having no particular relevance apart from whatever interest it may have in and of itself. Information of this kind can possess determinate relevance *potential*, however. Remembering a long-forgotten fact about the accused, a fact of no particular relevance, say that he was in Athens in 1944 (not 1943), may, once remembered, secure a conviction in the criminal courts.[26] *Utter* irrelevance is better reserved for information that doesn't get processed at all, or not enough to be noticed or remembered. It is worth noting that psychoanalysts (for example) may have a more generous appreciation than others of the relevance potential of what the laity would regard as utterly irrelevant information. It matters here whether we are speaking of Harry, say, or his belief-adjustment device f. Information utterly irrelevant *for* Harry might be relevant *to* f.

The distinction inchoately at hand might be brought out more sharply by attending to some central issues which require consideration in their

[26]For a charming example of what we are calling relevance potential, see [Latour, 1987, pp. 11–12]. Latour tells us of James Watson, hot on the discovery of the double helix: 'To his amazement [Watson] realizes that the shapes drawn by pairing adenine with thymine and guanine with cytosine are superimposable. The steps of the double helix have the same shape. Contrary to his earlier model, the structure might be complementary instead of being like-with-like. He hesitates a while, because he sees no reason for this complementarity. Then he remembers what was (sic) called 'Chargaff laws' ... These 'laws' stated that there was always as much adenine as thymine and as much guanine as cytosine, no matter which DNA one chose to analyze. This isolated fact, devoid of any meaning in his earlier like-with-like model, suddenly brings new strength to his emerging model. Not only are the pairs superimposable, but Chargaff laws can be made a consequence of his model'.

own right. Relevance is defined for triples of items of information, cognitive agents and agendas. Agendas we have recently been considering, and there is more to come in the following section. We should now say something about cognitive agents.

7.7 Cognitive Agency

We have been thinking of cognitive agents in ways that suggest competent human reasoning. This is part of the story, but not all. For reasons that will shortly appear, it is inadvisable to cleave to the competent-human-reasoner paradigm. The reason for this is that relevance is not restricted to information in relation to its conscious consumption by human beings. Not all consumers of information are human, not all are primates, and not all are organisms. A laptop computer or a thermostat might well figure in a fuller story of how the relevance relation gets deployed. A cognitive agent could be thought of as an information-processing system that is capable of transforming analogue information into digital information. So as a first pass, we have

♡ **Proposition 7.2 (Cognitive Agency)** *A cognitive agent is an information-processor capable of analogue–digital conversion.*

Here we try a suggestion of Dretske. Most information-processing devices are awash in information. Information comes to such a device by way of its sensors, by way (as Quine says) of sensory irritation. In the case of the thermostat, the information which floods in comes from the molecular turbulence of the air upon its bimetallic strip. Dretske would say that this is information for the thermostat in analogue form. For a human perceptor, analog information flow is his field of vision. A smart thermostat makes something of this unbounded and continuous flow. It makes something discrete of it; it classifies it as 'warm' or 'cold'. Or, in another case, Helen notices that Sarah is taller than Harry. In each case information has been digitized. This is what we mean by cognition — or, more carefully, digitization of information is a necessary condition, and large part, of cognition.

So what is it that the digitizer can do that the non-digitizer cannot? It can abstract, classify and edit information. It can code information in a particular way. If you look at a photograph of Harry and Sarah you can notice, as Helen did, that Sarah is taller than Harry. If it is a good picture, you might make a fair guess about how much taller she is. If they were in their swimming togs when snapped, you might also notice that Sarah is longer in the trunk than he, but not longer in the leg. But consider, now, that you are unacquainted with our couple and that no photo of them has come your way. Someone informs you that Sarah is taller than Harry by uttering 'Sarah is taller than Harry' — this is the form in which you have the information that Sarah is taller than Harry. It does not inform you of other things as the photo does. It embeds no information about how much taller she is or about what parts of her are longer. In the first case, the photo gives you information in analogue form. In the other case, you have a digitization of it.

A piece of information is our infon. In this, we follow Devlin notationally. We might consider going further with Devlin, as follows. Information is analogue information. *Items* of information — infons — might be thought of as digitizations of information.[27] Although it seems unnecessary, in fact, undesirable to invoke the distinction between information and infons in the general scheme for relevance, it is quite clear that from time to time the theory will need to attend to it, as we have lately seen. Utter irrelevance we attributed to information that doesn't get processed at all, or not enough, to be noticed or remembered. We can try to be more precise:

♡ **Definition 7.3 (Utter irrelevance)** **I** *is utterly irrelevant for* **X** *with regard to* **A** *iff* **I** *cannot be digitized by* **X**.

Two conceptions of relevance potential now suggest themselves.

♡ **Proposition 7.4 (Relevance potential)** **I** *has relevance potential for* **X** *with respect to* **A** *if* **I** *is analogue information for* **X** *and there is a digitization of it* **I*** *of which* **X** *is capable such that* **I*** *is relevant for* **X** *with regard to* **A**, *and* **X** *has not converted* **I** *to* **I***.

And,

♡ **Proposition 7.5 (Relevance potential)** **I** *has relevance potential for* **X** *with regard to* **A** *if* **I** *is a digitization of analogue information for* **X** *and, given* **X***'s capabilities* **I** *could come to be relevant for* **X** *with respect to some future* **A**.

It is a nice question as to what qualifications to attach to 'could'. In a modally promiscuous world virtually any digitization *could* be relevant for any agent with regard to virtually any agenda. It is all a matter of the causal success that an item of information might come to enjoy with regard to agenda-closure or agenda advancement. Proposition 7.5 seeks to moderate the promiscuity by reference to the totality of actions available to him.

[27] [Devlin, 1991, p. 107]. See also [Dretske, 1986, p. 142] and [Barwise, 1989a; Seligman, 1990].

This determines, as we shall see, the totality of agendas he can define. No agent is capable of everything, but even cognitive agents are capable of a great deal that we (and they) would not rejoice in. In particular, agents are capable of horrendous blunders; and proposition 7.5 leaves it open that information might possess relevance potential the realization of which by any agent for given agendas would be nothing but a blunder. More realistically, proposition 7.5 encompasses the following kind of situation. Perhaps it is not far-fetched to assume that Harry possesses all sorts of digitized information which advances no agenda he currently has. If this is so, such information has relevance potential to the extent that Harry could come to have agendas that would be advanced by it. Intuitively, this seems a cogent notion of relevance potential. Harry possesses the information, having read it in the *Times*, that the Nikkei has fallen by some 630 points. Later Lou proposes that Harry join him in purchasing shares in a company listed in Tokyo. Harry now has something to decide. He decides not to bother. Seen this way, it is hard to impose *a priori* bounds on relevance potential. It is hard to think of information for which no agenda could be taken up that would make it relevant to it. Perhaps inconsistent information would fit the bill, but there is, as we will see in due course, reason to resist the suggestion.

It is important that intuitions tug in opposite directions. Doing so places substantial weight on the idea of agendas. Taken one way it seems a plausible conjecture that all of Harry's information carries relevance potential. In that case, the distinction between information for Harry and potentially relevant information for Harry is, in Hume's words, a distinction of reason; 'potentially relevant' is redundant in the context $\ulcorner$**I** is potentially relevant information for **X**$\urcorner$. On the other hand, it may be that anything that qualifies as information for Harry advances or closes an agenda in virtue of which it gets to be so. Does Harry have an agenda to digitize information? Does he have an agenda to acquire analogue information? And could it be that the having of such information depends upon Harry's having those agendas? If so, a contrary intuition is cashed. All information for Harry is relevant for him with respect to those agendas necessary for his having that information in the first place. As we proceed, it will become clear that we want to make rather liberal use of the idea of agendas. It will emerge that any information processed by an information-processing agent is relevant with respect to its information-processing agendas. This may strike us as countenancing far too much relevance. It is not radically excessive provision for relevance, but it is quite a lot of it all the same. We want, nevertheless to stick with the idea and to try to make good on it. Success implies that information, all of it, qualifies as relevant and potentially relevant (hence irrelevant) at once. But this is no bother. We know it already.

Information is both relevant and (only) potentially relevant relative to different agendas. It is precluded only that information be both relevant and (only) potentially relevant with respect to identical agendas under strictly monitored identity conditions. The information that the Nikkei had fallen 630 points was relevant for Harry with respect to his agenda to digitize information but, as before, it was only potentially relevant with respect to the unactivated agenda to decide whether to purchase shares in that Tokyo company.

♡ **Proposition 7.6 (Relevance potential)** *Information* **I** *has relevance potential for* **X** *just in case it would be made relevant for* **X** *upon the emergence of the appropriate agenda. (We note that Proposition 7.6 is preserved in the formal model of Part III. See Remark 15.15 of Chapter 15.)*

We also now have it that in a rather intuitive way the idea of utter irrelevance is substantially deflated, whereupon definition 7.3 is derailed. If any information that Harry manages to process is relevant for Harry with respect to information-processing agendas, then no information that Harry has is utterly irrelevant (and the idea that irrelevance has something principled to do with analogue information lapses).

Utter irrelevance is tricky. It invokes the idea of information somehow received but not processed, fully or at all. We seem to be speaking of what psychologists call *attention*. Attention theories take note of the fact that, at any given time, of the information received only some is attended to and less still is reacted to or remembered. The theorist might conjecture that some is analogue only; others are digitizations held in readiness for action; and still others are digitizations that are indeed acted on. He might go on to propose that the middle group invites a further refinement. Some digitizations are those for which action is not contextually appropriate and others are those for which action is not contextually inappropriate but unperformed. In each case the theorist can postulate the absence of attention. In the one case the inattention is little more than what would be expected; in the other the theorist is right to be regretful, for the relevance of information has been lost on our agent.

We have been making it appear as if, short of relevance potential, analogue information sustains no actual case of relevance. But consider the following case.

Sarah, distracted by Freddie's death, is driving her car. The traffic light turns red and, not paying attention, Sarah drives on. The information signalled by the red light seems to have been utterly irrelevant for Sarah. But it caused her pupils to contract. It was a factor in the causal matrix affecting a change in pupillary disposition, and so it might be said to have been relevant to *that*. It seems unobjectionable, in fact desirable, that a causal account of relevance provides for the red light's relevance in this way. On reflection, one should want a causal theory to generalize beyond the sway of changes of mind. But now the question is, how do we demarcate information involved in changes of mind and information, causally efficacious information, not thus involved? That we have need of such a demarcation may be reflected in the idiomatic difference between 'relevant for' and 'relevant to'. The changing of the light to red proved not to be relevant for Sarah, though it was a factor relevant to the change in her vision, which may be relevant to another agent.

We might think that Sarah's situation is elucidated by the analogue/digital distinction. Sarah's pupil contracted in response to analogue information. The information embedded the information that the light was red. So perhaps Sarah's failure to attend or to notice was her failure to digitize that unattended information. If that were so, we could suggest an amplification of the distinction between relevant to and relevant for. We might decide to say that **I** was relevant *to* (what happened to) **X** just in case **I** was analogue information (only) for **X** and yet **I** was absorbed by **A** in ways that induced the thing that happened to it. We might say that **I** was relevant *for* **X** just in case **I** was a digitization for **X** and **I** played a role in advancing or closing some agenda of **X**. Underlying these speculations is the idea that digitization suffices for attentiveness. So Sarah didn't pay attention to the red light, even though it impacted on her retina, because she didn't digitize the information at hand, so to speak.

It won't do. As Dretske concedes, 'every signal carries information in both analogue and digital form'[Dretske, 1986, p. 137]. For one thing, Sarah's retinal action itself involves a digitization of analogue information. There is lots of digitized information which agents like Sarah will not and cannot attend to. Another more general reason for discounting present suggestions is that if they were sound, then a good psychological theory of attention would be one in which the analogue/digital distinction plays deep and central explanatory roles. There is, however, no good reason at present to think that it would make any such use of this distinction. (See e.g., [Shiffrin *et al.*, 1974] and [Shiffrin and Grantham, 1974].) So we must be careful not to overload it with unrealistic expectations. The analogue/digital distinction has its uses, but it will not elucidate Sarah's running the light and, so, will not serve in the explication of the distinction between relevant to and relevant for. Neither will it endorse our definition 7.3 of utter irrelevance.

This is not to say that the analogue/digital distinction is inapplicable to cases of the Sarah kind. Sarah's mishap is made interesting because there is so little difference in information-theoretic terms between an episode of normal competent driving for Sarah, and the episode in which she runs the light. 'I just didn't see it', she says afterwards, her way of underscoring the slightness of the difference from her standard driving performance. So let us consider the standard case, the case in which Sarah shows herself to be an attentive driver. How is it to be characterized information-theoretically? The answer is that by and large analogue processes are involved, not digital; the flow of information in continuous and 'curvey' rather than discrete and step-like. If this is right, then it cannot be true that Sarah's inattentiveness in the case in which she ran the light is explicable as a function of her failure to digitize information which, in the standard case, she would have digitized. For in the standard case she does not digitize it.

It is necessary again to consider levels of description. As we see, at one level of description, at the level (say) of human psychology, the attention-inattention matrix is largely an analogue arrangement. It may be that at other — as we say, lower — levels the attention-inattention matrix is largely a digital affair. This would be true at the quantum mechanical level if, as some make so bold to say, everything is digital. So we might imagine that corresponding to Sarah's noticing the light, as she does in a standard driving situation, there is a microphysical counterpart whose information-theoretic structure is digital. But it would not be true that the difference between her standard and her light-running situations is that in the latter the analysis of the corresponding microphysical system is analogue in character. For, at that level, there aren't any analogue structures.

In a well-known study, researchers present a computer model for attention and problem solving, similar in many ways to Anderson's ACT* [Anderson, 1983, Ch. 1 *et passim*]. The model contains productions linked together in a network which allows activation to spread from node to node. In this model, the extent to which something is attended to is represented by the extent to which its node (representation) is active, and this is an analogue function (approximately) [Hunt and Lansman, 1986]. In a later study, Cohen, McClelland and Dunbar designed a computer model to mimic the Stroop[28] effect in people, using PDP architecture [Cohen *et al.*, 1990]. Considerable success was reported, matching or exceeding the performance of the programs of rival theories. The present program used an on/off

[28]The Stroop effect: Subjects see a colour word (e.g., 'RED') printed in a given colour (e.g. green). Subjects who are instructed to attend to the word can readily identify it, even when it is printed, as here, in a 'conflicting' colour. However, attending subjects find the process of naming it easier (the response times are faster) when the colour matches the word, and more difficult (much slower RTs) when the colour conflicts with the word. 'RED' in red is easily handled either for colour name or for word name. Word names are readily given for colour names in green, but colour names are not.

model of attention arousal, but this was because degrees of arousal were not under study. It was concluded that the presumed dichotomy between controlled tasks (requiring conscious attention) and automatic tasks was in fact a continuum from tasks with indirect input to output links to tasks with very direct links. This is a result that bears on our question. Could the analogue/digital distinction, we asked, elucidate the intuitive distinction between inattention and attention? There is further reason now to think not. The analogue/digital distinction is strewn all along the continuum between controlled attention and automatic attention.

It is worth noticing that the notion of relevance is well-embedded in statistical studies of causation. The Norwegian study, lately touched on, of the causes of smoking sought to explain the following puzzle. If cigarette smoking causes lung cancer, why do so few smokers contract it? The study went on to suggest that, whereas levels of dietary vitamin A was a relevant factor, the incidence of smoking was probably not. Leaving to one side the question of the study's accuracy, we see how effortlessly the relevance idiom spills over onto causal milieux beyond an agent's being affected by information in ways that advance an agenda. For our purposes here we wish to stay mainly on the far side of the divide, and so the demarcation question recurs. How are we to understand the demarcation? Understand it we can, we believe, and in ways that call the analogue/digital distinction back into play. But it plays obliquely.

♡ **Definition 7.7 (Relevance-to)** *Information is relevant to an information processing agent* **X** *just in case it was processed by* **X**, *but in processing it,* **X** *was not functioning as a cognitive agent.*

Here, for ease of exposition, we take some abstract liberties. **X** is the sample of smoking Norwegians and **I** is dietary intakes of vitamin A. **I** was certainly digitized twice over, both collectively and severally, in that sample and in its individual smokers. So by our present test for cognitive agency, cognitive agency is at work at some levels of description — at the level of biochemistry, for example. But in that situation no individual Norwegian digitized the information; no individual Norwegian was a cognitive agent with respect to those biochemical conversions, and still less the collective sample. We note in passing that definition 7.7 begins to redeem the pledge of pages ago to try to fix the idea that any information an agent might process is relevant information, and yet at the same time to discourage the objection that in saying so we make promiscuous provision for relevance. The distinction between relevance-to and relevance-for is now a theoretically motivated one. We would expect relevance-to to have a more liberal provenance than relevance-for; and it does.

It may strike us as odd to speak of human beings as incorporating devic(that qualify as cognitive agents with regard to processes concerning whic they themselves fail the same qualifications. It shouldn't. Recall the ro assigned to f. It is perfectly straightforward that one is not a cogniti\ agent with regard to, say, the pupillary responses of one's eye. One's eye another matter. We have it here that the eye is a cognitive agent with regaı to its processing of photons. Perhaps this is too odd for comfort. Reli(is available once it is recalled that capacity for the digital conversion (analogue information was offered only as a necessary condition on cogniti\ agency. We ourselves might be prepared to accommodate to the oddne: provisionally, but we do not insist upon it for others. Either way there aı problems. If we go this way, we are left with the chore of accounting for tl difference between parts and wholes in such a way that, for certain kinds (information processing, the parts count as cognitive agents and the whol(do not. If we go the other way, cognitive agency is unanchored to sufficieı conditions.

7.8 Propositional Relevance Revisited

In chapters 5 and 6 we repeatedly asserted that if one is looking for conceptual analysis of the common notion of relevance, it is a mistake t define relevance as a propositional relation. In support of this claim, w tried to cite difficulties that arise in the various propositional approach(examined so far.

Our main complaint has been that, in one way or another, the prop(sitional accounts have been too 'coarse-grained' to capture the essence (what we see as the core notion of relevance. This is a complaint which w see no reason to abandon. But care needs to be taken in persisting wit it. For one thing, the propositional accounts that we have criticized coı stitute a sample which we have done nothing to show even comes close t exhausting the type. Accordingly, we are far from having established th: propositional analyses of relevances are inherently defective realizers of tl common notion of relevance. A second matter that calls for caution is tha in some criticisms of theories of propositional relevance, we have claime to have discerned the presence of internal difficulties. These are difficulti(that typically afflict, not a theory's basic programme, but rather its pa ticular mode of execution. A clear example of this contrast is afforded t disputes about implication. The general programme is to represent implic: tion as a relation on propositions. Some theorists reject classical analyses (implication as inadequate (or worse). Right or wrong, they are not rejectin the general idea that implication is a propositional relation. They are sa ing (rightly or wrongly) that there are difficulties with partiuclar features of the account — e.g., that in certain respects it contradicts what we all understand the common notion of implication to be.

It is no less true of relevance that problems with a particular version of it may do nothing at all to overturn the basic idea that relevance is propositional.

Our own point of departure is *not* that relevance is not a propositional relation and not that propositional relevance is no part of relevance as commonly conceived. Ours is the more circumspect (and, we think, accurate) claim that, in tracking the common analysis of relevance, it is ill-advised to *begin* with propositional relevance or to think of it as the *basic idea.*

Although we stand by our criticisms of the various propositional systems we have reviewed, we do not say that relevance is not in any way propositional. We do not want to make light of our criticisms. They have been mustered against most of the known ways in which theorists have tried to see relevance as propositional. If our criticims have been just, they do amount, therefore, to a significant indictment of the general project of propositional relevance. But, as in a court of law, indictments are one thing and convictions are another. For one thing, indictments are in general easier to answer than convictions are to overturn.

Our indictment of the propositional approach is indeed answerable. We ourselves intend to answer it. We see it as one of the tasks for the formal part of this book to resuscitate a propositional conception of relevance. This we deal with in the formal model developed in chapters 14 and 15. Lest anyone think that our venture into propositional relevance is sheer abandonment of earlier criticisms, it should be said that the propositional relevance of these later chapters will emerge as abstractions from the core ideas whose conceptual analysis we are now in the process of presenting. This leads us to say that a propositional conception of relevance might be all right if two conditions are met: first, that it not be taken for all of what relevance is; and, second, that the basic conception of relevance of which propositional relevance is an abstraction not itself be a propositional conception of it.

In our view, we lie much closer to this desired basicness by seeing relevance as agenda relevance, in which there is a linkage between information, agents, and agendas. This may be right, but it is rightness that comes with a cost. We must try to be clear about the three relata of relevance so conceived — information, agendas and agendas. The chapters to come, on top of what has been said so far, is reserved for agendas.

Chapter 8

Agendas

> *Tasks* ... [are] ... certain-two-place-relations-in-intension between persons and moments ... To say that x *performs* the task R at t is to say that x bears the relation-in-intension R to t.
>
> [Montague, 1974, p. 151]

8.1 Plans

Intuitively, agendas resemble Michael Bratman's plans [Bratman, 1987, esp. Ch. 3]. Plans, says Bratman, are like intentions, only more complex. Plans, like intentions, resist reconsideration — they possess inertia. They are both 'conduct controllers'. They 'provide crucial inputs for further practical reasoning and planning' [Montague, 1974, p. 29]. Plans enable us to make prior deliberations which shape future behaviour.

> In the search for coordination and effective action we simply are not capable of constantly redetermining, without inordinate cost, what would be the best thing to do in the present, given an updated assessment of likelihoods of our own and other future actions. [Montague, 1974, p. 28]

We are not, as Bratman says, 'frictionless deliberators'.

The greater complexity of plans over simple intentions is revealed in further and special features of them. For example, plans are partial. They are not the total strategies governed by what Savage calls 'look before you leap' principles, which provide that a 'person decides 'now' once for all;

there is nothing for him to wait for, because his one decision provides for all contingencies' ([Savage, 1972, p. 17], cf. [Bratman, 1987, p. 178, n. 2]).

Plans are also hierarchal. 'Plans concerning ends embed plans concerning means and preliminary steps; and more general intentions (for example, my intention to go to a concert tonight) embed more specific ones (for example, my intention to hear the Alma Trio)' [Bratman, 1987, p. 29]. The partial and hierarchal character of plans suit the make-up of cognitive and deliberative agents especially well. On the one hand we have neither the time nor the information to make complete plans, by and large, yet if we did not have some access to prior deliberation we would be overwhelmed by the unplanned-for immediacy of every undeliberated moment. The more partial a plan is, the more it is likely to be general. General plans Bratman likens to 'projects' that structure lives 'in a way analogous to the way in which more specific plans for a day structure deliberation and action that day'. Very general plans are 'radically partial' and have to be filled in as events turn, and that 'is a virtue of such plans' [Bratman, 1987, p. 30].

Bratman believes, over-hastily we think, that plans cannot support coordination and cannot influence future action unless they conform to the requirements of consistency with respect to what the planner believes and of means–end coherence. The consistency of a plan makes it completely implementable should the planner's beliefs be true and a plan's means–end coherence provides that the plan fills in efficiently over time in ways that realize the end in question. It is clear that there are pragmatic constraints on plans, considerations in virtue of which normally they are practically implementable. Thus they are also defeasible [Bratman, 1987, p. 32]. Plans are a filter on admissible options for consideration about what to consider and how to act.

Bratman's notion of plan has affinities to some of the main developments in AI. Much of contemporary planning theory in computer science is extensions or adaptations of *state-based planning systems*, implemented as STRIPS in [Fikes and Nilsson, 1971]. Alternative approaches include the *situation calculus* of [McCarthy and Hayes, 1969] and a *dynamic logic for semantic programs* developed in [Harel, 1984] and [Rosenschein, 1981]. Common to all going theories of planning is the idea that plans require intentions, that they are goal-oriented.

As we develop the idea here, plans will turn out to bear some resemblance to only a proper subset of what we call agendas. For one thing, Bratman's plans and AI plans are (or contain) mental entities whereas our agendas mostly are not and do not (see below, section 8.3.1). Pending further clarification, perhaps eyes are cognitive agents. If so, there is a principled reason to attribute agendas to them, but none at all to attribute minds. The figure of the mind's eye may be all right for certain purposes. But we will have no use for the figure of the eye's mind.

Whether it is desirable to postulate unconscious or tacit agendas might be influenced, though not determined, by the same question for plans. It seems clear that Bratman's plans won't stretch to such limits, and it is here especially that a decision is required: Shall we allow freer reign to agendas? Our answer must give due weight to the presumptions about relevance which our theory attempts to acknowledge. We have already suggested that there might be no radical discontinuity between the role of information in changes of mind and its role beyond the sway of mind as when the colour of the changed traffic light which was information causally significant to Sarah's retina. If this is right, it might be that there is no radical difference between agendas that underwrite relevance for and those that underwrite relevance-*to*. So agendas are not always plans.

8.2 Representation

Subject to a qualification, the following seems to us to be a plausible conjecture. Lots of organisms have biologically controlled mechanisms for the operation of which the idea of information is intelligible. These, it may be said, are information-program systems. If we wanted to restrict the idea of relevance to relevance *for* a cognitive agent then we can define for information-program systems in which it is a condition that the information is that it be *represented*. Representation we take in Millikan's way [Millikan, 1984, pp. 12–13]. For example, '[s]entences, and thoughts are representations; bee dances, though they are information-programme systems', are not [Millikan, 1984, p. 12]. What makes representations special is that when they function properly their referents are identified.[1] On the other hand, 'Von Frisch knew what bee dances are about, but it is unlikely that bees do.' [Millikan, 1984, p. 13].

Relevance-to puts us in mind of compiled programs and, by extension, of compiled agendas. Think of a procedure written in some logic for calculating the amount of tax a citizen pays. After years of experience, the tax office decides that it would be advantageous (a saving of labour and public relations costs) if they simply accepted all tax returns without ever checking them. The agenda of collecting taxes is now *compiled* to an essentially stimulus-response program. (Of course, the authorities must take care to keep the public unaware of the compilation.)

[1]This too is disputed. We appear to understand utterances (e.g. those includig talk of 'beeches' and 'elms') wihtout being able to identify the denotations.

We know of no entirely satisfactory way of putting an *à priori* lower bound on relevance defined for non-representational information-program systems. Perhaps we lack a settled body of intuitions here, if that mattered greatly. A bee spots some nectar and does a bee dance. Its movements 'bear a certain relation to or are a certain function of the direction (relative to the sun), distance, quality, and/or quantity of the nectar spotted.' [Millikan, 1984, p. 39]. Interpreter bees take the bee dance information into a direction of flight which reflects the observed dance and the whereabouts of the nectar. This is not representation. 'Bee dances ... do *not* contain denotative elements, because interpreter bees do not identify the referents of these devices but merely react to them appropriately' [Millikan, 1984, p. 71]. Even so, we might wish to say that the information of the bee dance was relevant *to* the interpreter bees with respect to the design of their flight plans. If so, the notion of representation (and the related notion of change of mind) now defers to the notion of appropriate response, as suggested at the close of the previous section. It should be noted that the concept of representation-talk is problematic for informational semantics in other ways. If representations are held to be items in causal matrices, it is necessary to ask whether their ontological status permits them such roles. If representations are concrete they can be expected to be causally unproblematic; but this leaves us with the chore of specifying their concreteness in ways that are compatible with their representational (and truth-value-bearing) character. If representations are abstract, they would seem to fall prey to Benacerraf's Dilemma. For how can abstract entities enter into causal relations? The short answer is that we don't know. A longer answer would involve resisting the suggestion that they can't. We leave the development of this point for another occasion. (But see Woods [2002c]. See also [Benacerraf, 1973, p. 662].) The Dilemma is approvingly discussed by, e.g., [Bonevac, 1982]. For resistance to the Dilemma, see [Maddy, 1990].

Should we then reserve the notion of relevance for those non-representational information-program systems that are also biological systems? The temperature in the room descends to 18 degrees C and the thermostat responds by telling the furnace to go on; and it does. Was that information relevant for the thermostat with regard to its furnace-management program? We have our doubts. Even so (this is the qualification mentioned above), we don't want to lose sight of the case that is made against universal representationalism in cognitive processing, briefly discussed in section 3.2.6. If the case for anti-representationalism is correct, certain cognitive states are non-representational, and yet are also states for which relevance is an applicable notion.

We are inclined to think that the information is better said to be relevant *to* what the thermostat does rather than relevant *for* it. But it is not clear what, even if it were true, such betterness would show. Once you admit thermometer-thermostat systems into the relevance family, it becomes very hard indeed to block the admissibility of any causal system. Any causal transaction is interpretable information-theoretically, and any causal outcome can be interpreted as programmed output of informational input. So, in a high Chicago (or worse, Lethbridge) wind, the bough breaks and falls to the ground. We will not want to say that the wind was relevant for the bough with regard to its gravitational programme, but we may agree to say that it was relevant to what happened. Our own suggestion is that we reserve the relevance idiom for those causal systems whose information-theoretic description seem most natural and of significant explanatory value. This will not permit us to draw fine lines, but it will capture the clear cases. While it is all right, it is also rather quaint to speak of the wind's breaking the bough and causing it to fall as information relevant to the bough with regard to its gravitational agenda; and you certainly don't, in talking this way, get a better explanation of what happened.

Though the falling rain causes the creek to rise, it is hardly plausible that this is one of its 'Proper Functions'. (See chapter 10 below.) It is unconvincing to suggest that making creeks rise is part of the explanation of why, historically, rain falls. We can now see at least some congruence with our former rough criterion; relevance is definable for causal systems whose information-theoretic description is both natural and explanatorily useful. But we don't pretend to have found an exact solution to the cut-off problem for relevance-attributability.

The deliberative character of agendas is sometimes problematic. All sorts of things get our agent to perform all sorts of cognitively competent routines without it being obvious that there is anywhere on the scene an antecedently organized agenda searching for closure. Sarah says, 'Salt, please', and Harry passes the salt. Sarah's utterance was relevant to what Harry did, and to what was on his mind when he did it, but what agenda of *Harry's* did Harry's response close? Or, glancing out of the window, Harry notices that it is starting to sprinkle. He runs out and takes the clothes off the line. One could conjecture that cognitive agents are possessed of standing agendas that are for the most part implicit and unarticulated, the advancing of which is in the responses made to relevant information. There is some support for such a conjecture in after the fact self-examination. 'What were you about?', asks Sarah. 'I wanted to get the clothes in before the rain'. True, the notion of agenda pales somewhat in such contexts, but no more perhaps than the notion of decision.

Other explanations tug in other directions. Instead of postulating standing and largely implicit agendas of interpersonal felicity and domestic orderliness (and standing agendas to process information, come to that) we might forgo such talk on grounds that in each case the supposed agendas are merely read off from the contextually appropriate thing to have done. Because it was appropriate for Harry to have rescued the clothes, we posit for him an implicit agenda to that very effect. But here, it might be argued, the more central notion that explains the relevance of the information that it was starting to sprinkle is that it got Harry to respond to it (and perhaps that the response was appropriate). Perhaps agendas need not enter such stories; perhaps they are bypassable without cost. If this is so, it would appear that a stripped down causal notion will suffice: **I** was relevant for **X** to the extent that **I** affected **X** in ways that led to the fulfilment of conditions on appropriateness of response.

Either way, relevance stays causal and it stays definable over triples, though to be sure they are (slightly) different triples: if we opt for the implicit agenda conjecture, then relevance is, as before, definable for the ordered threesome

$$\langle \mathbf{I}, \mathbf{X}, \mathbf{A} \rangle$$

If we opt for the second approach, agendas drop out of the analysis but they are replaced by responses to stimuli, thus recurring to the idea of a compiled program

$$\langle \mathbf{I}, \mathbf{X}, \mathbf{R} \rangle$$

It could be proposed that the second threesome is the more general, perhaps also the more basic of the two. For agendas are advanced or closed always and only on the basis of *some* response to relevant information. Should we not, then, forgo the less general approach for the more general? One possibility, of course, is that the more general is too general, as when R is 'Stop bothering me with irrelevancies!" So we want to resist this line of thought. Its promise of economy is a false one. Or rather it is too economical by half. It costs us our theoretical purchase on relevance. There is a saving of a kind involved in assimilating agenda-closure to appropriateness of response (or advancing a compiled agenda). Taken thus, it seems that we can do without tacit agendas. But tacit agendas are nothing to worry about, never mind that they present challenges to the theoretical understanding. We see them as in the same boat with tacit knowledge and deep memory and the like. The proposal under view saves us an affordable cost, but this is not the main thing wrong with it.

This is a particularly damaging concession, this assimilation of relevance as information that closes agendas to relevance as information inducing the

INFORMATION PROCESSORS

Non-Cognitive Processors	Cognitive Processors
Appropriateness of response definable; **advancement of agendas** not definable.	**Appropriateness of response** and **advancement of agendas** both definable.
Relevance to definable; **relevance for** not definable.	**Relevance to** and **relevance for** both definable.

Figure 8.1

appropriate response. For isn't agenda relevance now dispossessed of its central place in theory? Shouldn't we instead be speaking of response relevance? This will depend on the starkness of the inequivalencies between the two theories. The truth is that we don't know the answer to this question. We do not know this because we do not know, for example, whether the idea of appropriate response embeds the idea of an agenda. If 'agenda' were given broad latitude, it could be that appropriateness of response for a system is always a matter of the degree of closure (one or other of) its agendas. Not knowing is one thing. Conjecturing is another. Perhaps appropriate responses are agendas that have been compiled, whether by convention or by evolution, on account of scarce resources. In any case, provided we are tolerant of tacit agendas, and bearing in mind that we have not yet foreclosed, if ever we do, on a fairly general and abstract notion of agenda proper, a strategy comes to mind.

We may take it as given that any account of appropriateness of response that makes essential use of the idea of tacit agendas advanced in fulfilment of conditions that would *intuitively* count as appropriately responsive, is an account that solicits the idea of agenda for promiscuous ends. If this is granted, it is necessary to specify for the pair *appropriate response*, *advanced agenda* a *principium divisionis* that reserves the relation of relevance for as a trait of advanced agendas, and not of appropriate responses.

It is tempting to think that, whatever else we make of it, the inequivalence between our two notions shouldn't outrun the inequivalence between information-processing systems and cognitive agents. Appropriateness of response is definable for any information-processor. Advancement or closure of agendas we might reserve for information-processors that are also cognitive agents. Doing so would give us occasion to marshall similarities and differences somewhat as follows:

Figure 8.1 is all right provided that we have an independently endorsable *principium divisionis* for the distinction between cognitive and noncognitive agents. The pressure on this would-be distinction is considerable, if only because there seems to be nowhere else to look for a plausible *principium.* Lately considered was a distinction between digitizing and non-digitizing information processors, but apparently to no avail. It would be well, then, to abandon our earlier cavalierness which put the notion of cognitive discrimination in the embrace of digitization. Now we have a reason to discourage such latitude, for we want to preserve a distinction between relevance for and relevance to, and the related difference between appropriateness of responses and advancement of agendas.

There is an intuition about such things. We would do well to cash it. It provides that at least a good part of the story as to why Harry is a cognitive agent — never mind that he is often a silly ass — and Harry's VCR is not, is that Harry has beliefs and his VCR doesn't, and can't. When it comes to cashing the intuition a certain economy is achievable if we stay with the framework of informational semantics; though doing so will require us to make do with about half of the intuition, so to speak. False beliefs and, more generally, misinformation are serious problems for informational semantics. We have occasion, below, to speak further of this. For now it suffices to cut our intuition in half, and to make do with the half that informational semantics can plausibly handle. So we will replace Proposition 7.2 about cognitive agency with

♡ **Definition 8.1 (Cognitive agency)** **X** *is a cognitive agent iff* **X** *is an information-processor capable of belief. (Definition 8.1 is preserved in the formal model, seen in section 15.1.)*

If we stick with Dretske we can give an account of true belief. False belief is a problem for Dretske. We reserve consideration of this problem for chapter 9. True belief is for now. True belief calls back into play the idea of digitization. Consider a signal S carrying information in digital form. S carries that information in the form that-p, for example, that a is F. When S carries information in digital form on an occasion that is the semantic content of S on that occasion [Dretske, 1986, p. 177]. Given that S's carrying the information that-p requires that-p be the case, we might identify true beliefs with semantic contents.[2] On the face of it and

[2]Dretske doesn't do this. He needs a conception of belief that allows for false beliefs. The belief that a is F is an instantiation of a type of state that developed as way of carrying information in that form, i.e., in the form that a is F. A belief is any instantiation of such a structure irrespective of whether it manages to carry the appropriate information. There is something amiss with this approach, as we will see in due course.

quite apart from the problem of accounting for false beliefs, it looks as though this will do for us. Recall that the main business of section 7.3 of the previous chapter was to secure a notion of belief and a notion of truth conditions such that for certain types of information and certain types of information processor, information could be processed in ways that qualify for belief and in ways that qualify for the satisfaction or violation of truth conditions. The constraint over-all was that when information is processed in such ways it was not to be assumed that symbol manipulation was going on, it was not to be assumed that an information processor is a semantic manipulator when it possesses beliefs. Ambiguities attaching to 'semantic' may make it appear that when Dretske ascribes semantic contents to states of information processors he is assuming that linguistic information is being manipulated. He is not assuming this, in fact, nor need he assume it. 'Semantic' here refers to that in virtue of which information qualifies as belief. It is a structure insinuated by Quine's 'keystone of the mental', the 'content clause that-*p*'. We don't know what this information-forming structure is. We doubt that anyone does at present. This makes it possible that one is wrong in thinking that cognition is not centrally a linguistic affair. But this is what we do think, and Dretske's use of 'semantic' as in 'semantic content' is no discouragement of the idea. False beliefs are another thing, as we will see, and a substantial discouragement all their own.

There are some reasons to like this approach. It makes belief a central concept and organizing principle of our theory. It puts the idea of belief to work in nicely efficient ways. Belief regulates the definitions between cognitive and non-cognitive agency; between agenda-advancement and appropriateness of response; between relevance-for and relevance-to; and, as we now see, between attributions of agenda-possession that are natural and have explanatory value and those that aren't and don't.

8.3 Agendas Again

Dretske proposes

♡ **Definition 8.2 (Belief)** *Belief is information carried in completely digitized form [Dretske, 1986, p. 184].*

The definition is damaged, as we have seen, by Dretske's own admission that there is no such thing as a structure or state that carries information in completely digitized form and none that carries it in completely analogue form. We concede this as (part of) a problem for any information theoretic approach to cognitive agency and intentional cognitive states. It is an inherited problem for agenda relevance, in so far as relevance is defined for cognitive agents and cognitive agents are defined as information processors, capable of belief.

Agendas have been assigned a large role in the present account. It is desirable that they be well understood. We ourselves would settle for a lexical relief reduction by virtue of which we could say that agendas are 'nothing but' this, that, or the other well-understood thing. We have already noted a certain affinity with plans, but it is clear that agendas outreach plans in certain ways. We want to allow for unconscious or tacit (i.e. compiled) agendas and it seems unconvincing to speak so of plans.

Perhaps agendas are strategies. We don't doubt that strategies are sometimes agendas, but this is not enough to be getting on with. Although there is abundant theoretical appropriation of the idea of strategy, there is by and large no theory of what it is to *be* a strategy. 'By and large' is a needed qualification. There are exceptions. One is that in various, and influential, biological writings a strategy is just a phenotype [Smith, 1989, p. 126]. We won't say (yet) that no phenotype is an agenda, but it is clear that many agendas won't be phenotypes. Another exception has it that strategies are complete sets of instructions concerning what choice to make for every contingency that might arise. But it is also apparent that in general our agendas are not strategies in this game-theoretic sense [Brams, 1975, p. 5, fn. 6]. For the rest, strategies seem most often to be assimilated to plans

> A strategy is a unified comprehensive and integrated plan that relates the strategic [sic] advantages of the firm to the challenges of the environment. It is designed to ensure that the basic objectives of the enterprise are achieved through proper execution by the organization. [Jauch and Glueck, 1982, p. 18]

And

> [strategy] is a plan of action designed in order to achieve some end; a purpose together with a system of measures for its accomplishment. [Wylie, 1967, p. 13]

With the exceptions noted, strategies are not the subject of much theoretical attention. Perhaps they might be accommodated in a theory of plans. But it won't be Bratman's theory. 'Strategy' is not to be found in Bratman's index. Strategies afford little prospect of lexical relief for agendas. If agendas are to serve their assigned theoretical roles, we will have to strike out on our own in an effort to say what they are.

Agendas are artifacts of theory. They are abstractions in various ways from plans, intentions, strategies, tactics, functions, designs, programs, scripts, tasks, undertakings, conventions and dispositions. Their abstractness constitutes one respect in which 'agenda' is a term of theory. At certain levels of description, agendas approximate to common features of these things. There is another feature which qualifies agendas as theoretical. It is the creative dimension of our account of them. For reasons that will appear, it is theoretically convenient to fill out agendas in a certain way, to endow them with traits that exceed what pre-analytic data would seem to call for.

8.3.1 Agendas: Transparent and Tacit

We have been at pains to make the point that significant portions of our cognitive tasks are transacted down below. This means that these aspects of cognition that occur without many of the factors listed on the right-hand column of a list of distinctions printed at the end of chapter 2. The full list is: *unconsciously, automatically, inattentively, involuntarily, non-linguistically, non-semantically* and *deep down* (rather than at the surface). We noted in chapter 2 a body of opinion among psychologists according to which these factors need not be thought of as equivalent or, for that matter, co-terminous. But when some are missing, typically others are; and where this is the case when some cognition is going on, we say that this is cognition 'down below'.

It is only natural to extend the metaphor of down below to an agent's agendas.

Often an agent is fully aware of his agendas and wholly disposed towards its advancement in the most psychologically transparent of ways. But we also find it desirable to acknowledge that sometimes an agent's agendas are implicit and that they are successfully advanced or closed under conditions that escape the agent's notice. What is more, information is relevant in relation to an agent when it acts upon him in ways that facilitate the closure of his agendas, we must also leave it open that relevance of information for an agent is something of which the agent may be unaware. Thus the having of agendas, the closing of agendas and the relevance of information that facilitates their closure are all in principle part of our cognitive lives down below. Under such conditions, an agent's agendas are said to be *implicit*.

We must shape our account of agendas so as to take note of these points.

We shall say that an agenda is a *causal* or *constitutive matrix*, $\langle E, N \rangle$, in which N is a state of affairs called an *endpoint* and E a set of states of affairs called *effectors* of N. The states of affairs in $\{S_1, \ldots, S_2\} = E$ are jointly sufficient for N. Sufficiency is understood in two ways, causally and constitutively. For the purposes of this book, causal sufficiency is whatever satisfies the causal algebra of Suppes [1970a] and [1970b], but the reader is free to substitute any preferred construal of this notion. We understand constitutive sufficiency as the property possessed by E when, under certain conditions, the S_i are just the endpoint. So, for example, if there is an endpoint for Harry realized by Sarah's having been apologized to, it suffices for this under normal conditions that Harry utter the words 'I apologise, Sarah'. (Austin [1961] cf. Anscombe [1957].) Constitutive conditions resemble what Aristotle called *formal causes*, whereas causal conditions in our present sense are what Aristotle called *efficient causes.* For expository ease we shall use the word 'cause' ambiguously as between the efficient causality and the constitutive condition senses, and will leave it to context to sort out which is intended. Typically, however, their disjunction is intended.

We also allow in principle for cases of *direct action* in which an agent's agenda is $\langle \Theta, N \rangle$, where N is a causally realizable endpoint and Θ is the empty set of prior conditions.

Agendas bear a certain resemblance to how classical decision theorists interpret actions. Relative to a decision problem D, an action is a function from all possible states of nature that bear on D to all decision-relevant consequences of them. An action therefore is a states-to-consequences mapping. Similarly, we can say that an agenda is a function from sets of realizable states of affairs to endpoints for which they are causally or constitutively sufficient. Agendas therefore are effectors-to-endpoint mappings.

With respect to any decision problem D, there can be a great many acts, as many as there are possible consequences of possible states of affairs bearing on D. The cardinality of actions, while large, should not be seen as daunting. Even when abstractly considered, the number of acts that an actual agent will consider is a stark subset of this capacious totality. Various factors conduce to this effect. One, no doubt, is the agent's subjective utilities, but that is only part of the story (and not at all a transparent part of it either).

As conceived of here, agendas are as plentiful, and then some, as decision theoretic actions. An endpoint is any state that can be realized. An agenda is a function from anything that can realize that state to that state. The cardinality of agendas *is* striking. This is of no matter so long as we are prepared to acknowledge a distinction between agendas and agendas *for.* We said that information is relevant to an agenda when it realizes states of affairs in the argument of the agenda-function. There is a natural adaptation of a well-established conception of *causal relevance* that fits the bill for this general case. What is causally relevant with respect to a certain state of affaris or sequences of states of affairs is (part of what is) causally sufficient for it. In the adaptation, a state of affirs or sequence thereof is constitutively sufficient for its realization. At the present level of abstraction, this is relevance-*to*. Information is relevant to such an agenda when it has the effect of realizing an effector. Relevance-to is the least interesting apsect of relevance, partly no doubt, because it lies so open to the charge of redundancy or mere lexical relief. So, why talk of causal (or constitutive) relevance when talk of causality (or constitutivity) will do just as well?

Relevance-*for* is more interesting. It is defined for cognitive agents in relation to agendas that meet an important condition. They are agendas *of* those agents in a sense that we shall shortly come to. Thereupon we will also go on to explain that subsets of agendas are also agendas-*for*.

For any realizable state of affairs there exists an agenda. Agendas in this broad sense are just states of affairs waiting to happen, linked to the conditions that might make them happen. Bearing in mind the conceptual precariousness of the purported divide between causal forces and causally effective information, we have judged it expedient to allow for a concept of relevance-to with which to represent energy flows that, e.g., get a thermostat to do what it is supposed to do. Central to this conception is that given what thermostats *are* supposed to do, there are numbers of agendas in this abstract sense whose endpoints are the states that the thermostat is supposed to be in and whose effectors are the causal forces, or the causally effective flow-throughs of information, that bring these ends about. The main idea of relevance-for, on the other hand, is that it is relevance of a kind defined for beings (or devices) capable of belief, that is, for cognitive agents. It is easy to see that associated with beings capable of belief are all kinds of realizable states induced by the action of causal powers or causally effective pieces of information. Harry's getting the measles is a case in point. We don't want to say that the measles virus was relevant for Harry with regard to his measles-getting agenda, never mind that such an agenda exists and that the measles virus is interpretable as causally effective information in a chain of events that bring the measles-endpoint about.

We go part of the way in evading this conclusion by requiring that information that is relevant for a cognitive agent is so not just because the being in question happens to be a being capable of belief, but rather *in virtue of* the fact that he is. Harry is such a being, a cognitive agent. Associated with Harry is an agenda for measles, a function from virus to spots. If Harry actually gets the measles, there are causal powers, or pieces of causally effective information that bring the measled state about. Although Harry is a cognitive agent, his measles do not come about in virtue of that fact.

What we require is to make the relevance that our theory seeks to caputre sensitive to this fact. To do this, it will help if we also bring the concept of agenda to heel. Much of what we have said in previous chapters bears on the desired contrast between relevance-to and relevance-for. What we must try to do now is draw a distinction between agendas and agendas-*for*.

We might observe in passing that our attempts to mark a distinction between relevance-to and relevance-for, and a distinction between agendas and agendas-for do not require us to have a principled command between the purported distinction between energy-to-energy transductions (or causal forces) and energy-to-information conversions (or causally effective information). So we will happily take the agnostic position on this matter.

The basic abstract idea of agendas owes nothing to the crude anthropormorphism suggested by its ordinary meaning. (So, while we seek for an analysis of the ordinary meaning of 'relevance', 'agenda' for us is a theoretical term.) The basic idea merely connotes a world that is causally susceptible to its every future state, usually just one among very many causally possible alternatives. In its most basic sense, the postulation of agendas is hardly more than recognition that the world is a causal order, that in all its multivarious particularity ours is a causally receptive world that lies in wait for causal fullfilment.

A further condition on agendas is that the states of affairs that occur in E be realizable by actions that are in the power of any agent whose agendas they are. It follows from this that endpoints are similarly realizable. This might strike us upon reflection as over-restrictive, since it follows from the characterization to date that an agent's agendas are always in his power to close. This presents us with two options neither of which justifies a lengthy discussion. The first option is to stick with the present characterization, and to observe that we now have a principled distinction between *agendas* and things such as *plans* and *strategies*. The other option is to alter the characterization of agendas so as to allow for the existence of agendas that an agent cannot close. In that case it would suffice to identify the endpoint N of any such agenda with θ, the causally impossible state of affairs relative to agent X. Since our aim is to say something useful about relevance, rather than to develop a detailed theory of agendas, we shall exercise option one of the present pair. Accordingly, we have the following

Definition 8.3 (Agendas: first pass) *An agenda A for an agent X is a causal matrix $\langle E, N \rangle$ of effectors jointly sufficient for an endpoint N, where N is realizable by actions causally possible, in principle, for X. Alternatively, an agenda is a function from effectors to* **X***-realizable endpoints.*

It is possible for an agent X to believe mistakenly that an endpoint is within his capacity to achieve. Thinking so, he might also believe that infon I gives him guidance as to how to bring this off. As things presently stand with relevance, I cannot be said to be relevant for X, since the agenda that

X thinks that he has, to whose realization the information certainly seems helpful, does not exist. Hence that information is not relevant for that agent with respect to that agenda.

If this seems over-harsh, let us note the following interesting pair of facts.

Fact 8.4 *Even impossible outcomes are subject to the condition that if they weren't impossible, such and so would be reasonable things to do to bring them off. If, for example, I believe mistakenly that I can achieve a 3-minute mile, it would be reasonable to run as quickly as I can rather than hop forward furiously. Steps that it would be reasonable to take with a view to attaining an endpoint that (in fact) cannot be attained can be called 'bona fide counterfactual effectors" of that endpoint.*

This gives us our next fact.

Fact 8.5 *If N is a causally impossible endpoint for an agent X and $E = \{E_1, \ldots, E_n\}$ is the set of its causally realizable bona fide counterfactual effectors, then although $\langle E, N\rangle$ does not exist as an agenda for X, it is possible that agendas do exist for the proper subendpoints E_i of $\langle E, N\rangle$. So it is perfectly possible for an agent to set out to fulfil conditions (and to have an agenda to do so) which are themselves realizable and are at the same counterfactual effectors of an endpoint which the agent mistakenly takes to be possible. Accordingly, whereas it is not possible for information to be relevant for the fulfilment of an impossible endpoint, it is possible (and common) for information to be relevant for the attainment of subendpoints embedded in counterfactual effectors.*

Fact 8.5 pre-supposes what is sometimes, though not always, true of causal matrices $\langle E, N\rangle$, viz. that E is structured in such a way that its states S_i are realized by succeeding with proper subagendas $\langle E', S_i\rangle$ in which E' is causally sufficient for those conditions S_i that are causally sufficient for the original endpoint N. Accordingly,

Proposition 8.6 (No relevance without agendas) *If N is an unrealizable endpoint for X, there can be no $\langle E, N\rangle$ that is an agenda for X and no information I that is relevant for X with respect to agenda $\langle E, N\rangle$.*

Proposition 8.7 (Relevance in relation to subagendas) *If N is an impossible endpoint for X and E^* a set of its causally realizable counterfactual effectors, then if there is any S_i^* in E^* that is realizable by virtue of actions by X that realize effectors E' of S_i^*, then $\langle E', S_i^*\rangle$ is a subagenda for X, and I is relevant for X with regard to his agenda $\langle E', S_i^*\rangle$ if X's processing I advances or closes that agenda.*

As indicated pages ago, there is a respect in which the evolving account of agendas is less than satisfactory. As things stand, we lack a distinction between sequences of states of affairs which an agent's behaviour chances to realize and which themselves happen to have causal outcomes, and instances of such sequences for which we want to reserve the name of agenda-*for*. A case in point: Harry accidentally tipped over his coffee into his keyboard, causing a short-circuit, which caused his computer to crash, and his current file to be lost. No one wants to call this one of *Harry's* agendas, an agenda *for* Harry.

The difficulty can be dealt with as follows. We stipulate that no such matrix is an agenda for X unless it can be said that N is a state of affairs in whose attainment X has an *interest* and, correspondingly, that the realization of *a* causal route E is something which X is *disposed* to bring about. Since it is possible for agents to possess interests and dispositions unawares, this keeps it open that agendas are sometimes implicit. Thus

Definition 8.8 (Agendas) *A matrix* $\langle E, N \rangle$ *is an agenda* for X *when the conditions of Definition 8.3 are met and, moreover,* N *is something in whose realization* X *has an interest and there is an effector-set* E *toward the realization of which* X *is disposed. (Definition 8.8 is preserved in chapter 15.)*

We shall say that an agent has such an interest and has such a disposition if in principle there is a later time (even after his agenda has closed) at which he is *able* to acknowledge expressly that N is (or was) his endpoint and actions which could be taken (or were taken) are actions that could (or did) constitute a route to N and are actions in which, on that account, the agent is able expressly to acquiesce. We have it, then, that whereas agendas can be implicit, and therefore psychologically opaque, they are not as such intractably hostile to psychological transparency. At the same time, however, our account of agendas leaves plenty of room for agents acting on agendas that they will never succeed in bringing to the surface. (They might not have tried; or they might suddenly have dropped dead, and so on.) Although psychological transparency is in principle possible for agendas, it is a contingent liability of the lives lived by beings like us that sometimes our agendas will remain dark. This seems about right for agendas.

Intuitively, a cognitive agent is a non-linear agent in the manner, e.g., of [Tate, 1977; Vere, 1983] and [Wilkins, 1988]. We represent this fact by imposing partial orders on agendas. Further structure will sometimes be discernible within E itself, whose subsets can also be seen as posets, partially ordered by a relation such as contributes-to-the-satisfaction of (endpoint N). At a further level of abstraction, sentential agendas bear some resemblance to closed Henkin models, but there is not resemblance enough between them to justify working out the comparison in any detail here.

Let $\langle E, N \rangle$ be an agenda for Harry. Then we will coin the term *sentential agendas* as follows: $\langle S^E, S^N \rangle$ is a sequence in which S^E is a set of sentences whose satisfaction concurs with the realization of the states in E, and S^N is a unit set of sentences bearing the same relation to N, the endpoint of $\langle E, N \rangle$. In other words, the sentences in S^E 'report' the realization of the states in E and the sentence in S^N 'reports' the realization of the state N. Sentential agendas resemble proofs from hypotheses, in which endpoints are sentences to be proved, and effectors are the hypotheses from which they are proved. A deducible wff is a formula waiting to be deductively realized. The other lines of the proof bring this off. In standard proof theories, whether a proof of a wff Φ exists from a set of hypotheses $\{H_1, \ldots, H_a\}$ has nothing to do with whether someone has actually constructed the proof or has it in mind to, or is in process of attempting to do so. Proofs are sequences of sentences meeting certain conditions. Proofs are sentential structures. Anyone wanting to construct a proof must find a way of assembling some sentences that satisfy those conditions. Proof theory itself doesn't tell us how to do this.

Sometimes a proof requires a lemma. Someone proving the lemma is said to have contributed to the main proof. We could also say that he advanced the main proof. The parallel with agendas speaks for itself.

In non-classical proof theories, there are additional restrictions on what counts as proof. If a proof is relevant in the Anderson–Belnap way, then the hypotheses $\{H_1, \ldots, H_a\}$ from which its conclusion is derived must each have an occurrence. Where the H_i constitutes a multiset, a proof from them may show more than one occurrence of one or more of them. Proofs from multisets mimic a feature of Sperber–Wilson relevance. It is the feature they call strengthening. If a proof is irredundant, then no hypothesis can be omitted (or withdrawn) and now can be repeated. Aristotle imposed an irredundancy condition in his theory of syllogisms.

There is no reason why similar constraints could not be entertained for sentential agendas. On reflection there is something to be said for irredundancy. So taken, agendas denote causal minima sufficient for the realization of realizable endpoints. It is a consequential constraint. It endows sentential agendas with full-use relevance in the manner of Anderson and Belnap and with premiss-irredundancy relevance in the sense of Aristotle's logic. If we decided to lighten up, and to permit agendas that repeat previously used effectors, then we could speak of multiagendas on the analogy of proofs from multisets; and this would enable us to give some kind of formal representation of the Sperber–Wilson notion of strengthening, as we said. Of course, our own account of relevance is none of these. But it is defined on triples of which one element is a structure that embeds features of those other conceptions of relevance. So it would appear that ours is an account that need not be hostile to such alternative conceptions. Consider an endpoint N. It is not proposed that in the general case there is just one agenda for N, although sometimes this will be so. There will also be cases in which alternative and not always comparable sets of effectors are available for service in agendas terminating in N. This is as it should be, given that realizable states of affairs sometimes have alternative and not always comparable minima that suffice for this realization.

As we have it so far, there is a certain indeterminacy in our concept of agenda. Among the issues that we have not yet discussed are these three (Gabbay, Nossum and Woods [2002a]):

1. whether effectors must be satisfied in the order in which they are listed

2. whether effectors can be repeated in which case the further issue of whether each occurrence must be satisfied separately

3. whether an agent can be affected in ways that satisfy an effector oftener than is listed in the agenda.

These issues call to mind substructural logic. If, for example, effectors must be satisfied exactly the number of times they are listed, then closing agendas will turn out to resemble proof-constructions in relevant logic.

When information plays on a cognitive agent relevantly, he processes it in ways that induce him to act or that put him in a state such that effectors of an agenda are satisfied. Given the way in which agendas have been conceived of, the agenda with regard to which some information is relevant for an agent need not be an agenda that the agent has consciously set out to advance. He need not be conscious of it as an agenda that it would be desirable to have satisfied. He need not be conscious of it at all. No need to be aware that the information in question is facilitating the agenda's closure.

Agendas, then, are not *intrinsically* owned. Of course, this is not to say that they can't be consciously adopted. There are no general recipes for the contingent ownership of agendas. But certain more or less clear cases stand out. If Harry has a goal, say to open the jar of pickles, it is not unreasonable to postulate for Harry a disposition to act in ways that, as it happens, might or would satisfy the requisite sentences. Harry himself might even have a plan of action: Step one, immerse the jar in boiling water; step two, let the jar cool slightly; step three, twist the cap. In being thus disposed, Harry may be said to have an agenda in our sense, and may know it. Yet in other cases, Harry's pursuit of his goals might display two features at once. One is that he has in hand, or in mind, nothing that he himself would characterize as a plan of action. The other is that his behaviour and/or his mental state is such that he is satisfying the right sentences; that is to say, advancing an agenda. Since it is an agenda that Harry chances to engage, in the process of pursuing a goal, we may fairly say that it was an agenda of Harry, provided that we do not say that it had to be an agenda that Harry consciously had in mind and consciously set out to advance, step by conscious step.

If we took the S_i of an agenda to be productive minima of the endpoint N, then an action agenda would be linear in the sense of linear logic. If repetitions of an S_i were allowed, we could speak of multiagendas in the sense of multisets. In this same spirit, we must also require that the action/state of affairs components of an agenda are non-monotonic. For it is not the case that any set of actions or states eventuating in a given state eventuates in that same state when supplemented arbitrarily many times by arbitrarily selected new actions or states. And of course, if we wanted our agendas to be linear, this would be automatic provision for them to be relevant in the sense of Anderson and Belnap. The *agendas* would be relevant, even though the *relevance* would not be agenda relevance in our sense.

It is also desirable to emphasize that agendas are not intentional objects in the sense of being the objects of conscious choice or conscious intent. They are however intentional objects in Husserl's sense (Husserl [1900–1913]). They possess actions or states that are objects of an agent's disposition to realize or interest in realizing, where the disposition and the interest need not be consciously held or present. Even so, those actions or states are what the relevant dispositions are dispositions *toward* and the relevant interests are interests *in*. So they are Husserlian intentionalities.

Finally, it is easy to extend agendas by addition of the appropriate temporal indicators.

Closed agendas are intractably closed, but they need not be inert. A closed agenda stays closed no matter what sets of states of affairs are subsequently realized, with the exception — if that is what it is — of backward causation. No subsequent state of affairs will bring it about that the endpoint of a previously closed agenda has not been realized. But ensuing states of affairs may sometimes disrealize a realized endpoint. If an endpoint is the state of affairs in which Harry is married to Sarah, a subsequent divorce or death will disrealize it. Nothing, however, will conspire to disrealize the realized state of affairs in which Harry married Sarah on July 13th, 1956. Agendas are inert just in case they are closed and their endpoints are not disrealizable.

Agendas are sometimes embedded in other agendas. It is largely a matter of decision to count embedded agendas as many or one. Harry's agenda is to marry Sarah. To that end he pays her court, with engagement in mind. At a time deemed appropriate Harry pops the question. Sarah accepts. That closes the agenda (or subagenda) of getting engaged to Sarah. Harry's engagement improves his chances of marriage, such is its place as a conventional prelude to it. The realized endpoint of the closed agenda advanced the other.

Embedment is a prickly notion. It raises questions about logical closure. Do we want to say that information closing an agenda likewise closes every deductive consequence of it? By present lights, there is no denying it. Let C be a set of realized conditions causally sufficient for the realization of a state of affairs E, and let $K_1, \ldots, K_n$ be sets of states of affairs logically implied by $C \cup \{E\}$. It is clear that for each i, $C \cup K_i$ is a closed agenda. So too is $C \cup K_1 \cup \ldots \cup K_n$. This is getting to be rather a lot of agendas.

Disposition is also a term of art. We don't want it to be the case that anything towards whose realization an agent is disposed is something whose realization he would be happy about or would approve. Desperate to straighten himself out and to quit the bottle altogether, Harry is having a difficult time. Not knowing this, Lou says. 'There's beer in the fridge, if you'd like some', and leaves the house on an errand. Harry is disposed to take up the invitation, such is the nature of his difficulty. He is also disposed to pass up Lou's hospitality. He wants his problem solved. Lou's invitation is relevant for Harry with respect to both agendas to the extent that it changes the causal nexus in certain ways. If Harry's will breaks and he helps himself, the relevance of the invitation is obvious. If it only tempted Harry, it was relevant in another way, for it increased the likelihood that he would drink, never mind that he didn't. Concerning the agenda of not drinking, Lou's invitation was negatively relevant. It reduced the likelihood that he wouldn't. In the case in which Harry succumbs, Lou's invitation was even more deeply negatively relevant. It played a role in the closure of the I-want-a-drink agenda which precludes the closure of I-don't-want-a-drink agenda.

Human agency is made interesting in considerable part for its involvement with incompatible agendas. 'Incompatible' is meant robustly and intuitively. Agendas are robustly incompatible when they have concurrently unsatisfiable endpoints.[3] Incompatible agendas remind us that agendas are susceptible to a certain kind of negative closure, for which we will appropriate the term 'defeated'. Conditions defeat an agenda when they preclude the realization of its endpoint. Where agendas are incompatible the closure of the one constitutes the defeat of the other. Unlike defeat, closure comes in degrees. Advancement is closure of a degree less than 1. Incompatible agendas might sometimes be such that conditions that advance the one to some degree also advance the other to that same degree, but not to the point of closure, of course. Their incompatibility need not be revealed in their respective advancement histories until near or at the point of closure of the one and defeat of the other. This is part of what makes life interesting.

It is worth emphasizing that agendas-for are definable for any device that qualifies as a cognitive agent. We want to leave open the question as to whether human beings are multiply endowed with cognitive agency. A device is a cognitive agent if it is capable of having beliefs. It is clear that human beings are corporations. Human agency comprehends various subagencies and there are subagencies of these. Any subagency of a human being is an information-processing device. Let M be an informational state that any such device D is in. If M satisfies a truth-predicate then D is a cognitive agent. It may be that subagencies such as the perceptual analyser, PI, also qualify. We can suppose the PI has informational states which record the orientation of the eyeballs or gradient texture. If these states have truth conditions then they qualify for cognitive agency. It would then be permissible to speak of PI as having true beliefs (about orientation and texture). We have no wish to join the throng of those who wrestle endlessly with such questions. It is enough for our purposes that we not forclose upon the possibility, short of showing cause to do so.

We take some solace in knowing that speaking of PI having beliefs is not conspicuously more obscure than speaking of Kurt Gödel having beliefs. We concede that there are people for whom that fact is more a *reductio* than a comfort; but that can't be helped. One person's *reductio* is another person's surprising fact.

The openness of the possibility is consequential. It is true that Harry's PI has beliefs; it does not follow that Harry does. It all but follows that Harry does not. Although Harry might not believe what his PI believes, the

[3] Of course, if we do not insist on realizing the endpoints at the same time then we may be all right on the score of compatibility. Harry can't marry Sarah and Louise in the same ceremony. But he may, after ditching Sarah, tie the knot with Louise.

information that PI stores under conditions that qualify it as having those beliefs, may well stand in a pointful relation to an agenda for Harry. If Harry can be said to be favourably disposed toward having veridical perceptions, that information will clearly enough count as relevant for Harry with respect to that agenda. This is quaintly latitudinarian. We need to do better. Better we can do once we recognize that the information that PI processes in ways that qualify it for belief Harry cannot process in ways that qualify for a belief *of Harry*.

This suggests that relevance-for be redefined in the light of further conditions. One is that **X** be a being capable of processing **I** in ways that qualify it as a belief for **X**. When this condition is satisfied, **I** may be said to be *live* information for **X**. **I**, then, is relevant for **X** with regard to **A** only if **I** is live for **X**. A similar constraint is wanted for agendas-*for*. Consider the contrary. As things now stand, an endpoint of an agenda for a cognitive agent is an unrealized state of affairs toward the realization of which the agent is disposed. Now Harry's protein-synthesizing subsystems are disposed to the realization of the state of affairs in which the codon on the *m*RNA immediately adjoining the initiating AUG codon interacts with the large ribosomal subunit in ways that position the codon for interaction with another *t*RNA molecule. Harry's protein synthesizer agency is disposed toward the realization of this state of affairs. If so, it is an endpoint of an agenda for it. But is it also an agenda *for* Harry?

It remains true nevertheless that all sorts of information will be relevant for Harry — that Harry would deny was relevant and whose agendas Harry would deny having. For he might not have processed that information in ways that qualify it for belief (though he could have) and he might not have represented that to which — in fact — he was disposed as something whose realization he might try to facilitate (though he could have done that, too). For the horn sounded and Harry stepped back onto the curb.

It is evident from the past several paragraphs that we have been trying to work with a generous notion of cognitive agency. A cognitive agent, we said, is an information-processor capable of belief. So conceived of, it is easier to draw a principled line between causal systems and cognitive agents. A capacity for belief is part of the difference. So is the ability to represent a state of affairs as something to the realization of which one is disposed. Trailing along is the necessity to distinguish relevance-to and relevance-for. We would go some way toward simplifying matters if we tightened the concept of cognitive agency. One of the benefits of tightening the definition of cognitive agency is that we can secure the suggestions of the past several pages with greater sure-footedness. For example, the proposals of figure 8.1 seem especially plausible now, untroubled by the difference between responsiveness and relevance.

8.4 MEM and KARO-agendas

8.4.1 MEM Agendas

Something like our agendas is evident in the concept of agenda that operates in Multiple Entry Modular (*MEM*) memory systems, concerning which there is a huge literature. (A small sample: Johnson [1983; 1990; 1992]. For an accessible exposition see [Johnson and Reeder, 1997].)

MEM postulates a three-level information-processing structure. At the lowest level P_i, there are perceptual processes, such as locating, extracting, resolving and tracking. This interacts with a second perceptual level P_2, involving placing, structuring, identifying and examining. Next step up is the lower, R_1, of two reflective subsystems, involving reactivating, noting, refreshing (memories), and shifting. At level R_2 we have processes such as retrieving, discerning, rehearsing and imitating. The *MEM* model then postulates the existence of *agendas* at both level R_1 and R_2. These are stylized anthropomorphically as *superior* and *executive*. The various components of *MEM* achieve considerable functional significance when they are controlled and monitored. This is the function of agendas.

> The component processes derive great functional power from the fact that they can be marshalled and executed by agendas. Agendas recruit processes in the service of goals — a combination of goals and component processes constitutes what we call an *agenda*. An agenda can be thought of as a script, or recipe. That is, a recipe is somewhat more flexible than a program; its instantiations allow for opportunistic flexibility and improvisation. Most agendas are learned through experience.
>
> [Johnson and Reeder, 1997, p. 271]

As we see, *MEM*-agendas bear a significant affinity to the agendas of agenda-relevance, which can be seen as a generalization of them.

To some extent, our concept of agenda also bears a resemblance to a concept of the same name in a practical reasoning structure known as *KARO* ([van der Hoek *et al.*, 1994a; van der Hoek *et al.*, 1994b], [van Linder *et al.*, 1994; van Linder *et al.*, 1995; van Linder *et al.*, 1997], and [Meyer and van der Hoek, 1995; Meyer *et al.*, 1999]). These authors seek a framework in which to model propositional attitudes that motivate the actions of agents.

The model reflects a basic BDI (belief–desire–intention) approach to agency. Based on its goals and the relevant practical possibilities, the model predicts that an agent may commit itself to actions that it knows (or believes) to be correct and feasible in realizing certain of its known goals. If, as events turn, an agent finds that his commitments no longer conduce to the realization of that goal or fail to be practically possible to implement, it is able to suspend or terminate some or all of these commitments. In *KARO*, the making and undoing of commitments is represented as a particular model-transforming action, by extension of the usual state-transition description conveyed by propositional dynamic logic. In this context, an action could be judged to be correct and feasible for the realization of a goal at a time by implanting in the *KARO* architecture a classical planner such as STRIPS [Fikes and Nilsson, 1971]. The basic form of practical reasoning that *KARO* formalizes by way of the making of commitments is the following:

1. Agent **X** knows that Φ is one of its goals
2. Agent **X** knows that α is correct and feasible with respect to Φ.
3. Therefore, **X** has the opportunity to commit to α [Meyer *et al.*, 1999, p. 17].

In the *KARO* approach, committing to an action is itself a full-blown action. Accordingly an agent **X** so situated as to perform the action commits to α if and only if **X** knows that α is correct and feasible as regards the goal in question. An agent's commitments in turn, are represented by an *agenda function*. Informally, the value of this function is what an agent is committed to for a given agent and its states as arguments. As Meyer *et al.* [1999] makes clear, the 'actual formal definition capturing this fairly unsophisticated idea is itself rather complicated [owing to the number of desiderata that commitments should be expected to meet]' [1999, p. 18]. The interested reader can find the formal complexities at pages 21 and 22 of [Meyer *et al.*, 1999]. It suffices for our purposes to point out that whenever an agent **X** performs a commit-to-α-action, **X**'s agenda is updated with α, and so too with all states 'epistemically equivalent' to **X**'s input states Δ. The actions that **X** is committed to are entered in its agenda ' in such a way that commitments are closed under prefix-taking and under practical identity, i.e., having identical computation runs' [Meyer *et al.*, 1999, p. 31].

Relevance in the theory of agenda relevance is a set of sequence of infons, agents and agendas. Agendas in turn are sequences of effectors terminating in an endpoint. Information is relevant for an agent when it advances or closes an agenda. Information advances an agent's agenda when it operates on the agent in ways that satisfy one or more effectors. It closes an agenda when it plays upon the agenda in ways that satisfy effectors that are sufficient for the attainment of the requisite endpoint. Although *KARO*-agendas are not the same as *AR*-agendas, there is sufficient structural similarity to warrant our thinking of *KARO*-agendas as a special case of their *AR* counterparts.

8.5 A Formal Interlude

This section is for readers who at this stage might like a glimpse of the formal model to come.

The basic idea of agenda relevance

Consider a state of affairs s and an agent **X** who is not satisfied with this state of affairs. Let us say that the state s is fully described by some theory Δ_s in some logic **L**. So if $\Delta_s \vdash_{\mathbf{L}} B$ then B holds in the state. A logical agent is identifiable by the actions available to him, say $\mathbf{a}_1, \ldots, \mathbf{a}_k$, reminiscent of an action-agenda. An action has the form $\mathbf{a} = (B, C)$, i.e., it has preconditions B and postconditions C. If $\Delta_s \vdash B$, then the preconditions hold and the action can be taken. Then the postcondition becomes true; and we move to a new state s'. We have $\Delta_{s'} = \Delta_s \circ C$ where $\Delta \circ X$ indicates the result obtained by *revising* Δ by X. (We can use any revision process for now, say AGM) [Alchourrón *et al.*, 1985]. So intuitively, if our agent wants to effectuate endpoint S and he knows that $\Delta \circ C \vdash_{\mathbf{L}} S$ (with $\Delta \not\vdash_{\mathbf{L}} S$), then he would want to take action $\mathbf{a} = (B, C)$. To perform this action he must have $\Delta_s \vdash B$. Thus any wff $A \in \Delta_s$ which may participate in any proof of B from Δ_s is relevant to our agent. It advances the associated agenda. (Note in passing that A may not actually be in Δ but that some *abduction* process might predict that A *needs* to participate in the proof.) Let us repeat the last sentence in a different way:

Any wff A which is *AB-relevant* to B (from Δ_s) is *SW*-relevant to our agent; it has *contextual effect* in the *contextual* schema $\vdash_{\mathbf{L},\mathbf{a}}$ where:

$$\Delta \vdash_{\mathbf{L},\mathbf{a}=(B,C)} S$$

iff either $\Delta \vdash_{\mathbf{L}} S$ or ($\Delta \vdash_{\mathbf{L}} B$ and $\Delta \circ C \vdash_{\mathbf{L}} S$).

So to prove S from Δ using actions means that there is some course of action associated with an agenda which can prove S. See [Gabbay, 2001].

The above example illustrates the connection between *AB*-relevance, *SW*-relevance and our own *AR*-relevance.

The reader should note the following:

(1) We do not claim that the AB-logic fits into our scheme 'as is', but we accept their idea of A being relevant to B when A is *used in the proof* of B. We shall propose what we take to be a better logic and a clearer notion of '*use in a proof*'.

(2) We shall also show (perhaps in a way compatible with SW-examples) that for 'inferential effects' the 'inference' can be taken as some sort of inference with actions and other mechanisms (abduction + presupposition + whatever else). Such consequences, $\Delta \vdash_{\text{mechanisms}} X$ will allow us to define *inferential effects* $(\Delta, A) = \{X | \Delta \circ A \vdash_{\text{mechanism}} X\}$.

(3) We also note that the *interpolation theorem* plays a role here. When we write $\Delta \circ A \vdash_{\text{mechanism}} Y$ we want Y to be in the common language of $\Delta \circ A$. This will be sufficient if and only if for all Y s.t. $\Delta \circ A \vdash Y$ there exists an X in the common language of $\Delta * A$ and Y with $\Delta \circ A \vdash X$ and $X \vdash Y$.

The following are required to develop the requisite formal model:

(1) A suitable base logic $\vdash$ in which to express the theories Δ_s associated with state s.

(2) A suitable notion of formal relevance $\mathbf{R}$ with which to express the notion of 'A is needed in the proof of B' and hence the idea that A is *locally relevant* to B. This means that A is relevant in some sense which is a more suitable variation of AB-relevance. We therefore have

$$\Delta \vdash_{\mathbf{R}} A \text{ implies } \Delta \vdash_{\mathbf{L}} A$$

i.e., $\mathbf{R} \subseteq \mathbf{L}$.

(3) A suitable notion of revision such that if Δ, A are wffs then $\Delta \circ A$ is the result of revising Δ with A. We expect $\circ$ to be given by an algorithm and to satisfy the main AGM postulates for revision among them.

$$\Delta \circ A = \Delta \cup \{A\} \text{ if } \Delta, A \text{ are consistent (i.e., } \Delta \cup \{A\} \nvdash_{\mathbf{L}} \bot$$

and

$$\Delta \circ A \vdash_{\mathbf{L}} A$$

and (this is new!) some reasonable interactions with $\mathbf{R}$; e.g., if X is not relevant to the contradiction $\bot$ from $\Delta \cup \{A\}$ then $\Delta \vdash_{\mathbf{L}} X$ implies $\Delta \circ A \vdash_{\mathbf{L}} X$ any X which is not relevant to the contradiction which A causes will not get thrown out by the revision process.

(4) A definition of actions $\mathbf{a}_i = (B_i, C_i)$ = (preconditions, postconditions) and define a suitable notion of

$$\Delta \vdash_{\mathbf{L},\mathbf{a}_1 \ldots \mathbf{a}_n} X.$$

(5) The definition of a suitable notion of *contextual effects* using $\Delta_{\mathbf{L},\mathbf{a}_1 \ldots, \mathbf{a}_n}$ and $\vdash_{\mathbf{R}}$,

(6) A check of the above notions against the intuitive motivating examples.

Notwithstanding the sheer sketchiness of this description of the formal model we trust that one important fact is already evident. It is its ecumenical intention: for here are early formal intimations not only of agenda relevance, but also of *AB*-relevance and *SW*-contextual effects.

Chapter 9

Adequacy Conditions Fulfilled?

> Detective Inspector George Headingley had a reputation for being a by-the-rules, straight-down-the-middle cop who treated hunches with embrocation and gut feelings with bismuth.
>
> Reginald Hill, *Dialogues of the Dead*

In this chapter we shall begin the attempt to test the conceptual model of AR against the adequacy conditions set out in chapter 7. We start with a brief aside about subjective relevance.

9.1 Subjective Relevance

A principal distinction for the purposes at hand is that between *de facto* relevance and objective relevance. *De facto* relevance is the target of a descriptive theory, and the previous chapter, together with this one, are offered as contributions to it. Objective relevance is thought of, for now, as what a normative theory of relevance quests after. It is the main business of the next chapter.

As presently drawn, the *de facto*/objective distinction obscures a further one; a pair struggles to make a discrimination better made by a triple. We might well expect a theory of relevance to differentiate among the following cases:

1. **X** *judging* that **I** is relevant for him with regard to **A**.
2. **I**'s *being* relevant for him with respect to it.

3. **I**'s being relevant for him with respect to it in fulfilment of the condition that things are happening as they *should*, i.e., **I**'s being *rightly* relevant for **A**.

In an earlier chapter, we reserved 'subjective' for case one. It is well to note that judgements of relevance will typically involve attributions of relevance in our third sense, for which 'objective' will serve well enough, until further notice. But there is no reason to think that the maker of judgements of subjective relevance might not sometimes be attributing *de facto* relevance.

In these pages we won't have much to say about the now re-worked conception of subjective relevance. It is prudent to distinguish it all the same. Subjective substance will be wanted for accounts of compliance with Grice's maxim. 'Be relevant'. Put to such uses, it might be thought that subjective relevance resists the embrace of our causal theory. What would it be to judge that **I** is causally efficacious with respect to fulfilment of the cooperative canons of conversation?

This asks the wrong question. If something is subjectively relevant for someone just when he judges it to be relevant in some way, then subjective relevance turns out to be definable for contexts in the form ⌜**X** judges that **I** is relevant for himself⌝. 'Himself' is important. It wins the case for subjectivity. The contexts for which subjective relevance is definable are opaque contexts. They resist the free interchange of equivalent idioms in the scope of the operator ⌜**X** judges that...⌝. It should be no surprise that there are people who judge that something is relevant for them but who do not judge — who may deny — that that something is or has affected them in ways that advance or close agendas. So contexts of subjective judgement aren't interesting for the abundant counterexamples they appear to occasion to causal agenda relevance. Counterexamples do not present themselves on that account; the opacity of 'judges-that' guarantees it.

Subjective relevance is interesting in other ways. We said a moment ago that the subjectivity of subjective relevance requires the relativity of relevance attribution: Harry *judges* that something is relevant for him, and so it *is* subjectively relevant for him. But consider. Sarah asks, 'I wonder where Harry Jr. is?' Harry replies. 'There's a hockey game tonight', judging that this is a relevant response.[1] He judges, that is, that it will be relevant for Sarah, that it will contribute to the closure of Sarah's agenda of wanting to know the whereabouts of their son. We might wish to think that Harry's

[1]Here is a defter example from Sperber and Wilson (slightly adapted):

Harry: Where are my chocolates?
Sarah: The dog is looking very sleepy.
[Sperber and Wilson, 1986, 121–122]

answer is subjectively relevant for Harry, since he judges that it will be relevant for Sarah. But the reflexivity of subjective relevance makes no provision for such a case. It is a case that invites iteration. That there is a hockey game tonight is information inducing Harry to think that its transmission to Sarah will be relevant for her; and so it induces him to think in ways that advances his agenda of transmitting information that will advance Sarah's own. It is possible for Harry to think of that information in these ways, as information that induces him to think that its transmission will induce Sarah to think, 'I know where Harry Jr. is.' If he does think so, that information is subjectively relevant for Harry with regard to his agenda to furnish information that will be objectively relevant for Sarah with regard to her interest in her son's whereabouts. Depending on what she does think, that information might be subjectively relevant for Sarah, too. The causal account can accommodate subjective relevance in contexts of Grice-compliant conversations. It will be an abiding feature of them. Saying so doesn't, however, offer much theoretical elucidation. We can take it as given that a Grice-cooperator would wish to conduct himself in ways that 'ground' subjectively relevant information. Information is groundedly subjectively relevant just when the judgment 'That information was relevant for me' is true. In Grice-conversations each party has an agenda to fulfil, among others, the maxim, 'Be relevant'. A party's information is *groundedly* subjectively relevant with respect to that agenda if he is right in thinking that its conveyance to his *vis-á-vis* fulfiled the maxim. It begins to look like the epicycles of Ptolemy: relevance within relevance. But there is a clear question that can be asked: is a Grice-cooperator ever in a position to know that information subjectively relevant for him with respect to the relevance maxim is grounded? Let us see.

9.2 Meta-agendas

People have an interest in dealing with their agendas efficiently and in a timely fashion. They have an interest in the fast and the frugal. As far as they know, they might be disposed to this sort of thing largely unawares.

Couldn't there be agendas concerning how to bring about the efficient and timely closure of agendas? Such might be a standing and general agenda to determine how to construct good scientific theories or to determine how to do philosophy well. By their fruits shall we know them. The methodology of theory construction (i.e., that agenda) will take as input what we know of the good theories we have constructed including the reasons we hold them as good. The agenda in question involves an effort to make a generalization from these. These things are done with greater and less sure-footedness.

Manuals of experimental procedure are fairly determinate successes with respect to the provision of information that will get the investigator to do well with a particular experiment. Conspicuously less successful is an agenda we might call metaphilosophy. We will have difficulty in writing a manual on how to do philosophy well, how to produce good philosophy theories, because

(i) the induction is harder to make

and

(ii) there is no *à priori* guidance.

Factor (i) is explained by the fact that it is uncertain as to what particular philosophical accomplishments qualify as good or successful theories. Factor (ii) allows us to make a more general point. Platitudes aside (e.g., be careful and get plenty of rest), could the possessor of a meta-agenda plausibly be supposed to have a clue about how to set about closing it, independently of any consideration about how the object agendas are or have been closed?

Meta-agendas appear to be worked out after the fact or concurrently with the working out of their object-agendas. There may seem to be an exception to this. Meta-agendas close independently of the closure histories of object-agendas when they close on analytic information. Agendas such as these thus constitute *à priori* knowledge concerning the closure conditions on object-agendas. Meta-agendas that close independently of any information about how their object-agendas close are detached meta-agendas.

So we might ask: Is there a detached meta-agenda for knowledge (or for induction, etc.)? There are two cases to consider, one analytic and one procedural.

Analytic: An analytic detached meta-agenda $\mathbf{M}^d$, for e.g., knowledge is one whose closure is accomplished only on information about the meaning of the word 'knowledge'. Essentially it produces a definition: **X** knows that Φ iff ... The definition in turn provides information for an agent whose object-agenda **A** is to know whether p, for some particular p. The agent $\mathbf{X}'$ of this agenda can be said to know whether p if the conditions under which the agenda advanced to 'Yes, p' or 'No, not-p' complies with that definition. Notoriously we have no way of determining whether this is so in the general case. $\mathbf{X}'$ needn't know that the definition is satisfied in order that it be satisfied. So the KK hypothesis is not upheld here.[2] This is as it should be, of course.

[2]The KK hypothesis asserts that, for any Φ, someone knows that Φ iff he knows that he knows that Φ.

Procedural: A procedural detachment meta-agenda $\mathbf{M}^d$, for e.g., knowledge produces information (which may include a definition) in ways that constitute either

(a) an (approximately) effective recognition procedure for knowledge

or

(b) an (approximately) effective acquisitions procedure for knowledge

or

(c) both.

There is no reason whatever to think that a human agent could advance or close any procedural agenda like $\mathbf{M}^d$. The theory of knowledge therefore cannot consist in the closure of $\mathbf{M}^d$. This is one meaning of anti-foundationalism in epistemology, but not a very interesting one. There is no epistemologist who ever lived who thought of his task as closing $\mathbf{M}^d$, not even Descartes himself on a fair reading.

One might think that the failure (or non-existence) of theories of knowledge of the $\mathbf{M}^d$-closing sort calls into question the possibility of analytic information. It does not. If there is trouble with analytic information, it lies elsewhere. The culprit is *à priori* knowledge. A condition on the closure of $\mathbf{M}^d$ is this: whatever information closes $\mathbf{M}^d$, any information about how any object-agenda of $\mathbf{M}^d$ closed would be hyper-relevant, or parasitically relevant (both shortly to be discussed) for the $\mathbf{M}^d$-theorist.

The interesting cases are those of meta-agendas $\mathbf{M}^c$ called *connected.* They are agendas whose closure conditions require the presentation of information concerning closure conditions of object-agendas. Analytic information is not precluded. It is only that analytic information linking terms $\tau_1, \tau_2, \ldots, \tau_n$ hold to the condition that any agent for whom $\mathbf{I}$ is analytic information has prior or concurrent information about the extensions of the τ_i.[3] If there *is* any analytic information, it makes the case for the analytic *à posteriori.*

Possessing a meta-agenda is possessing a kind of thing sometimes instantiated when some metareasoning is going on. Metareasoning is reasoning about reasoning. Many researchers think that metareasoning is characteristic of advanced intelligence, and it has attracted the attention of workers in AI. Metareasoning carries with it a metalevel problem. It is a problem concerning what decisions an agent should make about what to think.

[3]But don't we sometimes have analytic information by hearsay? No, we have non-analytic information $\mathbf{I}'$ to the effect that $\mathbf{I}$ is analytic information (for someone).

Metalevel problems contrast with object-level problems. The object-level problem is that of deciding what 'external' actions to take in the wake of certain information. In each case, the level problem is a decision problem. In reasoning and metareasoning alike a levels-function implements choices, of external actions in the case of object-level operation, and of 'internal' or cognitive actions in the case of metalevel operation. Some writers think that

> Like the object-level decision problem (that is, the problem of what external action to take), the metalevel decision problem can be solved by a variety of methods ranging from full-scale decision-theoretic deliberation to simple condition-action rules and routine procedures. [Russell and Wefald, 1991, p. 24]

Thinking this way leaves plenty of room for the relevance theorist to reflect on the kinds of information that a metareasoner would require, or be glad to have, with regard to his meta-agenda of metareasoning. It is interesting that 'by and large [AI researchers] have ignored the general question of what metaknowledge to insert into their systems. Metaknowledge is viewed as consisting of domain-specific heuristics ...' [Russell and Wefald, 1991, p. 24].

Russell and Wefald demur from this view. They 'argue that metareasoning can be viewed as entirely domain-independent' [Russell and Wefald, 1991, p. 24]. All that needs to be known on the metalevel is how object-level decisions procedures work, what decisions they produce, and 'this knowledge is independent of what those decisions are about'. Domain independence is an attractive assumption for the metareasoning decisions problem because 'metalevel control provides a way of defeating complexity' [Russell and Wefald, 1991, pp. 26–27]. It is fair to say that the domain-dependence/domain-independence question is still open for solutions of the metareasoning decision problem in AI. This matters for meta-agendas, too. Detached meta-agendas resemble the metareasoning decision-problem under the assumption of domain-independent metaknowledge. Connected meta-agendas resemble the metareasoning decision-problem under the assumption of domain-dependent meta-knowledge. In neither case is the resemblance exact, but it is close enough to be interesting.

People who want to see logic naturalized are all but guaranteed to adopt connected meta-agendas. Whether this is the better way of proceeding is, of course, disputed. We can say that it is also an open question in the theory of relevance.

There is (an inequivalent) variation on Grice's maxim, 'Be relevant'. It is, 'Seek for relevant information'. Anyone inclined to comply with this might be said to possess a meta-agenda for relevance. We ourselves are not much attracted by the idea that we all have a meta-agenda for relevance. It is another unruly notion. Much of the time and in most circumstances the meta-agenda for relevance will not be accessible. It will resemble the putative agenda to process information. There is nothing 'meta' about the agenda to process information, and if all processed information is relevant to the agenda to process it, we might think that there is nothing 'meta' about the meta-agenda for relevance. It hardly seems possible to seek for information in fulfilment of the conditions that it advance agendas short of the specification of those agendas. Once the agendas are specified — object-agendas, as we could say — it is difficult to see in what the effort to advance the meta-agenda could consist other than the effort to advance those object-agendas.

But consider a case. Harry is a barrister. He wants to construct a winnable case from a weak defence for his client charged with insider trading. Months of detailed work lie ahead, and mountains of documents to be analysed. He seeks out information that will cause him to think that he has such a case. Thinking it is not having it; but thinking may advance the prospects of having. We can imagine that there will be numerous occasions on which Harry has doubts about how things are going. Am I doing this right, he wonders? Is there something else I should be doing? A kibitzer of Gricean proclivities tries to help: 'You should be looking for relevant information'. But that precisely is what he *is* looking for. Harry's worry is about how well he is doing with it. 'Yes', says his kibitzing friend, 'I understand your difficulty. Let me make myself clear. You should supplement your efforts with a good normative theory of agenda relevance'.

Harry's friend goes on to say that although such a theory, NAR, is unlikely to constitute an effective procedure for acquiring information that will advance Harry's object-agenda, it could nevertheless be expected to facilitate its advancement. So perhaps we can think of a relevance meta-agenda as a NAR that facilitates the closure of object-agendas. More carefully, if Harry has a NAR, we can speak of him as running NAR (in his head) much as a computer runs a program. The relevance meta-agenda would be that for which the running of NAR counts as advancement of it.

If there were no NAR, then there would be no relevance meta-agendas in the sense in question. We are at a loss to know in what other sense such a meta-agenda might exist. If there were no relevance meta-agendas, it would not follow that there are no NARs. But it would follow that nothing that counts as a NAR would be of material assistance in facilitating the advancement of object-agendas. It might still be the case that a NAR is dominantly or exclusively the set of truth conditions on sentences in the form ⌜**I** is objectively relevant for **X** with respect to **A**⌝. *NAR* would tell us what it is for something to be 'normatively relevant', but it could do this without giving any means of recognizing the extension of the predicate ⌜**I** is objectively relevant for **X** with respect to **A**⌝. In this respect *NAR* is in distinguished company. Tarski's theory of truth (i.e., objective truth) determines the extension of the predicate '... is (objectively) true'. But it is notorious how bad we are in recognizing the members of that class. Grice told us that in order to understand something it is not necessary to have an analysis of it. We are going Grice one better. We are saying that having an analysis of objective relevance is no guarantee of being able to fulfil Grice's injunction, 'Be relevant'. Grice was genuinely perplexed that he had made so little headway with relevance over the years. An explanation comes to mind, though it is conjectural. It is this: that *nothing counting as an analysis of agenda relevance will suffice for compliance with Grice's maxim.* (Cf. adequacy condition 8.)

9.3 Comparative Relevance

It seems evident to many people that some information is more or less relevant than other information. It is tempting to think of relevance and irrelevance as coming in degrees. We can capture this intuition, as required by AC3.

Proposition 9.1 (Degrees of relevance) **I** *is relevant for* **X** *with regard to* **A** *to the extent that it closes* **A**.

Proposition 9.2 (Degrees of relevance) **I** *is relevant for* **X** *with regard to* $\mathbf{A}_1, \ldots, \mathbf{A}_n$ *to the extent that* **I** *closes* i *agendas,* $i = 0, \ldots, n$. *(Proposition 9.2 is preserved in the formal model at section 15.4.)*

It has been said that degrees of relevance are best thought of in terms of the number of belief-changes it induces and the length of time it takes to process them [Sperber and Wilson, 1986, p. 126].

But, as we have seen, there are difficulties for SW-relevance posed by these economic considerations. We again follow [Levinson, 1989]; see too [Gazdar and Good, 1982]. SW-relevance is a measure of contextual effects E in the light of processing costs C. Let T be the task of providing the best interpretation of an interpreter's utterance. SW propose that the best interpretation is one that makes the utterance most relevant. So the best interpretation in a particular context will depend on the solution for the equation $R = E/C$. Suppose that there is an interpretation of an interpreter's utterance such that the value of C is n and of E is m, and for further interpretation, these values respectively are $n+1$ and $m+1$. Then the cost on each interpretation is the cost of their comparison, $2n+1$. But this means that the interpretation in which the value of E is higher should be selected no matter what the cost. But this guts the idea of cost of any empirical significance.

Perhaps it lies closer to what Sperber and Wilson intend when they think of processing time merely as a measure of the ease or difficulty of integrating information into belief-inventories. Integrability won't quite do either. It is neither necessary nor sufficient for degrees of relevance. In particular, the following claim is untrue: **I** is relevant to degree n for **X** with respect to **A** just in case **I** integrates to degree n (with other information possessed by **X**), which advances or closes **A**. Harry (again) wants to know whether it snowed overnight. He looks out the window and sees that it has. His agenda closes. It is hard to imagine that that information was not of utmost relevance for Harry with respect to that agenda. We don't say that a case to this effect can't be made; it is just that one has to struggle to do it. That information — the evidence of his senses — would have been of less relevance for Harry than it was in fact were Harry to have had reason to (or just did) distrust his vision or if he were uncertain about how to manage the snow/sleet distinction, or some such thing. What seems clear, in any case, is that utmost relevance is cotenable with minimal integrability.

Integrability, here, mimics the structure of linked arguments. A linked argument α is one in which for some target relation R, α's premiss-set bears R to α's conclusion but no proper subset of the premiss-set does [Thomas, 1977, pp. 36–38]. Where R is the entailment relation, then α is linked just in case its premisses jointly entail its conclusion and no proper subset does. Linked arguments resemble Aristotle's syllogisms.[4] Linkage portends a certain notion of maximality. The premiss-sets of linked arguments are the largest set of sentences sufficient for the conclusion, and which also obey a redundancy condition. There is no redundant premiss in a linked argument. If there were, a proper subset of the premisses would suffice for the conclusion, in violation of the linkage constraint. Linked arguments are therefore non-monotonic. They do not tolerate arbitrary supplementation of their premiss-sets. Another way of saying this is that a linked argument is a *premissorily irredundant* argument. By a plausible extension information

[4]Aristotle defines syllogisms in such a way that they are intrinsically linked. Aristotle requires that if α is a syllogism then no proper subset of α's premisses can necessitate α's conclusion. One might think that linear logic satisifes this concept of linkage, but it doesn't quite. Consider

$$A \rightarrow (A \rightarrow A), A, A, A \rightarrow A \vdash A.$$

A is still derivable even after deletion of the first two wffs.

is linked with respect to a given task if it plays its role in the achievement of that task and no proper part of it does the same. We will say for short that linked information is *irredundant information.*

A specification of degrees of integrability now suggests itself. The greater the number of premisses in a linked argument the greater the integrability of each of them in that premiss-set relative to the argument's conclusion. It is easy enough to abstract from our case a sufficiently pliable notion of integrability to enable its broader and more versatile application. The degree of integrability of some information **I** is a matter of the complexity of the total information **I′** sufficient for a task, and for whose insufficiency **I′**-**I** itself is sufficient. By these lights what Harry saw on looking down at the street from his bedroom window has an integrability value of next to zero, if not zero outright, relative to his agenda. But its relevance is maximal. So again, we conclude that integrability does poorly as a necessary condition on degrees of relevance.

Integrability does no better as a sufficient condition. Harry's agenda closed outright with the information that the neighbourhood was heavily snowed on, even if we allow that **I** itself was insufficient for closure, that it had to be integrated with something — if only Harry's remembering that the streets were bare when he retired last night and perhaps also his recognizing the regularity that snow-coverage comes by way of snowfall. This is too little integration for so much relevance to make the case for a correlation between degree of integration and degree of relevance.

Integrability, so conceived, is a matter of complexity. Complexity is not the issue; efficacy is what really signifies. Information is relevant the more it advances the agenda. It is not in general a condition on this happening that there be quite a lot of information conniving to the desired outcome. Perhaps, then, integrability has been assimilated to the wrong paradigm. We might say instead that information is relevant the more it advances agendas, the more agendas the better. There are two subcases to consider.

Subcase One: Harry possesses numerous agendas at any given time. Wanting to know if it snowed overnight might be embedded in Harry's wanting to decide whether to drive his car to the office. He might also want to decide whether to go skiing after work. It is easy to think of the evidence of his senses as closing both these agendas — and so three in all — and that it was on that account more relevant than it would have been had Harry merely been interested in how the weather was overnight or in how best to negotiate the trip to his office that morning. Here complexity and quantity get a useful grip. Information is relevant the more an agent's agendas are nested and/or the greater the number of his agendas that the information advances or closes.

Subcase Two: It is also possible to define agendas for populations. The world-wide population of stock-market speculators is interested in knowing how the Nikkei did overnight. The information that it fell 630 points closed thousands of agendas. Investors backed out all over the place. This was quite a lot of relevance. We shan't concern ourselves further here with relevance for populations, interesting though that question is.

As we have it now, relevance is a property of a piece of information irrespective of how that information is structured. Now that we have the concept of linked or irredundant information, we have the means to take account of certain structured features of the information that AR must press into action. The question of structure is forced on us by the fact that often the information that turns the trick for an agenda is a complex of infons. In its complexity lies the need to consider structure.

Not only is it the case that sometimes information that turns the trick for an agenda is a bundle, i.e., information that is integrated but it also frequently happens that the information that turns the trick for an agenda is not just new information, but rather new information in combination with old. Here the idea of integration serves us well. Let K be everything that Harry knows at time t. Suppose that at t Harry has an agenda to which new information $\mathbf{I}$ is relevant when *combined* with K. No one wants to say that all of K is involved in the partnership. The more intuitive idea is that the information that is relevant at t for Harry's agenda, is the union of $\mathbf{I} \cup \mathbf{I}'$, where $\mathbf{I}'$ is a proper subset of K.

Yet another fact of some importance is the generally good record of beings like us not to lose ourselves in masses of redundancy. This makes it true to say that part of the effectiveness in the use we make of information is our comparative success in avoiding redundancies.

We have the means to tie these points together in terms of integration. Bearing in mind that

Proposition 9.3 (Integration) *Integrated information is linked information.*

Definition 9.4 (Linkage) *Linked information is irredundant information.*

Proposition 9.5 (Maximal irredundancy) *Irredundant information is the largest quantity of information sufficient for some contextually indicated eventuality such that no proper subset of it is likewise sufficient.*

So we can now propose

Definition 9.6 (Relevance) *Where* $\mathbf{I}'$ *is a possibly empty proper subset of what* $\mathbf{X}$ *already knows, new information* $\mathbf{I}$ *is relevant for* $\mathbf{X}$ *with regard*

to **A** *to the extent both that* $\mathbf{I} \cup \mathbf{I}'$ *is integrated, i.e., linked, i.e., maximally irredundant, and* $\mathbf{I} \cup \mathbf{I}'$ *advances* **A**.

We see that definition 9.6 retains what previous definitions provided. Like 9.6, they defined relevance for **I**. But as 9.6 also makes clear, there are lots of cases in which it is not **I** but $\mathbf{I} \cup \mathbf{I}'$ that turns the trick for the agenda at hand. Why, when this is the case, do we not define relevance for $\mathbf{I} \cup \mathbf{I}'$? What is it that makes **I** stand out? The answer is by virtue of the fact that $\mathbf{I}'$ is *background* information. Giving the relevance nod to **I** (honourifically, as it were) is a means of emphasizing the backgroundedness of $\mathbf{I}'$. Some readers may find this an unconvincing rationale. It doesn't matter. There is no harm done in altering 9.6 so as to define relevance for $\mathbf{I} \cup \mathbf{I}'$ if this is what some readers would prefer.

As we will see in chapter 15, the base logic for our formal model of agenda relevance is a labelled deductive adaptation of relevance logic in the manner of Anderson and Belnap. While this ecumenism is a virtue, relevance logic cannot deliver our concept of linkage, nor indeed can linear logic, as we saw in footnote 4. This means that further refinements would need to be made to the base logic if we were to preserve definitions 9.4 and 9.6 in the formal model. Work to this end is currently underway in our paper 'Strong Relevance Logic' [Gabbay and Woods, 2004b]. The notion of strong relevance is discussed in [Diaz, 1981]. A strongly relevant logic would be one capable of handling the linkage condition on agenda relevance. No currently available system we know of can handle this requirement.

This would be a good point at which to pause. At this stage of the book, we are producing a conceptual analysis of agenda relevance. Alternatively, we are constructing a conceptual model of it. In due course (in Part III) we shall turn to the taks of formalizing agenda relevance. In so doing, it is desirable that the conceptual account of relevance be preserved in the formal modeel. It is quite possible, of course, that some features of the conceptual account will not make the cut formally. When this happens, two diagnoses are generally possible. One is that the conceptual feature that is not upheld in the formal model should be retained and we must recognize that the formal model is not strong enough to accommodate it. But it is also sometimes possible that the reverse of this diagnosis is correct, viz., that the fact that the conceputal feature didn't make the cut formally indicates that the conceptual claim was too strong or implausbile, or incorrect in other ways. Whenever the theorist is confronted with these two diagnostic options, he should look for reasons to select one or other of them. If he is unable to decide, he should declare his agnosticism.

Here is how we stand on the linkage question for relevance. Relevant information can't be linked information in the formal model, because the logic of the formal model can't handle irredundancy in the required ways. But we think that it *should* be possible for a logic to do this, i.e., for a logic to handle strong relevance. So we are not prepared to fault the conceptual account in this regard. We acknowlewdge, however, that others might see it differently.

We now have the means to characterize the following kind of case.

It is one thing to say that human beings are disposed to minimize redundancy; it is another thing to suggest that they do so perfectly. As we might expect, therefore, there will be lots of cases in which there is some redundancy in $\mathbf{I} \cup \mathbf{I}'$. More tellingly there will be lots of cases in which the agenda that $\mathbf{I} \cup \mathbf{I}'$ advances or closes will stay advanced or closed under replacement of $\mathbf{I}'$ with larger and larger subsets $\mathbf{I}^*$. In such cases, as far as agenda-closure is concerned, hence as far as relevance is concerned, there is a lot of redundant information in $\mathbf{I}^*$ that goes along for the ride (the free-rider problem for agenda relevance). W can make something of this if we chose.

Definition 9.7 (Parasitic relevance) *If the conditions of definition 9.6 are met except for the linkage of* $\mathbf{I} \cup \mathbf{I}'$*, then* $\mathbf{I}$ *is parasitically relevant for* X *in relation to* A *to the extent that* $\mathbf{I} \cup \mathbf{I}'$ *fails the linkage condition.*

Here, too, it might be objected that the definition pins the rap for parasitism not where it belongs, viz. on $\mathbf{I} \cup \mathbf{I}'$ but rather on $\mathbf{I}$ itself. Of course $\mathbf{I}$ itself could be redundant, but since the only place in which redundancy can be attributed safely is $\mathbf{I} \cup \mathbf{I}'$, that is where to pin the blame. Strictly speaking this is right, and is easily corrected. We ourselves admit to an aversion to the Fair-Weather Friend Principle. Why, bearing the backgroundedness of $\mathbf{I}'$ in mind, do we give the relevance-nod to $\mathbf{I}$ when 9.6 is satisfied, yet not pin the blame on $\mathbf{I}$ when definition 9.6 fails for reasons of redundancy? Still, as we say, readers not liking this rationale can easily make the requisite adjustment to Definition 9.7.

Given that Definition 9.6 fails in our base logic in chapter 15, definition 9.7 is trivially satisfiable there. Thus the model is not strong enough to preserve the distinction between relevance and parasitic relevance. This too need not be seen as a setback. It may indicate, again, that the linkage requirement imposed on relevance by the conceptual model is too strong.

9.4 Hyper-relevance

Linkage of information plays a role in the conceptual elucidation of parasitic relevance. Convergence of information serves a different end. An argument is said to be *convergent* [Thomas, 1977, pp. 38–39], just in case, for some target relation R (here, too, we can think of R as entailment), its premiss-set bears R to its conclusion and every non-empty subset likewise bears R to it. Convergent arguments are an *embarras de richesse* with regard to premissory sufficiency. They are also, to vary the figure, object lessons in premissary overkill.

Convergence, like linkage, can also be defined for information and agenda-advancement. Information **I** is convergent for **X** with respect to agenda **A** iff **I** advances or closes **A** to degree n and every non-empty proper subset **I**′ of **I** likewise advances or closes **A** to that same degree, with n sufficiently high.

There are, of course, approximations to convergence. Information approximates to convergence to the extent that it advances agendas and some subsets also do to a lesser degree. Convergence should not be confused with *cumulativeness.* Thus

Definition 9.8 (Cumulative relevance) I *is cumulatively relevant for* **X** *with regard to* **A** *to the extent that* **I** *is the consistent union of subsets* $\mathbf{I}'_1$, ..., $\mathbf{I}'_n$ *such that for each* $\mathbf{I}'_i$, $\mathbf{I}'_i$ *is relevant for* **X** *with regard to* **A** *to some or other degree* k, *where in each case* k *is less than the degree to which* **I** *itself is relevant to* **X** *with regard to that same agenda but with* k *sufficiently high throughout. (Cumulative relevance is preserved in the formal model at section 15.4.)*

Intuitively, cumulativeness falls midway between linkedness and convergence with respect to agenda closure. Cumulativeness is an approximation to convergence. In a certain respect, cumulative relevance is a good thing. It is defined for summations of intuitively relevant items of information that jointly increase the degree of relevance.

A theory of relevance should be expected to deal with the following kind of case. Harry sees Lou, with whom he has only a slight acquaintance. 'How are you?', Harry asks. Given conventional agendas, it is likely that the information that Harry recruits he will expect to be drawn from the quintet of colloquially conventional responses {'Great', 'Fine', 'Fair', 'Not so hot', 'Lousy'}. Suppose, however, that Lou replies:

> The cheque at the butcher bounced. My sinuses are acting up. They've discovered a heart murmur. I think Wanda's having an affair. I can't shake the arthritis in my shoulder. I'm probably not going to get my promotion. My anxiety attacks are becoming more frequent. Georgina was arrested for speeding.

Now it can't be said that Harry doesn't know which answer to pick from the quintet. Lou's answer is decisive for Harry's agenda. Still, we may think that Lou's was hardly the most apt reply. How so? Certainly Lou's answer took longer to give than 'Lousy' would have taken. This suggests that something like the length of processing time criterion might need to be reconsidered. The suggestion, initially attractive, doesn't bear much scrutiny. Lou's answer, well before it is completed, is decisive for Harry's agenda. This means that Lou's answer overdetermines Harry's agenda; it is *hyper-relevant.* Lou has told Harry much more than he needed to know; most of what he said was unnecessary. Thus

Definition 9.9 (Hyper-relevance) **I** *is hyper-relevant for* **X** *with respect to* **A** *iff there is a subset of* **I** *that is convergent for* **X** *with respect to* **A** *and no proper subset of* **I** *is parasitically relevant for* **X** *with respect to* **A**. *(Definition 9.9 is preserved in the formal model at chapter 15.)*

There is an important conceptual difference between parasitic relevance and hyper-relevance. Each involves the factor of redundancy but in structurally different ways. A complex of information is parasitically relevant when parts of it aren't relevant at all. A complex of information is hyper-relevant when it is relevant and every part of it is also relevant.

We may expect, in turn, that proper subsets of hyper-relevant information will sometimes be cumulative. Hyper-relevance is cumulative relevance taken to extremes. A young barrister is pleading his case before the local magistrate. It is an impressively strong case, but, callowness being what it is, the rooky-lawyer goes on and on. The judge intervenes. 'Would counsel be good enough to pause so that I might find for him?' It is a common enough mistake among the dialectically anxious. Cumulative relevance gives way to convergence and thence to hyper-relevance. We note in passing that if one's base logic is linear, then there can be no hyper-relevance, since in such a logic all premisses must be used exactly once.

Never mind that it is altogether common, hyper-relevance is offensive. It sometimes offends against something like Grice's maxims of quantity.

> The category of Quantity relates to the quantity of information to be provided [by a co-operative interlocutor], and under it falls the following maxims:
>
> 1. Make your contributions as informative as is required (for the current purposes of the exchange).[5]
> 2. Do not make you contributions more informative than is required.[6]

[5]So we may volunteer information if we are interacting with another agent who (say) might have some control of our actions. 'How are you?', the supervisor asks Harry. Harry replies in detail, hoping the supervisor will not ask him to do inventory on the weekend.

[6][Grice, 1991, p. 308].

Grice is unsure about whether a violation of (2) is to be thought of as uncooperative or inefficient ('a waste of time', as he says). We see no harm in seeing it both ways, especially in cases as extreme as Lou's reply to Harry. Either way, it is a dialogical infelicity, and there is reason to suppose that the maxim it violates has a counterpart in nature herself. We conjecture that the information-processing devices of cognitive agents conspire to minimize hyper-relevance. Even if this is so, it would be overdoing it to insist that hyper-relevant information is not relevant information. The offence, to speak loosely, that hyper-relevant information commits suggests a kind of cognitive dissonance. Cognitive dissonance can be created by the marshalling of information aimed at closing agendas that are already closed. Having decided that his newly purchased lawnmower is the best buy for the money, Harry goes on consulting the consumer literature for additional reassurance. If Harry takes this too far, his quest takes on a pathological aspect. But that is a fact about Harry, not about the information that he marshalls.

9.5 Hunches

It is inadvisable to mix up relevance with evidence. This is supported by a consideration of hunches. Detective Brown has learned that Spike was released from prison in San José four days before a murder in Montréal. Considered to have the best instincts on the force, Brown finds himself smitten by the inference that Spike did the deed. Brown has had a hunch. Hunches fit the causal idiom especially well. Brown was made to think, he couldn't shake the idea, and so on. Essential to hunches is that they persist and dominate in the face of weak evidence or of counter-evidence. A person who 'plays his hunch' is taking a specific kind of risk. Hunch-players need to be distinguished from cranks and crackpots.[7] We might respect Brown's, 'I just know Spike did it', but we will have no truck with the Southern Californian cultist's, 'I just know that the earthquake in San Francisco resulted from Thor's displeasure.' It has something to do with the following things. A respected hunch-player tends to have a good track record, whereas a crackpot, even where his confidences are testable, is constantly discredited. Credible hunches involve the skills of judgement, like those involved in assessing fine paintings and the related skills of attentiveness to detail and nuance. Such skills are learnable and perfectible. It is not likely that the same hunch from a rookie would be found credible at all, for he has no experience. It should be noted that the daily routine of

[7]More easily said than done. Cf. Copernicus.

ordinary human beings is filled with hunch playing, though usually of an undramatic kind. Concerning most of life's turnings, people lack the time for syllogisms, even if they knew how to make them.

The basic question is whether Brown's information **I** about Spike is relevant for Brown. We may think it was because it produced an ingenious hunch. It caused Brown to reflect in ways that made him think that his agenda was closed ('Spike did it'). But that cannot be the end of the matter, since Spike might not have done it after all. (In fact, Ike did it.) Brown has the agenda, **A**, to ascertain who the guilty party is. He cannot manage that agenda without also having a second agenda **A*** (or, identity conditions on agendas being what they are, a subagenda **A*** of **A**) to come to a stable belief as to who the guilty party is. These things are nested. Given his cognitive finitude, the best that Brown can hope for in numbers of cases like the present one is closure of **A*** in ways that also close **A**. For closure of **A*** it is sufficient that Brown follow procedures that bring him to the stable belief that Spike did it. For closure of **A**, Spike had to have done it; and thinking doesn't make it so. There is the natural question as to whether information that advances agendas must always be true. The answer is this: For some agendas, closure requires the agent to have beliefs of a certain sort. For some of *those* agendas closure requires that the beliefs be true. Not all agendas so turn. Harry, in asking Sarah whether she had found his tie, thought he heard her say, 'Your grey suit isn't back from the cleaners.' His agenda closed; he decided to wear his brown suit. What Sarah in fact did say was 'You'll have to send your grey suit to the cleaners', suggesting that after yesterday it is unwearable. Harry's agenda was closed by misinformation, but close it did. (Hunches appear in the formal model at section 13.2.4.)

Hunches can be particularly good examples of what might be called negative relevance. AC4 (the negative relevance condition) now enters the picture. Hunches are negatively relevant when they go wrong in certain ways. It may well have been that Brown's hunch about Spike had the effect of sending Brown off on a wild goose chase in which the investigation was significantly set back. If positive relevance is a matter of advancing agendas, negative relevance is a matter of impeding them. Thus

Definition 9.10 (Negative relevance) **I** *is negatively relevant for* **X** *with regard to* **A** *to the extent that* **I** *bears upon* **X** *in ways that impede the closure of* **A**. *(Definition 9.10 is satisfied in the formal model at section 15.4.)*

It should also be noticed that the career of information **I** reflects the causal vagaries of its complete relevance-history. The information **I** about Spike, initially negatively relevant ('a wild goose chase'), may nevertheless be part of a causal chain, even a meandering and branching chain, concerning which two things could be true: first, **I** is a necessary condition of the formation of subsequent links of the chain and nodes of the branches; and second, **I*** is a subsequent link or node which proved decisive for Brown's case. Thus, provided that one is careful, one can say that **I** was both positively and negatively relevant, relativized to different subprogrammes of the agenda in question.

9.6 Misinformation

We need at this point to say something about misinformation. If we are to take the idea of information, which is central to the present account, in the manner of most going informational semantics, we land ourselves with a nasty problem. It is the problem of explaining how a representation can take on determinate content and yet be false [Fodor, 1984]. Peter Godfrey-Smith has emphasized how persistent and troubling a problem this is.

> ... I pause to stress the gravity of the issue. Informational semantics is almost the only theory in an important philosophical market. The market is the naturalistic explanation of intentionality, and ultimately, of truth and reference. Some versions of conceptual role semantics and theories based on biological function are competitors, but none of these is as highly developed as informational semantics. The causal theory of reference is certainly highly developed, but only attempts to tell part of the story about meaning. [Godfrey-Smith, 1989, p. 534]

In our example, Harry misheard Sarah. One might say that Harry was seized by a wayward representation-token of a type to which determinate content has been causally assigned, and that, more generally, misinformation will be a matter of wayward tokens. But this will hardly do. 'We must then explain how an inner state type can acquire the content that *p*, when the connection between this state type and *p* obtaining in the environment is imperfect enough for there to be wayward tokens' [Godfrey-Smith, 1989, p. 534].

Now it is true that our account of relevance turns on an agent's or a system's response to his or its representation of information **I**, and the theory acknowledges, as it should, that sometimes a faulty representation of **I** is no bar to satisfying agenda-closure. Sometimes an agenda will close appropriately on misinformation, sometimes not, and it is precisely this that critics of informational semantics complain about: How can there *be* such a thing? Intuitively all right, the concept of misinformation would seem to be theoretically disabled, and its deficiencies cannot be stopped from invading relevance theory.

It might be thought that the problem is averted by taking representation not in Dretske's way but Millikan's, and so in a way 'not squarely within the informational program' [Godfrey-Smith, 1989, p. 542]. For an approach such as Dretske's to do the required job, it would need to be true that the idealization toward what the receptor-organism is designed for is one toward circumstances in which there is reliable correlation between classes of representation-tokens and their truth conditions.[8] Misrepresentation could then be said to be subideal in the appropriate ways. But it doesn't quite work. There are counterexamples.

> Stich's favorite example involves rats. Rats make very broad and hasty generalizations about what is poisonous. They will inflexibly avoid any food tasting like any food eaten shortly before any illness. Stich says that this probably leads to more false beliefs than true, but this strategy nevertheless is favoured by evolution. Similarly, many birds have a hair trigger flight response to dark fluttering shapes that could be predators.
> [Godfrey-Smith, 1989, p. 547]

Millikan, on the other hand, needs it to be true that the episodes which explain the selection of a cognitive device are episodes in which the organism tokened truths. Yet the 'natural circumstances' during which these episodes occurred could be circumstances in which truths are very hard to come by. The truths could be selectively salient without being common and if they are not common then there need be no reliable correlation between classes of representation tokens and their truth conditions.[9]

Perhaps, as Godfrey-Smith suggests, it would be advisable to abandon any notion of reliable representation of information in favour of 'the biological functions of the representational states themselves' used 'to direct thought to object' [Godfrey-Smith, 1989, pp. 548–549]. Such a theory we do not yet have[10] and until we do, relevance defined our way carries with it a theoretical liability. (Recall, here, the skepticism of [Wheeler, 2001].)

---

[8]Cf. Millikan: '... presumably it is a proper function of belief-manufacturing mechanisms in John to produce beliefs that p only if and when p, for example, beliefs that Jane is in Latvia and beliefs that it is raining only if and when it is raining. Turning this around, a belief that Jane is in Latvia is, and is *essentially*, a thing that is not normally in John unless Jane is indeed in Latvia'. See [Millikan, 1986, pp. 69–70]. Emphasis in the original.

[9]We are indebted to Ruth Millikan and Peter Godfrey-Smith for helpful correspondence on this point.

[10]'Dretske ... seems to be halfway to such a theory, and Millikan ... is closer to it again'. [Godfrey-Smith, 1989, p. 549]. That said, we are prepared to stay the course.

9.7 Dialectical Relevance

We expect a theory of relevance to answer to conditions such as AC8 and, more broadly, AC9, the semantic distribution condition. Consider, for example, dialectical conversations of conflict resolution. They are an attractive possibility if only because dialectical exchanges often incorporate well-defined agendas. In as much as they are conversational agendas, they are subject to the over-arching conversational maxim, 'Be relevant'. As devices of conflict-resolution, they are also held to more specific relevance requirements. In [van Eemeren and Grootendorst, 1992] three particular kinds of relevance requirements are distinguished. These we might call

1. The requirement of stage relevance

2. The requirement of pointfulness

3. The requirement of efficacy.[11]

Stage relevance. Conversations of conflict resolution proceed in stages. The conflict is identified, arguments pro and contra are advanced, concessions are registered, main points are reconsidered, and so on. Without procedural fidelity to the stagedness of such things, conflict-resolution can quickly lapse into a squabble. Here, again, is one way that requirement (1) might be violated. Harry and Sarah are in a disagreement about creationism. Harry states the case for evolution. Sarah states the case for creation science. Then Harry says: 'Very well, I concede'. Now it is possible that Harry saw the light on the mere statement of the creationist's position. Even so, Harry's task is to put maximum pressure on Sarah's thesis, never mind that he now believes it. So it seems right to say that he has made his response at the wrong stage of the discussion. He has quit the argument, not advanced it.

Why call this procedural infelicity a case of irrelevance? The causal theory can account for thinking it so. Harry's response **I** is irrelevant for Sarah with respect to his agenda **A** (answering Sarah's challenge) just because it is not information for Sarah that advances the argument. There is a difference here between advancement and giving up.

The requirement of pointfulness. This requirement is violated when the disputant presents information which the other can't integrate. His inability to integrate it does not ensue from his inability to understand it, but rather from his not knowing how to put it to use. In the creationism example, if

[11] van Eemeren and Grootendorst, [1992]. The terminology that we here employ is not theirs. We trust that it does their account no violence.

Sarah were to say that lions *could* be striped, Harry might well not know what Sarah's point is. Violations of the present requirement are construable in the account of agenda relevance. They involve information that does not advance the agenda.

The requirement of efficacy includes the requirement that information exchanged in conversations of conflict-resolution be clear and credible. If Harry's information is sufficiently unclear to Sarah, then Sarah cannot integrate it. If Harry's information is sufficiently incredible to Sarah, then Sarah *will* not integrate it. Either way, the irrelevance is unmistakable. Such information is inert in the agenda at hand.

Thus the account of agenda-relevance integrates with dialectical accounts, a circumstance that the causalist will be tempted to take as confirming, and it responds to adequacy conditions AC8 and AC9 the requirements that our theory investigate the claim that relevance is intrinsically a dialectical notion, and that it should attempt an analysis of relevance as a common concept.[12]

A somewhat different approach is Douglas Walton's account of dialectical relevance [Walton, 2003] (pre-publication draft).

> The kind of relevance defined in the new theory can be called *dialectical relevance*, meaning that an argument, a question, or other type of speech act, is judged to be relevant insofar as it plays a part or has a function in goal-directed conversations, that is, a dialogue exchange between two participants who are aware of each other's moves in the exchange.

The ultimate aim of the theory is to be useful in judging cases of material relevance.

Material relevance in turn is understood as follows:

> An argument (or other speech act) is *materially relevant* in a conversation if it bears directly or strongly on the issue so that it is worth prolonged or detailed consideration in relation to the specific problem or issue that the conversation is supposed to resolve. [Walton, 2003, p. 142 of ms]

Thus, material relevance contrasts with topical relevance, which formed part of our discussion in chapter 1.

Walton takes legal relevance to be a special case of material relevance [Walton, 2003, p. 131 of ms].

[12]Relevance as an enhancer of dialectical agendas is discussed by M. Agnes Van Rees in [1989, esp. sec. 3].

> Thus in theory, anything is relevant in a legal case that could be used as evidence to prove or disprove a statement at issue in that case.[13] However the law adds restrictions to this general notion of relevance, by ruling kinds of evidence inadmissible in a trial.[14]

We note in passing the narrowness of these definitions. Consider the following moves in a criminal trial, *Regina* vs. Smith.

Crown (rising): My lord, owing to developments overnight, the Crown stays the charges against the accused.

Judge: Very well. [To the accused] Mr Smith, you are free to go.

Neither materially nor legally relevant according to Walton's definition, what the Crown Attorney said was relevant according to The Laws of Evidence (see section 5.3 above) and was relevant in the sense of agenda-relevance. It influenced (decisively) the judge in determining whether the trial could properly proceed, which is a standing duty of the sitting Bench.

Of more central concern is how dialectical relevance works in general.

> According to the pragmatic definition of dialectical relevance, an argument, or other move in a dialogue, is *dialectically relevant* (in that type of dialogue) if and only if it can be chained forward using either the method of profile reconstruction or argument extrapolation (whichever is more applicable to the given case) so that the line of argumentation reaches one or other of the pair of propositions that defines the issue of the dialogue [Walton, 2003, p. 219 of ms.].[15]

Forward chaining is a notion that Walton borrows from AI. He illustrates it as follows. Let Σ be a set of statements. Let C be a statement. Then there is a forward chaining from Σ to C if $\Sigma \Vdash C$, if, that is to say, the argument from Σ to C is deductively valid. Forward chaining contrasts with backward chaining. Let C be a statement, which a reasoner wishes to deduce. For no Σ known to the reasoner is there a forward chain to C. The reasoner assumes a statement S and decides to accept it if there is a forward chaining

[13] Here Walton cites [Strong, 1992; Mueller and Kirkpatrick, 1995; Imwinkelried, 1993; Roberts, 1993].

[14] Concerning the rather spotty record of coherence concerning this practice, see [Fisher, 1986, p. 8].

[15] Think also, for example, of proof theory, in which a line is used in an elimination rule.

from $\Sigma \cup S$ to C. In such a case, the reasoner has *abduced* S. In the former case, the reasoner has *deduced* C.

These are highly simplified characterizations of forward and backward chaining (see, for example, [Gabbay and Woods, 2004a]). But for present purposes it suffices to examine the role played in the definition of dialectical relevance by the general idea of forward chaining.[16]

By argument extrapolation Walton understands a generalization of procedures for the resolution of enthymeme problems.[17] By profile reconstruction Walton understands a generalization of rules for conversational coherence in the manner of Jacobs and Jackson [Jacobs and Jackson, 1983; Schegloff, 1988; Levinson, 1981; Walton and Krabbe, 1995]. With forward chaining as our example, we may suppose that a move M is dialectically relevant in a dialogue D with respect to a disputed issue F if either

1. there is an extrapolation that produces a set of moves S such that $\{M\} \cup S$ forward chains to $\pm F$, or

2. there is a coherent conversation C from M such that $\{M\} \cup C$ forward chains to $\pm F$. ($\pm F$ is F or its negation, as the case may be.)

Readers of [Walton, 2003] may be disappointed to discover that the procedures for extrapolation and profiling are not expounded here, so readers must try to make do with the main idea. For our purposes, the main idea is all we need. We take it to be obvious that the basic approach to dialectical relevance can, without too much strain, be absorbed into the more general theory of agenda relevance. This would appear to be so in the sense that for a direction of movement of a certain kind, relevance is anything which enhances it.

On the other hand, and notwithstanding that our present discussion is very general, we find core features of Walton's account to be problematic, all the more so if we assume, as he himself appears to do, that a condition on the success of forward chaining is the production of a deductively valid argument.

Any move will fail the extrapolation test if it fails to have an extrapolation that delivers the goods deductively. Thus M will fail to be relevant in a dialogue D with respect to an issue F, unless for some S, $\{M\} \cup S \Vdash \pm F$. We will restrict our comments to two. One is that we take it to be methodologically ill-advised to hold the presence or absence of relevance to procedures

[16] In the definition of dialectical relevance, Walton seems to have forgotten about backward chaining, concerning which 'The key to the new pragmatic theory of relevance is [in part] the chaining of argumentation (backward and/or forward chaining) to the ... issue'. [Walton, 2003, p. 200 of ms.]. We take the omission to have been unintentional.

[17] [Walton, 2003, pp. 209–211 of ms.]. See for details, [Walton and Krabbe, 1995].

which, themselves, are awash in theoretical dissensus, as anyone familiar with the literature on enthymemes will (or should) appreciate.[18] A second worry is that Walton leaves the structure of forward chaining underdescribed in key respects. Is forward chaining monotonic? If so, then any move is relevant in any D with respect to any F. For every F, there is an S that implies it. Hence for every F, there is an M such that $\{M\} \cup S \Vdash F$; and the same is true for every M, and for the negation of any F. Monotonic forward chaining therefore makes excessive provision for relevance and in so doing fails our adequacy condition AC1 (the anti-excessiveness condition). On the other hand, we may put it that forward chaining is non-monotonic. That alone will not solve the problem of excessive relevance, but let that pass. A more interesting problem is that it does not suffice to abduce on the mover's behalf anything which in concert with M delivers the goods in D with respect to the contested issue F. This is not to say that we are wholly in the dark about how to proceed. One way of proceeding is to abduce on the mover's behalf commitments that are relevant to the task at hand. Not a bad idea, just so, it is problematic in the context of Walton's theory. It makes the definition of dialectical relevance viciously circular, and it leaves the tacit deciderutum of achieving *material* relevance ill-provided for. It's material relevance is what bears on the truth of F; satisfying the extrapolation test is insufficient for material relevance (hence, by definition, for dialectical relevance).

The conversational coherence test bears on our question somewhat differently. M passes this test if from M there is a coherent conversation C such that there is a forward chaining to $\pm F$ from $\{M\} \cup C$.

Consider the following conversation.

Harry: M

Sarah: M? What has M to do with it?

Harry: Well doesn't M imply G, which in turn implies not-F?

Sarah: No. It's N that implies G.

Harry: (slapping his forehead) By golly, you're right. It's N, and not M.

Sarah: Good.

Harry: But anyhow, N.

[18] See [Gabbay and Woods, 2004a, Ch. 10]. See also [Hitchcock, 2000], [Hitchcock, 1987] and [Woods, 2003, ch. 19].

Sarah: So, I suppose it's not-F.

Harry: Right you are.

By the conversational coherence test, M is relevant in D with respect to F, even though M bears no weight in the forward chaining to not-F. It takes little ingenuity to show ranges of such cases in which the values of M are intuitively as irrelevant to $\pm F$ as could be imagined.

So we conclude that while Walton's basic idea of dialectical relevance is all right (in fact, it is easy to see it is an instance of agenda relevance), certain of its fundamental details require further attention. As it stands, the account of dialectical relevance is met with internal difficulties which damage its would-be contribution to the theory of argument. Still repairs might be possible. With or without them, we see Walton's dialectical theory as a suitable candidate for our ecumenical aspirations.

We turn now to a third way of approaching relevance dialectically. In dialectical settings a prominent role is played by *irrelevance claims*. In fact, the same is true for dialogical exchanges generally. If we understand dialectic in one of its modern senses as an argument between two or more parties in which some disputed claim is attached and defended then a standard way for Harry to defend his position against a proposition, q, which has been advanced against it by Sarah is to put it that p is irrelevant; that is it is irrelevant even *if it is true*. The principal dialectical significance of the irrelevance-rejoinder is that it (purports to) shift the burden of proof back to the utterer of q. This matters. It annuls the objection presented by p without having to show *semantic* cause; for if p is indeed irrelevant, it is perfectly possible for it to be true. There is no satisfactory answer to a charge of p's irrelevance except

1. to withdraw p

or

2. to make the case that p is not irrelevant.

Rejoinders in the form 'It certainly *is* relevant!' are the dialectical equivalent of high dudgeon, and they beg the question. Accordingly as the original utterer of q, Sarah is better advised not to *answer* Harry's irrelevance-charge, but to *question* it. ('Why do you say it's irrelevant?') In so doing, Sarah is refusing the burden of proof that purportedly shifts to her with Harry's irrelevance claim. Can this example be absorbed by the AR approach?

Let us say that p is relevant to the matter at hand iff for an arbitrarily selected agent $\mathbf{X}$ whose agenda $\mathbf{A}$ is to determine whether q, and for $\mathbf{I} = p$, $\mathbf{I}$ impinges on X in ways that advances (or closes) his agenda. If p is relevant in this way its utility may have manifested itself variously.

1. It may persuade **X** that q is false.

2. It may *also* persuade him that q is true. (Perhaps the utterer of p failed to see that p together with something implied by something else she has concedes implies q.)

3. In varying degrees **X** may feel more or less strongly with respect to the question whether q.

All of this is compatible (though not compossible) with the following.

1. p entails q (not-q).

2. p together with some other concession or concessions entails q (not-q).

3. p raises the probability of q (not-q).

4. p raises **X**'s subjective probability with regard to q (not-q).

5. p is evidence for q (not-q).

We see in this a distinction between *grounds* for p's relevance and what it is for p to *be* relevant. We could have it, for example, that p actually does entail q without its being the case that p is relevant in the matter at hand. For **X** may not see that p entails q.

We are speaking, of course, of de facto relevance. De facto relevance is such that a (sincere) utterance of 'That's irrelevant' has a very high likelihood of being true, for the right ranges of agendas. Since dialectical exchanges are dynamic interactions, what is true now could be untrue afterwards. If Harry sincerely says 'irrelevant' to p, then he is in effect reporting that his agenda has not advanced even on the supposition of p. Harry's agenda was to *determine* or *decide* whether q is the case. Sarah's uttering p was tantamount to a belief-revision prediction for Harry. She supposes that Harry will be so disposed to p as to modify in some way his disposition toward q. Harry falsifies Sarah's prediction (or presupposed prediction) if he is in fact unmoved.

Needless to say, Sarah may elect to persist. Perhaps she will now show Harry a proof of q from p. In that case, we may safely suppose that Harry will withdraw his charge of irrelevance.

Our discussion draws attention to two consequential points. One is that relevance is a dynamic notion. What is irrelevant at t_1 may be relevant at t_2. The other is that we may be left with a certain wistfulness about *normative* relevance. We may think that de facto relevance is too fugitive a thing to be all there is to relevance. Can we not therefore say that, precisely because

Harry's situation was one in which de facto irrelevance metamorphosed into de facto relevance, that p was normatively relevant all along?

We return to the question of normativity in chapter 10

9.7.1 Fallacies of Relevance

One of the challenges for a theory of relevance is that it go some way toward elucidating the fallacies of relevance, some of which (but not all) are of an expressly dialectical character. Let us ask, therefore, how the grand-daddy of the fallacies of relevance — the *argumentum ad hominem* — fares in AR. It is customary to distinguish two modern conceptions of the *ad hominem*, the circumstantial and the abusive. We shall here discuss the circumstantial type.[19]

Harry and Harry Jr. are having a tense chat about smoking (let us suppose that neither knows about the Norwegian study discussed earlier).[20] Harry presents the standard case, and the kitchen reverberates with direness: cancer, heart disease, wrinkling skin, premature aging, and so on. Harry Jr. listens patiently and then says, 'But you smoke, Dad.' It is astonishing that in many an introductory logic text, Harry Jr. would be taken, without ado, to have committed a fallacy of relevance at precisely this point in the discussion. It is hardly so on the causal account. Harry knows very well that his son's response signals trouble for the early or easy resolution of their dispute. That response causes Harry to reconsider his position tactically. Harry might take his son to be thinking that since Harry doesn't practise what he preaches — that he doesn't really believe what he preaches — then Harry's own behaviour may be evidence that the real case against smoking is a good deal less dire than Harry is making it out to be.

If he is dialectically astute, Harry will turn the complaint to his own advantage. 'Look, that's just the point. Smoking is so pernicious that I'm hooked on it. I'm a cigarette addict. So it's not just that it's very bad for you. Millions of people know its further destructiveness, since, for them, once you start, you can't quit.' It is a good thing that people don't always believe what they read in logic textbooks. If they did, then Harry would have found himself in the imbecilic position of saying. 'Son, that doesn't disprove what I'm saying. My behaviour isn't relevant, and your thinking that it is is a logical *fallacy*!'[21]

[19]Aristotle and Locke have a quite different appreciation of *ad hominem* manoeuvres [Woods, 2002a] and [Woods, 2003, ch. 6].

[20]This sort of case is discussed in greater detail in [Woods, 1993b].

[21]Jonathan Adler has expressed (personal communication) an interesting reservation. Couldn't we suppose that Harry Jr. has two agendas, a specific one (whether to smoke) and a standing one (to cognitively economize). The *ad hominem* can be seen advancing

A retort *ad hominem* is neither fallacious nor irrelevant just because it is *ad hominem*. It is irrelevant when it doesn't advance agendas. In such cases there is a certain theoretical efficiency in characterizing the *ad hominem* as fallacious. So described, part of the traditional wisdom is preserved. An *ad hominem* is fallacious just when it is irrelevant. If this is right, 'But you're a Gemini, Dad', would likely stand convicted; not because it is an *ad hominem*, but because it is irrelevant. It ill-serves the dialectical objectives at hand. Thus not all of the traditional account is preserved[22]; but enough has been said to qualify for fulfilment of adequacy condition AC6 (that the theory elucidate the fallacies of relevance).

A reader might think that this was hardly a standard account of the *ad hominem*. Perhaps it was rigged to better its prospects of satisfying AC6. This is not the place for wrangles about fallacy theory. So let us yield the field to Locke. Locke speaks of '*four sorts of arguments* that men, in their reasonings with others, do ordinarily make use of to prevail on their assent, or at least so as to awe them as to silence their opposition' [Locke, 1961]. Italics in the original. Of the four only one pertains to 'true instruction'; it involves 'the using of proofs drawn from any of the foundations of knowledge or probability.' [Locke, 1961, p. 279]. Locke calls this the *argumentum ad judicum*. The others, says Locke, are arguments that fail the cause of true instruction. Arguments *ad verecundiam* forward the opinions of reputed personnages. Arguments *ad ignorantiam* press an opponent to accept *his* opponents's opinion or produce a better one. Arguments *ad hominem* 'press a man with consequences drawn from his own principles or concessions'.

Locke recognizes that his three underdetermine the quest for truth which 'must come from proofs and arguments and light arising from the nature of things themselves, and not from my shamefacedness, ignorance, or er-

---

the second agenda. We agree with this.

[22]The transparent mistake of attempting to convict every *ad hominem* manoeuvre, just so, of fallaciousness, can be seen from the following aggressive bit of advocacy.

> Rorty ... is a philosopher who claims to know nothing about knowledge but uses *historical* knowledge to make good the claim that those philosophers who thought they knew something about knowledge are wrong, thus assuming for his proof that historical knowledge, unlike all other knowledge, can be had for asking. How, one must ask, can one use knowledge to prove that one knows nothing about knowledge? [Munz, 1987]

Whether Munz's *ad hominem* is decisive or not, it is clear that it is intended as decisive. For Rorty is offered up as constructing his own counterexample; and the ancient links between the *ad hominem* and the *reductio ad absurdum* are called down with menacing and relevant effect. Actually Munz's attack is unfair to Rorty. Rorty is leery of Knowledge and Truth, not of knowledge and truth. He is prepared (how could he not be) to use knowledge and truth in the construction of his case against Knowledge and Truth. But, if this is a criticism of Munz, it is more than modestly significant that it is *not* the complaint that Munz has employed an *ad hominem*.

ror.' But nowhere does Locke say or suggest that questing for the truth is the only legitimate function of argument. He expressly mentions two others: prevailing on the assent of an interlocuter and reducing him to silence concerning which, of course, getting at the truth of things is *one* way of proceeding.

Still, the person who does engage in argument and inquiry for the purpose of instruction has an agenda to that effect. Sentiments of shamefacedness (*ad verecundiam*), ignorance (*ad ignorantiam*) or error, that is, an opponent's inconsistency (*ad hominem*) may well produce strong beliefs. But they will not advance the agenda in question unless they meet the requirements of 'the foundation of knowledge or probability'. Locke holds that such arguments plainly do not fulfil *those* conditions, and by the account of agenda relevance they convey information irrelevant for agents having the instruction agenda. Locke's trio are paradigms of the so-called fallacies of relevance. Any sentence of the form 'Argument α commits a fallacy of relevance in Locke's sense', is easily re-expressed in a truth-preserving way in the vocabulary of agenda relevance with regard to *that* agenda. So the theory makes good progress with AC5.

It is easy to see that although AR satisfies AC5, it doesn't do so in a theoretically deep way. (Besides, for the other agendas, e.g., dialectical disputes resolution, an effective *ad hominem* is clearly relevant for the person against whom it is pressed, since it tells him that he has landed himself with a convergence he is unwilling to accept.) Even in the instruction case, it doesn't expose the structure of failed instruction in ways that deepen very much Locke's own account, which is also rather abrupt and superficial. So it might be said that AR, in the form in which we have it presently, provides little more than lexical relief for the idiom of 'fallacy of relevance'. But haven't we disdained lexical relief? Isn't a lexical relief fulfilment of AC5 a Phyrric achievement? No. We said that an analysis of relevance that defined relevance in the minimum vocabulary of a theory T provided 'mere' lexical relief if the truth-preserving interpretations of the relevance idiom in T failed to occasion novel developments in T itself and failed to motivate novel insights into relevance. This would be so when no new T-theorem, whether about T's target concept or about relevance, was other than any immediate consequence of the lexical relief definition itself.

In the case at hand, AR is a fledlging theory of relevance which makes, or so we say, some headway with both conditions. The relevance idiom is interpretable in the union of subsets of the minimum vocabularies of probabilistic causal theory, information theory (including inference theory), cognitive science and agenda theory. It is not required that AR sponsor new theorems in every theory where minimum vocabulary figures in the analytic reconstruction of relevance, but it is agreeable that it do so in some of them. If what is said in e.g., [Woods, 1993b] and [Woods, 1992b] is right, then AR is extendible even more deeply. AR would then prompt new theorems in fallacy theory itself. A case in point is the irrelevance attributed in cases of the circumstantial *ad hominem*. Suppose again that Harry is lecturing his son, Harry Jr., on the perils of cigarette-smoking. When Harry is well-launched, his son intervenes with 'But you smoke, Dad'. If the boy is right, Harry has been shown to be pragmatically inconsistent. The received wisdom among fallacy theorists is that there is a fallacy involved in *attributing* pragmatic inconsistency at this point in the discussion. The fallacy is the fallacy of introducing an irrelevancy.

In what way, then, does it do any good to point out to a preachy anti-smoker his own pragmatic inconsistency? What is this information irrelevant *to*? A rather common answer is that his pragmatic inconsistency doesn't establish the falsity of Harry's anti-smoking thesis. But why attribute to the boy this intention? It is obvious that someone's pragmatic inconsistency with regard to his policy P is no indictment of P. Neither is one's state of *logical* inconsistency with respect to P an indictment of P. So we conclude that the standard analysis of the irrelevance of the boy's *ad hominem* retort against his father is itself an *ad ignorantiam* or straw man fallacy.

What accounts for the utter prevalence of the straw man fallacy in the analysis of the circumstantial *ad hominem*? We conjecture that the standard analysis involves the following chain of reasoning.

1. Relevance is the propositional semantic relation of bearing on the truth or falsity of statements or claims.
2. Harry's pragmatic inconsistency does not bear on the truth or falsity of his anti-smoking thesis P.
3. In his failure to appreciate (2), Harry Jr.'s charge of inconsistency is irrelevant, hence fallacious.

We have already remarked that assuming the son's insensitivity to (2) may already be a straw man fallacy against him. But there is also reason to query (1), which as we have been at pains to show, is a vexed, and in some variations wholly discredited, conception of relevance. We propose instead the agenda approach to relevance. The boy is asking his father whether he can explain his inconsistency. He asks for the explanation because different things *would* explain it. One is that Dad has overstated his own thesis, that he is saying that no one should smoke *heavily* or that no one should smoke who is not yet an *adult*. Another explanation of Harry's defection from his own policy is that he is a nicotine addict. In all of these respects the son has a competent agenda with regard to which he has asked a competent question (assuming the equivalency or 'But you smoke, Dad.' with 'Then why do you smoke, Dad?').

On the agenda-relevant approach, the standard analysis of the circumstantial *ad hominem* is mistaken in both of its premisses. What is more, it leaves space for an answer from Dad which in turn is negatively relevant. Ironically, it is an answer of a kind prompted by the standard analysis. In colloquial form, it is the 'Don't do what I do, but what I say'-answer, at the dismissive core of which is the claim

* No one should smoke, and that I do smoke is for me of no moment.

But, this is a blind-spot, a claim bearing an unmistakable resemblance to Moore's Paradox.

** P, but I don't believe it.

Moore's Paradox is a blind-spot in the sense that in the absence of further information it is not possible to determine the utterer's position with regard to P [Sorenson, 1988]. The same is true of Dad's dismissive response to his son: *No one* should smoke, but the fact that someone *does* smoke is a matter of no moment. In the absence of additional information, Harry's utterance makes it impossible for his son to fathom his father's position on smoking.

On the other hand, the fledgling 'theory' of agendas is entirely *de novo* and expressed in the idiom of causal sufficiency in ways hardly likely to produce new theorems in causal theory apart from immediate consequences of the analysis of agendas there.

9.8 Semantic Distribution

We now ask: How well does AR satisfy AC9, the semantic distribution condition? Does AR preserve the range of the common notion of relevance? A test case for AR is the extent to which it can accommodate our eight cases from an earlier chapter. They are also a test case for SOR. Let us see.

1. *That it will rain today is relevant to the fact that the picnic was scheduled for today.*

Scheduled picnics have been scheduled by someone having an interest in them. The would-be picnicker has a picnic-arranging agenda. The information at hand is relevant for anyone having such an agenda. It might get him to cancel the picnic and, so, to act in ways that disclose the relevance by way of agenda override. Or it might induce the picnic-planner to move the event indoors.

2. *A patient's wishes are relevant to a surgeon's entitlement to operate.*

Wishes run the gamut from legal consent to mere preference. Since entitlement is at issue, wishes here are what a patient consents to. A surgeon, knowing that he has his patient's consent, may be moved to proceed with his surgical agenda. Knowing that consent has been withheld may make him desist. If, as in certain sorts of emergencies, he does not desist, he will need to close post-operatic agendas in certain ways. He will need to make the case that circumstances of the emergencies voided the patient's refusal.

3. *That Harry decided to go to the movies was relevant to the question of whether he favours light entertainment over theatre of the absurd.*

Someone having that question in circumstances in which the claim is true will be made to ponder whether Harry's preference in that case is evidence one way or the other. Perhaps it isn't, and perhaps our questioner comes to think that it isn't. But it is relevant to her question if she is made to consider its evidential potential.

4. *Recent findings in archeominerology are relevant to Sarah's interest in pre-Columbian civilization.*

It depends on the findings and the interest, too, of course. Suppose that she is curious about the accuracy of the Chilam Balam of Chumayel concerning the dates of the first tall pyramids. The Chilam Balam records their construction in the second and third centuries BCE. The researcher reads Roy's *The Book of Chilam Balam of Chumayel* [Roy, 1967]. The archeological evidence presented there is striking. She was made to see that the Chilam Balam account was probably right. Her agenda closes.

5. *Be relevant!*

(See again the discussion of section 9.2.)

6. *An arts & science degree is irrelevant in today's world.*

For an employer, knowing that a job-applicant has a B.A. could lead him to think that the applicant is not qualified to fill the vacancy, or is, but because of qualifications other than the possession of a B.A. If proposition (6) is true, it would be true for an appropriate generalization from the present case: A B.A. won't get a company to hire you. For the B.A.-holder, the information that his degree has furnished him with has little or no occasion for use in his worldly pursuits.[23]

[23]Assertion 6 is, of course, notoriously false. It is used here for exemplary purposes only.

7. *Harry always peppers his stories with mindless irrelevancies.*

Harry's stories abound in information that doesn't advance the story's point. Perhaps they get in the way of the story. Perhaps, that is, they are negatively relevant.

8. *Harry is the most irrelevant guy I know.*

Nothing he says or does is helpful in advancing the speaker's agendas. People wouldn't dream of asking Harry's advice about next month's bond issue or about how to fix the carburetor or even how to get from Strasbourg to Amsterdam by the most direct route. Neither would he fit in with the company's plans for a leveraged merger or be kept in mind for the next Cabinet shuffle; etc.

It is easy to see that the pull of the idiom of agenda relevance on these eight cases is not perfectly truth-preserving. Agenda relevance does a pretty good job of it all the same. The eight yield to the canonical pull of agenda relevance in a non-trivial way. This in turn counts as fair conformability to AC10. It does so in ways that verify and exemplify an earlier claim. We said in chapter 1 that there would be uses of 'relevant' that occupy a kind of twilight zone. They would fulfil truth conditions on agenda relevance only approximately, and yet their failure to do so perfectly would be insufficient to validate a judgment of counterexample or to motivate strategies of ambiguation. Their approximate satisfaction of truth conditions on agenda relevance would show two things. It would reveal what we knew from the outset, that in so far as relevance is a common sense concept, a concept-in-use, it would have fuzzy edges, that it would satisfy truth conditions only approximately. The second thing that our eight suggest is the weight of the canonical pull of agenda relevance. It is enough to make one think that there is a semantic core to the ordinary idioms of relevance, and that agenda relevance is that core. And our invocation of SOR was neither vacuous nor mistaken.

9.9 Relevant Logic, Pittsburgh Style

All of this bears on a lively and still unsolved contention between classical and relevant logicians. Though relevant logicians offer no theory of relevance,[24] it would be interesting to know whether our account gets a non-trivial purchase in the contention.

[24]What they have to say by way of an analysis of relevance boils down to two things. One is the specification of a necessary condition on a necessary condition of implication [=entailment]. We have it, first, that relevance is a necessary condition on implication

The disagreement centers on the classical theorem, *ex falso quodlibet*, according to which any self-contradiction implies any proposition whatever. Supporters of *ex falso quodlibet* take refuge in a celebrated proof [Lewis and Langford, 1932, 250 ff.]:

1.	$A \wedge \neg A$	assumption
2.	A	1, simplification
3.	$A \vee B$	2, addition
4.	$\neg A$	1, simplification
5.	B	3,4, disjunctive syllogism
6.	$(A \wedge \neg A) \rightarrow B$	1-5, conditionalization

Relevant logicians demur. They abhor the execrable theorem and they distrust disjunctive syllogism, 'which commits a fallacy of relevance ...'. We therefore reject it as an entailment and as a valid principle on inference [Anderson and Belnap, 1975, p. 164].

Disjunctive syllogism: not an entailment and not a valid rule of inference. Anderson and Belnap may or may not be right about entailment ([Woods, 1989, pp. 77–86]; see also [Woods, 2002b].), but they are certainly right about inference. Inference, taken Harman's way, is a species of the adjustment of belief inventories under the dynamic press of new stimuli. The rules of inference are thus the rules by virtue of which some such adjustments are made correctly. Harman is careful to say that the rules of deductive logic misdescribe good inference strategies. (See also [Woods, 1989, pp. 81–82 and p. 86, n. 15].) If we take *modus ponens* (or it's equivalent, disjunctive syllogism), as a rule of inference, then it provides that if **X**'s belief inventory contains $P, \ulcorner P \rightarrow Q \urcorner$, then it is always allowable to add to it the new belief Q. But this is not so. **X** might realize that Q is false, and might thereupon deny or withdraw P or deny or withdraw $\ulcorner P \rightarrow Q \urcorner$, or both. **X**'s rational inference options thus significantly exceed what *modus ponens* tells him it is always all right to do. Another difference is this: Implication can be monotonic and inference cannot. (See chapter 5.)

That said, there is no point in worrying about *particular* deductive rules, about disjunctive syllogism for example, since none of them is a correct rule of inference. And neither is the rule derived from the classical theorem, for from a contradiction it is not all right to infer everything whatever. Deductive logic (classical or relevant, it doesn't matter) is not a tenable

---

and, second, that propositional variable-sharing is a necessary condition on relevance. Jointly, it is provided that $\ulcorner (A \wedge \neg A) \rightarrow B \urcorner$ fails because $\ulcorner (A \wedge \neg A) \urcorner$ and B fail to share at least one propositional variable. The other, as we have seen, is a conception of relevant proof from a set of hypotheses, in which all the hypotheses must be used in the proof.

theory of rational inference. How it fares as a theory of implication is another matter about another question.

The point is easily captured in the theory of agenda-relevance. For any cognitive agent **X**, **X** possesses no agenda (nor could he) the closure of which requires the filling of **X**'s mind with everything, and no agenda, therefore, whose closure implies boundless doxastic clutter.[25] There being no such agendas, there is no case in which contradictory information will induce a cognitive agent to adjust his beliefs in ways that close them. In this precise sense is contradictory information guaranteed the status of causal irrelevance. This seems not at all to be what, historically, the relevant logician had in mind, but it is true and worth knowing.

9.10 Revision and Update

Consider the database or belief-set Δ and **I** some new information. There are two kinds of abductive problem occasioned by situations of this sort [Aliseda-LLera, 1997]. **I** is an *anomaly-trigger* with respect to Δ iff **I** is incompatible with Δ. The abducer's task is to modify Δ in a certain sort of way so as to accommodate **I**. On the other hand, **I** is a *novelty-trigger* with respect to Δ iff there is some desired relation that Δ fails to bear to **I**. (For expository convenience, think of this relation as that of *providing an explanation of*.) Here the abducer's task is to supplement Δ in ways that achieves the desired explanation (and meets other conditions). It is easy to see that the agenda created by an anomaly-trigger belongs to a class of problems known as belief-revision problems, and that the agenda prompted by a novelty-trigger belongs to a class of problems known as belief-update problems.

We shall confine our remarks to anomaly resolutions. It may be that this is the trickier of the pair, concerning which we have discussed at some length the conjectured roles of Seer of Trouble Coming and Putter of Things Right (which counts as at least partial compliance with AC8, which requires that AR have something helpful to say about belief revision). On the whole, we have given the nod to Putter over Seer, although the matter cannot be said to have been settled. Anomaly problems are, as we say, a further reason to like the Putter option. Here is why. Anomaly problems are a special case of belief-revision problems. What makes them special is that the inconsistency in question is a noticed inconsistency and the database with respect to which the inconsistency has arisen is often no larger than a

[25] Such agendas would, in fact, give ultimate and radical offense to Harman's Clutter Avoidance Principle. [Harman, 1986, p. 12]. The Clutter Principle resembles Clark's The 007 Principle. [Clark, 1989, p. 64].

given scientific theory. Even so, given that the abducer's task is to replace Δ with a restriction or restriction-extension of it Δ^* such that Δ^* bears to **I** the explanation relation $\Rightarrow$ that Δ alone failed to provide, Δ^* can be much larger than Δ by virtue of the number of inputs to $\Rightarrow$ that actually delivers the desired consequence **I**. In abductive reasoning, the required adjustments to Δ are accomplished by way of *conjecture*, in which deletions from Δ are propositions now conjectured not to hold, and in which additions to Δ are proposition now conjectured to hold. The propositions of such conjectures are thus *hypotheses* H. The number of hypotheses that solve an anomaly problem are without theoretical limit. True, their number is somewhat constrained by the requirement that no hypothesis be admitted which alone bears $\Rightarrow$ to **I**; but still the number of winners is arbitrarily large.

The abducer's agenda is to conjecture his way to the derivation of **I**. There are more ways of doing this than he has the capacity to entertain. We may take it that the H_i that occur in the domain D of the explanation relation exceed what the abducer's agenda requires him to select. He is required to select not just any H that gets the job done, but rather the H that gets the job done subject to some conditional constraints. This turns out to be a hugely important fact in the manner of agenda-specification. If Harry is our abducer, it turns out that he is not in the least disposed to pick randomly from this domain of $\Rightarrow$. Harry's agendas are typified by the sorts of things that he can actually bring off, notwithstanding his status as a practical agent, his status as a deployer of scarce resources. Harry must, in effect, select an H from this huge domain D. He must do so without there being the slightest question of a search of its members. Abetting him in this task is a structural fact about D. D is the set of proper subsets of Δ and extensions of proper subsets of Δ that, unlike Δ itself, bear $\Rightarrow$ to **I**. In each such case, one or more Hs is involved, either driving the deletions or constituting the additions. Let D^* be the proper subset of all *irredundant* explainers of **I**. In the full-use of hypotheses sense, D^* is the set of relevant inputs to $\Rightarrow$ with regard to **I**. (Actually, D^* is the set of linear, hence relevant, inputs.) D^* is free for the taking. It exists whether or not Harry has ever thought of it, irrespective of whether Harry has had any interest in identifying it. This is explicable. Harry's agenda is not to specify D^*, or to make a random selection from it.

There is a further structural fact that we would do well to take note of. We said that the anomaly-trigger that we are presently discussing is the inconsistency created by addition of new information **I** to a database Δ. In the general case, the inconsistency will be preserved by proper subsets of Δ (and, if requisitely complex, by proper subsets of **I**). This allows us to speak of the smallest subsets Δ' of Δ (and possibly of **I**) for which the inconsistency persists. This, too, presents the abducer with a smaller target (smaller here in the sense of tractible), irrespective of whether he had ever thought of performing the contractions in question.

Abductive reasoning presents the theory of agenda-relevance with an interesting peculiarity. Relevance is defined for quadruples of new and backgroud information cognitive agents and agendas. In the general case the new information is presented to the agent rather than by him. In abductive problems, the abducer must *collapse* this distinction. He presents information to *himself* for consideration by himself. How does he do this? Given abduction's good track record, especially in everyday 'figuring out what gives' situations, it is safe to postulate that an abducer's hypotheses are drawn from D' rather than D and that his adjustments are made not to Δ but to Δ'.

Some writers are of the view that abducers, in effect, perform a further operation on those compacted sets. In one way of telling it, the abducer considers all hypotheses that he considers plausible and picks the one that is more plausible than any other. It is sometimes noted that plausiblity is ambiguous as between the plausibility of what an H says and the plausibility of an H as solver of an abduction problem. We might call the first *content plausiblity* and the other *instrumental plausiblity.* A case in point is Planck's original conjecture of quanta. On the score of content-plausibility Planck had nothing but scorn for the quantum hypothesis. But it did facilitate the derivation of some decently unified laws of black body radiation, and that was reason to judge it instrumentally plausible. The question remains. What are the mechanisms that explain our facility in thinking up problem-solving hypotheses? Peirce chalked it up to instinct [Peirce, 1931–1958, 5.591, 5.604, 6.476, 7.508, 7.220]. Others have tried to give an analysis of plausibility [Rescher, 1976; Gabbay and Woods, 2005]. This is not our task here. Our task is to explain the role of relevance in the production of solutions of a certain class of belief-revision problems. The theory of agenda-relevance claims that Planck's information, 'Maybe quanta', was relevant if it advanced or closed one of Planck's agendas. We know that Planck wanted a unified set of laws for black body radiation. That was certainly part of his agenda, some but not all of it. What he also wanted was a conjecture that delivered the goods so well that its conjectural character could be dropped in favour of categorical assertion. What Planck wanted was an hypothesis that he could de-hypothesize. This is a transition involving the various criteria of scientific trial. Part of his agenda, therefore, was to find an H that delivered the unificational goods that he was also prepared to submit to the full-court press of scientific skepticism. It is in this, and this alone, that the relevance of the quantum hypothesis **I** consisted. **I** was relevant for Planck because it was implicationally adequate and because it disposed Planck to submit it to trial.

What the successful abducer does, in effect, is to engage in successive stages of Cut Down. He appears to take very large sets of possible solutions, sets as large as D, into a smaller subset of (full-use) relevant possibilities, and these in turn to proper subsets of plausibilities, and thence (if he is lucky) to a unit set of these. This anyhow was the story we entertained earlier on. It facilitates the telling of that story that the reduction of a space S of possibilities to a space of real possibilities is already achieved by a partition on S via the $\Rightarrow$-relation, and that relevant possibilities in turn are filtrations R of an irredundancy condition. Of course, this is not our relevance; and its sole significance is that it is a structural relation that locates the sought-for hypothesis in a smaller search space. This *would* be relevance in our sense if abductive agents had search agendas for such spaces, but nothing in the empirical record indicates any such disposition. So we conclude that full-use relevance is irrelevant to what an abductive agent wants to do. Everything we know of learning theory suggests that for the general range of abduction problems, practical agents are *cut-to-the-chase* abducers. They play their hunches and make their determinations as if these structural contractions didn't exist. This is not to say that the structural facts are of no interest. But such interest as they possess is for the theorist of abduction rather than the abducer at ground zero. It is helpful to the theorist to be able to show that where the abducer does his real business is in small subspaces of an arbitrarily large superspace and that the small subspaces come by way of elementary logic and set theory: deducibility, inconsistency and subsets. Let R be the smallest subset achievable from the original set of arbitrarily many possibilities. R will be much smaller than its predecessor spaces, and it will contain a still smaller subset P of plausibilities. We again note that P is not got from R by our elementary Cut Down devices, and that there is no evidence of a general disposition in abducers to search R, even though we know that they do have a disposition to search P.

The question that Peirce answered with his instinctual conjecture was the wholly captivating question of what it is that enables beings like us to cut to the chase, and hence to avoid the engagement of possibilities that do them no good, or worse. It is the question, in other words, of what it is about beings like us that draws them to *relevancies*.

It is not the job of a theory of relevance to provide a complete answer to this question. What it must do, at a minimum, is say what it is that a reasoner is drawn *to* when he is drawn to relevancies.

It would be well here to pick up a suggestion made late in chapter 3, in which we developed the idea of a practical logic as a disciplined description of (aspects of) the cognitive behaviour of practical agents. We noted that in classical decision theory the soundness of an agent's decision is a matter of its comporting or approximately comporting with a mathematical structure *MS* generated by a decision tree. It is, of course, an open question as to the extent to which real-life decision-makers actually execute the provisions of *MS*. This struck us as carrying an interesting suggestion for making our commitment to psychologism respectable. Part of the problem that critics find with psychologism is that it fails to produce a principled division of labour for the logician and the cognitive scientist. We ourselves had suggested earlier that the desired distinction is to be discusssed operationally, in the difference between what logicians and psychologists are interested in and good at. But in section 3.2.6, we were able to make a further suggestion. There is the kindred question in decision theory as to what is fit work for the logician (or mathematician) and what falls in the ambit of the psychologist. Our tentative answer was this: let the logician construct *MS*, and let the psychologist determine whether, or to what extent, they are psychologically real.

The same suggestion can be made for the Cut Down problem. Whenever an abducer makes a successful or plausible choice of an hypothesis; there is a space of possiblities, structured by successive subset operations furnished by considerations of relevance and plausibility, in which the chosen hypothesis has a determinate place. Here, too, we might say that constructing such spaces is the logician's task. Testing them for psychological reality falls to the cognitive scientist.

Fine as far as it goes, but we find it necessary to add a caveat. If the psychologist were to determine that effective real-life abduction does *not* consist in the execution of the logician's structures, then the logician must allow that one cannot *just so* insist that the provisions of his structure are canonical for the correctness of an individual's real-life abductions, and that his abductions are therefore defective or otherwise subpar (to say nothing of dead-wrong). See the chapter to follow.

9.11 The Relevant Thing

Grice says, 'Be relevant'. This is something that someone might be favourably disposed to do, if he knew how. How would he do it? Sarah hands Harry a beaker of olive oil as Harry prepares to dress the Neapolitan spaghetti. Harry dresses the Neapolitan spaghetti. Sarah did the relevant thing. What made it so? If a person fulfils Grice's injunction she also does the relevant thing. What makes it so?

Years earlier, before they married, Harry had the agenda of favourably impressing Sarah's mother at Sunday dinner. He minded his manners, kept his tie knotted, accepted a second helping and laughed heartily at Mrs. Thing's jokes. On the face of it this has nothing to do with relevant information. True, we can, without too much effort, construe Harry's actions as information for Mrs. Thing, relevant for her with respect to *her* agenda of finding out what kind of fellow Harry is.

Another case, previously touched on: Harry wants to open a jar of pickles. Called into play is the panoply of sensory-motor mechanics that gets this done. Harry did the relevant things. But is it far-fetched to say that those doings were relevant for Harry with regard to his jar-opening agenda. It is true that the sensory-motor mechanical matrix of opening a jar of pickles is awash in information that guides the process. This is information that is input for the various sensory-motor devices whose operations jointly constitute Harry's opening the jar. It is doubtful that much of this is information for Harry. *Some* of it could be. Harry might be a sensory-motor misfit or he might be pathologically and nervously attentive. ('Yes, I think that this is going pretty well'.) It will not be true in any event that those doings, every one of which was a relevant thing to do, will be information affecting Harry in ways that caused him to open the jar. Those doings didn't cause Harry to open the jar. They caused the jar to be opened.

It seems then that Harry's dinner with Mrs. Thing and his opening of the jar of pickles are counterexamples to the theory of agenda relevance. If this were so, it would be a gentle irony. For didn't we say, in effect, that these cases were counterexamples to the theory of Sperber and Wilson?

In chapter 6 we noted an interesting feature about classes of contexts for 'relevant'. (Contexts, here, are sentential environments, not the sets of beliefs of Sperber and Wilson. For example, the string 'That was a ____ option' is a context for 'relevant'. 'That was a relevant option' is a well-formed sentence of English.) The interesting feature is that in those contexts 'relevant' is redundant. There is a test for this. NP is the noun phrase marker and Adj is the adjective marker. If

$$\text{NP} \vdash \text{AdjNP}$$

then Adj is semantically redundant in the context $\ulcorner \ldots \text{NP} \urcorner$. Semantic redundancy doesn't preclude other kinds of redundancy. An utterance of an AdjNP string might serve better than an utterance of its NP component for reasons of emphasis, or some such thing. But by this test, 'relevant' will be semantically redundant in contexts such as '...option', '...consideration', and so on.

Sometimes the relevant options aren't just the options, but the options that we've been talking about. In other uses still, the relevant options are just the right or the best options.

These are all uses of 'relevant' that seem destined to join the dinner party and the jar opening as counterexamples to agenda relevance. Saying so requires that we resurrect a question that occupied us earlier. What, we wanted to know, counts as a counterexample to a theory of relevance? It was suggested there that something like the following might do as a first pass:

♡ **Proposition 9.11 (Counterexample)** *A fact that a is F is a counterexample to a theory T iff that a is F is not derivable in T or of any consistent extension of it, and there exists insufficient grounds for postulating that the fact that a is F insinuates a sense of 'F' different from the sense of 'F' to which T is targeted.*

A counterexample, here, is a fact that your theory can't consistently honour and for which you lack good reasons to invoke the strategy of ambiguation. It is interesting that *Grice* or the generalization of it, AC9, obliges a theory of relevance to try to honour as many contexts as possible for 'relevant'. This was the semantic distribution condition. We can now be more specific: AC9 requires a theory of relevance to honour any context for 'relevant', the failure to do so for which would constitute a counterexample to the theory. Seen this way, AC9 makes it important that we be more thoughtful about Semantic Occam's Razor (SOR). SOR bids us to use the strategy of ambiguation as sparingly as we can. If SOR were made a condition of adequacy for a theory of relevance, it together with AC9 would conspire to make the theory especially vulnerable to counterexample. This is as it should be. It holds a theory to realistically rigorous expectations. Any theory incorporating a common analysis of a target concept will, trivially, be bound by something like AC9. What is wanted is an analysis which is faithful to the pre-theoretical data, or which gives a principled reason for giving some of them up. Wanting is not getting, of course. One needs a clear policy governing the not getting. We don't know what that policy should be in any detail, but of this much we are sure: it is disallowed to implement the strategy of ambiguation just on the grounds that not doing so will create counterexamples to the theory in question.

Redundancy pre-empts the question of ambiguation. If a term τ is redundant in a sentence Φ the question doesn't arise as to whether τ shows itself as having some new or different sense. So a negative constraint on counterexamples is straightforwardly formulable. Let T be a theory for which K is a target concept and let Φ be a K-claim, that is, a sentence attributing to something an instantiation of K. (We might remark in passing that most of the pre-theoretical data for T are K-claims taken for true without benefit of T.) A K-claim Φ is recalcitrant for T just in case Φ is true and inconsistent with T.

Proposition 9.12 (Redundancy) *If Φ is recalcitrant for a theory T with target concept K and τ is a K-term that is redundant in Φ, then Φ is not a counterexample to T.*

Proposition 9.12 takes care of some of our cases. It disarms cases of the 'relevant alternative' kind for all uses in which 'relevant' is redundant. For recalcitrant cases involving uses in which 'relevant' is not redundant, something else is required.

Proposition 9.13 (Ambiguation) *If Φ is recalcitrant for T with target concept K and τ is a K-term in Φ, if τ is lexically substitutable for τ^* and τ^* is not in the primitive vocabulary of T and is not definable there, then there is sufficient reason to ambiguate τ in such a way that Φ is not a counterexample to T.*

By these lights, uses in which 'relevant NP' means 'NP that I have been talking about', or 'causally sufficient NP', or 'causally necessary NP', or 'appropriate NP', and so on, ambiguation is underwritten by lexical substitutivity, and ambiguation denies these cases the status of counterexamples. For generality, where τ is a term for which lexical substitutivity for τ^* produces a new sense $K*$ of some concept K, then $K*$ becomes a concept of some theory $T*$, a theory for τ^*, if there is one. If 'a relevant factor' goes onto 'a causally sufficient factor', or 'a relevant variable' goes onto 'a potentially falsifying variable', it could turn out that $T*$ will be a theory of causality or a theory of inductive strength, or some such thing. Intuitively, these are not theories of relevance. That they are not indeed theories of relevance is reinforced by the fact that the synonymy between τ and τ^* which makes $T*$ a theory for τ sends τ^* to no theory with antecedently established *bona fides* as a theory of relevance and makes no provision for the truth of τ-claims in any such theory.

This suggests that ambiguating 'relevant' is a long way from producing a sense of 'relevant' for which an adequate theory would count as a theory of relevance. We don't suppose that it will be possible to produce algorithms for this kind of discrimination. When a theory counts as a theory of relevance, or more problematically when it doesn't, even though it is a theory of a sense of 'relevance', is not something that sits well with necessary and sufficient conditions. But there is something to the distinction, however intuitive and inchoate. Perhaps there is enough to it to make us want to make something of it. For example

♡ **Proposition 9.14 (SOR-satisfaction)** *If the ambiguation strategy is legitimately applied to sentences* Φ *recalcitrant for a theory* T*,* T *is a theory of* K*-hood,* Φ *are lexical substitutes that underwrite the ambiguation and* Φ *are sentences of a theory* T^**, then if* T^* *is not a theory of* K*-hood, the ambiguation strategy on* Φ *with regard to* T *satisfies SOR (Semantic Ockam's Razor).*

SOR-satisfying ambiguations are desirable. They disarm counterexamples in ways that recognize new senses; but they are semantic byproducts that don't matter of a process that does matter. They don't matter because they don't matter for theory. SOR-satisfying strategies are, thus, ambiguation strategies that try to conform to AC9. The uses of 'relevant' for which a SOR-satisfying ambiguation is invoked won't be honoured by the theory of agenda relevance. This is a violation of AC9, but it is a violation that could be called 'technical'. The non-conforming uses of 'relevant' are precisely uses that don't matter for a theory of relevance.

We return to Harry's dinner with Mrs. Thing, and the opening of the jar. In each case, what Harry did were the relevant things to have done. A verdict of redundancy presses for a hearing. 'The relevant thing to have done' is surely just 'the thing to have done'. If so, the counterexamples are disarmed by way of proposition 9.12. Some people might have contrary intuitions. Harry's performance at dinner involved his doing the relevant things, but, here, this just means that Harry did the socially correct things. So perhaps we have a case for lexical substitution. If so, ambiguation (proposition 9.13) disarms the counterexamples. And if we think that a theory of etiquette is not a theory of relevance, and that a theory of sensory-motor manual dexterity is not a theory of relevance, then twice-over the ambiguation will prove to have been SOR-satisfying (proposition 9.14).

There is a further thing to take note of. The sentences we have been examining are recalcitrant for the theory of agenda relevance. Even if they are not counterexamples to it, they remain recalcitrant. Recalcitrant sentences don't honour the account of relevance put forward by that theory. What does 'honour' mean here? It means that, e.g., 'Having a second helping was a relevant thing to have done' and 'Having a second helping was information for Harry that affected him in ways that advanced his agenda of trying to impress Mrs. Thing' have different truth conditions. And so they do. What we cannot say is that a recalcitrant sentences fails to honour our account of relevance just in case there is no sentence in the form $\ulcorner$**I** affected **X** in ways **I**$'$ that advanced **A**$\urcorner$ for which it and the recalcitrant sentence have the same truth conditions. In fact, we think that for any recalcitrant sentence Φ there will be at least one sentence of the $\langle$**I**, **X**, **I**$'$, **A**$\rangle$ sort that is true just when Φ is true. Whether opening a jar of pickles or being charming to Mrs. Thing, these are things that could not happen in the absence of some information impacting on Harry in ways that make some contribution to the desired outcome. People who study human behaviour are much too carelessly disposed to attribute the Mayor Koch modality in which most human experience is filtered through a How am I doing? device. It takes little reflection to see that people are not Mayor Koch-ers in anything like the general case. Not even Mayor Koch was a Mayor Koch-er across the board.[26]

Most of the information that gets processed in the matter of Harry's opening the jar, some of which being indispensible for the task at hand, has no chance of being live for Harry. But mustn't some of it be live for Harry if what he did is to count as *Harry's* having opened the jar? Perhaps not. Perhaps it is possible that Harry opened the jar strictly on the basis of a chain of information none of which was live for him. This would mean that it was information that Harry couldn't conceptualize. If Harry opened the jar, he opened the jar not having a clue as to what was going on. We don't much care whether we count this as an action of Harry's or something of a lesser metaphysical grade. It will suffice to say that any time somebody does something with some idea of what's going on, there will be some sentence of the $\langle \mathbf{I}, \mathbf{X}, \mathbf{I}', \mathbf{A} \rangle$-sort that is true. In those cases, the Mayor Koch modality will be somewhat in evidence.

This can be true without there being any cause to query the judgements of recalcitrance as applied to those sentences about Harry. For, again, it won't be true of all the things that were the relevant things for Harry to have done that doing *them* was information that affected Harry in such ways as to get it to be the case that Mrs. Thing is impressed or the jar is open. That this is so is further confirmation of an earlier claim. If no sentence of the form $\ulcorner \mathbf{I}$ is relevant for $\mathbf{X}$ with regard to $\mathbf{A} \urcorner$ which is true just when it is true that Harry is doing the relevant things suffices to undo the recalcitrance for the theory of agenda relevance of sentences attributing relevance to the things that Harry is doing, then we can say this: Whenever 'relevant thing to do' is correctly attributed to $\mathbf{X}$, there is always some true sentence $\ulcorner \mathbf{I}$ is relevant for $\mathbf{X}$ with respect to $\mathbf{A} \urcorner$ in the absence of which the attribution could not be correct. Agenda relevance is therefore a condition on the relevant thing to do. But the relevance of the relevant thing to do is not in general the agenda relevance that is a condition of it.[27]

[26]Ed Koch was Mayor of New York in the period 1978–1989. He was especially effective in walkabouts where he would ask his fellow citizens, 'How am I doing?'.

[27]'In the general case'. Harry has stitches in his tongue. He wants to know whether he can pronounce 'Spuistraat'. He utters 'Spuistraat'. That was the relevant thing to do. Doing it also closed his agenda. Here the thing that was the relevant thing to do was such that the doing of it was agenda-relevant for Harry.

If this is right we must revise some things previously said. Let **C** be the class of sentences of the relevant-thing-to-do sort, recalcitrant forAR, the theory of agenda relevance. Now should it prove to be the case that for every $\Phi \in \mathbf{C}$ there is some set S of sentences in the form ⌜**I** affects **X** in ways that advance or close **A**⌝ such that the truth of these sentences are all and only what it takes for Φ to be true, that would be a reason for proposing that the sentences of S constitute a contextual definition of Φ. Since, for the most part, we don't know how to specify the members of S, we won't in general to able to produce the conceptual definition of 'relevant thing to do'. It could, however, be proposed that

♡ **Proposition 9.15 (Contextual eliminability of relevant things to do)** *There exists in* AR *a contextual definition of every sentence of* **C**.

If proposition 9.14 were true, this would leave us with three strategies for counterexamples, inconsistent on their face. The inconsistency can be remedied. Each is a strategy relative to an interpretation of Φ. So we have (1) a strategy modulo redundancy; (2) a strategy modulo lexical substitutivity; and (3) a strategy modulo contextual eliminability. It is interesting that for some Φ our strategies are jointly inapplicable. The use of (2) and (3) together is especially interesting. (2) provides ambiguation as the escape from counterexample. (3) provides contextual elimination as a more direct escape. Must it follow that Φ is ambiguous? This would be true in case the strategies were equally applicable, if there were nothing to favour the one over the other. But there *is* a reason to favour the one over the other. It is SOR.

Chapter 10

Objective Relevance

> [Decision] theory can be taken as a theoretical account of the nature of rational or 'coherent' action. Alternatively, it can be regarded as a normative guide to how actual decision-making can be made more reasonable.
>
> [Cooper, 2001, p. 44]

10.1 Normative Theories

Normative theorists come in two stripes, sometimes both at once. Let us say normative theory N^m is a *melioristic* theory with respect to some target concept K iff K is such that instantiations of it are performable by an agent, and N^m provides rules for competent, rational (rational, best) performance. Historically, inference has drawn the interest of meliorists, and theories of inference have liberally trafficked in rules of competent (etc.) inferential performance.

Not all normative theories are melioristic. There are two quite different reasons for this. One is that the target concept K might not be one whose instantiations are intelligibly characterized as performable by an agent. Another is that although instantiations of K are intelligibly described as performable, the theory in question is unable to specify rules for competent (etc.) performance. Theories of either sort have a way of being analytically normative or explicational. They undertake authoritatively to answer the question 'What is it to be a K?' (though perhaps only after adding a condition that the norms of normative K be computationally dischargeable by beings like us. See here [Stanovich, 1999].). Theories such as these place a strain on the notion of normativity. True, they invoke the idea of giving a 'right' account of K, but all theories try to do that for their target concepts.

Sometimes a normative account of something is the same thing as a set of prescriptions. If the equation held good here, then in providing a normative treatment of agenda relevance one would, among other things, be specifying prescriptive rules for getting information to act on agents as it should. Speaking for ourselves, we haven't the slightest confident idea of how to do this. Without some adroit paraphrasing it doesn't make sense to talk this way. Apart from some banal admonitions, such as 'Be careful and attentive; get plenty of rest and watch your diet', the prescriptive task is beyond us, and we think that we are not alone in this. Worse still is the prescription, 'Select information that is relevant to the task at hand' (for recall the previous chapter).

Melioristic theories frequently make use of talk about ideal types and normative models. This is loose talk and it needs some careful tightening. Here is one way in which it should not tighten. If we introduce the notion of an ideal reasoner, we might mean (as some theorists have meant) a reasoner who, among other things, adjusts his deductive practice by conforming proper subsets of his inferences to the demonstrably valid rules of deduction. We might also put it that he will close his beliefs under consequence, and also that his beliefs will be transparent, i.e., he will believe that he believes what he believes, etc. If we now want to introduce the idea of a normative model of reasoning, we might cash the notion of normativity as follows: reasoning in the normative model is reasoning done by ideal reasoners. The normativity of the normative model is secured by the ideality of its ideal participants. (This is how reasoning *should* be transacted by ordinary reasoners because this is how reasoning *is* transacted by ideal reasoners, who, among other things, choose deductive strategies licensed by demonstrably valid rules of deduction). If a skeptic asks, 'Why *these* rules?', he can be told that they are provably valid and, in standard elementary formulations, complete.

But this is wrong. Any real reasoner who even attempted to fulfil this deductive ideal would quickly paralyse thought.

So a condition on our normative model — a negative condition — is this: beyond a certain point, do *not* approximate to the behaviour of ideal deducers. Alternatively: constrain your notion of an ideal reasoner in such a way that ordinary reasoners can realistically approximate to him or her (or it). But what are the positive conditions that we should expect the normative model to honour? How do we know that the participants in our model are reasoning as they should? This we do not get by positing rules and procedures that hold in a model that we've decided to call a 'normative' model. The sentence 'Response R to occasion O is correct in the normative model' does not imply that R is a correct response to O. Having it otherwise is the ancient fallacy of *secundum quid*, i.e., the fallacy of 'omitting a qualification'.

For this reason, among others, we are reluctant to pursue the question of when information should be relevant for cognitive agents by way of talk of ideal reasoners. Whether the reluctance is something that we should try to subdue is something we will come back to shortly.

The call for normativity gives additional pause. There is something tendentious about normative prescriptions of cognitive performance. Consider Harman's Clutter Avoidance Principle: one should not clutter one's mind with trivialities. It is less a maxim for the rationally well-behaved than a registration of approval of how things happen anyway. The mechanisms of belief management are largely automatic, as we keep saying.[1] Taken at face value, principles such as this bid the human agent to do what is in any case done automatically. Subscription to its provisions cannot be volunteered for the most part and so cannot sensibly be enjoined either. Changes of mind under relevant information is largely like this, too. Given the psychological literature it is entirely unsurprising that this should be so.

10.2 Relevance Naturalized?

It is worth reviewing what a descriptive and a normative account of relevance might be expected to look like. A descriptive theory has two parts. Part one is an explication or conceptual analysis or definition of *de facto* relevance. Part two is a psychological account which specifies conditions under which *de facto* relevance is actually realized for quadruples $\langle \mathbf{I}, \mathbf{X}, \mathbf{I}', \mathbf{A} \rangle$. A normative theory also comes in two parts. As before, part one gives an explication, but this time of objective relevance, and it is followed by a specification of conditions under which objective relevance is actually or counterfactually realized for quadruples $\langle \mathbf{I}, \mathbf{X}, \mathbf{I}', \mathbf{A} \rangle$.

It is far from obvious that descriptive theories of relevance are likely to come thick and fast (and right). In fact, a good descriptive theory would be a major and welcome accomplishment. A good normative theory would be a miracle. For recall that there is some doubt as to whether part one (the explication component) can be brought off non-trivially and non-vacuously.

[1]For some philosophical opinions to the same effect, see [Williams, 1973; Bennett, 1990]. For reasons favouring a contrary view (which we find unconvincing) see [Moser, 1989, p. 18 and 210–211]. See also [Shiffrin, 1997], and the discussion in section 2.6.1 above.

By what has been called the Replacement Thesis in epistemology, the following two questions are linked in an interesting way.

> Q1: How ought we to arrive at our beliefs?
> Q2: How do we arrive at our beliefs?

The Replacement Thesis asserts that answers to Q2 entirely exhaust the admissible answers to Q1 [Kornblith, 1985, pp. 2–3]. A parallel suggests itself. Naturalized epistemology is made interesting and worthwhile to the extent that answers to Q1, that are not also answers to Q2, or that are reached indifferently to Q2, have been produced by a degenerating research programme. This is precisely what is claimed by philosophers and others hostile to *à priori* methods and foundationalist presumptions in the theory of knowledge. We need not here attempt to take the measure of epistemology naturalized or, in particular, of attempts to trounce *à priori* foundationalism. But with relevance theory, there is *some* reason to fear that the normative account is indeed lashed to the decks of a degenerating research programme. This suggests the wisdom of naturalizing relevance theory. It is precisely this that option two proposes. It is proposed not in the rather harsh and categorical terms of the Replacement Thesis, but rather as a tentative methodological variant of it. In its more cautious form, option two proposes acceptance of the following procedural rule. This is the **Actually Happens Rule**.

> **Actually Happens Rule**
> In seeking to discover rules for the acceptability of cognitive performance in human agents, seek always and first for a description of what characteristically human beings actually do. What is actually done makes a defeasible first claim on what ought to be done.

The *Actually Happens Rule* is intended to convey the idea that once a good descriptive theory is up and running there is nothing further that a normative theory would need, or could legitimately have — except, that is, for cause. For all its modesty, the *Actually Happens Rule* is a tough sell. Some people will not like it at all. It gives no guidance for the recognition of defeasing conditions.

There is the intuition that sometimes, perhaps typically, when a cognitive agent processes information that proves *de facto* relevant for him he performs in ways that qualify the process as rational. We could say that a theory of relevance is a normative theory when it offers an account of rational performance, since this is a notion which adumbrates the idea of cognitive tasks dealt with as they should be dealt with, or in the right ways. A contrast is intended between performance as it should be and performance as it is. We have difficulty with this. It is not a difficulty with persuasiveness of the intuition that underlies the distinction, for we too have the same intuition. Our worry is about whether we have any clear idea about how to construct theories that elucidate it. If difficulty there is, it has not been for want of trying. Considerable effort has been made to explicate the notion of rational practice by way of conditions that justify it. So let us look at justification.

> Principles of eductive inference are justified by their conformity with accepted deductive practice. Their validity depends upon accordance with particular deductive inferences we actually make and sanction. If a rule yields unacceptable inferences, we drop it as invalid. Justification of general rules then derives from judgments rejecting or accepting particular deductive inferences. [Goodman, 1983, pp. 63–64]

It is the same way with induction.

> ... rather than being able to justify our confidence in inductive inference or in the procedures for taking fair samples, we look to the confidence itself for whatever justification there may be for these procedures. ... We have seen, on the contrary, that rightness of categorization, which enters into most other varieties of rightness, is a matter of fit with practice; that without the organization, the selection of relevant kinds, effected by evolving tradition, there is no rightness or wrongness of categorization, no validity or invalidity of inductive inference, ..., no fair or unfair sampling, and no uniformity or disparity among samples. [Goodman, 1978, pp. 138–139]

We can generalize from this. Rules for, or principles of, rational performance are justified by their fit with confident practice and practice is something to be confident about by its fit with justified rules. It is 'the only justification needed for them' [Goodman, 1983, p. 64].

10.2.1 Reflective Equilibrium

Goodman's view has attracted its fair share, and more, of disapproval, earnest and sanctimonious by turn.[2] It is objected that what is sanctioned

---

[2]A good summary of the disapproval can be found in the far from sanctimonious [Siegel, 1992, pp. 27–46].

as rational practice and what is taken as justified performance cannot be equated with rational or justified performance. Goodman thinks that our confidence constitutes the justification, but surely our confidence is sometimes misplaced.

'[R]eflective equilibrium — Goodman's fit between inferential practice and normative principles — is not itself a source of justification of the principles' [Thagard, 1982, p. 40]. See also [Woods, 2002b, Ch 8]. Why not? Because, it is said, there is experimental evidence that some of our settled cognitive practices are faulty and lots of good principles of rational performance fail to conform to settled confident practice (for example [Stich, 1988; Stich and Nisbett, 1980]). People endorse principles which conform to, are in reflective equilibrium with, their cognitive practice but which are bad principles. Such principles drive the gambler's fallacy, regression-to-the-mean mistakes and covariation blunders, and there is reason to think that these errors are common, easy to make and practically incorrigible [Stich and Nisbett, 1980, pp. 192–295].[3] Nor are they the result of pathological or circumstantial degradation in those who commit them. They are made by people of high intelligence and superior education, who are in good health, well-rested, and so on.

We are not so sure. For a countervailing view (the view of bounded rationality) see e.g., [Gigerenzer and Selten, 2001a] and the discussion of section 2.6 above.

Let us not forget that we are speaking of justification. It is not enough that a critic of justification-by-balance produces the experimental results which promote the intuition (rightly or not) that balanced practice could in some respects be routinely mistaken. He should tell us what it is that justifies the intuition — validates it well enough to give it the heft of a solid counterexample to equilibrium theories. If we see things in Goodmanian ways, we will be troubled by the possibility, or the likelihood, that the perch

[3]The factor of incorrigibility is important. Without it, reflective equilibrium fanciers could say what Goodman himself has said, that balanced practice is not once for all. It evolves and corrects itself. In the fullness of time such errors will cease or we will change our conception of error. But not if they are incorrigible mistakes. Not if, even under welcome and trusted instruction and in unqualified recognition of their badness, people who commit them go on committing them. That they are so is precisely what is thought to be indicated by the experimental data. In other writings Woods has characterized fallacies as mistakes that are commonly made, are easy to make (i.e., they seem all right intuitively), and stoutly resistant to correction. If this is right, a fallacy is an error that is preserved, not eliminated, by the evolving and self-correcting processes of settled practice. See [Woods, 1992b]; for a further and somewhat different discussion, see [Gabbay and Woods, 2004a, Ch. 3]. It is there suggested that not being eliminated from settled practice can be explained by putting it that fallacies aren't mistakes, or aren't mistakes that count.

from which critics are hostile to the equilibrium approach, and who see it as open to experimental refutation, is the 'view from nowhere'. Having a lever, they lack a fulcrum. It won't do to press probability theory and logic into supporting roles since it is precisely they that are in disequilibrium with the experimental data. Perhaps we could propose them as analytically self-justifying or as somehow justified independently of how the balance of deductive and inductive practice actually lies. But, as we have said before to the point of tiresomeness, their rules don't prescribe good inferential practice. *Modus ponens* is not a good rule of inference; conditionalization is not a good rule of inference; and on and on. Goodman himself is equivocal. He routinely confuses arguments with inferences. 'How do we justify a deduction? Plainly, by showing that it conforms to the general rules of deductive *inference*. An *argument* that so conforms is justified or valid, even if its conclusion *happens to be false*' [Goodman, 1983, p. 63].[4] McGee is especially good on this point. 'One of the aims of logic is to teach us how to reason well by showing us patterns of inference that are reliable. Two *prima facie* requirements that a logical system must satisfy in order to secure this goal are the following':

> The patterns of reasoning sanctioned by the system must be reliable, that is, they must never permit us to infer an untrue conclusion from true premises.
>
> It must be possible for human reasoners to learn the patterns of inference and to follow them. [McGee, 1991, p. 95]

And so a rule such as

> From Φ and $\ulcorner\Phi \rightarrow \Psi\urcorner$ one may infer Φ, provided that Ψ is true 'is reliable, but it is not learnable, since we have no way of telling whether the restriction 'provided Ψ is true' is met'.
> [McGee, 1991, p. 95]

It may be that, apart from what actually happens, normative rules exist, self-justifying or justified independently of the more or less settled practice of real-life human beings. But now the question is: What are these rules, how do we have access to them, and how do we know that they are reliable and learnable?[5] The short answer is that we don't know. Not knowing

[4] Emphasis in the original omitted; emphasis here added.

[5] Other manoeuvres have been tried. One is to deny the need of a fulcrum by denying the intuition that the standard rules are compromised by settled practice. Cohen argues to this effect against certain of the psychological findings. Experiments purporting to show that people routinely violate the conjunction axiom of the calculus of probability actually show that the experimental subjects were working with a Baconian rather than

makes us think kindly toward the *Actually Happens Rule.* The rule says that until we have reason to think otherwise we should look to actual cognitive performance as an indicator of good cognitive performance, in fact, as a first approximation of it. It is possible to see the *Actually Happens Rule* as reflecting Goodman's insistence, in the words of Putnam, that '*any* proposed solution [to problems of justifying our cognitive practices] be judged by its ability to systematize what we actually do' [Putnam, 1983, p. xiii]. This says more than we intend by the *Actually Happens Rule*, and less, too. More: because discovering cases in which what we actually do is wrong can fall far short of identifying principles in virtue of which what we do when it is not wrong *isn't* wrong. Less: because systematizing what we actually do is not, by an intuition we share with Siegel and others, justifying what we actually do.

The point is not unchallenged. Cohen produces a subtle and ingenious argument to the opposite effect, in which he proposes that, understood the right way, to systematize is to justify. Cohen's argument is especially interesting. It engages the question of epistemology naturalized. The 'neo-Goodman project' of reflective equilibrium is a standing invitation to naturalization. The rightness of what we do is wholly a matter of what we do. Cohen is an equilibriumist with a difference. Give Cohen his head, and before you know it, normativity has made a vigorous recovery and the project of 'analytic epistemology' is restored to philosophical primacy [Cohen, 1981]. So we must ask: Should we give Cohen his head?

Cohen says that a normative theory of reasoning is a theory that systematizes bodies of intuitions — the 'immediate and untutored inclinations ... to judge' that this, that or the other thing is rational. Let C be the set of intuitions which the theorist undertakes to systematize in a normative theory N. N will be an idealization of interlinking principles such that for a great many $\Phi \in C, N \vdash \Phi$, the more the merrier. Intuitions $\Phi_1, \ldots, \Phi_n$ not entailed by N or incompatible with it can be tolerated or not tolerated by N. They will be untolerated when they are overridden by theoretical provisions we think too well of to give up. They will be tolerated when it

a Pascalian concept of probability, for which the standard conjunction axiom is untrue, and which, moreover, is a concept of probability rationally appropriate to the tasks they were asked to perform. Stich and Nisbett pull in the other direction. They allow that the experimental data are violations of good and appropriately applied rules, and hold that those practices, settled and confident as they surely are, are unjustified. Some equilibria are justified and some are not. An equilibrium is justified when it reflects the practices of people who know better, of people with the right expertise, the right stuff. See [Cohen, 1989, p. 13], and [Stich and Nisbett, 1980, pp. 201–202]. Stich changes his mind about the 'right stuff' approach in [Stich, 1988]; he jettisons the 'neo-Goodmanian project' of 'analytic epistemology', and opts for relativism or skepticism. A detailed discussion can be found in [Woods, 2002c, chapter 8].

can be established independently that they fail the idealized presumptions of N itself.[6] Idealization can be troublesome. It is too easy to go off the tracks entirely and propose rules, such as

From Φ, $\ulcorner \Phi \rightarrow \Psi \urcorner$, one may infer Φ, provided that Ψ is true

which may be fine for an ideal performer but are no good for us. But there is reason to think that Cohen intends his N-rules to be humanly learnable. An ideal N-performer will be one whose practice conforms to N and is free from 'performance-errors'. Performance-error is now a technical notion. It encompasses errors arising from pathological or circumstantial degradation. Performance-error is nevertheless not a well-behaved notion. It leaves open the question of whether cognitive practices which were, counterfactually, wholly unblemished by performance-errors, could still count as recognizably human performance to the approximation of which actual human performance could be held as a standard of rationality. We will not go on with this here, and will assume that Cohen's idealizations are unproblematic.[7]

A normative theory N systematizes intuitions. There are those who think that intuitions are just mistakes waiting to be discovered. This is certainly Quine's view of intuitions in set theory, for example. There is a great deal to be said before intuitions can convincingly be given the theoretical deployment that Cohen reserves for them. We ourselves have made liberal use of the notion of intuition in these pages — they are the pre-theoretical data that a theory of relevance should try to honour. We have not said anything in particular to make the idea clear, and so we won't worry over much about Cohen's intuitions as a central concept of metatheory [Cohen, 1986].

Even so, it is appropriate to ask to what do intuitions owe their canonical place in theories such as N or AR. Some people will say that they are all we have to go on, and that is all there is to it. Cohen has a different answer. They are all we have to go on, but that is not all there is to it. Our intuitions about how people should reason are the output of a good descriptive theory. It is a psychological theory which describes and predicts

> a competence that human beings have — an ability, uniformly operative under ideal conditions and often under others, to form

[6] We may note in passing that this is a variation on what we have been calling the strategy of ambiguation. Intuitively good inferences incompatible with N would be good inferences in a different sense of 'good' (or perhaps a different sense of 'inference') than is recognized by N.

[7] And so we leave some disagreements unresolved. Cohen thinks that inconsistency is confined to performance-errors. We are not so sure, to put it mildly. See again [Woods, 2002b, Ch. 8].

> intuitive judgments about particular instances of ... right or wrong, deducibility or nondeducibility, probability or improbability. This theory will be just as idealized as the normative theory.
>
> [Cohen, 1981, p. 321]

It becomes noticeable that D and N are the same theory. The descriptive theory, D, describes an underlying idealized cognitive competence which people must be presumed to have if our intuitions about what constitutes rational practice are to be honoured. Given the way that the normative theory, N, is engineered, it too reconstructs the same underlying competence in recognition of the same intuitions. In neither case is there much occasion to grub about with experimental data, for in each case competence is an idealized construct that efficiently underwrites the entailments from N to C. If it appeared initially that Cohen's argument was lavish endorsement of the *Actually Happens Rule*, it is also clearly a constraint on it. It implies the further methodological principle that experimental findings appearing to contradict N don't. They record performance-errors arising from design limitations, fatigue, inattention, inadequate access to needed information, and so on.

Cohen's thesis has met with some heavy weather. Stich again is a case in point. Stich points out that the competence/performance distinction which is central to Cohen's position was tailor-made for linguistics. There is reason to think that it resists his normative designs. There is no difficulty in recognizing a diversity of linguistic competences — French, Urdu, Dutch, and all the rest. There is also experimental evidence that there is a diversity of cognitive competences, individual, social and cultural.

> ... although there are obviously great variations in linguistic competence, there is no such thing as a normative theory of linguistics (or at least none that deserves to be taken seriously). There is no problem about which of the many linguistic competences abroad in the world corresponds to the normatively correct one. [Stich, 1988, p. 131]

Why should it be otherwise with cognitive competence? Stich says, and we agree with him, that the existence of cognitive diversity at the level of competence is an empirical question, although hardly a straightforward one. (It is a contested point. See, for example, [Davidson, 1974].) For our purposes here, it doesn't matter. The hypothesis of cognitive diversity is true or not. If true, it mandates a silly question, 'Which cognitive competence corresponds to the normatively correct one?' If it is not true, we know what the correct normative theory is. It is the correct psychological theory of a universal cognitive competence. Either way, something like the *Actually Happens Rule* is endorsed.

If Cohen is right, a normative theory of relevance is a set of interlinking claims that entails a good many pre-theoretical data, the more the merrier, guided by a policy on what to do with recalcitrant data, by a policy, e.g., on counterexamples. We make to propose that AR, the theory of agenda relevance is, warts and all, just such a theory. Either normative theories of relevance, like normative linguistic theories, can't be got, and it is no reflection on *AR* that it isn't one. Or they can be got in the kinds of ways favoured by Cohen, and *AR* is a normative theory after all. Isn't that the end of the matter? No. J.A. Blair writes that

> we once suggested that to assert that a premise is relevant is to hold that 'either alone or in conjunction with other accepted propositions, should cause me to be ... more inclined ... to accept the conclusion than one would otherwise be.' The point brings out the causal connection between one's recognition of a proposition's premissary relevance and one's disposition to accept the proposition it supports, but it applies to any attribution of relevance, incorrect ones as well as correct ones, so it does not account for actual relevance ... So ... *relevance must be a property that is independent of its causal influence on the alteration of cognitive attitudes.* [Blair, 1992, p. 207], emphasis added

For many people, Blair is unquestionably right. For them, we could say that Blair's thesis is an intuition that a theory of relevance must honour. As we have it now, it is clear that *AR* doesn't account for Blair's intuition. If so, *AR* fails to accommodate a datum which, if honoured, would show unreservedly that *AR* is a normative theory in Cohen's sense. We propose to adopt Blair's intuition until further notice. Having done that, we have work to do. We must try to extend *AR* in ways that honour the intuition. Since doing that would be to produce a normative theory, we should speak of our task as the extension of *AR* to *NAR*. How is this to be done? We are not sure.

There is, we think, something right about the reflective equilibrium approach to rationality. But, as it is conventionally formulated, it is just the community standards approach to rationality, which has nothing more going for it than, say, the community standards approach to pornography. According to the reflective equilibrium criterion what is rational is *constituted* by the community standards that it meets. What we find wanting in this view is that it leaves it unexplained as to how community standards manage to play so ontologically audacious a role. (Here, by the way, is the classical *Euthyphro*-problem in modern dress.)

This is not to say that community standards are good for nothing. They clearly suffice for linguistic acceptability (e.g., grammatically) and they also suffice for fashionability. They do not suffice for rationality, lest the very idea of basic rational performance — elementary reasoning skills, for example — is subject to the same degree of striking transformation over time that any natural language happens to exhibit, to say nothing of the spiky history of the rise and fall of ladies' skirts. What makes it plausible to suggest that community standards of competent reasoning are presumptively authoritative is that the reasoning behaviour that those standards call for are already competent prior to and independently of the community's disposition to endorse them. The *Euthyphro* problem was a dilemma constructed by Socrates in the Platonic dialogue of the same name. It is said that what is holy is what the gods decree. But, asks Socrates, do they command what they command because it is holy? (First horn.) Or is it holy because they command it? (Second horn.) If it is the first, the gods' endorsement have nothing to do with what it is to *be* holy. If the second, there is no constraint whatever on what might turn out to be holy; for the gods are free to say anything they like in this regard.

Once transformed into the question of reflective equilibium, it is clear that of the two horns, the second is far the less plausible. It evacuates the notion of the holy of any stable content, apart from the utter contingencies of what the gods chance to think; equally it leaves the notion of rationality devoid of stable content, apart from the utter contingencies of what a community of would-be reasoners chances to think. Though not problem-free, the better option is the first horn. It kills the divine-command theory of the holy, which is hardly a theological or ethical disaster, and it kills the 'community-command' theory of rationality. What it leaves is the proposition that normativity inheres in how we act and behave, that normativity in descriptively imminent rather than transcendent. It is a view for which there are at least some favourable indications. One is that how we actually reason doesn't kill us. Another is that it doesn't even keep us from prospering. So we are not inclined to make light of the *Actually Happens Rule*.

10.3 Objective Relevance

Objective relevance. What might it be? It is not for want of some good ideas — five of them by actual count. None is quite good enough to produce the desired result here and now. Still, they are all worth considering, and some are less dismissible than others.

First Idea. Consider a community cognitively at home with the practice of trial by ordeal. The jurists of the community, on seeing that the accused drowned after having been submerged in the moat, are made to conclude that he was not guilty ([Tewksbury, 1967, p. 269]: 'the guilty floated and the innocent sank'). True, *AR* makes no provision except for the irrelevance of that information. In thinking that it closed or advanced their agenda [=*established* the victim's innocence], they couldn't have been more wrong. So we don't have in this case a case in which information is *de facto* relevant when it shouldn't have been. But such a case is construable. We may suppose that jurists of yore would attribute subjective relevance: 'That he drowned got us to see that he was guilty' or, in effect, 'That information was objectively relevant for us'. Of course, they would be wrong each time.

Second Idea. There is the famous story of Auguste Kerkulé who, in one account, was suffering from the D.T.s. When he saw snakes dancing across the flames of his fireplace, one snake suddenly made a ring by biting its own tail, whereupon Kerkulé saw that the long sought-after structure of the benzene molecule was a ring. Here are the ingredients of relevance: Agenda: to ascertain the structure of the molecule; Information: Seeing the ring formed by the snake; Change of Mind: Kerkulé was made to realize that benzene is a ring compound, which is true and closed an agenda. Do we want to say that seeing an hallucinated snake bite its tail was relevant for Kerkulé's advance in organic chemistry?

Information may strike different people in different ways. *In extremis*, some information **I** may give rise to deviant causal chains that end up, strictly by chance as we might say, in genuinely advancing an agenda. In such cases, we might wish to say that though **I** did in fact cause a change of mind that somehow advanced the agenda, it did do so in a deviant way and so the information **I** wasn't 'really' relevant. Think of the case in which Sarah says to Harry, 'We should try to pick the Derby winner'. Assenting, Harry dons his coat and drives to the local abattoir, where he is known and indulged. Harry examines some entrails. On his return, he tells Sarah to bet the farm on Charlie-Boy. Sarah does and Charlie-Boy wins. On the descriptive account, Sarah's request was relevant for Harry with respect to his trip to the abattoir, and what he learned there was relevant for his selection of the winning horse. This is too much relevance for serious belief. Harry's's cognitive equipment didn't function as it should. Normatively, **I** is objectively relevant for **X** with regard to **A** to the extent that **I** caused **X** to change his mind in ways that advanced or closed agenda **A**; *and* **X**'s cognitive-conative processes were functioning as they should.

We might say, here following Cummins' exposition of Millikan, that 'x performs a Proper Function in a system S when it does the sort of thing the doing of which has been, historically, responsible for the replication of x's type'.[8] The circulation of the blood is one of the heart's Proper Functions, since that hearts circulate blood in the way that they do historically accounts for the fact that hearts get replicated. Similarly, the Proper Functions of cognitive and conative devices are such that their contribution to epistemic and decisional life are historically responsible for such devices being replicated.[9]

A Normal Case is one in which 'the function is performed *successfully* — i.e., a case in which the [device] in question does its stuff and everything else conspires to produce the kind of result that is responsible for that item's replication' [Cummins, 1989, p. 77]. In the example of the bee dance, a Normal Case is one in which the interpreter bees orient their flight plans appropriately. Such cases need not be statistically average. For consider, to change the example, 'how few sperm have historically managed to realize any but the most immediate functions (say swimming) proper to them?' [Millikan, 1984, p. 34].

We can now characterize the idea of cognitive and conative processes functioning properly.

Definition 10.1 (Normal performance) *A process performs Normally to the extent that its performance conduces to its replication in the descendent class of the type of being whose process it is.*

Then

♡ **Definition 10.2 (Proper function)** *A process functions properly to the extent that it operates Normally. (Definition 10.2 is satisfied in the formal model. See remark 15.5.)*

Though helpful in certain ways, it may seem that the normative account of causal relevance as involving the properliness of cognitive and conative functions is nevertheless inadequate. Consider Sherlock Holmes and any information relevant for him with regard to solving the case of the so-and-so. Take all others privy to the same information and equipped with the

[8] [Cummins, 1989, p. 76]. See also, [Cummins, 1989, p. 163, n. 2]: 'I have changed Millikan's formulation somewhat in order to simplify the exposition. I don't believe any of the subsequent discussion is materially affected by the liberties I have taken' [Millikan, 1993, pp. 33–34].

[9] Here is Millikan on the same point: 'There must, after all, be a finite number of general principles that govern the activities of our various cognitive-state-making and cognitive-state-using mechanisms and there must be explanations of why these principles have historically worked to aid our survival. To suppose otherwise to to suppose that our cognitive life is an accidental epiphenomenal cloud hovering over mechanisms that evolution designed with other things in mind'. ([Millikan, 1986, p. 55].)

same agenda. Now it is notorious that in that whole population the penny will drop for Holmes alone. Descriptively there is no problem in saying that the information was not (then) relevant for the others and that it was relevant only for Holmes. Normatively, however, it doesn't seem wrong to say that the information was relevant all along for them all, but that only Holmes picked up on it.

On our present position, we cannot accede to this. It is perfectly possible that Watson's cognitive devices were functioning Normally in our sense and for the penny not to have dropped. The information was not relevant for him. Watson is not here revealed as a cognitive misfit, and still less the rest of us. Holmes' accomplishment was spectacular or anyhow out of the ordinary. Holmes is cognitively interesting precisely because he functions as others don't. Perhaps he is a genius. Holmes' equipment performs more than just Normally; it performs, as we might say, *Hyper-Normally.* We can thus capture Holmes' gift in the idiom of Proper Functions. It is precisely because his cognitive devices perform at levels beyond what is required for those sorts of devices historically to be lodged in the repertoires of his descendents that we can say that Holmes' particular achievements are more than the result of his devices operating Normally. They operate Hyper-Normally, beyond the Norm. Holmes is, so to speak, a lot smarter than he needs to be. That said, a further suggestion proposes itself. Let the notion of proper functioning defer to that of Hyper-Normal functioning. And so, we revise the conditions on objective relevance.

Definition 10.3 (Hyper-Normal performance) *A process functions Hyper-Normally to the extent that it operates beyond its Norm.*

And

♡ **Definition 10.4 (Objective Relevance)** **I** *is objectively relevant for* **X** *with regard to* **A** *to the extent that* **I** *is* de facto *relevant for* **X** *with regard to* **A** *and* **X***'s cognitive and conative devices are functioning Hyper-Normally. (Definitions 10.3 and 10.4 are satisfied in the formal model. See remark 15.5.)*

There are several things wrong with our first two ideas. One is that cognitive devices fulfil conditions on Normal functioning in ways compatible with the production of a good deal of error in thought and action. Some of the time it will strike us as intuitively clear that such errors arise from or incorporate failures of relevance. More generally, it is clear that an agent's cognitive devices could routinely be doing two things at once. They could be failing (i.e., producing a lot of error and failing to discern lots of irrelevance), and they could be working Normally. So the Normal functioning of cognitive devices is too weak a notion to serve as a truth condition on objective relevance. We could attempt to repair this difficulty by recourse to Hyper-Normalcy, but doing so is problematic in other ways. One is that if Hyper-Normalcy is taken as cognitive performance beyond the Norm then, unless we are prepared to admit that most of us most of the time are normative misfits, it must be allowed that most of us most of the time perform Hyper-Normally. So it is wrong to make of Sherlock Holmes the paradigm of Hyper-Normalcy. It is wrong to think of hyper-properliness as reserved for prodigies.

On the other hand, if we non-geniuses were routinely Hyper-Normal in our cognitive performances, it would be desirable that Hyper-Normalcy be specified in some suitably independent way. We might venture that Hyper-Normal performance involves the operation of cognitive mechanisms fashioned in some way on the designs of *Just* and *modus tollens* (see chapter 7). If *Just* and *modus tollens* were part of the story of human cognitive design, it is extremely unlikely that the story that they tell would be one of Normal functions. Cognitive devices function Normally when they facilitate the replication of those devices in our descendants. Nothing that is so far known of such things lays convincing claim on our having internalized the complexities of, e.g., the calculus of probability.

Perhaps it would be less of a strain to make these postulations for Hyper-Normal performance. But once done, Hyper-Normalcy won't do for the analysis of relevance, since *Just* in particular is a partial analysis of that very thing. Apart from this it is clear that, given what we want Hyper-Normalcy to do for us in the account of normative relevance, we will need it to be true that Hyper-Normal performance is, among lots of other things, objectively relevant performance. Saying it this way is unavailable to us without circularity. Yet we know of no other way of saying it to the same effect. So we conclude that we must abandon — or anyhow postpone — the Hyper-Normal account of objective relevance.[10]

[10]We desert hyper-normalcy with a certain wistfulness. A definition of objective *propositional* relevance is denied us:

> Proposition P is objectively relevant to proposition Q iff for any cognitive agent whose agenda targets a question $\ulcorner ?Q \urcorner$, P is *de facto* relevant for him with respect to that agenda, and his cognitive devices are functioning Hyper-Normally.

Then if it were thought that the relevance relation could obtain in agentless worlds, these would include worlds in which it would still be true that Newton's Laws have explanatory relevance to Kepler's Laws. (George Schlesinger, personal communication.) The definition could be recast subjunctively. Here the counterfactual agenda would be to secure an explanation of Kepler's Laws.

Similar devices would also seem to be available for absorbing Cohen's account of relevant variables and Bas van Fraassen's account of Why-questions [Cohen, 1977, pp.

What do we want from a normative theory of relevance? We have been assuming that it is two things:

(1) an analysis which provides in a suitably general way truth conditions for open sentences ⌜**I** is objectively relevant for **X** with regard to **A**, given **I**′⌝

and

(2) an account of the competence in virtue of which cognitive agents are efficient and reliable recognizers of objective relevance and avoiders of objective irrelevance or would be under appropriate (and specified) conditions.

Theoretical component (2) is approachable in two ways. One way is to specify performance rules in a meliorist theory NAR^m. Seen this way, an agent's competence as a detector of objective relevance and an avoider of objective irrelevance would be a matter of his fidelity of those rules. In the other approach the theorist would seek to embed his analysis in a broader theoretical context in hopes that the broader context would elucidate, short of specifying performance rules, how it is that an agent manages to situate himself in a way that satisfies the truth conditions of objective relevance. That is, given the truth conditions TC of open sentences ⌜**I** is objectively relevant to **X** with respect to **A**, given **I**⌝, we suppose that an agent tries (in effect) to situate himself in such a way that he gets to be a value of **X** in fulfilment of TC for appropriate values of **I**, **A** and **I**′. We have been assuming that the place to look for theoretical guidance about such things is a pragmatic theory of informational competence in which the analysis of objective relevance is embedded.

We have been experimenting with a certain approach to these things. Twice now we have postulated kinds of cognitive performance (Normal performance and Hyper-Normal performance) which were offered as constituents of truth conditions for sentences of the form, ⌜**I** is objectively relevant for **X** with regard to **A**, given **I**′⌝. The idea of the experiment was a simple one: **I** is relevant (really relevant) for **X** with respect to his agenda **A** to the extent that **X** employs **I** or responds to it in ways that, given **I**′, advance or close his agenda *and* in so doing **X** is functioning as he should. We don't doubt that if **X** does function as he should he will employ information that is relevant and resist it when it is not. But, as we have seen, though both Normal performance and Hyper-Normal performance are reasonably postulated for practical agents, Normal performance is too weak

144–157] and [van Fraassen, 1980, pp. 141–146].

to serve as a truth condition on objective relevance, and, though it may do all right as a truth condition, Hyper-Normal performance comes to us unanalysed and as a notion whose analysis, if we knew how to give it, would almost certainly pre-suppose a notion of relevance.

We could, of course, brazen it out and say that **I** is objectively relevant for **X** with respect to an agenda **A** to the extent that **I** is *de facto* relevant for him with regard to it and **A** objectively *did* advance or close (not just that **X** thinks that it did).

This is our *Third idea.* It is not one to be entirely contemptuous about. It seems to get some things nearly right. It catches the case of trial by ordeal, but it probably doesn't handle the case of serendipitous causal response. Recall that Brown was our detective for whom some information **I**, hardly relevant in itself (as the lawyers say), proved to be a trigger of events that eventuated in the solving of the case. Some people think that such cases don't count as the genuine article — as objective relevance of high assay. Nor is it likely that our third idea will accommodate the Kerkulé example, which is a case of serendipity of another kind. Kerkulé got madly drunk, thought he saw in the fire a snake bite its tail and had a flash of insight: the benzene molecule is a ring. And so it is. Kerkulé *did* solve that problem.

We have, thus, two types of case, each fully conforming to our third idea, yet from which many would withhold the laurel of objective relevance. The causal serendipity case, as we might call it, is a classic example of getting the right result the wrong way. Detective Brown was doubly lucky. Not only did his mistake not hinder him, in the final analysis it actually helped him. The other case — the flash of insight example — reminds us that Kerkulé committed no mistakes about benzine. What happened was that in experiencing something as ring-like, Kerkulé found himself analogizing about the benzene molecule. Ah yes, we say, but not everyone would have done so.

The two cases motivate two further passes at objective relevance. The *Fourth idea* suggests that we define ⌜**I** is objectively relevant for **X** with regard to **A**, given **I**′⌝ as fulfilment of the condition that **I** is *de facto* relevant for **X** with regard to **A**, given **I**′ and in processing and/or responding to **I**, **X** has made no error.

The Kerkulé example suggests a *Fifth idea*, according to which ⌜**I** is objectively relevant for **X** with regard to **A**, given **I**′⌝ is true just in case it is also true that **I** is *de facto* relevant [etc.], and, for any agent **X*** with interests and competencies approximating to those of **X**, and who possesses an agenda **A*** type-identical to **A**, if **X*** were to process **I** then **I** would be *de facto* relevant for **X*** with regard to **A***, given **I**′.

The definition of idea four withholds from **I** in Detective Brown's solution of his case the standing of objective relevance; and the definition of idea five grudges objective relevance to Kerkulé. So they do some things right. What is doubtful is whether they do enough things right to serve as anchors of serious normative accounts.

Mindful that *de facto* relevance admits of cases in which the mismanagement of information is causally fortuitous by giving rise to successor stages of enquiry and reflection that 'get' **X** to hit upon the right answer (and so the answer that objectively advances or closes **A**), we might stipulate further that **I**'s role in the objective advancement or closure of **X**'s agenda not to be fortuitous in this way. Fine as far as it goes, this would be hopeless as an analysis of relevance so long as there were no satisfactory way of characterizing freedom-from-mistake without invoking considerations of relevance. For our part, we don't see how the invocation could be avoided short of trivializing the role of freedom-from-mistake in the truth conditions for objective relevance.

We see that the definition of idea five is menaced by Charybdis and Scylla alike. Charybdis threatens triviality and Scylla forebodes vacuousness. If the definition is interpreted in ways that overload the similarity relations, triviality trails along. If, short of overloaded-similarity, the similarities aren't specified the definition courts vacuity.

10.4 Modularity

The decision to lodge an account of relevance in a pragmatic theory was a fateful one. It bears directly on the question of whether a normative theory of relevance is possible. We have been assuming all along that a theory of inference is a pragmatic theory. That may give some people a start. So we should say something further about it; in doing so we will be able further to elucidate the bearing of pragmatics on normativity. Inference is a case in point.

When Harry infers *this* from *that*, he bears some relation R to *this* and *that*. We may also assume that if Harry's inference is correct then *that* bears some semantic relation R^* to *this* independently of whether Harry bears R to them. In large part, a theory of inference is the specification of R and R^* and the provision of truth conditions. There is a strong tradition in philosophy that 'semanticizing' *this* and *that* is necessary for an understanding of inference. By semanticizing we mean processing information in ways that qualify it for truth conditions. By information's qualifying for truth conditions we mean that, once qualified, the processing system has a belief. In chapter 8 we spoke of live information. Information is live for an agent when it is information he is capable of processing in ways that qualify it for truth conditions. So live information is information that an agent *can* semanticize.

Concerning the information-processing that attends (or constitutes) inferences, something like the following picture emerges. Having semanticized *this* and *that*, it is possible to define semantic relations over them. R will be such a relation. We can specify conditions under which *that* implies *this* and we can specify conditions (or try to) under which *that* is evidence for *this*. It signifies that in the standard philosophical approaches evidence is a set of sentences having truth values or truth-approximation values, for example, probabilities. In other places, evidence is not thought of in this way. For the policeman and the cancer experimenter, evidence is physical evidence.

We see that the philosopher is drawn to what Quine has called 'semantic ascent' met with briefly in chapter 8. Semantic ascent is the 'shift from talking in certain terms to talking of them'. It 'applies anywhere', but it is 'more useful in philosophical connections than most' [Quine, 1960, pp. 271–272]. 'The strategy of semantic ascent is that it carries the discussion into a domain where both parties are better agreed on the objects (viz., words) and on the main terms concerning them.'[11]

The great appeal of semantic ascent is that it facilitates the articulation of theory at agreeable levels of abstraction and with significant economy and generality. Interpretations stand ready for linguistic entities by way of functions. Functional interpretations abet recursive specification with mechanical reliability. They sometimes make for the effective recognizability of a theory's target properties.

Interpretation functions are, thus, algorithms, albeit sometimes from ideal perspectives inaccessible to the theorist. They are the theorist's analytical conveniences. They are often supposed to be the subject's own dynamic devices. The subject is assumed to have internalized them.

It is a commonplace among linguists that a subject's integration of a sentence is the output of such algorithms. Those who think so sometimes speak of algorithms as modules. The most frequently discussed modules include the subject's grammar or his grammatical process, and these are processes deployed to recover the semantic representation of the sentences of the subject's language. When this is done the subject is said to have

[11][Quine, 1960, p. 272]. Semantic ascent, Quine's way, is a pragmatic principle of procedure. It helps make difficult things easier to do. There are metaphysical variations of it which seem to us altogether wild. Here is Lycan on Dennett: 'Beliefs are identified by sentential complements because it is sentences over which the epistemic norms of logic and probability theory are defined, and it is these normative sciences that (according to Dennett) make beliefs beliefs.' [Lycan, 1988, p. 70, n. 18].

specified the meanings of those sentences.[12] When his 'grammar' interacts with his 'logic', algorithms will specify meaning(s) of a sentence that is implied by a sentence for which meanings have been specified, or it will determine that a sentence with this meaning contradicts a sentence with that meaning; and so on. The grammatical and the logical processes of a subject are jointly his semantic processes or his semantics. The subject's semantics is a module, or is modular, because and to the extent that it is algorithmic.

If, intuitively speaking, semantic processing determines the meaning and/or logical implications of a sentence, a subject's pragmatic processes will interpret what an utterer means in uttering a sentence on an occasion, and what the utterer implies by it on that occasion. It is a matter of considerable controversy as to whether a subject's pragmatic processes are modular. To ponder this is to ponder whether the interpretation of the utterer's meaning and the utterer's implication lies in the embrace of algorithms. Fodor characterizes a non-modular process as having unfettered access to contextual information. They are, as he says, informationally unencapsulated. Semantic processes, being modular, are informationally circumscribed. For example, they are indifferent to a subject's beliefs (that is, his non-linguistic beliefs). As we saw in chapter 2, Fodor's and Wheeler's anti-modularism about central cognition turns on its holistic character, which (in Fodor's case) is inferred from the holism of science, and which (in Wheeler's case) is inferred from the existence of intelligent behaviour in the face of continuous reciprocal causation. We have already said that we distrust Fodor's inference; and we took note of the efforts of some theorists, notably evolutionary psychologists, to modularize central processes. We do not think that is a settled issue, especially in light of the case developed by Wheeler; and we are prepared to examine how a non-modular approach bears on the question before us.

People who think of pragmatic processes non-modularly find it implausible that there should be effective routines for the interpretation of utterers' meanings and implications, for figuring out what Harry meant by 'Boiling eggs is easy if you've had the right training' on a given occasion of its utterance. Here is Fodor.

---

[12]Such views comport badly with Quinean strictures about meanings. Elsewhere in this book, we have capitulated to Quine. Here we won't be so accommodating. It doesn't matter that certain linguists might be wrong about sentential meaning. It matters whether they are right about utterers' meaning. Their being right about this, if they are, comports with Quinean reservations about sentential meaning.

> ... the limits of modularity are also likely to be the limits of what we are going to be able to understand about the mind, given anything like the theoretical apparatus currently available.
> [Fodor, 1983, p. 126]

If this were so, we should expect to find that pragmatics is in an underdeveloped and intractable condition. We should expect to find that normative theories of information deployment and information use are in especially bad shape. This is what we do find, and it sets up an inference *modus tollendo tollens* with regard to the modularity of pragmatics. Those who draw the inference include formal pragmaticists, such as Montague, for whom pragmatics is a branch of metamathematics. These pragmatists want to assimilate pragmatics to semantics and in so doing to recover the reassurance of algorithms.

Pragmatics in this book is an encompassing perspective for relevance. Having analysed the notion of objective relevance, our pragmatic theory attempts to elucidate how a subject situates himself in ways that satisfies the analysis. Suppose then that Sarah is **X** and that she has the agenda **A** of interpreting what Harry meant in uttering something on some occasion. What factors **I** will facilitate Sarah's bringing this off? Part of what Sarah is up to will depend in how we interpret the schema

(1) **I** is relevant for Sarah with respect to her Harry-figuring-out agenda.[13]

If pragmatic processes are non-modular then no limits can be set on the possible values of **I**. That is, it will be beyond the powers of a speaker of English to specify a particular set of interpretations of **I** for which (1) comes out true prior to the speaker's contingent engagement of conditions under which (1) does come out true.

Concerning (1), there is no information that is ruled out in advance that conduces to Sarah's figuring out what Harry meant in uttering 'Boiling eggs is easy if you've had the right training'. Of course, Sarah can produce truth conditions for (1).

(1*) (1) is true iff **I** is information that helps of gets Sarah to figure out what Harry meant in uttering 'Boiling eggs is easy if you've had the right training'.

But producing the truth conditions doesn't constitute an interpretation of **I**.

It may seem that Harry is an exception to this. After all, Harry might know what he meant by that utterance on that occasion. Knowing this,

[13]For a considerably more detailed discussion of these issues, see the chapter on 'Interpretative Abduction' in [Gabbay and Woods, 2004a].

he might throw out hints. Suppose Harry had said, as he and Sarah, out for their evening stroll, were passing Lou's house, that boiling eggs is easy if you've had the right training. Sarah looks at Harry blankly. Now as it happens, Lou works for the federal government in the department of labour. He heads up the re-training division. Lou is a man of celebrated gravity. In fact, he is a bit of a prig. Lou is always telling people at the drop of a hat that there's nothing a person can't do if he's had the right training. People run when they see Lou. He is a certain kind of optimistic simpleton. What he keeps on saying is so obviously false yet so desirably true.

Harry says, 'Whose house did we just pass?' Sarah replies, 'Lou's', and then, 'Oh, *you*!' and titters. Harry was sending Lou up. Harry provided information that makes (1) true.

To hold that Sarah could not have constrained the interpretation of **I** in advance, is tantamount to subscribing to the non-modularity of Sarah's pragmatic process. Sarah's agenda, recall, was to interpret what Harry meant, to engage her pragmatic processes with regard to his utterance. Some people will not be so inclined to postulate for Sarah so loose a control on interpretation. It is vanishingly likely that she will give consideration to the prime factorization theorem or try to remember the year of the publication of Kepler's third law. It is implausible to say that she possesses no filter against arbitrary informational invasion. We have no doubt of this. Sarah will try to find interpretations of **I** which make (1) true. But she will do much better in predicting values for **I** for which (1) comes out false than in predicting values for **I** for which (1) comes out true. What she will or will not try to do is consistent with the information afforded by the prime factorization theorem doing the job after all. (We leave details to the reader's creative imagination.) The prime factorization theorem says that all whole numbers can be expressed as the products of primes, and that such expressions are (essentially) unique. Let it be the case, our readers' fruitful imaginations being what they are, that Sarah's thinking of that got her to figure out what Harry means by 'Boiling eggs is easy if you've had the right training'. A normatively minded critic will be strongly disposed to insist that this is a pathological case, that the prime factorization theorem wasn't really relevant in the case at hand. The intuition is attractive. If it is right, we can say what a normative theory of relevance must do. It must specify constraints on admissible values for **I** in our schema (1). It must do this in ways that avert prime factorization problems, as we might call them for short. It is perhaps too much to expect such a theory, *NAR*, to determine values of **I** for which (1) is true, but it seems undeniable that *NAR* must find values for **I** for which (1) *might* be true. This is what we will now mean by 'admissible values for **I**'. Admissible values for **I** are those for which (1) could be true and in ways that avert the prime factorization problem. Apart from constraints on **I** required by the analysis of relevance *for* (*viz.*, that **I** be live and **A** be accessible), it may appear that no theory can do that.

Notice that saying that no theory could specify values for **I** that might make (1) true (short, that is, of a finding for all values of **I**) is tantamount to Fodor's claim about non-modular processes: there can be no scientific theory about them, given present resources.

We are considering what a normative theory of relevance would be and whether there is any reason to think that there might actually be such theories. In the previous chapter, we saw reason to say that no analytic *NAR* could provide the wherewithal for fulfiling Grice's maxim, 'Be relevant'. What we are saying here is that no *NAR* will ever succeed in restricting values of **I** in such a way that guarantees the possible truth of (1).

For expository convenience we propose to say that normativity and the non-modularity of pragmatics come together in the following way.

Proposition 10.5 (Normativity and non-modularity) *There is no NAR that could specify the admissible values of* **I** *in (1). This makes of agendas of the type instantiated in (1) non-modular agendas.*

Sarah's agenda in (1) was to engage her pragmatic processes with regard to Harry's utterance. We are saying that those processes—her pragmatics—we have reason to think of as non-modular.

As we have been using the term, pragmatics is a theory of information-deployment. It includes theories of reasoning, inferential and otherwise. It comprehends any use of information by an agent for whom the information counts as live and for whom it is intelligible to postulate an accessible agenda. So conceived, pragmatics will range well beyond the pragmatic processes we have lately discussed since those were processes reserved for determining utters' meanings on shifting occasions of utterance. It would be helpful to have a way of marking this distinction. Let pragmatics^u be the study of the processes that interpret utters' meaning; and let pragmatics, without a superscript, be our broader theory of informational competence. It is easy to see that

Proposition 10.6 (Pragmatics^u/Pragmatics) *Even if it is true that nothing could be a pragmatic^u* NAR, *it doesn't follow that nothing could be a pragmatic* NAR.

To show this stronger thing, we would need to show that

♡ **Proposition 10.7 (Pragmatic *NAR*)** *Unless we draw the metalevel into the object level, for no arbitrary specification of* **X** *and* **A**, *is it possible* *to set the admissible values for* **I** *in the schema:* **I** *is relevant for* **X** *with regard to* **A**, *given* **I**′.

On the face of it, proposition 10.7 is seriously mistaken. We have only to consider (sentential) inference to see that this is so. Sentential inference is inference from sentence meaning, as opposed to inference from utters' meaning. After all, sentential meaning is in the embrace of semantic processes and strictly semantic processes appear to be modular. What is more, pragmatics, unsuperscripted, includes the study of those processes, never mind that saying so muddies the terminological waters. So let us again turn to inference.

10.5 Inference

It will be convenient to revisit our stories of f as a Putter of Things Right and as a Seer of Trouble Coming. For reasons previously discussed, we will confine our remarks to the former story; but what we say of it might extend readily enough to the other. This trades heavily on the phenomena of perceptual information-processing. The stories require it to be intelligible that perceptual information be processable in ways that qualify as having truth conditions. We supposed that in Putting Things Right the belief-adjuster device interpreted perceptual flow semantically. This is what a belief-adjuster does, after all. New information arrives and displaces old. There is an incompatibility between old and new which displacement connives to remove. Though it is possible that f might recognize such incompatibilities and construe them semantically ('Ah, inconsistency here'), it is insufficient to suppose that it does this in the general case. The incompatibility is causal. New information causes the displacement of old without the need to postulate meta-causal commentary from f. Displacement just happens. It is largely a matter of the electrochemistry of neural nets, no doubt. In our stories we imagined that f routinely semanticized the states of electrochemical flow. There would be reason to do this if we thought that in general that information flow were routinely processed in ways that qualify for truth conditions. Thought of this way, information-processing would in general be a matter of exchanging old beliefs for new and it would always be intelligible to characterize the dynamics of informational exchange in terms of inconsistency elimination, among other things. A considerable efficiency is involved in subdoxastic, subsemantic processing. For one thing, the regulating device needn't code up information semantically; it needn't process it in ways that qualify for truth conditions. Subsemantic processing has less work to do. So why not postulate it? Why postulate that the displacement dynamic is controlled by f, a belief-adjustment device? This is precisely the wrong thing to postulate if PDP theorists are right in saying that propositional information-processing is peripheral, biologically eccentric, and superficial [Churchland, 1989, p. 16]. In the case of the man walking his dog, we allow ourselves to say that the observer, in seeing what he saw, believed his own eyes, but this is a turn of phrase. It does not mean, or not obviously, that the observer formed the following sequence of beliefs: Now they are there, now the other place, now yet another; and so on. What is interesting about this kind of case is that it allows for belief formation, selectively as it were. It does not require that successive belief-formations be the very stuff of perceptual flow. 'Where was Laurie Walker at 7:30 a.m. on May 30th?', he is asked. He replies 'He was walking his dog in front of my house.' 'Which way did he go?' 'He went north and then turned west onto 10th avenue A', I reply, believing what I say each time. Though my visual flow at 7:30 a.m. on May 30th causally underwrites those beliefs, it is too much to suppose that the dynamic visual record of that part of that day is constituted by, or sufficient for, ordered strings of beliefs in the form 'Now, they are at place P.' It doesn't, of course, follow from this that f doesn't have those beliefs. But we are suggesting now that there is no explanatory virtue in ascribing them even to it. Allow, as we might, that the information flow negotiated on that occasion was information susceptible of processing in ways that qualify for truth conditions, it doesn't follow that this is the way it was processed on that occasion. It doesn't follow that f negotiated the flow.

What we have been saying about the flow of perceptual displacement has consequences for memory. The output of the mechanism regulating perceptual flow is available as input to memory. Memory too is in a constant process of upgrading, current information being supplemented and sometimes displaced by incoming information. It is natural to speak of our trying to keep our memories as consistent as possible. This is all right as long as we don't suppose that the memory regulation device routinely inspects for the semantic property of inconsistency. It bears on the question of modularity whether the memory upgrading device is distinct from the perceptual upgrading device. Same or different, it doesn't matter for the point at hand. It does matter that, on grounds of efficiency if nothing else, there is reason to think that this device too is not f.

We also imagine that informational flow is often like this: information states are causally cotenable but incompatible together with some other. Schematically, state A might be cotenable with state B and their joint realization might be causally incompatible with state C. The device might displace A or B, but it might do neither and admit K, a contrary of C. A, B

thus induces K. This begins to look a lot like inference. It *is* inference.[14] Inference is describable subdoxastically and subsemantically. Harry, let us say, has a street-crossing agenda. He has it while he is furiously explaining to Sarah his million dollar inheritance. Even if the agenda is accessible to Harry none of it need be or have been doxastically coded up. They are in the middle of the road, Harry is jumping up and down trying to make a point. The signal turns amber and they scurry to the other side. They inferred that they'd better hurry up. This could be true in the absence of any doxastic coding up. In fact, we have to work hard to make a case for it here. Cases such as these are routine. So inference is not routinely a matter of doxastically coding up in the right ways. Here too the information that got Harry to hurry is patterned in ways that render it processable in ways that qualify for truth conditions. Perceptual information, reminiscential information and inferential information is often codable in this way. But it is no more attractive to suppose that inferential information *is* doxastically coded in the general case than to suppose that perceptual information is or that reminiscential information is. Thus inferential information is not, as such or routinely in the ambit of f. Inference does not come about by checking the deployment of information against truth conditions. Inference has nothing centrally to do with (standard) logic.

How well does this story comport with what cognitive sciences know (or conjecture) about perceptual information flow? How, in particular, does the factor of accuracy play here? Here is Shiffrin on this point:

> In summary, the points I am trying to make on the basis of the accuracy results are the following. First, there are many demonstrations that the subject can process many sensory inputs, on many channels, simultaneously and without loss, if care is taken to insure [sic] that neither memory loss nor decision time will limit performance. Second, limitations on the perception of many near threshold stimuli are often seen when short-term memory loss can occur before decisions can be made about all relevant inputs. Third, limitations on the perception of, or memory for, above-threshold stimuli can be seen when multiple stimuli are presented at too fast a rate for decisions to be made, or for coding to be completed, for all current stimuli before new stimuli appear. Fourth, both types of limitations may be bypassed if sufficient training is given that the target becomes 'distinct'

[14] Cf. [Lycan, 1991, p. 275]: Perhaps we can live with the idea that inference is 'associationist rather than proof theoretic. (An advantage of that view is that subsymbol-relating associationist *norms* are far less often violated than are the inference-rules of the predicate calculus, though some of them would be violated in cases of network damage).'

> from the background stimuli and automatic search takes place; in such an event, decisions are made concerning the target, or coding carried out for the target, before other stimuli are considered. Fifth and last, most, if not all, attentional limitations may be a result of search and decision processes occurring in postperceptual short-term memories. [Shiffrin, 1976, p. 194]

Philosophers have a standing interest in truth conditions. They are their stock in trade. Truth conditions serve their normative proclivities especially well. Philosophers are interested in saying how things should be done, how human beings should behave. It is attractive to think that human beings should get things right, not wrong. Beliefs have truth conditions. If human beings had beliefs then it would be straightforward to say that beliefs 'should' satisfy their truth conditions. We could then set out to specify conditions under which this happens and rules for getting this to happen. With that done, it could be said that human beings behave as they should when, among other things, they follow those rules or when their behaviour is structured in ways that instantiate compliance models of them.

Standard logic looms as a kind of Holy Grail. Logic regulates with normative force the fulfilment of truth conditions. It is noticed that when someone infers something from something else it is sometimes true that the something else implies the something. So it becomes natural to think that the theorems and rules that characterize the implication relation will turn out to be canonical for inference. (Notice, by the way, that what we are presently going on about is not logic in the sense of Part I; logic as an account of cognitive agency.)

It is admitted that standard logic trades in abstractions and idealizations. But this is of no mind; every serious science does the same thing. Implication is defined over sets of abstractions from information assumed to have been doxastically coded up. Thus are propositions contrived from beliefs. Propositions, in their turn, have properties that are largely responsive to closure conditions. So every proposition in the deductive closure of a true proposition will itself be true. This is a godsend. It is a huge encouragement to a really deep theory of truth. It is granted that any account of correct inference offered by the logic of implication will make use of inferers' idealizations. No human is able to conform his inferences just as the ideal inferer does. Yes, but no smooth surface ever manages to be frictionless. Mechanics is still approximately true, and fruitfully so, of smooth surfaces, and logic is approximately true, and fruitfully so, of human inferers. A human inferer does what he should to the extent that his inferences do conform to those of the ideal inferer. One doesn't however come to learn what inferences are good by making inductions from what human inferers actually do. One learns what inferences are good by consulting standard logic. This was Frege's point against psychologism. No psychological account of inference-behaviour, no matter how rich, will tell you how to infer correctly. No such account can have normative authority. No mere law of thought can qualify as canonical. There is only one place to look, the place where normative authority is earned by proof. One must look to logic.

Human inferers then are approximations to ideal inferers. Ideal inferers apply rules that have been defined for information doxastically coded up and abstracted to the status of propositions. It follows that human inferers are manipulators of semanticized information. They are to some degree manipulators of beliefs in the light of truth conditions. They manipulate in approximate fulfilment of implication rules with which they are innately endowed or which they have somehow acquired. Human inferers have internalized, however imperfectly, the logic that regulates their inferences.

Not every one is sanguine about this picture. Rebels lurk about. Harman is one. We are two more. The approximation of human inferers to ideal inferers is much less impressive than one might have thought. The rule of *modus ponens* is a case in point. It is by now an old story. If Harry believes that P and that P implies Q then, at a minimum, believing Q is all right for him, under the provenance of *modus ponens*. But if Q is incompatible with something else Harry believes, say with R, he has many more inference options. He might admit $\ulcorner \neg Q \urcorner$ and erase R. He might admit $\ulcorner \neg Q \urcorner$ and erase P. He might admit $\ulcorner \neg Q \urcorner$ and erase $\ulcorner$If P then $Q\urcorner$; he might reject Q and erase P (or $\ulcorner$If P then $Q\urcorner$); and so on. Although *modus ponens* is not a good rule of inference (for not even the ideal inferer will abide by it), Harman's inferer is one who 'notices the entailments' and who conforms his inferences as best he can in ways that honour them. In short, he adjusts his belief-set B in such a way that no member of it contradicts any other in B. If a belief of his entails a belief inconsistent with a belief of his, he would do well to notice the entailment and to undo the inconsistency it leads to.

'Frege' re-enters the picture. What, he asks, are the rules which now govern inference? If not *modus ponens* and the others, then what? Harman says, in effect, that he doesn't know. One of Harman's rules is, loosely paraphrased: 'The rational agent is one who sometimes closes some of his beliefs under consequence.' 'Frege' turns away disappointed. There is nothing in this sort of whimsy that qualifies as a theory, and nothing that answers to the imperious interests of normativity. Our hypothetical 'Frege' here gives way to the real Hintikka. Harman's rules are fine as 'a heuristic idea', says Hintikka. Yet they have 'scarcely led to anything remotely like a satisfactory theory of reasoning in general' [Hintikka, 1989, p. 4].[15]

[15]More particularly, '[t]he following are among the most glaring weaknesses: (1) No

There are two issues to consider. Both are interesting and difficult. One involves the question of normativity. What would count, if standard logic doesn't, as a normative theory of inference? The other involves the question of the rôle of the human inferer as a manipulator of truth conditions. The issues link. We grant that logic requires an ontology of semantic items over which the logical relations are defined. Any being, abstractly considered, who was a performance model of logic would perforce be a manipulator of truth conditions. But standard logic is not a theory of inference worthy of the name. Not even its simplest rules are credible rules of even ideal inference. Why then assume, as Harman and nearly everyone else does, that human inference is routinely and dominantly semantic and that a good theory of inference, when we have one, will respect the competent inferer as a manipulator of semantic information in accordance with rules whose normativity (let us charitably suppose) will somehow have been established?

Our disposition to think of inference as semantic information-processing of a certain kind is encouraged by two considerations. The first is that sometimes when someone infers *this* from *that* he does so thinking that *this* is true and that *that* is true and that *that*'s being true has something principled to do with *this*'s being true. Moreover, it is helpful to think that all our inferences are semantically codable since it is in that form that they are most lucidly presentable to theory; e.g., they are presentable as sentences taken to denote or to express propositions. How else is inference to be theoretically divined if the inferential flow of information is not made efficiently recognizable in the ontology of the divining theory?

A second reason for liking to think that inferential flows of information are semantically encodable is that it seems to be required by theories of inference appraisal.

Concerning the first point, let it simply be said that, apart from a supplementary argument to show it in the present case, it is not generally the case that the ontology of theories is made up of semantic items. The ontology of physics isn't and the ontology of the continuum isn't. Of course, it will fall upon the theorist to represent the ontology of his theory in language and to do so in ways that invite semantic construal. But to suppose that this makes of the real numbers linguistic objects is as sharp a betrayal of use and mention as there could be. Though the theorist's theory of inference can be

theory has been developed as to where the new evidence itself is to be found. Nor is this new approach capable of handling questions of reasoning strategies in any other size, shape, or form. (2) It does not present any explanation of the true element in the traditional conception of logic as a general theory of inference. (3) This type of approach often relies on notions like 'inference to the best explanation.' Such notions seem to be either too vague, too complicated, or too little understood to sustain as yet a genuine theory of the subject.' [Hintikka, 1989, p. 4].

thought of as an interpreted language closed under certain operations, it is the same fallacy to conclude that the ontology of his theory must be made up of entities bearing semantic relations. So we conclude that no need has been demonstrated to construe the ontology of inferential flow semantically as a condition of there being such a thing as a theory of inference.

A related thing can be said about the second consideration. If it can be shown that a condition on something counting as a theory of inference appraisal is that the theory's ontology be stocked with semantic entities, then well and good. We would then say that an inference is good to the extent that information flow is semantically encodable in ways that fulfil the requirements of the appraising theory. We would also consider saying that whenever an inferer makes a good non-semantic inference he tacitly mimics a semantic inference approved by the appraising theory. That is, we would consider conceding that non-semantic inference just is tacit semantic inference. But, note, these impressive conditions are spectacularly unmet. It may be that, considered as a theory of inference appraisal, standard logic requires an ontology of semantic entities. But standard logic is a terrible theory of inference appraisal. Nothing else pretends (convincingly) to the status of an adequate theory, and so nothing else demands (convincingly) that inference appraisal require that inference be understood semantically.

Of course one is free to ignore such things. Our own view is that there had better be good reasons for doing it.

We will not press this point further. It is possible to deflate prospects for a normative theory of inference even if we are seriously mistaken in thinking that inference should not be thought of as irreducibly semantic. For the purpose at hand, we can give up entirely on such a view. What we want to show is that even considered as a semantic process, prospects for a normative theory of inference are not at all good. If this can be shown, it will follow that prospects for a normative theory of relevance are even worse.

We have said many times over that we agree with Harman that the rules of traditional deductive logic are not good rules of inference. If true this is a normative setback for the theory of (deductive) inference. Perhaps we were over-hasty in casting our lot with Harman. Hintikka is someone who would think so. Hintikka distinguishes definatory rules from strategic rules [Hintikka and Bachman, 1991, pp. 31–33].

A definatory rule of inference is a rule on what qualifies an episode of reasoning or belief-adjustment as an inference. When an agent satisfies a definatory rule, it follows that what he is doing is making an inference. It does not follow that he is making a good inference, that he is reasoning well. Inferring efficiently, fruitfully, correctly and so on involves the satisfaction of supplementary rules. These are Hintikka's strategic rules. Take *modus ponens*, for example. On Hintikka's account

(**MP**) $\Phi, \ulcorner\Phi \rightarrow \Phi'\urcorner \vdash \Phi'$

is a valid definatory rule, but it is not a strategic rule. This means that an agent who modified his beliefs in fulfilment of **MP** would not be guaranteed to have made a correct inference. He would only be guaranteed to have made an inference. Strategic rules are needed for goodness of inference. Here is a possibility.

> (**SR**): Whenever $\Phi \vdash \Phi'$ is a definatory rule, then for any agent **X** who holds that Φ, and holds no Ψ that he recognizes to be inconsistent with Φ, and if in the belief-adjustment interval in question **X** does not change his mind, then **X** must infer Φ' (alternatively and more weakly: inferring Φ' would be a good thing for **X** to do).[16]

When we apply strategic rule **SR** to the definatory rule **MP**, we get the following result. If Harry believes that the cat is on the mat, and if he believes that the cat is on the mat implies that a feline is on the mat, then so long as he detects no inconsistency between 'a feline is on the mat' and those prior beliefs, and given that he persists with them, then inferring that some feline is on the mat is a good thing for Harry to do. When these conditions are variously unfulfiled, different strategies suggest themselves along lines noted earlier in this chapter.[17]

Someone eager to have a normative theory of inference might think that he has found one here. Definatory rules tell you what you must do to make an inference; strategic rules tell you what you must do to make the inference adroitly.

Say what we like, the theory in question is not truth-preserving, owing to the effective unrecognizability of inconsistency. In fact, we can give a reformulation of **SR** which both strengthens and simplifies it; doing so reinforces the point at hand.

> (**SR***): Any agent who believes $\Phi, \ulcorner\Phi \rightarrow \Phi'\urcorner$ and believes his beliefs are consistent, and doesn't change his mind, would do well to infer Φ'.

---

[16]**SR**; we should emphasize, is not a Hintikkian strategic rule. (We are borrowing the label and the idea, not the rule). Hintikka's rules assume a greater degree of ideality than we think justified.

[17]In fact, there is a good deal of intuitive overlap between Harman's approach and Hintikka's. There is no reason for Harman not to agree that **MP**, e.g., is a perfectly good definatory rule. Still, there are substantial differences between the two writers that come out in details that need to occupy us here.

SR*, as we say, is not truth-preserving. It is not, anyhow, so long as there are no rules for the production and maintenance of consistent belief-sets. And none there are, not in the sense of prescriptions compliance with which guarantees the production of consistent belief-sets. Fragmentary heuristics there may be, but they are neither definatory rules nor strategic rules for the composition of consistent belief-sets.

We don't say that further heuristics could not be unearthed, but it is ludicrous to think that how people should adjust for consistency might be discernible independently of how they do adjust for it. At a minimum, a theory of inference that tried to account for adjustment for consistency would be a principled response to a connected meta-agenda. Constructing such a theory, moreover, would not guarantee it the status of normativity. Such a theory might be got by vigorous compliance with the *Actually Happens Rule.*

Relevance is like inference and consistency, only worse. Consistency, the relational property, is easily defined over semantic entities. There are rather deep theories of this property. Despite some celebrated disputes, there is not much doubt as to what consistency really is. We possess *analytically* normative accounts of it, to stretch (again) the idea of normativity. A good deal less settled are questions of how a competent user of information is to check for, determine the presence of, eliminate or 'reason around' inconsistency. There is no normative theory of *that.*

People have tried to make relevance, too, a propositional relation. Doing so has a certain appeal. If relevance is a propositional relation, just as consistency is, perhaps we can look for a logic of relevance that would be normative for it just as we looked for and found a logic of consistency that is normative for consistency. Whatever the prospects for an analysis of relevance as a propositional relation, nothing to date remotely approaches the success of analytic theories of consistency, and it may be that none will be forthcoming.

Better, we say, to define relevance over quadruples $\langle \mathbf{I}, \mathbf{X}, \mathbf{I}', \mathbf{A} \rangle$ and make of it a causal relation. It is not customary to think of relevance in this way, and that alone goes some way towards explaining why we have no theory of relevance, that is, no analytic account of it that approaches theories of consistency for maturity and completeness.

Consistency analyses as a docimatic concept; it is as such a desirable thing for a rational being to instantiate in his cognitive and optative practice. We would use 'probative' had it not been appropriated by Walton's theory of probative relevance. 'Docimatic' comes from *docimacy* ('to examine', in the ancient Greek). In antiquity, docimacy was a judicial examination of worthiness to serve in public office or to acquire citizenship. In modern uses it is the assaying of metals and/or drugs, and so is a test of purity. A concept is docimatic in our sense if its instantiation in cognitive practice is a positive factor in its passing muster.

It is harder to make out that relevance is a docimatic concept just as it stands. Our quest for objective relevance is interpretable as a quest for a conception of relevance which is a desirable thing to have instantiated in our cognitive and conative practice. Some readers may reject agenda relevance precisely because it proves so difficult to qualify it as a docimatic concept. If anything is antecedently clear, they will say, it is precisely that relevance is docimatic. The failure of the theory of agenda relevance to preserve and elucidate this insight is a substantial setback.

What we have been trying to demonstrate in these pages is that there is occasion to resist the insight. There is a better way of putting this. If *de facto* relevance is not docimatic, no conception of it is. This is a thought on which several unsettled threads of argument converge. Here they are. Relevance mistakes are possible, we said. That suggests a distinction between *de facto* and objective relevance. Objective relevance, we thought, was *de facto* relevance in fulfilment of a condition on things happening as they should. We have not done well in formulating such a condition, and objective relevance has suffered in consequence. That this should have proved to have been so puts pressure on the very idea of a normative theory for relevance, analytic and melioristic alike. That this should *be* so is reinforced by considerations suggesting that pragmatics^u is non-modular and, as such, a bad candidate for a normative theory. Pragmatics, in our broader sense, was found to run into unexpected trouble. It is not clear what would constitute a good normative theory even of inference. And if inference doesn't do well normatively, why should we think that relevance would?

10.6 Reconsidering Normative Relevance

We would go some way towards knitting up these ravelled threads if we could defeat the idea that there are relevance mistakes. In so doing, we would override Blair's Intuition, that relevance is independent of its causal influence in the alteration of cognitive attitudes. We aren't sure that we can do this cleanly, but there is no doubt that we can exert considerable pressure on it. The idea is given a boost once it is recalled that we are not speaking here of subjective relevance, that is, of judgements in the form 'this was relevant for me'. It is very unclear what are the truth conditions for sentences that make judgements in this form. Even so it is plainly a fact that sometimes such judgments are mistaken and sometimes we know that they are.

That there can be mistaken judgements of relevance goes without saying. The elusiveness of their truth condition explains why we have not tried to produce a normative theory of subjective relevance, a theory that makes such judgements proof against error.

The question for us is whether an agent who is so situated as to be the value of **X** in satisfaction of the truth conditions of ⌜**I** is relevant for **X** with respect to agenda **A**, given **I**′⌝ is one for whom the idea of a relevance-defeating circumstance is definable. On the face of it, it could not be denied that our question carries the presupposition that, given **I**′, **I** is relevant for **X** in those circumstances. We could press the idea of relevance-defeat even in those circumstances provided we were prepared to ambiguate with respect to 'relevant'. This is precisely what the proposed distinction between *de facto* and objective relevance amounts to. And what we are now suggesting is that there is some reason to think that the distinction collapses, that there is no need of the distinction between *de facto* and objective relevance. Whether or not this is so will pivot on our problem cases (and some others that we will introduce). Let us see.

Case One (Trial by Ordeal): We said that the jurists wanted to establish whether the accused was guilty. He drowned and was thought to be not guilty. By our account his drowning was not *de facto* relevant with respect to that agenda. The jurists thought otherwise, and *that* was a mistake. Agendas are sometimes attended by what their possessors regard as criteria of closure. It is no condition on the accessibility of agendas that the proposed closure criteria be correct. The mistake here lies in the closure criteria. It had nothing to do with information closing an agenda which it shouldn't have closed.

Case Two (Kerkulé): Kerkulé got drunk and hallucinated in ways that provoked the insight that the benzene compound is a ring. Now this was an oddity. Kerkulé wasn't routinely visited by the D.T.s and it is not hard to imagine that on no arbitrary occasion on which he hallucinated as he did here would he have had this particular insight. There was something peculiar to this particular occasion. We might have great difficulty in seeing what the details of the situation were. But this is a long way from establishing that what Kerkulé 'saw' on that occasion wasn't relevant for him. Of course something was cognitively amiss; he was hallucinating. His agenda closed on misinformation, but as we have seen this does not preclude its relevance.

Case Three (Inexplicable Connections): Holmes was remarkable in having amassed a substantial record of agenda closure in the light of information that failed to close the same agendas of interested third parties (Watson, Lestrade and Doyle's readers). Holmes was particularly good at two additional things: (i) his judgements of subjective relevance about such cases and (ii) his ability to explain them to others after the fact.

Could we imagine a situation in which such a record existed for an agent, the record was inexplicable to the rest of us, the agent purported to do well with (i), that is, with judgements of subjective relevance, but he was not good at all in performing (ii) that is, in explaining the connection? Let us stipulate that there is no one else on Earth who, in the absence of such explanations, could see anything but irrelevance in the correlations that made up the agent's astonishing record. Does this case justify a finding of lack of objective relevance?

Our case covers a more commonplace one. Harry says that information **I** made him realize that Φ and Sarah says that she can't see the connection. Sometimes she says that with a confidence that suggests that there is something fishy about **I** having worked on Harry in that way. Perhaps Sarah might also think that no one else, no one in his right mind, would have responded to **I** as Harry did. These are judgements of subjective relevance. They are about me and about people generally. They may be correct. Nothing in their correctness makes the case that **I** wasn't 'really' relevant for Harry with respect to his interest in Φ.

Our case is made interesting when the agent in question attributes relevance to himself but, like everyone else, can offer not a whiff of an explanation of the connection. Our agent has a record of correlations that resembles the one in which Harry reads the entrails and then picks the Derby winner. Winning the Derby admits of two interpretations, only one of which concerns us here. So let us quickly dispose of the one interpretation. In it, Harry sees the entrails in some perceptual configuration PC. Harry carries the belief that if the entrails display PC then Charlie-Boy will win. They do, and Harry bets the farm, and Charlie-Boy wins. There is something wrong with Harry, but it is not his ability to respond to relevant information. His error is the belief that if the entrails display PC, Charlie-Boy will win. For this to *be* the error we think it is, we would expect the PCed entrails to be relevant for Harry with respect to that agenda, given that false belief.

Another interpretation of the Charlie-Boy situation more nearly resembles the present case. In it Harry reads the entrails which, as anyone can see, displays the configuration PC. Then Harry bets the farm on Charlie-Boy, who later wins. Harry has no belief in the form 'PCed entrails mean that Charlie-Boy will win'. He has contrary beliefs. Even so, after the fact he solemnly promises that it was those entrails that made him pick that horse. Suppose now that Harry finds himself encumbered with these sorts of mystifying correlations all over the place. Lou suddenly gives forth with 'Spring is Busting Out All Over' and Harry completes his proof of Fermat's theorem, saying afterwards (and puzzled), that the song somehow was the key to his completing the proof. We don't doubt that such people would lead very troubled lives. They would be chock-a-bloc with illucidity just where other people do more or less well. Is it a case that forces upon us the strategy of ambiguation? Do we need here to speak of a lack of objective relevance?

No. The more widespread these inexplicable correlations become, the less reason there is to believe Harry when he says that this got him to see that, and so on. There is, in short, no more reason to posit the want of objective relevance than there is to deny *de facto* relevance. The more these astonishing and sprawling correlations are inexplicable even to Harry, the less there is reason to credit his judgements, 'This was relevant to that'.

Case Four (The Undropped Penny): Lou, as we said, is a serious man. He is also a bore about job training. And he is humourless; he doesn't get jokes. Harry tells Lou the story about the logician and the used-car salesman. Everyone laughs uproariously. Everyone except Lou. This is discussed. Sarah is of the view that even though Lou didn't find it funny, it was funny and ought to have made Lou laugh.[18] This is tantamount to thinking that the joke was objectively funny for Lou, never mind that he didn't find it so. The question is: Would we ever say this of such a case?

Perhaps the most common example of information that people fail to respond to relevantly is that of the missed clue. These are situations in which the penny doesn't drop. Situations like this are common. People say, 'How could he not have seen it?', leaving the suggestion that since they themselves did, or would have in his place, there is a sense in which the penny that failed to drop was pertinent for him.

People for whom the penny doesn't drop are sometimes obtuse, or more comprehensively stupid, or distracted, or tired, or drunk, and on and on. These circumstances make the absence of *de facto* relevance effortlessly explicable. Do they also motivate the postulation of objective relevance? We want to say not. Having the penny drop is like being able to figure out what Harry meant by 'Boiling eggs is easy if you've had the right training', in the light of the hint 'Whose house did we just pass?' (Lou, recall, is always boring people about the efficacy of job-training. Sarah is meant to see that Harry is sending Lou up.) Well, let's now say that she doesn't get it. Harry chides Sarah. 'How could you not get it!' Harry can be pretty

[18] There is no question here of Lou's not 'understanding' the joke. It is rather that he fails to find it funny.

offensive at times. He says, 'Here is information that is objectively relevant for Sarah.' Perhaps this is not exactly offensive, but he has no call to think it all the same. Harry is confusing objective relevance with relevance potential. Here is information with relevance potential. Its potential is not realized for Sarah in circumstances which defeat Harry's expectation that it will be. That does not suffice to define a relational property over 'Whose house did we just pass?', Sarah, and her desire to figure out what Harry meant by his remark about boiling eggs, a property that obtains even when it didn't help her figure it out. 'Relevant' is more like 'funny' than like 'consistent'. Objective relevance for Sarah in the case at hand is like objective funniness for Lou, never mind that Lou doesn't laugh.

The burden of the past few pages is not that the idea of relevance-errors cannot be made good on, only that it is much harder to do so than we were initially supposing, and hard enough to warrant some tolerant skepticism. Suffice it to say that if the notion of relevance-errors is hard to make out, so too is the intended kind of distinction between objective and *de facto* relevance. That being so, the determination to explicate a conception of cognitive devices functioning properly as a deep construct of relevance theory loses much of its motivation. The putative distinction between a descriptive theory and a normative theory threatens to collapse, adding further fuel to reservations about normative pragmatic theories more generally.

This is not to say that agenda relevance lacks normative nuance. We want again to suggest that *de facto* relevance is a docimatic notion, that *de facto* relevance is a desirable thing as such to have instantiated in our cognitive and conative practice. It gets things done; it closes agendas that we want closed. Some of these agendas qualify for fairly direct normative classification. Desiring to know the truth about the Big Bang is, we suppose, a rather splendid ambition but, no information will be relevant for Harry in that regard unless he does get to know (some of) the truth about the Big Bang, never mind what he might think about it. Or, Harry might want to crush Sarah's feelings, and his remembering her sensitivities about so-and-so might turn the trick for him. We might regret the relevance of that information for him but, as in the prior example, this will be parasitic upon what we normatively think of the agenda in question. The desirability of relevance, just so, is instrumental, and that suffices for its docimaticity.

10.7 Schizophrenia

Not getting it is theoretically interesting. Information that Sarah doesn't get and which we say she should have got, makes no claim on objective relevance in our sense. Objective relevance for Sarah is *de facto* relevance for her, subject to some conditions. In penny non-dropping cases, there is no *de facto* relevance. The question of objective relevance doesn't arise. A critic will find this telling. Any theory of relevance in which penny non-dropping is something other than a failure to twig to relevant information must be a bad theory of relevance.

We want to acknowledge the tenacity of intuitions that our account fails to honour. Blair's Intuition is not just there for the dismissing. There is simply no doubt that we very often make the judgements in the form ⌜**I** was relevant information⌝ in circumstances that fulfil two conditions. One is that there are or might be people for whom **I** is *not* relevant. The other is that the judgement is transparently true. Granting people who didn't get it use of the label 'de facto irrelevance', ambiguation presses for recognition of an additional sense, and objective relevance applies for the job. We have been at pains to argue that we should give up on objective relevance as a bad job, that objective relevance is not a theoretically fruitfully idea, and that it lacks a convincing motivation. Should these things prove to be so, the relevance of **I** needs to be reconciled with the plain fact that it is not relevant for Harry, short of the postulation of objective relevance. So what is it that makes true the judgement that **I** was relevant even though it was not relevant for Harry? It is that the information would be relevant for others having the same agenda as Harry and being similarly positioned with regard to that information. What is it that makes true the judgement that **I*** is irrelevant even though it was relevant for Harry? It is that the information would not be relevant for others having the same agendas as Harry and being similarly positioned with respect to that information. Those judgements could be true, though it would be a great mistake to underestimate their trickiness. They possess elusive truth conditions even apart from their subjective character. What, for example, are the conditions on 'similarly positioned'? And, as presented, they have no obviously normative cachet. Perhaps the omission could be repaired by reformulating: **I** is relevant if it would be relevant for anyone possessing Harry's agenda and being similarly positioned with respect to it, except for those who are somehow defective. Schizophrenics come to mind.

> Normal individuals perceive mainly task-relevant information, while irrelevant information does not reach awareness. A schizophrenic individual, however, is hypothesized to process too little relevant, or too much irrelevant information.
>
> [Hirt and Pithers, 1991, p. 140]

Hirt and Pithers report experimental results concerning where in the cognitive process schizophrenics mishandle information. Schizophrenics and 'normals' were shown two letters on a screen. The letters shown could be the same or different. Subjects were measured for responses. Schizophrenics were slower overall, but as judgement-tasks become more complex, ranging from visual identification to name identification to category identification, schizophrenics had increasingly slower response times than normal. This the researchers attributed to difficulties in mapping iconic information onto verbal representations of it. It was also suggested the schizophrenia may impair information-processing at several other junctures of the cognitive process.

In related work, in which it is hypothesized that schizophrenics are unable to ignore irrelevant information, subjects were exposed to a negative priming experiment. In negative priming, a distractor in one trial becomes the target in the next. Here subjects were asked to name the colours of words flashed at them in a variation of the Stroop experiment. The distractor was the word itself, which generally was the name of a colour. It was found that schizophrenics were unaffected by negative priming, whereas the psychiatric control group (previously hospitalized, but without major psychosis) was sensitive to it; that is, it impaired its performance. The experimenters concluded that schizophrenics do not inhibit awareness of irrelevant information in the manner of normals; and they concluded that their work supports an earlier proposal that schizophrenic symptoms are caused by 'awareness of processes that normally occur preconsciously' ([Beech *et al.*, 1989, p. 116]. See also [Pishkin and Williams, 1984]).

Here then are cases presented by the experimental record of a connection between relevance and normativity. Schizophrenics don't do well at avoiding negatively relevant information, information that inhibits the performance of tasks. We could say that schizophrenics do badly when it comes to Harman's Clutter Avoidance Principle; for theirs are minds, precisely, cluttered with trivialities. Consumption of irrelevance is had because schizophrenia is bad. And non-consumption of relevance is bad; it is, so to speak, the other side of schizophrenia. The cognitive agent who fails to consume relevant information has a mind that conforms to the obverse of the Clutter Principle: Do not permit your mind to have too little in it. We might be emboldened to say

♡ **Proposition 10.8 (Objective Irrelevance)** *Objectively irrelevant information is information which, when processed by* **X**, *is negatively (de facto) relevant for* **X** *with respect to some agenda. (Proposition 10.8 is preserved in the mormal model at section 15.5.)*

And

♡ **Proposition 10.9 (Normativity)** *Since processing lots of objectively irrelevant information leads to psychological aberration, it is desirable that cognitive agents avoid (and do what they can to avoid) objectively irrelevant information.*

A caricature awaits: Objectively irrelevant information is bad for mental health; objectively relevant information is good for mental health. Not getting it is a kind of empty-headedness. Irrelevance consumption is a case of clutter-mindedness. Empty-headedness and clutter-mindedness are each pathologically significant. And this is normativity enough for us.

So we have it. There is, after all, a conception of objective relevance different from the one we have been proposing (and, once proposed, trashing as well), and it calls down in a natural and unforced way normative shadings. Objectively irrelevant information is processed in ways that tend to make you sick, and it is that that makes it irrelevant. Objectively relevant information is information whose failure to be processed in just those kinds of ways also tends to make you sick, albeit in a very different way. It is all the difference between clutter-mindedness and empty-headedness, the two sides, *in extremis*, of schizophrenia.

Objectivity of relevance and irrelevance is now a property of the design of the processes that process it. Objective irrelevance is got when processes deviate from their design in the direction of lavish inclusion. Objective relevance is now allowed to be *de facto* irrelevant. When that happens processes deviate from design in the other direction, to the point of miserly exclusion.

Perhaps this restores prospects for a normative theory of objective relevance and irrelevance. Whatever it turns out to be, it will be a response to a connected meta-agenda. It will, in a deep and central way, be a psychological theory. In this we stand with Lycan:

> ...the normative force of epistemological terms comes from the value notions implicit in design-stance psychology. What Mother Nature provides is *good design* and it is that evaluative notion that is the ultimate source of our ordinary superficial evaluative ideas of 'better explanation', 'rational inference' and so forth.
> [Lycan, 1988, p. 142]

To that we say Amen, and we add to this list the ordinary superficial idea of 'objective relevance'.

This is an attractive arrangement. We can revive the distinction between objective and *de facto* relevance, and we can give modest recognition to the modest normativity of the objective side. We can also formulate an idea of what a normative theory of objective relevance would be. It would be a branch of design-psychology, or psychobiology (see here [Wouters, 1999, ch 8]). This requires the qualification or abandonment of certain of the critical terms that dot the previous section of this chapter. But the essentials are left in tact. Most of objective relevance is *de facto* relevance. That is, it is a fact that most of the time most of us are neither empty-headed nor clutter-minded. Objective or *de facto* relevance is irreducibly tied to agendas, information and processors of it. There is no stand-alone normative theory of relevance. What normativity there is attaches to one side of the objective/*de facto* distinction. The distinction is well-recognized and accommodated in a common theory. It is, again, the theory we know as design-psychology. This is relevance naturalized.

10.8 Reprise

In its most general sense, information is relevant for a cognitive agent when it proves helpful in a certain way. 'In a certain way' is a necessary qualification. Nothing is just plain helpful. Anything helpful is so in relation to some factors or condition or state of affairs with respect to which helpfulness is an intelligible notion. In a rough and ready way, any process can in principle be said to come to a halt. In principle, any such procedure can be interfered with or aborted. Thus there is a working equivalence between susceptibility to facilitation and susceptibility to interference.

Practical agents are awash in changes to their information states which, in turn, are reflections of even greater dynamisims in the outer world. In some sense that is not yet understood, energy-to-energy transductions get transformed into energy-to-information conversions. At every moment there is more information available to information-processing beings like us than we will ever need. Somehow we manage to discount such information, to filter it out in various ways. In chapter 2 we took note of the fact, or what appears to be the fact, that consciousness itself is a massive depressor of information, that consciousness is a kind of informational-filter. Given that human cognition is informationally driven and that it operates in ways that allow us both to reproduce and prosper, it is easy to see that (if not *how*) consciousness is a device that filters out unhelpful information. Additional filtrations presuppose different structures for helpfulness. In what we have here proposed an essential part of such structures are what we have called agendas. Thus it is in relation to agendas and to the condition of their advancement and closure that the flow of information is sorted and channelled. Agendas too filter out information. They inhibit information that would be unhelpful in the realization of what agendas require for advancement or closure. Seen in this way, it is evident that our account of relevance manages to preserve the two primordial beliefs which we introduced at the beginning of chapter 2. Preserved is the idea that irrelevance inhibits cognitive halting; also preserved is the idea that irrelevance is wasteful. The one idea has it that irrelevance clogs the cognitive arteries, and echoes Harman's Clutter Avoidance Principle not to clutter up our minds with trivialities. The other idea has it that dealing with irrelevancies takes too long and produces too many complexities for timely, executable cognition. Taken together, we have it that irrelevance inhibits the timely execution of *agendas*. And since it is plain that in general and overreaching ways agendas are successfully advanced and closed by beings like us, it must be the case that, by and large, the information that drives the processes of cognition is not irrelevant information, but relevant. Capturing this fundamental fact is the first business of a theory of relevance and, unless we are badly mistaken, a chief virtue of AR.

AR says that information is relevant for Harry when it helps in a certain way with Harry's agenda. Some will think this analysis too close to the ground, especially so given the eccentricities to which actual agents are sometimes prone. Various abstractions are, however, routinely available to those who wish to have them. We can, for example, define counterfactual relevance as relevance with respect to agendas that aren't actually possessed by any agent, but could be. Or, we could revive propositional relevance by saying that information **I** is relevant to proposition $P_1, \ldots, P_n$ just in case **I** is agenda relevant for agents whose agendas are of a type to be closed by it and the P_i denotes those states of affairs occasioned by those closures. These turn out to be very much the right sort of abstractions, since they are built from, so to speak, the *ground up*.

Part III

Formal Models for Relevance

Chapter 11

A Logic for Agenda Relevance — Overview

> Even if it be true that the propositions of logic are in any sense laws in accordance with which we do, or must, or ought to think (and it is highly doubtful whether this is true), it is quite certain that they can be completely defined without mentioning this fact.
>
> G. E. Moore, 'Russell's *Principles of Mathematics*', unpublished

11.1 Conceptual Analysis

In the preceding chapters we have developed an analysis of a common concept. The common concept is relevance, and our treatment of it is what philosophers call a *conceptual analysis* (though subject to Fodor's and our own qualifications in section 4.3 above). A conceptual analysis lies open to two sorts of difficulty. The analysis may turn out to be locally troubled or globally troubled. The alternation is not exhaustive, of course. A locally troubled account is a theory that gets particular things wrong; a given argument is a non sequitur; a particular claim is brought down by a counterexample; and so on. An example of a locally troubled theory is the Sperber and Wilson account of relevance. Although we think this treatment is defective in particular (and non-trivial) ways, we also think that their book is an overall success. It is, so to speak, a global winner, in contrast with accounts that could be thought of as globally troubled.

Globally troubled theories are afflicted by difficulties intrinsic to their underlying methodologies. In a somewhat unrealistic example, creation science is a globally troubled account not just because it gets particular things wrong, but because it is the wrong way in which to approach cosmology scientifically (or, anyhow, as its critics say). In the case of theories produced by conceptual analyses, global difficulties are those intrinsic to the methods of analysis.

We won't take the time to review in detail how the methods of conceptual analysis have played out in the first seven chapters of this book, but we shall mention a few of the most important methodological features of such theories; and we shall indicate what it is about these features that make for global liability.

1. Conceptually analytic theories are rooted in the theorist's intuitions about the theory's target concepts. 'Intuition' is a theoretician's term of art. Intuitions are what the theorist believes 'going in'. They are the beliefs he takes to the table prior to the theory's articulation, and to which he (initially and defeasibly) pledges the theory's loyalty.

2. It is important that these intuitions not be mere fragments of the theorist's intellectual autobiography, that they not be beliefs peculiar to him and his circumstances and concerns. The intuitions of a conceptually analytic theory are also required to be part of the common knowledge of some relevantly situated community of cognitive agents (e.g., speakers of English; work-a-day category theorists; actuaries; mums and dads; and so on). Thus a condition K on a theorist's subscription to an intuition is that he believe it, that he believe that others believe it as well, and that they believe that he too believe it. Of course, notoriously, common knowledge is sometimes more common that it is knowledge. In common knowledge, 'knowledge' is applied from the inside. Common knowledge is what common believers commonly believe their beliefs to be.

3. Condition K is some guarantee that intuitions selected under its providence will be about common things, or about things in their common signification, as Locke might say. In a rough and ready way, the bigger the community whose belief B satisfies K, the more common B will be. By this test, the wetness of water is more commonly known than the colour of Australian swans.

4. Having seeded his theory with his fundamental intuitions about a target concept, the theorist sets about to develop his account of it, an account which, within limits, leaves the target concept recognizably

> common. In constructing his account, the theorist will in large measure also be governed by what he antecedently believes and takes for common knowledge. He may also specify adequacy conditions which reflect his intuitions about what an analytic theory of his target concept should look like. The methodological or procedural beliefs are also in general what the theorist assumes others believe (including his readers) and what they in turn are disposed to attribute to him. So the theorist's procedural beliefs are also common, and being so their commonality is roughly proportional to the size of the communities in which the commonality condition K are observed.

Common beliefs are beliefs widely held in communities. Very common beliefs are beliefs very widely held in very large communities. At the limit, a common belief is a belief widely held in every community. There exist elaborate technologies which test for the commonality of beliefs, largely through the application of sampling theory. By and large the costs of such enquiries are high; they are sufficiently high to make it unlikely that beyond a comparatively narrow range of issues (whether from politics or show-biz), samplings of this sort will actually be made. It bears on this that, after a fashion, it lies in the nature of intuitions that those who hold them are not much disposed to think that their provenance is something that needs to be established by polls.[1] For to hold a belief of the of this sort is to hold it under conditions in which it is believed also to hold in the relevantly situated communities. They are beliefs such that anyone believing them believes that 'everyone' believes them. The feedback mechanisms that structure such loops are an important feature of the dynamics of shared views, but they need not detain us here.

Even so, it remains true that practitioners of the methods of conceptual analysis float their intuitions without the benefit, if that is what it is, of independent verification of their commonness.

We are speaking here of global difficulties attaching to the methods of conceptual analysis. The list is longer than two, but we shall confine our discussion to this number.

First global problem
In chapter 3, we introduced the

> *Heuristic Fallacy*: Let H be a body of heuristics with respect to the construction of some theory T. Then if B is a belief from

[1] In the heyday of Oxford Linguistic Philosophy, Arne Naess was actually derided for insisting that claims about what 'we' would say admitted of empirical test.

> H which is indispensable to the construction of T, then the unsupplemented inference that T is incomplete unless it sanctions the derivation of B is a fallacy.

The problem for the conceptual analyst is this. For some concept C, he comes to the task of constructing a theory of C-hood armed with a set of confident and enduring convictions about what it is to be a C-thing, hence about what his theory should say about C-things. If he had no such beliefs, he should not proceed to construct his theory. They are beliefs indispensable to that task. If he expects to be taken seriously, he must also suppose that his beliefs are *intuitions*; that is, beliefs widely held in the relevant communities. This is so because their wide acceptance is a guarantee that the theorist is not a doxastic eccentric and is some further indication — though not a guarantee — that the belief in question is some encouraging approximation of truth. The difficulty for the theorist is not only that he might be mistaken in thinking that his confident and enduring convictions are intuitions; he might well have fallen prey to the Heuristic Fallacy. In its most basic sense the Heuristic Fallacy tells us that it is often not discernible in advance whether the fundamental beliefs with which the theorist stocks his theory involve him in the fallacy.

Second global problem

Not knowing whether you've committed the Heuristic Fallacy is a global problem. It is a difficulty inherent in the method of conceptual analysis. It is not a vitiating difficulty, but it is far from trivial or inconsequential.

There is a second problem which is tougher. The methods of conceptual analysis are important in contexts of basic conceptual disagreement. *Ex falso quodlibet* is a case in point. *Ex falso quodlibet* ascribes a property to the implication relation. It says that omniderivability is triggered by inconsistent inputs. As the history of logic amply attests, *ex falso* divides theorists sharply.

There are those for whom *ex falso* is counterintuitive and others for whom it gives no such offence. It is unnecessary to dwell on details.[2] It is sufficient to list the resolution options and to indicate how each is problematic for the method of conceptual analysis.

Option 1. Ex falso is false for those whose intuitions it contradicts and true otherwise. (But not only does this sharply relativize a core part of logic, it sows doubt as to whether the contending beliefs are in the technically intended sense intuitions. If Harry has the intuitions that *ex falso* offends, then he has it believing that you have it too. But if *ex falso* doesn't offend

[2]These are furnished amply in [Woods, 2002b].

you, you don't have the belief that Harry ascribes to you when he takes it to be one of his intuitions.)

Option 2. Look for a more dominant intuition shared by both camps, which resolves the original conflict. (Even were this possible, it would show that it is possible that our most confident and enduring beliefs could be false and are shown so by another most confident and enduring conviction, which might also turn out to be false.)

Option 3. Try to negotiate a resolution of the disagreement by tracking the economic costs of the contending positions. For example, logics not admitting *ex falso* are vastly more complicated than those that do. Perhaps, then, we might settle for *ex falso.* (But this is tantamount to giving up the method of conceptual analysis, in the form anyhow in which we have described it so far.)

The global problems that affect the method of conceptual analysis suggest the wisdom of a certain circumspection. As the discussion of the Heuristic Fallacy previously acknowledges, no theorist (especially about matters lacking a direct empirical check) can be expected not to operate on the basis of what he thinks is so and what he thinks others also think. But care should be taken not to overindulge prior conviction. Theory construction is a fallibilist enterprise, and, especially when there is no access to such determination as empirical checkpoints provide, it is an enterprise subject to a convention that requires the theorist to put what he is prepared to say up against what others say or are disposed to say. However this desired concurrence is dressed-up, it remains a fundamental fact that the theorist is selling a view of things to his fellows, and that he does more or less well at doing so depending on what his fellows actually do think.

11.1.1 Complexity, Approximation and Consequence

At this juncture it is appropriate to ask whether we have succeeded in handling the three problems cited in chapter 3: the complexity problem, the approximation problem, and the consequence problem. Let's see.

Logic is an account of the behaviour of a cognitive agent. When the agent is an individual, his (or its) associated logic is a practical logic. Practical agents are individuals. They transact their cognitive affairs under conditions of scarcity. They are pressed for information and time; and they have limited computational powers.

Our logic is a theory about how such agents go about their cognitive business. Like any theory, ours takes liberties; it trades in idealizations. Our idealizations aren't beyond the reach of the dociamatic norms, however they are abstractions in the sense of systematicity and generality. See below, section 11.2. Even at the level of conceptual analysis, there are elements of idealization. In examining how relevance plays on practical agents in ways that advance agendas, we assumed, for one thing, the absence of what Cohen and others call performance errors; we did not take into account the influence of fatigue, illness, injury, intoxication, and so on. Even so, it is clear that our theory should not ascribe to a practical agent protocols that are too complex for any real individual to execute in a timely way (or at all) and for which there is no compensating factor of approximation. Defining an approximation relation was, in turn, our second problem.

As we saw earlier, it is important not to confuse metamathematical and operational complexity. Systems of relevant logic are very complex metamathematically; they have very hard decision problems. But it is one thing that a routine that would pronounce on the relevant validity of any arbitrarily selected object, and do so mechanically, infallibly and in finite time, is a computationally intractable problem. It is another thing as to whether a cognitive agent is able (sometimes) to deploy (some of) the virtual rules of relevant logic; (and, if so, as to how he does it). Even if we pretended that a practical agent had no difficulty in implementing the rules of relevant logic if he (or it) were a perfect embodiment of it, so to speak, it would not follow that such a being is a decision procedure for relevant validity or that it would run relevant logic's semantic programme

It remains true nevertheless that in a practical sense the rules of relevant logic are too complex for the likes of us. Virtually everyone now concedes this; but often with a 'but'. One is: 'But beings like us approximate to devices that run the rules of relevant logic'. Another 'but' is: 'But beings like us, while we don't use the rules, do employ heuristics to the same effect, by and large'. We shall say something about approximation in a moment, and not until we have had our say about heuristics.

Those who invoke the heuristics-rule distinction or, relatedly, the heuristics-theory distinction often have a certain picture in mind of how beings like us operate. According to this picture the rules (or theory) tell us what we should do. But, for one reason or another, we don't do what we should. It might even be the case that we *can't* do what we should. However, wonder of wonders, we are able to do *something* which nets out as saving us from the unqualified disgrace (and ruinous consequences) of not doing as we should. These saving graces come to us from heuristic devices that enable us to do on the cheap less well than we would have done had we followed the rules, but well enough even so. Furthermore, whereas it is the job of the logician to identify the rules that we should be following, it is left to the psychologist to figure out the heuristics. Finally, corresponding to this division of labour is our old friend the normative-descriptive distinction.

It is a popular view of such things, but it is not our view. Early on, we decided to smudge the distinction between logic and psychology. In that same spirit we propose the attenuation of the other two. Our first principle of normativity is the *Actually Happens Principle.* What people actually do is defeasibly the sort of thing that they should be doing. Exceptions have to be argued for; and the burden of proof is on him who claims the exception. This emphasis on the normative presumptiveness of what people actually do not only puts pressure on the old normative-descriptive distinction; it also makes headway with the approximation problem. The approximation problem was to specify conditions under which unachievable ideal conditions could safely be supposed to be achieved approximately. As things stand now, at the end of the section of the book that deals with conceptual models, an approximation achiever is identified as an actual reasoner sans performance errors. If this does not adequately explain how actual agents approximate to the behaviour that they are unable to produce, this will not be for the reason that our notion of approximation is inadequate; but rather for the reason that we have not postulated for them routines that actual agents cannot run. Of course, much of this is guessing. No one knows in detail how cognition works. This is as true for ideal-model theorists as it is for us. Even so, there is a difference between the two camps. The ideal modelist thinks that there is something else he *needn't* guess at, namely, the ideal rules that the actual agent can't honour. We are differently minded. In what we have examined so far, we haven't seen the need for such idealizations. So we haven't yet encountered the necessity of explaining how beings like us approximate to their fulfilment.

The rules–heuristics distinction attracts a like judgement. If an agent's cognitive heuristics are his net capacities for getting through his cognitive tasks, we see no explanatory purpose in specifying a bunch of conditions, knowing in advance that our agent can only fail them. Of course, it is also true that there is much that we don't know about these heuristic devices; a certain amount of guesswork is unavoidable. Like it or not, no relief is achieved by thinking up rules that actual reasoners can't comply with. But people can't stop themselves, such is the pull of the *Can Do Principle.*

We are now at the juncture where we seek formal models of the outputs of the conceptual analyses undertaken in the past few chapters. As we proceed, we may find it necessary to revisit the complexity and approximation problems. For, whatever else they are, formal models are abstractions.

It remains to say a further word about the consequence problem. What, we wanted to know, was the role of a consequence relation in a practical logic of cognitive agency. In this book, we relativize that question to the practical logic of agenda relevance. As we see, a consequence relation figures prominently in this account. More precisely, it is two relations. One is a causal consequence relation that instantiates Suppes' causal algebra. Information that is relevant for Harry is information that *puts him* in the requisite state. The requisite state is one which constitutes or causes (as the case may be) an advance in Harry's agenda. This is the second of our two relations. But here, too, we sound an admonition. It remains to be seen how little or much remains of these consequence relations under the formalizations that we have in mind.

Consequence also enters the picture with the analysis of anomaly-triggers, as when new information **I** contradicts old information Δ. If an abductive solution is sought, then, as we have seen, the agent in question must adapt Δ to Δ^* in fulfilment of a number of conditions. Δ^* is either a consistency-restoring restriction of Δ, in which some Δ-wffs are removed by the hypothesis that they no longer hold; or an extension of such a restriction, in which case an added wff is also introduced as an hypothesis. A further requirement is that, for some target wff $\mathcal{T}$, and a consequence relation $\mid\!\sim$, $\Delta^* \mid\!\sim \mathcal{T}$. Thus $\mid\!\sim$ could be a relation of deductive consequence, or explanatory consequence, or predictive consequence, and so on; and $\mathcal{T}$ is the wff that describes the new information, the new fact, **I**. A central part of the abducer's task is to think up and deploy from an arbitrarily large group of possibilities that deliver the desired abductive goods. A minimal condition on doing so is that the, up to massively, many possibilities that occur in the domain of the designated consequence relation be subjected to what, in effect, is the Clutter Avoidance Principle. Since the domain of the $\mid\!\sim$-relation is usually so large, it is not in general a good idea to see truth conditions on $\mid\!\sim$ as even virtual rules for clutter avoidance. What the abducer wants, of course, are possibilities that are also relevant and plausible. As for relevance, AR provides that a wff in the domain of $\Rightarrow$ is relevant for an abducer, when it advances his abductive agenda. But what *is* his agenda? Certainly it is not just to find a member of the domain of $\Rightarrow$. What he requires is a wff from that domain which also answers to various conditions of betterness (thus, the best explanation, the shortest proof, the strongest prediction, and so on). As we have seen, little is known of how beings like us actually hit such targets. The theory of agenda relevance leaves it open that a given possibility might advance the abducer's agenda without his being aware of it. This is a desirable result. It helps make the point that clutter avoidance is largely an automatic and sub-symbolic affair. It also helps explain why so little is known about how actual reasoners achieve their abductive targets. But one thing is clear; they do not do so by running the virtual rules for $\Rightarrow$-derivations. So in the present instance, the consequence problem draws a negative solution.

11.2 Formalization

This is the spirit in which the first ten chapters have been crafted. They are an offering to the interested research communities. They are an invitation to subscribe to our views, to come on board, as it were. Given the perilous history to date of theoretical accounts of relevance, ours is a risky venture. It asks for concurrence, but it risks rejection, or worse, indifference.

We take formalization to be a hedge against rejection and indifference. In less dramatic terms, it is a form of discipline that does conceptual theories nothing but good, if it comes off.

This is a good place to reinforce something briefly discussed in chapter 9. Our conceptual model of agenda relevance is what our formal model seeks to model. Accordingly, the modelling process is subject to two conditions, never mind that they pull in different directions. On the one hand, once the formal model is produced the conceptual account must be recognisably preserved in it. The other is that the formal model should refine or augment — and even in some cases correct — features of the conceptual account. The first condition speaks for itself. If the conceptual account is not recognizably preserved in the formal model, then the formal model will not have modelled its intended target. In that case, instead of a unified account of relevance, we would have two possibly disjoint accounts, the conceptual theory of Part II of this book, and the formal theory of some other set of intuitions, which would be the formal account of Part III of this book. Clearly the second condition bears on this issue, since among other things, it allows for exceptions. Beyond that it reflects the fact that when we formalize a conceptual theory, in addition to the things in the conceptual theory that we must include in the formal account, there are also things not in the conceptual account that we should put in the formal account. Thus formalizing a more or less unified body of conceptual data is not just giving a formal re-expression of it. It is also a way of producing a *theory* for those conceptually organized data. As such, the formal model should try to systematize those conceptual inputs, to generalize upon them where possible, and to unify them with existing theories not dealt with at the conceputal level. Given that there is a gap between data and theory, it is important to note that a datum does not have the automatic right of veto over what the theory may propose. So it is to be expected that to some extent the formal account will change the story told by the conceptual account.

All of this gives rise to an eleventh adequacy condition:

AC11 The formal model of relevance should preserve at least the central propositions and definitions of the conceptual account. Where it does

> not it should try to determine whether this represents a weakness of the formal model or a defect in the conceptual model.

See again the discussion of definitions 9.6, 9.7 and 9.9.

A formal model, then, is an idealized description of a thinking agent. A formal model of relevance is an idealized description of the play of information on an agent **X** (in relation to **X**'s agenda) under conditions in which that information is relevant for X. All idealized descriptions take liberties. They are in various ways empirically untrue. Provided that the gap is not too large between how formal models represent what an agent does and what the agent actually does, the formal models methodology is widely recognized to have virtues difficult to come by in more descriptively dense accounts.

Idealizations are abstractions. They subdue the number of parameters that enter the formal model's descriptions and they reduce contextual complexity. Abstraction is a kind of liberation. It frees the theorist to weave a tightly connected account around formal representations of the main features of the conceptual account. When the formal model is already itself a well-understood structure, there is value in squeezing into it any other theory that will reasonably fit. For in so doing, the squeezed-in theory adapts to, and amplifies the interpretation of a structure that is antecedently well-understood. What the ensuingly formalized account gains by way of systematicity and precision, it may lose by way of literal accuracy. But it is a winning cost–benefit strategy if the formal model in turn elucidates connections that were not initially apparent in the conceptual account.

A further benefit that sometimes accrues to formalization is an appreciation that it brings of systematic connections between and among rival theories. It also sometimes happens that at certain levels of abstraction apparent rivalry gives way to integration. At the beginning of Chapter 4 we quoted as follows:

> The topic of relevance has suffered much from those who have taken a part of the topic as the whole. [Cohen, 1994, p. 1]

And in 7,

> The relevance [problem] is too fundamental and too general to be dealt with in one stroke.
>
> [van Eemeren and Grootendorst, 1992, p. 141]

The formal modelling of the next chapters is designed to reflect the spirit of the remarks. We aim to integrate our approach with apparent rivals. We mean to embed AR in a more general theoretical environment, an environment whose generality makes AR especially conducive to the abstractions of our formal models. Formal models of the sort presently discussed are taken to be logics. On this view, a logic is a formal idealized description of how a practical agent reasons. A reasoning agent in turn is characterized as a being who commands, more or less, resources necessary for the discharge of his (or its) cognitive agendas. A reasoning being is an agent *of a type* depending on the extent of his cognitive resources. *Practical* agents are beings whose command of resources such as information, time and computational capacity is comparatively scarce. Individual human beings are practical agents in this sense. Theoretical agents are agents whose command of resources is comparatively abundant. NASA is a theoretical agent in this sense. Individual — or practical — agents are reasoning beings who must do things on the cheap. Institutionistical — or theoretical — agents can afford to travel business class or better.

A theory of reasoning can be seen as a set of algorithms which an agent is presumed to run. We have seen that some theories of reasoning (e.g., first-order classical logic and the Anderson and Belnap relevant systems) cannot be run by practical agents, by beings like us. But it is not ruled out that they might be run by theoretical agents, by beings like NASA but with lots more still of the requisite resources.

AR is a theory of relevance for practical agents. It is a theory for reasoning beings who must do things on the cheap. This is an important qualification. It needs some approximate reflection in our formal model, or, as we can now say, our *relevance logic.*

Part of what the mathematically oriented logician is interested in and adept at is the construction of formal models. The degree of latitude the logician has in producing his models bears directly on the nature of his contribution to a theoretical description of the behaviour of a practical cognitive agent. The psychologism to which we have committed ourselves suggests a general kind of answer. It suggests that our formal models should not idealize beyond the reach of the theoretical models of psychology itself, especially those models that stand a good chance of handling approximation to real-life performance in a realistic way.

Since the time of its founding, logicians have been sensitive to such constraints, especially as regards deductive reasoning. Aristotle was the first to adjust a logical theory to the fact that in making deductions from a body of data, or a set of premisses, real-life reasoners neither infer nor ought to infer anything whatever that chances to be a consequence of those data. Underlying this constraint is the distinction between what the consequences of a body of data *are* and what consequences of those data are to be *drawn.* Aristotle's view was that what the consequences are, are fixed by what we would call a classical consequence relation (nearly enough, it is classical entailment); whereas the consequences that are (to be) drawn are fixed by what he calls *syllogistic* consequence. Syllogistic consequence is classical consequence (or 'necessitation', as Aristotle has it) constrained in certain ways. Accordingly, a syllogism is a classically valid argument meeting those constraints, two of the most prominent of which are premiss-irredundancy and non-circularity. Two others are the consistency of premiss-sets and a ban on multiple conclusions. Taken together, syllogistic is the first non-monotonic, paraconsistent and intuitionist (-like) system in the history of logic. (Woods [2001, Chapter 6] and Woods and Irvine [2003].)

It is quite clear that Aristotle has in mind the distinction between what the consequences are and what consequences are (to be) drawn. Equivalently, he was aware of the difference between what *follows from* a database or premiss-set, and what is (or should be) *inferred* from it. It was a fateful recognition, since it led the founder of logic to the insight that deduction reasoning (or inference) is both a lesser and at the same time more complex thing than what unfettered logical consequence allows. The syllogistic reflects this awareness. It is Aristotle's attempt to *inferentialize* the consequence relation.

Aristotle thought that he could come close to getting a psychologically realistic set of rules for deductive thinking by beginning with truth conditions on unfettered consequences and adjusting them to the task of reasoning by imposing syllogistic constraints. There are two parts to this task. The syllogistic logician requires a theory of consequence, and he requires a theory of inference which will be spelled out in the constraints he imposes. It is noteworthy that Aristotle left the first of these tasks unperformed, concentrating his efforts upon the second. But this is far from showing that the first is not also essential.

How does this tie in with our disucssion of the degree of latitude the logician has in constructing formal models? If we stay with our present example for a moment, one clear task of the logician is to model consequence formally. Another, if we follow the lead of Aristotle himself, is to inferentialize the consequence relation by constraining the model in appropriate ways. It falls to the cognitive scientist to determine whether the inference model solves the approximation problem. If so, the logician's task is at an end. But if psychological experimentation shows respects in which the formal model's inferences are not plausible approximations of the real thing, the logician has the remedial task of refining his model further.

Much the same can be said for the formal modelling of agenda relevance. Here, too, it is open to the theorist to begin at a certain level of abstraction, prior to the imposition of more realistic constraints. Thus, as pointed out in section 7.8, it is open to the formal theorist to operate initially with a notion of propositional relevance, considered as an abstraction of agenda relevance. In these first stages of formal reconstruction, it would be wholly reasonable for the model-builder to fashion a conception of propositional relevance with a view to its susceptibility to the requisite constraints yet to be imposed. For example, suppose that the model-builder is able to capture a notion of propositional relevance that avoids some of the difficulties of the Anderson–Belnap approach, and suppose further that this model of propositional relevance is able without undue strain to capture a conception of contextual effects that avoids some of the difficulties of the Sperber–Wilson approach. Then we might say that here is a model of propositional relevance that augurs well for eventual adaptation to agents and agendas. This is precisely what we ourselves do say, and is the course we have set for ourselves in the chapters to follow. If the task of the inference-minded logician is to try to inferentialize propositional consequences, we might also say (for brevity) that a task of the agenda relevance-minded logician is to attempt to 'agendize' propositional relevance.

11.3 Overview of the Model

We now proceed with an overview of our formalization. Our basic definition of relevance has the form $(\mathbf{I}, \mathbf{X}, \mathbf{A})$, such that information $\mathbf{I}$ is relevant to agent $\mathbf{X}$'s agenda $\mathbf{A}$, in the sense that $\mathbf{I}$ helps towards (or hinders) closing his agenda. In order to model this concept we need the following components:

I. A base logic for basic reasoning, since logic, as we see it, is an account of what reasoning agents do;

II. A dynamic axis of evolution to enable the modelling of (dynamically evolving) agendas, since relevance is information that helps an agent's agenda advance;

III. Mechanisms that can detect and define relevance.

Our base logic will be a sophisticated labelled logic rich enough to accommodate and interact with whatever II and III may demand from it. (See chapters 12 and 13 to follow.)

Our dynamic axis will be a time and action model.

Since we want our logic to have a degree of psychological reality, our main mechanisms will be abduction, non-monotonicity through negation as failure and revision.

We will define the above notions in the following chapters. After we accomplish I–III, we can then present the notion of

IV. agenda relevance.

We note here with some emphasis that the devices in I–III are rather sophisticated and require an advanced notion of a logical system. So even before we start presenting our model we need a chapter on 'what is a logical system'.

To summarize, we need

1. An advanced theory of logical systems which includes the known major systems of logic that arise in AI in general and in AI agents and planning theories in particular.

The logic in (1) must have a data structure and proof theory. This gives rise to a further requirement:

2. A notion of input of information and the mechanisms of abduction, non-monotonicity and of belief revision for the logics in (1) to enable us to define how (whatever we are going to model as) agents absorb information and revise their beliefs.

The above components (1) and (2) are static. At best they would help us choose a suitable logic and define an improved propositional relevance (in which, for example to solve some of the difficulties of SW relevance). We have not so far included any *actions, change* or *dynamics* relative to some evolving directional axis (such as passage of time, or the progress of a friendly conversation or a sequence of information updates, etc.). We therefore must supply the following:

3. A directional dynamical axis of evolution involving sequencing of information states and a notion of abstract actions which can shift any given state into another new state.

4. A definition of what it means to be an agent capable of belief and action and what resources and mechanisms are available to him (or it).

Components (1)–(4) do not necessarily model relevance. They arise independently in the context of modelling the notion of an agent and developing the new notions of logic and logical mechanisms needed for applications in AI and computer science.

So we now outline what else we need to add if we want to model agenda relevance:

5. A definition, in the context of (1)–(4) above, of the notion of agenda and of execution agendas, compatible with section 8.3.2.

6. A definition of an improved notion of propositional relevance for states in the spirit of chapter 5 on propositional relevance.

7. A definition of agenda relevance using (5)–(6) in the spirit of chapter 7.

8. An account of the various nuances in relevance discussed earlier in this book, showing how they manifest themselves in the model. For example, the model should take note of

   - degree of relevance,
   - positive/negative relevance
   - hunches and accidental luck
   - *de facto* relevance
   - relevance to versus relevance for
   - relevance potential, etc.

Finally, having done all that, we critically discuss the limitation of the model.

Again we must emphasize that to be able to achieve all the above we will need to develop a lot of logical machinery. This machinery is independently motivated to explain what systems are needed in AI, but it is also within this machinery that we shall define agendas and agenda relevance.

Fortunately, our general approach to this new logical machinery is that it is built up from the bottom and intuitively reflects common human practical reasoning. Our readers are already using and are familiar with these logics, through their daily activities, even though they may not be aware of them in a formal (mathematical) sense. Given this situation, we can tell the reader right now, very quickly, how our relevance model is going to work. Of course to make the notions precise we will have to go through the subsequent chapters. It is good, however, for the reader to intuitively get a feel for the sequence of steps involved in building the model. It is also instructive to keep a familiar example in mind. We start with such an example.

Example 11.1 Harry is a policeman. He wants to arrest Joe for a crime committed on January 1st, 2003, and put him in jail. The acceptable sequence of events for such a goal is the following:

1. Gather enough evidence to be able to persuade a magistrate to issue a warrant to arrest Joe.

2. Together with a prosecutor get a legal case strong enough for conviction.

3–?. Secure a conviction and a jail-sentence.

Our directional axis is *time*; to simplify matters we assume that it is discrete. Let us review the situation at four points of time $t_1 < t_2 < t_3 < t_4, \ldots$.

Let Δ_t be the logical description of the state of affairs at time t. Thus Δ_{t_1} contains the information available at time t_1 about the case. Δ_{t_2} contains the information at a later time when more evidence was gathered. In fact, let us assume that enough information is available to be able to make an arrest. Δ_{t_3} is a description of the situation after the arrest was made and $\Delta_{t_4} \ldots$ are the states of affairs sometime later.

The Δ are expressed in some logic, which we schematically denote by $\vdash$. The logic could be classical logic. We know, however, that since we are dealing here with complex day-to-day common reasoning, that one of the new logics would do better. Joe's arrest is an action **a** which changes the state of affairs, and therefore it can take us from Δ_{t_2} to Δ_{t_3}. The arrest action has preconditions. We cannot arrest a person without making a case for it. Let α be the evidence needed to persuade the magistrate to make an arrest. So if $\Delta_{t_2} \vdash \alpha$, we can execute the action **a** and make the arrest. This will change the world and we will pass from Δ_{t_2} to Δ_{t_3}. The action has postconditions β, describing what is going to be in Δ_{t_3}. What we know for sure is that after the arrest Joe is in custody. There may be other things in β. However, we must have it at least that $\Delta_{t_3} \vdash \beta$.

This us our simplified story. Let us see what logical machinery we need to enable us to model it.

1. We need a serviceable logic $\vdash$. The logic must allow us to record for reasoning all the important features of this case. It must handle belief revision and inconsistency in a sophisticated way (i.e., be able to handle the passage from Δ_{t_1} to Δ_{t_2} when more information is uncovered, sorting contradictory evidence, and making a good case for proving $\Delta_{t_2} \vdash \alpha$).

2. We need a system of logic allowing for actions to be performed and for the passage of time and the sequencing of actions to be integrated in the logic.

3. A lot more is needed, but for the purpose of this preliminary example let us stop here.

Our choice for the logical methodology is that of Labelled Deductive Systems (*LDS*). It is general enough to incorporate many logics in it, and it is flexible enough to adjust to the needs of modelling relevance. Thus LDS will accommodate both (1) and (2). Having an LDS for the logic, we can formally define Harry's agenda as follows (at time t_1):

time $x < t_1 : \alpha$
time y: execute action **a**
time z: prepare case ...
⋮
etc.

Let us now see how we can add the notion of agenda relevance to this model.

Suppose we are given a piece of information **I** at time t_1. This should be a declarative unit in our LDS logic. Is it relevant to some other declarative unit **J** at that time?

The propositional theories of relevance will define a metapredicate $\mathbb{R}$ involving $\vdash, \Delta_{t_1}, \mathbf{I}$ and **J** and use $\mathbb{R}$ to define the notion. This was discussed in chapters 7 and 8 above. Various additional metapredicates were used in defining $\mathbb{R}$. The logical base was not a sophisticated *LDS*, but classical logic. We have seen that the models developed in chapters 5 and 6 have weaknesses. However we thought the SW idea was good; and we now hope that with LDS as the underlying logic many of those difficulties will disappear. We will also be able to define a good notion of (LDS) contextual effects and thus give (as a by-product) better foundations for SW relevance.

So, for example, adopting the SW spirit of contextual effects we define $\mathbb{R}(\Delta_{t_1}, \mathbf{I}, \mathbf{J})$ to be $\Delta_{t_1} + \mathbf{I} \vdash \mathbf{J}$ and $\Delta_{t_1} + \mathbf{I}$ has maximal LDS-contextual effects.

If **J** is α, the precondition of the action, then **I** can also be relevant to the *agenda* of arresting Joe, it enables the action **a**.

So the difference between propositional relevance and agenda relevance runs along three tracks:

1. The extent of our conceptual analysis of relevance
2. The quality, complexity and adequacy of our logic $\vdash$ and its related concepts (consistency, revision, etc., ...)
3. The setting up of a directional axis, time, action and agendas.

These give us a set-up in which we can say something about contextual effects. But we should also need chapters on

(a) The new notion of a logical system

(b) Labelled deductive systems

(a) and (b) will give us $\vdash$. But we shall also

(c) define the notion of a logical agent, and a time/action/revision logical model, using LDS.

(c) will allow us to define agendas and their properties and, only after all of that, to deal with agenda relevance.

Accordingly we shall

(d) model relevance in the logic thus built up. It will explain formally what $(\mathbf{I}, \mathbf{X}, \mathbf{A})$ means, and will examine the various nuances of agenda relevance.

11.4 How to Proceed

It is useful at this juncture to say something further about the *Can Do Principle*, discussed in chapter 3. We said that the

> *Can Do Principle* bids an investigator of a question Q in a domain D to invest his resources in answering questions $Q_1^*, \ldots, Q_n^*$ from domain D^* where the following conditions appear to have been met. First, the investigator is adept at answering the Q_i^*; and second, he is prepared to attest that answering the Q_i^* facilitates the answering of the initial question Q.

The *Can Do Principle* has two principal advantages. One is that it recognizes the virtue of trying to exploit what one already knows how to do in the process of determining whether he also knows how to do some further thing. Thus if our yet-to-be achieved task were a theory of, say, economic rationality, then it would fall within the providence of *Can Do* at least to consider whether grafting the probability calculus (in which one is adept) onto some assumptions about rational performance might facilitate the ongoing development of the economic theory, which at present is the theorist's yet-to-be achieved end. A second virtue of *Can Do* is itself economic. It counsels against re-inventions of the wheel, and counsels for making use, where possible, of expertise and information that already exists.

As we say, *Can Do* also has a vulnerable side. It lies open to a slide into what we call the *Make Do Principle. Make Do* is a degenerate case of *Can Do* and a standing liability for it. In plain terms, *Make Do* is in play when the work that a theorist is doing is not the work that he purports to be doing, but rather some other; and that the explanation of this detour is that the work he purports to be doing he doesn't know how to do, whereas the work that he is actually doing is work that he does know how to do. In subtler variations, *Make Do* is masqued by the undemonstrated assumption or the simple assertion that the work at hand does indeed facilitate the theorist's more central task. The trouble is sometimes such assumptions and such assurances are wrong; sometimes they are innocently wrong.

How does all this bear on the task of formalizing our conceptual account of relevance? Aside from appearing a rather general admonition against choosing models *simply* because they are things that we already known how to build, the *Can Do Principle* requires that the empirical liberties that our formal model takes with relevance-behaviour not be excessive, i.e., that they not outreach a reasonable notion of approximation. Even so, the *Principle* also bids us to at least start (if not always stay) with what we know, and this is advice we are happy to accept. But we do so by picking up a point late in chapter 7. Right from the beginning, we showed little enthusiasm for propositional models of relevance. The principal purpose of chapter 5 was to expose what we take to be the shortcomings of such an approach. As the reader will be quick to see, the logical structures that we have begun with in this chapter are straightforwardly propositional structures. This would seem an unpromising move (and a potential slide into *Make Do*) if it were our view that relevance is not satisfactorily catchable in any propositional structure. This is not our view, however. What we tried to show in chapter 5 is that propositional accounts of the sort we examined there don't do well for relevance. If this is right, it leaves us with two possibilities. One is that there is no propositional model in which relevance can thrive. The other is that relevance might well be elucidated by propositional models *if they have the requisite complexity*. This is in fact what we do think. Accordingly, we shall proceed in the following way.

In chapter 12 we shall develop a general answer to the question of what it is to be a logical system. As we proceed, it will become clear that, on our approach, the basic idea of a logic exhibits a good deal more structure than one finds in the more traditional treatments. As that model unfolds, we will enrich it further with purpose-built mechanisms for *time, action and belief-revision*. So the logic of chapter 12 will be a *TAR*-system.

Next, in chapter 13, we shall build in further structure. Our *TAR*-logic will be extended by addition of our *algebra of labels*. Thus the *TAR*-logic will be given the structural overlay of a Labelled Deductive System. The ensuing system, a *TAR–LDS*, will display resources enough to rehabilitate the *SW*-notion of *contextual effects*, as well as to elucidate the concept of hunches, which we discussed conceptually in chapter 9.

After some refinements, chapter 14 shows how to revive the fortunes of *AR*-relevance, answering again to the ecumenical spirit with which we have endeavoured to develop the theory of agenda relevance. And, in chapter 15, agenda relevance itself finally comes to the fore in a suitably formal way.

11.4.1 Bidirectional Coverage and Fit

In judging the success of a formalisation $\mathcal{F}$ of a conceptual model $\mathcal{C}$ of a notion n, efforts should be made to answer two main questions. One is the question of *bidirectional coverage* and the other is the question of *fit*. A formal model $\mathcal{F}$ of a conceptual model $\mathcal{C}$ does well or badly on the score of bidirectional coverage to the extent that provisions originating in $\mathcal{C}$ have counterparts in $\mathcal{F}$ and provisions originating in $\mathcal{F}$ can be accommodated in unforced extensions of $\mathcal{C}$. $\mathcal{F}$ does well or badly with respect to its fit with $\mathcal{C}$ to the extent that $\mathcal{F}$'s counterparts in $\mathcal{C}$ (or an unforced extension of $\mathcal{C}$) solve the approximation problem. It is also worth repeating that a failure of coverage, whether by $\mathcal{F}$ or $\mathcal{C}$, or an extension of $\mathcal{C}$ of $\mathcal{F}$, is not necessarily fatal. The fact that a provision of $\mathcal{C}$ (a $\mathcal{C}$-fact, so to speak) is unmatched in $\mathcal{F}$ (has no corresponding $\mathcal{F}$-fact) could be reason to adjust $\mathcal{C}$ rather than to fault $\mathcal{F}$. Similarly, that an $\mathcal{F}$-fact has no counterpart in an unforced extension of $\mathcal{C}$ might show only that $\mathcal{F}$ has a conceptual or mathematical richness that $\mathcal{C}$ need not have.

It is not desirable that the question of how well $\mathcal{F}$ fits $\mathcal{C}$ be restricted to how well $\mathcal{F}$-counterparts of $\mathcal{C}$-facts solve the approximation problem. Formalisation is at its best when there is genuine reciprocity between $\mathcal{F}$ and $\mathcal{C}$. It is possible, therefore, that the $\mathcal{F}$-fact that is counterpart to some $\mathcal{C}$-fact will *deepen* the analysis of the subject of the enquiry beyond what the $\mathcal{C}$-fact, and others like it, are able to do. So it must not be automatically supposed, just because an $\mathcal{F}$-fact 'says more' than its correpsonding $\mathcal{C}$-fact, that the fit of $\mathcal{C}$ to $\mathcal{F}$ is inadequate or defective (alternatively, that $\mathcal{F}$ does poorly with the aproximation problem).

Perhaps it would be prudent to give some idea of how well we think the formalisations of Part III have made out with the bidirectional coverage and fit. To some extent, this is putting the cart before the horse — after the conceptual model has been produced but before the reader has had a chance to inspect the formal developments. Even so, there are advantages to proceeding in the way that we propose. One is that it offers the reader advance notice of where to look for salient connections between the conceputal and the formal. Another (and related) consideration is that the proferred signposts may help to motivate the formal chapters, especially for readers not wholly at home with formal techniques. A third factor is the converse of the second. It is that before going in, formally minded readers are again reminded that the formal models that we develop in Part III are held to substantial conceptual and methodological preconditions, and that the ensuing formalisms satisfy them, if not perfectly, then significantly. What we propose to concentrate on are the factors of bidirectional covereage and adequacy conditions, but we won't here attempt a complete accounting.

Considerations of fit are harder to judge, and are, we think, more properly left for the reader to deal with, after the formalities have been concluded. Where there are failures of either coverage or fit, we also leave it to the reader to determine where the fault, if any, lies — with $\mathcal{F}$ or with $\mathcal{C}$.

The basic conceptual idea, forwarded by definition 7.1, of relevant information as agenda-advancing information is captured in the formal model at Definition 15.4. In so doing, $\mathcal{F}$ satisfies adequacy condition $AC2$, which requires that a theory of relevance recognize the context-sensitivity of relevance. Proposition 7.6 proposing the existence of potentially relevant information is preserved in remark 15.15. Definition 8.1 defines a cognitive agent as an information-processor that is capable of belief. This finds formal expression in definition 15.3. Definition 8.8 (which absorbs definition 8.3) defines an agenda as a function from effectors to endpoints. The formal counterpart is developed in sections 15.2 and 15.3. Propositon 9.2 has it that the more agendas a piece of information advances, the more relevant it is, and definition 15.4 stipulates to the same effect; and, in so doing, provides that $\mathcal{F}$ meets $AC3$, which requires a theory of relevance to honour the comparative notion of that relation. Definition 9.8 has it that information is cumulatively relevant when it is the sum of pieces of information also relevant, but less so one by one. Chapter 15 sees things the same way. Definition 9.9 provides that a piece of information is hyper-relevant to a certain degree when all its parts are also relevant to (close to) that same degree, and Chapter 15 preserves this provision. Adequdacy condition $AC4$ requires that a theory of relevance recognize a notion of negative relevance. The conceptual model obliges at definition 9.10 and the formal model does the same at definition 15.4. Hunches are disucsssed conceptually in section 9.5 and they reappear formally in section 13.2.4. Contextual effects are the principle business of chapter 6. An adaptation of them can be found in section 13.2.5 of the formal model Proper functions, which are defined by definition 10.2, recur in remark 15.5, as do hypernormativity (conceptually proposed by definition 10.3) and objective relevance (captured by definition 10.4). The same is true for objective irrelevance, proposed in proposition 10.8.

Adequacy condition $AC8$ asks for an answer to the question as to whether relevance is an inherently dialogical notion. The burden of chapter 9 was to say No, and nothing in the formal model says otherwise. Even so, it is proposed in chapter 9 that dialogical conceptions of relevance can be absorbed by the conceptual model, a fact that is easily modelled but not here. The same may be said for $AC5$, which bids the theorist to say something about fallacies of relevance. We haven't given their discussion in chapter 9 formal expressions in Part III, but we see no structural or technical bar to doing so. $AC9$ calls for an analysis of the common idea of relevance, and $AC10$ plumps for a theoretical ecumenism. The sheer variability attaching to information, agents and agendas, and the fact that this variabilty is preserved in the formal model, speaks well for the model in relation to $AC9$. That the model gives us adaptations of contextual effects and Anderson–Belnap relevance speaks well for it in relation to $AC10$. The conceptual model apeaks at length about belief-reorganization (thus satisfying $AC7$) and the formal model does the same. Chapter 14 does formally what was done in section 9.8 *et passim*; and twice-over is satisfied the requirement ($AC6$) to say something useful about dispute about relevant logic ($AC6$). Finally, $AC1$ requires a theory of relevance to be non-excessive. It is theoretical discouragement of both omni-relevance and null relevance in which, respectively, everything is relevant to everything and nothing is relevant to anything. The condition holds both conceptually and formally.

This is a fair bit of compliance, and is nothing to sneeze at. But formal coverage of conceptual providence is not perfect. We said in the conceptual model that when information is relvant it integrates with existing or background information in a certain way. This was the way of maximal irredundancy or some near thing. We have not been able to find a formal home for a suitably robust notion of irredundancy, and will pursue the task in work in progress. This is a non-trivial omission. It nullifies the definition of linked information as irredundant information (definition 9.4). It does the same to definition 9.6, which tried to build the idea of the integration of new information and background information with the analysis of relevance itself. And we lose the distinction purported by definition 9.7 of parasitic relevance.

These are methodologically important failures of coverage. What makes them so, as we have already suggested, is the pressure they exert on the question of where the fault lies. Shall we say that in their failure to find a home in the formal model, the formal model provides inadequate cover for conceptually verified truths about relevance? Or should we agree that their lack of formal coverage show these provisions of the conceptual model in a new light, in which, at a minimum, they cannot be seen as conveying what is essential to the analysis of relevance. It is not simply obvious as to which of these alternatives is the more plausible. Our own present position is that, short of our having been able to do it up to now, there is no especially good reason to think that their formal expression is a bad idea.

Chapter 12

A General Theory of Logical Systems

> We could define the intelligence of a machine in terms of the time needed to do a typical problem *and* the time needed for the programmer to instruct the machine to do it.
>
> John Nash [1954, p. 119]

12.1 Introduction

The present chapter investigates the notion of a logical system. We imagine that there are lots of our readers who may think that tutelage on this subject is not necessary for them. These readers are, of course, free to skip to chapter 13 or beyond. But, with respect, we counsel against doing so precipitately. There is more to the present chapter than one might think.

The structure of the chapter is such that it leads the reader from the traditional notion of a logic as a *consequence relation* to the more complex notion of what we call a *practical reasoning system*. We shall make a choice of one such logical system in which to develop our agenda relevance model. In fact, the next chapter develops the particular notion of LDS.

In general, to specify a logical system in its broader sense we need to specify its components and describe how they relate to each other. Different kinds of logical systems have different kinds of components which bear different kinds of relationships to each other.

The following components are identified.

1. *The language*
   This component simply defines our stock of predicates, connectives, quantifiers, labels, etc.; hence all the kinds of symbols and syntactical structures involved in defining the basic components of the logic.

2. *Declarative unit*
   This is the basic unit of the logic. In traditional logical systems (such as classical logic, modal logics, linear logic, etc.) the declarative unit is simply a well-formed formula. In more complex logics, such as *Labelled Deductive Systems*, it is a labelled formula or a database and a formula, etc.

3. *Databases*
   This notion is that of a family of declarative units forming a *theory* representing intuitively the totality of our *assumptions*, with which we reason. In classical and modal logics this is a set of formulas. In linear logic it is a multiset of formulas. In the Lambek calculus it is a sequence of formulas. In *Labelled Deductive Systems* it is a structured labelled family of formulas.

   Databases can contain as few wffs as a simple declarative unit. More complex databases are built up compositionally.

   Other notions need also be defined for databases. Among these are:

   - *Input* and *deletion*, dealing with how to add and remove declarative units from a database. In classical and modal logic these are union and subtraction.
   - *Substitution* of a database Δ for a declarative unit φ inside another database containing φ. We need this notion to define *cut*.
     These notions are purely combinatorial and not logical in nature.[1]

4. *Consequence*
   Now that we have the notion of a database, we define consequence.

[1]To clarify, consider the Lambek calculus. A declarative unit is any formula φ. A database is any sequence of formulas $\Delta = (\varphi_1, \dots, \varphi_n)$. Input of φ into Δ can be either at the end of the sequence or the beginning, forming either $(\varphi_1, \dots, \varphi_n, \varphi)$ or $(\varphi, \varphi_1, \dots, \varphi_n)$. Similarly the corresponding deletion. Substitution for the purpose of Cut can be defined as follows:

The result of substituting $(\beta_1, \dots, \beta_m)$ for α_i in $(\alpha_1, \dots, \alpha_n)$ is the database $(\alpha_1, \dots, \alpha_{i-1}, \beta_1, \dots, \beta_m, \alpha_{i+1}, \dots, \alpha_n)$.

Note that no logical notions are involved, only sequence handling is needed.

In its simplest form it is a relation between two databases of the form $\Delta_1 \mid\!\sim \Delta_2$. This means that Δ_2 *follows* in the logic from Δ_1. Of special interest is the notion $\Delta \mid\!\sim \varphi$, between a database Δ and a declarative unit φ.

$\mid\!\sim$ can be specified set theoretically or semantically. Depending on its various properties, it can be classified as monotonic or non-monotonic.

As part of the notion of consequence we also include the notions of consistency and inconsistency.

5. *Proof theory, algorithmic presentation*
One may give, for a given $\mid\!\sim$, an algorithmic system for finding whether $\Delta \mid\!\sim \varphi$ holds for a given Δ and φ. Such an algorithm is denoted by a computable metapredicate $S^{\mid\sim}(\Delta, \varphi)$. Different algorithmic systems can be denoted by further indices, e.g.

$$S_1^{\mid\sim}(\Delta, \varphi), \ldots, S_i^{\mid\sim}(\Delta, \varphi)$$

One view, however, is to regard $S_i^{\mid\sim}$ as a mere convenience in generating or defining $\mid\!\sim$ and that the real logic is $\mid\!\sim$ itself.

However, there are several established proof (algorithmic) methodologies that run across logics, and there are good reasons to support the view that at a certain level of abstraction we should consider any pair $(\mid\!\sim, S^{\mid\sim})$ as a logic. Thus classical logic via tableaux proofs is to be considered as a different logic from classical logic via Gentzen proofs.

6. *Mechanisms*
The previous items (1)–(5) do not exhaust our list of components for a practical logical system. We shall also require additional mechanisms such as *abduction, revision, aggregation* and *actions*. Such mechanisms make use of the specific algorithm S (of the logic $(\mid\!\sim, S^{\mid\sim})$) and define metalevel operations on a database. The particular version of such operations we present as part of the logic. Thus a logic can be presented as $(\mid\!\sim, S^{\mid\sim}, S_{\text{abduce}}, S_{\text{revise}}, \ldots)$.

The notion of a database needs to be modified to include markers which can activate these mechanisms and generate more data. The language of the logic may include connectives that activate or refer to these mechanisms. Negation by failure is such an example.

We shall see later that it is convenient to present the metapredicate $S^{\mid\sim}$ as a three-place predicate, $S(\Delta, \varphi, x)$, where $x \in \{0, 1\}$ or $S(\Delta, \varphi) = x$.

$S(\Delta, \varphi, 1)$ means that the computation succeeds and $S(\Delta, \varphi, 0)$ means that the computation finitely fails. The definitions of some of the $S_{\text{mechanism}}$ will make use of this fine tuning of the S predicate.

In the rest of this chapter we motivate and exemplify the above notions.

12.2 Logical Systems

We begin by presenting general answers to:

What is a logical system?
What is a monotonic system?
What is a non-monotonic system?
What is a (formal) practical reasoning system?

and related questions.

Imagine an expert system running on a personal computer, say the *Sinclair QL*. You put the data Δ into the system and ask it questions Q. We represent the situation schematically as:

$$\Delta?Q = \text{yes/no depending on the answer}$$

We understand this expert system because we know what it is supposed to be doing, and we can judge whether its answers make reasonable sense. Suppose now that we spill coffee onto the keyboard. Most personal computers will stop working, but in the case of the *QL*, it may continue to work. Assume however that it now responds only to the symbol input and output, having lost its natural language interface. We want to know whether what we have here is still 'logical' or not. We would not expect that the original expert system still works. Perhaps what we have now is a new system which is still a logic.

So, we are faced with the question:

What is a logic?

All we have is a sequence of responses:

$$\Delta_i?Q_i = \text{yes/no}$$

How do we recognize whether this makes for a logic at all?

This question was investigated by Tarski and Scott, who gave an answer for monotonic logic systems. If we denote the relation

$$\Delta?Q = \text{yes} \qquad \text{by } \Delta \vdash Q$$

then this relation must satisfy three conditions to be a *monotonic logic*:

1. *Reflexivity*:
   $\Delta \vdash Q$ if $Q \in \Delta$.

2. *Monotonicity* :
   If $\Delta \vdash Q$ then $\Delta, X \vdash Q$.

3. *Transitivity (Lemma Generation, Cut)*:[2]
   If $\Delta \vdash X$ and $\Delta, X \vdash Q$ then $\Delta \vdash Q$.

To present a monotonic logic it is necessary to mathematically define a relation '$\vdash$' satisfying conditions 1, 2, and 3. Such a relation is called a *Tarski consequence relation.* Non-monotonic consequence relations are obtained by restricting condition 2 as follows:

2*. *Restricted Monotonicity:*
   If $\Delta \vdash Q$ and $\Delta \vdash X$ then $\Delta, X \vdash Q$.

We discuss this condition later in the present section.

Example 12.1 Let our language be based on atomic formulas and the single connective '$\Rightarrow$'. Define $\Delta \vdash_C Q$ to hold iff by doing classical truth tables for the formulas in Δ and Q, we find that whenever all elements of Δ get *truth*, Q also gets *truth*. We can check that conditions 1, 2, 3 hold. If so, we have defined a logic. In this particular case, we also have an algorithm to check for a given Δ and Q, whether $\Delta \vdash Q$. In general, consequence relations can be defined mathematically without an algorithm for checking whether they hold or not.

Example 12.2 For the same language (with '$\Rightarrow$' only) define $\vdash_I$ as the smallest set theoretical relation of the form $\Delta \vdash Q$ which satisfies conditions 1, 2, 3, together with the condition DT (*Deduction Theorem*):

DT: $\Delta \vdash A \Rightarrow B$ iff $\Delta \cup \{A\} \vdash B$.

We want to prove that this is a good definition. First notice that '$\vdash$' is a relation on the set $Powerset(Formulas) \times Formulas$ where $Formulas$ is the set of all formulas. We now have to show that the smallest consequence relation '$\vdash$' required in the example does exist.

[2] Cut has many versions. In classical logic they are all equivalent. In other logics they may not be. Here is another version:

4. *Second Version of Cut* :
   If $\Delta_1 \vdash X$ and $\Delta_2, X \vdash Q$ then $\Delta_1, \Delta_2 \vdash Q$.

We must be careful not to take a version of cut which collapses condition 2* to condition 2.

Exercise 12.3

(a) Prove that $\vdash_I$ of the previous example 12.2 exists. (It actually defines intuitionistic implication.)

(b) Let $\Delta \vdash Q$ hold iff $Q \in \Delta$. Show that this is a monotonic consequence relation. (We call this civil servant logic, *Beamten Logik*.)[3]

(c) Similarly for $\Delta \vdash Q$ iff $\Delta = \{Q\}$. (This is the literally minded Beamten Logik.)

The difference between examples 12.1 and 12.2 is that example 12.2 does not provide us with an algorithm as to when $\Delta \vdash_I Q$. The $\vdash_I$ is defined implicitly. For example how do we check whether (see example 12.14)

$$(((b \Rightarrow a) \Rightarrow b) \Rightarrow b) \Rightarrow a \vdash_I ?a$$

This motivates the need for algorithmic proof procedures.

We now have at hand the relationships depicted in figures 12.1, 12.2 and 12.3.

Logics

Monotonic **Non-Monotonic**

Figure 12.1

Monotonic Logics

Consequence Relation $\vdash_1$ defined mathematically in any manner.	**Consequence Relation $\vdash_2$** defined mathematically in any manner.

Figure 12.2

$S_i^{\vdash}(\Delta, Q)$ is an algorithm for answering whether $\Delta \vdash Q$. Two properties are required:

[3]'Beamter' means *civil servant* in German.

Consequence Relation $\vdash$

Algorithmic System	Algorithmic System
$S_1^{\vdash}(\Delta, Q)$	$S_2^{\vdash}(\Delta, Q)$

Figure 12.3

Soundness If $S_i^{\vdash}(\Delta, Q)$ succeeds then $\Delta \vdash Q$.

Completeness If $\Delta \vdash Q$ then $S_i^{\vdash}(\Delta, Q)$ succeeds.

We assume of course that the algorithmic system is a recursive procedure for generating (with repetition) all pairs (Δ, Q) such that $\Delta \vdash Q$ holds.

There can be many algorithmic systems for one and the same logic. For example, for classical logic, there are resolution systems, connection graph systems, Gentzen systems, semantic tableaux systems, Wang's method, among others.

It bears on the practical aspects of a logic such as *PLCS* that an algorithmic system $S_i(\Delta, Q)$ may not be optimizable in practice. It may be, for example, double exponential in complexity. There are, however, several *heuristic* ways of optimizing it. If we try these optimizing methods we obtain different automated deduction systems for the algorithmic system S_i, denoted by: $O_1S_i, O_2S_i, \ldots$

In this case only soundness is required, to wit:

if $O_1S_i(\Delta, Q)$ succeeds then $S_i(\Delta, Q)$ succeeds

But we do not necessarily require completeness (e.g., the automated system may loop, even though the algorithmic system does not). (In fact, if the relation $\vdash$ is not recursively enumerable (RE), we may still seek an automated system. This will be expected to be only sound.)

So far we have been talking about monotonic systems. A *PLCS* is non-monotonic. How do we characterize a non-monotonic system? There is a problem: Can we characterize $\mid\!\sim$ as a non-monotonic system by imposing conditions on ? (We will use $\vdash$ for monotonic systems and henceforth $\mid\!\sim$ for non-monotonic systems.) To seek this answer we must look at what is common to many existing non-monotonic systems. Do they have any common features, however weak these common features might be? Before proceeding, we state the main recognizable difference between monotonic and non-monotonic systems. Consider a database (1), (2), (3) and the query $?B$

(1) $\neg A$ $\quad\quad\quad ?B$
(2) $\neg A \Rightarrow B$
(3) *other data.*

B follows from (1) and (2). It does not matter what the other data are. Thanks to monotonicity, we do not need to survey the full database to verify that B follows. In non-monotonic reasoning, however, the deduction depends on the entire database. If we introduce more data, we get a new database, and the former deduction may no longer go through. Suppose we agree to list only positive atomic facts in the database. Then negative atomic facts are non-monotonically deduced simply from the fact that they are not listed. Thus a list of airline flights from Vancouver to London which lists an 11:05-flight Monday to Saturday, would imply that there is no such flight on Sunday. This is negation-as-failure, one of the economizing devices of a *PLCS*. Thus following this agreement, clause (1) of the database can be omitted provided the database is consistent, i.e., A is not listed in (3). We can deduce B by first deducing $\neg A$ (from the fact that it is not listed) and then deducing B from (2). To make sure A is not listed we must check the entire database.

Our original question was: What are the conditions on $\mid\!\sim$ that make it a non-monotonic logic?

We propose to replace condition 2 on $\vdash$ of monotonicity by condition 2* already mentioned, namely:

2*. *Restricted Monotonicity*:
If $\Delta \mid\!\sim X$ and $\Delta \mid\!\sim Q$ then $\Delta, X \mid\!\sim Q$.

This means that if X, Q are 'expected' to be true by Δ (i.e., $\Delta \mid\!\sim X$ and $\Delta \mid\!\sim Q$) then, if X is actually assumed true, it remains the case that Q is expected to be true (i.e. $\Delta, X \mid\!\sim Q$).

In section 12.3 we will return to the question of finding a correct definition for a non-monotonic consequence relation. We will see in that context that it might also be interesting to replace Cut by weaker rules. We will claim that it is best to regard the term 'non-monotonic' as expressing the absence of monotonicity and that many different features fall under this umbrella, among them resource considerations of a kind essential to a *PLCS*. Some of these features are orthogonal and complementary to each other.

Accordingly, we advance

The Gabbay-Schulz–Zimmermann proposal (1988):

> Non-monotonicity is not a positive property. It is the absence of monotonicity. We should therefore look for several separate versions of non-monotonic systems in order to cover the main types of non-monotonicity.

Given a non-monotonic system $\mid\!\sim$, we can still seek for algorithmic systems $S_i^{\mid\sim}(\Delta, Q)$ for $\mid\!\sim$. In the non-monotonic case these are rare. Most non-monotonic systems are highly non-constructive, and are defined using complex procedures on minimal models or priority of rules or non-provability considerations. So the metatheory for $\mid\!\sim$ is not well developed. There is much scope for research here. Later on we will introduce the notion of *Labelled Deductive Systems* (*LDS*), which will yield in a systematic way a proof theory for several non-monotonic systems.

We are now ready to answer provisionally the question of what a logical system is. We propose a first answer which may need to be modified later on.

Definition 12.4 (Logical system version 1) *A logical system is a pair* $(\Vdash, S^{\Vdash})$, *where* $\Vdash$ *is a consequence relation (monotonic or non-monotonic, according to whatever definition we agree on) and* $S^{\Vdash}$ *is an algorithmic system for* $\Vdash$. $S^{\Vdash}$ *is sound and complete for* $\Vdash$.[4]

Different algorithmic systems for the same consequence relation give rise to different logical systems. So classical logic presented as a tableau system is not the same logic as classical logic presented as a Hilbert system.

Here are some examples of major proof systems:

- Gentzen
- Tableaux
- Semantics (effective truth tables)
- Goal directed methodology
- Resolution
- Labelled Deductive Systems.

Definition 12.4 is supported by the following two points: First, we have an intuitive recognition of the different proof methodologies, and show individual preferences to some of them depending on taste and the need for

[4]Of course, there are other requirements such as the notion of what a theory (database) is, input into a theory, consistency/inconsistency, etc.

	Truth tables	Gentzen
Łukasiewicz infinite valued logic	•	??
Classical logic	•	•
Intuitionistic logic	??	•

Figure 12.4 Logics landscape

applications. Second, slight variations in the parameters of the proof systems can change the logics *significantly*. Figure 12.4 is an example of such a relationship.

In the truth table methodology, classical logic and Łukasiewicz logic are slight variations of each other. They resemble intuitionistic logic less closely. In the Gentzen approach, classical and intuitionistic logics are very similar, while Łukasiewicz logic is difficult to characterize.

This evidence suggests strongly that the landscape of logics is better viewed as a two-dimensional grid.

The reader may ask why we need $\Vdash$, if we have $S^{\Vdash}$ from which $\Vdash$ can be obtained? The answer is that $\Vdash$ is introduced via a mathematical definition which reveals the intended meaning of $\Vdash$ as separate from the algorithmic means of computing it. So in saying a logical system is a pair $(\Vdash, S^{\Vdash})$ we do not intend only a set theoretical definition of $\Vdash$ and an algorithm $S^{\Vdash}$, but also an expression of the intended meaning for $\Vdash$ as well.

The reader should note that definition 12.4 is a pivotal definition and a serious departure from current conceptual practice. It will be properly motivated throughout these chapters. Let us use the notation $\tau = (\Vdash_\tau, S^{\Vdash}_\tau)$ for a logical system τ. $\Vdash_\tau$ is its consequence relation and $S^{\Vdash}_\tau$ is an algorithmic system for $\Vdash_\tau$. We also note that in case $\Vdash_\tau$ is not RE, recursively enumerable (as may happen often in non-monotonic logics), we will make do with $S^{\Vdash}_\tau$ which is only sound for $\Vdash$.

Here is a further example:

Example 12.5 (Modal logic S4)

1. Consider a language with atoms p, q, r, ... the classical connectives $\neg, \wedge$ and the unary connective $\Box$. Let h be a function assigning to each atom a set of points in the Euclidean plane $\mathcal{R}^2$. Let:

   - $h(A \wedge B) = h(A) \cap h(B)$.
   - $h(\neg A) =$ complement of $h(A)$.
   - $h(\Box A) =$ topological interior of $h(A)$.

   Let $\models A =_{df} \forall h[h(A) = \mathcal{R}^2]$.

   Let $A_1, \ldots, A_n \models B$ iff $\forall h(\bigcap_i h(A_i) \subseteq h(B))$.

   Then $\models$ is a consequence relation.

   Let $A \Rightarrow B$ be defined as $\neg(A \wedge \neg B)$ and let $A \leftrightarrow B$ be defined as $(A \Rightarrow B) \wedge (B \Rightarrow A)$. Then we have for example: $\models \Box(A \wedge B) \Leftrightarrow \Box A \wedge \Box B$.

2. Let * be a translation from the previous language into classical logic. For each atom q_i associate a unary predicate $Q_i(t)$, with one free variable t. Let R be a binary relation symbol. Translate as follows (note that the translation function depends on t):

   - $(q_i)^*_t = Q_i(t)$.
   - $(A \wedge B)^*_t = A^*(t) \wedge B^*(t)$.
   - $(\neg A)^*_t = \neg A^*(t)$.
   - $(\Box A)^*_t = \forall s(tRs \Rightarrow (A)^*_s)$.

   Let $A_1, \ldots, A_n \Vdash A$ hold iff in predicate logic one can prove:

   $$\textit{classical logic} \vdash [\forall x(xRx) \wedge \forall xyz(xRy \wedge yRz \Rightarrow xRz)] \Rightarrow \forall t(\textstyle\bigwedge_i (A_i)^*_t \Rightarrow (A)^*_t).$$

   Although the two consequence relations $\models$ and $\Vdash$ are defined in a completely different way, they are the same from the mathematical point of view, i.e., $\Delta \Vdash A$ iff $\Delta \models A$ holds. However, their meaning is not the same.

   To define an algorithmic system for $\Vdash$ or $\models$ we can modify the system in example 12.9 below by adding to it the Restart Rule. We can also use any theorem prover for classical logic, and obtain yet another algorithmic system.

3. It is possible to give a Hilbert formulation for this consequence relation with the following axioms together with modus ponens (necessitation is derivable):

   (a) $\Box A$, where A is an instance of a truth functional tautology

   (b) $\Box(\Box(A \Rightarrow B) \Rightarrow (\Box A \Rightarrow \Box B))$

   (c) $\Box(\Box A \Rightarrow \Box\Box A)$

   (d) $\Box A \Rightarrow A$

   (e) $\Box(\Box A \Rightarrow A)$

We have $A_1, \ldots, A_n \vdash B$ iff $\bigwedge_i A_i \Rightarrow B$ is a theorem of the Hilbert system.

This example illustrates our point that even with the same S, $(\models, S)$ and $(\Vdash, S)$ as defined are *not the same logic*!

Let us revisit monotonicity's three levels of presentation. These were:

Mathematical definition of $\vdash$	$\Delta \vdash Q$
Algorithmic procedures (recursively enumerable)	$S_i^{\vdash}(\Delta, Q)$
Optimizing automated systems (polynomial time)	$OS_i^{\vdash}(\Delta, Q)$

Experience shows that if we take $S_i^{\vdash}$ and change the computation slightly, to S_i^*, we may get another logic. For example, $S(\Delta, Q)$ is an algorithmic system for intuitionistic logic. Change S a little bit to S^*, and $S^*(\Delta, Q)$ gives you classical logic. These types of connections are very widespread, to the extent that we get a much better understanding of a logic $\vdash$, not only through its own algorithmic systems, but also (and possibly even chiefly) through its being a 'changed' version of another automated system for another logic.

It may be difficult to appreciate fully what is being said now because we are proceeding abstractly, without examples. There is no choice but to talk abstractly *in the beginning*. (We will consider some examples later on.)

Another important point is the role of failure. Assume that we have an algorithmic system for some logic. The algorithmic system can be very precise; in fact, let us assume it is an automated system. Suppose we want to ask $\Delta?Q$. We can look at the rules of the automated system and see immediately that it is looping (a loop checker is needed; we can record the history of the computation and so can detect that we are repeating ourselves) or possibly finitely failing (i.e., we try all our computation options and in each case we end up in a situation where no more moves are allowed). We add new connectives to the logic, denoted by $loop(Q)$ and $fail(Q)$ and write formulas such as $loop(Q) \Rightarrow R$ or $fail(Q) \Rightarrow P$. This is similar to Prolog's negation by failure. In this way we get *new* non-monotonic logics out of old monotonic logics. Here we are connecting the monotonic hierarchy of logics with the non-monotonic one. The abduction mechanism can also be viewed in this way, as $fail(q) \Rightarrow q$. However, this kind of metalevel/object level mixing deserves a fuller treatment.

Our final point here concerns the general nature of theorem proving (or automated reasoning). We have already mentioned $S_i^{\vdash}(\Delta, Q)$. All our automated rules have the form, e.g., $S_i^{\vdash}(\Delta, Q \Rightarrow R)$ if $S_i^{\vdash}(\Delta \cup \{Q\}, R)$; in other words, the success of $\Delta \vdash Q \Rightarrow R$ reduces to that of $\Delta, Q \vdash R$ *in the same logic* $\vdash$. This suggests the need for taking the logic as a *parameter*, in view of the fact that we get things like $S(\Delta, Q, \text{logic } 1)$ if $S(\Delta', Q', \text{logic } 2)$.

We thus have an automated system defining several logics by mutual recursion.

12.3 Examples of Logical Systems

This section discusses a number of examples of logical systems. We begin with the definition of a Kripke model which we shall use to define several logics. Note that a consequence relation can be presented via several completely unrelated semantical interpretations. A single semantical interpretation can be slightly changed to give rise to different logics.

Definition 12.6

1. *A Kripke model (structure) for modal logic has the form* $\mathbf{m} = (T, R, a, h)$, *where* T *is a set of possible worlds,* $a \in T$ *is the actual world and* $R \subseteq T \times T$ *is the accessibility relation.* h *is an assignment giving for each atomic* q *a subset* $h(q) \subseteq T$.

   h *can be extended to all wffs as follows:*

   - $h(\neg A) = T - h(A)$
   - $h(A \wedge B) = h(A) \cap h(B)$
   - $h(\Box A) = \{t \mid \text{for all } s, \text{ if } tRs \text{ then } s \in h(A)\}$
   - *We say* $\mathbf{m} \models A$ *iff* $a \in h(A)$

   The following holds for the logic $\mathbf{K}$*:*

   - $\mathbf{K} \models A$ *iff for all* $\mathbf{m}, \mathbf{m} \models A$

2. *The modal logics* **T**, **B**, **K4**, **S4**, *and* **S5** *are defined by the class of all Kripke models where the accessibility relation R takes the following interesting properties:*

   T *Reflexivity*

   B *Symmetry and reflexivity*

   K4 *Transitivity*

   S4 *Reflexivity and transitivity*

   S5 *Reflexivity, transitivity and symmetry*

3. *Kripke models can be used to characterize intuitionistic logic as well* ($\vdash$ *of example 12.2) as follows:*

   Consider models of the form (T, R, a, h) *as above, with* R *reflexive and transitive and* h *satisfying the following persistence condition for all* q

   - $t \in h(q)$ *and* tRs *imply* $s \in h(q)$

   We now associate with each wff A *two subsets* $[A]^{\text{Beth}}$ *and* $[A]^{\text{Kripke}}$ *as follows:*

   - $[q]^{\text{Kripke}} = h(q)$
   - $[q]^{\text{Beth}} = \{x \in T|$ *every maximal chain* Π *through* x *intersects* $h(q)\}$, *where a maximal chain* π *through* x *is a maximal* R *linearly ordered subset of* T *containing* x. *In this case we say that* $h(q)$ bars x.
   - $[A \wedge B]^{\text{Beth}} = [A]^{\text{Beth}} \cap [B]^{\text{Beth}}$
   - $[A \wedge B]^{\text{Kripke}} = [A]^{\text{Kripke}} \cap [B]^{\text{Kripke}}$
   - $[A \Rightarrow B]^{\text{Beth}} = \{x \in T|$ *for all* y, tRy *and* $y \in [A]^{\text{Beth}}$ *imply* $y \in [B]^{\text{Beth}}\}$

     Similarly for $[A \Rightarrow B]^{\text{Kripke}}$

   - $[\neg A]^{\text{Beth}} = \{x|$ *for all* y, xRy *implies* $y \notin [A]^{\text{Beth}}\}$

     Similarly for $[\neg A]^{\text{Kripke}}$

   - $[A \vee B]^{\text{Kripke}} = [A]^{\text{Kripke}} \cup [B]^{\text{Kripke}}$
   - $[A \vee B]^{\text{Beth}} = \{x|$ *every maximal chain through* x *intersects* $[A]^{\text{Beth}} \cup [B]^{\text{Beth}}\}$

- *Define* $\mathbf{m} \models_{\text{Beth}} A$ *iff* $[A]^{\text{Beth}} = T$
  $\mathbf{m} \models_{\text{Kripke}} A$ *iff* $[A]^{\text{Kripke}} = T$

- *Define consequence relations* $\Vdash_{\text{Beth}}$ *and* $\Vdash_{\text{Kripke}}$ *by:*

  $A_1, \ldots, A_n \Vdash_{\text{Beth}} B_1, \ldots, B_k$ *iff for each model* $\mathbf{m}$ *there exists* B_j *such that* $\mathbf{m} \Vdash_{\text{Beth}} \bigwedge A_i \Rightarrow B_j$

  Similarly for $\Vdash_{\text{Kripke}}$.

Example 12.7 Consider a language with $\wedge$, $\Rightarrow$, $\neg$, $\vee$ and $\Box$. Define a Hilbert system for a modal logic **K** for modality $\Box$. **K**'s axioms and rules are as follows:

1. Any instance of a truth functional tautology
2. $\Box(A \Rightarrow B) \Rightarrow (\Box A \Rightarrow \Box B)$
3. The rules:

$$\frac{\vdash A, \vdash A \Rightarrow B}{\vdash B} \quad \text{and} \quad \frac{\vdash A}{\vdash \Box A}$$

Define $A_1, \ldots, A_n \vdash_{\mathbf{K}} A$ iff $\vdash \bigwedge A_i \Rightarrow A$. It is complete for all Kripke structures.

Consider the additional condition on Kripke structures that only the actual world is reflexive (i.e., we require aRa but not generally $\forall x(xRx)$). The class of all models with aRa defines a new logic. Call this logic **K1**. We cannot axiomatize this logic by adding the axiom $\Box A \Rightarrow A$ to **K** because this will give us the logic **T** (which is complete for the reflexivity of every possible world, not just the actual world). We observe, however, that $\vdash_{\mathbf{K}} A$ implies $\vdash_{\mathbf{K1}} \Box A$. If we adopt the above rule together with $\vdash_{\mathbf{K1}} \Box A \Rightarrow A$, we will indeed get, together with modus ponens, an axiomatization of **K1**.

The axiomatization of **K1** is obtained as follows:

Axioms:

1. Any substitution instance of a theorem of **K**.
2. $\Box A \Rightarrow A$.

Rules: Modus ponens (only).

We can define an extension of **K1** (call it $\mathbf{K1}_{[2]}$) by adding a $\Box^2$ necessitation rule

$$\frac{\vdash A}{\vdash \Box^2 A}$$

This yields the logic mentioned in section 2.4.4.

Example 12.8 (Classical logic with restart) The following is an algorithmic (possibly a phantom algorithm in a sense similar to the notion discussed conceptually in *The Reach of Abduction* [Gabbay and Woods, 2004a]) presentation of classical propositional logic. (See [Gabbay, 1998a] for more details and compare with section 14.2.) We choose a formulation of classical logic using $\wedge, \to, \bot$. We write the formulas in a 'ready for computation' form as the following clauses:

1. q is a clause, for q atomic, or $q = \bot$.
2. If $B_j = \bigwedge_i A_{ij} \to q_i$ are clauses for $j = 1, \ldots, k$ then so is $\bigwedge_j B_j \to q$, where q is atomic or $q = \bot$.
3. It can be shown that every formula of classical propositional logic is classically equivalent to a conjunction of clauses.

We now define a goal directed computation for clauses.

4. Let $S(\Delta, G, H)$ mean the clause G succeeds in the computation from the set of clauses Δ given the history H, where the history is a set of atoms or $\bot$.
   (a) $S(\Delta, q, H)$ if $q \in \Delta$ for q atomic or $\bot$.
   (b) $S(\Delta, q, H)$ if $\Delta \cap H \neq \varnothing$.
   (c) $S(\Delta, \bigwedge_j (\bigwedge_i A_{ij} \to q_j) \to q, H)$ if $S(\Delta \cup \{\bigwedge_i A_{ij} \to q_j\}, q, H)$.
   (d) $S(\Delta \cup \{\bigwedge_{j=1}^{k} (\bigwedge_{i=1}^{m_j} A_{ij} \to q_j) \to q)\}, q)$ if $\bigwedge_j S(\Delta \cup \{A_{ij} \mid i = 1, \ldots, m_j\}, q_j, H \cup \{q\})$.
5. The computation starts with $S(\Delta, G, \varnothing)$, to check whether $\Delta \vdash G$.

We have the following theorem:

$$S(\Delta, q, H) \text{ iff } \Delta \vdash q \vee \bigvee H.$$

The next example is a challenging example of a modal intuitionistic algorithmic system defined for the modality $\Diamond$, $\Rightarrow$, $\vee$, and $\bot$. To understand the intuition behind this example, imagine a family of possible worlds of the form (T, R, now), where T is the set of worlds, R the accessibility relation and now is the actual world. Syntactically we write $t : A$ to mean that A is assumed to hold at world t. A theory is a set $\Delta = \{t_i : A_i\}$ together with some relation R among the labels $\{t_i\}$ of Δ. So, for example (Δ, R), with $\Delta = \{t_1 : A_1, t_2 : A_2\}$ and $R = \{(t_1, t_2)\}$ is a theory which says that there are two worlds t_1 and t_2, t_2 accessible to t_1 and A_1 holds at t_1 and A_2 at t_2.

For a given world t the local reasoning is intuitionistic. Thus $S(\Delta, T, R, t, Q)$ reads that the theory (Δ, R) based on labels from T and accessibility R has the property that at the point t the wff Q can be proved.

In our example $S(\Delta, T, R, t_1, A_1)$ holds.

Example 12.9 (Challenge) *Intuitionistic Modal Logic:*

Consider a language with $\wedge$, $\Diamond$, $\Rightarrow$ and $\bot$, and atoms $\{p, q, \ldots\}$. Define the notion of a clause as follows:

1. $\bot$ is a clause and an atom.
2. If A_i are clauses then $(\bigwedge A_i \Rightarrow \text{atom})$ is a clause.
3. If A_i are clauses then $\Diamond \bigwedge A_i$ is a clause.

Define the following algorithmic system for this modal language: the basic predicate is $S(\Delta, T, R, t, Q)$ (which reads: 'the goal $t : Q$ succeeds from the labelled database (Δ, T, R))', where Δ is a set of labelled clauses of the form $s : A$, where A is a clause, s is a label. T is the set of labels. $R \subseteq T \times T$, $t \in T$, is a binary relation on the labels. Q is the current goal to prove. Note: These are virtual rules and reflect something of the same notion discussed conceptually in section 3.2.5 above.

Rule 1 The computation starts with $S(\Delta, T, R, t, Q)$. Q is said to be the *original goal* for the label t. t and T are said to have been *introduced* at the beginning.

Rule 2 $S(\Delta, T, R, t, Q)$ if Q is atomic and for some $t : A \Rightarrow Q$ or $t : A \Rightarrow \bot$ in Δ we have $S(\Delta, T, R, t, A)$.

Rule 3 $S(\Delta, T, R, t, Q)$ if Q is atomic and $t : Q \in \Delta$ or if $s : \bot \in \Delta$, for any s.

Rule 4 $S(\Delta, T, R, t, Q \wedge Q')$ if $S(\Delta, T, R, t, Q)$ and $S(\Delta, T, R, t, Q')$.

Rule 5 $S(\Delta, T, R, t, Q \Rightarrow Q')$ if $S(\Delta \cup \{t : Q\}, T, R, t, Q')$.

Rule 6 $S(\Delta, T, R, t, \Diamond Q)$ if for some $s \in T$ such that tRs, $S(\Delta, T, R, s, Q)$.

Rule 7 $S(\Delta, T, R, t, \Diamond Q)$ if for some $(t : \Diamond \bigwedge A_i) \in \Delta$ and some *new* label r, $S(\Delta \cup \{r : A_i\}, T \cup \{r\}, R \cup \{(t, r)\}, r, Q)$. r is said to have been introduced at this stage of the computation and Q is said to be the *original goal* for r.

Rule 8 $S(\Delta, T, R, t, Q)$ if for some $(s : B \Rightarrow \bot) \in \Delta$ we have $S(\Delta, T, R, s, B)$.

Rule 9 $S(\Delta, T, R, t, \bot)$ if $S(\Delta, T, R, t, \Diamond \bot)$.

(a) Show that the relation $\vdash$ defined by

$$\{A_i\} \vdash B \text{ iff } S(\{t : A_i\}, \{t\}, \emptyset, t, B) \text{ succeeds}$$

is a consequence relation.

(b) (Challenge) Write a Prolog interpreter for the above algorithmic system.

(c) We can add the Restart Rule:

Rule 10 $S(\Delta, T, R, t, Q)$ if $S(\Delta, T, R, t, Q')$, where the goal Q' is the original query associated with the label t when the label t was first introduced. See Rules 1 and 7 for this notion.

With the restart rule we get (we think) the modal logic **K**.

Exercise 12.10 Prove that the above computation with the Restart Rule is sound and complete for **K**.

Example 12.11 Show

$$\begin{array}{ll} (1) & \Box a \\ (2) & \Box(a \Rightarrow b) \\ \hline (3) & \Box b \end{array}$$

in the modal logic **K**.

We use the computation of example 12.9. We have to translate $\Box a$ as $\Diamond(a \Rightarrow \bot) \Rightarrow \bot$.

Translate:

$$\begin{array}{ll} (1) now: & \Diamond(a \Rightarrow \bot) \Rightarrow \bot \\ (2) now: & \Diamond((a \Rightarrow b) \Rightarrow \bot) \Rightarrow \bot \\ \hline (3) now: & \Diamond(b \Rightarrow \bot) \Rightarrow \bot \end{array}$$

now is the label for the actual world.

Our computation starts with $S(\{(1),(2)\},\{now\},\emptyset,now,(3))$

Computation:

Ask for ? (3) at *now* and get the new database and query as indicated below:

Database		*Query*
(1)	as above	? *now*: $\bot$
(2)	as above	
(4)	*now*: $\Diamond(b \Rightarrow \bot)$	

From Rule 9 we ask $?\Diamond\bot$

From (4) we ask $?t : \bot$, where t is a new label, with the relation $nowRt$, and where we add to the database clause 5, with label t:

(5) $t : b \Rightarrow \bot$

Continue from (5) and ask

$$?t : b$$

We cannot go on, so we try to get a contradiction from (2)

$$?now : \Diamond((a \Rightarrow b) \Rightarrow \bot)$$

Continue

$$?t : (a \Rightarrow b) \Rightarrow \bot$$

Add to data

(6) $t : a \Rightarrow b$

and ask

$$?t : \bot$$

Using (5) and (6) get

$$?t : a$$

Try to get a contradiction from (1).

$$?now : \Diamond(a \Rightarrow \bot)$$

Continue

$$?t : a \Rightarrow \bot$$

Add (7) to the data

(7) $t : a$

and ask

$$?t : \bot$$

From (5) ask $?t : b$.
From (6) ask $?t : a$.
From (7) we succeed.

Exercise 12.12 Consider the language with $\Rightarrow$ and $\neg$ and the many valued truth tables below. Define:

$A_1, \ldots, A_n \vdash B$ iff $A_1 \Rightarrow (A_2 \Rightarrow \ldots (A_n \Rightarrow B) \ldots)$ gets always value 1 under all assignments

What consequence relation do we get? What logic is it?

TABLE 1

$\Rightarrow$	1	1/2	0
1	1	1/2	0
1/2	1	1	1/2
0	1	1	1

	$\neg$
1	0
1/2	1/2
0	1

TABLE 2

$\Rightarrow$	1	2	3	4
1	1	2	3	4
2	1	1	3	3
3	1	2	1	2
4	1	1	1	1

	$\neg$
1	4
2	3
3	2
4	1

Exercise 12.13 Define a Horn clause with negation by failure as any wff of the form $\bigwedge a_i \wedge \bigwedge \neg b_j \Rightarrow q$, where a_i, b_j, q are atomic; q is called the head of the clause. Define a computation as follows:

1. $\Delta ?q = success$ if $q \in \Delta$.

2. $\Delta ?q = failure$ if q is not head of any clause in Δ.

3. $\Delta ?q = success$ if for some $\bigwedge a_i \wedge \bigwedge \neg b_j \Rightarrow q$ in Δ we have that $\Delta ?a_i = success$ for all i and $\Delta ?\neg b_j = success$ for all j.

4. $\Delta ? \neg b = success$ (respectively failure) if $\Delta ? b = failure$ (respectively success).

5. $\Delta ? q = failure$ if for each clause $\bigwedge a_i \wedge \bigwedge \neg b_j \Rightarrow q \in \Delta$ we have either for *some* i, $\Delta ? a_i = failure$ or for some j, $\Delta ? \neg b_j = failure$.

(a) Show that propositional Horn clause Prolog with negation by failure is a non-monotonic system, i.e., if we define $\Delta \mid\!\sim Q$ iff (definition) Q succeeds in Prolog from data Δ, then $\mid\!\sim$ is a non-monotonic consequence relation according to our definition. (To show (3) and (2*) assume X is positive.)

(b) *(Challenge)* Prove in Prolog $\mid\!\sim$ that:

$$\text{if } \Delta \mid\!\sim q \text{ and } \Delta, d \mid\!\sim \neg q \text{ then } \Delta \mid\!\sim \neg d \text{ (for } d \text{ atomic).}$$

Similarly,

$$\text{if } \Delta \mid\!\sim \neg q \text{ and } \Delta, d \mid\!\sim q \text{ then } \Delta \mid\!\sim \neg d.$$

Example 12.14 Recall the definition of $\Phi \vdash_I A$ as the smallest Tarski relation on the language with $\Rightarrow$ such that the equation DT holds.

DT: $\Phi \vdash A \Rightarrow B$ iff $\Phi, A \vdash B$.

According to Exercise 12.3 from this chapter, $\vdash_I$ exists.

Our algorithmic problem is how do we show for a given $\Phi \vdash_I ?A$ whether is holds or not.

Take the following (Hudelmaier):

$$(((b \Rightarrow a) \Rightarrow b) \Rightarrow b) \Rightarrow a \vdash_I ?a$$

We can only use the means at our disposal, in this case DT. Certainly, for cases of the form $\Phi \vdash_I A \Rightarrow B$ we can reduce to $\Phi, A \vdash_I B$. This is a sound policy, because we simplify the query and monotonically strengthen the data at the same time.

When the query is atomic we cannot go on. So we must look for patterns.

Out of a, b we can make the following possible formulas with at most one $\Rightarrow$:

$a \Rightarrow b$
a
b
$b \Rightarrow a$
$a \Rightarrow a$
$b \Rightarrow b$

The following are possible consequences:

$a, b \vdash ?a \Rightarrow b$
$a, a \Rightarrow b \vdash ?b$
$a \Rightarrow b \vdash ?a \Rightarrow b$
$a \Rightarrow a \vdash ?b \Rightarrow b$

Shuffling around and recognizing cases of reflexivity we can get:

1. $a, a \Rightarrow b \vdash b$ (from reflexivity and DT)

2. $\vdash a \Rightarrow a$

3. $b \vdash a \Rightarrow b$

Back to our example:

$(((b \Rightarrow a) \Rightarrow b) \Rightarrow b) \Rightarrow a$	$\vdash_I ?a$
same	$\vdash_I ?((b \Rightarrow a) \Rightarrow b) \Rightarrow b$
add $(b \Rightarrow a) \Rightarrow b$	$\vdash_I ?b$
same	$\vdash_I ?b \Rightarrow a$
add b	$\vdash_I ?a$
same	$\vdash_I ?((b \Rightarrow a) \Rightarrow b) \Rightarrow b$
same	$\vdash_I ?b$ (*success*: you already have b)

12.4 Refining the Notion of a Logical System

In what we have covered so far, the wholly general notion of a logical system makes a much more plausible claim on capturing essential features of a *PLCS* than is the case with standard logics *as customarily presented.* All the same, bearing in mind the kind of applications studied in this book, we see that we need an even more refined notion of a logical system, to enable us to cope with the needs of the applications. This section surveys some options.

12.4.1 Structured Consequence

The next move in the notion of a logical system is to observe that part of the logic must also be the notion of what the logic accepts as a theory. Theories have structure; they are not just sets of wffs. They are structures of wffs. Different notions of structures give rise to different logics, even though the logics may share the same notion of consequence for individual wffs.

In ways that tie up with the fact that the agendas of *AR* often have significant internal structure, we need a

1. Notion of structure to tell us what is to be considered a theory for our logic. For example, a theory may be a multiset of wffs or a list of wffs or a more general structure. The best way to define the general notion of a structure is to consider models M of some classical structure theory τ and a function $\mathbf{f} : M \mapsto$ wffs of the logic. A theory Δ is a pair $(M, \mathbf{f})$. We write $t : A$ to mean $\mathbf{f}(t) = A$.

2. In the spirit of belief revision and belief update required by a *PLCS* and developed conceptually in *AR* itself, we require a notion of insertion into the structure and deletion from the structure. i.e., if $t \in M$ and $s \notin M$ we need to define $M' = M + \{s\}$ and $M'' = M - \{t\}$. M' and M'' must be models of τ. When theories were sets of wffs, insertion and deletion presented no problems. For general structures we need to specify how it is done.

3. Bearing in mind the role of analogy in a *PLCS*, discussed conceptually in Part I, we also must have a notion of substitution of one structure M_1 into another M_2 at a point $t \in M_2$. This is also needed for the notion of cut. If $(M_2, \mathbf{f}_2) \mid\!\sim A$ and for some $t \in M_2, (M_1, \mathbf{f}_1) \mid\!\sim \mathbf{f}_2(t)$, we want to 'substitute' '$(M_1, \mathbf{f}_1)$' for 't' in M_2 to get $(M_3, \mathbf{f}_3)$ such that $(M_3, \mathbf{f}_3) \mid\!\sim A$.

Example 12.15 Let the structure be lists. So let, for example, $\Delta = (A_1, \ldots, A_n)$. We can define $\Delta + A = (A_1, \ldots, A_n, A)$ and $\Delta - \{A_i\} = (A_1, \ldots A_{i-1}, A_{i+1}, \ldots, A_n)$. Substitution of $\Gamma = (B_1, \ldots, B_k)$ for place i in Δ (replacing A_i) gives $\Delta[i/\Gamma] = (A_1, \ldots, A_{i-1}, B_1, \ldots, B_k, A_{i+1}, \ldots, A_n)$.

The cut rule would mean

- $\Delta \mid\!\sim C$ and $\Gamma \mid\!\sim A_i$ imply $\Delta[i/\Gamma] \mid\!\sim C$.

We need now to stipulate the minimal properties of a structured consequence relation. These are the following:

Identity $\{t : A\} \mid\!\sim t : A$

Surgical Cut $$\frac{\Delta \mid\!\sim t : A; \Gamma[t : A] \mid\!\sim s : B}{\Gamma[t/\Delta] \mid\!\sim r : B}$$

Typical good examples of structured consequence relations are algebraic labelled deductive systems based on implication $\rightarrow$.

The basic rule is modus ponens.

- $$\frac{s : A \rightarrow B; t : A; \varphi(s, t)}{f(s, t) : B}$$

- $s : A \to B$
- $t : A$ $\quad\quad\quad\quad \mid\!\sim f(s,t) : B$

$\varphi(s,t)$

Figure 12.5

t, s are labels, φ is a compatibility relation on labels and $f(s,t)$ is the new label.

What the rule means for databases is given in figure 12.5.

The labels can be resource, time, relevance, strength/reliability, complete file. See [Gabbay, 1996]. Thus there are precise connections now emerging between *LDS* and certain features of *PLCS* (e.g., resource-sensitivity) and *AR* (e.g., relevance).

12.4.2 Algorithmic Structured Consequence Relation

Just as in the case of ordinary consequence relations, different algorithms on the structure are considered as different logics. The general presentation form of most (maybe all) algorithms is through a family of rules of the form

- $\Delta \mid\!\sim ?\Gamma, \Pi$ reduces to $\Delta_i \mid\!\sim ?\Gamma_i, \Pi_i, i = 1, \ldots, n$;

if we use a traditional method of display we will write:

- $\dfrac{\Delta_1 \mid\!\sim \Gamma_1, \Pi_1; \ldots; \Delta_n \mid\!\sim \Gamma_n, \Pi_n}{\Delta \mid\!\sim \Gamma, \Pi}$.

We need the notion of a formula $t : A$ in the structure Π *being used* in the rule. We further need to have some complexity measure available which decreases with the use of each rule. $\Delta, \Gamma, \Delta_i, \Gamma_i$ are structured theories and Π, Π_i are parameters involved in the algorithm, usually the history of the computation up to the point of application of the rule. There may be side conditions associated with each rule restricting its applicability.

Some rules have the form

- $\Delta \mid\!\sim ?\Gamma, \Pi$ reduces to *success*

or in a traditional display

- $\overline{\Delta \mid\!\sim \Gamma, \Pi}$.

These are axioms.

Having the rules in this manner requires additional (decidable) metapredicates on databases and parameters. We need the following:

1. $\Psi_0(\Delta, \Gamma, \Pi)$ recognizing that $\Delta \mid\!\sim \Gamma, \Pi$ is an axiom.

2. $\Psi_1(\Delta, \Gamma, \Pi)$ recognizing that $\Delta \mid\!\sim \Gamma, \Pi$ is a failure (no reduction rules apply).

3. $\Psi_2(\Delta, \Delta_1, \Delta_2, \Pi, \Pi_1, \Pi_2)$ says that Δ is the result of inserting Δ_2 into Δ_1 (also written as $\Delta = \Delta_1 + \Delta_2$, ignoring the parameters).

4. $\Psi_4^n(\Delta, \Delta_1, \ldots, \Delta_n, \Pi, \Pi_1, \ldots, \Pi_n)$ says that Δ is decomposed into $\Delta_1, \ldots, \Delta_n$. The decomposition is not necessarily disjoint. So for example, the reduction rule $\Delta \mid\!\sim ?\Gamma$ if $\Delta_i \mid\!\sim ?\Gamma_i, i = 1, \ldots, n$ may require that $\Psi_4^n(\Delta, \Delta_1, \ldots, \Delta_n)$ and $\Psi_4^n(\Gamma, \Gamma_1, \ldots, \Gamma_n)$ both hold (ignoring the parameters).

There may be more Ψs involved.

The Ψs may be related. For example $\Psi_4^n(\Delta, \Delta_1, \ldots, \Delta_n)$ may be $\Delta = (\Delta_1 + (\Delta_2 + (\ldots + \Delta_n) \ldots)$.

The reader should note that with structured databases, other traditional notions associated with a logic change their relative importance, role and emphasis. Let us consider the major ones.

Inconsistency

As we have seen, AR is highly tolerant of inconsistency, which on the Putter-of-Things-Right model discussed in section 6.4 is a standard precondition of belief-revision. Traditional logics reject inconsistent theories. They do not permit having both A and $\neg A$ among the data. In structured databases, there is no such problem with that. If, for example, a system must be inconsistent before it can be put through belief-revision procedures, inconsistency must be as acceptable in that system as its role in triggering revision. Thus the more fundamental question is not whether a system is inconsistent. The prior question is whether it is (in some way or other) an *acceptable* inconsistency. Thus the structural database approach answers in a direct way to our argument that a $PLCS$ be paraconsistent.

We can have $\Delta = \{t : A, s : \neg A\}$, and what we prove from Δ depends on the logic. Even when we can prove everything from a database, we can use labels to control the proofs and make distinctions on how the inconsistency arises. A new approach to inconsistency is needed for structured databases. Some databases are not acceptable. They may be consistent or inconsistent.

We have, for example, the notion of integrity constraints in logic and commercial databases. We may have as an integrity constraint for a practical database that it must list with each customer's name also his telephone number. A database that lists a name without a telephone number may be consistent but is unacceptable. It does not satisfy integrity constraints. See [Gabbay and Hunter, 1991] and [Woods, 2002b] for more discussion.

Deduction theorem

If a theory Δ is a set of sentences we may have for some A, B that $\Delta \not\mid\!\sim B$ but $\Delta \cup \{A\} \mid\!\sim B$. In which case we can add a connective $\twoheadrightarrow$ satisfying $\Delta \mid\!\sim A \twoheadrightarrow B$ iff $\Delta \cup \{A\} \mid\!\sim B$.

If Δ is a structured database, we have an insertion function $\Delta + A$, adding A into Δ and a deletion function, $\Delta - A$, taking A out of Δ. We can stipulate that $(\Delta + A) - A = \Delta$.

The notion of deduction theorem is relative to the functions $+$ and $-$. Let $\twoheadrightarrow_{(+,-)}$ be the corresponding implication. Then we can write $\Delta + A \mid\!\sim B$ iff $(\Delta + A) - A \mid\!\sim A \twoheadrightarrow_{(+,-)} B$.

We can have many $\twoheadrightarrow$s and many deduction theorems for many options of $(+, -)$ pairs.

Take, for example, the Lambek calculus, in which databases are lists, $(A_1, \ldots, A_n)$ of wffs. We can have two sets of $+$ and $-$, namely we can have $+_r, -_r$ (add and delete from the right hand side) and $+_l, -_l$ (add and delete from the left). This gives us two arrows and two deduction theorems

$$(A_1, \ldots, A_n) \mid\!\sim A \rightarrow_r B \text{ iff } (A_1, \ldots, A_n, A) \mid\!\sim B$$

and

$$(A_1, \ldots, A_n) \mid\!\sim A \rightarrow_l B \text{ iff } (A, A_1, \ldots, A_n) \mid\!\sim B$$

The Lambek calculus is the smallest bi-implicational logic with $\rightarrow_r, \rightarrow_l$ only and databases which are lists which satisfy the two deduction theorems.

12.4.3 Mechanisms

Our notion of logical systems so far is of pairs $(\mid\!\sim, S^{\mid\sim})$, where $\mid\!\sim$ is a structured consequence relation between structured databases and $S^{\mid\sim}$ is an algorithm for computing $\mid\!\sim$. The data items in any database $\Delta = (M, \mathbf{f})$ are wffs, i.e., for $t \in M, \mathbf{f}(t)$ is a wff. We know from many applications that items residing in the database need not be the data itself but can be

Δ

official
data
with structure

algorithm

Goal

more data

Figure 12.6 Mechanisms extend data

mechanisms indicating how to obtain the data. Such mechanisms can be subalgorithms which can be triggered by the main $S^{\vdash\!\sim}$ algorithm or in the most simple case just a link to another database.

We regard such mechanisms as part of the logic. They are ways of extending our databases Δ with more data without having to put them explicitly into the structure of Δ.

Among the well-known mechanisms are

- abduction
- default
- other non-monotonic mechanisms (circumscription, negation as failure, etc.).

Figure 12.6 shows what a database looks like. Formally a database $\Delta = (M, \mathbf{f})$ can be such that for $t \in M, \mathbf{f}(t)$ is a mechanism. Of course these mechanisms depend on $S^{\vdash\!\sim}$.

These mechanisms are well studied in the literature but the traditional way of perceiving them is that they depend on $\vdash\!\sim$ and not necessarily on the proof method ($S^{\vdash\!\sim}$). Our view is that

1. they are part of Δ;

and that

2. they depend on $S^{\vdash\!\sim}$.

Thus a database may be a list of the following form.

$$\Delta = (A_1, A_2, \text{ use abduction algorithm } \mathbf{Ab}_1, A_4, \\ \text{use default algorithm } \mathbf{D}_1, A_6)$$

3. In fact each item of data in Δ may come with a little *algorithmic patch*, giving the main algorithm $S^{\vdash\!\sim}$ extra or less freedom in using this item of data. A well-known example of such a 'patch' is the exclamation mark in linear logic. $!A$ means 'you can use A as many times as you need'. The patch can interact with the *mode* (see subsection 12.4.4 below) and change it to a new mode.

The algorithm $S^{\vdash\!\sim}$ may approach the third item in the list with a view to trying to succeed. Instead of a data item it finds an algorithm $\mathbf{Ab}_1$. It exchanges information with $\mathbf{Ab}_1$ and triggers it. What $\mathbf{Ab}_1$ does now depends on the state of the $S^{\vdash\!\sim}$ algorithm when it 'hits' $\mathbf{Ab}_1$. $\mathbf{Ab}_1$ returns with some additional data, say $(B_1, \ldots, B_k)$. The $S^{\vdash\!\sim}$ algorithm can now continue *as if* the database were $(A_1, A_2, (B_1, \ldots, B_k), A_4, \mathbf{D}_1, A_6)$. There are two ways of looking at mechanisms. One way is that they are some sort of algorithmic shorthand for additional data, like links to other places where data can be found. Thus according to this view $\Delta +$ *mechanism* $= \Delta + \Delta'$, where $\Delta' =$ data obtained by *mechanism* applied to Δ. This is a traditional view, since a theory Δ is still a (structured) set of data. The second view, which is the one we want to adopt, is that procedures are themselves data. This view is better because:

1. The mechanisms may yield different results depending on when in the computation they are used ('hit'), which makes it difficult to specify the declarative content of the theory.

2. Since we attach the proof theory as part of the logic, we can go all the way and accept additional mechanisms and patches to the proof theory as part of the data. Thus different databases may include additional rules to be used to prove more (or prove less) from themselves. In fact each item of data (declarative unit) can carry as part of its label a patch on the computation $S^{\vdash\!\sim}$.

This idea is somewhat revolutionary. It gives up the current received view that theories (data) must have a declarative content.

12.4.4 Modes of Evaluation

When we present logics semantically, through say Kripke models, there are several features involved in the semantics. We can talk about Kripke frames of the form (S, R, a), where S is a set of possible worlds, $R \subseteq S^{n+1}$ is the accessibility relation (for an n-place connective $\sharp(q_1, \ldots, q_n)$) and $a \in S$ is the actual world. We allow arbitrary assignments $h(q) \subseteq S$ to atomic variables q and the semantical evaluation for the non-classical connective $\sharp$ is done through some formula $\Psi_\sharp(t, R, Q_1, \ldots, Q_n), Q_i \subseteq S$ in some language. We have:

- $t \vDash \sharp(q_1, \ldots, q_n)$ under assignment h iff $\Psi_\sharp(t, R, h(q_1), \ldots, h(q_n))$ holds in (S, R, a).

For example, for a modality $\Box$ we have

- $t \vDash \Box q$ iff $\forall s(tRs \rightarrow s \vDash q)$.

Here $\Psi_\Box(t, h(q)) = \forall s(tRs \rightarrow s \in h(q))$. Different logics are characterized by different properties of R.[5]

We can think of $\Psi_\sharp$ as the *mode of evaluation* of $\sharp$. The mode is fixed throughout the evaluation process.

In the new concept of logic, mode shifting during evaluation is common and allows for the definition of many new logics. We can view the mode as the recipe for where to look for the accessible points s needed to evaluate $\Box A$.

Consider the following:

- $t \vDash \Box A$ iff $\forall n \forall s(tR^n s \rightarrow s \vDash A)$
  where $xR^n y$ is defined by the clauses:
  - $xR^0 y$ iff $x = y$
  - $xR^{n+1} y$ iff $\exists z(xRz \wedge zR^n y)$.

Clearly $\{(t, s) \mid \exists n tR^n s\}$ is the transitive and reflexive closure of R.

Thus in this evaluation mode, we look for points in the reflexive and transitive closure of R.

We can have several evaluation modes available over the same frame (S, R, a).

Let $\rho_i(x, y, R), i = 1, \ldots, k$, be a family of binary formulas over (S, R, a), defined in some possibly higher-order mode language $\mathcal{M}$, using R, a and h as parameters.

We can have a mode shifting function $\varepsilon : \{1, \ldots, k\} \mapsto \{1, \ldots, k\}$ and let

- $t \vDash_i \Box A$ iff for all s such that $\rho_i(t, s, R)$ holds we have $s \vDash_{\varepsilon(i)} A$.

Example 12.16 Consider now the following definition for $\vDash$ for two modes ρ_0 and ρ_1 and $x = 0$ or 1:

[5] Some logics presented axiomatically cannot be characterized by properties of R alone, but require the family of assignments h to be restricted. This is a minor detail as far as the question of 'what is a logic' is concerned.

- $t \vDash_x q$ for q atomic iff $t \in h(q)$
- $t \vDash_x \neg A$ iff $t \nvDash_x A$
- $t \vDash_x A \wedge B$ iff $t \vDash_x A$ and $t \vDash_x B$
- $t \vDash_x \Box A$ iff for all s such that $\rho_x(t, s)$ holds we have $s \vDash_{1-x} A$.

We now see that, as we evaluate, we have a change of modes, so we are not defining $\vDash_0$ independently on its own, but together with $\vDash_1$ in an interactive way.

We repeat here example 1.5 of [Gabbay, 1998b].

Example 12.17 We consider two modes for a modality $\Box$.

$$\begin{array}{rcl} \rho_1(x,y) & = & xRy \vee x = y \\ \rho_1(x,y) & = & xRy. \end{array}$$

Define a logic $\mathbf{K1}_{[2]}$ as the family of all wffs A such that for all models (S, R, a) and all assignments h we have $a \vDash_0 A$.

In such a logic we have the following tautologies.

$$\begin{array}{l} \vDash \Box A \to A \\ \nvDash \Box(\Box A \to A) \\ \vDash \Box^{2n}(\Box A \to A) \end{array}$$

It is easy to see that this logic cannot be characterized by any class of frames. For let (S, R, a) be a frame in which all tautologies hold and $\Diamond(\neg q \wedge \Box q)$ holds. Then aRa must hold since $\Box A \to A$ is a tautology for all A. Also there must be a point t, such that aRt and $t \vDash \neg q \wedge \Box q$. But now we have $aRaRt$ and this falsifies $\Box^2(\Box A \to A)$ which is also a tautology.

This logic, $\mathbf{K1}_{[2]}$, can be axiomatized. See example 12.7.

The idea of a mode of evaluation is not just semantical. If we have proof rules for $\Box$, then there would be a group of rules for logic $\mathbf{L}_1$ (say modal $\mathbf{K}$) and a group for $\mathbf{L}_2$ (say modal $\mathbf{T}$). We can shift modes by alternating which group is available after each use of a $\Box$ rule.

This way we can jointly define a family of consequence relations $\mid\!\sim_\mu$ dependent on a family of modes $\{\mu\}$.

We believe mode evaluation and mode shifting is an important concept in proof theory and semantics.

The notion of mode can be attached to data items. Since mode means which proof rules are available, data items can carry mode with them and when they are used they change the mode. This is fully compatible with our approach that procedures are part of the data.

For more details about mode, see [Gabbay, 2002].

12.4.5 TAR-Logics (Time, Action and Revision)

We are now ready to introduce TAR-logics. First let us summarize what we have got so far, all of which are grist for the mills of a *PLCS* into which we want to embed *AR*.

Logical Systems

- structured data;
- algorithmic proof theory on the structure;
- mechanisms that make use of data and algorithms to extend data;
- the idea that inconsistency is no longer a central notion. There are contexts in which it is respectable and welcome.
- a deduction theorem that is connected with cut, and the notions of insertion and deletion.

Notice the following two points about the current notion of a logical system:

- time and actions are not involved;
- proofs and answers are conceptually instantaneous.

Our new notion of logic and consequence shall make the following points:

- proofs, like ordinary reasoning generally, take time (real time!);
- proofs , like ordinary reasoning generally, involve actions and revisions;
- logics need to be presented as part of a mutually dependent family of logics of various modes.

We explain the above points.

In classical geometry, we have axioms and rules. To prove a geometrical theorem may take 10 days and 20 pages, but the time involved is not part of the geometry. We can say conceptually that all theorems follow instantaneously from the axioms.

Let us refer to this situation as a *timeless* situation.

Our notion of a logic developed so far is timeless in this sense. We have a structured database Δ, we have a consequence relation $\mid\!\sim$, we have an algorithm $\mathcal{S}^{\mid\sim}$, we have various mechanisms involved and they all end up giving us answers to the timeless question: does $\Delta\mid\!\sim ?\Gamma$ hold?

In practice, in many applications where logic is used, time and actions are heavily involved. The deduction $\Delta\mid\!\sim ?\Gamma$ is not the central notion in the application, it is only auxiliary and marginal. The time, action, payoffs, planning and strategic considerations are the main notions and the timeless consequence relation is only a servant, a tool that plays a minor part in the overall picture. In such applications we have several databases and queries $\Delta_i \mid\!\sim ?\Gamma_i$ arising in different contexts. The databases involved are ambiguous, multiversional and constantly changing. The users are in constant disagreement about their contents. The logical deductive rules are non-monotonic, common sense and have nuances that anticipate change and the reasoning itself heavily involves possible, alternative and hypothetical courses of action in a very real way. The question of whether $\Delta_i \mid\!\sim ?\Gamma_i$ hold plays only a minor part, probably just as a question enabling or justifying a sequence of actions.

It is therefore clear that to make our logics more practical and realistic for such applications, we have no alternative but to bring in these features as serious components in our notion of what is a logic.

Further, to reason and act adequately we need to use a family of different logics at different times, $\Delta_i \mid\!\sim_i ?\Gamma_i$, and where their presentation and proof theory are interdependent. We anticipate a heavy use of modes in its deduction.

Let $\{\mathbf{a}_1, \ldots, \mathbf{a}_n\}$ be a family of actions of the form $\mathbf{a}_i = (\alpha_i, \beta_i)$, where α_i is the precondition and β_i is the postcondition. Let $*$ be a revision operation such that for a given Δ and α $\Delta * \alpha$ is the result of inputting α into Δ and then revising the new theory into an *acceptable* new theory $\Delta * \alpha$.

We define by induction on n the notion $\Delta \mid\!\sim_{(\mathbf{a}_1, \ldots, \mathbf{a}_n)}$ as follows:

- $\Delta \mid\!\sim_{\varnothing} A$ iff $\Delta \mid\!\sim A$.
- $\Delta \mid\!\sim_{(\mathbf{a}_1, \ldots, \mathbf{a}_{n+1})} A$ iff $\Delta \mid\!\sim_{\varnothing} \alpha_1$ and $\Delta * \beta_1 \mid\!\sim_{(\mathbf{a}_2, \ldots, \mathbf{a}_{n+1})} A$.

In $\mid\!\sim_{(\mathbf{a}_1, \ldots, \mathbf{a}_n)}$ the sequence $(\mathbf{a}_1, \ldots, \mathbf{a}_n)$ acts as a *mode of provability*. See Gabbay [2001].

Note that an agent with scarce resources can be modelled by limiting the following parameters in $\mid\!\sim(\mathbf{a}_1, \ldots, \mathbf{a}_n)$.

1. Allow the actions $\mathbf{a}_i$ to be used a limited number of times, i.e., to have a 'cost'.

2. To use an action or to process an input, an agnt needs to prove preconditoins or check consistency and revise. This can also have cost or be limited in processing time.

   Thus if 'relevance' means 'effect on agendas' and the latter requires resources and processing ability then relevance is influenced by agents assets.

Chapter 13

Labelled Deductive Systems

Post tot logicas nondum Logica qualem desidero scripta est.

Leibniz, *Philosophische Schriften*

13.1 Introduction

This chapter introduces possible base logics for agenda relevance. The purpose of this introductory section is to explain all the components which play a part in the logic. A suitably general framework for our base logics is the methodology of Labelled Deductive Systems (LDS). Some readers will find this chapter 'old hat'; others may find it a trifle heavy-going. The former can skip to the next chapter. The latter are asked to be patient. The machinery described here really does help deliver the goods (in chapters 14 and 15) for the formal analysis of agenda relevance.

In its most basic conceptual sense, the labels methodology helps direct traffic right in the logic itself. In terms of everyday human reasoning it gives the reader guidance on when to use or re-use assumptions and when it is sensible (not just truth-preserving) to apply a rule. Provided labels are properly integrated into the structure of derivation systems having them are both more psychologically real and economical. They have the effect of elevating what in traditional language are called *heuristics* to the structure of logical rules. Thus, just as with a *PLCS*, an *LDS* approach puts some pressure on the traditional dichotomy between heuristics and rule (or theory).

Our starting point is a simple natural deduction system for implication $\Rightarrow$. We shall use this system to make some important distinctions in the proof theory.[1]

$\Rightarrow$ has two rules, $\Rightarrow E$, the $\Rightarrow$-elimination rule and $\Rightarrow I$, $\Rightarrow$-introduction rule. In textbooks they are usually presented as follows:

$$\Rightarrow E \qquad \frac{A; A \Rightarrow B}{B}$$

$$\Rightarrow I \qquad \frac{\begin{array}{c} A \\ \vdots \\ B \end{array}}{A \Rightarrow B}$$

This presentation does not tell us how to use these rules. Let us turn to an example.

Example 13.1 Show $A \Rightarrow (A \Rightarrow B) \vdash A \Rightarrow B$.

Solution 1

1. $A \Rightarrow (A \Rightarrow B)$, assumption
2. Assume A
3. From (1) and (2) get $A \Rightarrow B$ by $\Rightarrow E$
4. From (3) and (2) get B, by $\Rightarrow E$
5. Discharge A and we have proved $A \Rightarrow B$.

We need to write the above proof more precisely. We imagine we are progressing in the proof line by line. We read $\Rightarrow E$ as a rule applying to two previous lines with A and $A \Rightarrow B$ and yielding B. We read $\Rightarrow I$ as a *subcomputation*, starting with a new line #1 assuming A, and ending in a line deriving B. We thus write our proof as follows:

[1]We use the notation $\Rightarrow$ for the implication because it is a general $\Rightarrow$ for LDS formulation and not any particular $\rightarrow$ for our model of agenda relevance. When we talk about particular systems the notation will be more specific e.g., $\rightarrow$ or $\supset$, etc.

Solution 2

1. $A \Rightarrow (A \Rightarrow B)$, assumption
2. $A \Rightarrow B$, follows from the following subcomputation:
   2.1. A, assumption
   2.2. $A \Rightarrow B$, from lines 2 and 2.1, using $\Rightarrow E$
   2.3. B, from lines 2.2 and 2.1, using $\Rightarrow E$.

Solution 2 in Example 1 is not formal enough for our purposes. Many logics such as linear logic, relevance logic, etc., want to make distinctions in the proof steps allowed in the subcomputation, such as whether the assumption (i.e., the A in the $A \Rightarrow B$) is being 'used' and how many times. So we need to be stricter in our notation.

Example 13.2 (Example 13.1 continued) We can now write solution 2 of example 13.1 more strictly:

Solution 3

1. $A \Rightarrow (A \Rightarrow B)$ assumption.
2. $A \Rightarrow B$ from the following box (subcomputation)[2]

	$\underline{B}$
(2.1)	A, box assumption
(2.2)	$A \Rightarrow B$, from line 2 and line 2.1, using $\Rightarrow E$. Line 2 is available inside this box from outside the box in this logic
(2.3)	B, from lines 2.2 and 2.1, using $\Rightarrow E$

Exit: $A \Rightarrow B$, since we started with A and showed B in the box.

The above is still not good enough. We have to be able to observe that A (i.e., 2.1) was used twice in the box and so if we want (as in, e.g., linear logic) we can block the Exit and thus line 2 will fail. To achieve this we need to use atomic names for all assumptions and accumulate the names as we progress in the proof. Thus modus ponens ($\Rightarrow E$) becomes:

$$\text{Labelled} \Rightarrow E: \quad \frac{\alpha : A; \beta : A \Rightarrow B}{\beta\alpha : B}$$

[2]The top right hand underlined formula in the box (i.e., $\underline{B}$) is the goal of the box.

where β, α are the current accumulated labels. Our proof now becomes the following:

Solution 4

1. $a : A \Rightarrow (A \Rightarrow B)$, assumption named a.

2. $a : A \Rightarrow B$, from the box below:

	$\underline{a : B}$
(2.1)	$b : A$, box assumption, named by the new atomic name b
(2.2)	$ab : A \Rightarrow B$, from lines 1 and 2.1, using the labelled $\Rightarrow E$. The logic box discipline looked at the position of line 1 and line 2.1 relative to the box and considered their labels; and permission is granted to use $\Rightarrow E$.
(2.3)	$(ab)b : B$ from lines 2.1 and 2.2.

Exit: $a : B$.
The box discipline examined the label of the box assumption (i.e., $b : A$) and the box conclusion (i.e., line 2.3 $(ab)b : B$). The box discipline allows the exit of $A \Rightarrow B$ from the box and assigns the label a to this Exit. (The exit fucntion is as follows:
Exit (γ, x) = the result of stripping all occurrences of x from γ.)

This kind of labelling already occurs in [Anderson and Belnap, 1975]. Of course, for them it is just a convenient (side effect) annotation to check their notion of relevance. Gabbay [1996] developed general labels as part of the logic itself, that of *LDS*. In this book we will apply the *LDS* approach to labels defining the notion of agenda relevance. Section 13.2 defines labelled natural deduction in a more formal way. For our purpose, we need the goal directed approach of section 14.3. This approach we now proceed to explain, by means of the same example.

Example 13.3 (Goal directed solution) Our problem is

$$A \Rightarrow (A \Rightarrow B) \vdash^? A \Rightarrow B$$

Since the goal $\vdash^? A \Rightarrow B$ is in implicational form we *input* the antecedent A into the database using a given input algorithm (in this case, the database is a set of wffs, so the input algorithm just puts A in), and ask for the consequent, namely

$$\left[\begin{array}{l}\text{the rest of the database is}\\ \text{implicitly available}\end{array}\right], A?B$$

Since B is atomic, we look for a clause with head B and ask for the formulas in the body of the clause:

$?A$	$?A$
Success since A is available	Success since A is available

When we have labels, as in solution 4 of example 13.2, the label calculations should also be taken into account. The following is the goal directed computation corresponding to solution 4:

$$a : A \Rightarrow (A \Rightarrow B) \vdash^{?} a : A \Rightarrow B$$

Input $b : A$ into the database and prove B with a label $\gamma(b)$ such that $\mathbf{Exit}(\gamma(b), b) = a$. So we proceed:

$$b : A?\gamma(b) : B, \text{ and } \mathbf{Exit}(\gamma(b), b) = a$$

Unify B with $a : A \Rightarrow (A \Rightarrow B)$ and ask

$$?x : A \qquad ?y : A$$

such that $\mathbf{Exit}((ax)yb) = a$.

Thus we must have, given our Exit function, that we must ask for $x = y = b$. We continue:

$$?b : A \qquad ?b : A$$

which succeeds, since $b : A$ is in the database.

Example 13.4 (The compatibility predicate $\mathcal{F}$) In the box of solution 4, if the logic is linear logic, then Exit from the box is not allowed because A is used *twice* in the proof of B.

When we execute $\Rightarrow E$ in the form:

$$\frac{\alpha : A; \beta : A \Rightarrow B}{\beta\alpha : B}$$

if β and α share an atom x in common, we may as well give up on B, because anything obtained using this B will have used the wff named by x more than once. We may as well save our time and effort and restrict the $\Rightarrow E$ by the predicate

$$\mathcal{F}(\beta, \alpha) = \text{(definition): } \alpha \text{ and } \beta \text{ share } no \text{ atoms}$$

Thus the general form of $\Rightarrow E$ becomes:

$$\Rightarrow E \text{ with } \mathcal{F} : \frac{\alpha : A; \beta : A \Rightarrow B; \mathcal{F}(\beta, \alpha)}{\beta\alpha : B}$$

13.2 Labelled Deduction

Let us summarize. A *PLCS* reflects how practical agents reason. For the most part, practical reasoners reason *economically*. Consider a case in which a practical reasoner revises his database on the strength of its assertion by another party. For large classes of actual cases, knowing that this was the warrant for the proposition that the reasoner accepted just *is* knowing how that proposition was derived. In still other cases it may follow from the knowing-precisely condition that in order to know precisely how a new proposition was derived a reasoner may need also to know something of how it came to be derived for his informant. But the basic idea is that of a proof that is subject to conditions of observation and control. When we say that from $A_1, \ldots, A_n$ we can prove B (i.e., $A_1, \ldots, A_n \vdash B$), we may want to know exactly *how* B was derived. For example, we can ask which of the A_i were used in the derivation, which rules were used and in what form. When we perform *modus ponens* A, $A \Rightarrow B \vdash B$, then both A and $A \Rightarrow B$ are used; A is the minor premiss, and $A \Rightarrow B$ is the major premiss.

To keep track of the assumptions used in proofs, we annotate all formulae appearing in the proof. New assumptions are annotated by new atomic *labels* and the labelling is propagated through the deduction.

Here is how this works. We have a stock of atomic labels, which is a set (or a multiset, as defined later) $\mathbb{A} = \{a_1, a_2, a_3, \ldots\}$. The labels can be finite subsets of this set, or sequences of elements from this set. If α, β are set labels, then we can perform the operations $\alpha \cup \beta$ to get new labels. If α, β are labels of sequence labels, we can perform the operation $\beta * \alpha$ to get new labels (where '$*$' denotes concatenation of sequences). Assume we have defined that our labels are labels of some operation $f_i(\beta, \alpha), i = 1, 2, \ldots$, giving new labels from old. Suppose further that we agree on how to label our assumptions and, as we progress in the proof, how to create new labels using the operation f_i.

Modus ponens will take the following form:

$$\frac{\alpha : A; \quad \beta : A \Rightarrow B}{f_{\mathrm{MP}}(\beta, \alpha) : B}$$

We now present some natural deduction rules for labelled formulae.

13.2.1 Labelled Deduction Rules

The labelled rules for $\Rightarrow$ Here are the standard rules for introducing and eliminating implication

$$(\Rightarrow E)$$

$$\frac{\begin{array}{c} A \\ A \Rightarrow B \end{array}}{B}$$

and

$(\Rightarrow I)$: If $\dfrac{\Delta, A}{B}$ is shown to be valid then $\dfrac{\Delta}{A \Rightarrow B}$ is also valid

The labelled versions of these rules are as follows (we assume labels are sets α, β of atomic labels and the operation on labels is union $\cup$; we write $a : A$ instead of $\{a\} : A$, for a atomic):

$$(\Rightarrow E)$$

$$\frac{\begin{array}{c} \alpha : A \\ \beta : A \Rightarrow B \end{array}}{\alpha \cup \beta : B}$$

and

$(\Rightarrow I)$: If $\dfrac{\Delta, a : A}{\alpha \cup \{a\} : B}$ is shown to be valid with a not in α then

$\dfrac{\Delta}{\alpha : A \Rightarrow B}$ is also valid

The labelled rules for $\wedge$ We can use the rules below for introducing and eliminating conjunctions:

$$(\wedge\text{I})\ \frac{\begin{array}{c}\alpha : A\\ \alpha : B\end{array}}{\alpha : A \wedge B} \qquad (\wedge\text{E})\ \frac{\alpha : A \wedge B}{\alpha : A}$$

But note that the introduction rule can be applied only when both formulae in the conjunction rely on exactly the same set of assumptions. Another possibility exists for conjunction, which (since the new labelling rule makes it different from $\wedge$) we might denote by $\sqcap$:

$$(\sqcap\text{I})\ \frac{\begin{array}{c}\alpha : A\\ \beta : B\end{array}}{\alpha \cup \beta : A \sqcap B} \qquad (\sqcap\text{E})\ \frac{\gamma : A \sqcap B}{\begin{array}{c}\alpha : A\\ \beta : B\\ \alpha \cup \beta = \gamma\end{array}}$$

where α, β are new variable labels, satisfying $\alpha \cup \beta = \gamma$. Here when we eliminate $\sqcap$ we obtain *both* $\alpha : A$ and $\beta : B$, $\alpha \cup \beta$ being a decomposition of γ whose exact value is to be determined later in the proof.

The labelled rules for $\vee$ There are no special changes necessary to the natural deduction rules for disjunction, except to add the labels:

$$(\vee\text{I})\ \frac{\alpha : A}{\alpha : A \vee B} \qquad (\vee E)\ \frac{\begin{array}{c}\alpha : A \Rightarrow C\\ \beta : B \Rightarrow C\\ \gamma : A \vee B\end{array}}{\alpha \cup \beta \cup \gamma : C}$$

The labelled rules for $\neg$ In many logics $\neg A$ can be defined using $\bot$. Thus we could use $A \Rightarrow \bot$ instead of $\neg A$, provided we had a rule for $\bot$. Thus we need

$$\frac{\alpha : \bot}{\alpha : B}$$

We can also add the classical rule:

$$\frac{\alpha : (A \Rightarrow \bot) \Rightarrow \bot}{\alpha : A}$$

As a consequence of the above rules, $\bot$ can be derived from different parts of the database; in particular, we may be able to derive several of the $\bot$, each labelled differently.

Example 13.5 Suppose we have a labelled database:

$$\begin{array}{ll} \text{(i)} & \alpha : A \\ \text{(ii)} & \beta : A \Rightarrow B \\ \text{(iii)} & \gamma : A \Rightarrow \bot \\ \text{(iv)} & \delta : B \Rightarrow \bot \end{array}$$

Using ($\Rightarrow$ E) on (i) and (ii), and on the results of that and (iv), we derive $\alpha \cup \beta \cup \delta : \bot$. By using ($\Rightarrow$ E) on (i) and (iii), we again derive falsity, but with a different label, i.e., $\alpha \cup \gamma : \bot$.

The usual classical negation rules can be written as

$$(\neg I)\ \frac{\alpha : A \Rightarrow B,\ \beta : A \Rightarrow \neg B}{\gamma : \neg A} \qquad (\neg E)\ \frac{\alpha : \neg A \Rightarrow B,\ \beta : \neg A \Rightarrow \neg B}{\gamma : A}$$

but we have to decide how to label the deduction, γ. The simplest choice is to take $\gamma = \alpha \cup \beta$.

We now have two label disciplines for negation, one through the use of $\bot$, and one through $\neg$. The two disciplines concur. This we can verify by deriving the labelled ($\neg$I) and ($\neg$E) in the $\bot$ discipline. We translate $\neg A$ as $A \Rightarrow \bot$. Thus the premisses for the ($\neg I$) rule are

$$\alpha : A \Rightarrow B,\ \beta : A \Rightarrow (B \Rightarrow \bot)$$

Using the ($\Rightarrow$I) rule and two applications of *modus ponens*, we can derive the conclusion $\alpha \cup \beta : A \Rightarrow \bot$, which is what our $\neg$ discipline would require. Let us now repeat this same proof for $A = (A' \Rightarrow \bot)$. We get

$$\frac{\begin{array}{c}\alpha : (A' \Rightarrow \bot) \Rightarrow B \\ \beta : (A' \Rightarrow \bot) \Rightarrow (B \Rightarrow \bot)\end{array}}{\alpha \cup \beta : (A' \Rightarrow \bot) \Rightarrow \bot}$$

Note that we have the expected $\alpha \cup \beta$ as the label on the conclusion. This second rule really says

$$\frac{\gamma : (A \Rightarrow \bot) \Rightarrow \bot}{\gamma : A}$$

Example 13.6 We want to show that $B \Rightarrow (A \Rightarrow C)$ follows from the assumption $A \Rightarrow (B \Rightarrow C)$. We therefore label the data with $\{a_1\}$. We want to show $B \Rightarrow (A \Rightarrow C)$. We have to say with which label. An obvious choice is $\{a_1\}$. The first two lines of the proof will be

$$\begin{array}{lll} (1) & \{a_1\} : A \Rightarrow (B \Rightarrow C) & \text{data} \\ (2) & \text{Show } \{a_1\} : B \Rightarrow (A \Rightarrow C) & \end{array}$$

We proceed by assuming that B is in the database, and attempting to show $A \Rightarrow C$. We have to decide what labels to attach to each formula. The B is a new assumption, with no past dependencies, so it should have a new label, a_2, say. The choice of label to be placed on our goal of $A \Rightarrow C$ is slightly more complicated. The labelled version of the implication introduction rule indicates that if we can show $\alpha \cup \{c\} : D$ by assuming $\{c\} : C$, with c not in α, then we can show $\alpha : C \Rightarrow D$. Thus if we are assuming $\{a_2\} : B$, then we show $\{a_1\} : B \Rightarrow (A \Rightarrow C)$ by showing $\alpha \cup \{a_2\} : A \Rightarrow C$, i.e., our label is $\{a_1\} \cup \{a_2\}$, which is $\{a_1, a_2\}$.

(2.1)	$\{a_2\} : B$	assumption with a new label
(2.2)	Show $\{a_1, a_2\} : A \Rightarrow C$	

We show $\{a_1, a_2\} : A \Rightarrow C$ by going to another subcomputation in which we assume A, and show C with the appropriate labels. Again we give the assumption a new label, a_3 say, and give the goal C the label which is the union of the label of the new assumption and the end goal, $\{a_1, a_2\}$. We can now proceed to complete the proof:

(2.2.1)	$\{a_3\} : A$	assumption for subcomputation (2.2)
(2.2.2)	$\{a_1, a_3\} : B \Rightarrow C$	(2.2.1) and from (1) and ($\Rightarrow$ E)
(2.2.3)	$\{a_1, a_2, a_3\} : C$	from (2.1) and (2.2.2) and ($\Rightarrow$ E)

Note that in steps (2.2.2) and (2.2.3) we constructed the label for the formula obtained by implication elimination from the union of the labels on the premisses to the elimination.

As with the non-labelled formulae, we can draw the subcomputations as nested boxes:

$\{a_1\} : B \Rightarrow (A \Rightarrow C)$

(1) $\{a_1\} : A \Rightarrow (B \Rightarrow C)$
(2) $\{a_1\} : B \Rightarrow (A \Rightarrow C)$

$\{a_1, a_2\} : A \Rightarrow C$

(2.1) $\{a_2\} : B$
(2.2) $\{a_1, a_2\} : A \Rightarrow C$

$\{a_1, a_2, a_3\} : C$

(2.2.1) $\{a_3\} : A$
(2.2.2) $\{a_1, a_3\} : B \Rightarrow C$
(2.2.3) $\{a_1, a_2, a_3\} : C$

13.2.2 Non-classical Use of Labels

We shall now illustrate the use of the labels to perform computations in non-classical logics. Our labels are multisets as defined in Definition 13.7 below. Multisets are like sets except that elements may appear in them more than once. The use of multisets allows us to keep track of how many times an assumption is used in *modus ponens.*

Definition 13.7 (Multisets) *Let $\mathbb{A}$ be a set of atoms. A multiset based on $\mathbb{A}$ is a function α on $\mathbb{A}$ giving for each element $a \in \mathbb{A}$ a natural number $\alpha(a) \geq 0$. $\alpha(a)$ tells us how many copies of a we have in the multiset α. Let $\gamma = \alpha \cup \beta$ be defined as the function $\gamma = \alpha + \beta$ (i.e., for each $a, \gamma(a) = \alpha(a) + \beta(a)$). Let $\gamma = \alpha \dot{-} \beta$ be the function defined for each a by $\gamma(a) = 0$, if $\alpha(a) \leq \beta(a)$, and $\gamma(a) = \beta(a) - \alpha(a)$, otherwise.*

We shall consider a propositional language with implication only, and reason forwards using *modus ponens.* The proof will be of $(B \Rightarrow A) \Rightarrow ((A \Rightarrow B) \Rightarrow (A \Rightarrow B))$. We have two options for the labels: we can regard them either as sets or as multisets.

In the derivation with labels as sets, we will end up with the empty label $\varnothing$, showing the formula to be a theorem. If the labels are multisets, we do not end up with the empty label; hence the formula is not a theorem of the logic whose labels are multisets.

We begin by using the ($\Rightarrow$I) rule to assume $\{a_1\} : B \Rightarrow A$ and try to show $\{a_1\} : (A \Rightarrow B) \Rightarrow (A \Rightarrow B)$. This will succeed only when the labels are sets, not when they are multisets. However, let us go on. Further assume $\{a_2\} : A \Rightarrow B$ and show $\{a_1, a_2\} : A \Rightarrow B$. Further assume $\{a_3\} : A$ and show $\{a_1, a_2, a_3\} : B$. We thus end up with the following problem (the strange line numbers have to do with the box proof later on):

Assumptions

1. $\{a_1\} : B \Rightarrow A$

2.2 $\{a_2\} : A \Rightarrow B$

2.2.1 $\{a_3\} : A$

show $\{a_2, a_1, a_2, a_3\} : B$

Derivation

2.2.2 $\{a_2, a_3\} : B$ by *modus ponens* from lines (2.1) and (2.2.1).

2.2.3 $\{a_1, a_2, a_3\} : A$ from (2.2.2) and (1).

2.2.4 $\{a_2, a_1, a_2, a_3\} : B$ from (2.2.3) and (2.1), note a_2 is used twice.

2.2 $\{a_2, a_1, a_2\} : A \Rightarrow B$ from (2.2.1) and (2.2.4) by ($\Rightarrow$I).

2. $\{a_2, a_1\} : (A \Rightarrow B) \Rightarrow (A \Rightarrow B)$ from (2.1) and (2.2) by ($\Rightarrow$I).

0. $\{a_2\} : (B \Rightarrow A) \Rightarrow ((A \Rightarrow B) \Rightarrow (A \Rightarrow B))$ from (1) and (2).

Note the following three conventions:

1. Each new assumption is labelled by a new atomic label. An ordering on the labels can be imposed, namely $a_1 < a_2 < a_3$. This is to reflect the fact that the assumptions arose from our attempt to prove $(B \Rightarrow A) \Rightarrow ((A \Rightarrow B) \Rightarrow (A \Rightarrow B))$ and not, for example, from $(A \Rightarrow B) \Rightarrow ((B \Rightarrow A) \Rightarrow (A \Rightarrow B))$, in which case the ordering would be $a_2 < a_1 < a_3$. The ordering can affect the proofs in certain logics. Some logics allow us to insert, anywhere in the proof, theorems of the logic with the empty label and allow their use in the proof. Other logics do not allow this.

2. If in the proof A is labelled by the multiset α and $A \Rightarrow B$ is labelled by β then B can be derived with a label $\alpha \cup \beta$ where $\cup$ denotes multiset union.

3. If B was derived using A as evidenced by the fact that the label α of A is a singleton $\{a\}$, a atomic and a is in the label β of $B (\alpha \subseteq \beta)$ then we can derive $A \Rightarrow B$ with the label $\beta \dot{-} \alpha$ ('$\dot{-}$' is multiset subtraction).

   In case our labels are sets, we use $\beta - \alpha$, where '$-$' is set subtraction. The labels of the derivation above become, in this case, the following:

2.2.4	$\{a_1, a_2, a_3\}$
2.2	$\{a_1, a_3\}$
2	$\{a_1\}$
0	$\varnothing$

The derivation of 2 from 1 can be represented in a more graphic way:

$$\{a_2, a_1\} : (A \Rightarrow B) \Rightarrow (A \Rightarrow B)$$

(1) $\{a_1\} : B \Rightarrow A$

(2) $\{a_2, a_1\} : (A \Rightarrow B) \Rightarrow (A \Rightarrow B)$

$$\{a_2, a_1, a_2\} : A \Rightarrow B$$

(2.1) $\{a_2\} : A \Rightarrow B$

(2.2) $\{a_2, a_1, a_2\} : A \Rightarrow B$

$$\{a_2, a_1, a_2, a_3\} : B$$

(2.2.1) $\{a_3\} : A$

(2.2.2) $\{a_2, a_3\} : B$

(2.2.3) $\{a_1, a_2, a_3\} : A$

(2.2.4) $\{a_2, a_1, a_2, a_3\} : B$

The above is the box method of representing the deduction. Note that in leaving the inner box for $\{a_2, a_1, a_2\} : A \Rightarrow B$, multiset subtraction was used and only one copy of the label a_2 was taken out. The other copy of a_2 remains and cannot be cancelled, so that the entire computation finishes with the label of $\{a_2\}$. We thus have scope here to define different logics by saying when a labelled proof is acceptable. For linear logic, the final label at the end of the computation must be empty, signifying that formulae have only been used once. Hence this formula is not a theorem of linear logic because the outer box does not exit with label $\varnothing$. In relevance logic, the discipline uses sets and not multisets. Thus the label upon leaving the inner box in this case would be $\{a_1\}$ and that upon leaving the outermost box would be $\varnothing$.

Note that different conditions on labels correspond to different logics, given informally in the following table:

condition:	**logic:**
ignore the labels	intuitionistic logic
accept only the derivations which use all the assumptions	relevance logic
accept derivations which use all assumptions exactly once	linear logic

The conditions on the labels can be translated into reasoning rules.

Exercise 13.8 Construct box derivations for the formulae below and indicate which logic (linear, relevance or intuitionistic) allows a derivation with the empty label.

1. $A \Rightarrow A$

2. $(A \Rightarrow (A \Rightarrow B)) \Rightarrow (A \Rightarrow B)$

3. $(C \Rightarrow A) \Rightarrow ((B \Rightarrow C) \Rightarrow (B \Rightarrow A))$

4. $(C \Rightarrow A) \Rightarrow ((A \Rightarrow B) \Rightarrow (C \Rightarrow B))$

5. $(A \Rightarrow (B \Rightarrow C)) \Rightarrow ((A \Rightarrow B) \Rightarrow (A \Rightarrow C))$

6. $A \Rightarrow (B \Rightarrow A)$

7. $((A \Rightarrow A) \Rightarrow A) \Rightarrow A$

13.2.3 The Theory of Labelled Deductive Systems

Previous sections have only touched slightly on the powerful use of labels in logic. We used the labels to control the forward proofs of a given system. Labels can have many roles and this section will hint at some of them. First note that by using sequences as labels we can have a better control of the proof. Thus $a : A$, $b : A \Rightarrow B$ should yield $(b, a) : B$ and not $\{b, a\} : B$. From the sequence (b, a) we know that b was the label of the ticket $A \Rightarrow B$ and a was the label of the minor premiss.

Consider the following argument:

Example 13.9 (Labels as resource)

Assumptions:
$a_1 : A$
$a_2 : A \Rightarrow B$
$a_3 : C$
$a_4 : C \Rightarrow B$
$a_5 : D \Rightarrow \neg B$
$a_6 : B \Rightarrow E$
$a_7 : D$

The labels just name the assumptions. We perform deduction with the rule of *modus ponens* ($\Rightarrow$ elimination rule). We use the labels to record the sequence of deduction steps. For example, from these assumptions we can deduce E in two different ways. We can record that by concatenating the labels in the following way:

$$\begin{array}{c} \beta : X \Rightarrow Y; \gamma : X \\ (\beta * \gamma) : Y \end{array}$$

where $*$ is concatenation. Notice that we put β first; it labels the 'ticket'.

We can get

$a_2 * a_1 : B$
$a_4 * a_3 : B$
$a_5 * a_7 : \neg B$

and therefore by another step of *modus ponens*:

$a_6 * (a_2 * a_1) : E$
$a_6 * (a_4 * a_3) : E$

Note that by looking at the labels we can tell exactly how each formula is derived. We can also determine from which parts of the data an inconsistency is derived. Thus B and $\neg B$ can be obtained either from $\{a_1, a_2, a_5, a_7\}$ or from $\{a_3, a_4, a_5, a_7\}$. We can double check those assumptions for errors.

The $\Rightarrow$ introduction rule has the following form:

> To introduce $t : A \Rightarrow B$ we further assume the labelled formula $y : A$, where y is a *new* arbitrary label, and show $t * y : B$.

The above used the labels as names used for resource considerations. However, we can use labels in much more profitable ways. The labels can be more complex annotations of the assumptions. For example, the labels can be names of the persons putting forward the assumptions together with a measure (number?) of their reliability, such as (john, 0.7). The label can be an entire chain of reasoning justifying the assumption. For example, the context of the argument of the previous example may be legal:

A = The prisoner has terminal cancer.
B = The prisoner should be freed.

In this case the label a_2 of $A \Rightarrow B$ can be a reference $a_2 = l_1$ to some legislation or precedent and the label a_1 of A can be a medical file $a_1 = m$ which involves medical evidence and argument.

In fact, C may be:

C = The prisoner was illegally arrested.

The label for $a_3 = r$ for C could be a report r from an internal investigative body of the police and the label $a_4 = l_2$ of $C \Rightarrow B$, another legal reference. We can thus write:

$m : A$
$l_1 : A \Rightarrow B$
$r : C$
$l_2 : C \Rightarrow B$

and B can be derived in two ways with two labels. '$\cup$' reads union of databases, giving the cumulative support of what is deduced:

$l_1 \cup m : B$
$l_2 \cup r : B$

A person wishing to attack the conclusion B will have to attack the derivation. In the labelled deductive system where the labels are names or people who recorded the assumptions, there is no recourse. In the *LDS* where the labels are themselves justifications to the assumptions, one can 'attack' the label. Thus one can question the medical argument which supports A, or the police report which supports C. Note that it is convenient to put the medical and police support in the label and not as further data because their reasoning is different in nature from the master deduction.

There are practical examples, such as arguments having to do with abortion, where one cannot label the data so easily. Medical, religious, social, legal and political considerations all intermingle. However, a neat theory of labelling can help the practical reasoner in presenting and studying the arguments and counterarguments.

There is much more to be done with labels, as the next example shows.

Example 13.10 (Aggregation, priorities and flattening) Assume that in the previous example we have another implication

$b_1 : C \Rightarrow \neg E$
$b_2 : D$

We can now derive $\neg E$ with the label

$$b_1 * a_3 : \neg E$$

and derive $\neg B$ with $a_5 * b_2 : \neg B$.

The data may appear inconsistent. Certainly without the labels we get an inconsistent set of assumptions and in many logics nothing can be done.[3] In the LDS what we do depends on the nature of the labels. First we must

[3]Recall that in our system for classical logic, any goal succeeds immediately if $\bot$ is in the database. This is not realistic. A practical database may contain data on several individuals. Getting the address of one individual wrong should not logically imply any statement about any other individual.

aggregate labels supporting the same formula. Let $\uplus$ be the aggregation symbol. We thus have

$$\begin{aligned}&(a_2 * a_1) \uplus (a_4 * a_3) : B\\&a_5 * b_2 : \neg B\\&(a_6 * (a_2 * a_1)) \uplus (a_6 * (a_4 * a_3) : E\\&b_1 * a_3 : \neg E\end{aligned}$$

Obviously $\uplus$ must be associative and commutative, and $*$ must distribute over plus.

In practice *modus ponens* may have compatibility restrictions. For example, the b_1, b_2 labels may be political files and we may not wish to intermingle political and legal considerations. Thus we need a predicate $\mathcal{F}(\beta, \gamma)$, which, when it holds, licenses the *modus ponens* between $\gamma : X; \beta : X \Rightarrow Y$.

In general, there is no way to decide whether to accept B over $\neg B$ or E over $\neg E$ and with what label, without more information about the labels. For example, if we give general priority to b_1, b_2 labels over $a_1, \ldots, a_6$ labels, we get priority for deriving $\neg B$ over B and $\neg E$ over E.

However, if the labels are reliability numbers then since B can be derived in two different ways it might end up with a higher reliability than $\neg B$. Everything depends on our policy.

A policy of deciding with which label and which X or $\neg X$ to emerge given a variety of derivations of $t_i : X$ and $s_j : \neg X$ is called a *flattening policy*.

For mathematical clarity, we can now give a formal definition.

Definition 13.11 (An algebraic LDS for implication and negation) *Let* $\mathbf{L}$ *be a propositional language with* $\Rightarrow, \neg$ *and atoms. Let* $\mathcal{A}$ *be an algebra of labels with relations* $x < y$ *for priority among labels,* $\mathcal{F}(x, y)$ *of compatibility among labels and functions,* $f(x, y)$ *for propagating labels and* $\uplus$ *for aggregating labels.*

1. *A* declarative unit *is a pair* $t : A$*, where* A *is a formula and* t *a term on the algebra of labels (built up from atomic labels and the functions* f *and* $\uplus$*).*

2. *A* database *is a set containing declarative units and formulae of the form* $t_i < s_i$ *and* $\mathcal{F}(t_i, s_i)$ *for some labels* $t_1, \ldots, s_i, \ldots$

3. *The* $\Rightarrow$ *elimination rule,* modus ponens, *has the form*

$$\frac{t : A; s : A \Rightarrow B; \mathcal{F}(s, t)}{f(s, t) : B}$$

4. *The $\Rightarrow$ introduction rule has the form*

   - *To introduce $t : A \Rightarrow B$*
     Assume $x : A$, for x arbitrary in the set $\{y \mid \mathcal{F}(t, y)\}$, and show $f(t, x) : B$.

5. *Negation rules have the form*

$$\frac{t : B; s : \neg B}{r : C}$$

   We are not writing any specific rules because there are so many options for negation.

6. *A family of* flattening rules **Flat** *of the form*

$$\frac{t_1 : A, \ldots, t_k : A; s_1 : \neg A, \ldots, s_m : \neg A; y_i < y_j, i = 1, 2, \ldots, j = 1, 2, \ldots}{\mathsf{Flat}(\{t_1, \ldots, t_k, s_1, \ldots, s_m\})}$$

   where γ is the result of applying the function Flat *on the set containing t_i, s_j and where y_j, y_i range over $\{t_1, \ldots, t_k, s_1, \ldots, s_m\}$.*[4]

7. Aggregation rule

$$\frac{t : A; s : A}{t \uplus s : A}$$

8. *$\uplus$ is associative, commutative and f is distributive over $\uplus$.*

9. *A proof is a sequence of expressions which are of the form $t < s$, $\mathcal{F}(t, s)$ or $t : A$ such that each element of the sequence is either an assumption or is obtained from previous elements in the sequence by an elimination rule or is introduced by a subcomputation via the $\Rightarrow$ introduction rule. Flattening rules are used last.*

Remark 13.12 Note that since $<$ is an ordering appearing positively in a database we can always consistently lower the priority of any label in the database.

Example 13.13 Consider the following database

[4] Flat is a function defined on any set of labels and giving as value a new label. To understand this, recall another function on numbers which we may call **Sum**. It adds any set of numbers to give a new number: their sum!

1.	$m : A$	5.	$r < m$
2.	$l_1 : A \Rightarrow B$	6.	$\mathcal{F}(l_1, m)$
3.	$r : X$	7.	$\mathcal{F}(l_2, r)$
4.	$l_2 : X \Rightarrow \neg B$		

where A, B mean as before and $<$ says that medical support for assumptions has higher priority (probably because it can more easily be reconfirmed) and the labelling propagation function is $\cup$.

$$\frac{\gamma : A; \beta : A \Rightarrow B; \mathcal{F}(\beta, \gamma)}{\beta \cup \gamma : B}$$

$\mathcal{F}$ is the compatibility function saying something like the supports γ, β are of a compatible kind, e.g., legal–medical, etc.

We can take the flattening rule

$$\frac{t : \neg B; s : B; t < s}{\mathsf{Flat}(t, s) : B}$$

and can thus prove $\mathsf{Flat}(l_2 \cup r; l_1 \cup m) : B$ from our data. If, however, the credibility of the label m is attacked (i.e., $r < m$ is questioned) then B may no longer be provable.

Example 13.14 (Flattening examples) Here are further examples of flattening.

1. Imagine the label α lists the independent sources confirming a statement A. Thus $\alpha : A$ means that A is confirmed by the sources in α. Then $\alpha_1 : A, \ldots, \alpha_n : A$ can be consolidated into $\alpha = \mathsf{Flat}(\{\alpha_1, \ldots, \alpha_n\})$. The consolidation process will take into account connections between the sources, etc.

2. Imagine we are dealing with a medical diagnosis system. $\alpha : A$ can mean that A is true with likelihood α, α being a number. There are various considerations involved in obtaining such numbers and we may have estimates $\alpha_1 : A, \ldots, \alpha_n : A$ coming from various directions. These can be flattened into $\alpha : A$ according to some statistical or probabilistic model [Gabbay, 1996].

13.2.4 Hunches and Guesses

We show how our labelled framework allows us to deal with hunches and inspired guesses, in satisfaction of AC11, which requires that the conceptual theory be fairly preserved in the formal account (see section 9.5). The essence of such a step is that it does not necessarily follow from available data but is a leap of faith possibly driven by some experience and subconscious mechanism. We must assume that such leaps are dependent on context, the total information available at the moment of the inspiration. We denote such leaps by

$$(\mathbb{N}) \quad \Delta \leadsto D.$$

Δ is the context, D is the result of 'inspiration'.

We need coherence requirements, namely

1. If $\Delta \vdash D$ then we *cannot* have $\Delta \leadsto \neg D$, i.e., we want no truck with *stupid* inconsistent 'hunches'.

2. If $\Delta \leadsto D_1$ and $\Delta \leadsto D_2$ then $\Delta \wedge D_1 \leadsto D_2$, i.e., we maintain our other hunches when some of them come true!

We now have to say how we represent context in our proof theory. The simplest way is to have as context of level 0 all the assumptions available at the start of the proof and whenever we open a box subcomputation, the context is augmented by the new assumption of this new box, but *not* by what is dynamically proved in the box (which may involve inspirations).

Example 13.15 (Inspired forward deduction) Consider the intuitionistic logic fragment with $\wedge$ and $\Rightarrow$ and the monotonic rules $(\wedge I), (\wedge E), (\Rightarrow E)$ and $(\Rightarrow I)$. Let $\vdash$ be the monotonic intuitionistic consequence for this fragment. Consider the following specific additional inspiration rules for $i = 1, 2$ with $\beta = A_1 \Rightarrow (A_2 \Rightarrow C)$.

$(\mathbb{N}_1)$ $\beta \wedge A_1 \leadsto D_1$

$(\mathbb{N}_2)$ $\beta \wedge A_1 \wedge A_2 \leadsto D_2$.

Let $\mid\!\sim$ denote the new inspiration consequence (which has not yet been defined formally) based on $\vdash$ and $\mathbb{N}_i, i = 1, 2$.

We show that $\beta \mid\!\sim \alpha$ where

$$\alpha = A_1 \Rightarrow (D_1 \wedge (A_2 \Rightarrow C \wedge D_2))$$

The following box deduction shows that $\beta \mid\!\sim \alpha$.

$\underline{A_1 \Rightarrow (D_1 \wedge (A2 \Rightarrow C \wedge D_1))}$

(1) $A_1 \Rightarrow (A_2 \Rightarrow C)$ data
(2) $A_1 \Rightarrow (D_1 \wedge (A_2 \Rightarrow C \wedge D_2))$
subcomputation

$\underline{D_1 \wedge (A_2 \Rightarrow C \wedge D_2)}$

(2.1) A_1 assumption
(2.2) D_1 from (1) (2.1) and ($\mathbb{N}_1$) and ($\wedge I$)
(2.3) $A_2 \Rightarrow C \wedge D_2$ subcomputation

$\underline{C \wedge D_2}$

(2.3.1)	A_2	assumption
(2.3.2)	D_2	from ($\mathbb{N}_2$) and (1) (2.2) and (2.3.1) and ($\wedge I$)[5]
(2.3.3)	$A_2 \Rightarrow C$	from (2.1) and (1) using ($\Rightarrow E$)
(2.3.4)	C	from (2.3.1) an (2.3.3) using ($\Rightarrow E$)
(2.3.5)	$C \wedge D_2$	from (2.3.2) and (2.3.3) using ($\wedge I$)

(2.4) $D_1 \wedge (A_2 \Rightarrow C \wedge D_2)$
from (2.2) and (2.3) using ($\wedge I$)

The reader may well ask where these hunches and inspirations come from? One mechanism for such extra data is *abduction*.

Suppose we have the context Δ and a new unprovable fact q is discovered or added to the database. Since $\Delta \nvdash q$ we may believe that q holds because of other reasons p such that $\Delta + p \vdash q$. So our abductive guess is p. We can write this as an abduction rule

($\mathbb{N}$) $\Delta + q \leadsto p$.

The simplest abduction process is as follows:

Given $\Delta = \{p \Rightarrow q\}$ and we observe q, then we abduce p. We need as part of our logic to have an abduction mechanism and to have a good

[5](2.2) D_1 is not in the context for $\mathbb{N}_2$, since it was obtained by inspiration.

one, we must formulate our logic in an implicational goal directed way (see Section 13.4).

Another source of 'hunches' is the non-monotonicity of negation as failure. If we fail to establish A, we deduce $\neg A$. If a Sunday flight to Timbuktu from Heathrow is not listed on the Web then there is no such flight. Negation as failure is a basic mechanism in AI and logic programming, and we can incorporate it into our basic logic if we give the logic a goal directed formulation. This we indeed do in section 14.3, definition 14.21.

13.2.5 Contextual Effects

The precise naming of assumptions and the propagation of labels allows us to define precisely the contextual effects of any assumption. This notion was put forward by Sperber and Wilson as part of their notion of relevance. This satisfies the ecumenism constraint called for by adequacy condition AC10. (See chapter 7 above.) In order to model this idea, we need to be able to keep track of exactly how formulas are proved. Here is the definition:

Definition 13.16 *Let Δ be a labelled database, in a language with $\Rightarrow$ only and possibly a special additional constant $\bot$. We assume some labelled rules of the form $\Rightarrow E$ and $\Rightarrow I$. We define the notion of $\Delta \vdash_{\alpha,m,n} A$, where α is a complex label and m, n natural numbers counting the way A is proved. m measures the complexity of nested boxes in the proof and n counts the total number of uses of $\Rightarrow E$ in the proof.*

1. $\Delta \vdash_{\alpha,0,0} A$ *iff* $\alpha : A \in \Delta$

2. $\Delta \vdash_{\gamma,m,n} A$ *if for some* $C, C \Rightarrow A$, *we have that* $\Delta \vdash_{\alpha,m_1,s_1} C$ *and* $\Delta \vdash_{\beta,m_2,s_2} C \rightarrow A$ *and* $\gamma = (\beta\alpha)$ *and* $n = 1 + s_1 + s_2$ *and* $m = max(m_1, m_2)$.

   Note that since the $\Rightarrow E$ rule is being used in the proof it must be licenced, i.e.,, $\mathcal{F}(\beta, \alpha)$ holds, see example 13.4.

3. $\Delta \vdash_{\alpha,m+1,n} A \Rightarrow B$ *if* $\Delta \cup \{x : A\} \vdash_{\beta(x),m,n} B$, *where x is a completely new (to Δ) atomic label and where* $\alpha = \mathbf{Exit}(\beta(x), x)$. *See solution 4 in example 13.2.*

The precise labelling of proofs afforded by definition 13.16 allows us to define the notion of contextual effects of a wff A in a context Δ, and to handle inconsistency as well.

Definition 13.17

1. *Let* Δ *be a labelled database and let* A *be a new wff. Define the database* $\Gamma = \Delta \cup \{x : A\}$, *where* x *is a new atomic label. Then the contextual effects of* A *on* Δ *is the set*

   $$\mathbb{C} = \{E | \Gamma \vdash_{\alpha(x),m,n} E, \textit{ for some } m,n \textit{ and } \alpha(x) \textit{ genuinely containing} x\}$$

   An important point to note is that each $E \in \mathbb{C}$ *has possibly several* $(\beta(x), m, n)$ *which show exactly from what assumptions and at what complexity it is proved.*

2. E *is in the contextual effects of* A *on* Δ *using only* elimination rules *if for some* $\beta(x)$ *genuinely containing* x *and some* n *we have* $\Gamma \vdash_{\beta(x),o,n} E$.

Remark 13.18 The notion of contextual effects works even if A is not consistent with Δ. If the logic allows Δ and A to prove any E, we still know exactly how any E can be proved and so we can discuss/prove/evaluate these proofs. Δ and A is not just an inconsistent black box that proves everything. The next example illustrates this point.

Example 13.19 In this example $\bot$ is falsity and any database proving $\bot$ is inconsistent. Let Δ be the following:

$$\begin{array}{ll} t_1 : & A \\ t_2 : & A \Rightarrow B \\ t_3 : & A \Rightarrow (C \Rightarrow D) \\ t_4 : & A \Rightarrow (C \Rightarrow E) \\ t_5 : & D \Rightarrow A_1 \\ s : & A \Rightarrow (A_1 \Rightarrow \bot) \end{array}$$

We have

$$\begin{array}{l} \Delta \vdash_{t_2 t_2,0,1} B \\ \Delta \vdash_{t_3 t_1,0,1} C \Rightarrow D \\ \Delta \vdash_{t_4 t_1,0,1} C \Rightarrow E \\ \Delta \cup \{x : C\} \vdash_{t_3 t_1,x,0,2} D \\ \Delta \cup \{x : C\} \vdash_{t_4 t_1 x,0,2} E \\ \Delta \cup \{x : C\} \vdash_{s t_1 t_5 t_3 t_1 x,0,3} \bot. \end{array}$$

Thus although $\Delta \cup \{x : C\}$ is not consistent, it can prove E with $y_1 = (t_4 t_1 x, 0, 2)$ and prove D with $y_2 = (t_3 t_1 x, 0, 2)$ and we have that $\Delta \cup \{y_1 : E, y_2 : D\}$ is consistent.

Also $\Delta \cup \{x : C\} \vdash_{t_2 t_1,0,1} B$ and $(\Delta - \{t_1 : A\}) \cup \{x : C\}$ is consistent with B and D.

Remark 13.20 (The use of Introduction rules) This remark will elaborate on the Sperber–Wilson idea of using only elimination rules in order to obtain contextual effects, as well as motivate the goal directed formulation of the next chapter. See section 6.2.

SW proposed that we use only elimination rules to generate contextual effects. Their motivation is good and healthy: to keep the number of effects in check. If we allow for introduction rules, we can get a lot of irrelevant junk. Take, for example, the assumption A. Using introduction rules we can get $(A \Rightarrow A), A \Rightarrow (A \Rightarrow A)$, etc. Using only elimination rules keeps the number of contextual effects in check.

The restriction, however, is too strong. Consider:

1. $A \Rightarrow (B \Rightarrow C)$
   To get a PhD degree (C), a student needs to pay his fees (A) and to successfully defend his thesis (B).

If we have the input:

2. B, i.e., the student defended his thesis successfully,

then this input does have a clear contextual effects, namely:

3. $A \Rightarrow C$.

However, without introduction rules, $A \Rightarrow C$ cannot be derived from the input (not under the usual formulation of elimination rules)[6]. So we do need some safe use of introduction rules.

Our solution is to move to a goal directed formulation which will not only solve this problem but also allow for non-monotonicity (through failure) and abduction.

Let us see how the goal directed computation will work.

Our data has the form

[6] The reader may wish to strengthen the elimination rule by letting

$$\frac{\Delta(A), A}{\Delta(\top)}$$

giving

$$\frac{A \Rightarrow (B \Rightarrow C), B}{A \Rightarrow (\top \Rightarrow C)}$$

with $A \Rightarrow (\top \Rightarrow C)$ being simplified to $A \Rightarrow C$. However, this is not good enough. We may have cases like

$$\frac{E \Rightarrow (A \Rightarrow (B \Rightarrow C)), E \Rightarrow B}{E \Rightarrow (A \Rightarrow C)}$$

How do we do these?

(1) $A \Rightarrow (B \Rightarrow C)$

The *head* of this clause is C.
Let us ask for the head $?C$
Working backwards, we need to ask in parallel for $?A$ and $?B$:

$?A$ $?B$

Any input which has contextual effects must help with our parallel queries.

(i) input B
This makes $?B$ succeed and we are left with $?A$. Thus we have that when asking $?C$ we were reduced to asking for $?A$, and hence the contextual effects of input B is $A \Rightarrow C$.

(ii) input $B \Rightarrow A$
Use this new input to continue with $?A$ of our parallel queries. We now ask $?B$.

Hence the contextual effect of the second input is $B \Rightarrow C$.

Note that we cannot get an explosion of contextual effects because all goal directed steps go through bodies of *existing clauses* (strong *cut* property).

This idea will be developed in detail in the next chapter, section 14.2.

Remark 13.21 (The need for Abduction) Let us build further on the example of the previous remark. Assume our data are:

1. $A \Rightarrow (B \Rightarrow C)$,
   to get a PhD (C), a student needs to pay his fees (A) and to submit and successfully defend his thesis (B).

2. $B \Rightarrow P$.
   If the student successfully submits and defends his thesis (B) his parents organize a big party (P).

   The input we get is:

3. P

What are the contextual effects of (3)?

Clearly we must use our common sense and abduce

4. B
   and then continue as in the previous remark and also get

5. $A \Rightarrow C$.

Hence we need an abduction mechanism.

As we said earlier, the goal directed formulation is also good for abduction.

Remark 13.22 (Contextual effects short of relevance) It is well to be clear about what we have been up to in the past few pages. We have attempted to answer in a formally adequate way those critics of SW who allege that the concept of contextual effects is not expressly enough articulated in [Sperber and Wilson, 1986] to make it clear that it can do the work asked of it in the account of relevance. We take those criticisms now to have been answered. It remains a separate question, of course, whether the account of relevance itself that can now be made to flow through our adjusted notion of contextual effects is one that will satisfy the SW-critics of relevance.

Chapter 14

Relevance Logics

> When you have assembled what you call your 'facts' in logical order, it is like an oil-lamp you have fashioned, filled and trimmed; but which will lead to no illumination until you first light it.
>
> Saint-Exupéry, *The Wisdom of the Sands*

14.1 Introduction

Let us briefly visit the question of relevance logic. Let us again ask why an agenda-relevance theorist should be interested in producing systems of relevant logic? If we succeed with the objectives which we have set for ourselves in this chapter, then we may fairly claim certain technical improvements over earlier AB-systems. But why should this matter for agenda-relevance?

We would have an acceptable answer to this question if it could be shown

1. that the original AB conceptions of relevance resonate appropriately in AR;

2. that the technical developments provided here support these conceptions.

Concerning (1), Anderson and Belnap have two main (inequivalent) conceptions of relevance. (We ignore the question of the adequacy of their formal representations in standard AB-systems.) On the one conception, relevance is a connection of meaning between the antecedent and consequent of a statement of (relevant) implication. If it could be shown that an interpolation theorem holds for a given implication relation, that would be some (though quite weak) indication of some kind of semantic connection. One would get a tighter connection if we actually required that a common element have an occurrence in both antecedent and consequent. No matter what we might find ourselves saying about the present point, there is no doubt that the meaning-connection conception of relevance is not at all the conception of relevance that motivates AR. What we want to know is whether the meaning-connection *conception* stands in interesting relations, other than identity, to the agenda *conception*. The answer is yes. For whole classes of agendas it is helpful for a cognitive agent to know what follows from what. In certain cases (e.g., Sperber and Wilson's non-introductive synthetic implications) implications are driven by direct meaning connections between antecedent and consequent. For other kinds of case, the closest that one comes to such a connection is by way of the requisite interpolation theorem. For still further cases, there is not even that connection. Now there is some empirical evidence that when it comes to spotting implications, human beings are more adept at spotting direct connections of meaning rather than implications that lack this tie. Accordingly, we should expect the theory of agenda relevance to predict that the former kind of implications are more helpful (i.e., more accessible and more quickly recognized) than otherwise. If this is right, then the theory of agenda relevance attributes to cognitive agents a particular interest in AB-relevance. This being so, the theory of agenda relevance itself motivates an adequately detailed study of AB-relevance.

The second conception of AB-relevance shows a perhaps more direct affinity to agenda relevance. According to this second conception, relevance is a property of proofs from hypothesis. A proof is relevant when it makes use of each of those hypotheses. As worked out in the standard AB-systems, this turns out to be a rather weak condition, for a proof that is relevant in the present sense can be as (finitely) redundant as you please. A much more agenda relevance-friendly conception is provided by a logic, to whcih linear logic approximates, in which relevance is retained and all redundancy is eliminated. But even in its original AB-form, the idea of relevant proof resonates in the theory of agenda relevance. If we think of proof as a kind of stand-in for reasoning in general, then a rule of use comes rather naturally to mind. It tells the would-be reasoner to (try to) confine his attention to considerations that he is actually prepared to use in the process of working out the various steps of his reasoning. It is a rule (actually, it is more a virtual rule in the sense of section 3.2 above) of central importance for practical agents who labour in cognitive economies of scarce resources. It is a rule or virtual rule that tells the agent two things we would do well to mind. One is that information is of no value unless it is used. The other is that attending to considerations that you are not prepared to make use of is a waste of cognitive effort. The AB-full-use conception of relevance models this rule, albeit somewhat crudely. But here, too, there is a phenomenon for the agenda relevance theorist to take note of, and the more so if its structure could be given a detailed and refined articulation. The interest that an agenda-relevance theorist can rightly take in full-use relevance, is not that full-use relevance is the same *conception* of relevance as agenda relevance, but rather that if full-use phenomena have an articulable logical structure, it behoves the AR-theorist to be aware of it.

With these things in mind, the present chapter introduces a base logic for our model of agenda relevance. Our choice is a modified version of Anderson and Belnap relevance logic. Since the methodology we are using is that of Labelled Deductive Systems (LDS), the base logic can be easily modified or even be replaced by another logic (also formulated in LDS). The formal model of agenda relevance introduced in the next chapter will not use any specific properties of the base logic, only general properties, common to many logics. However, any system of relevance specially tailored for some specific application area may well benefit from fine tuning of the specific properties of the base logic.

Relevant implication is introduced in section 14.2. This is basically the Anderson–Belnap notion of relevance, namely to get $A \Rightarrow B$, we need to prove B by actually using A in the proof. Section 14.3 formulates a goal directed algorithmic proof procedure for this logic and can therefore also introduce the notion of failure and the mechanism of abduction. Here we are already departing from the traditional formulation and capabilities of the AB logic. Section 14.4 studies some move properties of the system and finally Section 14.5 shows how to vary the system, into the system of deductive relevance.

Let us conclude this section with a brief explanation of deductive relevance. Ordinary AB relevance logic requires us, in order to show that $A \Rightarrow B$ holds, that A be used in the proof of B. This 'use' is technical. The physical wff 'A' needs to be used in a *modus ponens* operation involved in the proof of B.

Such a technical definition has two weaknesses.

1. A may be used even though it is not needed.

2. An A' may be used, which from the point of view of content and meaning is related to A, but this use of A' does not count, because 'A'' is not 'A'.

To illustrate (1) consider

(a) $B \Rightarrow A$

(b) $A \Rightarrow B$

(c) A

(b) and (c) can prove B but we can deliberately go and use (a) (and hence (b) again) and involve it in the proof.

To illustrate (2) consider

(a) A (or any Δ such the $\Delta \vdash A$)

(b) $A \Rightarrow B$

(c) A

(a) and (b) can give B, but (c) is not used, though the 'contents' of (c) are used.

Deductive relevance uses an additional logic which decides, given a use of any wff 'A' in the data which other (logically equivalent?) items of data are to be considered 'used'.

We may wish to modify the logic a bit by allowing wffs in the data that may be used but are not required to be used. See Definition 14.5.

14.2 Anderson–Belnap Relevant Logic

The previous chapter introduced labelling and box discipline into our logics. We still need to choose the particular base logic we want for our model of agenda relevance. Our choice is going to be a modified goal directed version of Anderson and Belnap relevant implication. The Anderson–Belnap relevant implication is introduced in this section.

There will be several versions of this system. The original AB-system simply modified the $\Rightarrow I$ rule to require that:

- To show $A \Rightarrow B$, we assume A and prove B by actually using A in the proof.

In the labelling system, this requirement manifests itself in the form:

- Assume A with a new atomic label x and prove B with a label $\gamma(x)$, actually containing x.

The labelled rule still allows options for deciding on what label to exit with. $\delta = \mathbf{Exit}(\gamma(x), x)$ may have more than one option. One thing we know: x must not be free in δ; it must be discharged.

Definition 14.1 *Let our language be propositional with falsity $\bot$ and the binary connective $\rightarrow$. Consider another language of atomic labels $S = \{t_1, \ldots, t_n, \ldots\}$. A label is a subset $\alpha \subseteq S$. A declarative unit is a pair $\alpha : A$, where α is a label and A a wff of the language with $\rightarrow$ and $\bot$.*

A database *is a set of labelled wffs $\{x_i : A_i\}$, where all the labels are atomic and all x_i are pairwise different.*

Definition 14.2 *There are two labelled rules for $\rightarrow$.*

$\rightarrow$-Elimination

$$\frac{\Delta \vdash \alpha : A; \beta : A \rightarrow B}{\Delta \vdash \beta \cup \alpha : B}$$

$\rightarrow$-Introduction

To show $\Delta \vdash \alpha : A \rightarrow B$, show $\Delta \cup \{x : A\} \vdash \alpha \cup \{x\} : B$, where x is a completely new atomic label.[1]

Rule for $\bot$

$$\frac{\Delta \vdash \alpha : \bot}{\Delta \vdash \alpha : A}$$

Definition 14.3 *Let Δ be a database and $\alpha : A$ a labelled wff. We define by induction the notion of $\Delta \vdash \alpha : A$:*

1. *For $\alpha : A$ atomic, $\Delta \vdash \alpha : A$ if $\{\alpha : A\} = \Delta$ or $\{\alpha : \bot\} = \Delta$.*

2. *$\Delta \vdash \alpha : A \rightarrow B$ iff $\Delta \cup \{x : A\} \vdash \alpha \cup \{x\} : B$ where x is a new atomic label.*

3. *If $\Delta = \Delta_1 \cup \Delta_2$ and $\Delta_1 \vdash \alpha : A$ and $\Delta_2 \vdash \beta : A \rightarrow B$ then $\Delta \vdash \alpha \cup \beta : B$*

4. *$\Delta \vdash \alpha : A$ if $\Delta \vdash \alpha : \bot$.*

Example 14.4

$$x : A \rightarrow B \vdash x : A \rightarrow B$$

[1] The fact that we require that B be proved with label $\alpha \cup \{x\}$ indicates that A is used in the proof of B.

iff by rule (2)

$$x : A \to B, y : A \vdash xy : B$$

which holds by rule (3).

Definition 14.5 *Let $\Delta = \{A_1, \ldots, A_n\}$ be a multiset[2] of wffs without labels. Let $\Delta' = \{x_1 : A_1, \ldots, x_n : A_n\}$, where x_i are all different atomic labels. We define the following consequence relations:*

(1) $\Delta \vdash_{\mathbf{1R}} B$ *iff* $\Delta' \vdash \{x_1, \ldots, x_n\} : B$

(2) $\Delta \vdash_{\mathbf{2R}} B$ *iff for every* $x_i : A_i \in \Delta$ *there exists* α *such that* $x_i \in \alpha$ *and* $\Delta' \vdash \alpha : B$.

(3) $\Delta \vdash_{\mathbf{3R}} B$ *iff for some* $\alpha \subseteq \{x_1, \ldots, x_n\}, \Delta' \vdash \alpha : B$.

Remark 14.6 Note that $\vdash$ is a relevant consequence relation in the sense that if $\Delta' \vdash \alpha : B$ then the labels in α indicate what was used in the proof of B. Thus for Δ and B, $\Delta \vdash_{\mathbf{1R}} B$ gives the Anderson–Belnap notion of relevance in ways that satisfy the deduction theorem

$$\Delta = \{A_1, \ldots, A_n\} \vdash_{\mathbf{1R}} B \text{ iff } A_1 \to \ldots \to (A_n \to B) \ldots)$$

For this reason, Δ must be multisets. E.g.,

$$\vdash_{\mathbf{1R}} A \to (A \to B) \text{ iff } \{A, A\} \vdash_{\mathbf{1R}} B$$

$\Delta \vdash_{\mathbf{1R}} B$ means that all assumptions in Δ are used in the proof of B.
$\Delta \vdash_{\mathbf{2R}} B$ says that for every assumption $A \in \Delta$ it can be used in some proof of B.
$\Delta \vdash_{\mathbf{3R}} B$ simply means that for some $\Delta_1 \subseteq \Delta, \Delta_1 \vdash_{\mathbf{1R}} B$.

Example 14.7 Consider

$$\begin{array}{ll} x_1 : & A_1 \\ x_2 : & A_1 \to B \\ x_3 : & A_3 \\ x_4 : & A_3 \to B \end{array}$$

Thus $\Delta \nvdash_{1R} B, \Delta \vdash_{\mathbf{2R}} B$ and $\Delta \vdash_{\mathbf{3R}} B$.

[2]We use multisets because we want to allow the same wffs to appear more than once. This allows us the deduction theorem.

Add $x_5 : C$ to form Δ_5. Then $\Delta_5 \vdash_{\mathbf{3R}} B$, but $\Delta_5 \not\vdash_{\mathbf{2R}} B$ and $\Delta_5 \not\vdash_{\mathbf{1R}} B$. Hence $x_5 : C$ is not relevant to B.

Critics of Anderson and Belnap relevance have complained that the explicit use of A in the proof of B does not make it necessarily relevant to B. How, then, does this formal notion connect with the real life cases of relevance? Consider the following example:

Example 14.8

$$\begin{array}{ll} (x_1): & A \\ (x_2): & A \to (A \to B) \\ (x_3): & (A \to B) \to C \\ (x_4): & C \to A \end{array}$$

B can be proved from $\{x_1, x_2\}$ with x_1 used twice. But that would not be accepted by AB-R because x_3 and x_4 are not used. However, x_1 and x_2 give $A \to B$ and $\{x_1, x_2, x_3\}$ give C, which together with x_4 gives A. We can then use x_2 again to get B, and thus *use* all the assumptions.

Criticism of SW- heory, as we have said, complains about the lack of adequate formal machinery, though the basic intuitions are sound in a general way.

The formal model of AR combines both approaches.

The next definition gives a Hilbert formulation of relevance implication with $\to$ and $\bot$.

Definition 14.9 (Hilbert formulation) *Consider the following axioms and rules for a propositional language with $\to$ and $\bot$.*

1. $A \to A$
2. $(A \to B) \to ((C \to A) \to (C \to B))$
3. $(A \to (B \to C)) \to ((B \to (A \to C)))$
4. $(A \to (B \to C)) \to ((A \to B) \to (A \to C))$
5. $\bot \to A$
6. $\dfrac{\vdash A \to B}{\vdash (B \to C) \to (A \to C)}$
7. $\dfrac{\vdash A; \vdash A \to B}{\vdash B}$

These axioms define relevant implication with $\to$ and $\perp$. The notion of $\vdash A$ is defined in the usual manner. Compare with subsection 13.2.2.

Definition 14.10 *Let $\Delta = \{A_1, \ldots, A_n\}$ be a multiset of wffs. Define $\Delta \vdash B$ as $\vdash A_1 \to \ldots \to (A_n \to B) \ldots$*

By axiom 3 of the previous definition $\Delta \vdash B$ is well defined, and does not depend on the ordering.

Exercise 14.11

1. Show that all axioms and rules of definition 14.9 can be proved in the labelled system of definitions 14.3, 14.5.

2. Show that if $\Delta \vdash B$ then $\Delta \vdash_{1R} B$.

3. Let Δ_{set} be Δ regarded as a set. Show that $(\Delta \to B) \vdash \Delta_{\text{set}} \to B$.

Theorem 14.12 (Cut theorem for the Hilbert system) *Let Δ, Γ be multisets of wffs. If $\Delta, A \vdash B$ and $\Gamma \vdash A$ then $\Delta \cup \Gamma \vdash B$.*

Proof. We first examine the case where Δ or Γ are $\varnothing$.

Case $\Gamma = \varnothing$ *and* $\Delta = \varnothing$
This is obvious

Case $\Gamma = \varnothing, \Delta = \{A_1, \ldots, A_n\}$
We have $\vdash A_1 \to \cdots \to A_n \to (A \to B) \ldots)$ and $\vdash A$.

We note by axiom 4 of definition 14.9 that $\vdash A \to (A_1 \to \cdots \to (A_n \to B) \ldots)$ and we use *modus ponens* to get $\Delta \vdash B$.

Case $\Gamma = \{D_1, \ldots, D_m\}, \Delta = \varnothing$
We have $\vdash A \to B$ and $\vdash D_1 \to \cdots \to (D_m \to A)$. We need to show $\vdash D_1 \to \cdots \to (D_m \to B) \ldots$. We prove this by showing by induction on m that the following generalization of axiom 6 holds

$$\frac{\vdash A \to B}{\vdash (D_1 \to \cdots \to (D_m \to A) \ldots)) \to (D_1 \to \cdots \to (D_m \to B) \ldots))}$$

We now turn to the case where both Γ and Δ are non-empty. We need to show that (1) and (2) implies (3):

1. $\vdash_{\mathbf{L}} (A_1 \to \ldots \to (A_n \to (A \to B)) \ldots)$

2. $\vdash_{\mathbf{L}} D_1 \to \ldots \to ((D_m \to A) \ldots)$

3. $\vdash_{\mathbf{L}} A_1 \to \ldots \to (A_n \to (D_1 \to \ldots \to (D_m \to B))\ldots)$

We can do that without using axioms (3), (4) and (5) of definition 14.9. Let **L** be the logic thus defined (it is known as *concatenation logic*):

We use induction on m and n.

Case $m = n = 1$

We have to show that (1) and (2) imply (3):

1. $\vdash_{\mathbf{L}} A_1 \to (A \to B)$
2. $\vdash_{\mathbf{L}} (D_1 \to A)$
3. $\vdash_{\mathbf{L}} A_1 \to (D_1 \to B)$

From rule (6), we get using (2) that

4. $\vdash_{\mathbf{L}} (A \to B) \to (D_1 \to B)$

and using axiom (2) we get

5. $(A_1 \to (A \to B)) \to (A_1 \to (D_1 \to B))$

we get (3) by *modus ponens* of (1) and (5).

Case $m = 1, n$ **arbitrary**

From $\vdash_{\mathbf{L}} D_1 \to A$ we get $\vdash_{\mathbf{L}} (A \to B) \to (D_1 \to B)$ and by induction on n we prove:

$$\begin{gathered}\vdash_{\mathbf{L}} (A_1 \to \ldots \to (A_n \to (A \to B)\ldots)) \to \\ (A_1 \to \ldots \to A_n \to (D_1 \to B)\ldots)\end{gathered}$$

For $n = 1$ this follows from axiom (2). Assume the above for n and get it for $n + 1$ by another application of axiom (2).

Case $m + 1, n$ **arbitrary**

We have

$$\vdash_{\mathbf{L}} (A \to B) \to ((D_{m+1} \to A) \to (D_{m+1} \to B))$$

hence

$$\begin{gathered}\vdash_{\mathbf{L}} A_1 \to \ldots \to (A_n \to (A \to B))\ldots) \\ \to ((A_1 \to \ldots \to (A_n \to ((D_{m+1} \to A) \to (D_{m+1} \to B))\ldots)\end{gathered}$$

and therefore

$$\vdash_{\mathbf{L}} A_1 \to \ldots \to (A_n \to (D_{m+1} \to A) \to (D_{m+1} \to B)\ldots)$$

On the other hand, we have

$$\vdash_{\mathbf{L}} D_1 \to \ldots (D_m \to (D_{m+1} \to A)\ldots)$$

hence by the induction hypothesis we get

$$\vdash_{\mathbf{L}} A_1 \to \ldots \to (A_n \to (D_1 \to \ldots (D_m \to (D_{m+1} \to B) \ldots)$$

This completes the proof of the theorem. ■

Definition 14.13 (Semantics for relevant implication) *Let $\mathcal{S}$ be a family of sets closed under set union and assume $\varnothing \in \mathcal{S}$.*

Let h be an assignment associating with every subset $X \in \mathcal{S}$ and every atomic q a value $h(X, q) \in \{0, 1\}$. Assume $h(X, \bot) = 0$. Then $(\mathcal{S}, h)$ is a model.

Define the notion of $X \vDash A$, for a wff A by induction as follows:

1. *$X \vDash q$ if $h(X, q) = 1$, for q atomic or $\bot$.*
2. *$X \vDash A \to B$ iff for all Y in $\mathcal{S}$ such that $Y \vDash A$ we have $X \cup Y \vDash B$, where $\cup$ is set union.*
3. *We say A holds in the model if $\varnothing \vDash A$.*
4. *We say $\vDash A$ iff A holds in all models.*

Theorem 14.14 $\vdash A$ *iff* $\vDash A$

Proof.

1. Soundness is proved by checking that all axioms and rules hold in all models.
2. For completeness, let $\mathcal{S}$ be the set of all theories Δ (sets of wffs) such that $\Delta \nvdash \bot$.

   Define for atomic q,

   - $\Delta \vDash q$ iff $\Delta \vdash q$

   We show by structural induction that for any theory Δ and any wff A

   - $\Delta \vDash A$ iff $\Delta \vdash A$.

   (i) Case A atomic holds by definition.

   (ii) Assume $\Delta \vDash A \to B$. Then for any $\Delta' \vDash A$ we have $\Delta \cup \Delta' \vDash B$. By the induction hypothesis since $A \vdash A$, we get $\Delta \cup \{A\} \vdash B$, i.e., $\Delta \vdash A \to B$.

   (iii) The converse follows from the cut theorem. Assume $\Delta \vdash A \to B$ and that $\Delta' \vDash A$, then $\Delta' \vdash A$ by the induction hypothesis and by cut $\Delta \cup \Delta' \vdash B$ and hence $\Delta \cup \Delta' \vDash B$. Hence $\Delta \vDash A \to B$. ■

14.3 Goal Directed Formulation of *AB* Relevance

This section gives a goal directed formulation for the AB-relevance logic of the previous section. We need this formulation in order to add the mechanisms of *abduction* and *failure.*

A database in AB-relevance logic will have the form for a labelled set of wffs. The labels are atomic name labels a_i for different assumptions but are annotated as $+a_i$ or $-a_i$, the sign signifying whether the assumption has been used in the proof or not.

Let us explain again (see examples 12.9 and 13.3) the idea of a goal directed proof in our context, before giving the formal definition.

Suppose we have a database of formulas of the form

1. $(c \to a) \to c$
2. $(c \to a)$

and we want to prove a. We can go forward and use *modus ponens* between (1) and (2) and get

3. c

and then use *modus ponens* again between (2) and (3) and get

4. a

This is a forward proof, and corresponds to definition 14.3.

To go goal directed, we observe that every wff B of the logic has the form $A_1 \to (A_2 \to \ldots \to (A_n \to q)\ldots)$, where q is atomic or $\bot$. q is called the *head* of the formula and $A_1, \ldots, A_n$ comprise the *body.*

If we want to prove q from the database, we can take the goal-directed approach, and look for clauses in the database with head q and try to prove the wffs in the body. The body wffs may have the form $Y = (X_1 \to \ldots \to (X_m \to r)\ldots))$. To prove Y we use the deduction theorem, add $X_1, \ldots, X_m$ to the database and try and prove r.

Such an algorithm is given in definition 14.9. The algorithm is indeed complete for the known $\to, \bot$ fragment of relevance logic and gives a very strong *Cut theorem,* built in by definition.

Let us see how our example will prove a in a goal directed way. We write the comptuation in the following form: data?goal.

Example 14.15

$$(c \to a) \to c, c \to a?a$$

from the second clause we get

$$(c \to a) \to c, c \to a?c$$

from the first clause we get

$$(c \to a) \to c, c \to a?c \to a$$

from the deduction theorem we get

$$c \to (c \to a) \to c, c \to a, c?a$$

from the second clause we get:

$$(c \to a) \to c, c \to a, c?c$$

and we can succeed using the third clause.

Since we need to use *all* data in relevance logic, we must annotate the data as used. Let $+B$ mean that B was used and $-B$ mean that B has not yet been used. The following is the computation with these annotations.

$$\begin{array}{l} -((c \to a) \to c), -(c \to a)?a \\ -((c \to a) \to c), +(c \to a)?c \\ +((c \to a) \to c), +(c \to a)?c \to a \\ +((c \to a) \to c), +((c \to a), -c?a \\ +((c \to a) \to c), +(c \to a), -c?c \end{array}$$

Success by using $-c$ and indeed all the other data have been used.

Note that we have two options for declaring immediate success of $?c$. We need $+c$ to be in the database. We also need to watch whether the rest of the data has been used. If we insist on that we get $\vdash_{1R}$ of definition 14.5. If we do not insist on that we get $\vdash_{3R}$ of definition 14.5.

Definition 14.16

1. *A database Δ is a set of signed labelled formulas of the form $\pm a_i : A_i$, where a_i are all pairwise disjoint atoms.*

2. *We define the predicate* Success$(\Delta, A) = 0$ *or 1 where Δ is a database, A a wff. We also keep implicit the complexity of the computation.*

   (a) *Immediate success (one step success)*
   Success$(\Delta, A) = 1$ *immediately if $A = q$ is atomic and $\pm a : q' \in \Delta$ where q' is either q or $\bot$. This condition corresponds to $\vdash_{3R}$. If we want $\vdash_{1R}$ we must insist here that all other clauses in Δ are of the form $+b : B$, i.e., with positive labels. We also say that $\pm a : q'$ was used at this step.*

(b) *Immediate failure*
Success$(\Delta, q) = 0$ *immediately if the following holds: for the case of* $\vdash_{1R}$ *we want either (i) or (ii) to hold. For the case of* $\vdash_{3R}$ *we want clause i to hold.*

i. $\pm a : A_1 \to (A_2 \to \cdots \to (A_n \to q') \cdots)$ *is not in* Δ *for any sequence* A_i.
This means that q' *is not the head of any clause in* Δ, *where* q' *is either* q *or* $\perp$.

ii. *Although* q' *is not the head of any complex clause in* Δ *(i.e.,* $A_1 \to (\cdots \to (A_n \to q') \cdots)$, *with* $n \geq 1$*),* q' *is in* Δ *in the form of* $\pm a : q'$, *but there are other unused clauses in* Δ *of the form* $-b : B$, *and so we cannot declare success nor can we continue with other clauses in the hope that the other unused data will be used. In this case all clauses of the form* $\pm a : q'$ *are said to be used. Again,* q' *is either* q *or* $\perp$.

(c) *Deduction theorem case for success/failure for* $\to$
Success$(\Delta, A_1 \to (\cdots \to (A_n \to q) \cdots)) = x$ *iff* Success$(\Delta + A_1 + \ldots + A_n, q) = x$ *where* $x = 0$ *or* $x = 1$ *and* $\Delta + A_1 + \ldots + A_n$ *is the database obtained from* Δ *by inserting into it the items* $-a_1 : A_1, \ldots, -a_n : A_n$, *where* a_i *are* completely new *atomic names. No clause is used in this case.*

(d) Unification case for success
Success$(\Delta, q) = 1$, *using at most* $n + 1$ *steps, if for some* $\pm a : A_1 \to (\ldots \to (A_n \to q') \ldots)$ *(called the* deduction clause*) in* Δ, *(where* $q' = q$ *or* $q' = \perp$*) the following holds:*

- *The database* Δ *can be split into* n *databases (not necessarily disjoint)*[3] *such that* $\Delta = \bigcup_i \Delta_i$ *and for each* i Success $(\Delta'_i, A_i) = 1$ *using at most* n *steps, where* Δ'_i *is obtained from* Δ_i *by switching the label* $\pm a$ *of the deduction clause into* $+a$ *(should it appear in* Δ_i*).*[4] *We say the deduction clause was used in this step.*

(e) Unification case for failure
Success$(\Delta, q) = 0$, *using at most* $n+1$ *steps if for* each *candidate deduction clause* $\pm a : A_1 \to (\ldots \to ((A_n \to q') \ldots)$ *(where* q' *is* q *or* $\perp$*), the following holds:*

- *for* each *decomposition* $\Delta = \bigcup \Delta_i$, *as described in the preceding item (d) there exists an* $1 \leq i \leq n$ *such that* Success

[3] For the case of linear logic, we can give up the signed labels and accept at this stage the requirement that Δ_i are disjoint and $\Delta - \{a : A_1 \to \ldots \to (A_n \to q') \ldots)\} = \bigcup_{i=1}^{n} \Delta_i$.
[4] At this point we can allow for other adjustments, to obtain different logics.

$(\Delta'_i, A_i) = 0$ *using at most* n *steps.*

We say this step has used all *the candidate deduction clauses.*

The next example will show how the computation works.

Example 14.17 Let $\Delta = \{-a_1 : A_1, -a_2 : A_1, -a_3 : A_1 \to (A_2 \to B)\}$. Then success (Δ, B) if $\bigvee_{i=1}^{2} \bigwedge_{j=1}^{2} Success(\Delta^i_j, A_j)$ where

$$\Delta^1_i = \{-a_i : A_1, +a_3 : A_1 \to (A_2 \to B\}$$
$$\Delta^2_1 = \varnothing, \Delta^2_2 = \{-a_1 : A_1, -a_2 : A_1 + a_3 : A_1 \to (A_2 \to B)\}$$

Both options $i = 1, i = 2$ of division fail to yield success. The reason for this is that there are two copies of A_1 in the database and no copy of A_2.

We need a lemma for future reference

Lemma 14.18 *Assume* $\text{Success}(\Delta \cup \{+y : C\}, q) = 1$. *Then either also* $\text{Success}(\Delta \cup \{-y : C\}, q) = 1$ *or* $\text{Success}(\Delta, q) = 1$.

Proof. The idea of the proof is simple: if $+y : C$ is used in the computation then we can replace $+y : C$ by $-y : C$, or if $+y : C$ is not used at all, then we can throw it out altogether. The proof is by induction on the computation.

1. *Case one step success*
   In this case for some $\pm a' : q' \in \Delta \cup \{+y : C\}$, we have $q' = q$ or $q' = \bot$ and in the case of $\vdash_{1R}$ all other members of $\Delta \cup \{+y : C\}$ have positive labels. If $\pm a' : q' \neq +y : C$ then also $Success(\Delta, q) = 1$ in one step. If $\pm a' : q' = y : C$, then we also have a one step success of $Success(\Delta \cup \{-y : C\}, q) = 1$.

2. *Case m step success*
   In this case for some $\pm a : A_1 \to (\ldots \to (A_n \to q')\ldots)$ with $q' = q$ or $q' = \bot$ we have $Success(\Delta'_i, A_i) = 1$ where $\Delta \cup \{+y : C\} = \bigcup_i \Delta_i$ and Δ'_i is obtained from Δ_i, by switching Δ_i the label $\pm a$ into $+a$ in case the deduction clause is in Δ_i. We distinguish several subcases.

   (a) In this subcase we have that $+y : C$ is used in the computation and the deduction clause $\pm a : A_1 \to (\ldots \to (A_n \to q')\ldots)$ is the same as $+y : c$. In this case it is clear that $Success(\Delta \cup \{-y : C\}, q) = 1$, because $-y$ turns into $+y$ immediately.

   (b) In this subcase $+y : C$ is used, but it is not the deduction clause. Let $\{\Delta'_j\}$ be the sets in which $+y : C$ appears. If $+y : c$ is not used in the computation of $Success(\Delta'_j, A_n) = 1$ then by the induction hypothesis it can be deleted to form $\Delta''_j = \Delta'_j - \{+y : C\}$ and we have *Success*$(\Delta''_j, A_j) = 1$. If $+y : c$ is not used in the computation then let $\Delta'_j = (\Delta'_j - \{+y : C\}) \cup \{-y : C\}$. By the induction hypothesis *Success*$(\Delta''_j, A_j) = 1$. Note that $+y : C$ *must* be used in at least one *Success*(Δ'_j, A_j) for otherwise it is not used at all.

We now have that *Success*$(\Delta \cup \{-y : C\}, q) = 1$, using the deduction clause $\pm a : A_1 \to \ldots \to (A_n \to q')$ and the *new* partition

$$\Delta^*_i = \begin{cases} \Delta_i & \text{if} \quad +y : C \notin \Delta_i \\ \Delta''_i & \text{if} \quad +y : C \in \Delta_i \end{cases}$$

Clearly $\bigcup \Delta^*_i = (\cup \Delta_i - \{+y : C\}) \cup \{-y : C\}$.

(c) In this subcase $+y : C$ is not used at all in the computation. The proof of (b) above shows that if $+y : C$ is not used then it is not used in any *Success*$(\Delta_i, A_i) = 1$, and hence can be deleted.

3. *Case deduction theorem step*
The case of q not atomic reduces to the case of q atomic by the deduction rule. ■

The goal directed computation allows for metalevel mechanisms to be added to the logic by following the inductive definition of the computation. First we add negation as failure.

Definition 14.19 *Let us add the connective* $\neg B$ *to the language. We thus allow for wffs of the form* $\neg B$ *as well as* $(B \to \bot)$. *These are not the same. We modify definition 14.16 by adding case (f) in item (2) as follows:*

(f) Case of negation $\neg$
Success$(\Delta, \neg B) = x$ *iff* Success$(\Delta, B) = 1 - x$.

No clause is used in this step.

Example 14.20 We have

$$q, q \vdash_{1R} \neg q$$

because q fails from $\{q, q\}$, since not all data is used.

The above definitions and example suggest that we work with $\vdash_{3R}$ and not insist on all data being used, as long as we keep a record of what was used. We should also supply a definition of what it means to be used during a proof of failure. This can be done by induction since definition 14.16 says explicitly what is being used at each stage of the computation. Note that if

$\Delta?q$ fails, then each candidate deduction clause (see definition 14.16, item 2(e)) must be used in order to ascertain that each avenue that might lead to success indeed fails. So in the previous example of $q, q \vdash_{1R} \neg q$ both copies of q are used. We try the first q and fail because the second q is not used; and similarly for the second q.

We now turn to abduction. Consider $A?B \to A$. This query fails, since $A, B \nvdash A$. This example is one of the main non-theorems of relevance logic and it is important that it remains a non-theorem.

However, suppose we receive reliable information that $\Delta = \{A\}$ should prove $B \to A$. This means that Δ is not exactly right and it really should be Δ'. How do we find Δ'? The process of abduction is supposed to help us to do that.

In other words, the abduction process is a multifunction algorithm which takes a database Δ and a goal G such that $\Delta \nvdash G$ and yields a family $\{\Delta'_1, \Delta'_2, \ldots\}$ of *related* databases (to Δ) such that for each Δ'_i we have $\Delta'_i \vdash G$. A detailed study of abduction is worked out in the next volume of this series of books [Gabbay and Woods, 2004a] but meanwhile let us agree on a policy for the case $\Delta = \{A\}$ and $G = (B \to A)$. As we mentioned,

$$A \vdash B \to A \text{ iff } A, B \vdash A.$$

To make amends, we can delete B, but doing so has two weaknesses.

1. It is against the *spirit* of relevance to delete B

2. Since we need to modify $\Delta = \{A\}$, so that $B \to A$ becomes provable, we would need to add to Δ the instruction to delete B when it appears (Say, by adding *Delete*(B) to Δ; but then we need a logic of deletion. This is tackled in [Gabbay and Woods, 2004a]).

We can avoid difficulties (1) and (2) as follows:

Since $B \to A$ is supposed to succeed from Δ and A can be proved from $\Delta_1 \subseteq \Delta$ without B, it must be that B is relevant to support the base Δ_1 which yields A. Hence we must add to our database the datum $B \to \Delta_1 = \{B \to X | X \in \Delta_1\}$.

So, the abduced database will be $\{A, B \to A\}$.

We need to get

$$A, B \to A \vdash ?B \to A$$

This still does not succeed because

$$B, A, B \to A \nvdash A$$

since only one copy of A is used. One can of course add $A \to (A \to A)$ so as to use the additional A,[5] but we think it is better to pass to a logic where 'used' is interpreted by 'content' rather than by form. This we do in section 14.5.

Now let us give the formal definition which does the job. Observe carefully clause (1) of the definition.

Definition 14.21 (The abduce function) *The function* $\mathbf{Ab}^+(\Delta, A)$ *tells us what to add to the database to make* A *succeed from* Δ. *For convenience we record the new databases as* $\Delta'_i, = 1, 2, \ldots$. *Therefore what we add is* $(\Delta'_i - \Delta)$.

$\mathbf{Ab}^+(\Delta, A)$ *is a set of alternative update actions, each of which changes* Δ *to a new database* Δ' *which proves* A. *We write it as*

$$\mathbf{Ab}^+(\Delta, A) = \{\Delta'_i\}.$$

The definition of $\mathbf{Ab}^+$ *is recursive on the computation stages of* Success $(\Delta, A) = 0$.

For notational convenience we let $\mathbf{Ab}^+(\Delta, A) = \{\Delta\}$, *when* $\Delta \vdash A$, *i.e., when* $\text{Success}(\Delta, A) = 1$.

1. *Consider the case of immediate failure of atomic* q *from* Δ. *We need to define* $\mathbf{Ab}^+(\Delta, q)$. *Let* Δ *be* $\{\pm x_1 : A_1, \ldots, \pm x_n : A_n\}$. *In this case let* y *be a new atomic label and add the clause* $y : A_1 \to (\ldots \to (A_n \to q) \ldots)$ *to* Δ *to form* Δ', *the abduced set.*

2. *Consider* $\text{Success}(\Delta, (A_1 \to (\ldots \to (A_n \to B) \ldots))$. *This fails iff Success*
   $(\Delta + A_1 + \cdots + A_n), B)$ *fails.*
   $\mathbf{Ab}^+(\Delta + A_1, + \cdots + A_n, B)$ *gives us options* $\Delta'_1, \ldots, \Delta'_m$ *of how to extend* $\Delta + A_1 + \cdots + A_n$ *to make* B *provable. Let* $\Delta'_i = \{\pm a^i_j : X_{i,j}\}$.
   Then let $A_1 \to \ldots \to (A_n \to \Delta'_i) \ldots)$ *be the theory*

$$\Delta^*_i = \{\pm a^i_j : A_1 \to (\ldots \to (A_n \to X_{i,j}) \ldots)\}.$$

---

[5]We want to ensure

$$A \vdash ?B \to A$$

we abduce

$$B \to A, A \to (A \to A).$$

We thus have

$$B \to A, A \to (A \to A), A \vdash ?B \to A$$

iff

$$B \to A, A \to (A \to A), A, B \vdash ?A$$

which indeed holds.

Then we define

$$\mathbf{Ab}^+(\Delta, A_1 \to \ldots \to (A_n \to B)\ldots) = \{\Delta_i^*\}$$

3. *Assume* $\text{Success}(\Delta, q) = 0$ *because for every candidate deduction clause* $Z = \pm a : (A_1 \to \ldots \to (A_n \to q)\ldots)$ *in* Δ *and any division of* $\Delta = \bigcup_i +\Delta_i^Z$ *there exists some* i *such that* $\text{Success}(\Delta_i, A_i) = 0$. *Let* $\mathbf{Ab}^+(\Delta_i, A_i)$ *be the abduced family for this case and recall that we can let* $\mathbf{Ab}^+(\Delta_i, A_i) = \{\Delta_i\}$ *if* $\Delta_i \vdash A$.

   We let $\mathbf{Ab}^+(\Delta, q)$ *be* $\bigcup_{\text{all clauses } Z \text{ and all divisions}} \bigcup_i \mathbf{Ab}^+(\Delta_i, A_i)$.

Theorem 14.22 (Soundness of abduction) *Let* $\Delta' \in \mathbf{Ab}^+(\Delta, A)$. *Then* $\text{Success}(\Delta \cup \Delta', A) = 1$.

Proof. By induction on the recursive definition of $\mathbf{Ab}^+$. ■

Note that the abduction function offers us several options of what we can add to the database. We need a special logic for deciding which option to take. We call this logic the *background logic* (for the abduction mechanism). Volume 2 of our current series *A Practical Logic of Cognitive Systems*, deals exclusively with abduction and, as we have mentioned, is entitled *The Reach of Abduction*. For the moment the reader should note that the notion of relevance is involved in the background logic. We choose to abduce a set which is relevant. This now involves a circularity of concepts. To explain relevance we need a basic logic which involves the mechanism of abduction, which in turn needs the notion of relevance for its background logic.

This circularity is not a problem for our model construction. We begin with a simple notion of abduction, say $\mathbb{A}_1$ and use it to model relevance $\mathbb{R}_1$. Then we use $\mathbb{R}_1$ to improve the notion of abduction to $\mathbb{A}_2$, etc., and we get better and better notions of relevance and abduction.

Suppose $\Delta \nvdash A$. Let $\Delta'_1, \ldots, \Delta'_k$ be the abduced sets according to definition 14.21. Let $\Theta'{}_i = \Delta'_i - \Delta$ be our options of what we need to add to Δ to make A provable. If our language contains $\to$ only, then we need not worry about conjunctions and can count the number of wffs in each Θ'_i. Let B be a new wff and consider $\Delta \cup \{B\}$. Let $\Theta''_i \subseteq \Theta'_i$ be the subset of all wffs of Θ'_i that are not provable from $\Delta \cup \{B\}$. We can use the difference $\Theta'_i - \Theta''_i, i = 1, \ldots$ to measure how 'helpful' B is in getting (proving) A. This notion can be used later (section 15.2) to define the notion of *degree of relevance* (of B).

14.4 Properties of the Goal Directed Formulation

We begin by proving the cut theorem for the goal directed formulation of relevance implication. Using cut we will show that the goal directed formulation defines the same logic as the Hilbert system of definition 14.9. We will also show that the system is complete for the semantics of definition 14.13. Having the semantics for the logic will allow us to introduce conditionals and the modalities into our logic without having to extend the goal directed computation to these connectives. This will enable us to use the logic in the model of agenda relevance of definition 15.16 below.

If we look at the algorithm of definition 14.16, we see that a database Δ is a set of signed wffs of the form $\pm b : B$. We must bear this in mind when we formulate the cut theorem. $-y : C$ is the cut formula and because we are dealing here with relevance logic, we assume it has a negative label, i.e., it is actually being used in the proof.

Note that we use set theoretic union for labelled databases, so $\Gamma \cup \Gamma = \Gamma$.

Theorem 14.23 *Let* $\text{Success}(\Delta, A) = 1$ *be the metapredicate of definition 14.16. Then (1) and (2) imply (3):*

1. $\text{Success}(\Delta \cup \{-y : C\}, q) = 1$

2. $\text{Success}(\Gamma, C) = 1$

3. $\text{Success}(\Delta \cup \Gamma, q) = 1$

Proof.

1. To prepare the ground for the proof, we examine (1). The computation in (1) has to 'use' a formula $\pm d : D \in \Delta \cup \{-y : C\}$. Write D as $D_1 \to (\ldots \to (D_k \to q')\ldots)$, with $q' = q$ or $\bot$ and with the understanding that $D_1, \ldots, D_k$ may not appear (i.e., $k = 0, D = q$). There are two possibilities for $\pm d : D$. $\pm d : D = -y : c$ or $\pm d : D \neq -y : c$. Our proof will distinguish these two cases. We use induction on the complexity, namely on the number of stages (unifications) in the proof of (1) and the structural compexity of C.

2. *Case (1) succeeds immediately and C arbitrary*
   In this case for some $\pm d : q'$ we have $\Delta \cup \{\pm y : C\} = \Delta_1 + \{\pm d : q'\}$ and all labels of Δ_1 are positive.

   Subcase $\pm d : q$ uses $\pm y : C$. In this subcase $d = y$ and $C = q$ or $C = \bot$ and all labels in Δ are positive. Hence (3) follows from (2).

Subcase $\pm d : q \in \Delta$
This case is not possible since the label $-y$ of C is negative.

3. *Case* C=*atom* p *or* $\bot$ *and the computation of (1) is arbitrary*
This case is proved by induction on the number of stages in the computation of (1).

Subcase a: (1) succeeds in one step
This follows from case (2)

Subcase b: q *unifies with a formula* $\pm d : D$ *as described in case (1).*

Subsubcase b1: $\pm d : D = -y : C$
In this subsubcase we have $C = p = q$ or $C = p = \bot$ and $d = y$ and

$$Success(\Delta \cup \{-y : q\}, q) = 1$$

since the computation goes through $D = -y : p$, it must succeed in one step and hence we are back to subcase (1).

Subsubcase b2: $\pm d : D \neq -y : C$
Let $D = D_1 \to (\ldots \to (D_k \to q')\ldots)$ with $q' = q$ or $q' = \bot$ and we know that the database $\Delta \cup \{-y : C\}$ can be presented as $\Delta_1 \cup \ldots \cup \Delta_k$ such that $Success(\Delta_i^+, D_i) = 1$ for $i = 1, \ldots, k$, where Δ_i^+ is like Δ_i except that $\pm d : D$ is now $+d : D$. By the induction hypothesis on the computation we have that for all i, $Success(\Delta_i', D_i) = 1$ where $\Delta_i' = \Delta_i^+$if $-y : C$ is not in Δ_i and $\Delta_i' = (\Delta_i^+ - \{-y : C\}) \cup \Gamma$, for the case that $-y : C \in \Delta_i$.

But since $\pm d : D \neq -y : C$, the above shows that (3) of the theorem holds.

4. *Case* C *is arbitrary and the computation in(1) is arbitrary*
Assume by induction that the cut theorem holds for any subformula C' of C and any complexity of computation and for the case of C for any lesser complexity of computation of (1). We now prove the theorem for C and the complexity of (1).

Subcase $\pm d : D \neq -y : C$

This subcase proceeds as in subsubcase (b2) of (3)
Subcase $\pm d : D = -y : C$
In this case we have $d = y$ and $D = C$ and for each $1 \leq j \leq k$

(*) $Success(\Delta_j^+, D_j) = 1$

where $\bigcup \Delta_j^+ = \Delta \cup \{+y : C\}$.

Assume without loss of generality that $+y : C \in \Delta_j^+, j \leq r$ and that $\Delta_j^+ \subseteq \Delta$ for $r < j \leq k$.

Let us take a closer look at (2) of the theorem, knowing that $D = C$. This means that

$$Success(\Gamma, D_1 \to \ldots \to (D_k \to q') \ldots)) = 1$$

where $q' = q$ or $q' = \perp$.

Therefore for some new labels $-d_1, \ldots, -d_k$ we have

(**) $Success(\Gamma \cup \{-d_j : D_j\}, q') = 1$

We are now ready to use the induction hypothesis. First consider (*) for $i \leq j \leq r$. We have in this case

$$\Delta_j^+ = \Delta_j^0 \cup \{+y : C\}$$

where $\Delta_j^0 \subseteq \Delta$.

By a previous lemma 14.18 we have because of (*) that either

(*1) $Success(\Delta_j^0 \cup \{-y : C\}, D_j) = 1$

or

(*2) $Success(\Delta_j^0, D_j) = 1$

hold.

For $r \leq j \leq k$ we have that (*2) holds.

In case (*1) holds, we can use the induction hypothesis for a simpler computation on (1) of the theorem and get[6]

(*3) $Success(\Delta_j^0 \cup \Gamma, D_j) = 1$

Now armed with either (*2) or (*3) for each j, we can join with (**) and the induction hypothesis for subformulas of C and get by simultaneous (or repeated) use of cut that

$$Success(\bigcup_{j \leq r} \Gamma \cup \Delta_j^0 \cup \bigcup_{r \leq j} \Delta_j, q') = 1$$

i.e., $Success(\Gamma \cup \Delta, q') = 1$.

If $q' = q$ we are finished. If $q' = \perp$ then we also have $Success(\Gamma \cup \Delta, q) = 1$, and we are also finished. ■

[6](1) is for atoms, but using the induction step will not increase complexity!

Definition 14.24 *Consider the notion of* $\{A_1, \ldots, A_n\} \vdash_0 B$ *if* Success$(\{-x_1 : A_1, \ldots, -x_n : A_n\}, B) = 1$ *where* x_i *are all different atomic labels and* $\{A_1, \ldots, A_n\}$ *is a multiset. Let* $\vdash$ *be as defined in definition 14.10. Then* $\vdash_0 = \vdash$.

Proof. First show that $\vdash_0$ holds for all the axioms and rules of $\vdash$. This shows that $\vdash \subseteq \vdash_0$.

We now show that if $\Delta \not\vdash_0 B$ then $\Delta \not\vdash B$.

Let $\mathcal{S}$ be the family of all sets Δ of wffs including the empty set. Define $\models_0$ on $\mathcal{S}$ by

- $\Delta \models_0 q$ iff $\Delta \vdash_0 q$

using the cut rule for $\vdash_0$ we show that for any A

$$A \models_0 A \text{ iff } \Delta \vdash_0 A.$$

Since $\Delta \not\vdash_0 B$, we have $\Delta \not\models_0 B$ and hence since we have a model of $\vdash$ as well (see definition 14.13) we get $\not\vdash B$. ■

Definition 14.25 (Adding modality to relevance logic) *Since we have a semantical interpretation for our system, we can define a logic with* $\rightarrow, \bot$ *and* $\Box$. *It is easy to do it semantically though some effort may be required to extend the goal directed proof theory and show completeness. Consider a tree of models of the form* $(T, <, t_0, \mathcal{S}_t, h_t)$ *with* t_0 *the root of the tree and where for each* $t, (\mathcal{S}_t, h_t)$ *is a relevance model (a family of sets). We need to assume that* $t < s$ *implies* $\mathcal{S}_t \subseteq \mathcal{S}_s$.

Define satisfaction as follows

- $(t, X) \models q$ *iff* $h_t(X, q) = 1$ *for* q *atomic.*
- $(t, X) \models A \rightarrow B$ *iff for any* $Y \in \mathcal{S}_t$ *such that* $(t, Y) \models A$, *we have that* $(t, X \cup Y) \models B$.
- $(t, X) \models \Box A$ *iff for all* $s > t, (s, X) \models A$.
- *We say the model satisfies* A *iff* $(t_0, \varnothing) \models A$

Remark 14.26 We can define a conditional $A \twoheadrightarrow B$ in the model of the previous definition by $(t, X) \models A \twoheadrightarrow B$ iff for any point s of the same height as t from the root t_0 we have that if $(s, X) \models A$ then $(s, X) \models B$.

Theorem 14.27 (Interpolation for relevance) *Let $\mathbb{L}_1, \mathbb{L}_2$ be two languages based on two sets of atoms with some non-empty common language $\mathbb{L}$ and the connectives $\to, \bot$. Let Δ_1, Δ_2 be two theories in $\mathbb{L}_1$ and $\mathbb{L}_2$ resp. and let q_1 be an atom in language $\mathbb{L}_1$. Assume that $\Delta_1 \cup \Delta_2 \vdash_0 q_1$. Then for some Θ in the common language we have $\Delta_2 \vdash_0 \Theta$ and $\Delta_1 \cup \Theta \vdash q_1$, where $\Delta_2 \vdash_0 \Theta$ means that for each $\alpha \in \Theta$ there exist $\Delta_\alpha \subseteq \Delta_2$ such that $\Delta_\alpha \vdash_0 \alpha$ and $\bigcup_{\alpha \in \Theta} \Delta_\alpha = \Delta_2$.*

Proof. By induction on the goal directed complexity of the proof of q_1 from $\Delta_1 \cup \Delta_2$.

(1) *Immediate success*
q_1 unifies with $q_1' = q_1$ or $q_1' = \bot$.
If $\pm a : q_1' \in \Delta_1$ then $\Delta_2 = \varnothing$ and $\pm a : q_1 = \Delta_1$.
If $\pm a : q_1' \in \Delta_2$ then $\pm a : q_1' = \Delta_2$ is in the common language and $\Delta_1 = \varnothing$ and q_1' is the interpolant.

(2) *General case*

Subcase 1
q_1 unifies with a clause $\pm a : A_1 \to (\ldots \to (A_n \to q_1') \ldots)$ in Δ_1 with $q_1' = q_1$ or $q_1' = \bot$. Then there are $\Gamma_1, \ldots, \Gamma_n$ as in definition 14.16 item (d) such that *Success*$(\Gamma_i', A_i) = 1$ and Γ_i' is related to Γ_i as in that definition. We know that

$$\Gamma_i = \Delta_{1,i} \cup \Delta_{2,i}$$

where $\Delta_{1,i}$ is in $\mathbb{L}_1$ and $\Delta_{2,i}$ is in $\mathbb{L}_2$.

By the induction hypothesis there exist interpolants Θ_i in the common language. Our interpolant is $\Theta = \bigcup_i \Theta_i$.

Subcase 2
q_1 unifies with $\pm a : A_1 \to \ldots \to (A_n \to q_1') \ldots)$ from Δ_2. This means that either $q_1' = q_1$ is in the common language or $q_1' = \bot$.

Again by the induction hypothesis there are $\Theta_1', \ldots, \Theta_n'$ in the common language such that $\Delta_{1,i} \vdash \Theta_i'$ and so

$$\Delta_1 \vdash \bigcup \Theta_i' = \Theta$$

and

$$\Theta + \Delta_2 \vdash q_1'$$

and

$$q_1' \vdash q_1.$$

By the deduction theorem

$$\Delta_2 \vdash \Theta \to q_1'$$

Since $\Delta_1 \vdash \Theta$ we have $\Delta_1 \cup \{\Theta \to q_1'\} \vdash q_1'$ and hence

$$\Delta_1 \cup \{\Theta \to q_1'\} \vdash q_1$$

■

Remark 14.28 Interpolation is important for relevance. It says that if $A \vdash B$, then there is some C in the common language such that $A \vdash C$ and $C \vdash B$. So A has something in common with B.

14.5 Deductive Relevance

This section introduces a modified version of relevance logic, the logic of *deductive relevance*, briefly touched on in Section 14.1. We start by further motivating it. Consider a non-empty database. Assume that from time to time the database is updated. The reason for the updating is that there seems to be a change of mind concerning whether a certain formula should be in the database. For example A could be 'Harry paid the invoice' and at different times there might be a change of view as to whether A is true or not. We can play it safe and insert into the database all updates, with the appropriate labels indicating when they were received. Thus the formulas A and $negA$ may both appear in the database with different time labels

$$\begin{array}{ll} t_i : A & i = 1, \ldots, k \\ s_i : \neg A & i = 1, \ldots, m \end{array}$$

where t_i, s_i are different time labels.

In general, a database of this sort will have the form $\Delta = \{t_i : A_i\}$ where t_i are labels and A_i are formulas. This database looks just like any other labelled database we have considered so far in this chapter. When we prove a formula B from the database, we want to keep track of exactly what labelled formulas were used. If we do that, we can know which version of the data was used in the derivation. The labelled deduction process is the same as in the case of AB-relevance logic. In AB-relevance logic we are interested in resource considerations, we want to make sure that all assumptions are used; we are also interested in making sure that the most recent updates were used. Consider the example below:

Example 14.29

Data:

$t_1 : A$

$t_2 : \neg A$

$s_1 : A \to B$
$s_2 : B \to \neg A$
$s_3 : \neg A \to (C \to B)$

Query: $C \to B$?

We can understand the above data as t-labelled updates of the data and s-labelled updates of the rule.

We assume $t_1 < t_2$ and $s_1 < s_2 < s_3$. We seek a derivation of $C \to B$ using the most recent data. This we do by modus ponens, which gives $s_3 t_2 : C \to B$.

			$\underline{B}$
	$a : C$	assumption	
	$s_3 t_2 : C \to B$		
	$s_3 t_2 a : B$		
Exit	$s_3 t_2 : C \to B$		

We can pretend that we are operating in relevant logic, if we agree that we are dealing with relevant classes of data, namely $\{t_1, t_2\}$ and $\{s_1, s_2, s_3\}$. Whenever a label x is used from a given class, this 'use' of the label is considered as using all lower ('past') labels. Thus in the above proof, $C \to B$ can be considered as a relevant derivation, because all labels were used. t_2 and s_3 were directly used, while t_1, s_1 and s_2 were 'used' because a more recent update of that class was consulted.

The above example suggests that we can divide the labels into classes according to some agreed 'Labelling Logic', **LL**. **LL** helps us organize the classes of labels. When we prove any $\alpha : B$ from the database with label α, the logic **LL** will tell us whether α is considered as a relevant use of the database labels. In fact, **LL** may come as part of a package deal together with a labelling scheme. We label the data in some agreed manner compatible with the application area (e.g., Δ is a knowledge representation database for the application area). **LL** is a suitable logic for the labels of the application area.

The next example shows how the labels can be used as *degrees of certainty*.

Example 14.30 Consider the assumptions:

1. $a \wedge b \to d$

2. $a \to d'$

3. $a \wedge b \wedge c \to d'$

4. a

5. b

6. c

Let $\mathbf{P}(n)$ give the degree of certainty we attach to clause n. $0 \leq \mathbf{P}(n) \leq 1$. To deduce d' we can follows two paths: We can use clauses 3,4,5,6 and get $\{3,4,5,6\} : d'$, or we can use 4 and 2 and get $\{2,4\} : d'$. In each case we can get the requisite degree of certainty using $\mathbf{P}$.

The label indicates which clauses were used. In the second case, we can apply the relevance deduction theorem and get

$$\{clauses\ 1,3,4,5,6\} \vdash \{4\} : (a \to d') \to d'$$

But the proof of $d'_{\{2,4\}}$ does not justify:

$$\{clauses\ 1,2,3,4,5\} \vdash c \to d'.$$

The latter does hold, however, thanks to the other proof of $\{3,4,5,6\}$: d'.

Note therefore that we do *not* require that the assumption (for application of the deduction theorem) be used in *all* proofs but only in *at least one*.

In each case the degree of certainty is obtained from the labels. Obviously what we need is a general system of deductive relevance which depends generally on a labelling scheme and on a labelling logic **LL**, which can be specialized to the various familiar systems (such as relevance logic, fuzzy logic, etc.) by a suitable choice of the labels and the logic **LL**. The system in its full generality needn't have an intrinsic intuitive meaning, beyond that of having some logic or other on the labels. Each choice of labels and logic **LL** will, however, model some known system and some body of intuitions.

As a first step, we ask what logic **LL** would correspond to relevance logic itself. Let us recall the essential principle of the relevance labelling.

The relevance labelling follows the following principles:

1. All assumptions are named (labelled) using different atomic names. The *same* wff A may be put in with more than one name: e.g.,

$$n_1 : A$$

$$n_2 : A$$

This can arise, e.g., in failed attempts to prove $\vdash A \to (A \to A)$.

2. If A is labelled α and $A \to B$ is labelled β, then using *modus ponens* we emerge with B labelled $\alpha \cup \beta$ (because B uses in its proof both A and $A \to B$).

3. If we want to show $A \to B$, we assume A with name α (usually $\alpha = \{a\}$, with 'a' a new name). We prove forward B, which ends up, at the end of the proof, with label β. Then if $\alpha \subseteq \beta$, we can conclude $A \to B$ with label $\beta - \alpha$.

Thus in diagram

$$\begin{array}{l} \{a\} : A \\ \ldots \\ \ldots \\ \beta = \{a, b, c, \ldots\} : B \end{array}$$

allows us to deduce $A \to B$ with label $\{b, c\ldots\} = \beta - \{a\}$.

We can now make the following observation.

It is possible to regard $a \in \alpha$ as $\alpha \vdash a$ in the Boolean logic of the atomic labels $a, b, c, \ldots$. Since all labels involved are atoms, or sets of atoms, the set theoretic relation $\alpha \subseteq \beta$ is identical with the logical relation $\beta \vdash \alpha$, in any logic, e.g., classical logic.

The relevance logic procedure generalizes by allowing a *logic* **LL** (Labelling Logic) on the labels of the formulas. Imagine that each formula assumption gets a label a. When we use *modus ponens* we get:

$$\frac{\begin{array}{l} \alpha : A \\ \beta : A \to B \end{array}}{\alpha \wedge \beta : B} \quad \text{in the logic } \mathbf{LL}$$

To prove $A \to B$ with label γ we assume:

$$\frac{\begin{array}{l} \alpha : A \\ \ldots \\ \ldots \\ \beta : B \end{array}}{\gamma : A \to B}$$

We argue from A to B and want to exit with $A \to B$ with label γ. For A to be used in the proof of B we need

$$\beta \vdash_{\mathbf{LL}} \alpha$$

γ would then be

$$\gamma = \bigwedge \{\text{names of assumptions } x \mid \beta \vdash_{\mathbf{LL}} x \text{ and } \alpha \nvdash_{\mathbf{LL}} x\}$$

So, to be able to get γ effectively, we need **LL** to be computable, and of course that the number of assumptions be finite.

In the case of ordinary relevance logic, the general definition reduces to the old definition. To see this, note that if:

$\alpha = \{a_1, ..., a_n\}$ old definition

$\alpha^* = a_1 \wedge \ldots \wedge a_n$ new definition

Thus

$$(\alpha \cup \beta)^* = \alpha^* \wedge \beta^*$$

Since a_i, b_j are atoms, then if $\alpha \subseteq \beta$,

$$\beta - \alpha = \{a \mid \beta \vdash a \text{ and } \alpha \nvdash a\}$$

in the logic **LL** of classical conjunctions and classical truth tables.

Let us call the logic obtained from labelling on **LL** '**DR**(**LL**)', which denotes deductive relevance *based on* the labelling logic **LL**.

It may be convenient to name a formula A by the symbol 'a'. If A is syntactically different from B then 'a' and 'b' are considered different atomic names. If A is put in the database twice, then we must use different atomic names, rather than using 'a' twice. E.g., 'a_1' and 'a_2'.

Important remark

There is no reason why the labelling logic **LL** should be monotonic. It can be any non-monotonic system which allows for conjunctions, i.e., allows us to form

$$\frac{\alpha : A, \beta : A \to B}{\alpha \wedge \beta : B}$$

and which is decidable. Decidability is needed in order to form γ as shown:

$$\begin{array}{ll} \alpha : A & \\ \ldots & \beta \mid\!\sim \alpha \\ \ldots & \\ \beta : B & \\ \hline \gamma : A \to B, \ \gamma = \bigwedge\{x \mid \beta \mid\!\sim x \text{ and } \alpha \not\mid\!\sim x\} & \end{array}$$

$\mid\!\sim$ is the non-monotonic **LL**

Example 14.31

Show that $\vdash (B \to A) \to ((A \to B) \to (A \to B))$ in relevance logic.

To show that, we show that the assumptions

$a_1{:}B \to A$

$a_2{:}A \to B$

$a_3{:}A$

prove B with label $(a_1 a_2 a_3)$.

We leave this as an exercise.

To illustrate what we have in mind for our labelling logic, we use *relevance logic* itself as the labelling logic. Thus **R** is relevance logic and **D** = **DR**(**R**) is the resulting logic when relevance logic is used on the labels. We use the formulas themselves as their names: We thus want to show:

$$B \to A, A \to B, A \vdash_{\mathbf{D}} B \text{ with label } (B \to A) \wedge (A \to B) \wedge A.$$

Since $(B \to A) \wedge (A \to B) \wedge A \vdash_{\mathbf{R}} A$, we use the deduction theorem in **D** = **DR**(**R**) and obtain:

$$B \to A, A \to B \quad \vdash_{\mathbf{D}} A \to B \quad \text{with label } \gamma,$$

where

$$\gamma = \bigwedge\{x \mid x \text{ is a name and } (B \to A) \wedge (A \to B) \wedge A \vdash_{\mathbf{R}} x \text{ and } A \not\vdash_{\mathbf{R}} x\}$$

We have three names. $A \not\vdash_{\mathbf{R}} A \to B$ and $A \not\vdash_{\mathbf{R}} B \to A$, hence $\gamma = (A \to B) \wedge (B \to A)$. We can use the deduction theorem again and get:

$$B \to A \vdash_{\mathbf{D}} (A \to B) \to (A \to B) \text{ with label } B \to A$$

and again

$$\vdash_{\mathbf{D}} (B \to A) \to ((A \to B) \to (A \to B)).$$

Example 14.32 **DR**(**R**) is not the same as **R**. Consider the formula:

$$(A \to A) \to ((A \to A) \to (A \to A))$$

This is a theorem of **R**, because $A \to A, A \to A, A \vdash_{\mathbf{R}} A$ with label $(A \to A, A \to A, A)$ (using modus ponens twice). We also have by the deduction theorem

$$A \to A, A \to A \vdash_{\mathbf{R}} A \to A \text{ with label } (A \to A, A \to A)$$

$$A \to A \vdash_{\mathbf{R}} (A \to A) \to (A \to A) \text{ with label } (A \to A)$$

However in **D** = **DR**(**R**) the exit label is computed differently. This gives

$$A \to A \vdash_{\mathbf{D}} (A \to A) \to (A \to A) \text{ with label } \emptyset \text{ (emptyset \#)}$$

In fact, any theorem of **R** of the form $\vdash_{\mathbf{R}} A \to (B \to C)$ such that $\vdash_{\mathbf{R}} B \to A$ will not be a theorem of **D**.

Example 14.33 We now employ intuitionistic logic Int as the labelling logic in example 14.31, and abbreviate $\mathbf{D} = \mathbf{DR}(Int)$. This gives:

$$B \to A, A \to B, A \vdash_{\mathbf{D}} B \text{ with label } (B \to A) \wedge A \wedge (A \to B)$$

We here use the deduction theorem
$B \to A,\ A \to B \quad \vdash_{\mathbf{D}} A \to B$ with label γ.
$\gamma = \bigwedge\{x \mid (B \to A) \wedge A \wedge (A \to B) \vdash_{Int} x \text{ but } A \not\vdash_{Int} x\}$
Clearly $\gamma = \{A \to B\}$. In intuitionistic logic $A \vdash_{Int} B \to A$, which is not true in relevance logic. Thus we get
$B \to A \vdash_D (A \to B) \to (A \to B)$ with label γ
$\gamma = \bigwedge\{x \mid A \to B \vdash_{Int} x \text{ and } A \to B \nvdash_{Int} x\} = truth.$
We cannot use the deduction theorem any further. Hence, for the logic $\mathbf{DR}(Int)$, where the labelling logic is intuitionistic logic, we do *not* have:

1. $\vdash_{\mathbf{DR}(Int)} (B \to A) \to ((A \to B) \to (A \to B))$

On the other hand we *do* have

2. $\vdash_{\mathbf{DR}(Int)} A \to ((A' \to A') \to A)$

(1) is a theorem of relevance logic while (2) is not. We can see that we are getting something new. We have not proved yet that what we get is a logic. In fact we must show that for any monotonic logic **LL**, the logic **DR**(**LL**) is indeed a consequence relation. At the moment I have proof only for the case of $\mathbf{DR}(Int)$. The difficult part to prove is the cut:

$$\Delta \vdash_{\mathbf{DR}(Int)} A \text{ and } \Delta, A \vdash_{\mathbf{DR}(Int)} B \Rightarrow \Delta \vdash_{\mathbf{DR}(Int)} B$$

14.6 The Cut Rule for Deductive Relevance

To investigate the relationship between a logic **Z** and its deductive relevance counterpart **DR**(**Z**) in general and **DR**(Int) in particular we need to proceed to go through a series of definitions and lemmas.

Definition 14.34

1. *Define for a Hilbert system* **H**, *the notion* $\vdash_{\mathbf{H}} A$ *as follows:*
   $\vdash_{\mathbf{H}} A$ *iff there exists a sequence* $B_1, B_2, \ldots, B_n = A$ *such that each member of the sequence is either an instance of an axiom or is obtained from the two previous formulas of the sequence by modus ponens.*

2. *Define* $A_1, \ldots, A_n \vdash_{\mathbf{H}} B$ *as*

$$\vdash_{\mathbf{H}} A_1 \rightarrow (A_2 \rightarrow \ldots \rightarrow (A_n \rightarrow B)\ldots)$$

Note that this definition is independent of the order of A_i *because of the axiom*

$$\vdash (A \rightarrow (B \rightarrow C)) \rightarrow (B \rightarrow (A \rightarrow C))$$

Also note that $\vdash_{\mathbf{H}}$ *is non-monotonic, i.e.,* $A \vdash_{\mathbf{H}} A$ *may hold, but* $A, B \vdash_{\mathbf{H}} A$ *might not hold, because its meaning is* $\vdash_{\mathbf{H}} A \rightarrow (B \rightarrow A)$.

3. *To define a monotonic consequence relation based on* $\mathbf{H}$, *let* $A_1, \ldots, A_n, \Vdash_{\mathbf{H}} B$ *be defined to hold iff there exists a sequence of formulas* $B_1, \ldots, B_n = B$ *such that each member* B_i *is either an assumption* A_j *or a theorem,* $\vdash_{\mathbf{H}} B_i$, *or is obtained from two previous elements of the sequence by modus ponens.*
Note that in this case we will have a monotonic consequence relation $A, B \Vdash_{\mathbf{H}} A$ *will hold.*
We do have however:

$$\varnothing \Vdash_{\mathbf{H}} B \textit{ iff } \varnothing \vdash_{\mathbf{H}} B \textit{ iff } \vdash_{\mathbf{H}} B.$$

Definition 14.35

(a) A set of assumptions has the form $\Delta = \{a_i : A_i\}$, *where* A_i *are formulas and* a_i *are all different atomic labels.*

(b) We define by induction the notion of a proof tree of $\Delta \vdash t : B$, *where* t *is a label.*

(1) $\tau = \{\Delta \vdash t : B\}$ *is a one node tree if* $t : B \in \Delta$. *This node is the bottom node of the tree.*

(2) If τ_1 *is a proof tree with bottom node* $\Delta \vdash t : A$ *and* τ_2 *is a proof tree with bottom node* $\Delta \vdash s : A \rightarrow B$ *then*

$$\begin{array}{cc} \tau_1 & \tau_2 \\ \\ \\ \multicolumn{2}{c}{\Delta \vdash st : B} \end{array}$$

is a tree with bottom node $\Delta \vdash st : B$.

(3) If τ *is a tree with bottom node* $\Delta \cup \{a : A\} \vdash t : B$ *and* a *appears in the string* t *then:*

$$\begin{array}{c} \mathcal{T} \\ | \\ \Delta \vdash t - a : A \to B \end{array}$$

is a tree with bottom node $\Delta \vdash t - a : A \to B$.

(c) *We say* $A_1 \ldots A_n \vdash B$ *if for some distinct atomic labelling* $a_i : A_i$ *we have a proof tree for* $\{a_i : A_i\} \vdash a_1 \ldots a_n : B$

Theorem 14.36 *$A_1, \ldots, A_n \vdash B$ in the sense of (c) of definition 14.35 iff $A_1, \ldots, A_n \vdash_{\mathbf{H}} B$, for $\mathbf{H}$ being relevance logic in the sense of definition 14.34.*

Definition 14.37

1. *Let $\vdash$ be a non-monotonic consequence relation. $\vdash$ is said to be a* labelling logic *if it satisfies the following conditions:*

   (a) $\dfrac{\Delta \vdash B \,;\, \Delta' \vdash B \to C}{\Delta, \Delta' \vdash C}$

   (b) $\dfrac{\Delta, \Delta' \vdash D_2 \,;\, D_1 \vdash \bigwedge \Delta'}{\Delta, D_1 \vdash D_2}$

   (c) $\dfrac{\Delta, D_1 \vdash D_2}{\Delta \vdash D_1 \to D_2}$

2. *A Hilbert system I is said to be a* labelling logic *if $\vdash_I$ is a labelling logic. A labelling logic I (or $\vdash$) is said to be* monotonic *if $\vdash_I$ (resp. $\vdash$) is monotonic.*
   Note that for $\mathbf{H}$ = Relevance logic, $\vdash_{\mathbf{H}}$ is a labelling logic. $\Vdash_{\mathbf{H}}$ is a monotonic labelling logic.

3. *A* database *is a set of pairs of the form:*

$$\begin{array}{ccc} a_1 & : & A_1 \\ \ldots & & \\ \ldots & & \\ a_n & : & A_n \end{array}$$

   where a_i are all different atomic labels.

4. *Let I be a labelling logic, on the same language as the data. A function h on $\{a_i \mid a_i : A_i \in \Delta\}$ is a* logical support function *if $h(a_i)$ is a set of wff and $h(a_i) \vdash_I A_i$.*

Definition 14.38 *Let Δ be a database and h a support function and B a wff. We define the provability $\vdash^h_{n\mathbf{DR}(I)}$ by induction of n. The basic notion we are defining is*

$$\Delta \vdash^h_n B, \alpha, \pi$$

where Δ is a database with labelled wffs, B is the proved wff, α is a set of labels used in the proof and π is a set of wff of I, the logical support of $B; n = 0, 1, 2, \ldots$

Case n = 0

$\Delta \vdash^h_0 B, \alpha, \pi$ iff there exists a sequence $(B_i, \alpha_i, \pi_i), i = 1, \ldots, k$ with $(B_k, \alpha_k, \pi_k) = (B, \alpha, \pi)$ and each element in the sequence satisfies the following:

Condition 1:

$$a_i : B_i \in \Delta \text{ and } \pi_i = h(a_i) \text{ and } \alpha_i = \{a_i\}.$$

Condition 2:

There exist $B_j, B_m, j, m, < i$ such that $B_m = B_j \rightarrow B_i$ and $\alpha_i = \alpha_m \cup \alpha_j$ and $\pi_i = \pi_m \cup \pi_j$.

Case n+1

We now define $\Delta \vdash^h_{n+1} B, \alpha, \pi$.

The above holds if there is a sequence satisfying any of the above conditions (1) and (2) or the following additional condition (3):

Condition 3:

$B_k = D_1 \rightarrow D_2$ and

$\Delta' = \Delta \cup \{d : D_1 \mid d$ a new label $\} \cup \{b_j : B_j \mid b_j$ new labels and $j < k\}$,

$h' = h \cup \{(d, D_1)\} \cup \{(b_j, \pi_j)\}$

and

$\Delta' \vdash^{h'}_n D_2, \gamma, \pi_0$, for some $m \leq n$ and $\pi_0 \vdash_I D_1$ and $\alpha_k = \gamma - \{d\}$ and $\pi_k = \{x \in \pi_0 \mid D_1 \not\vdash_I x\}$.

Case n=∞:

Let $\Delta \vdash^h_n B, \alpha, \pi$ if for some $n, \Delta \vdash^h_n B, \alpha, \pi$.

Lemma 14.39 *Let Δ be a labelled database and let h be a support function. Let $U = U(\Delta, h)$ be $U = \bigcup_{(a:A)\in\Delta} h(a)$. For any α let $U_\alpha = \bigcup_{a\in\alpha} h(a)$. Then if $\Delta \vdash^h_n B, \alpha, \pi$ we have $\pi \subseteq U$ and $\pi \vdash_I B$. (In fact $\pi \subseteq \bigcup_{a\in\alpha} h(a) = U_\alpha$.)*

Proof. The proof is by induction on the definition of $\vdash^h_n$.

Case n=0:

Assume $\Delta \vdash^h_0 B, \alpha, \pi$. Then there is a sequence as in the definition. If $a_k : B_k \in \Delta$ then $\alpha_k = \{a_k\}$ and $\pi_k = h(a_k)$ and $\pi_k \vdash_I B_k$ and $\pi_k \subseteq U_{\alpha_k}$. If $B_m = B_j \rightarrow B_k$ then $\alpha_k = \alpha_m \cup \alpha_j$ and $\pi_k = \pi_m \cup \pi_j$ and since by the induction hypothesis $U_{\alpha_m} \supseteq \pi_m \vdash_I B_m$ and $U_{\alpha_j} \supseteq \pi_j \vdash_I B_j$ we get $U_{\alpha_k} \supseteq \pi_k \vdash_I B_k$.

Case n+1:

Assume $\Delta \vdash^h_{n+1} B, \alpha, \pi$. We check the case of $B = B_k = D_1 \to D_2$. We have $\Delta' = \Delta \cup \{(d : D_1)\} \cup \{(b_j : B_j) \mid j < k\}, h' = h \cup \{(d, D_1)\} \cup \{(b_j, \pi_j) \mid j < k\}$ and $\Delta' \vdash^{h'}_m D_2, \gamma, \pi_0$ for $m \le n$, and $U_\gamma \supseteq \pi_0 \vdash_I D_1$ and $\alpha_k = \gamma - \{d\}$ and $\pi_k = \{x \in \pi_0 \mid D_1 \not\vdash_I x\}$ and $U_{\alpha_j} \supseteq \pi_j \vdash_I B_j$, for $j < k$. We have to show that $U_{\alpha_k} \supseteq \pi$ and $\pi \vdash_I D_1 \to D_2$.

Consider all wffs in π_0. Classify them into two sets $\{x_i\}, \{y_j\}$, where $D_1 \vdash_I y_j$ and $D_1 \not\vdash x_i$, hence $\pi = \{x_i\}$. Clearly $\pi \subseteq U_{\alpha_k}$ since $D_1 \notin \pi$. We know that by the induction hypothesis we have:

$$\pi_0 = \bigwedge_i x_i \wedge \bigwedge_j y_j \vdash_I D_2.$$

Also since $D_1 \vdash_I \bigwedge y_j$ we get $\bigwedge x_i \wedge D_1 \vdash_I D_2$ and hence $\bigwedge x_i \vdash_I (D_1 \to D_2)$. ■

Lemma 14.40 *Assume that I is a monotonic labelling logic. Let $\underline{h} \supseteq h$ mean that for any label $a, \underline{h}(a) \supseteq h(a)$. Assume $\Delta \vdash^h_n B, \alpha, \pi$ then $\Delta \vdash^{\underline{h}}_n B, \alpha, \underline{\pi}$, where $\underline{\pi}$ satisfies $(\pi \cup U^*) \supseteq \pi_0 \supseteq \pi$ and $U = \bigcup_a \underline{h}(a)$ and $U^* = \bigcup_a (\underline{h}(a) - h(a))$.*

Proof. By induction on the proof of $\Delta \vdash^h_n B, \alpha, \pi$.

Case n=0:

$\Delta \vdash^h_n B, \alpha, \pi_i$. Then there exists a sequence as in the definition. Replace h by $\underline{h}$ and use the same sequence. We get a sequence with $\underline{\pi}$ satisfying the lemma.

Case n+1:

To show the lemma for $\Delta \vdash^h_{n+1} B, \alpha, \pi_i$ we use the second half of the definition. We need to consider the case $B = B + k = D_1 \to D_2$, with

$$\Delta' = \Delta \cup \{(d : D_1)\} \cup \{(b_j : B_j) \mid j < k\},$$

$$h' = h \cup \{(d, D_1)\} \cup \{(b_j, \pi_j) \mid j < k\}.$$

and the following holds:

$$\Delta' \vdash^{h'}_m D_2, \gamma, \pi_0,$$

$$\pi_0 \vdash_I D_1, \alpha_k = \gamma - \{d\},$$

$$\pi = \{x \in \pi_0 \mid D_1 \nvdash_I x\}.$$

By a previous lemma $\pi_o \vdash_I D_2$. By the induction hypothesis the same proof sequence will give:

$$\underline{h}' = \underline{h} \cup \{(d, D_1)\} \cup \{(b_j, \underline{\pi}_j) \mid j < k\}.$$

Since B_j has a shorter proof we get:

$$\pi_j \cup U^* \supseteq \underline{\pi}_j \supseteq \pi_j$$

Again by the induction hypothesis:

$$\Delta' \vdash^{h'}_{m} D_2, \gamma, \underline{\pi}_0$$

$$(\pi_0 \cup U^*) \supseteq \pi_0 \supseteq \pi_).$$

Since $\pi_0 \vdash_I D_1$ we get $\underline{\pi}_0 \vdash_I D_1$. Since by the previous lemma $\pi_0 \vdash_I D_2$, we get $\underline{\pi}_0 \vdash_I D_2$.

Define $\underline{\pi} = \{x \in \underline{\pi}_0 \mid D_1 \nvdash_I x\}$. Clearly then $\Delta \vdash^{h}_{n+1} B, \gamma, \underline{\pi}$. Clearly $(\pi \cup U^*) \supseteq \pi_0 \supseteq \pi$. ■

Lemma 14.41 *For a monotonic labelling logic, the following holds: If* $\Delta \vdash^h A$ *and* $\Delta, A \vdash^h B$ *then for some* $h_1 \supseteq h$ $\Delta \vdash^{h_1} B$.

Proof. Assume $\Delta^h_n \vdash A, \alpha, \pi_1$ and $\Delta, A \vdash^h_m B, \beta, \pi_2$. Let h_1 be defined by $h_1(x) = h(x) \cup \pi_1$. By the previous lemma, since $U^* \subseteq \pi_1$ we get $\Delta \vdash^{h_1}_{n} A, \alpha, \underline{\pi}_1$ with $\pi_1 \subseteq \underline{\pi}_1 \subseteq (\pi_1 \cup U^*) \subseteq \pi \cup \pi_1$. We also have $\Delta, A \vdash^{h_1}_{m} B, \beta, \underline{\pi}_2$.

We can now string the two proofs together:

Δ

...

proof as in $\Delta \vdash^{h_1} A$

...

A

...

proof as in $\Delta, A \vdash^{h_1} B$.

...

B

The crucial reason that we can indeed string the proofs together is that the label $\underline{\pi}_1$ of A at the end of the proof of $\Delta \vdash^{h_1} A$ is the same as the label h_1 gives to A as an item of data in the proof of $\Delta, A \vdash^{h_1} B$. The construction of h_1 from h by adding $\underline{\pi}_1$ to all labels was designed to ensure this. ■

Lemma 14.42

1. *If* $a : A \in \Delta$ *then* $\Delta \vdash^h A$.

2. *If* $\Delta \vdash^h A$ *then* $\Delta, B \vdash^h A$.

Proof. By definition. ■

Theorem 14.43 *Let I be a monotonic logic and $\Delta \subseteq J$ be a set of wffs. Let $\Delta \vdash^J_{\mathbf{DR}(I)} A$ iff for some h (with $U(h) \subseteq J)\Delta \vdash^h_{\mathbf{DR}(I)} A$. Then $\vdash^J_{\mathbf{DR}(I)}$ is a consequence relation.*

Proof. From previous lemmas. ■

Example 14.44 (Relevance Logic) Let $\Delta = \{a_i : A_i\}$ with a_i new and different atoms. Let $h_R(a_i) = a_i \wedge (\bigwedge_j A_j)$. then, provided $h(a_i) \vdash h(a_j)$ iff $i = j$, we get:

Lemma 14.45 $\vdash^h_{\mathbf{R}}$ *is relevance logic.*

Proof. Show by induction that $\Delta \vdash^h_{\mathbf{R}} A, \alpha, \pi$ iff $\pi = \bigwedge \alpha \wedge \Delta$. ■

Theorem 14.46 *Let I = Relevance logic and let $h(a : A) = A$. Then* $\mathbf{DR}(\mathbf{R}) = \mathbf{R}$.

Proof. Show that if $\Delta \vdash^h A, \alpha, \pi$ then $\pi = \{A \mid a \in \alpha$ and $a : A \in \Delta\}$. ■

Chapter 15

Formal Model of Agenda Relevance

> ... perfect reasoning is a perilous plan for living. Perfection has no safety net. One slip and it shatters.
>
> Reginald Hill, *Pictures of Perfection*, 1999

15.1 Introduction

This chapter forwards a generic formal model of agenda relevance. The model is presented schematically in terms of components. The exact details can be fine-tuned for any application area. The generic model will explain conceptually how agenda relevance is supposed to work. We develop the model in two steps. We first present a simple model in section 15.2 and then an intermediate more complex model in section 15.3. To develop a full fine-tuned model in full detail we require more logical machinery than we have at present and we must postpone such a model to a later, more technical volume ([Gabbay and Woods, 2005], in preparation). However, our two models are more than enough to explain the technical aspects of agenda relevance.

We are dealing with a single agent. The logical machinery describes his belief states and actions, thus preserving definition 8.1, which says that a cognitive agent is an information-processor capable of belief. If we have two agents, we need three states, the belief sets of each agent and a common (reality) state. Here are the basic components. This satisfies definition 8.1 of cognitive agency in the conceptual account.

Component 1: Base logic

The base logic has the following resources:

1. A language $\mathbb{L}$ in which the notions of a declarative unit (wff) A and a database Δ are defined. We require that a single wff A is a database and that the empty database is a database.

2. A notion of consistent database is available.

3. A consequence relation of the form $\Delta \mid\!\sim A$ is available satisfying certain conditions. We need not specify the exact axioms, but certainly $A \mid\!\sim A$ holds.

4. Note that we are not saying what it means for one database to *extend* another. We do not need this concept for our generic model. Also note that a set of wffs $\mathbb{E}$ is not necessarily a database, nor have we defined what it means for a database Δ *to contain* $\mathbb{E}$. We can define, however, $\Delta \mid\!\sim \mathbb{E}$ by:

$$\Delta \mid\!\sim \mathbb{E} \text{ iff } \Delta \mid\!\sim A, \text{ for all } A \in \mathbb{E}$$

Component 2: Consistent input operator

Given a consistent database Δ and a set of wffs $\mathbb{E} = \{A_i\}$, we have a function '+' which forms a new consistent database $\Delta + \mathbb{E}$. If A is consistent, then

(a) $\Delta + A \mid\!\sim A$

(b) If A in itself is not consistent then $\Delta + A = \Delta$.

Note that $\Delta + A$ is a combined revision + abduction + non-monotonic adjustment operation. We could put more restrictions on '+'; for example, if $\Delta \cup \{A\}$ is consistent then

$$\Delta \cup \{A\} \subseteq \Delta + A$$

However, in a general logic, $\Delta \cup \{A\}$ may be meaningless (for example if the data-structures are lists). Let us leave the fine tuning of '+' for later.[1] However we offer three comments:

[1] We shall see in the next section that the language of the basic logic should contain operators that restrict the future. This may cause the postconditions of some actions to be forbidden. Therefore the requirement $\Delta + A \mid\!\sim A$ may no longer be useful. When we take an action, the new state may or may not satisfy the postcondition.

1. If the language of Δ contains $\Rightarrow$, we should *not* expect any necessary connection between $\Delta |\!\!\sim A \Rightarrow B$ and $\Delta + A |\!\!\sim B$.

2. $+$ is not necessarily a pure revision operator. It may be a combination of abduction and revision and non-monotonic default, all done together. So for example, even when A and Δ are consistent, we may have

$$\Delta \cup \{A\} \not\subseteq \Delta + A$$

but no equality, since $+$ may involve additional abductive consequences of the input.

Nor do we necessarily expect

$$(\Delta + A) + B = \Delta + \{A, B\}.$$

3. $+$ might not always be single valued. $\Delta + A$ could be a set of databases.

Component 3: Basic actions

We assume our language contains notation for basic action of the form $\boldsymbol{a}$, $\boldsymbol{b}$, etc. An action has a precondition $\alpha_{\boldsymbol{a}}$ and a postcondition $\beta_{\boldsymbol{a}}$. We allow for an empty precondition (think of it as $\alpha_{\boldsymbol{a}} = \top$) and the empty postcondition ($\beta_{\boldsymbol{a}} = \top$, note that we may not know what $\Delta + \top$ is going to be) and for the empty action $\varnothing$.

Given a situation or state adequately described by a database Δ, if $\Delta |\!\!\sim \alpha_{\boldsymbol{a}}$ then the action $\boldsymbol{a}$ can be taken and we move to a new state $\Delta_{\boldsymbol{a}} = \Delta + \beta_{\boldsymbol{a}}$.

Note that $\Delta_{\boldsymbol{a}} |\!\!\sim \beta_{\boldsymbol{a}}$, i.e., the result of the action is guaranteed to hold.

The above actions are *deterministic*. We may have non-deterministic actions whose postconditions are sets of wffs

$$\beta_{\boldsymbol{a}} = \{B_1^{\boldsymbol{a}}, \ldots, B_k^{\boldsymbol{a}}\}$$

and once the action is taken, at least one of the postconditions will hold.

Given a Δ, we may also allow for a probability distribution (dependent on Δ) on the outcomes of the actions.

We leave all these details to the fine-tuning of our model.

Note that we may extend $+$ to revise actions: Let $\mathbf{a} = (\alpha, \beta)$ be an action. Then let $\mathbf{a} + \mathbb{E}$ be the action $(\alpha, \{\beta\} + \mathbb{E})$.

15.2 The Simple Agenda Model

We assume that we have the components described in section 15.1. We now define some basic concepts. It is well here to keep in mind our notion of *sentential agenda*, discussed in section 8.3 above.

Definition 15.1

1. *Universe*
   Let $\mathcal{S}$ *be the set of all consistent databases. Let* $\mathbb{A}$ *be a set of actions. Define* $\Delta R_{\mathbb{A}}\Theta$ *iff for some* $\boldsymbol{a} \in \mathbb{A}, \Delta \mid\!\sim \alpha_{\boldsymbol{a}}$ *and* $\Theta = \Delta + \beta_{\boldsymbol{a}}$. *This means that* Θ *is the result of an action in* $\mathbb{A}$ *performed on* Δ.

2. *The model* $(\mathcal{S}, \{R_{\mathbb{A}}\})$ *is called* the universe.

Definition 15.2 (Agendas)

1. *A simple agenda is a sequence of sets of formulas of the form* $(\mathbb{E}_1, \ldots, \mathbb{E}_n)$.[2] *Recall that a set of wffs may not be necessarily a database* Δ, *though we can write* $\Delta \mid\!\sim \mathbb{E}$ *as* $\Delta \mid\!\sim X$ *for all* $X \in \mathbb{E}$.

2. *A sequence* $(\Delta_0, \ldots, \Delta_n)$ *of databases satisfies the agenda* $(\mathbb{E}_1, \ldots, \mathbb{E}_n)$ *if for each* $i, \Delta_i \mid\!\sim \mathbb{E}_i$. *Think of* Δ_0 *as* now *and* $(\Delta_1, \ldots, \Delta_n)$ *as a future sequence.*

3. *A sequence of databases* $(\Delta_0, \ldots, \Delta_n)$ *is said to be a possible* real history (from the universe) *iff for some actions* $(\boldsymbol{a}_1, \ldots, \boldsymbol{a}_n)$ *and for each* $1 \leq i \leq n$, *we have:*

$$\Delta_{i-1} \mid\!\sim \alpha_{\boldsymbol{a}_i} \text{ and } \Delta_i = \Delta_{i-1} + \beta_{\boldsymbol{a}_i}.$$

4. *We can also say, if all actions are deterministic, that* $(\Delta_1, \ldots, \Delta_n)$ *is generated by* $(\boldsymbol{a}_1, \ldots, \boldsymbol{a}_n)$ *starting at* Δ_0.

5. *We can also say that* $(\Delta_0, (\boldsymbol{a}_1, \ldots, \boldsymbol{a}_n))$ satisfy *the agenda* $(\mathbb{E}_1, \ldots, \mathbb{E}_n)$ *if* $(\Delta_1, \ldots, \Delta_n)$ *satisfies the agenda, where* $(\Delta_1, \ldots, \Delta_n)$ *is generated by* $(\Delta_0, (\boldsymbol{a}_1, \ldots, \boldsymbol{a}_n))$.

[2] Again, consider the discussion of *sentential agendas* in section 8.3. These sentential agendas were presented in 8.3 in the form (S^E, S^N) where $S^E = (S^E_1, \ldots, S^E_n)$, and $S^N = S^E_n$. S^N is the target of the agenda and S^E_i are sentences which help achieve the target if true in sequence. Thus in our formal notation, $S^E_i = \mathbb{E}_i$ and $S^n = \mathbb{E}_n$.

There is the problem of how the agent views $\mathbb{E}_1, \ldots, \mathbb{E}_{n-1}$. Are these just enabling intermediate sentences towards the real goal target $\mathbb{E}_n$ or perhaps some of them are also targets in themselves. This could make a difference when an input comes and causes the agents to drop some of the $\mathbb{E}_i$s and simplify his means of achieving $S^n = \mathbb{E}_n$.

6. *Let* $\mathbb{D} = (\mathbb{D}_0, \ldots, \mathbb{D}_n)$ *and* $\mathbb{D}' = (\mathbb{D}'_1, \ldots, \mathbb{D}'_n)$ *be two sequences of sets of wffs. Let* $\mathbb{E} = (\mathbb{E}_1, \ldots, \mathbb{E}_n)$ *be an agenda and let* Δ_0 *be a theory and* $\mathbf{a}_1, \ldots, \mathbf{a}_n$ *be actions. We say that* $(\Delta_0, (\mathbf{a}_1, \ldots, \mathbf{a}_n))$ satisfies $\mathbb{E}$ with the assistance of the input $(\mathbb{D}, \mathbb{D}')$ *iff the following holds:*

   (a) $\Delta_0 + \mathbb{D}_0 \mid\!\sim \alpha_{\mathbf{a}_1}$ *and* $\Delta_1 = (\Delta_0 + \mathbb{D}_0) + (\beta_1 + \mathbb{D}'_1)$

   (b) *For each* $1 \leq i \leq n-1$ $\Delta_i + \mathbb{D}_i \mid\!\sim \alpha_{\mathbf{a}_i}$ *and* $\Delta_{i+1} = (\Delta_i + \mathbb{D}_i) + (\beta_{\mathbf{a}_i} + \mathbb{D}'_i)$

   (c) *For each* $1 \leq i \leq n, \Delta_i \mid\!\sim \mathbb{E}_i$

   The meaning of (a)–(c) is that we revise the action $\mathbf{a}_i$ *to be* $\mathbf{a}_i + \mathbb{D}'_i$ *and that at each stage* i *the new theory* Δ_i *is boosted by the additional information* $\mathbb{D}_i$ *which enables the action* $\mathbf{a}_i + \mathbb{D}'_i$ *and this sequence realizes the agenda* $\mathbb{E} = (\mathbb{E}_1, \ldots, \mathbb{E}_n)$.

Definition 15.3 (Simple agents) *A simple agent* $\boldsymbol{X}$ *has the following components*

1. *A set* $\mathbb{A}$ *of actions which he can execute.*

2. *A family* $\boldsymbol{A}$ *of simple agendas of the form* $\mathbb{E}^i = (\mathbb{E}^i_1, \ldots, \mathbb{E}^i_{n_i})$, $i = 1, 2, \ldots$.

3. *A* 'now' *point* Δ_0 *(a database).*

4. *Let* $(\Theta_1, \ldots \Theta_n)$ *be a sequence of databases. We say agent* $\boldsymbol{X}$ *generates this sequence as a future history if for some* $\boldsymbol{a}_1, \ldots, \boldsymbol{a}_n$ *available to* $\boldsymbol{X}$ *(i.e.,* $\boldsymbol{a}_i \in \mathbb{A}$*),* $(\Delta_0, (\boldsymbol{a}_1, \ldots, \boldsymbol{a}_n))$ *generates* $(\Theta_1, \ldots, \Theta_n)$.

5. *We say* $\boldsymbol{X}$ *can potentially satisfy the agenda* $\mathbb{E} = (\mathbb{E}_1, \ldots, \mathbb{E}_n)$ *if the agent can generate a future history* $(\Theta_1, \ldots, \Theta_n)$ *which satisfies the agenda.*

6. $\boldsymbol{X}$ *can partially satisfy* $\mathbb{E} = (\mathbb{E}_1, \ldots, \mathbb{E}_n)$ *if he can generate* $(\Theta_1, \ldots, \Theta_m)$ $m < n$ *which satisfy* $(\mathbb{E}_1, \ldots, \mathbb{E}_m)$.

7. *The agendas in* $\mathbf{A}$ *are the agent's* explicit *agendas* Δ. $\mathbf{A}$ *generates a family* $\mathbf{A}_{\text{tacit}}$ *of* tacit *agendas of the form* $\mathbb{E} = (\mathbb{E}^1_1, \ldots, \mathbb{E}^k_k)$, *whenever* $\mathbb{E}^i = (\mathbb{E}^i_1, \ldots, \mathbb{E}^i_{n_i}), i \leq n_i$ *is in* $\mathbf{A}$.

8. *We say agent* $\mathbf{X}$ *has a* disposition *towards an agenda* $\mathbb{E} = (\mathbb{E}_1, \ldots, \mathbb{E}_k)$ *if for some* $1 \leq i_1 \leq i_2 \leq \ldots i_n \leq k$ *we have that* $(\mathbb{E}_{i_1}, \ldots, \mathbb{E}_{i_n}) \in \mathbf{A} \cup \mathbf{A}_{\text{tacit}}$.

   Let $\mathbf{D} = \{\mathbb{E} | \mathbf{X}$ *has a disposition towards* $\mathbb{E}\}$.

9. *Not that any two agendas are compatible in the sense that we can interleave them. This is possible since our formulas speak only about the local present and not about the past or future. So* $(\mathbb{E}_1, \ldots, \mathbb{E}_n)$, $(\mathbb{E}'_1, \ldots, \mathbb{E}'_m)$ *can always be interleaved in any way we want, for example* $(\mathbb{E}_1, \mathbb{E}'_1, \mathbb{E}_2, \mathbb{E}'_2, \ldots)$.

10. *In items 4 and 5 above we implicitly assumed that the world changes (i.e., we move from a database* Θ *to* Θ'*) only as a result of actions taken by our agent. There is no need to have our model that simple. We can assume that our agent can sit back taking no actions and actions may be taken by nature or by other agents. If our agent has an agenda* $\mathbb{E} = (\mathbb{E}_1, \ldots, \mathbb{E}_n)$ *he may satisfy this agenda by lying back and having nature execute the requisite actions.*

We are now ready to define a simple notion of relevance. Our agent $\boldsymbol{X}$ assumes he is at a state ('now') Δ_0. However, he may be mistaken. If he receives input A which is verified, he must assume his state is $\Delta_0 + A = \Delta_1$. Now the agent may think he can satisfy some agenda $\mathbb{E}$ because a sequence of actions $(\boldsymbol{a}_1, \ldots, \boldsymbol{a}_n)$ is available to him to create a suitable history.

This means that $\Delta_0 \not\mid\!\sim \alpha_{\boldsymbol{a}_1}$. However, $\Delta_1 \mid\!\sim \alpha_{\boldsymbol{a}_1}$. Thus the input A is relevant to his agendas. It can also work the other way round, more agendas may be satisfiable.

Definition 15.4 (Simple agenda relevance) *Let* $\boldsymbol{X} = (\mathbb{A}, \boldsymbol{A})$ *be rooted at a state* Δ_0. *Let* A *be a wff. Let* $\Delta_1 = \Delta_0 + A$. *Then* A *is relevant (positively or negatively) to* $\boldsymbol{X}$ *at* Δ_0 *iff for some agenda* $(\mathbb{E}_1, \ldots, \mathbb{E}_n)$ *and some sequence of actions* $(\boldsymbol{a}_1, \ldots, \boldsymbol{a}_n)$ *from* $\mathbb{A}$ *we have that for* $y \in \{0, 1\}$ *we have* $(\Delta_y, (\boldsymbol{a}_1, \ldots, \boldsymbol{a}_n))$ satisfies $(\mathbb{E}_1, \ldots, \mathbb{E}_n)$ *while* $(\Delta_{1-y}, (\boldsymbol{a}_1, \ldots, \boldsymbol{a}_n))$ *does not satisfy* $(\mathbb{E}_1, \ldots, \mathbb{E}_m)$ *for some* $(\mathbb{E}_1, \ldots, \mathbb{E}_n) \in \boldsymbol{A}$.

Note that we have satisfied definition 9.10 of negative relevance.

Note that the agent may still be able to satisfy all of his agendas but through a different sequences of actions.

It is clear that our definition allows for a notion of a degree of relevance, if we pay attention to how many agendas and action preconditions an input can affect. This can model proposition 9.2 and definition 9.8 of cumulative relevance.[3]

Remark 15.5 We conclude this section by explaining why we prefixed all our concepts by the word 'simple'.

[3] Proposition 9.2 says that the more agendas an infon advances or closes the more relevant it is.

First, the language $\mathbb{L}$ was not assumed to be able to talk about the future, i.e., we did not require a construct of the form $\Box A$, with

$$\Delta \mid\!\sim \Box A \to \forall B(\Delta + B \mid\!\sim A)$$

We are also not allowing actions as part of the data or more complex logics as in Section 12.4.5.

Second, our present ('now') Δ_0 has no history. We can define relevance relative to a history say $(\Delta_{-3}, \Delta_{-2}, \Delta_{-1}, \Delta_0)$ and allow actions to have as preconditions the closing of agendas, i.e., $\alpha_{\boldsymbol{a}} = (\mathbb{E}_{-3}, \mathbb{E}_{-2}, \mathbb{E}_{-1}, \mathbb{E}_0)$ and we can apply the action $\boldsymbol{a}$ if $\Delta_{-i} \mid\!\sim \mathbb{E}_{-i}$, $i = 0, 1, 2, 3$ and only then can we move to $\Delta_1 = \Delta_0 + \beta_{\boldsymbol{a}}$.

This allows the closing of agendas to be preconditions for actions.

Thirdly, agendas require only satisfaction of wffs. We do not require certain actions to be performed. It may be part of the agenda, for example, that John be home but the agenda does not specify by what action this is achieved.

The next section will add these features to our higher level concepts.

Remark 15.6 Let us indicate how the logics already defined in chapters 13 and 14 can provide us with the needed components for a simple model for agenda relevance.

1. *Base logic*
   We take for simplicity the goal directed formulation of relevance $\to$ without $\bot$ and without negation as failure of section 14.3. We are taking the pure $\to$ so that we can define the revision $+$ easily. Otherwise we need deletion which is more complex.

2. *Consistent input operator*
   Because we have no negation, everything is consistent. However, we take $\Delta + A$ to be not just $\Delta \cup \{A\}$ but any theory $\Delta' \in \mathbf{Ab}^+(\Delta, A)$ of definition 14.21.

3. *Basic actions*
   These can have the form $\mathbf{a} = (A, B), A, B$ wffs.

   Note that applying an action to Δ means that if $\Delta \mid\!\sim A$ then move to $\Delta + B$. Compare this action with the non-monotonic hunch rules of the form $A \rightsquigarrow B$ of section 13.2.4.

Given the above then agendas will be like sequences of wffs we wish to prove using hunch rules (actions).

We now have the formal machinery available even in this simple model to define some of the concepts of relevance mentioned in chapters 8 and 9.

Consider a theory Δ_0 and an agenda $E = (E_1, E_2)$. To be able to satisfy this agenda we need two actions $\mathbf{a}_1 = (\alpha_1, \beta_1), \mathbf{a}_2 = (\alpha_2, \beta_2)$ such that

$$\begin{aligned} &\Delta_0 \mid\!\sim \alpha_1 \\ &\Delta_0 + \beta_1 \mid\!\sim E_1 \\ &\Delta_0 + \beta_1 \mid\!\sim \alpha_2 \\ &(\Delta_0 + \beta_1) + \beta_2 \mid\!\sim E_2 \end{aligned}$$

Several things may go wrong which will not enable us to satisfy the agenda using the above actions.

Case 1

Δ_0 fails to prove α_1. In this case, depending on the base logic $\mid\!\sim$, we may have an *abduction process* (see section 14.3) which may tell us that if we were to add say $\Theta_i = \{A_1^i, \ldots, A_{k_i}^i\}$, to Δ_0, then $\Delta_0 \cup \Theta_i$ would prove α_1. This addition will enable us to execute the action $\mathbf{a}_1$ and hopefully we can assume that $(\Delta_0 \cup \Theta_i) + \beta_1 \mid\!\sim E_1$.

In this case we can say that the addition of Θ_i *advances positively* the agenda $E = (E_1, E_2)$.

In fact, any contribution of the form $A_j^i \in \Theta_i$ *partially advances* the agenda E.

Case 2

We do have $\Delta_0 \mid\!\sim \alpha_1$ but $\Delta_0 + \beta_1$ do not prove E_1. Similarly to case 1, a Θ_i' may be found by abduction such that $(\Delta_0 + \beta_1) \cup \Theta_i'$ can prove E_1 and therefore any $B_j^i \in \Theta_i'$ can partially advance the closure of the agenda E.

We can even talk about degrees of advancement by recording some measure of how easy it becomes to satisfy the agenda E. In fact the notion of degree should be put forward in the context of abduction, namely how much of the abduced sets Θ_i we can put forward and make the gap between what we have and what we need to have smaller. See the end of section 14.3 for discussion.

Another form of input which may be relevant is to add to the postcondition of actions. We may add information about the action $\mathbf{a}_1 = (\alpha_1, \beta_1)$ that its postcondition should be $\beta_1 \wedge \beta_1'$ and indeed, although $\Delta_0 + \beta_1 \not\mid\!\sim E_1$, we do have that $\Delta_0 + \{\beta_1, \beta_1'\} \mid\!\sim E_1$

We are now ready for a formal definition.

Definition 15.7

1. *An input stream of information has the form $(\mathbb{D}, \mathbb{D}')$ where $\mathbb{D} = (\mathbb{D}_0, \ldots, \mathbb{D}_n)$ and $\mathbb{D}' = (\mathbb{D}_1', \ldots, \mathbb{D}_n')$.*

2. *Let* $(\Delta_0, (\mathbf{a}_1, \ldots, \mathbf{a}_n))$ *be a theory and some actions and let* $\mathbb{E} = (\mathbb{E}_1, \ldots, \mathbb{E}_n)$ *be an agenda. Then we already defined in definition 15.2 item 6 how the input* $(\mathbb{D}, \mathbb{D}')$ *can assist* $\mathbf{a}_1, \ldots, \mathbf{a}_n$ *close the agenda* $\mathbb{E}$ *at* Δ_0.

   We define the notion of $\mathbf{I} = (\mathbb{D}, \mathbb{D}')$ *being relevant to agent* $\mathbf{X}$ *at* Δ_0 *if it assists in closing some agenda at* Δ_0.

15.3 Intermediate Agenda Model

The last section concluded remark 15.6 with a discussion of three possible options for defining more complex agendas and therefore a richer notion of relevance. This section will offer a better model. We begin our considerations with the second option. The following example illustrates our needs.

Example 15.8 (Hiring example) Professor X is a very successful and wise university researcher and administrator. In fact, he is president of his university. As part of a general effort to expand, he submitted a very strong research proposal for a centre of excellence in practical logic and has even politically lobbied to have it funded. In a meeting with directors of the main funding bodies, it was promised that funding is very imminently forthcoming and a positive decision will be officially announced 'very soon'. Professor X was very keen to hire Professor Y, who is the best person to run the centre. The problem was that Professor Y got a firm offer from Silicon Valley and unless Professor X makes a commitment now, Professor Y will have to go. Professor X considered various options of persuading Professor Y to wait because funding was coming 'very soon', but upon reflection decided that the best course of action was to make a firm offer to Professor Y, based on the expectation of the 'very soon' government funding.

Unfortunately the government funding did not come through and Professor Y was appointed without any additional funds. The university was quite honourable about it and made the effort to absorb the costs by adjusting its budget, thus creating some difficulties in other areas of activity.

Three years later, the university finance policy was audited by (the same) government. An auditor was going through the books and hit upon the appointment of Professor Y, and the difficulties it caused in other university sectors, and it seemed to the auditor that this appointment was either corrupt or at best a result of misadministration, having caused budgetary difficulties in subsequent years.

The university needed to explain to the auditors the following two points:

1. At the time of the appointment there was a very strong expectation that the funding was forthcoming.

2. There was no other course of action, if the centre were to be a success. It was absolutely necessary to appoint Professor Y to head the centre.

   Figure 15.1 below explains the action flow of the case:

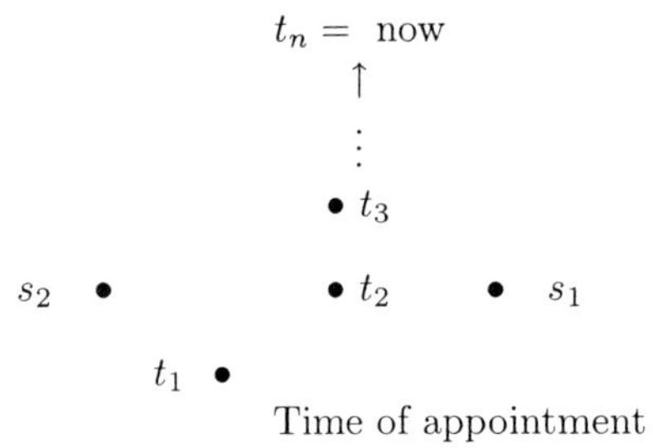

Figure 15.1

s_1 is a future of t_1 in which funding is forthcoming and Professor Y is in place. s_2 is a future where funding is forthcoming but Professor Y is not in place.

t_2 is what actually happened: no funding but with Professor Y landing in the university 'lap'.

The reasoning at time t_1 was that state t_2 had a very low probability. State s_1 was in a high probability zone and utility-wise was much better than s_2.

On the basis of these considerations Professor Y was hired at time t_1.

The reader should note that in the simple language of the previous section none of the points in the above example can be expressed. All we have at time t_1 is a language talking about time t_1. We need at least to be able to say something like:

(i) $\Box$ (get funding), holds at time t_1

(ii) $\neg$ Hire Professor Y $\twoheadrightarrow$ centre not successful, holds at time t_1 where $\twoheadrightarrow$ is some sort of subjunctive conditional.

In other words, we need special connectives in our language that can talk about alternative histories and alternative worlds.

In fact, hypothetical information about the success of the centre without Professor Y is highly relevant to the action of hiring him at time t_1. This makes the base logic much more complex.

Example 15.9 (Hiring example, continued) Let us continue with our story. Suppose the auditor at time t_n criticized the university for not putting pressure on the funding bodies asking them to at least pay for the hiring of Professor Y. After all, they did give the university to understand that they are going to fund the project and did not even hint that some change of plans might take place. So, claims the auditor, although university actions at time t_1 may be understandable, their failure to put pressure on the government at time t_2 (e.g. hold a press conference) is not acceptable. To this the university might reply that such pressure would have been counterproductive. The auditor might disagree, and produce some relevant information to show that had the university insisted, the government in all probability would have found ways to ease their difficulty.

Examining the above argument, our model needs to be able to do the following:

(i) Represent past counterfactuals of the form:

- Had a sequence of actions $\mathbf{a}_1, \ldots, \mathbf{a}_{n-1}$ been initiated at time t_1, while all other actions remain the same, then a new sequence of states $t'_2 < t'_3 < \ldots < t'_n =$ *new now*, would have obtained in which B is true.
  This has the form
- $(\mathbf{a}_1, \ldots, \mathbf{a}_{n-1})$ at $t_1 \twoheadrightarrow B$ at *new now*

(ii) Similarly we can say

- had Silicon Valley not offered a position to Professor Y, he would have been still waiting now.

This has the form

- A at $t_1 \twoheadrightarrow B$ at *new now*

Let us analyse what formal machinery we need to accommodate (i) and (ii).

First note that $(\mathbf{a}_1, \ldots, \mathbf{a}_{n-1})$ initiated at t_1 looks awfully like an agenda $\mathbb{G}$.

Thus at time t_n, the auditor is saying that had you initiated the agenda $\mathbb{G}$, B would have been true at the new $t'_n =$ new *now*.

If we define an agenda as having the form

$$\mathbb{G} = ((\mathbf{a}_1, B_1), \ldots, (\mathbf{a}_{n-1}, B_{n-1}))$$

with the understanding that we want the sequence of actions $\mathbf{a}_1, \ldots, \mathbf{a}_{n-1}$ to cause $B_1, \ldots, B_{n-1}$ to hold in the respective states, then our new conditionals have the form $\mathbb{G} \twoheadrightarrow B$.

To define the notion of satisfaction for $t_n \vDash \mathbb{G} \twoheadrightarrow B$, we must have a model of time as a tree and be able to identify equal distance of two points from the latest common past (see figure 15.2).

t_n t'_n

distance n from t_0 distance n from t_0

t_0

Figure 15.2

Such a new modal connective was studied in [Gabbay and Malod, 2002].

The preconditions of actions must also change. Imagine a state theory Δ and an action $\mathbf{a} = (\alpha_{\mathbf{a}}, \beta_{\mathbf{a}})$. Our previous definition was that $\mathbf{a}$ is enabled if $\Delta \mid\!\sim \alpha_{\mathbf{a}}$ then we perform the action and the new theory state is $\Delta + \beta_{\mathbf{a}}$.

However, now that Δ can talk about the future, it may be that $\Delta \mid\!\sim \Box\neg\beta_{\mathbf{a}}$ and hence the action cannot be executed. We therefore need to say the following:

(*) $\mathbf{a} = (\alpha_{\mathbf{a}}, \beta_{\mathbf{a}})$ is executable at Δ iff $\Delta \mid\!\sim \alpha_{\mathbf{a}}$ and $\Theta = \{\beta_{\mathbf{a}}\} \cup \{\gamma \mid \Delta \mid\!\sim \Box\gamma\}$ is consistent.

The result of the action is the theory $\Delta + \Theta$.

We have already mentioned the possibility that a precondition for actions can be agendas $\mathbb{G}$. We also saw that agendas can participate in conditional, as antecedents ($\mathbb{G} \twoheadrightarrow B$). We therefore need a notion of $\Delta \mid\!\sim \mathbb{G}$. We must use a sequence

(**) $(\Delta_1, \ldots, \Delta_n) \mid\!\sim \mathbb{G} = ((\mathbf{a}_1, B_1), \ldots, (\mathbf{a}_{n-1}, B_{n-1})$ iff for each $i = 2, \ldots, n$ we have $\Delta_i \mid\!\sim B_i$ and Δ_i is the result of executing $\mathbf{a}_{i-1}$ on Δ_{i-1}. Execution can be in the sense of (*) above.

The reader may ask if the components of the agenda $\mathbb{G}$ are $((\mathbf{a}_1, B_1), \ldots, (\mathbf{a}_n, B_n))$ and say $\mathbf{a}_1 = (\alpha_1, \beta_1)$, then when we execute $\mathbf{a}_1$ at Δ_1 we get $\Delta_1 + \Theta_1 \mid\!\sim B_1$, where $\Theta_1 = \{\beta_1\} \cup \{X | \Delta_1 \mid\!\sim \Box X\}$, then can't we dispense with B_2 by taking a new action $(\alpha_1, \beta_1 \wedge B_2)$? The answer is that revising with Θ_1 may not be the same as revising with $\Theta_1 \cup \{B_1\}$.

We can now define conditionals.

(***) $(\Delta_1, \Gamma_2, \ldots, \Gamma_n) \mid\!\sim \mathbb{G} \twoheadrightarrow B$ iff for every $\Delta_1, \ldots, \Delta_n$ such that $(\Delta_1, \ldots, \Delta_n) \mid\!\sim \mathbb{G}$ we have that $(\Delta_1, \ldots, \Delta_n) \mid\!\sim B$. (If B is a wff this means $\Delta_n \mid\!\sim B$.)

In fact, B can be replaced by an agenda and so we can talk about $(\Delta_1, \Gamma_2, \ldots, \Gamma_n) \mid\!\sim \mathbb{G}_1 \twoheadrightarrow \mathbb{G}_2$.

One last remark. Our examples show that conditionals can be relevant to agendas because if the auditor could show that a conditional $\mathbb{G} \twoheadrightarrow B$ was true (available) for the university, then they have been negligent. This means that the language of Δ must contain agendas *in the object level.*

Definition 15.10

1. *Let $\mathbb{L}$ be a language with various connectives, among them $\twoheadrightarrow, \Box, \Diamond$ and $\boxplus$ and $\diamondplus$, as well as conjunction $\wedge$.*

   Assume that a notion of a wff and a database Δ is given as well as a notion of consistency of databases and also assume that a single wff is a database. Further assume that a consequence relation of the form $\Delta \mid\!\sim A$ is given such that $A \mid\!\sim A$ holds.

2. *Assume that a revision operation is given such that for each theory Δ and a set of wffs Θ which are consistent, a new consistent theory $\Delta + \Theta$ can be created. It is expected but does not necessarily hold that $\Delta \mid\!\sim \Theta$, or at least $\Delta \mid\!\sim X$ for most $X \in \Theta$.*

Definition 15.11 (Actions, conditions and agendas)

1. *A basic action $\mathbf{a}$ is a pair of sets of wffs $(\alpha_{\mathbf{a}}, \beta_{\mathbf{a}})$. $\alpha_{\mathbf{a}}$ is the precondition and $\beta_{\mathbf{a}}$ is the postcondition.*

2. *A basic agenda has the form $((\mathbf{a}_1, \gamma_1), \ldots, (\mathbf{a}_n \gamma_n))$ where $\mathbf{a}_i$ are basic actions and γ_i are sets of wffs.*

3. *A basic conditional wff is any wff of the form* $A \twoheadrightarrow B$.

4. *If* $\mathbb{G}$ *is an agenda or a set of complex conditionals or a set of both and* β *is a set of simple wffs then* $(\mathbb{G}, \beta)$ *is an action.*

5. *If* $\mathbf{a}_i$ *are actions and* γ_i *are sets of wffs then* $\mathbb{G} = ((\mathbf{a}_1, \gamma_1), \ldots, (\mathbf{a}_n, \gamma_n))$ *is an agenda.*

6. *If* $\mathbb{G}_1$ *and* $\mathbb{G}_2$ *are agendas then* $\mathbb{G}_1 \twoheadrightarrow \mathbb{G}_2$ *is a complex conditional wff. [It is not a simple wff and hence cannot be a postcondition of an action.]*

7. *Note that the notions of action, agenda and conditional are not part of the object language* $\mathbb{L}$ *in which databases and wffs and consequence are defined. They are metalevel notions using constructs from* $\mathbb{L}$.

Definition 15.12 (Extending consequence) *The consequence notion* $\Delta \mid\!\sim A$ *is defined only for databases* Δ *and wffs* A. *This definition extends* $\mid\!\sim$ *to agendas and conditionals.*

Let $(\Delta_1, \ldots, \Delta_n)$ *be a sequence of databases and let* $\mathbf{a}$ *be an action and let* $\mathbb{G}$ *be an agenda. We define inductively the following notions:*

(*) $(\Delta_1, \ldots, \Delta_n, \Delta_{n+1})$ *is the result of executing* $\mathbf{a}$ *at* Δ_n.

(**) $(\Delta_1, \ldots, \Delta_{n+1}) \mid\!\sim \mathbb{G}$.

1. *For a simple action* $\mathbf{a}$ *we have (*) holds iff the following holds:* $\Delta_n \mid\!\sim \alpha_{\mathbf{a}}, \Theta = \{Y | \Delta_n \mid\!\sim \Box Y\} \cup \{\beta_{\mathbf{a}}\}$ *is consistent and* $\Delta_{n+1} = \Delta_n + \Theta$.

2. *For a simple agenda* $((\mathbf{a}_k, \gamma_k), (\mathbf{a}_{k+1}, \gamma_{k+1}) \ldots (\mathbf{a}_n, \gamma_n))$, $1 \leq k < n$, *we say (**) holds if for each* $k \leq i \leq n$ *we have that* Δ_{i+1} *is the result of executing* $\mathbf{a}_i$ *at* Δ_i *and* $\Delta_{i+1} \mid\!\sim \gamma_i$.

3. *For any action* $(\mathbb{G}, \beta)$ *and* $(\Delta_1, \ldots, \Delta_{n+1})$ *with* n *sufficiently large we say (*) holds if* $(\Delta_1, \ldots, \Delta_n) \mid\!\sim \mathbb{G}$ *and* $\Theta = \{Y | \Delta_n \mid\!\sim \Box Y\} \cup \{\beta\}$ *is consistent and* $\Delta_{n+1} = \Delta + \Theta$.

4. *For a complex agenda* $\mathbb{G} = ((\mathbf{a}_k, \gamma_k), \ldots, (\mathbf{a}_n, \gamma_n)), 1 \leq k \leq n$, *we say* $(\Delta_1, \ldots, \Delta_{n+1}) \mid\!\sim \mathbb{G}$ *if for each* $1 \leq k \leq n$ *we have that* Δ_{i+1} *is the result of executing* $\mathbf{a}_i$ *at* $(\Delta_1, , \ldots, \Delta_i)$ *and* $\Delta_{i+1} \mid\!\sim \gamma_i$.

Definition 15.13 *Note that the language of theories* Δ *does not contain agendas and actions, nor does it contain complex conditionals. We therefore need to also define what it means to have*

(***) $(\Delta_1, \ldots, \Delta_n) \mid\!\sim \mathbb{G}_1 \twoheadrightarrow \mathbb{G}_2$

1. $(\Delta_1, \ldots, \Delta_n) \mid\!\sim A \twoheadrightarrow B$ *iff* $\Delta_n \mid\!\sim A \twoheadrightarrow B$ *for a simple conditional.*

2. $(\Delta_1, \ldots, \Delta_n) \mid\!\sim \mathbb{G}_1 \twoheadrightarrow \mathbb{G}_2$ *for* n *large enough is defined as follows.*

Let $\mathbb{G}_1$ *be* $((\mathbf{a}_1, \gamma_1), \ldots, (a_k, \gamma_k))$ *and* $\mathbb{G}_2$ *be* $((\mathbf{b}_1, \delta_1), \ldots, (\mathbf{b}_m, \delta_m))$ *with* $m, k < n$.

Then(***) holds if for any alternative sequence such that $(\Delta_1, \ldots, \Delta_{n-k}, \Gamma_1, \ldots, \Gamma_k) \mid\!\sim \mathbb{G}_1$ *we also have that the sequence* $\mid\!\sim \mathbb{G}_2$.

This means that any alternative history which satisfies $\mathbb{G}_1$ *also satisfies* $\mathbb{G}_2$.

We are now ready to define the notion of *agenda relevance*. Here is the idea. An agent is a pair $(\mathbb{A}, \mathbf{A})$, where $\mathbb{A}$ is a set of actions (available to the agent) and $\mathbf{A}$ is a set of agendas which the agent wishes to execute. The agent is rooted at a state Δ. The agent can advance his state by performing actions from $\mathbb{A}$, provided they are allowed. Let $\Delta_{\mathbf{a}_i}$ be the new state after the agent performs (the allowed) action $\mathbf{a}_i$. After some time the agent is at a state $\Delta_{\mathbf{a}_1\mathbf{a}_2,\ldots,\mathbf{a}_n}$ and his history is $(\Delta, \Delta_{\mathbf{a}_1}, \Delta_{\mathbf{a}_1,\mathbf{a}_2}, \ldots, \Delta_{\mathbf{a}_1,\ldots,\mathbf{a}_n})$.

Of course the agent chooses to execute the sequence $\vec{\mathbf{a}} = (\mathbf{a}_1, \ldots, \mathbf{a}_n)$ to satisfy his agendas. The agent's *full universe* is the set $\mathcal{S} = \{\Delta_{\vec{\mathbf{a}}} | \vec{\mathbf{a}}$ a sequence of actions which can be executed in sequence$\}$.

Consider the situation in figure 15.3

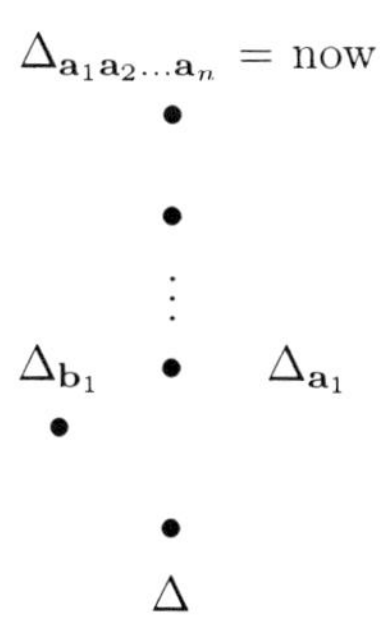

Figure 15.3

$\Delta_{\mathbf{b}_1}$ is a result of an action the agenda did not take. It does influence the possibility of executing the sequence $\mathbf{a}_1, \ldots, \mathbf{a}_n$ because preconditions of actions can contain complex conditionals.

An input is a consistent set of wffs coming into a theory in the universe such as $\Delta_{\mathbf{b}_1}$ and updating it. We now have $\Delta'_{\mathbf{b}_1} = \Delta_{\mathbf{b}_1} + \Theta$ instead. This might affect the preconditions in the sequence $\Delta_{\mathbf{a}_1}, \ldots, \Delta_{\mathbf{a}_1,\mathbf{a}_2,\ldots,\mathbf{a}_n}$ or the executability of actions in the future of $\Delta_{\mathbf{a}_1,\ldots,\mathbf{a}_n}$. If it does, then it is *agenda relevant.* If it does not, then it is not relevant.

Let us consider the situation with the auditor and the university. The auditor wants to show that the university could have put pressure on the government to fund Professor Y (say action $\mathbf{b}_1$). This is a precondition for the auditor to take action. The university claims that putting pressure would have been counterproductive. Thus the university claims that $\Delta_{\mathbf{b}_1} \mid\!\sim$ *counterproductive.* However, if new information changes $\Delta_{\mathbf{b}_1}$ to $\Delta'_{\mathbf{b}_1}$ which does not prove *counterproductive*, then the precondition for the auditor holds and he can take action.

We are now ready for the formal definition.

Definition 15.14

1. *Let* $\mathbf{X} = (\mathbb{A}, \mathbf{A})$ *with actions* $\mathbb{A}$ *and agendas* $\mathbf{A}$. *Let* Δ *be a theory. Then* $(\Delta, \mathbb{A})$ *generates a universe with root* Δ. *It is* $\mathcal{S}_{\Delta}^{\mathbb{A}} = \{\Delta_{\mathbf{a}_1,\ldots,\mathbf{a}_n} | \mathbf{a}_i \in \mathbb{A}\}$ *where* $\Delta_{\varnothing} = \Delta$. $\Delta_{\mathbf{a}_1,\ldots,\mathbf{a}_n,\mathbf{b}} =$ *the result of executing the (allowed) action* $\mathbf{b}$ *on* $\Delta_{\mathbf{a}_1,\ldots,\mathbf{a}_n}$.

2. *Let* Δ_{now} *be some* $\Delta_{\mathbf{e}_1,\ldots,\mathbf{e}_n}$. *This means that* $\mathbf{e}_1, \ldots, \mathbf{e}_n$ *are the actual course of executions of actions the agent choose to take. In this case the agent's history is* $(\Delta, \Delta_{\mathbf{e}_1}, \ldots, \Delta_{\mathbf{e}_1,\ldots,\mathbf{e}_n})$. *The agent's* open future universe *is* $\mathcal{S}_{\Delta_{\text{now}}}^{\mathbb{A}}$.

3. *An input information* $\mathbf{I}$ *is a triple* $(\mathbf{K}, \mathbf{b}_1, \ldots, \mathbf{b}_k, B)$ *where* B *is a wff and* $\mathbf{b}_1, \ldots, \mathbf{b}_k$ *is a sequence of actions and* $\mathbf{K}$ *is a piece of knowledge, being defined as* anything *for which* $\Delta \mid\!\sim \mathbf{K}$ *is meaningful, for databases* Δ.

   So $\mathbf{K}$ *can be a wff or an agenda or* Δ *itself. The meaning of* $\mathbf{I}$ *is that whenever we are at some* $\Delta_{\bar{\mathbf{a}}}$ *such that* $\Delta_{\bar{\mathbf{a}}} \mid\!\sim \mathbf{K}$ *and we execute* $\mathbf{b}_1, \ldots, \mathbf{b}_k$ *to get to* $\Delta' = \Delta_{\bar{\mathbf{a}}\mathbf{b}_1,\ldots,\mathbf{b}_k}$ *then we must have* $\Delta' \mid\!\sim B$. *Now if the actual* Δ' *does not prove* B *then we must replace it by* $\Delta' + B$.

   In its simplest form, the input is just (Δ', B) *and it replaces a certain* Δ' *by* $\Delta' + B$. *Now if in the universe* $\mathcal{S}_{\text{now}}^{\mathbb{A}}$ *changes, then the input is relevant. The agent may still be able to satisfy all of his agendas but he may need to chose a different course of actions.*

Remark 15.15

1. Note that our notion of agenda is too strong. We presented agendas as $\mathbb{G}_1 = ((\mathbf{a}_1, \gamma_1), (\mathbf{a}_2, \gamma_2), \ldots)$ and to satisfy the agenda we have to

execute the actions one after the other with *no time gaps.* A more reasonable notion is to allow for gaps.

Furthermore, we allow for only one action $\mathbf{a}_i$. It makes more sense to allow for a choice of actions $\mathbb{A}_i$. Thus an agenda can have the form $\mathbb{G}_2 = ((\mathbb{A}_1, \gamma_1), \ldots, (\mathbb{A}_n, \gamma_n))$ and the agenda can be executed if some $\mathbf{a}_i \in \mathbb{A}_i$ can be successful. So we define $(\Delta_1, \ldots, \Delta_n) \mid\!\sim \mathbb{G}_2$ iff for some $\mathbf{a}_i \in \mathbb{A}_i, (\Delta_1, \ldots, \Delta_n) \mid\!\sim \mathbb{G}_1$.

2. In this case as well we can allow the agent to lie back and have nature do the actions for him.

3. Also note that our stock of agents and actions and agendas is fixed. We can allow for input of new agendas into our system as we proceed unveiling the future in our model. The incremental nature of our systems allows us to handle additional agendas as they come along. In fact, new concepts can be defined under these circumstances such as the notion of relevance potential characterized by proposition 7.6.

4. Note that our model allows us to define a notion of rationlaity (or what in definition 10.2 we referred to as 'proper function') for an agent. If an agent $\mathbf{X}$ takes action $\mathbf{b}$, whose postcondition is not relevant nor potentially relevant to his agendas, then he is not rational . This gives us the wherewithal to satisfy definition 10.3 of hypernormal performance and definition 10.4 of objective relevance and proposition 10.8 on objective irrelevance.

15.4 Case Studies

Let us conclude with some case studies:

Example 15.16 (A relevant modal example) Let $\mathbb{L}$ be a language with atoms only and $\Box$ (necessity) and conditional $\twoheadrightarrow$.

1. We need to define consequence $\Delta \mid\!\sim A$ on this language. We use semantics to define $\mid\!\sim$. Consider a tree Kripke model of the form (S, R, a, h). S is the tree, a is the root and R is the tree successor function. h is the assignment giving each atom q a subset $h(q) \subseteq S$. Figure 15.4 shows what it looks like.

   We have
   $t \vDash q$ iff $t \in h(q)$, for atomic q
   $t \vDash \Box A$ iff for all higher points s in the tree $(tRs), s \vDash A$.

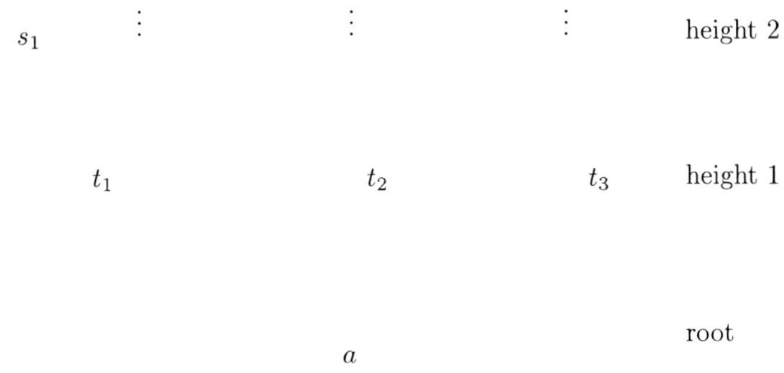

Figure 15.4

$t \vDash A \twoheadrightarrow B$ iff for all points s of the same height as t, if $s \vDash A$ then $s \vDash B$.

The reader should compare with definitions 14.25 and remark 14.26 of section 14.4.

2. Now that the consequence is defined, we can define actions and $+$. Since we want to concentrate on the actions, we did not include falsity $\bot$ in the language and therefore any set of wffs is consistent. Thus we can take $\Delta + A$ to be $\Delta \cup \{A\}$. In the general case, when $\bot$ is present, and $\Delta \cup \{A\}$ might be inconsistent, there is an easy 'wholesale' method for defining revision. This method works for any logic with a reasonable possible world semantics. We can define revision $+$ by translation into classical logic and by using an AGM revision operator $\circ$ in classical logic and then translating back. This is a quick way of doing revision in modal logic as worked out in [Gabbay *et al.*, 2000].

   The rest can continue as in definitions 15.11 onwards.

Let us just quickly check what actions would look like. Our simple actions are of the form $\mathbf{a} = (A, B)$, where A is the precondition and B is the postcondition. Thus if $\Delta \mid\!\sim A$ and $B \cup \{X | \Delta \vdash \Box X\}$ is consistent, which it is, then $\Delta_{\mathbf{a}} = \Delta \cup \{B\}$.

So the actions become simply $A \rightarrow B$, where $\rightarrow$ can be taken as ordinary (classical?) implication.

What is a simple agenda? It has the form $((\mathbf{a}_1, \gamma_1), \ldots, (\mathbf{a}_n, \gamma_n))$, i.e., the form $(((A_1 \rightarrow B_1), \gamma_1) \ldots ((A_n \rightarrow B_n), \gamma_n))$.

Given $(\Delta_1, \ldots, \Delta_{n+1})$, the sequence satisfies the agenda if for each $1 \leq i \leq n, \Delta_i \mid\!\sim A_i$ and $\Delta_{i+1} = \Delta \cup \{B_i\}$ and $\Delta_{i+1} \mid\!\sim \gamma_i$. Using the deduction theorem we get $\Delta_i \mid\!\sim B_i \rightarrow \gamma_i$. Note that since $\Delta_{i+1} \mid\!\sim \gamma_i$, we can replace the agenda above by the agenda $(\mathbf{b}_1, \ldots, \mathbf{b}_n)$, where $\mathbf{b}_i$ is $(A_i, B_i \wedge \gamma_i)$.

Thus we can assume our agenda contains no γ_is.

We now check what we get:

1. $\Delta_1 \mid\!\sim A_1$
2. $\Delta_2 = \Delta_1 \cup \{B_1\} \mid\!\sim A_2$. Hence $\Delta_1 \vdash B_1 \rightarrow A_2$
3. $\Delta_3 = \Delta_2 \cup \{B_2\} \mid\!\sim A_3$. Hence $\Delta_1 \mid\!\sim B_1 \wedge B_2 \rightarrow A_3$

   By induction we get

k. $\Delta_1 \mid\!\sim B_1 \wedge \cdots \wedge B_{k-1} \rightarrow A_k$,

   From this we conclude that:

   (1) an agenda is a sequence $(A_i, B_i), i = 1, \ldots, n$.

   (2) an agenda is implemented in Δ if $\Delta \mid\!\sim A_1$ and for all $2 \leq k \leq n$ we have $\Delta, B_1 \wedge \ldots \wedge B_{k-1} \mid\!\sim A_k$. Note that we are not using the classical $\rightarrow$ any more. It may not be in the language.

Example 15.17 (Blocks world example) Consider a blocks world example where we have two kinds of blocks: big blocks and small blocks. Think of them as wine barrels. Imagine a warehouse storing these blocks. The following are the warehouse rules:

1. The only allowable stacks of blocks are as in figure 15.5. Of course we

small	small	small			
big	small	small	big	small	small
big	big	small	big	big	small

Floor

Figure 15.5

   also allow single blocks on the floor

2. A state of the warehouse is a configuration of blocks. A state is *optimized* if one cannot rearrange the blocks in such a way that less floor space is used. Figure 15.6 shows an allowable but not optimized state of three blocks. To optimize the state of figure 15.6 one needs to put

small	
big 1	big 2

Floor

Figure 15.6

the small block on the floor then put the big block on top of the other one and then put the small block on top of the other two. Figure 15.7 shows two possible optimized states.

3. An input to a state is basically a delivery of blocks. Figure 15.8 shows an example of an input. It shows how some additional blocks were delivered to the optimized state of figure 15.7. Four big blocks were delivered, big 3–big 6 and the labourers dumped them as in figure 15.8. The situation in 15.8 is not allowable and a revision operator needs to be applied.

4. Let us assume that our revision algorithm simply takes blocks down from the top and puts them on the floor until a better allowable state is obtained. This is a simple-minded stylized way of operating.

   Thus figure 15.8 will be 'revised' to figure 15.9. Figure 15.9 is not optimized. An optimizing option is to put big 3 on top of big 6.

5. We can view our agenda as optimizing the warehouse. In formal terms

small	small
big 2	big 1
big 1	big 2

Floor

Figure 15.7

big 3	
small	big 6
big 2	big 5
big 1	big 4

Floor

Figure 15.8

small			
big 2		big 5	
big 1	big 3	big 4	big 6

Floor

Figure 15.9

we want to make true the statement 'The state is optimized with respect to space'. We can assume that some haulage company just delivers the blocks into the warehouse (input). The warehouse people 'revise"it in a simple way, as described, but do not optimize. the owner (our agenda agent) optimizes the warehouse himself, after the warehouse people have 'revised' the input. The actions available to him are the traditional actions of the AI blocks world, namely

- move(x, y), put block x on top of y, provided x is free and y is free and the result is allowed. (See condition (*) of example 15.9!)

6. Information (of the form) of what is on top of what and what is big or small) is relevant to the agenda if it affects optimization! So if a block on the floor is reclassified as 'small' this is relevant because we cannot put a big block on top of it, but if the middle big block 2 in figure 15.7 is reclassified as small, then this is not relevant because 15.7 is optimized even if big 2 is really small 2.

7. Let us now do the formal part.

Let $\mathrm{on}(x,y), \mathrm{big}(x), \mathrm{small}(x)$, **table** be the language of the basic state logic. We assume we have equality $=$. Let $\mathrm{move}(x,y)$ be a language for actions. Let Δ be the following theory (wff).

- $\forall x(\mathrm{on}(x,\mathbf{table}) \vee \exists y \mathrm{on}(x,y))$
- $\forall xy(\mathrm{on}(x,y) \to x \neq y)$
- $\forall x(\mathrm{big}(x) \vee \mathrm{small}(x))$
- $\forall x(\neg(\mathrm{big}(x) \wedge \mathrm{small}(x)))$
- $\forall xy\ (\mathrm{on}(x,y) \wedge \mathrm{on}(y,z) \to z = \mathbf{table})$
- $\forall xyz(\mathrm{on}(x,z) \wedge \mathrm{on}(y,z) \to x = y \vee z = \mathbf{table})$
- $\forall xy(\mathrm{on}(x,y) \to \neg\mathrm{on}(y,x))$
- $\forall x \neg\mathrm{on}(\mathbf{table},x)$
- $\forall xyz\neg(\mathrm{on}(x,y) \wedge \mathrm{on}(y,z) \wedge z \neq \mathbf{table} \wedge \mathrm{big}(x) \wedge \mathrm{big}(y) \wedge \mathrm{big}(z))$
- $\forall xy(\neg\mathrm{on}(x,y) \wedge \mathrm{big}(x) \wedge \mathrm{small}(y))$.

We are not saying whether big(**table**) holds but it makes sense to say that.

The preconditions for an action $\mathrm{move}(x,y)$ are as follows:

$$\begin{array}{l}\neg\exists z \mathrm{on}(z,x) \wedge x \neq \mathbf{table} \wedge \\ [y = \mathbf{table} \vee \neg\exists z \mathrm{on}(z,y)] \wedge \\ \neg[big(x) \wedge \mathrm{small}(y)] \wedge \\ \wedge\neg\exists uv(v \neq \mathbf{table} \wedge \mathrm{on}(y,u) \wedge \mathrm{on}(u,v))\end{array}$$

The post condition of $\mathrm{move}(x,y)$ is $\mathrm{on}(x,y) \wedge \neg\exists z \mathrm{on}(z,x)$.

The agenda is to minimize the number of blocks on the table. Here is how we express it.

Let

$$\begin{array}{l}\alpha(n) = \exists x_1,\ldots,x_n(\bigwedge_i \mathrm{on}(x_i,\mathbf{table}) \wedge \forall y(\mathrm{on}(y,\mathbf{table}) \to \bigvee_i y = x_i) \\ W(m) = \exists x_1,\ldots,x_m(\bigwedge_{i\neq j} x_i \neq x_j \wedge \forall y(\bigvee_i y = x_i))\end{array}$$

$W(m)$ is there are exactly m elements and $\alpha(n)$ says there are exactly n elements on the table.

Assume we are given the theory Δ and a $W(m)$, let size^m_β be a formula of the form $\mathrm{size}^m_\beta = \bigwedge_{i=1}^m \beta_i(x_i)$ where $\beta_i(x_i) = \pm\mathrm{big}(x_i)$ and $\beta = (\beta_1,\ldots,\beta_m)$. size^m_β says the size of each block.

Then there exists a first n, dependent on m and size_β^m, such that $W(m) \wedge \Delta \wedge \text{size}_\beta^m \vdash \neg\alpha_k$ for each $k < n$, but not for $k = n$.

For example, for three big blocks $n = 2$.

The agenda is then for each $W(m)$ and size_β^m to make sure by moving blocks that $\alpha(n)$ holds for this minimal n.

Chapter 16

Conclusion

16.1 Introduction

Der Ausgang giebt den Taten ihre Titel.

Goethe

Before we continue to the next section, let us recheck whether our theory has addressed the adequacy conditions listed at the beginning of chapter 7. We discuss these conditions one by one.

AC1: In the formal model relevance is not excessive, i.e., it is not derivable that either everything is relevant to everything or nothing is relevant to anything.

AC2: Given that circumstances include an agent's current state, current agenda and available actions then obviously relevance is context sensitive in the formal model.

AC3: The formal account models degrees of relevance enabling more or fewer actions and furthering more agendas.

AC4: In the formal model, negative relevance means hindering the closure of agendas.

AC5: The connection with fallacies of relevance will be studied in Volume 3 of our monograph series, *Fallacies and Other Seductions.* We will say now that the formal model is well-positioned for this task.

AC6: We have used a variant of relevance logic as our base logic.

AC7: Belief revision is central in our model.

AC8: Although our formal model extends in a natural way to a dialogue model, agenda relevance is not intrinsically a dialogical notion.

AC9: The formal system models agenda relevance, and the extent to which agenda relevance analyses the common notion of relevance the formal model captures a common notion.

AC10: An adaptation of AB-relevance logic is our own base logic, and we have tried to improve upon the notion of contextual effects. See section 13.2.5.

This chapter discusses further formal aspects of agenda relevance which we leave for the fourth, more mathematical, volume of our series entitled *Formal Models of Practical Reasoning.*

16.2 Quantification

The models for agenda relevance presented so far in this book are propositional. When we move to predicate logics we encounter all the known difficulties and options troubling traditional modal logic as well as some new ones characteristic to our way of modelling agenda relevance. The task of this section is to familiarize our readers with the kind of quantificational difficulties generated in our models of agenda relevance.

Our starting point is modal logic **K4**. Its semantics calls for possible worlds with domains. Modal **K4** can also be understood as a future temporal logic and this way of looking at it gives us a good base for comparison with our own models of agenda relevance. The **K4** models have the form (S, R, a, D_t, h_t), where S is the set of possible worlds, $a \in S$ is the actual world, D_t is the domain at world t and h_t is the assignment at world t to the predicates, constants and variables of the language. The relation R is an arbitrary transitive irreflexive relation on S. In our agenda relevance models the worlds arise from state theories and R is the transitive closure of the basic revision relation

- $s = t$ revised by input β (being the post-condition of some action).

Figure 16.1 describes a typical situation in the **K4** semantics.

In this context, we have the following options for constants and quantifiers:

1. Options on the relation between D_t, D_{s_1} and D_{s_2} (e.g., $D_t = D_{s_1} = D_{s_2}$, constant domains).

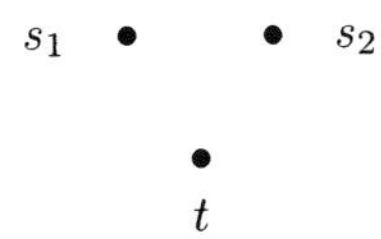

Figure 16.1

2. Options on the interpretation of the linguistic constants c (e.g., c is rigid) and predicates (e.g., does h_t assign extensions to predicates in D_t or in $D = \bigcup_{t \in S} D_t$?.)

3. Options on the definition of term forming operators such as ε-symbols (a simple way of dealing with $\varepsilon x A(x)$ is to index it with a world, i.e., $\varepsilon^w x A(x)$.)

The simplest arrangement for modal **K4** is constant domains where all constants are rigid designators and where the ε-symbol is indexed by world. So we write $\varepsilon^t x A(x)$ to be an $x \in D$ such that $t \vDash A(x)$, if such an x exists and to be arbitrary otherwise. This designator is *rigid*, so $s \vDash A(\varepsilon^t_x A(x))$ iff an element chosen at world t such that $A(x)$ holds at world t continues to satisfy A in the world s.

Thus, for example

$$\begin{gathered} t \vDash \Box A(\varepsilon^t x \neg \Box A(x)) \wedge tRs \\ \rightarrow s \vDash \Box\Box A(\varepsilon^s x \neg \Box A(x)) \end{gathered}$$

is equivalent to the Barcan formula of constant domains.

We can write it sloppily as

$$\Box A(\varepsilon x \neg \Box A(x)) \rightarrow \Box\Box A(\varepsilon x \neg \Box A(x))$$

We can use a device from the logic of nominals and write

$$\begin{gathered} \Box A(\downarrow_w \varepsilon^w x \neg \Box A(x)) \rightarrow \\ \Box\Box A(\downarrow_w \varepsilon^w x \neg \Box A(x)) \end{gathered}$$

where

$$\begin{gathered} t \vDash \downarrow_w B(\varepsilon^w x A(x)) \text{ iff} \\ t \vDash B(\varepsilon^t x A(x)) \end{gathered}$$

We have the ε axiom

$$\exists x A(x) \rightarrow \downarrow_w A(\varepsilon^w x A(x))$$

We can now describe the main difference between agenda relevance models and **K4** models. In **K4** models, when we 'stand' in world t, the worlds s_1, s_2 also exist before us. In fact the entire flow of time is available. In agenda relevance we have an evolving open future point of view. Thus at time t, s_1 and s_2 are two possible futures that have not occurred yet. So what then does $\Diamond \downarrow_w \varepsilon^w x A(x)$ mean? To see the problem, assume that $t \vDash \Diamond\exists x A(x)$, and let tRs hold with $s \vDash \exists x A(x)$ and $x_0 = \varepsilon^s x A(x)$. With this understanding, $\Diamond A(x_0)$ means that $A(x_0)$ is true in the future. In the **K4** semantics this is OK because the world s is laid out for us in the model and x_0 can be identified. However, the future has not yet happened in our agenda relevance model, and so x_0 cannot be identified at world t. So what does $\Diamond\exists x A(x)$ mean in agenda relevance models? Let us understand $\Diamond\exists x A(x)$ as meaning that we have an agenda to make $\Diamond\exists x A(x)$ true.

So we can talk about x_0, but we do not know which one it is!

Let us continue to develop this situtation. Imagine that we might have another agenda, to make $\Box B(x_0)$ always true, i.e., $\Box(\downarrow_w \varepsilon^w x A(x))$, as illustrated in the following example 16.1.

Example 16.1

1. John will buy a car.

2. Mary will always insure this car.

(1) can be written as

$$\Diamond\exists x[\text{John buys}(x) \wedge \text{ Car}(x)]$$

and (2) can be written as

$$\text{Insure Mary}(x_0)$$

where x_0 is what is chosen by $\Diamond \downarrow_w \varepsilon^w x(\text{John buys}(x) \wedge \text{Car}(x))$.

We can write

$$x_0 = \varepsilon y^{\varepsilon^t w \Diamond(\downarrow_w \varepsilon^w x(\text{John buys}(x) \wedge \text{Car}(x)))}(\text{John buys}(y) \wedge \text{Car}(y))$$

This is still a problem since there are alternative futures and we do not know which one will come to be and therefore what is x_0. Does Mary want to insure all of these cars, or only the one John will actually buy?

A detailed quantificational model will be presented in Volume 4, *Formal Models of Practical Reasoning.*

16.3 Some Tail Ends

In our disucssion in chapter 9 of definitions 9.6, 9.7 and 9.9, we saw that the formal resources of Part III would not be able to accommodate the notion of linked (or, equivalently, irredundant) proofs, and by extension of linked, or irredundant information. Definition 9.6 is a definition of relevance. It does not make the cut formally; it makes essential use of the notion of wholly irredundant information. Given the centrality of a definition of relevance to a theory of relevance, it cannot be regarded as a peripheral detail that 9.6 fails the cut. The idea behind 9.6 is that redundancy and relevance do not make especially good neighbours, although clearly enough in low doses redundancy can be an aid to relevance. We persist in the opinion that, since the irredundancy property is a perfectly fit target for logical investigation (after all, it is crucially tied to our concept of strong relevance), it is desirable that we seek to repair this omission, never mind what we may think of definiton 9.6. Once this work is accomplished 9.6 would have a fighting chance in a formal account of relevance.

For the present it seems prudent to take 9.6 as defining *strong relevance*, as we may now say, and to concede that the formal model as we have it now does not model strong relevance. This is far from saying that it models no definition of agenda relevance. At definition 15.4, the formal model gives us simple agenda relevance, which is a good approximation of definition 7.6. Information **I** is relevant for **X** with respect to agenda **A** iff in processing **I**, **X** is affected in ways that advance or close **A**.

Here is a second issue that we should pay some attention to. In earlier chapters we made much of the fact that some of what an agent does in discharging his cognitive agendas is done 'down below', and further that, at least some of the time, down-below cognition is subsymbolic. Consider a case. Harry is informationally stimulated in a certain way and is induced to make a certain inference. This he does subsymbolically. We want to be able to say that the information that induced Harry to make that subsymbolic inference was relevant if in drawing the inference one of Harry's agendas was advanced. (We can but need not assume that Harry's agenda was tacit.) On the other hand, the formal model of agenda relevance is thoroughly linguistic in character. Perhaps there are those who would conclude that this disparity between the formal model and the actual state of Harry's processes in this situation precludes the formalization of Harry's inference and of the relevance of the information that induced it. This would be a mistake. In representing something in a formal language it is certainly not necessary — or even typical — that what is represented is itself lingusitic. It is true that the state an agent is in when cognition is going on is usefully represented by propositions expressing sentences, but sentential represnta- tion is hardly out of place with respect to those states or processes that exhibit properties in which the formal model has a stake. In particular, if Harry drew a subsymbolic inference on being informationally stimulated in a certain way, and if, as we are supposing, this did not involve Harry in the processing of bits of language, it is still appropriate to represent both the stimulating information and the thing inferred from it sententially. For sentential structures, too, exhibit the properties in which the formal model has a state — *information, inference, consequence, consistency* and so on.

This leads us to a certain conjecture in the spirit of late in chapter 3. Let S be any state or process occurring down below. Then if that state or those processes are correctly describable in terms in which the formal logician has a stake, then we may say defeasibly that corresponding to that state or that process is a propositional sturcture describable in the same terms and, for this reason, that structure is at least a candidate for the job of representing the logical landscape of that particuar part of what has gone on down below. Think again of Harry's drawing an inference subsymbolically. Just because in *drawing* it, Harry engaged in no symbolic processing, it does not follow that in *describing* it, the theorist must likewise eschew symbolic representation.

The point on which the defeasibility of the current proposal is this. Since we know very little of what goes on inside Harry's black box, it is possible that although what happens there and what is presented in a logician's model can share in a common vocabulary, it cannot be ruled out that this commonality is disavowed by systematic ambiguity, that e.g., the inferences that go on inside Harry's black box are inferences in a different sense from those describable in a system of logic, and so different in fact, that the best that the formal model can do with respect to these black box inferences is seriously to misrepresent them.

We make two observations. *If* this were so, it would be so for Harry's inferences up above *as well as* for down below. *Whether* it is so depends upon black box facts that it is the role of the cognitive scientist, not the logician, to ferret out.

List of Main Propositions, Definitions and Theorems

Chapter 7

Chapter 8

Chapter 9

Definition 9.8, p. 236

Definition 9.9, p. 237

Definition 9.10, p. 239

Chapter 10

Definition 10.1, p. 282

Definition 10.2, p. 282

Definition 10.3, p. 283

Definition 10.4, p. 283

Proposition 10.8, p. 308

Proposition 10.9, p. 309

Chapter 12

Definition 12.4, p. 345

Definition 12.6, p. 349

Chapter 13

Definition 13.7, p. 379

Definition 13.11, p. 385

Definition 13.16, p. 390

Definition 13.17, p. 391

Chapter 14

Definition 14.1, p. 399

Definition 14.2, p. 399

Definition 14.3, p. 399

Chapter 15

Bibliography

[Adler, 2002] Jonathan Adler. *Belief's Own Ethics.* Cambridge, MA: MIT Press, 2002.

[Aizawa, 1994] K. Aizawa. Representations without rules, connectionism and the syntactic argument. *Synthese*, 101:465–492, 1994.

[Aizawa, 2000] K. Aizawa. Connectionist rules: A rejoinder to Horgan and Tienson's *connectionism and the philosoph of psychology. Acta Analytica*, 22:59–85, 2000.

[Alchourrón *et al.*, 1985] C. E. Alchourrón, P. Gardenfors, and D. Matkinson. On the logic of theory change: Partial meet functions for contraction and revision. *Journal of Symbolic Logic*, 50:510–530, 1985.

[Aliseda-LLera, 1997] A. Aliseda-LLera. *Seeking Explanations: Abduction in Logic, Philosophy of Science and Artificial Intelligence.* Amsterdam: Institute for Logic, Language and Computation, 1997. PhD dissertation (ILLC Dissertation Series 1997-4).

[Allen and Hayes, 1989] J. F. Allen and P. J. Hayes. Moments and points in an interval-based temporal logic. *Computational Intelligence*, 5:225–238, 1989.

[Allen *et al.*, 1991] J. F. Allen, H. A. Kautz, R. N. Pelavin, and J. D. Tenenburg. *Reasoning About Plans.* San Mateo, CA: Morgan Kaufmann, 1991.

[Anderson and Belnap, 1975] A. R. Anderson and N. D. Belnap, Jr. *Entailment: The Logic of Relevance and Necessity*, volume 1. Princeton, NJ: Princeton University Press, 1975.

[Anderson, 1983] J. R. Anderson. *The Architecture of Cognition.* Cambridge, MA: Harvard University Press, 1983.

[Anscombe, 1957] G. E. M. Anscombe. *Intention.* New York: Cornell University Press, 1957.

[Antoniou, 1995] G. Antoniou. *Non-Monotonic Reasoning.* Cambridge, MA: MIT Press, 1995.

[Atlas, 1989] J. Atlas. *Philosophy without Ambiguity.* Oxford: Oxford University Press, 1989.

[Audi, 1999] R. A. Audi. *The Cambridge Dictionary of Philosophy.* Cambridge: Cambridge University Press, 2nd edition, 1999.

[Austin, 1961] J. L. Austin. *How to Do Things with Words.* Oxford: Oxford University Press, 1961.

[Axelrod, 1984] R. Axelrod. *The Evolution of Cooperation.* New York: Basic Books, 1984.

[Axsom *et al.*, 1987] D. S. Axsom, S. Yates, and S. Chaiken. Audience response as a heuristic case in persuasion. *Journal of Personality and Social Psychology*, 53:30–40, 1987.

[Bach, 1984] K. Bach. Default reasoning: Jumping to conclusions and knowing when to think twice. *Pacific Philosophical Quarterly*, 65:37–58, 1984.

[Bar-Hillel and Carnap, 1952] Y. Bar-Hillel and R. Carnap. Outline of a theory of semantic information. Technical Report 247, Research Laboratory of Electronics, Massachusetts Institute of Technology, 1952. Reprinted in Bar-Hillel, *Language and Information*, Reading, MA: Addison-Wesley, 1964.

[Bar-Hillel, 1955] Y. Bar-Hillel. An examination of information theory. *Philosophy of Science*, 22:86–105, 1955.

[Bar-Hillel, 1964] Y. Bar-Hillel. Semantic information and its measures. In *Language and Information.* Reading, MA: Addison-Wesley, 1964. Article was originally published in 1955.

[Barringer *et al.*, 1996] H. Barringer, M. Fisher, D. M. Gabbay, R. Owens, and M. Reynolds. *The Imperative Future: Principles of Executable Temporal Logic.* Tauton, UK: Research Studies Press and New York: John Wiley and Sons, 1996.

[Barth and Krabbe, 1982] E. M. Barth and E. C. W. Krabbe. *From Axiom to Dialogue: A Philosophical Study of Logic and Argumentation.* Berlin and New York: de Gruyter, 1982.

[Barwise and Perry, 1983] J. Barwise and J. Perry. *Situations and Attitudes.* Cambridge, MA: MIT Press, 1983.

[Barwise, 1977] J. Barwise. *Handbook of Mathematical Logic.* Amsterdam, New York and Oxford: North Holland, 1977.

[Barwise, 1989a] J. Barwise. *The Situation in Logic.* Stanford: CSLI, 1989. Lecture Notes 17.

[Barwise, 1989b] J. Barwise. *The Situation in Logic.* Stanford, CA: Center for the Study of Language and Information (CSLI), 1989.

[Bechtel and Abrahamsen, 1991] W. Bechtel and A. Abrahamsen. *Connectionism and the Mind.* Oxford: Blackwell, 1991.

[Beech *et al.*, 1989] A. Beech, T. Powell, J. McWilliam, and G. Claridge. Evidence of reduced "cognitive inhibition" in schizophrenia. *British Journal of Clinical Psychology*, 28:109–116, 1989.

[Beer, 1995] R. D. Beer. Comptuational and dynamical languages for atuonomous agents. In R. Port and T. van Gelder, editors, *Mind as Motion: Explorations in the Dynamics of Cognition*, pages 121–147. Cambridge, MA: MIT Press/Bradford Books, 1995.

[Belke, 1975] E. Belke. Dietary vitamin A and human lung cancer. *Internation Journal of Cancer*, 15:561–565, 1975.

[Benacerraf, 1973] P. Benacerraf. Mathematical truth. *Journal of Philosophy*, LXX:661–679, 1973.

[Bennett, 1973] C. H. Bennett. Logical reversibility of computation. *IBM Journal of Research Development*, pages 525–532, November 1973.

[Bennett, 1990] J. Bennett. Why is belief involuntary? *Analysis*, 50:87–107, 1990.

[Berlin, 1939] I. Berlin. Verification. In *Proceedings of the Argumentation Society*. Oxford: Blackwell Publishers, 1939.

[Blackburn, 1994] S. Blackburn. *The Oxford Dictionary of Philosophy*. Oxford: Oxford University Press, 1994.

[Blair *et al.*, 1992] P. Blair, R.V. Guha, and W. Pratt. Microtheories: An ontological engineer's guide. Technical Report CYC-050-92, Microelectronics and Computer Technology Corporation, Austin, TX, 1992.

[Blair, 1992] J. A. Blair. Premissary relevance. *Argumentation*, 6:203–217, 1992.

[Blakemore, 1987] D. Blakemore. *Semantic Constraints on Relevance*. Oxford: Basil Blackwell, 1987.

[Block, 1995] N. Block. On a confusion about a function of consciousness. *Behavioral and Brain Science*, 18:227–247, 1995.

[Boden, 1987] M. A. Boden. *Aritifical Intelligence and Natural Man*. Cambridge, MA: MIT Press, 1987.

[Bonevac, 1982] D. A. Bonevac. *Reduction in the Abstract Sciences*. Indianapolis, IN: Hackett, 1982.

[Boole, 1854] G. Boole. *An Investigation of the Laws of Thought on which are Founded the Mathematical Theories of Logic and Probabilities*. Cambridge: Macmillan and London: Walton and Maberly, 1854. Reprinted by LaSalle, Ill: Open Court in 1952.

[Botterill and Carruthers, 1999] G. Botterill and P. Carruthers. *The Philosophy of Psychology*. Cambridge, U.K. and New York: Cambridge University Press, 1999.

[Bowles, 1990] G. Bowles. Propositional relevance. *Informal Logic*, XII:65–77, 1990. Originally presented as 'On Relevance' to the Conference on Critical Thinking, Newport, VA, 1987.

[Brams, 1975] S. J. Brams. *Game Theory and Politics.* New York: The Free Press, 1975.

[Brand and Walton, 1975] M. Brand and D. Walton. *Action Theory.* Dordrecht: Reidel, 1975.

[Brand, 1984] M. Brand. *Intending and Action: Toward a Naturalized Action Theory.* Cambridge MA: MIT Press, 1984.

[Brandom, 2000] R. B. Brandom. *Articulating Reasons.* Cambridge, MA: Harvard University Press, 2000.

[Bratman, 1987] M. E. Bratman. *Intention Plans and Practical Reason.* Cambridge, MA: Harvard University Press, 1987.

[Bratman, 1999] M. Bratman. *Faces of Intention: Selected Essays on Intention and Agency.* Cambridge: Cambridge University Press, 1999.

[Bringsjord and Zenzen, 1997] S. Bringsjord and M. Zenzen. Cognition is not computation. *Synthese*, 113:285–320, 1997.

[Brooks, 1991] R. A. Brooks. Intelligence without representation. *Aritificial Intelligence*, 47:139–159, 1991.

[Brown, 1993] B. Brown. Old quantum theory: A paraconsistent approach. *Proceedings of the Biennial Meetings of the Philosophy of Science Association*, 2:397–411, 1993.

[Bruza *et al.*, 2000] P. D. Bruza, D. W. Song, and K. F. Wong. Aboutness from a commonsense perspective. *The Journal of the American Society for Information Science*, 51(12):1090–1105, 2000.

[Burton, 1999] R. G. Burton. A neurocomputational approach to abduction. *Mind*, 9:257–265, 1999.

[Carlsen, 1982] L. Carlsen. *Dialogue Games.* Dordrecht and Boston: Reidel, 1982.

[Carlson and Pelletier, 1995] G. N. Carlson and F. J. Pelletier. *The Generic Book.* Chicago: Chicago University Press, 1995.

[Carston, 1987] R. Carston. Being explicit. *Behavioral and Brain Sciences*, 10:713–714, 1987.

[Cartwright, 1983a] N. Cartwright. *How the Laws of Physics Lie.* Oxford: The Clarendon Press, 1983a.

[Change and Lee, 1975] C. L. Change and R. C. T. Lee. Some properties of fuzzy logic. *Information and Control*, 19:417–431, 1975.

[Chater and Oaksford, 1999] N. Chater and M. Oaksford. The probability heuristics model of syllogistic reasoning. *Cognitive Psychology*, 39:191–258, 1999.

[Cheng and Holyoak, 1985] P. W. Cheng and K. J. Holyoak. Pragmatic reasoning schemas. *Cognitive Psychology*, 17:391–416, 1985.

[Cherniak, 1986] C. Cherniak. *Minimal Rationality*. Cambridge, MA: MIT Press, 1986.

[Churchland, 1989] P. M. Churchland. *A Neurocomputational Perspective: The Nature of Mind and the Structure of Science*. Cambridge, MA: MIT Press, 1989.

[Churchland, 1995] P. M. Churchland. *The Engine of Reason, The Seat of the Soul*. Cambridge, MA: The MIT Press, 1995.

[Clark, 1989] A. Clark. *Microrecognition*. Cambridge, MA: MIT Press, 1989.

[Clark, 1997] A. Clark. *Being There: Putting Brain, Body and World Together Again*. Cambridge, MA: MIT Press/Bradford Books, 1997.

[Coady, 1992] C. A. J. Coady. *Testimony: A Philosophical Study*. Oxford: Oxford University Press, 1992.

[Cohen and Nagel, 1934] M. R. Cohen and E. Nagel. *An Introduction to Logic and Scientific Method*. New York: Harcourt Brace, 1934.

[Cohen *et al.*, 1990] J. D. Cohen, K. Dunbar, and J. L. McClelland. On the control of automatic processes: A parallel distributed processing account of the stroop effect. *Psychological Review*, 97:332–361, 1990.

[Cohen, 1972] J. Cohen. *Psychological Probability, or the Art of Doubt*. London: Allen and Unwin, 1972.

[Cohen, 1977] L. J. Cohen. *The Probably and the Provable*. Oxford: Clarendon Press, 1977.

[Cohen, 1980] L. J. Cohen. Bayesianism vs. Baconianism in the evaluation of medical diagnosis. *British Journal for the Philosophy of Science*, 31:45–62, 1980.

[Cohen, 1981] L. J. Cohen. Can human irrationality be experimentally demonstrated? *The Behavioral and Brain Sciences*, 4:317–331, 1981.

[L. Jonathan Cohen, 1982] L. J. Cohen. What is necessary for testimonial corroboration? *British Journal for the Philosophy of Science*, 33:161–164, 1982.

[Cohen, 1986] L. J. Cohen. The corroboration theorem: A reply to Folk. *Mind*, XCV:510–512, 1986.

[Cohen, 1989] L. J. Cohen. *An Introduction to the Philosophy of Induction and Probability*. Oxford: Clarendon Press, 1989.

[Cohen, 1991] L. J. Cohen. Twice told tales: A reply to Schlesinger. *Philosophical Studies*, 62:197–200, 1991.

[Cohen, 1994] L. J. Cohen. Some steps towards a general theory of relevance. *Synthese*, 101:171–185, 1994.

[Cook, 1971] S. A. Cook. The complexity of theorem-proving procedures. In *Proceedings of the 3rd Annual ACM Symposium on Theory of Computing*, pages 151–158. New York: Association for Computing Machinery, 1971.

[Cook, 1983] S. A. Cook. An overview of computational complexity. In *Communications of the Association for Computing Machinery*, pages 400–408. New York: Association for Computing Machinery, 1983.

[Cooper, 2001] W. S. Cooper. *The Evolution of Reason: Logic as a Branch of Biology.* Cambridge: Cambridge University Press, 2001.

[Copeland, 1993] J. Copeland. *Artificial Intelligence.* Oxford: Blackwell, 1993.

[Corteen and Wood, 1972] R. S. Corteen and B. Wood. Autonomic responses for shock-associated words in an unattended channel. *Journal of Experimental Psychology*, 94:308–313, 1972.

[Cross and Wilkins, 1964] R. Cross and N. Wilkins. *An Outline of the Law of Evidence.* London: Butterworths, 1964.

[Cummins, 1989] R. Cummins. *Meaning and Mental Representation.* Cambridge, MA: MIT Press, 1989.

[Cuppens and Demolombe, 1988] F. Cuppens and R. Demolombe. Cooperative answering: a methodology to provide intellgient access to databases. In *Proceedings of 2nd International Conference on Expert Database Systems*, Tysons Corner, VA: 1988.

[Cuppens and Demolombe, 1989] F. Cuppens and R. Demolombe. How to recognise interesting topics to provide cooperative answering. *Information Systems*, 14(2), 1989.

[Davidson, 1963] D. Davidson. Actions, reasons and causes. *Journal of Philosophy*, 60:685–700, 1963. Reprinted in Donald Davidson editor, *Essays on Actions and Events*, Oxford: Clarendon Press 1980, 3–19.

[Davidson, 1967] D. Davidson. Truth and meaning. *Synthese*, 17:304–323, 1967.

[Davidson, 1974] D. Davidson. The very idea of a conceptual scheme. *Proceedings and Addresses of the American Philosophical Association*, pages 5–20, 1974.

[Davidson, 1980] D. Davidson, editor. *Essays on Actions and Events.* Oxford: Oxford University Press, 1980.

[Davis, 1991] S. Davis. *Pragmatics: A Reader.* New York: Oxford University Press, 1991.

[Dawson and Schell, 1982] M. E. Dawson and A. M. Schell. Electrodermal responses to attended and nonattended significant stimuli during dichotic listening. *Journal of Experimental Psychology: Human Perception and Performance*, 8:315–324, 1982.

[de Kleer, 1986] J. de Kleer. An assumption-based tms. *Artificial Intelligence*, 28:127–162, 1986.

[de Rijke, 2001] M. de Rijke. Computing with meaning. In Johan van Benthem, Paul Dekker, Jan van Eijck, Maarten de Rijke, and Yde Venema, editors, *Logic in Action*, pages 75–113. Institute for Logic, Language and Computation, Amsterdam, 2001.

[Demolombe and Jones, 1999] R. Demolombe and A. J. I. Jones. Sentences of the kind 'sentence p is about topic t. In H. J. Ohlbach and U. Reyle, editors, *Logic, Language and Reasoning*, pages 115–133. Dordrecht and Boston: Kluwer, 1999.

[Dennett, 1984] D. C. Dennett. *Cognitive Wheels: The Frame Problem in A.I.* Cambridge: Cambridge University Press, 1984.

[Dennett, 1988] D. C. Dennett. Quining qualia. In A. Marcel and E. Bisiac, editors, *Consciousness in Contemporary Science*, pages 43–77. Oxford: Oxford University Press, 1988.

[Devlin, 1991] K. Devlin. *Logic and Information.* Cambridge: Cambridge University Press, 1991.

[Dewey, 1938] J. Dewey. *The Theory of Enquiry.* Vol 12 of JoAnn Boydston (ed.), *John Dewey: The Later Works, 1925–1953*, Carbondale, IL: Southern Illinois University Press, 1981, 1938.

[Diaz, 1981] M. R. Diaz. *Topics in the Logic of Relevance.* Berlin: Philosophica Verlag, 1981.

[Doyle, 1979] J. Doyle. A truth maintenance system. *Artificial Intelligence*, 7:231–272, 1979.

[Dretske, 1981] F. I. Dretske. *Knowledge and the Flow of Information.* Cambridge, MA: MIT Press, 1981.

[Dretske, 1986] F. I. Dretske. Misrepresentation. In Radu J. Bogen, editor, *Belief: Form, Content and Function*, pages 17–36. Oxford: Clarendon Press, 1986.

[Eagly and Chaiken, 1993] A. H. Eagly and S. Chaiken. *The Psychology of Attitudes.* Fort Worth: Harcourt Brace Jovanovich, 1993.

[Eells, 1991] E. Eells. *Probabilistic Causality.* Cambridge: Cambridge University Press, 1991.

[Ehrenfeucht, 1961] A. Ehrenfeucht. An application of games to the completeness problem for formalized theories. *Fundamenta Mathematica*, 49:129–141, 1961.

[Epstein, 1979] R. L. Epstein. Relatedness and implication. *Philosophical Studies*, 36:137–173, 1979.

[Evans and Over, 1996] J. St. B. T. Evans and D. E. Over. *Rationality and Reasoning.* Hove, UK: Psychology Press, 1996.

[Fikes and Nilsson, 1971] R. E. Fikes and N. J. Nilsson. STRIPS: A new approach to the application of theorem proving to problem solving. *Artificial Intelligence*, 2:189–208, 1971.

[Fisher, 1986] L. Fisher. The rules of evidence. *Newsweek*, 108:8, 1986.

[Flach and Kakas, 2000] P. A. Flach and A. C. Kakas. *Abduction and Induction: Essays on Their Relation and Integration.* Dordrecht and Boston: Kluwer, 2000.

[Fodor, 1975] J. A. Fodor. *The Language of Thought.* New York: Thomas Y. Crowell, 1975.

[Fodor, 1983] J. Fodor. *The Modularity of Mind.* Cambridge, MA: MIT Press, 1983.

[Fodor, 1984] J. Fodor. Semantics Wisconsin style. *Synthese*, 59:231–250, 1984.

[Fodor, 1998] J. Fodor. *Concepts: Where Cognitive Science Went Wrong.* Oxford: Oxford University Press, 1998.

[Fodor, 2000] J. Fodor. *The Mind Doesn't Work That Way.* Cambridge, MA: MIT, 2000.

[Fraissée, 1954] R. Fraissée. Sur l'extension aup relations de quelques proprietes des ordres. *Annales Scientificques de L'E'cole Normale Superieure*, 71:363–388, 1954.

[Frankfurt, 1988] H. Frankfurt. *The Importance of What We Care About.* Cambridge: Cambridge University Press, 1988.

[Freeman, 1992] J. B. Freeman. Relevance, warrants, backing, inductive support. *Argumentation*, 6:219–236, 1992.

[Frege, 1884] G. Frege. *The Foundations of Arithmetic: A Logico-mathematical Enquiry into the Concept of Number.* Oxford: Blackwell, 1884. Originally published in Breslau by Koebner. [Translated by J.L. Austin].

[Gabbay and Hunter, 1991] D. M. Gabbay and A. Hunter. Making inconsistency respectable. In Ph. Jorrand and J. Kelemen, editors, *Proceedings of Fundamental of Artificial Intelligene Research (FAIR '91)*, volume 535 of *LNAI*, pages 19–32. Berlin: Springer-Verlag, 1991.

[Gabbay and Malod, 2002] D. M. Gabbay and G. Malod. Naming worlds in modal and temporal logic. *Journal of Logic, Language and Information*, 11:29–65, 2002.

[Gabbay and Woods, 1999] D. M. Gabbay and J. Woods. Cooperate with your logic ancestors. *Journal of Logic, Language and Information*, 8, 1999.

[Gabbay and Woods, 2001] D. M. Gabbay and J. Woods. Non-cooperation in dialogue logic. *Synthese*, 127:161–186, 2001.

[Gabbay and Woods, 2001d] D. M. Gabbay and J. Woods. More on non-cooperation in dialogue logic. *Logic Journal of the IGPL*, 9:321–339, 2001d.

[Gabbay and Woods, 2004a] D. M. Gabbay and J. Woods. *The Reach of Abduction*. Amsterdam: North-Holland, 2004. To appear in the series *Studies in Logic and Practical Reasoning*.

[Gabbay and Woods, 2004b] D. M. Gabbay and J. Woods. Strong relevance logic. In preparation, 2004.

[Gabbay and Woods, 2005] D. M. Gabbay and J. Woods. *Formal Models of Practical Reasoning*. 2005. In preparation.

[Gabbay *et al.*, 2000] D. M. Gabbay, O. Rodrigues, and A. Russo. Revision by translation. In B. Bouchon-Meunier, R. R. Yager, and L. A. Zadeh, editors, *Information, Uncertainty and Fusion*, pages 3–31. Kluwer Academic Publishers, 2000.

[Gabbay *et al.*, 2002a] D. M. Gabbay, R. Nossum, and J. Woods. Context-dependent abduction and relevance. Technical report, King's College London, 2002.

[Gabbay *et al.*, 2002b] D. M. Gabbay, O. Rodriguez, and J. Woods. Belief contraction, anti-formulae and resource-draft. *Logic Journal of the IGPL*, 2002.

[Gabbay *et al.*, 2003] D. M. Gabbay, G. Pigozzi, and J. Woods. Controlled revision. *Journal of Logic and Computation*, 13:3–27, 2003.

[Gabbay, 1990] D. M. Gabbay. Editorial. *Journal of Logic and Computation*, 10:1–2, 1990.

[Gabbay, 1994] D. M. Gabbay. *What is a Logical System?* Oxford: Clarendon Press, 1994.

[Gabbay, 1996] D. M. Gabbay. *Labelled Deductive Systems*. Oxford: Oxford University Press, 1996.

[Gabbay, 1998a] D. M. Gabbay. *Elementary Logic: A Procedural Perspective*. Upper Saddle River, NJ: Prentice Hall, 1998.

[Gabbay, 1998b] D. M. Gabbay. *Fibring Logics*. Oxford: Oxford University Press, 1998. Vol. 38 of *Oxford Logic Guides*.

[Gabbay, 2001] D. M. Gabbay. What is a logical system 2. In *Logical Consequence: Rival Approaches*, pages 81–104. Oxford: Hermes Science Publications, 2001. Proceedings of the 1999 Conference of the SEP. Vol 1.

[Gabbay, 2002] D. M. Gabbay. A theory of hypermodal logics: mode shifting in modal logic. *Journal of Philosophical Logic*, forthcoming, 2002.

[Gamut, 1991] L. T. F. Gamut. *Logic, Language and Meaning, volume 2 [= Intensional Logic and Logical Grammar]*. Chicago: University of Chicago

Press, 1991. L.T.F. Gamut is the collective pseudonym for Johan van Benthem, J. A. Groenendijk, D. H. de Jongh and M. J. Stokhoff.

[Gazdar and Good, 1982] G. Gazdar and D. Good. On a notion of relevance. In N. Smith, editor, *Mutual Knowledge*, pages 88–100. London: Academic Press, 1982.

[Geffner, 1992] H. Geffner. *Default Reasoning: Causal and Conditional Theories*. Cambridge, MA: MIT Press, 1992.

[Gigerenzer and Selten, 2001a] G. Gigerenzer and R. Selten, editors. *Bounded Rationality: The Adaptive Toolbox*. Cambridge, MA: MIT Press, 2001.

[Gigerenzer and Selten, 2001b] G. Gigerenzer and R. Selten. Rethinking rationality. In *Bounded Rationality: The Adaptive Toolbox*, pages 1–12. Cambridge, MA: MT Press, 2001.

[Girle, 1993] R. A. Girle. Dialogue and entrenchment. *Proceedings of the Sixth Florida Artificial Intelligence Research Symposium*, pages 185–189, 1993.

[Girle, 1996] R. A. Girle. Knowledge: Organized and disorganized. In *Proceedings of the International Conference on Formal and Applied Practical Reasoning*, pages 246–260. Bonn, 1996.

[Girle, 1997] R. A. Girle. Belief sets and commitment stores. In Hans V. Hansen, Christopher W. Tindale, and Athena V. Colman, editors, *Argumentation and Rhetoric*. St. Catharines, ON: Ontario Society of the Study of Argument, 1997.

[Globus, 1992] G. Globus. Towards a non-computational cognitive neuroscience. *Journal of Cognitive Neuroscience*, 4:299–310, 1992.

[Glymour and Cooper, 1999] C. Glymour and G. F. Cooper. *Computation, Causation, and Discovery*. Menlo Park, CA:AAAI Press and Cambridge, MA and London: MIT Press, 1999.

[Gochet, 2002] P. Gochet. The dynamic turn in twentieth century logic. *Synthese*, 130:175–184, 2002.

[Godfrey-Smith, 1989] P. Godfrey-Smith. Misinformation. *Canadian Journal of Philosophy*, 19:533–550, 1989.

[Goodman, 1978] N. Goodman. *Ways of Worldmaking*. Indianapolis, IN: Hackett, 1978.

[Goodman, 1983] N. Goodman. *Fact, Fiction, and Forecast*. Cambridge MA: Harvard University Press, 4th edition, 1983. First edition was printed in 1954.

[Govier, 1988a] T. Govier. *A Practical Study of Argument*. Belmont, CA: Wadsworth, 1988.

[Govier, 1988b] T. Govier, editor. *Selected Issues in Logic and Communication*. Belmont, CA: Wadsworth, 1988.

[Gray, 2000] J. Gray. *Two Faces of Liberalism*. New York: The New Press, 2000.

[Grice, 1991] H. P. Grice. Logic and conversation. In Steven Davis, editor, *Pragmatics: A Reader*, pages 305–315. New York: Oxford University Press, 1991.

[Grice, 2001] P. Grice. *Aspects of Reason*. Oxford: Clarendon Press, 2001.

[Groenendijk and Stokhof, 1991] J. Groenendijk and M. Stokhof. Dynamic predicate logic. *Linguistics and Philosophy*, 14:39–100, 1991.

[Groenendijk *et al.*, 1996] J. Groenendijk, M. Stokhof, and F. Veltman. Coreference and modality. In S. Lappin, editor, *Handbook of Contemporary Semantic Theory*, pages 179–213. Oxford: Blackwell, 1996.

[Guarini, 2001] M. Guarini. A defence of connectionism against the "SYNTACTIC" argument. *Synthese*, 128:287–317, 2001.

[Guha and Levy, 1990] R. V. Guha and A. Y. Levy. A relevance based meta level. Technical Report ACT-CYC-040-90, Microelectronics and Computer Technology Corporation, Austin, TX, 1990.

[Hacking, 1990] I. Hacking. *The Taming of Chance*. Cambridge: Cambridge University Press, 1990.

[Hájek, 1998] P. Hájek. *Metamathematics of Fuzzy Logic*. Dordrecht and Boston: Kluwer, 1998.

[Hamblin, 1970] C. L. Hamblin. *Fallacies*. London: Methuen, 1970.

[Harel, 1984] D. Harel. Dynamic logic. In D. M. Gabbay and F. Guenthner, editors, *Handbook of Philosophical Logic, Volume II: Extensions of Classical Logic*, pages 497–604. Boston: D. Reidel, 1984.

[Harman, 1986] G. Harman. *Change in View: Principles of Reasoning*. Cambridge, MA: MIT Press, 1986.

[Hartley, 1928] R. L. Hartley. Transmission of information. *Bell Technical Journal*, 7:535–563, 1928.

[Haugeland, 1987] J. Haugeland. *Aritificial Intelligence: The Very Idea*. Cambridge, MA: MIT Press, 1987.

[Hendriks-Jansen, 1996] H. Hendriks-Jansen. *Catching Ourselves in the Act: Situated Activity, Interactive Emergence, Evolution and Human Thought*. Cambridge, MA: MIT Press/Bradford Books, 1996.

[Henkin, 1950] L. Henkin. Completeness in the theory of types. *Journal of Symbolic Logic*, 15:81–91, 1950.

[Herzberger, 1982] H. G. Herzberger. Notes on naive semantics. *Journal of Philosophical Logic*, 11:62–102, 1982. Reprinted in *The Paradox of the Liar*, R. L. Martin, ed., pp. 134–174. Oxford: Clarenden Press, 1984.

[Hintikka and Bachman, 1991] J. Hintikka and J. Bachman. *What if ...? Toward Excellence in Reasoning*. Mountain View, CA: Mayfield, 1991.

[Hintikka and Pietarinen, 1966] J. Hintikka and J. Pietarinen. Semantic information and inductive logic. In Jaakko Hintikka and Patrick Suppes, editors, *Aspects of Inductive Logic*, pages 96–112. Amsterdam: North-Holland, 1966.

[Hintikka and Suppes, editors, 1970] J. Hintikka and P. Suppes, editors. *Information and Inference*. Dordrecht: Reidel, 1970.

[Hintikka, 1970] J. Hintikka. On semantic information. In J. Hintikka and P. Suppes, editors, *Information and Inference*, pages 3–27. Dordrecht: Reidel, 1970.

[Hintikka, 1973] J. Hintikka. *Logic, Language Games and Information*. Oxford: Clarendon Press, 1973.

[Hintikka, 1989] J. Hintikka. The role of logic in argumentation. *The Monist*, 72, 1989.

[Hirshberg, 1991] J. Hirshberg. *A Theory of Scalar Implicature*. New York: Garland, 1991.

[Hirt and Pithers, 1991] M. Hirt and W. Pithers. Selective attention and levels of coding in schizophrenia. *British Journal of Clinical Psychology*, 30:139–149, 1991.

[Hitchcock, 1987] D. Hitchcock. Enthymematic arguments. In Frans H. van Eemeren, Rob Grootendorst, J. Anthony Blair, and Charles A. Willard, editors, *Argument: Across the Lines of Discipline*, pages 289–298. Dordrecht and Providence: Foris Publications, 1987.

[Hitchcock, 1992] D. Hitchcock. Relevance. *Argumentation*, 6:189–202, 1992.

[Hitchcock, 2000] D. Hitchcock. Fallacies and formal logic in Aristotle. *History and Philosophy of Logic*, 21:207–221, 2000.

[Hogan and Tienson, 1996] T. Hogan and J. Tienson. *Connectionism and the Philosophy of Psychology*. Cambridge, MA: MIT Press, 1996.

[Holland *et al.*, 1986] J. H. Holland, K. J. Holyoak, R. E. Nisbett, and P. R. Thagard. *Induction: Processes of Inference, Learning and Discovery*. Cambridge, MA: MIT Press, 1986.

[Holyoak and Thagard, 1995] K. J. Holyoak and P. Thagard. *Mental Leaps: Analogy in Creative Thought*. Cambridge, MA: MIT Press, 1995.

[Honderich, 1995] T. Honderich, editor. *The Oxford Campanion to Philosophy*. Oxford: Oxford University Press, 1995.

[Horgan and Tienson, 1988] T. Horgan and J. Tienson. Settling into a new paradigm. *Southern Journal of Philosophy*, 26:97–113, 1988. *Connectionism and the Philosophy of Mind: Proceedings of the 1987 Spindel Conference*, special supplement.

[Horgan and Tienson, 1989] T. Horgan and J. Tienson. Representations without rules. *Philosophical Topics*, 17:147–174, 1989.

[Horgan and Tienson, 1990] T. Horgan and J. Tienson. Soft laws. *Midwest Studies in Philosophy: The Philosophy of the Human Sciences*, 15:256–279, 1990.

[Horgan and Tienson, 1992] T. Horgan and J. Tienson. Cognitive systems as dynamical systems. *Topoi*, 11:27–43, 1992.

[Horgan and Tienson, 1996] T. Horgan and J. Tienson. *Connectionism and the Philosophy of Psychology.* Cambridge, MA: MIT Press, A Bradford Book, 1996.

[Horgan and Tienson, 1999a] T. Horgan and J. Tienson. Authors' replies. *Acta Analytica*, 22:275–287, 1999.

[Horgan and Tienson, 1999b] T. Horgan and J. Tienson. Short précis of *connectionism and the philosoph of psychology. Acta Analytica*, 22:9–21, 1999.

[Horn, 1989] L. Horn. *A Natural History of Negation.* Chicago: University of Chicago Press, 1989.

[Howard, 1966] R. Howard. Information value theory. *IEEE Transactions on Systems Science and Cybernetics*, 2:22–26, 1966.

[Huhns and Singh, editors, 1998] M. N. Huhns and M. P. Singh, editors. *Readings in Agents.* San Francisco: Morgan Kaufmann, 1998.

[Hunt and Lansman, 1986] E. Hunt and M. Lansman. Unified models of attention and problem solving. *Psychological Review*, 93:446–46, 1986.

[Husbands and Meyer, 1998] P. Husbands and J. A. Meyer, editors. *Volutionary Robotics: Proceedngs of the First European Workshop, EvoRobot98*, volume Vol. 1468 of Lecture Notes in Computer Science. Berlin: Springer, 1998.

[Husserl, 1900–1913] E. Husserl. *Logical Investigations, six volumes.* 1900–1913.

[Imwinkelried, 1993] E. J. Imwinkelried. *Evidentiary Distinctions.* Charlottesville, VA: The Michie Company, 1993.

[Irvine, 1989] A. D. Irvine. Epistemic Logicism and Russell's Regressive Method. *Philosophical Studies*, 55:303–327, 1989.

[Irvine, 1992] A. D. Irvine. Gaps, gluts and paradox. In P. Hanson and B. Hunter, editors, *Return of the A Priori*, pages 273–299. Calgary, Canada: University of Calgary Press, 1992.

[Iseminger, 1986] G. Iseminger. Relatedness logic and entailment. *The Journal of Non-Classical Logic*, 3:5–23, 1986.

[Jackson, 1996] S. Jackson. Fallacies and heuristics. In R. Grootenborst J. van Benthem, F. H. van Eemeren and F. Veltman, editors, *Logic and Argumentation*, pages 101–114. Amsterdam: North-Holland, 1996.

[Jacobs and Jackson, 1983] S. Jacobs and S. Jackson. Speech act structure in conversation: Rational aspects of pragmatic coherence. In Rober T.

Craig and Karen Tracy, editors, *Conversational Coherence: Form, Structure, and Strategy*, pages 47–66. Newbury Park, CA: Sage, 1983.

[Jacobs and Jackson, 1992] S. Jacobs and S. Jackson. Relevance and digressions. *Argumentation*, 6:161–176, 1992.

[Jacobs *et al.*, 1985] S. Jacobs, M. Allen, S. Jackson, and D. Petrel. Can ordinary arguers recognize a valid conclusion if it walks up and bites them in the butt? In J. R. Cox, M. O. Sillars, and G. B. Walker, editors, *Argument and Social Practice: Proceedings of the Fourth SCA/FA Conference on Argumentation*, pages 665–674. Annandale, VA: Speech Communication Association, 1985.

[Jacquette, 1986] D. Jacquette. Intentionality and intensionality: Quotation contexts and the modal wedge. *The Monist*, 69:598–608, 1986.

[Jacquette, 2001] D. Jacquette. Assumption and mechanical simulation of hypothetical reasoning. 2001.

[Jamison, 1970] D. Jamison. Bayesian information usage. In J. Hintikka and P. Suppes, editors, *Information and Inference*, pages 28–57. Dordrecht: Reidel, 1970.

[Jauch and Glueck, 1982] L. R. Jauch and W. F. Glueck. *Business Policy and Strategic Management*. New York: Macmillan, 5th edition, 1982.

[Johnson and Blair, 1983] R. H. Johnson and J. A. Blair. *Logical Self Defence*. Toronto: McGraw Hill, 2nd edition, 1983.

[Johnson and Reeder, 1997] M. K. Johnson and J. A. Reeder. Consciousness as meta-processing. In J.D. Cohen and J.W. Schooler, editors, *Scientific Approaches to Consciousness*, pages 261–293. Mahawah, NJ: Erlbaum, 1997.

[Johnson-Laird and Byrne, 1991] P. N. Johnson-Laird and R. M.J. Byrne. *Deduction: Essays in Cognitive Psychology*. Hove and London: Lawrence Erlbaum Associates, 1991.

[Johnson, 1983] M. K. Johnson. A multiple-entry modular memory system. In G. H. Bowers, editor, *The Psychology of Learning and Motivation*, volume 17, pages 81–123. New York: Academic Press, 1983.

[Johnson, 1990] M. K. Johnson. Functional forms of human memory. In J.L. McGough, N.M. Weinberger, and G. Lynch, editors, *Brain Organisaton and Memory: Cells, Systems and Circuits*, pages 106–134. New York: Oxford University Press, 1990.

[Johnson, 1992] M. K. Johnson. Mem: Mechansims of recollection. *Journal of Cognitive Neuroscience*, pages 268–280, 1992.

[Johnson, 1996] R. H. Johnson. *The Rise of Informal Logic*. Newport News, VA: Vale Press, 1996.

[Josephson and Josephson, 1994] J. R. Josephson and S. G. Josephson, editors. *Abductive Inference: Computation, Philosophy, Technology.* Cambridge: Cambridge University Press, 1994.

[Kahneman and Treisman, 1984] D. Kahneman and A. Treisman. Changing views of attention and automaticity. In R. Parasuraman and D. R. Davies, editors, *Varieties of Attention*, pages 29–61. New York: Academic Press, 1984.

[Kanerva, 1987] P. Kanerva. *Sparse Distributed Memory.* Cambridge, MA: MIT Press, 1987.

[Karp, 1972] R. Karp. Reducibility among combinatorial problems. In R. Miller and J. Thatcher, editors, *Complexity of Computer Computations*, pages 85–104. New York: Plenum Press, 1972.

[Keynes, 1971] J. M. Keynes. *The Collected Writings of John Maynard Keynes.* New York: St Martin's Press, 1971.

[Kolmogorov, 1965] A. Kolmogorov. Three approaches to the quantitative definition of information. *Problemy Peredachi Informatsii*, 1:3–11, 1965. In translation.

[Kornblith, 1985] H. Kornblith. Introduction: What is naturalistic epistemology? In Hilary Kornblith, editor, *Naturalizing Epistemology*, pages 1–14. Cambridge, MA: MIT Press, 1985.

[Krifka *et al.*, 1995] M. Krifka, F. J. Pelletier, G. N. Carlson, A. ter Meulen, Godehard Link, and Germano Chierchia. Genericity: An introduction. In Gregory N. Carlson and Francis Jeffry Pelletier, editors, *The Generic Book*, pages 1–124. Chicago: The Univeristy of Chicago Press, 1995.

[Kyburg, 1987] H. E. Kyburg, Jr. The hobgoblin. *The Monist*, 70:141–151, 1987.

[Lakatos, 1970] I. Lakatos. Falsification and methodology of scientific research programmes. In I. Lakatos and A. Musgrave, editors, *Criticism and the Growth of Knowledge*, pages 91–196. Cambridge: Cambridge University Press, 1970.

[Latour, 1987] B. Latour. *Science in Action.* Cambridge, MA: Harvard University Press, 1987.

[Lee, 1972] R. C. T. Lee. Fuzzy logic and the resolution principle. *Journal of the Association of Computing Machinery*, 19:109–119, 1972.

[Lenat and Feigenbaum, 1991] D. B. Lenat and E. A. Feigenbaum. On the thresholds of knowledge. *Artificial Intelligence*, 47:185–230, 1991.

[Lenat and Guha, 1990] D. B. Lenat and R. V. Guha. *Building Large Knowledge-Based Systems: Representation and Inference in the CYC Project.* Reading, MA: Addison-Wesley, 1990.

[Levinson, 1981] S. C. Levinson. Some pre-observations on the modelling of dialogue. *Discourse Processes*, 4:93–116, 1981.

[Levinson, 1989] S. C. Levinson. A review of relevance. *Journal of Linguistics*, 25:455–472, 1989.

[Levinson, 2001] S. C. Levinson. *Presumptive Meanings: The Theory of Generalised Conversational Implicature*. Cambridge, MA: MIT Press, 2001.

[Lewis and Langford, 1932] C. I. Lewis and C. H. Langford. *Symbolic Logic*. New York: Dover Publications, 1932.

[Lewis, 1986] D. K. Lewis. *Philosophical Papers*, volume II. Oxford: Oxford University Press, 1986.

[Lewis, 1990] D. Lewis. What experience teaches. In William Lycan, editor, *Mind and Cognition*, pages 499–519. Oxford: Blackwells, 1990.

[Locke, 1961] J. Locke. *An Essay Concerning Human Understanding*. London: Dent, 1961. Originally publisher in 1690. Edited in two volumes with an introduction by John W. Yolton.

[Lorenzen and Lorenz, 1978] P. Lorenzen and K. Lorenz. *Dialogische Logik*. Darmstadt: Wissenschaft-liche Buchgesellschaft, 1978.

[Lorenzen, 1965] P. Lorenzen. *Formal Logic*. Dordrecht: D.Reidel Publishing Company, 1965.

[Lycan, 1984] W. G. Lycan. *Logical Form in Natural Language*. Cambridge, MA: MIT Press, 1984.

[Lycan, 1988] W. G. Lycan. *Judgement and Justification*. Cambridge: Cambridge University Press, 1988.

[Lycan, 1991] W. G. Lycan. Homuncular functionalism meets PDP. In William Ramsey, Stephen P. Stich, and David E. Rumelhart, editors, *Philosophy and Connectionist Theory*, pages 259–286. Hillsdale, NJ and London: Erlbaum, 1991.

[MacKenzie, 1990] J. MacKenzie. Four dialogue systems. *Studia Logica*, XLIX:567–583, 1990.

[Maddy, 1990] P. Maddy. *Realism in Mathematics*. New York: Oxford University Press, 1990.

[Manktelow, 1999] K. Manktelow. *Reasoning and Thinking*. Hove, UK: Psychology Press, 1999.

[Mautner, 1999] T. Mautner, editor. *Penguin Dictionary of Philosophy*. London: Penguin, 1999, revised edition.

[McCarthy and Hayes, 1969] J. McCarthy and P. J. Hayes. Some philosophical problems from the standpoint of artificial intelligence. In B.M.D. Mickie, editor, *Machine Intelligence 4*, pages 463–502. Edinburgh: University of Edinburgh Press, 1969.

[McCarthy, 1956] J. McCarthy. Measures of the value of information. *Proceedings of the National Academy of Sciences of the USA*, 42:654–655, 1956.

[McClelland *et al.*, 1988] J. L. McClelland, D. E. Rumelhart, and the PDP Research Group. *Parallel Distibuted Processing: Psychological and Biological Models*, volume 2. Cambridge, MA: MIT Press, 1988.

[McGee, 1991] V. McGee. *Truth, Vagueness and Paradox.* Indianapolis, IN: Hackett, 1991.

[McGinn, 1989] C. McGinn. *Mental Content.* Oxford: Blackwell, 1989.

[McGinn, 1999] C. McGinn. *The Mysterious Flame: Conscious Minds in a Material World.* New York: Basic Books, 1999.

[Meyer and van der Hoek, 1995] J. J. Meyer and W. van der Hoek. *Epistemic Logic for AI and Computer Science.* Cambridge: Cambridge University Press, 1995.

[Meyer *et al.*, 1999] J. J. Meyer, W. van der Hoek, and B. van Linder. A logical approach to the dynamics of commitments. *Artificial Intelligence*, 113:1–40, 1999.

[Mill, 1974] J. S. Mill. A system of logic. In J. M. Robson and J. Stillinger, editors, *The Collected Works of John Stuart Mill*, volume VII and VIII. Toronto, ON: University of Toronto Press, 1974. Originally published in 1843, London: Longman and Green. Volume VII was published in 1973 and Volume VIII was published in 1974.

[Millikan, 1984] R. G. Millikan. *Language, Thought, and Other Biological Categories.* Cambridge, MA: MIT Press, 1984.

[Millikan, 1986] R. G. Millikan. Thoughts without laws. *The Philosophical Review*, XLV:47–80, 1986.

[Millikan, 1993] R. G. Millikan. *White Queen Psychology and Other Essays.* Cambridge, MA: MIT Press, 1993.

[Minsky, 1975] M. Minsky. Frame-system theory. In R. C. Schank and B. L. Nash-Webber, editors, *Interdisciplinary Workshop on Theoretical Issues in Natural Language Processing.* Cambridge, MA: Yale University Press, 1975. Preprints of a conference at MIT, June 1975. Reprinted in P. N. Johnson-Laird and P. C. Wason (eds.), *Thinking: Readings in Cognitive Science*, pages 355–376. Cambridge: Cambridge University Press 1977.

[Minsky, 1981] M. Minsky. A framework for representing knowledge. In J. Haugeland, editor, *Mind Design: Philosophy, Psychology, Artificial Intelligence*, pages 95–128. Cambridge, MA: MIT Press, 1981.

[Montague, 1974] R. Montague. Formal philosophy. In Richmond H. Thomason, editor, *Formal Philosophy: Selected Papers of Richard Montague*, New Haven, CN: Yale University Press, 1974.

[Moore and Hobbs, 1996] D. Moore and D. Hobbs. Computational uses of philosophical dialogue theories. *Informal-Logic*, 18:131–163, 1996.

[Morris, 1971] C. W. Morris. *Writings on the General Theory of Signs.* The Hague: Mouton, 1971.

[Moser, 1989] P. K. Moser. *Knowledge and Evidence.* New York: Cambridge University Press, 1989.

[Mueller and Kirkpatrick, 1995] C. B. Mueller and L. C. Kirkpatrick. *Modern Evidence: Docrine and Practice.* Boston, MA: Little Brown, 1995.

[Munz, 1987] P. Munz. Philosophy and the mirror of rorty. In G. Radnitzky and W.W. Bartley, III, editors, *Evolutionary Epistemology, Rationality and the Sociology of Knowledge*, pages 345–398. La Salle, IL: Open Court, 1987.

[Murphy, 2000] P. Murphy. *Murphy on Evidence.* London: Blackstone, 7th edition, 2000. First published in 1980.

[Nash, 1954] J. Nash. Parallel control. *RAND/RM-1361*, 8–27–54, 1954.

[Nisbett and Ross, 1980] R. E. Nisbett and L. Ross. *Human Inference: Strategies and Shortcomings of Social Judgement.* Englewood Cliffs, NJ: Prentice-Hall, 1980.

[Nisbett, 1989] R. E. Nisbett. Conditional reasoning. In *Third International Symposium on Informal Logic.* University of Windsor, Canada, 1989.

[Oaksford *et al.*, 1997] M. R. Oaksford, N. Chater, B. Grainger, and J. Larkin. Optimal data selection in the reduced array selection task (rast). *Journal of Experimantal Psychology: Learnıng, Memory and Cognition*, 23:441–458, 1997.

[O'Connor, 2001] T. O'Connor. *Persons and Causes.* Oxford: Oxford University Press, 2001.

[O'Keefe, 1990] D. J. O'Keefe. *Persuasion: Theory and Research.* Thousand Oaks, CA: Sage, 1990.

[Otte, 1981] R. Otte. A critique of Suppes' theory of probabilistic causality. *Synthese*, 48:167–189, 1981.

[Parasuraman and Davies, 1984] R. Parasuraman and D. R. Davies. *Varieties of Attention.* New York: Academic Press, 1984.

[Paris, 1991] J. Paris. *The Uncertain Reasoner Companion.* Cambridge: Cambridge University Press, 1991.

[Pearl, 2000] J. Pearl. *Causality: Models, Reasoning and Inference.* Cambridge: Cambridge University Press, 2000.

[Peirce, 1931–1958] C. S. Peirce. *Collected Works.* Cambridge, Mass: Harvard University Press, 1931–1958. A series of volumes, the first appearing in 1931.

[Pereira, 2002] L. M. Pereira. Philosophical incidence of logic programming. In D. M. Gabbay, R. H. Johnson, H. J. Ohlbach, and J. Woods, editors, *Handbook of the Logic of Argument and Inference: The Turn Towards the Practical*, pages 421–444. Amsterdam: North-Holland, 2002. To appear in the series *Studies in Logic and Practical Reasoning.*

[Petty and Cacioppo, 1986] R. E. Petty and J. T. Cacioppo. *Communication and Persuasion*. New York: Springer-Verlag, 1986.

[Petty *et al.*, 1981] R. E. Petty, J. T. Cacioppo, and R. Goldman. Personal involvement as a determinant of argument-based persuasion. *Journal of Personality and Social Psychology*, 41:847–855, 1981.

[Pietroski, 2000] P. M. Pietroski. *Causing Actions*. Oxford: Oxford University Press, 2000.

[Pishkin and Williams, 1984] V. Pishkin and W. V. Williams. Redundancy and complexity of information in cognitive performances of schizophrenic and normal individuals. *Journal of Clinical Psychology*, 40:648–654, 1984.

[Popper, 1934] K. R. Popper. *The Logic of Scientific Discovery*. London: Hutchinson, 1934. In large part a translation of *Logik der Forschung*, Vienna: Springer, 1934.

[Priest, 1998] G. Priest. To be *and* not to be — that is the answer: On Aristotle on the law of non-contradiction. *Philosophiegeschichte und Logische Analyse*, 1:91–130, 1998.

[Prior, 1967] A. N. Prior. Logic, many-valued. In Paul Edwards, editor, *Encyclopedia of Philosophy*, volume 5, pages 1–12. New York and London: Collier Macmillan, 1967.

[Przełecki, 1976] M. Przełecki. Fuzziness as multiplicity. *Erkenntnis*, 10:371–380, 1976.

[Putnam, 1983] H. Putnam. Foreward to the fourth edition. In *Fact, Fiction,* and *Forecast*, pages vii–xvi. Cambridge, MA: Harvard University Press, 4th edition, 1983.

[Putnam, 1988] H. Putnam. *Representation and Reality*. Cambridge, MA: MIT Press, 1988.

[Pylyshyn and Demopoulos, 1986] Z. W. Pylyshyn and W. Demopoulos. *Meaning and Cognitive Structure: Issues in the Computational Theory of Mind*. Norwood, NJ: Ablex, 1986.

[Pylyshyn, 1984] Z. W. Pylyshyn. *Computation and Cognition: Toward a Foundation for Cognitive Science*. Cambridge, MA: MIT Press, 1984.

[Quine and Ullian, 1970] W. V. Quine and J. S. Ullian. *The Web of Belief*. New York: Random House, 1970.

[Quine, 1960] W. V. Quine. *Word and Object*. Cambridge, MA and New York: MIT Press and John Wiley, 1960.

[Quine, 1975] W. V. Quine. Empirically equivalent systems of the world. *Erkenntnis*, 9:313–328, 1975.

[Quine, 1990] W. V. Quine. Comment on Ullian. In R. B. Barrett and R. F. Gibson, editors, *Perspectives on Quine: Logic, Words and Objects*, page 348. Oxford: Blackwell, 1990.

[Quine, 1995] W. V. Quine. *From Stimulus to Science.* Cambridge, MA: Harvard University Press, 1995.

[Raiffa, 1968] H. Raiffa. *Decision Analysis.* Reading, MA: Addison-Wesley, 1968.

[Reiter, 1980] R. Reiter. A logic for default reasoning. *Artificial Intelligence*, 12:81–132, 1980.

[Rescher, 1964] N. Rescher. *Hypothetical Reasoning.* Amsterdam: North-Holland, 1964.

[Rescher, 1976] N. Rescher. *Plausible Reasoning: An Introduction to the Theory and Practice of Plausible Inference.* Assen and Amsterdam: Van Gorcum, 1976.

[Rey, 1997] G. Rey. *Contemporary Philosophy of Mind.* Oxford: Blackwell, 1997.

[Rips, 1983] L. J. Rips. Cognitive processes in propositional reasoning. *Psychological Review*, 90:38–71, 1983.

[Rips, 1994] L. J. Rips. *The Psychology of Proof: Deductive Reasoning in Human Thinking.* Cambridge, MA: MIT Press, 1994.

[Roberts, 1993] G. B. Roberts. Methodology in evidence — facts in issue, relevance and purpose. *Monash University Law Review*, 19:68–91, 1993.

[Robinson, 1966] A. Robinson. *Non-standard Analysis.* Amsterdam: North-Holland, 1966.

[Rosch, 1978] E. Rosch. Principles of categorization. In E. Rosch and B. B. Lloyd, editors, *Cognition and Categorization*, pages 27–48. Hillsdale, NJ: Erlbaum, 1978.

[Rosenschein, 1981] S. J. Rosenschein. Plan synthesis: A logical perspective. In P.J. Hayes, editor, *Proceedings of the International Joint Conference on Artificial Intelligence*, pages 331–337. Vancouver, BC: Morgan-Kaufmann Publishers, 1981.

[Roy, 1967] R. Roy. *The Book of Chilan Balam of Chumayel.* Norman, OK: University of Oklahoma Press, 1967.

[Rumelhart *et al.*, 1986] D. E. Rumelhart, J. L. McClelland, and PDP Research Group. *Parallel Distributed Processing: Explorations in the Microstructure of Cognition*, volume 2. Cambridge, MA: MIT Press, 1986.

[Russell and Wefald, 1991] S. Russell and E. Wefald. *Do the Right Thing: Studies in Limited Rationality.* Cambridge, MA: MIT Press, 1991.

[Salmon, 1971] W. Salmon. Statistical explanation. In Wesley Salmon, editor, *Statistical Explanation and Statistical Relevance*, pages 29–88. Pittsburgh, PA: University of Pittsburgh, 1971.

[Savage, 1972] L. J. Savage. *The Foundations of Statistics.* New York: Dover, 2nd edition, 1972.

[Schegloff, 1988] E. A. Schegloff. Presequences and indirection. *Journal of Pragmatics*, 12:55–62, 1988.

[Schiffrin, 1977] R. M. Schiffrin. Attentional control. *Perception and Psycholphysics*, 21:93–96, 1977.

[Schiller, 1912] F. C.S . Schiller. *Formal Logic: A Scientific and Social Problem*. London: MacMillan, 1912.

[Schlesinger, 1986] G. N. Schlesinger. Relevance. *Theoria*, LII:57–67, 1986.

[Schlesinger, 1988] G. N. Schlesinger. Why a tale twice-told is more likely to hold. *Philosophical Studies*, 54:141–152, 1988.

[Schneider *et al.*, 1984] W. Schneider, S. T. Dumais, and R. M. Shiffrin. Automatic and controlled processing and attention. In R. Parasuraman and D. R. Davies, editors, *Varieties of Attention*, pages 1–27. New York: Academic Press, 1984.

[Seligman, 1990] J. Seligman. Perspectives in situation theory. In K. Mukai R. Cooper and J. Perry, editors, *Situation Theory and Its Applications, Vol 1*, volume 1, pages 147–192. Stanford: CSLI Publications, 1990.

[Semb, 1968] G. Semb. The detectability of the odor of butane. *Perception and Psychophysics*, 4:335–340, 1968.

[Shagrin *et al.*, 1985] M. L. Shagrin, W. J. Rapaport, and R. R. Dipert. *Logic: A Computer Approach*. New York: McGraw-Hill Book Company, 1985.

[Shannon, 1948] C. Shannon. *The Mathematical Theory of Information*. Urbana, IL: The University of Illinois Press, 1948.

[Shannon, 1993] B. Shannon. *The Representation and the Presentational: An Essay on Cognition and the Study of Mind*. New York and London: Harvester Wheatsheaf, 1993.

[Shiffrin and Grantham, 1974] R. M. Shiffrin and D. W. Grantham. Can attention be allocated to sensory modalities? *Perception and Psychophysics*, 15:460–474, 1974.

[Shiffrin *et al.*, 1974] R. M. Shiffrin, D. B. Pisoni, and K. Casteneda-Mendez. Can attention be divided between the ears? *Cognitive Psychology*, 6:190–215, 1974.

[Shiffrin, 1976] R. M. Shiffrin. Capacity limitations in information processing, attention, and memory. In W.K. Estes, editor, *Handbook of Learning and Cognitive Processes: Attention and Memory*, volume 4, pages 177–236. Hillsdale, NJ: Lawrence Erlbaum Associates, 1976.

[Shiffrin, 1997] R. M. Shiffrin. Attention, automatism and consciousness. In Jonathan D. Cohen and Jonathan W. Schooler, editors, *Scientific Approaches to Consciousness*, pages 49–64. Mahwah, NJ: Erlbaum, 1997.

[Siegel, 1992] H. Siegel. Justification by balance. *Philosophy and Phenomenological Research*, LII:27–46, 1992.

[Simon, 1957] H. A. Simon. *Models of Man.* New York: John Wiley, 1957.

[Simpson, 1951] E. H. Simpson. The interpretation of interaction in contingency tables. *Journal of the Royal Statistical Society*, Series B, 13:238–241, 1951.

[Slater, 2002] H. Slater. *Logic Reformed.* Bern: Peter Lang, 2002.

[Smith and Medin, 1981] E. E. Smith and D. L. Medin. *Categories and Concepts.* Cambridge, MA: Harvard University Press, 1981.

[Smith, 1989] J. Maynard Smith. *Evolutionary Genetics.* New York: Oxford University Press, 1989.

[Smokler, 1966] H. Smokler. Information content: A problem of definition. *Journal of Philosophy*, 63:63 and 201–211, 1966.

[Smolensky, 1986] P. Smolensky. Information processing in dynamical systems: Foundations in harmony theory. In D.E. Rumelhart, J.L. McClelland, and PDP Research Group, editors, *Parallel Distributed Processing: Explorations in the Microstructure of Cognition*, volume 1, pages 194–281. Cambridge, MA: MIT Press, 1986.

[Smolensky, 1988] P. Smolensky. On the proper treatment of connectionism. *Behavioral and Brain Sciences*, 11:1–74, 1988.

[Sober, 1988] E. Sober. *Reconstructing the Past: Parsimony, Evolution, and Inference.* Cambridge, MA: MIT Press, 1988.

[Sorenson, 1988] R. A. Sorenson. *Blindspots.* Oxford: Clarendon Press, 1988.

[Sperber and Wilson, 1986] D. Sperber and D. Wilson. *Relevance.* Oxford: Basil Blackwell, 1986. 1st Edition.

[Sperber and Wilson, 1987] D. Sperber and D. Wilson. Precis of *relevance: communication and cognition. Behavioral and Brain Sciences*, 10:697–754, 1987.

[Stanovich, 1999] K. A. Stanovich. *Who is Rational? Studies of Individual Differences in Reasoning.* Mahawah, NJ: Erlbaum, 1999.

[Stein, 1996] E. Stein. *Without Good Reason: The Rationality Debate in Philosophy and Cognitive Science.* Oxford: Clarendon Press, 1996.

[Sterelny, 1990] K. Sterelny. *The Representation Theory of Mind.* Oxford: Blackwell, 1990.

[Stich and Nisbett, 1980] S. P. Stich and R. E. Nisbett. Justification and the psychology of human reasoning. *Philosophy of Science*, 47:188–202, 1980.

[Stich, 1983] S. P. Stich. *From Folk Psychology to Cognitive Science.* Cambridge, MA: MIT Press, 1983.

[Stich, 1988] S. P. Stich. Reflective equilibrium, analytic epistemology and the problem of cognitive diversity. *Synthese*, 74:391–413, 1988.

[Stillings *et al.*, 1987] N. A. Stillings, M. H. Feinstein, J. L. Garfield, E. L. Rissland, D. A. Rosenbaum, S. E. Weisler, and L. Baker-Ward. *Cognitive Science: An Introduction.* Cambridge, MA: MIT Press, 1987.

[Strong, 1992] J. William Strong. *McCormick on Evidence.* St Paul, MN: West Publishing, 4th edition, 1992.

[Suppes, 1970a] P. Suppes. A probabilistic theory of causality. *Acta Philosophica Fennica*, 24:121–124, 1970.

[Suppes, 1970b] P. Suppes. *A Probabilistic Theory of Causality.* Amsterdam: North-Holland, 1970.

[Suppes, 1984] P. Suppes. *Probabilistic Metaphysics.* Oxford: Blackwell, 1984.

[Tarski, 1956] A. Tarski. The concept of truth in formalized languages. In *Logic, Semantics, Metamathematics*, pages 152–278. Oxford: Clarendon Press, 1956.

[Tate, 1977] A. Tate. Generating project networks. In R. Reddy, editor, *Proceedings of the International Joint Conference on Artificial Intelligence*, pages 888–893. Cambridge, MA: Morgan-Kaufmann Publishers, 1977.

[Taylor, 1967] A. Taylor. Causation. In Paul Edwards, editor, *Encyclopedia of Philosophy*, volume 2, pages 56–66. New York and London: Collier Macmillan, 1967.

[Tewksbury, 1967] W. J. Tewksbury. The ordeal as a vehicle for divine intervention in medieval Europe. In Paul Hohannan, editor, *Law and Warfare*, pages 267–270. Garden City, NY: The Natural History Press, 1967.

[Thagard, 1982] P. Thagard. From the descriptive to the normative in psychology and logic. *Philosophy of Science*, 49:24–42, 1982.

[Thagard, 1988] P. Thagard. *Computational Philosophy of Science.* Princeton, NJ: Princeton University Press, 1988.

[Thagard, 1992] P. Thagard. *Conceptual Revolutions.* Princeton, NJ: Princeton University Press, 1992.

[Thelen and Smith, 1993] E. Thelen and I.B. Smith. *A Dynamic Systems Approach to the Development of Cognition and Action.* Cambridge, MA: MIT Press, 1993.

[Thomas, 1977] S. N. Thomas. *Practical Reasoning in Natural Language.* Englewood Cliffs, N.J.: Prentice-Hall, 1977.

[Thomason, 1974] R.. H. Thomason. Introduction. In R. H. Thomason, editor, *Formal Philosophy: Selected Papers of Richard Montague*, pages 1–69. New Haven and London: Yale University Press, 1974.

[Thomason, 1990] R. H. Thomason. Accommodation, meaning, and implicature: Interdisciplinary foundations for pragmatics. In Philip R. Cohen,

Jerry Morgan, and Martha E. Pollack, editors, *Semantics, Pragmatics, Conversation and Presupposition*, pages 325–364. Cambridge, MA: MIT Press, 1990.

[Toulmin, 1972] S. Toulmin. *Human Understanding*, volume I. Princeton: Princeton University Press, 1972.

[Treisman *et al.*, 1974] A. M. Treisman, R. Squire, and J. Green. Semantic processing in dichotic listening? A replication. *Memory and Cognition*, 2:641–646, 1974.

[Treisman, 1960] A. M. Treisman. Contextual cues in selective listening. *Quarterly Jounral of Experimental Psychology*, 12:242–248, 1960.

[Treisman, 1964] A. M. Treisman. Selective attention in man. *British Medical Bulletin*, 20:12–16, 1964.

[Turing, 1950] A. Turing. Checking a large routine. In *Rep. Conf. High Speed Automatic Calculating Machines*, Inst. of Comp. Sci. Univ. of Toronto, Ontario, Can., Jan 1950.

[Tye, 1990] M. Tye. Vague objects. *Mind*, 99:535–557, 1990.

[van Benthem *et al.*, 2001] J. van Benthem, P. Dekker, J. van Eijck, M. de Rijke, and Y. Venema, editors. *Logic in Action*. Amsterdam: Institute for Logic, Language and Computation, Amsterdam, 2001.

[van Benthem, 1988] J. van Benthem. *A Manual of Intensional Logic*. Stanford: CSLI Publications, 1988. CSLI Lecture Notes no. 1.

[van Benthem, 1991] J. van Benthem. *Language in Action: Categories, Lambdas and Dynamic Logic*. Amsterdam: North-Holland, 1991.

[van Benthem, 1993] Johan van Benthem. Modelling the kinematics of meaning. *Proceedings of the Aristotelian Society*, 93:105–122, 1993.

[van Benthem, 1996] J. van Benthem. *Exploring Logical Dynamics*. Stanford: CSLI Publications, 1996.

[van Benthem, 1999] Johan van Benthem. Resetting the bounds of logic. *European Review of Philosophy*, 4:21–44, 1999.

[van Benthem, 2001] J. van Benthem. Introduction. In J. van Benthem, P. Dekker, J. van Eijck, M. de Rijke, and Y. Venema, editors, *Logic in Action*, pages 1–6. Institute for Logic, Language and Computation, 2001.

[van der Hoek *et al.*, 1994a] W. van der Hoek, B. van Linder, and J.J. Meyer. A logic of capabilities. In A. Nerode and Yu V. Manyasevich, editors, *Lecture Notes in Computer Science*, volume 813, pages 366–378. Berlin: Springer, 1994. Proceedings of the Third International Symposium on the Logical Foundations of Computer Science.

[van der Hoek *et al.*, 1994b] W. van der Hoek, B. van Linder, and J.J. Meyer. Unravelling nondeterminism: On having the ability to choose. In P. Jorrand and V. Squrev, editors, *Proceedings of the Sixth International Conference on Artificial Intelligence: Methodology, Systems, Ap-*

plications, pages 163–172. Singapore: World Scientific, 1994. Extended abstract.

[van Eemeren and Grootendorst, 1992] F. H. van Eemeren and R. Grootendorst. *Argumentation, Communication, and Fallacies: A Pragma-Dialectical Perspective.* Hillsdale, NJ and London: Lawrence Erlbaum Associates, 1992.

[van Eemeren *et al.*, 1996] F. H. van Eemeren, R. Grootendorst, F. Snoeck Henkemans, J. A. Blair, R. H. Johnson, E. C. W. Krabbe, C. Plantin, D. N. Walton, C. A. Willard, J. Woods, and D. Zarefsky. *Fundamentals of Argumentation Theory: A Handbook of Historical Backgrounds and Contemporary Developments.* Mahwah, NJ: Erlbaum, 1996.

[van Fraassen, 1980] B. C. van Fraassen. *The Scientific Image.* Oxford: Clarendon Press, 1980.

[van Linder *et al.*, 1994] B. van Linder, W. van der Hoek, and J. J. Meyer. Tests as epistemic updates. In A. C. Cohn, editor, *Proceedings of the Eleventh European Conference on Artificial Intelligence*, pages 331–335. New York: Wiley, 1994.

[van Linder *et al.*, 1995] B. van Linder, W. van der Hoek, and J. J. Meyer. Actions that make you change your mind. In A. Laux and H.Wansing, editors, *Knowledge and Belief in Philosophy and Artificial Intelligence*, pages 103–146. Berlin: Akademie, 1995.

[van Linder *et al.*, 1997] B. van Linder, W. van der Hoek, and J. J. Meyer. Seeing is believing (and so are hearing and jumping). *Journal of Logic, Language and Information*, 6:33–61, 1997.

[Van Rees, 1989] M. Agnes Van Rees. Conversation, relevance, and argumentation. *Argumentation*, 3:385–394, 1989.

[Velleman, 2000] J. D. Velleman. *The Possiblity of Practical Reason.* Oxford: Clarendon Press, 2000.

[Veltman, 1996] F. Veltman. Defaults in update semantics. *Journal of Philosophical Logic*, 25:221–261, 1996.

[Venema, 1996] Y. Venema. A crash course in arrow logic. In M. Marx, M. Masuch, and I. Pólos, editors, *Arrow Logic and Multi-Modal Logic*, pages 3–34. Stanford: CSLI Publications, 1996.

[Vere, 1983] S. Vere. Planning in time: Windows and durations for activities and goals. *IEEE Transactions: Pattern Analysis Machine Intelligence 5*, 3:246–267, 1983.

[Von Eckard, 1993] B. Von Eckard. *What is Cognitive Science?* Cambridge, MA: MIT Press, 1993.

[von Wright *et al.*, 1975] J. M. von Wright, K. Anderson, and U. Stenman. Generalization of conditioned gsrs in dichotic listening. In P.M.A. Rabbitt and S. Dornic, editors, *Attention and Performance V*, pages 194–204. London: Academic Press, 1975.

[Walton and Krabbe, 1995] D. Walton and E. C. W. Krabbe. *Commitment in Dialogue*. Albany, NY: SUNY Press, 1995.

[Walton, 1982] D. Walton. *Topical Relevance in Argumentation*. Amsterdam: John Benjamins, 1982.

[Walton, 2003] D. Walton. *Relevance in Argumentation*. Erlbaum, to appear, 2003.

[Webb, 1994] B. Webb. Robotic experiments in cricket phonotaxis. In D. Cliff, P. Husbands, J.A. Meyer, and S. Wilson, editors, *From Animals to Animats 3: Proceedings of the Third International Conference on Simulation of Adaptive Behavior*, pages 45–54. Cambridge, MA: MIT Press/Bradford Books, 1994.

[Wells, 1961] R. Wells. A measure of subjective information. In *Structure of Language and Its Mathematical Aspects*, volume XII. Providence, RI: American Mathematical Society, 1961. Proceedings of Symposia in Applied Mathematics.

[Werth, 1981] P. N. Werth. The concept of relevance in conversational analysis. In P. N. Werth, editor, *Conversation and Discourse*, pages 155–178. London: Croom Helm, 1981.

[Wheeler and Clark, 1999] M. Wheeler and A. Clark. Genie representation: Reconciling content and causal complexity. *British Journal for the Philosophy of Science*, 50:103–135, 1999.

[Wheeler, 1994] M. Wheeler. From activation to activity: Representation, computation and the dynamics of neural network control systems. *Artificial Intelligence and Simulation of Behaviour Quarterly*, 87:36–42, 1994.

[Wheeler, 2001] M. Wheeler. Two threats to representation. *Synthese*, 129:211–231, 2001.

[Wilkins, 1988] D. Wilkins. *Practical Reasoning*. San Mateo, CA: Morgan Kaufmann, 1988.

[Williams, 1973] B. Williams. Deciding to believe. In Bernard Williams, editor, *Problems of the Self*. Cambridge: Cambridge University Press, 1973.

[Williams, 1982] A. G. P. Williams. *Applicable Inductive Logic*. London: B. Edsall and Co, 1982.

[Williamson, 1994] T. Williamson. *Vagueness*. New York: Routledge, 1994.

[Wimsat, 1986] W. Wimsat. Forms of aggregativity. In A. Donagan, N. Perovich, and M. Wedin, editors, *Human Nature and Natural Knowledge*, pages 259–293. Dordrecht: Reidel, 1986.

[Wolfram, 1984] Stephen Wolfram. Computer softwear in science and mathematics. *Scientific American*, 251:188, September 1984.

[Woods, 1980] J. Woods. What is informal logic? In *Informal Logic: The First International Conference*, pages 57–68. San Francisco: Edgepress Publishers, 1980. Reprinted in Woods and Walton *Fallacies: Selected Papers 1972-1982*, Berlin and New York: Foris de Gruyter, 1989.

[Woods, 1989] J. Woods. The maladroitness of epistemic TIT FOR TAT. *Journal of Philosophy*, LXXXVI:324–331, 1989.

[Woods, 1992] J. Woods. Public policy and standoffs of force five. In E. M. Barth and E. C. W. Krabbe, editors, *Logic and Political Culture*, pages 97–108. Amsterdam: North-Holland, 1992. Reprinted in *Death of Argument* as chapter 10.

[Woods, 1992b] J. Woods. Who cares about the fallacies? In F. H. van Eemeren, R. Grootendorst, J. A. Blair, and C. A. Willard, editors, *Argumentation Illuminated*, pages 22–48. Amsterdam: SicSat Press, 1992b. reprinted in *Death of Argument* as Chapter 1.

[Woods, 1993b] J. Woods. Dialectical blindspots. *Philosophy and Rhetoric*, 26:251–265, 1993b. Reprinted in *The Death of Argument* as chapter 6.

[Woods, 2000] J. Woods. Has informal logic anything to learn from fuzzy logic? In H. V. Hansen and C. Tindale, editors, *Argumentation at the Century's Turn*. St. Catharines, ON: OSSA, 2000. Compact Disc.

[Woods, 2001] J. Woods. *Aristotle's Earlier Logic*. Oxford: Hermes Science Publications, 2001.

[Woods, 2002a] J. Woods. John Locke. *Argumentation*, 2002. To appear.

[Woods, 2002b] J. Woods. *Paradox and Paraconsistency: Conflict Resolution in the Abstract Sciences*. Cambridge and New York: Cambridge University Press, 2002.

[Woods, 2002c] J. Woods. Standard logics as theories of argument and inference: Deduction. In D. M. Gabbay, R. H. Johnson, H. Jurgen Ohlbach, and J. Woods, editors, *Handbook of the Logic of Argument and Inference: The Turn Toward the Practical*. Amsterdam: North-Holland, 2002. To appear in the series *Studies in Logic and Practical Reasoning*.

[Woods, 2003] J. Woods. *The Death of Argument: Fallacies in Agent-based Reasoning*. Dordrecht and Boston: Kluwer, to appear in 2003.

[Woods and Irvine, 2003] J. Woods and A. D. Irvine. Aristotle's early logic. In D. M. Gabbay and J. Woods, editors, *Greek, Indian and Arabic Logic. Volume 1 of Handbook of the History and Philosophy of Logic*. North-Holland, Amsterdam, 2003. to appear.

[Woods and Walton, 1982] J. Woods and D. Walton. *Argument: The Logic of the Fallacies*. Toronto: McGraw-Hill, 1982.

[Woods and Walton, 1989] J. Woods and D. Walton. *Fallacies: Selected Papers 1972-1982*. Berlin and New York: Foris de Gruyter, 1989.

[Woods *et al.*, 2000] J. Woods, A. Irvine, and D. Walton. *Argument: Critical Thinking, Logic and the Fallacies.* Toronto: Prentice-Hall, 2000.

[Woodworth and Sells, 1935] R. S. Woodworth and S. B. Sells. An atmosphere effect in formal syllogistic-reasoning. *Journal of Experimental Psychology*, 18:451–460, 1935.

[Wouters, 1999] A. G. Wouters. *Explanation Without a Cause.* Utrecht: Zeno, 1999.

[Wylie, 1967] J. C. Wylie. *Military Strategy: A General Theory of Power Control.* New Brunswick, NJ: Rutgers University Press, 1967.

[Zadeh, 1975] L. A. Zadeh. Fuzzy logic and approximate reasoning. *Synthese*, 30:407–428, 1975.

[Ziff, 1960] P. Ziff. *Semantic Analysis.* Ithaca, NY: Cornell University Press, 1960.

[Zimmermann, 1989] M. Zimmermann. The nervous system and the context of information theory. In R. F. Schmidt and G. Thews, editors, *Human Physiology*, pages 166–175. Berlin: Springer-Verlag, 2nd edition, 1989. Translated by Marguerite A. Biederman-Thorson.

Index